Syria 2011–2013

Revolution and Tyranny before the Mayhem

With a Critical Account of Developments since 2013

Syria 2011–2013

Revolution and Tyranny before the Mayhem

With a Critical Account of Developments since 2013

Azmi Bishara

I.B. TAURIS
LONDON · NEW YORK · OXFORD · NEW DELHI · SYDNEY

I.B. TAURIS
Bloomsbury Publishing Plc
50 Bedford Square, London, WC1B 3DP, UK
1385 Broadway, New York, NY 10018, USA
29 Earlsfort Terrace, Dublin 2, Ireland

BLOOMSBURY, I.B. TAURIS and the I.B. Tauris logo are trademarks of Bloomsbury Publishing Plc

First published in 2013 in Arabic under the title Suwriyyah: Darb Āl-Ālām Naḥwa Āl-Ḥurriyyah Muḥāwalah Fy Āl-Tārykh Āl-Rāhin (Ādhār/Māris 2011 – Ādhār/Māris 2013) by The Arab Center for Research & Policy Studies. Translation © [The Arab Center for Research & Policy Studies (ACRPS)], 2022.

First published in Great Britain 2023
This paperback edition published 2024

Copyright © Azmi Bishara, 2023

Azmi Bishara has asserted his right under the Copyright, Designs and Patents Act, 1988, to be identified as Author of this work.

Cover design by Adriana Brioso
Cover image © Sepia Times/Universal Images Group/Getty Images

All rights reserved. No part of this publication may be reproduced or transmitted in any form or by any means, electronic or mechanical, including photocopying, recording, or any information storage or retrieval system, without prior permission in writing from the publishers.

Bloomsbury Publishing Plc does not have any control over, or responsibility for, any third-party websites referred to or in this book. All internet addresses given in this book were correct at the time of going to press. The author and publisher regret any inconvenience caused if addresses have changed or sites have ceased to exist, but can accept no responsibility for any such changes.

A catalogue record for this book is available from the British Library.

A catalog record for this book is available from the Library of Congress.

ISBN: PB: 978-0-7556-4546-6
ePDF: 978-0-7556-4543-5
eBook: 978-0-7556-4544-2

Typeset by RefineCatch Limited, Bungay, Suffolk

To find out more about our authors and books visit www.bloomsbury.com and sign up for our newsletters.

CONTENTS

List of illustrations	vi
List of abbreviations	vii
List of Fridays	ix
Preface	xi
Recollections: An introduction to the English edition	xii
Introduction	1
1 The bitter harvest: The first ten years of Bashar al-Assad	15
2 From spark to fire	39
3 Protests in the main squares	69
4 Masses in the cities: The revolutionary movement in Damascus and Aleppo	85
5 An armed revolution	95
6 The regime's strategy	115
7 Ruralization of the party and sectarianization of the army: The origins of sectarian discourse and violence	139
8 Sectarian violence unleashed	167
9 Between revolutionary violence and remnants from previous eras	181
10 The opposition	199
11 New actors	221
12 Political solutions and international positions	233
13 The effect of economic sanctions on Syria's macroeconomy	287
Conclusion	295
Supplement: A critical account of developments since 2013	303
Calculating the incalculable	369
Bibliography	377
Index	391

Illustrations

Figures

S.1	Actual and Counterfactual GDP change, 2011–2018 (per cent), and real GDP loss, 2011–2018 (billion dollars)	372

Maps

0.1	Syria: Administrative Divisions	x
C.1	Areas of Control	347
C.2	Regime-controlled Areas	348
C.3	SDF Areas of Control	355
C.4	North-Eastern Syria Oil Fields and Cross-Border Points (15 November 2019)	356
C.5	Areas under SNA Control	360
C.6	Areas under HTS Control	364

Tables

7.1	The Origins of Military Committee Members	155
7.2	Syrian State Revenue Pre-2011	160
9.1	Nusra Front Fighters by Nationality	191
9.2	Crime Statistics in Syria 2001–6	196
C.1	Sources of Employment in the SDF-controlled Areas	359
C.2	Population of Eastern Syria by Average Monthly Income	359
C.3	Sources of Employment in Northern Aleppo, ar-Raqqa and al-Hasakeh	363
C.4	Population of Western Syria by Average Monthly Income	363
C.5	Sources of Employment in Idleb Governorate	367

Abbreviations

AANES	Autonomous Administration of North and East Syria
ACRPS	Arab Centre for Research and Policy Studies
ACU	Assistance Coordination Unit
AKP	Justice and Development Party (Adalet ve Kalkınma Partisi)
AOHRS	Arab Organization for Human Rights in Syria
ASU	(Arab) Socialist Union Party
CAP	Communist Action (Labour) Party
CBS	Central Bureau of Statistics
CDF	Committees for Defense of Democratic Freedoms and Human Rights in Syria
DAD	Kurdish Organization for the Defense of Human Rights and Public Freedoms in Syria
DD	Damascus Declaration
ESCWA	United Nations Economic and Social Commission for Western Asia
EU	European Union
FAO	United Nations Food and Agriculture Organization
FOB	Free Officers' Brigade
FSA	Free Syrian Army
GCC	General Consultative Council
GCSR	General Commission of the Syrian Revolution
HDI	Human Development Index
HNC	Higher Negotiating Committee
HTS	Hay'at Tahrir al-Sham (new coalition dominated by Nusra)
IDF	Israel Defence Forces
IF	Islamic Front
IIC	Independent Islamic Current
ISI	Islamic State in Iraq (ISIS forerunner)
ISIS (Daʿesh)	The Islamic State of Iraq and al-Sham
KDP	Kurdish Democratic Party
KNC	Kurdish National Council
KRG	Kurdistan Regional Government
LCCs	Local Coordination Committees (tansiqiyat)
MAF	Human Rights Organization in Syria
MOC	Military Operations Command
MOM	Joint Operations Centre (from its Turkish name Müşterek Operasyon Merkezi)
NAG	National Action Group
NCB	National Coordination Body for Democratic Change

NCC	National Command Council
NDC	National Dialogue Conference
NDF	National Defence Forces
NDR	National Democratic Rally, also known as the National Democratic Gathering (NDG)
NPF	National Progressive Front
NSG	National Salvation Government
Observer	Kurdish Committee for Human Rights
OCHA	United Nations Office for the Coordination of Humanitarian Affairs
PFLP	Popular Front for the Liberation of Palestine
PKK	Kurdistan Workers' Party (Partiya Karkerên Kurdistan)
PLO	Palestinian Liberation Organization
PYD	Democratic Union Party (Partiya Yekîtiya Demokrat)
RCC	Regional Command Council
RMC	Revolutionary Military Council
RPS	Reform Party of Syria
SANA	Syrian Arab News Agency
SCC	Syrian Credit Company
SCIRI	Supreme Council of the Islamic Revolution in Iraq (Formerly the Islamic Supreme Council of Iraq ISCI)
SDC	Syrian Democratic Council
SDF	Syrian Democratic Forces
SIF	Syrian Islamic Front (was dissolved in 2013 and replaced by the Islamic Front)
SILF	Syrian Islamic Liberation Front
SMC	Supreme Military Council (the highest military leadership of the FSA)
SNA	Syrian National Army
SNC	Syrian National Council
SNHR	Syrian Network for Human Rights
SOC	National Coalition for Syrian Revolutionary and Opposition Forces
SQHC	Syrian-Qatari Holding Company
SSNP	Syrian Socialist Nationalist Party
SYRCU	Syrian Revolution Coordinators Union
TNC	Transitional National Council
UAE	United Arab Emirates
UAR	United Arab Republic
UN	United Nations
UNSC	United Nations Security Council
US	United States
USSR	Union of Soviet Socialist Republics
WHO	World Health Organization
YPG	People's Defence Units (in Kurdish: Yekîneyên Parastina Gel)
YPJ	Women's Protection Units (in Kurdish: Yekîneyên Parastina Jin)

List of Fridays

13 January 2012
Support the FSA Friday
18 March 2011
Friday of Dignity
25 March 2011
Friday of Honour
1 April 2011
Friday of Martyrs
8 April 2011
Friday of Resilience
15 April 2011
Friday of Determination
22 April 2011
Good Friday
29 April 2011
Friday of Rage
6 May 2011
Friday of Defiance
13 May 2011
Friday of Syria's Women
20 May 2011
Azadi Friday
27 May 2011
Friday of the Protectors of the Homeland
3 June 2011
Friday of the Children of Freedom
8 June 2012
Friday of Merchants and Revolutionaries… Hand in hand towards Victory
10 June 2011
Friday of the Clans
1 July 2011
Get Out Friday
22 July 2011
Friday of the Sons of Khalid bin al-Waleed
29 July 2011
'Your Silence Is Killing Us' Friday
23 September 2012
Friday of Opposition Unity

Map 0.1 Syria: Administrative Divisions

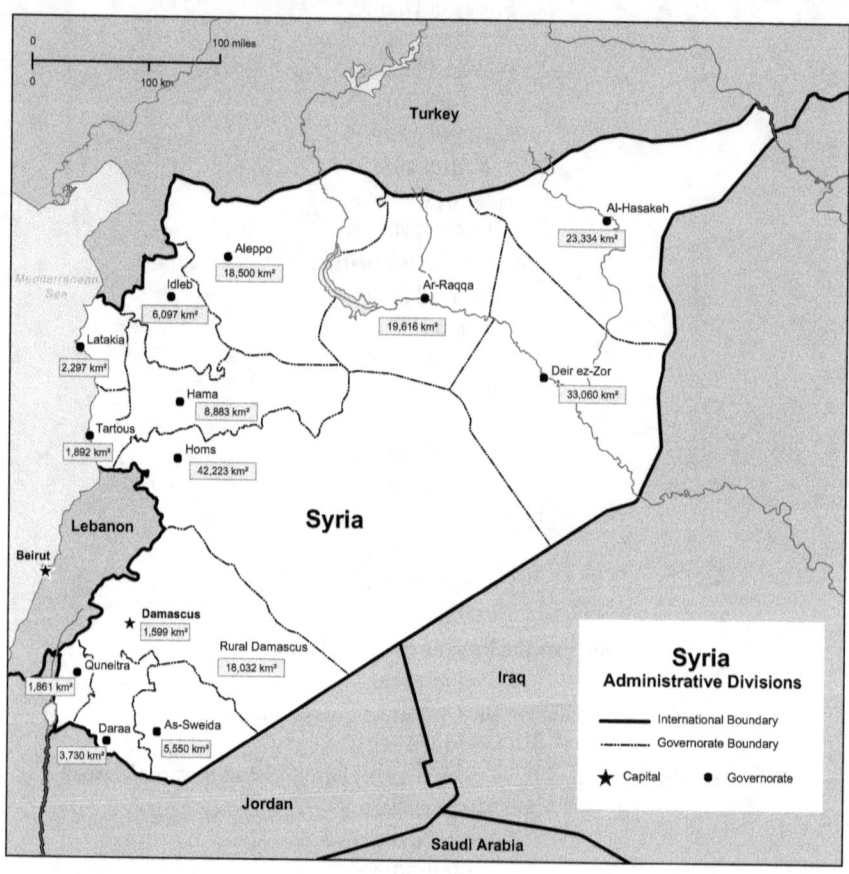

Preface

This book is the third and final volume of the *Understanding Revolutions* series. The Revolution Tribology discusses the social, economic and political backdrop to the Arab revolutions that began in 2011. It also represents an attempt to write contemporary history, documenting the trajectory of those revolutions and the subsequent political developments through to 2013. But as important as tracing the revolutions' day-to-day progress and analysing their dynamics is, this constitutes only one portion of a much broader effort that began with the theoretical portion of *Opening Acts in Tunisia* and continued with the analysis of the regime structure, politics and economies of three Arab countries: Tunisia, Egypt and Syria.

The Arabic edition of this book was released at a fairly early stage of the Syrian revolution, before many other studies had been published. The number of book-length monographs could be counted on the fingers of one hand, and there were very few articles available; it was thus an important source on developments in the country. By the time that it came to be translated into English, however, nine years had passed. I have thus updated it with a long introduction and a final chapter that offers a critical analysis of developments after 2013, while retaining the original introduction and conclusion. The other chapters have largely been left as they were, with some abridgement as required by the English edition. The few additions I have made are in the footnotes.

The book series is tied together by its interdisciplinary and analytical-historical approach, but each study represents a stand alone work.

Here I must thank the publishers, in particular Sophie Rudland, for all the work they have done to make this English edition a reality, allowing a much broader audience to access the product of many years of work, including some two years spent on the translation. I would also like to thank my assistants at the Arab Centre for Research and Policy Studies.

Recollections: An introduction to the English edition

Revisiting this book to add an updated introduction and conclusion is perhaps one of the most psychologically challenging writing tasks I have ever undertaken. It may be for this reason that I have taken great pains to avoid writing about Syria since the publication of the Arabic edition of this book at the end of 2013. To write about the period after 2013 is to confront the worst-case scenario, one in which all your worst fears have come true, with a grievous impact on people close to you. It is to watch the application of Murphy's law in living colour. Moreover, it forces you to engage in a painful reconsideration of the relationship between your moral position – standing with the Syrian people and their revolution – and the likely outcome based on all the data.

The rational prognosis for a direct revolutionary confrontation with the Syrian regime was always pessimistic. There was no public sphere separate from state institutions and no political frameworks other than those built by the regime. The efforts made to foment hostility between different components of Syrian society and tie the fate of particular groups to that of the regime and its security forces meant that there was a great risk of social fragmentation. And many Syrians were well aware of how the army had behaved in previous socio-political crises before the Ba'th came to power in March 1963.[1]

Nonetheless, that moral position was the correct one. In the revolutionary atmosphere that gripped the Arab world after the toppling first of former Tunisian President Zine el-Abidine Ben Ali and then of former Egyptian President Hosni Mubarak, people came out into the streets in defiance of reality and rational analysis. They defied, too, their own bitter memories of the regime's behaviour, in particular the events in Hama in 1982, the most

---

[1] The army was deployed against Syrians three times within the first decade of the country's independence: to put down Sulayman al-Murshid's 'rebellion' in Jabal al-Alawiyyin in 1946 and to crush political opposition in Jabal al-Druz in 1947 and 1954. All three were socio-political crises with an ethno-sectarian dimension. After 1963, the main direct intervention by the Ba'th regime's 'ideological army' was against the Muslim Brotherhood in Hama. In the course of that operation in Hama in 1964, the famous Sultan Mosque was shelled. Since most of the conscripts involved came from the mountainous rural districts and many of them were Alawis, the intervention was read as sectarian. Army involvement in Hama continued through to the massacre of 1982, which brought an end to one period of Syrian history and ushered in another.

recent and most horrifying of the massacres it had carried out. The peaceful revolution showed the remarkable depth of Syrians' bravery and solidarity, their morality and ideals. They demanded reform and got bullets instead – along with cosmetic changes that they knew were meaningless so long as the security regime was still in place. But they did not stop protesting. They began to call for the fall of the regime.

When unarmed people demonstrate *en masse* against a tyrannical regime, and when they are met by terrible violence, rational analysis is no substitute for a moral position. When people are sacrificing their lives for a cause, you, the intellectual who is fully aware of the risks of revolution, must choose the side you feel is right. Should that moral position be revised in light of the catastrophic outcome, when the main reason for that outcome is the conduct of the regime – conduct that, given the regime's nature, any rational analysis would have predicted?

When the regime rejected reform, the majority of Syrians chose confrontation. Its brutal response to the peaceful civil uprising sent Syria past the point of no return. A democratic intellectual must be mindful of potential outcomes but at the same time stand with the oppressed. He must defend them in order to be able to warn them of the dangers of sectarianism, militarization and foreign intervention. Criticism from those who play the role of neutral spectators – never mind those who take the side of a regime that opens fire on peaceful protesters or defend the use of barrel bombs against densely populated urban neighbourhoods – will go unheeded. Critique of a revolution in service of the regime's war on that revolution is not critique but inflammatory propaganda. The revolution has shown the true colours of those who have ignored the suffering and daily humiliations inflicted on Syrians and the crimes of the regime and who insist on seeing a genuine popular uprising as nothing but an imperialist conspiracy.

In the conclusion to the original edition, I said very clearly that the confluence of factors at play in the Syrian revolution 'may lead to catastrophic scenarios unless a political settlement is reached'.[2] Aside from the need to understand the Syrian revolution through an interdisciplinary, analytical approach to the Syrian state and society, I was concerned that the disastrous scenario looming on the horizon would allow the regime and its supporters to recast the revolution as an act of mass terror, a grand conspiracy of domestic and foreign forces. It was for precisely this reason that I set out to write the book at such an early stage, before any other works had been

---

[2] It is important to note that I issued many warnings about this in the past, including the Arabic edition of this book. Azmi Bishara, *Syria: A Path to Freedom from Suffering. An Attempt in Contemporary History (March 2011–March 2013)* [Arabic] (Beirut and Doha: ACRPS, 2013). Also see my original conclusion, reproduced here in the English edition, 300.

published that attempted to write the history of the revolution. I was convinced of the need to analyse and document the revolution's history before it could be rewritten. The signs of impending disaster were already all there and I felt that they needed to be recognized and addressed before it was too late. I predicted that years down the line, this disaster would provide the pretext for a historiographical war, as attempts would be made to erase the civil and peaceful nature of the revolution through to early 2012 and the subsequent escalation of armed action.

The revolution did not achieve its aims. More than a decade later, Syria is in a worse state than it was when the first protests began. Living standards are lower and the regime is more brutal. The war has broken the country into pieces and left deep divisions in society and individual psyches. At this point it is clear that the Syrian people have not become free of tyranny. But I believe there is also much evidence that *Syrians themselves* have become free. Not only have they overcome the paralysis of fear and realized what they are capable of, the millions of refugees driven out of the country have taken the opportunities for self-realization available to them in the diaspora. This is not to mention the dozens of civil society initiatives, the media projects that have proliferated thanks to the internet, or the continuation of critique and protest in the opposition areas.[3] It may seem counterintuitive given the sheer scope of the tragedy, the extent of social fragmentation, and the crimes of extremist forces, whose pernicious influence can also be seen in the discursive and cultural spheres, but we must recognize the fact that defying tyranny has served to emancipate Syrians in many ways.

The aim of my book was, quite simply, to outline the background to the revolution (the nature of the regime and society) and to trace and analyse its trajectory – morally, politically, economically, socially – as a *civil revolution* against a corrupt authoritarian regime whose tentacles extended into every part of life. I tried to show that militarization was not the conscious choice of the popular uprising, and that in fact it was a regime decision, part of a plan to change the course of the peaceful revolution by extreme force. It is the regime that must bear the brunt of the responsibility.

This uprising, as I showed in the book, was part of a broader revolutionary wave that swept across the authoritarian states of the Arab world – in this

---

[3] Robin Yassin-Kassab notes how the revolution dramatically changed Syrians' culture and encouraged acts of defiance. They began to question not only the regime's authority but that of those attempting to replace it: Islamists and secularists, traditional and new leaders, and the Democratic Union Party (Partiya Yekîtiya Demokrat or PYD). They were critical of the corruption and intolerance of local Free Syrian Army (FSA) militias and of the Islamic State of Iraq and al-Sham (ISIS). Robin Yassin-Kassab, 'Revolutionary Culture', *Critical Muslim* 11 (2017), at: https://bit.ly/3DY3Kuw (accessed 10 April 2022).

case, the most authoritarian state of all. It was driven by a longing for human dignity and a rejection of physical and psychological degradation. It was driven, too, by socioeconomic conditions in which immiseration was intimately bound up with enrichment and corruption, in which the fruits of economic liberalization were gobbled up by the strong.[4] It was also a reaction to the regime's retreat from its promises of reform – promises that politicized Syrians, fearful of the consequences of a full confrontation with the regime, still hoped to see met.[5]

Many believed, or wanted to believe, that those promises represented a historic opportunity for Syria to avoid the catastrophic splintering of society along vertical communal lines. They were especially anxious given that the majority of Syrians believed that the regime had a sectarian character, seen in its broad social base, the structure of its security institutions, and its rhetoric, its willingness to defy the United States (US) in Iraq and its continuing support for the Lebanese and Palestinian resistance notwithstanding. Indeed, even in the latter cases there were obvious ulterior motives having to do with regime survival, first and foremost the need to justify maintaining the state of emergency, the threat of US forces just next door and the desire to hold on to bargaining chips in Lebanon. It is an irony of history that a secular-nationalist party like the Baʻth – as a result of its dependence on the army and the security forces – has produced a regime in which the party is marginalized and regional and sectarian difference shapes the state and divides the people. Its nationalist rhetoric is hollow and derided by most Syrians as simply another form of propaganda.

By adopting reformist rhetoric, Bashar al-Assad hoped to root his own legitimacy in the idea of reform and the new, open-minded generation. He did so largely in order to skirt the embarrassing fact that he had essentially inherited the presidency from his father – a kind of dynasticism that would lack legitimacy in any republic, let alone one whose rulers are full of radical

---

[4] The long drought that affected many of Syria's agricultural regions played a role in the deteriorating conditions of farmers and the great wave of urban in-migration. It also contributed to the country's balance of payments problems. It thus added to the general sense of grievance. But a political event *par excellence* like the Syrian revolution cannot be reduced to the effects of global climate change, as some bodies keen to use it as a cautionary example try to do. In a detailed study on this issue, Marwa Daoudy notes that drought was not an inevitable outcome of climate change, and that agricultural planning and policy were also significant drivers. Moreover, she points out that Syria suffers from chronic water scarcity and that none of the other numerous droughts it has suffered in its modern history ever caused a revolution. Nor did the revolution begin in drought-stricken areas or among displaced peasants in the cities. The primary cause of the revolution, in her view, was 'structural inequalities of power and distribution of resources', as well as the general Arab political atmosphere. See: Marwa Daoudy, *The Origins of the Syrian Conflict: Climate Change and Human Security* (Cambridge and New York: Cambridge University Press, 2020), 11, 205–6.
[5] *The New York Times*, 18 July 2000, at: https://nyti.ms/3L6SIGg (accessed 20 April 2022).

bombast. But this does not mean that both popular and elite hope for reform as a way of avoiding the fate of Iraq and Lebanon was wrong.

There is great debate over the extent to which the regime is capable of reforming itself. At the beginning of his tenure, Syrian and Arab intellectuals and Western academics all hoped that Assad's rhetoric was more than just talk and that he would pursue genuine and substantial reforms.[6] That he would not should have been clear to everyone from the moment that the regime began to demonstrate a new self-confidence, having shaken off the international pariah status imposed on it after the 2005 assassination of Lebanese Prime Minister Rafiq al-Hariri. This self-confidence was on full, almost exhibitionist, display during the 2007 presidential 'elections',[7] after which it no longer even pretended to be reformist. Democracy is not created by revolution but by reform. Can revolution produce reform? This is what I was trying to get at when I described the events in Tunisia and Egypt as 'reformist revolutions'.[8] Could reform have resulted from a revolution – that is, by popular revolutionary pressure – in Syria? Perhaps if the peaceful civil revolution had been able to endure for longer, and if the regime had not chosen to crush it and push the country into an armed conflict. But there are no such 'ifs' in history.

It became clear that the regime wanted all or nothing. It offered Syrians a choice: concede defeat and accept the regime or take up arms against arms. In much the same vein, it offered its allies the choice between supporting it in its current form, without reform, or losing everything – that is, sustaining a geostrategic defeat at the hands of the West, the agent of the revolution according to these allies.[9]

But it is not correct to say that the Assad family does not retreat under pressure or show weakness.[10] In 2005, after the Hariri killing, a combination

---

[6] For just one of many examples, see: David W. Lesch, *Syria: The Fall of the House of Assad*, updated edn (New Haven and London: Yale University Press, 2013), 4.

[7] I said this in the original edition of the book, based on several meetings with Assad himself and other senior officials and on the evidence of Syrian policy after 2007. I subsequently discovered that the American academic David Lesch, who also met Assad during this period, had arrived at the same conclusion. See: Ibid., 31–3. Carsten Wieland, meanwhile, and perhaps others too, still hoped for a reformist Bashar al-Assad. In 2006, Wieland argued that the Mehlis report provided Bashar with a chance to 'ally with the Syrian people who still pin their hopes on him'. See: Carsten Wieland, *Syria: Ballots or Bullets? Democracy, Islamism, and Sectarianism in the Levant* (Seattle, WA: Cune Press, 2006), 184.

[8] In particular in the long theoretical introduction in: Azmi Bishara, *Understanding Revolutions: Opening Acts in Tunisia* (London and New York: I.B. Tauris, 2021), 1–36.

[9] Iran praised the Egyptian and Tunisian revolutions, describing them as anti-imperialist and the next act in the Islamic Revolution. But after the Syrian revolution, official discourse began to characterize all the Arab revolutions as the product of foreign conspiracy, with the exception of the revolution in Bahrain. Vladimir Putin's Russia, on the other hand, was always suspicious of events it saw as similar to the 'colour revolutions' that had swept the former Soviet states and undermined Russian influence there. It has consistently characterized the Arab revolutions as Islamist rather than democratic.

[10] Lesch, 213.

of mass demonstrations and international pressure forced Syria to withdraw from Lebanon in total disarray. In 1998, too, Hafez al-Assad's government caved to Turkish threats and handed over Abdullah Öcalan. And the Syrian government joined the Annapolis negotiations with Israel mere months after an Israeli strike destroyed a nuclear reactor under construction in Kibar in Deir ez-Zor.[11] But making concessions that touch on the nature of the regime is a different story altogether. Key regime figures are convinced that reform would be the beginning of the end and that the government would be unable to maintain control. The cosmetic reforms of 2011 and 2012, even the constitutional reforms, were introduced under pressure. But with Iranian and Russian support, the regime moved to a policy of total confrontation, especially once it became clear that the US would not intervene.

Since the revolution, Nikolaos Van Dam has written that he predicted[12] that the regime would not carry out substantive reform of the kind that might lead to democracy unless it was forced to do so[13] and that Hafez al-Assad and Bashar al-Assad had both rejected political reform outright.[14] But he finds himself in a dilemma when it comes to the revolution. He argues that the opposition should not have called for the fall of the regime so long as it was unable to defeat it militarily,[15] and accuses both sides of a failure to compromise.[16] But what is the point of compromising with a regime that can only be convinced of the need for reform by force? Van Dam says that there was no possibility of change without bloodshed, but since the opposition did not garner enough support to win, it should have lowered its expectations and reconciled itself to partial demands.[17] When the opposition did agree to negotiate without conditions, however, it got nowhere, and the regime continued to advance militarily.[18]

My own vision is rooted in the belief that gradual reform that guarantees an incremental and peaceful transition – beginning with expanded rights and freedoms and ending with political participation – is the only safe path to democracy. In a religiously and ethnically diverse country, this prevents the social fabric and the state from collapsing along with the dictatorship. We might add that Syria is a country whose regime has made no effort over the last fifty years to build a nation of citizens, emphasizing Arabness as a unifying factor for all Arabs, who comprise some 90 per cent of the

---

[11] Emile Hokayem, *Syria's Uprising and the Fracturing of the Levant* (London: Routledge; the International Institute for Strategic Studies, 2013), 109.
[12] Nikolaos Van Dam, *The Struggle for Power in Syria* (London: Croom Helm, 1979).
[13] Nikolaos Van Dam, *Destroying a Nation: The Civil War in Syria* (London: I.B. Tauris, 2017), 65–6.
[14] Ibid., 44.
[15] Ibid., 172.
[16] Ibid., 170.
[17] Ibid., 123–4.
[18] Ibid., 177.

population,[19] in such a way as to allow both Arabs and non-Arabs to live as full citizens. The regime has treated Arabness as an ideology rather than a unifying cultural identity within an even broader Syrian citizenship. It has bolstered subnational identities because it has found it easy to rely on regional and sectarian identities in struggles within and beyond the leadership – both because it has never been a stable regime[20] and because in the absence of citizenship rights, citizenship itself has become meaningless. Under a tyrannical, arbitrary and corrupt regime, the people themselves have become more attached to their own local identities. The regime has guaranteed the loyalty of a minority of citizens through their regional and sectarian identities. The majority has continued to seek protection via other channels, such as the party, the corporatist 'popular organizations' and traditional leaders and clerics. In the 2000 party elections, tribal and sectarian blocs within the party were clearly aligned with tribal and sectarian leaders outside the party, who exercised substantial influence over the vote. These elections were the first in fifteen years, and in the intervening period, the role of traditional elites had ossified and a sclerotic bureaucratic class had taken control of the party, in what some have described as the 'Brezhnevian period' of Syrian history.[21]

Syrian citizens came to feel that they were oppressed, marginalized and degraded. Moreover, they came to conclude – individually or in private settings – that the reason was systematic sectarian discrimination rooted in the sectarian nature of the regime. The more the regime rejected a public discussion of sectarianism, the more convinced Syrians became that it was itself sectarian, particularly given the predominance of Alawi officers in the security forces and the army and the ease with which Alawis secured state jobs and resources. In the beginning, the peaceful civil revolution sought to address this phenomenon by stressing the unity of all Syrians: 'one, one, the Syrian people are one!' But as those who had chanted this slogan were gunned down, imprisoned or driven out of the country, and as the revolution became increasingly militarized and sectarian in the face of a regime that refused to make any concessions, this slogan gave way to identitarian killings and a culture of hatred. This is the situation today.

---

[19] According to various pre-revolutionary sources, Kurds make up around 7 per cent of the population, while partially Arabized groups like Armenians, Assyrians and Turkmen account for another 3–5 per cent.

[20] I do not agree with the common assertion that Hafez al-Assad built a stable regime after 1970. There were major challenges to his rule after the intervention in Lebanon, during the conflict with the Brotherhood, and later with his brother Rifaat. It was only genuinely stabilized in the late 1980s, and then at the cost of fierce repression and general regime closure. Between this point and the Syrian revolution, it was stable for little more than twenty years.

[21] Muhammad Jamal Barout, *The Last Decade in the History of Syria: The Dialectic of Stasis and Reform* [Arabic] (Beirut and Doha: ACRPS, 2012), 36–7.

The more the regime arbitrarily bombarded cities whose safety it was supposed to guarantee, the stronger this feeling became. Sectarian grievance combined with a willingness to fall in with Salafi forces that described the regime in sectarian terms.[22] This was the secret to the success of first the Nusra Front (*Jabhat al-Nusra*) and then Islamic State of Iraq and al-Sham (ISIS), which was able to straddle the Syrian-Iraqi border and establish itself not only as a representative of Sunni grievance in both countries but as a force that slaughtered Shi'i and Alawi 'infidels' without mercy. It was not its ideology but its extreme sectarianism that allowed it to do this. Salafi-jihadi thought calls for the rule of the Shari'a; in a sectarian environment, it is often able to convince people that this means the rule of the Sunni majority. In reality, of course, it is the rule of a Salafi minority – itself divided into warring factions – that imposes its own interpretation of the Shari'a onto other Sunnis and the rest of the population. The vast majority of Syrians, like the vast majority of other Arabs and Muslims, live secularized lifestyles, and the forms of religiosity common among the religious majority have little in common with Salafi religiosity, never mind jihadi-Salafi religiosity.

One academic argues that the point at which the Syrian revolution turned dramatically towards armed conflict was the bombing of a meeting of ministers and senior security officials in Damascus on 18 July 2012.[23] Others place the turning point on 4–6 June 2011, when more than 100 regime operatives were killed in Jisr ash-Shughur. Still others prefer the destruction of Baba Amr in Homs in January 2012. I discuss all these occurrences in addition to highlighting the moment when the revolutionaries took control of Az-Zabdani and the regime's attempts to negotiate its return, ushering in the concept of the 'liberated area'. I do not believe, however, that there is a single decisive turning point. The regime was on the road to armed conflict from the very beginning, when it chose to deal with unarmed demonstrators as if they were terrorists. The people, on the other hand, took up arms only gradually, in very local contexts and without any central plan. At first – before February 2012, when the

---

[22] I agree with Roel Meijer that one of the main attractions of Salafism is its capacity to transform 'the humiliated, the downtrodden, disgruntled young people, the discriminated migrant, or the politically repressed into a chosen sect (*al firqa al-najiya*) that immediately gains privileged access to the Truth'. Roel Meijer, 'Introduction', in *Global Salafism: Islam's New Religious Movement*, ed. Roel Meijer (New York: Columbia University Press, 2009), 13, cited in: Aron Lund, 'Syria's Salafi Insurgents: The Rise of the Syrian Islamic Front', UI Occasional Paper, no. 17, Swedish Institute of International Affairs, March 2013, 10, at: https://bit.ly/3jK3qX9 (accessed 17 April 2022). In the case of rising political sectarianism, Salafism is additionally attractive as it sounds more militantly 'Sunni' than other identities.

[23] Teije Hidde Donker, 'Beyond Syria: Civil Society in Failed Episodes of Democratization', in *Social Movements and Civil War: When Protests for Democratization Fail*, ed. Donatella della Porta et al. (London and New York: Routledge, 2018), 61.

revolution developed into something approaching a civil war – peaceful action was combined with armed action.[24]

There are many regional, international and domestic forces that bear primary responsibility for the Syrian revolution's descent into warlordism. The Syrian opposition was unable to produce a critique of the fissiparous nature of the armed groups and the atrocities committed by many of them; fighting the regime granted immunity against criticism. But the regime alone is responsible for the resort to brute military force and before that for delaying reforms. The regime alone could have saved Syria from this terrible fate. Instead, it pursued a policy of brute, naked force, firing on peaceful protesters, besieging and destroying towns and cities with random airstrikes and barrel bombs (an Assad regime invention), and carrying out an unprecedented campaign of arrests and torture of a kind even the most twisted sadist would struggle to imagine. Torturing prisoners, of course, was nothing new. It is an old tradition in Syrian prisons, as the extensive pre-revolutionary prison literature attests.[25] But during the revolution it was no longer a way of extracting information from prisoners or teaching them a lesson. It became a tool of punishment, revenge and intimidation. The huge number of detainees rounded up during the peaceful and armed revolutions only exacerbated this development. This much is clear from the 55,000 pictures leaked by a defector from the Syrian military police, some of which document unimaginable forms of physical torture. These photos represent only a small part of the sufferings of tens of thousands of prisoners and detainees. Ongoing documentation efforts are continually revising the figure upwards. These images prompted Congress to pass the Caesar Act, which imposed stringent sanctions on Syria from 17 June 2017.[26] Nor has the Syrian regime been able to dispute their veracity. But the Caesar sanctions have not only affected the regime. They have had terrible repercussions for the living standards of normal people in Syria and raised the number of those at risk of poverty or absolute poverty to perhaps 70 per cent of the population. The regime itself, meanwhile, still

---

[24] Various researchers seem to agree on this definition, including Christopher Phillips, who believes that the transition to a civil war took place between mid-2011 and late 2012. He adds that Assad ordered the raid because he feared that Homs would become a new Benghazi. See: Christopher Phillips, *The Battle for Syria: International Rivalry in the New Middle East*, revised and updated edn (New Haven and London: Yale University Press, 2020), 84, 86.

[25] The most famous example is Mustafa Khalifa's *The Shell: Memoirs of a Hidden Observer*, first published in Arabic by Dar al-Adab in 2008, which enjoyed a renewed period in the spotlight after the revolution. Syria has produced more prison literature than any other country, including Yassin al-Haj Saleh's *Salvation O Boys: Sixteen Years in Syrian Prisons*, Mohamed Berro's *A Survivor from the Guillotine: Eight Years in Tadmor Prison*, Heba Dabbagh's *Just Five Minutes: Nine Years in Syria's Prisons* and Faraj Bayrakdar's *Betrayals of Language and Silence*.

[26] Howard J. Shatz, 'The Power and Limits of Threat: The Caesar Syrian Civilian Protection Act at One Year', RAND Blog, 8 July 2021, at: https://bit.ly/3rw7mia (accessed 17 April 2022).

has ways of obtaining necessities and of providing them to its own narrow support base. It has never shown much interest in the general socioeconomic situation, and it seems unlikely that deterioration in this sphere will force it to reconsider its options.[27]

The regime, then, bears the main responsibility for what has happened. That this is so, however, does not alleviate the anguish felt after being poised for so long between anxiety about the worst-case scenario and awe at Syrians' bravery in the face of a brutal regime. Thinking about Syria anew brings on the same sense of dread. But so long as I am alive and capable of writing, I cannot publish a translation of a book released in 2013 without including some reference to what has happened since.

In the Arab world, Syria is well-known for the comedies and dramas it produced in vast quantities prior to the revolution. It is famous for its cultural diversity, handicrafts, entrepreneurship, cuisine (Aleppan and Damascene) and its novelists and writers. If we include Mesopotamia as part of historical Greater Syria, it is also the birthplace of modern pan-Arabism. But it is also – less enviably – known for the suffering inflicted on its population by a uniquely corrupt and arbitrary despotic regime, one of the worst in the Arab world. Syrians have been subjected to mass killings and exterminations. Fully half of them have been displaced within or beyond the country. Those who remain in Syria are scattered across areas governed by four separate forces. The regime has shown itself quite willing to turn Syria into a pile of smoking rubble so long as it can remain in power. Along with the Russian forces and Iranian militiamen who support it, it has continued to govern using the same old tools, with one exception: gangs of *Shabbiha* – bands and individuals paid to provoke violent clashes – have replaced the party, which has lost its entire power base over the course of the revolution (a process that had already begun before). The regime continues to loom over the lives of a large part of a bloodied and immiserated people who – with nothing left to steal or loot – are no longer able to sustain it. And efforts are beginning, some sheepish and behind the scenes and others explicit, to rehabilitate it.

Because the regime has managed to avoid paying the price of its crimes, and because the wounds of the revolution are still fresh, self-criticism is difficult for Syrians, as important as it may be. The disappointment born of failure and the frustration of the regime's victims have caused a great build-up of violence in the Syrian psyche. This violence periodically explodes into nihilistic arguments and mudslinging between opposition figures,

---

[27] Ali Madouni and Hichem Derradji, 'The Caesar Law for the Protection of Civilians in Syria: Objectives and Ramifications', *Prizren Social Science Journal* 4, no. 3 (2020), 63–4.

who sometimes go so far as to accuse one another of betraying, profiteering off or conspiring against the revolution. No one is safe from these accusations. Mutual recriminations instead of sober, rational critique is the rule in the slough of despondency, but even that has an endpoint. Some critical retrospectives are being published, and a new generation of Syrian academics is in the rise.

Between mid-2013 and 2021, the signs of the catastrophe that I had feared and warned of if no transitional political settlement was reached proliferated rapidly. Although the regime has not fallen, the last decade has made a dramatic break with the rest of Syria's modern history. This period does not resemble any that came before it.

Introduction

The Syrian revolution cannot be understood or analysed apart from the revolutionary climate that swept the Arab world following the Tunisian and Egyptian revolutions, for these constituted its main trigger. The political causes of the revolution in Syria had been present for decades, and there had been times when the Syrian regime appeared weaker than it was in early 2011. New economic and social causes emerged due to the neoliberal policies of the last decade, but the Syrian revolution took place when the regime was particularly stable and finally emerging from its international isolation after the war on Iraq (2003) and especially after the assassination of Lebanese Prime Minister Rafiq al-Hariri (14 February 2005). The catalyst was the particular historical moment made relevant by Syrians' cultural, political and emotional identification with the events unfolding in the Arab region – one of many ironies in a revolution against a regime that had always stressed its Arab identity.

In the early stages of the Arab uprisings, the Syrian regime made little effort to hide its mixed feelings of glee and anxiety at the fall of Mubarak and Ben Ali. It took consolation from the fact that it maintained a different foreign policy than that of the fallen regimes – Syria was after all a 'resistance regime' on the front line of the battle against global imperialism. In Damascus, the fall of the Egyptian regime was put down to Mubarak's foreign policy, a discourse used to explain Egypt's popular revolt and to stress the difference between the regime in Damascus and those in Cairo and Tunis. This issue was not marginal to regime resilience. Mubarak and Ben Ali did not have ideological products to sell, but the Syrian regime had plenty in its populist discourse, and some people in the Arab world bought the idea of universal conspiracy against an anti-imperialist regime. But what really distinguished Assad's regime from its Arab counterparts was its categorical rejection of political reform and its readiness to employ unbridled violence against its people.

Many analysts fail to understand what drove the protest movement in Syria due to their exclusive focus on an immediate cause that spurred the people of Daraa to take to the streets in March 2011. But it is equally misguided to focus exclusively on economic factors and social policies to explain the eruption of protests in marginalized regions while ignoring the impact of the revolutionary upheaval in the Arab region starting at the end of 2010. Every conceivable trigger for revolt, direct and indirect, already existed, and the preceding years – if not decades – had witnessed abuses and repression far worse than what Daraa experienced in 2011. But none of it set off an uprising or a popular revolution. In other words, this 'routine' repression was not the immediate cause of the uprising. Rather, the Syrian revolution was part of the Arab revolutionary tide that started in Tunisia, ushering in a new era in which Arabs flocked to public spaces as citizens asserting demands, decrying corruption and despotism, and expressing their aspiration for change and democratic transition. The Syrian revolution was not a mere social protest. Even before it snowballed into a fully-fledged political revolution, demonstrators were already demanding political reform. From the early days, it was a political revolt against the way the Syrian people were governed.

The reverse, however, is also true. If aspirations for change spread easily across the Arab world, so too does the fear of change. The instability that follows revolutions, not unlike the chaos that often emerges during transitional phases, can generate an aversion to change among the populace, a vulnerability that Arab authoritarian regimes exploit so as to reinforce and reassert stability in their own countries. One need only look at the disintegration of the Iraqi state under the weight of foreign military invasion in order to conclude that it deterred neighbouring societies from seeking change and led them to choose 'stability' instead, even if under an unjust government. By contrast, the peaceful revolts in Egypt and Tunisia showed Syrians how their will could be expressed peacefully without fomenting civil war. The Libyan case, on the other hand, demonstrated a third path, at least before the slide into civil war and mayhem: foreign intervention after a revolution against an authoritarian regime.

Syrians felt change was feasible, particularly in the immediate aftermath of the revolutions, before the complications of the transitional phase began to unfold in Egypt and Tunisia.

Neighbouring Lebanon (since 1975) and Iraq (since 2003) naturally had a great influence on Syrians as crude examples of the civil strife that is likely to appear under a weak state. Syrian demonstrators thus initially demanded regime reform even though they were marching under the influence of other Arab revolutions that openly called for the overthrow of their despotic regimes. In part, this is why I argue that the Syrian revolution might have been avoided – or even contained after it had got underway – by reform. But this would have required the regime to understand the political mood of its people, their memories and fears, and their demands.

It would have had to change its entire approach to its people and undertake genuine reforms.[1]

Some factions within Syria's emigre opposition were insensitive to such distinctions. Influenced more by the Libyan revolution than events in Tunisia or Egypt, they were quick to call for foreign intervention to bring down the regime. In doing so they neglected the fact that it was the peaceful Arab revolts that had encouraged Syrians to rise up. Even more, they misunderstood that the Syrian regime was not wrong to believe that its apparently principled foreign policy (against imperialism, the US and Israel) genuinely did heighten its legitimacy in the eyes of its people. The emigres considered the regime's political claims to be meaningless propaganda, failing to see that most Syrians on the ground, witnessing the repercussions of such intervention still unfolding in Iraq, did not favour foreign intervention. Syrians also remembered that even after the war in Iraq, the regime found ways to come to an understanding with the West, especially the US, based on the regime's vital security role, which it usually proved by aggravating the very problems that it was later called to help in solving.[2] Any rational analysis of the dangers of instability in the crescent of Iraq, Syria Lebanon and the non-intervention policies of Barack Obama would conclude that American intervention in Syria was not on the agenda.[3] And while it is true that the repressive character of the Syrian regime is quite different from its Tunisian and Egyptian counterparts, conditions in Syria and Libya were also utterly different, particularly when it came to social structure and geopolitical position, and considering that Obama was dragged into the aerial intervention in Libya by France and Britain, which were already there.

This point about reform versus revolution, or peaceful versus armed revolution, must be stressed – not to prove some ideological claim, but in order to demonstrate the regime's historical responsibility for choosing the

---

[1] I said this prior to the revolution and made the same argument in an earlier media interview (28 March 2011) at a time when the idea of the departure of the president was not yet on the table, unlike the situation during the revolutions of Egypt and Tunisia. In that interview I wondered why, if the regime claimed that this was a Western conspiracy, it then promised, at least verbally, to implement reforms? No state would meet a foreign conspiracy with reforms unless the regime acknowledged that there were rightful popular demands. And was possible to proceed with reforms when there were no demands for regime change. See: YouTube, 29 March 2011, at: https://bit.ly/3IQUeLM (accessed 16 December 2021).

[2] In October 2005 when American-Syrian relations were in their lowest ebb, after the assassination of Hariri and when the US was still considered to be victorious in Iraq and had an overwhelming presence in the region, Former Secretary of State Condoleezza Rice said, 'What we have focused on is getting the Syrian regime to change its behavior.' See: US Department of State, 16 October 2005, at: https://bit.ly/3b2Jf5z (accessed 15 June 2022). This focus not on regime change, but attitude change was repeated several times by US officials.

[3] Joshua Landis, 'The Syrian Uprising of 2011: Why the Asad Regime is Likely to Survive to 2013?' *Middle East Policy* 19, no. 1 (Spring 2012), 77–8.

path of armed violence. It also allows for a more sophisticated analysis of the problematic Syrian 'we', enabling us to address questions of belonging and identity that are always present during revolutions and the intellectual debates surrounding them. Such questions are among the most important future challenges facing a diverse society like Syria.

Aside from a sense of shared identity fostered and cemented by Arab television, media and the internet, there are other commonalities that allow one to speak of a specifically *Arab* revolution or describe the revolutionary movement as Arab. Prime among these considerations is the shared sense among Arabs that they live in the shadow of corrupt dictatorships. Arabs are connected by their aspiration for freedom since they are all bound – to varying degrees – by the same dictatorial chains.[4] An awareness of this fact has long been building and is prior to any analysis of Arab regimes themselves, which came to resemble each other after the end of the Cold War with the neoliberal adjustment to globalization, the decay of populist authoritarianism, the incremental transition from party politics to neopatrimonialism and initiation of cosmetic reforms. Arab regimes became more similar in composition regardless of differences in social structure, foreign policy, and regional and international alliances.

In post-independence Arab states, the longevity of dictatorships has served to blur the lines between republics and monarchies. Almost invariably, Arab regimes came to consist of ruling families (with or without a ruling party) and security apparatuses loyal to them. These two pillars may be buttressed by a clique of businessmen either built or reshaped by the regime and closely bound to it by ties of kinship and political fealty. These states are usually controlled by the security services and through the management and distribution of political patronage or the management of diversity, which is a prime characteristic of the Arab Levant, including Syria.[5]

The fissures that may result from the politicization of the 'social mosaic', or the diverse confessional and ethnic identity groups in the Arab Levant, are not a new phenomenon. This existential threat has regularly reared its head during national crises and at critical historical junctures. Conversely however, the anti-colonial struggle for national liberation, for instance, gave rise to a unifying tendency among confessional communities in the Levant. The developing discourse of national liberation served to cement

---

[4] Azmi Bishara, *On the Arab Question: Preface to an Arab Democratic Manifesto* [Arabic], 2nd edn (Beirut: Centre for Arab Unity Studies, 2010), 9. Also see Azmi Bishara's lecture at Cairo University after the revolution titled, 'Yearning for Freedom after the Arab Revolutions' [Arabic], 10 June 2011. Available on: YouTube, 14 June 2011, at: https://bit.ly/3yumBuB (accessed 16 December 2021).

[5] My analysis of the composition of Arab regimes and Arab countries' susceptibility to revolution was published in Arabic before this book, but it can now be found in English: Bishara, *Understanding Revolutions*, 37.

modern political concepts that went a long way to surmounting sub- and pre-national identities, weakening their hold over individuals' attitudes and containing their potential to fragment society.⁶

Post-independence, however, nation states in the Levant have failed in their capacity as political regimes to exploit this unifying tendency to generate an inclusive national identity, creating instead new political mechanisms to manage identitarian diversity. All sorts of reasons – sometimes good ones – are cited for this failure, both foreign (colonial hegemony and control) and domestic (the rise of ideological religious or ethnic movements that have reinvigorated subnational and sectarian identities or advanced separatist claims that threaten the state's territorial and political integrity). In this way, the rich social canvass of the Arab Levant has become a minefield: the politicization of its diversity transformed it from a blessing into a curse.

Diversity is embedded in the social fabric of the Levant. Were it to be integrated into a well-considered strategy of state-building on the basis of equal citizenship and cultural commonalities – a strategy that encouraged communal interaction without erasing difference – it could become a source of strength and resilience. In short, diversity, if managed wisely, is not a driver of division and weakness, but if poorly managed, it can become a liability. This is especially the case when regimes resort to tacit deals and quotas among different sects and identity groups with the absence of equal citizenship, or when a regime that is not ideologically or structurally sectarian begins to politically manipulate subnational identities and to formulate policy towards them that reflects its own immediate interests. Intersecting regional, familial, tribal and sectarian or ethnic loyalties and identities can easily be exploited to secure fealty through – for instance – recruitment policies in the security agencies. There is enough evidence to suggest that this has been the policy in Syria in recent decades, especially under the Assads, a topic that will be covered more extensively in the section on sectarianism and social diversity in Syria.

One of the most significant characteristics shared by all Arab regimes on the eve of the revolutions was the expansive, all-encompassing role of the security establishment. A major pillar of both monarchic and republican

---

⁶ 'The best example of this would be that of modern Arab societies, which witnessed until relatively recently an exponential evolution of national allegiances and the political blocs representing them, before they fell victim to the modern regimes of despotism starting in the 1970s. These societies were no less traditional or diverse (religiously, ethnically and otherwise) than they are today; nevertheless, they produced impressive national movements whose birth and evolution constituted the first step towards independence and the expulsion of foreign occupation forces.' See: Burhan Ghalioun, *The Sectarian Question and the Problem of Minorities* [Arabic], 3rd edn (Beirut and Doha: ACRPS, 2012), 16.

regimes, the security apparatus closely monitored society as a whole and interfered with every aspect of citizens' lives.[7] In the Arab world, the security establishment has gone beyond its traditional repressive function to assume a more visible role, playing an active part in politics and involving itself directly in business investments. This has paved the way for a kind of corruption and misconduct without precedent even under older dictatorships. Security organs have in this manner shut down the public space for any opposition political activity, exploiting societal contradictions and cleavages to maintain their own social networks and sources of tribute. A mutual relationship of clientelism and favouritism was thus established between the regime and parts of the business community, supplanting a civic relationship based on laws and national economic policies that provide the framework for economic activity. While such a framework may be exploited by capital, likewise it may be used to impose restrictions on the movement of capital.

In Syria's case, this crony capitalism took the form of an alliance between the political regime and select circles within the urban bourgeoisie, who were given all manner of accommodations, privileges, grants, and public contracts and tenders in return for political fealty and commissions.[8] The

---

[7] The security agencies in Syria are divided into four main organs, with dozens of branches in the various Syrian cities and regions. Since Hafez al-Assad's ascension to power, these services have been under the direct control of the president, regardless of their formal administrative affiliations:

1) <u>The Military Intelligence Apparatus</u>: Also known as 'military security', it was led by Brigadier Abd al-Fattah Qudsiyyah, and before him Asef Shawkat, Hassan Khalil and Ali Duba. This organ is affiliated with the armed forces. Until the outbreak of the revolution it was considered the most influential among Syria's security services. Many senior leaders and security officials have come out of this institution. Military Intelligence has several subdivisions, most notably the Palestine Branch (or Branch 235), which though ostensibly devoted to combating Israeli espionage, ended up focusing on domestic political issues, such as Islamist movements in Syria. Few examples are more expressive of the state's demarche of conflating domestic and foreign adversaries, and its tendency to accuse political dissidents of being agents for Israel, than the fact that the Palestine Branch was charged with combating Syrian and Palestinian political opponents.
2) <u>The General Intelligence Apparatus</u>: Also known as the 'State Security Apparatus', with several sub-departments, such as the Internal Security Branch, which nominally specialized in the security of the capital, but expanded its influence under some of its stronger leaders to surpass the General Intelligence Apparatus itself, though formally speaking, it is but a branch of General Intelligence. The branch was especially powerful when managed by politically influential officials who were close to the president, such as Muhammad Nasif Khayrbek (and Bahjat Sulayman, for a shorter period). General Intelligence has other branches, such as the External Branch (Branch 279) and the Information Branch, which specializes in the media and monitors writers, journalists, and print, electronic and audio-visual media outlets.
3) <u>The Political Security Apparatus</u>: Theoretically affiliated with the Ministry of Interior. The director of the Political Security branch in any governorate is for all intents and purposes the most senior security official in the governorate.
4) <u>Air Force Intelligence</u>: This apparatus was designed to follow up on foreign military issues, but it has engaged in public political life in Syria since the 1982 Hama massacre, when it participated in the repression of civilians, becoming one of the organs involved in domestic surveillance and political repression.

[8] Bishara, *On the Arab Question*, 95.

profits were shared as part of a system of direct partnership or through more subtle networks of corruption, creating a complex network of interests which saw the intersection of political, security, economic, and even ideological and religious elements, especially when it came to the security services' relationship with the pro-regime intelligentsia and clerics. These networks tend to be difficult to penetrate or subvert as they operate beyond the purview of any court, law or professional standard.

A dictatorial, violent, corrupt regime cannot hold sway so absolutely without influencing society's values. A certain kind of astuteness – a culture of resourcefulness and guile without concern for moral probity – pervades even the smallest transactions, while social solidarity manifests itself on the level of local communities (or what remained from them), charity and family. Violence becomes a natural way of resolving problems, the rule rather than the exception. Shedding such deep cultural and psychological artifacts is difficult, and even a society rebelling against the regime will inevitably carry some trace of them within it. When corruption prevails and the security establishment is all-powerful, avenues for social and legal redress are narrowed, and people lose the ability to shield themselves from the abuse of authority by resorting to the mercy of a higher authority. Under such a regime, citizens simply flee one kind of corruption for another. They can only protect themselves from one security agency by appealing to another, and this 'service' comes at a cost. Or they find social and moral refuge in all kinds of local traditional or constructed communities.

The degree to which the security forces control the public sphere varies from one country to another, as does the margin of freedom they permit their citizens. We have many reasons to believe that, despite the ruthlessness they bring to their primary mission, security agencies generally have a more pragmatic understanding of politics than political decision-makers. They may be more brutal than required, but they also have an intimate knowledge of the social and political reality, and study the potential for crises and unrest more closely and objectively than regime 'theorists' or decision-makers.

With all this in mind, it might be argued that the motives and causes for protest in Syria were structurally similar to those of the other Arab revolutions: Syrians seek freedom and dignity, and yearn for the rights of citizenship just like other Arabs. However, Syria is a composite country containing multiple religious, sectarian and ethnic groups. The ruling elite's dependence on core, loyal identity groups in the internal struggles for power in the party and among officers fostered the creation of communal networks that blur the lines between the social and the political, intersecting both vertically and horizontally, and thereby enabling the regime to exploit the communal loyalty of the security services and army officers in its unchecked use of violence.[9]

The second difference concerns Syria's political and geostrategic position. Syria's regime is closer to an international axis that not only does not support any democratic transition anywhere in the world – never mind within its own sphere – but also considers any such transition to be a geostrategic expansion by the US and Western powers. The third difference is the regime's near-complete alienation from the populace it rules, which it approaches as a sort of domestic colonizer. The regime may successfully exploit its alliances with social forces and the commercial and capitalist classes in order to further its control, but it does not view itself as part of these groups nor as their representative. It considers any show of leniency, to say nothing of real reform, a weakness that can be used by the people to overthrow the regime and retaliate. This, in addition to the absolute loyalty of the security organs, helps to explain its unprecedented brutality in suppressing protests, which escalated to the bombardment of entire cities in the later stages of the revolution. Loyalty alone, however, cannot explain such brutality. There is no doubt that there exist other social and cultural factors that must be considered in order to explain regime violence.

The biggest threat facing complex societies in which the concepts of the modern nation state and citizenship have only tenuous purchase is when a

---

[9] I wish, once again, to take the opportunity to point to my early analyses of this reality, offered before events in Syria escalated to a quasi-civil war. While this has not been my practice in other books and writings on the Arab revolutions, in the case of Syria, I feel that citations of early analyses and warnings demonstrate that it was possible to predict the direction in which events were heading and that expressions of surprise at the outcome are disingenuous. I also view these quotations as one real-time account of the evolution of the revolution. In a May 2011 interview on the complexity of the societal make-up of Syria and the Arab Levant compared to Egypt and Tunisia, and how that affects the revolution, I stressed the following: 'In the Arab Levant the situation is much more complex because Western colonialism gained a foothold in the Ottoman Empire on the pretext of protecting minorities. In addition, despotism did not allow for the creation of a civic identity or the expansion of the reach of Arab culture to become a more open and inclusive cultural patrimony. Under these conditions, people turned in many cases to other entities such as tribes, clans, confessional communities (sects), etc. Of course, the sect is the most dangerous. It is more dangerous than tribalism because it can become the regional fuel for regional solidarities, transnational in some cases. Of course, sectarianism was fostered and exploited by regimes whenever they saw fit, and colonial powers exploited it as well whenever they wished, and now we have a problem that must be confronted. The first thing is to strengthen citizenship, in the relationship between citizens themselves and in their relationship with the state; moreover, a state of institutions must be built, one that deals with individuals as citizens, regardless of their national, ethnic, sectarian or tribal affiliation. This is what I term "the state of citizens" or the state for all its citizens, rather than the state of this group or that. Naturally, citizens may also harbour Arab nationalist solidarities with groups of citizens from different countries and sects developing a sense of unity through Arabism, while also feeling unity, through citizenship, with non-Arab citizens, say, Kurdish citizens. In other words, various citizens have intersecting identities. Individuals live with multiple identities and have intersecting identities, which actually enrich social life. Of course, what happened after the revolutions was that the power and stature of the state and its institutions weakened. In such instances of turbulence – turmoil in social and cultural life as well as values – people tend to cling to their closest affiliations.' See the interview titled 'The Fridays of Arab Revolutions' [Arabic], on 13 May 2011. Available at: *Al Jazeera*, 19 July 2011, at: https://bit.ly/3GIKkK8 (accessed 16 December 2021).

certain identity group, be it a minority or a majority, comes to believe it 'owns' the state, although in fact, it is the state that owns the loyalty of that community. In such circumstances, affirming other identities becomes dissident behaviour and an affront to the identity of the group that lays claim to the state (or whose supposed representatives act as if this were the case).[10] To make things worse, if this group is a minority with a sense of historical victimization even when its members are the victimizers, it is often more willing to act repressively. In the land of sectarianism every community is told by its own sectarians that it is the ultimate victim. Minorities must therefore exert more violence to deter the majority. Furthermore, victimhood can become a tool of vengeance, wielded for the purpose of avenging a history of suffering, real or imagined, and motivated as well by fear of the future. As a result of these dynamics, the politics of identity bleeds into politics and political activism more generally, which risks splitting struggles for justice or purely political conflicts on the basis of communal identity.

This is largely due to the state's failure to gradually develop its public and universalizing functions – meaning its ability to universalize law and citizenship, disassociate itself from sub-identities and imagine a universal citizenship that cuts across communal identities.[11]

Since the ruling regime keeps the loyalty of segments of society in times of crisis, what makes it difficult to separate the regime from communal ties is what makes it equally hard to separate the state from the regime. Achieving this separation is what enabled Egyptians and Tunisians to demand the overthrow of the regimes in their countries without splitting along identity lines. The ability to separate and distinguish the state from the regime was what led the army to refrain from employing military force in support of the regime in its struggle against the people in Tunisia and Egypt, notwithstanding the army's motivations to do so. In Syria, where such lines are blurred, the regime appeared simultaneously more coherent and more brutal, the pro-regime security agencies and the army having set no red lines in the use of violence.

When the Syrian people moved from protest to revolution aiming to overthrow the regime, the people split. The regime maintained the loyalty of its own community, which controls the security forces, thereby precluding the possibility of a coup or even the army's neutrality.[12] In addition, the

---

[10] Bishara, *On the Arab Question*, 190.
[11] Azmi Bishara, *Civil Society: A Critical Study* [Arabic], 6th edn (Doha and Beirut: ACRPS, 2011), 310.
[12] Joshua Landis considered the loyalty of a minority controlling the security forces a source of strength for the regime: 'Some analysts estimated that as many 80 per cent of Syria's officer corps is Alawi [...] The main strike forces, such as the Republican Guard led by Bashar's brother, are overwhelmingly Alawi. Many of the divisions made up of enlisted Sunnis have not been deployed to quell the uprising.' He concludes that 'Syria's feeble sense of political community has been the regime's greatest asset'. Landis, 'The Syrian Uprising of 2011', 73–4.

regime maintained the support of other confessional minorities that felt threatened and cross-sectarian segments of society that benefited from its neoliberal policies. That is why revolution in such a country forebodes a civil war.

From the start, the Syrian regime met the reformist protest movement with rhetoric about 'sectarian sedition', alleging it was a conspiracy targeting Syria's social stability which needed to be suppressed by any means necessary. The regime knew that many parts of Syrian society were scared that events would move in a sectarian direction. It would be wrong to say that this discourse has failed to achieve its purpose.

The regime thus sent its army into battle, a domestic battle it assumed would end quickly with the crushing of the popular revolution. The plan was to follow this victory with cosmetic reforms at its own convenience – over the course of decades, if not generations. Bashar al-Assad said as much to *The Wall Street Journal* on 31 January 2011, when he rejected the adoption of immediate, radical reforms. In his view, Syria was in need of institution-building and the improvement of education prior to the opening-up of the political system, because 'the rising demands for rapid political reforms could turn out to be counter-productive if Arab societies aren't ready for them'.[13] At the same time, Assad called upon Arab leaders to learn from the lessons of Ben Ali and Mubarak and to quickly respond to the economic and political aspirations of their populations. This was two months before the outbreak of the Syrian revolution, when the writing was already on the wall. Nevertheless, the only lessons he learned from the fall of Ben Ali and Mubarak is that they did not (or could not) use enough force in supressing the revolt.

Assad's interview showed the regime's palpable fear that any real reform could lead to regime breakdown. He cast these sentiments in a paternalist, orientalist language that targeted the Western ear, arguing that the people were not yet 'mature' enough for political reform.

Let us not forget that the regime that we see here belittling Arabs to a Western audience and casting doubt on their readiness not only for democracy but even for *reform* is the very same regime that claims to resist the West and its racism in propaganda directed to the Arab public. The Western orientalists and politicians who make such claims about Arabs and Muslims are at least democrats within their own societies, arguing that the other culture has not yet matured to their level. Assad, on the other hand, is not a democrat, neither in practice nor in theory. His 'concerns' about political reform in his country were nothing more than a cynical attempt to play to Western racism, luring the West closer to his position

---

[13] *The Wall Street Journal*, 31 January 2011, at: https://on.wsj.com/3GRvl0u (accessed 16 December 2011).

and turning it against his 'backward' society. Internally, demands for reforms and institution building were considered part of an imperialist conspiracy, but the same Western powers Assad called imperialists in his Ba'th speech to Syrians were cast as his allies against his own society.

Neither do Assad and his regime represent, in the historical sense, the rule of an aristocratic elite that sees itself as being above 'the plebs' and democracy. His regime continued to adopt a populist discourse even after it stopped being a populist regime, in economic terms at least. Syria's security services and businessmen are a far cry from a philosophical elite implementing an enlightened despotism while preparing the people for democracy. It is indeed too backwards to establish the kind of totalitarianism it craved – even when the regime of Hafez al-Assad attempted to mimic European totalitarian regimes through popular festivals, military parades, and statues and banners, these spectacles were tacky and embarrassing. Unlike totalitarian regimes, Assad's legacy failed to penetrate every level of society and culture. His regime lacked the administrative and technological ability to manage society as if it were a machine – even for the short period during which such regimes (fascist or communist) typically delude themselves that they have united the people, the state and the party. The Syrian regime could not achieve this level of totalitarianism, thriving instead on security repression, partisan and ideological demagoguery, and economic corruption.

Assad's regime adopted a condescending tone that patronized the people from its high ledge with paternalistic lectures reminiscent of an old-fashioned classroom (we will return to this tone in the next chapter).

The official Syrian media uses such discourse to communicate with Syrian citizens, as if they were children and its task were to educate them, using propaganda and lies when need be, all for their own good. The work of the media thus complements that of the security agencies, whose firmer brand of discipline teaches the people that they should never dare rebel against their 'masters'.

Damascus's public analysis of the Egyptian and Tunisian revolutions was that the governments of those countries had become alienated from the masses; as a staunch supporter of anti-imperialist causes, the Syrian regime was much closer to public opinion. After the uprising in Daraa, however, it drew a very different conclusion – that Mubarak and Ben Ali had been toppled because they had failed to crush the uprisings by brute force because the army was not blindly loyal to them. The Syrian regime, on the other hand, was immune to this 'problem', possessing more than enough enthusiasm for repression and the use of force. This conclusion determined its approach throughout the Syrian revolution, alongside its attempts to play on middle class and communal fears (especially of confessional minorities) of anarchy and sectarian strife. For a short period, the regime's gamble paid off. After long and heroic attempts to stay the course of peaceful protest – despite sustained and systematic violence against demonstrators from the army, the security forces and regime militias – the people finally took up arms.

This book attempts to trace the course of the Syrian revolution in broad strokes from the first stirrings of protest through its peaceful early stages. I will also examine the social dynamics of the revolution, its transformation into an armed revolution and the resulting violent revolutionary, criminal and sectarian phenomena that grew out of it. I will discuss the initiatives aiming for a political solution, especially the efforts of the Arab League and the accompanying Arab, regional and international engagements. One section is devoted to the description of the politics and conduct of the opposition during the revolution. Although this book does not aim to study the history of Syria and its society and economy, it is impossible to understand the Syrian revolution in an in-depth manner without an overview of the regime structure, its discourse and the rule of Bashar al-Assad since he took power in 2000, a phase during which the regime squandered the opportunity for political reform and gradual democratic transition and lost the social constituency of the Baʻth Party due to neoliberal economic reforms that harmed the peasants, the poor and the middle classes.

The peaceful revolution was active throughout 2011, producing civic organizations such as coordination committees and popular committees that led the local popular movement and eventually reached a degree of nationwide coordination. Day- and night-time solidarity demonstrations and popular gatherings became widespread, featuring songs and poems in the dialect of each region, in a display that surpassed other Arab revolutions. Amid this show of national solidarity and the ecstasy of experiencing dignity and freedom after years of humiliation – and against a constant background rhythm of violence and sacrifice – the features of a pluralistic Syrian national identity began to crystallize in a democratic manner through the struggle against dictatorship. However, it was given one year full of sacrifices, a relatively brief respite before the civil war broke out.

In this context, this book makes four critical points on the issue of Syrian identity:

First, the premise that it is the ideology and practice of the Syrian regime that has prevented the formation of a Syrian national identity needs to be outlined from the start. The notion of Syrian citizenship has never been enshrined in law, nor is it linked to rights. It is based on regional, tribal and sectarian affiliations, all the while propagating Arab identity as a state ideology.

Second, the experience of the Syrian revolution is the first moment since independence in which such a sense of national identity has taken shape – the first moment to join Daraa with Latakia, Hama with Idleb, Deir ez-Zor with Homs and Aleppo with Damascus, as mirrored in the omnipresent slogan 'Syrians are one people'. This nascent national identity is based on Syrians' experience of a 'homogeneous time' during the days and events of the revolution and on a sense of a shared destiny uniting all the regions of Syria in the face of the regime.

Third, ironically, the very revolution that has been so central to the formation of this Syrian national identity has also placed it at a vital crossroads. One path leads to sectarian schisms, which may lend this new national identity a sectarian Sunni character. The other path is that of democratic citizenship, which could underpin a national identity that is compatible with the Arab and Muslim identity of the majority of Syria's population.

Fourth, while the peaceful revolution took the latter path, the armed revolt that erupted in response to the military regime's choice to quell the revolution has been more inclined towards sectarianism, increasing its risks. An armed revolution cannot avoid playing the 'game of nations', which, in the Levant, usually produces consociational models that negate Arab and state-national identities in favour of various sub-identities while reflecting the interests of whatever other states are involved in brokering such settlements.

I will also discuss here the Syrian revolution against the social and political background of Bashar al-Assad's rule, going back to how the regime of Hafez al-Assad and later Bashar dissolved the Alawi sect into the state apparatus until the former was fully atomized and individual Alawis came to depend wholly on the state apparatus. I will discuss the influence of other Arab revolutions on Syrian society based on that existing background. I will also detail the history of the revolution (March 2011 until March 2013), or what I term 'current history', explaining its transformation from a group of regional uprisings into a revolution and analysing its political, social and military structure, as well as the sectarian question and international factors. In addition, I will look at the strategy employed by the regime against the revolution and consider various models to explain the regime's behaviour. In doing so I will show that the regime was responsible for turning the peaceful revolution into an armed one, leading to a civil war.

In other words, this book presents the readers with an attempt to analyse a complex psycho-socio-political phenomenon and to reconstruct it in a manner that makes it possible to recognize its features and better understand Syria's revolution.

1

The bitter harvest: The first ten years of Bashar al-Assad

Recapitulating the first decade of Bashar al-Assad's rule, this chapter provides an overview of the period between his ascent to power in July 2000 and the outbreak of the protest movement in Syria on 15 March 2011. The decade was marked by hastily broken promises of reform made by the president at the beginning of his tenure and sparks of protest, some of them making specific socioeconomic demands and others expressing political discontent. To understand these early protests, this chapter examines several individual cases, including the Hariqa Market incident of 17 February 2011 and the Libyan embassy sit-in of 22 February 2011.

I. Wasted opportunities

When the Arab revolutions began in December 2010 and January 2011, most Syrians – including those involved in the nascent protest movement – expected the regime to recognize the significance of the Arab revolutionary climate in the region. They hoped for a strategy of gradual reform with clear objectives: a pre-emptive settlement between the regime and its people. Such a strategy would have meant meeting Syrians' fundamental demands and starting a process of democratic transition. It might have prevented Syria from setting off down the perilous path that has since led to the collapse of its entire social environment and propelled it into a protracted phase of instability and sectarian realignment, a consequence of the diverse make-up of its society.

It was precisely because Syrians were aware of these lurking threats, and of the regime's unscrupulous harshness when facing political dissent, that protesters did not initially call for the overthrow of the regime, unlike their counterparts in Egypt or Tunisia.

The same anxieties were at work at the time of Bashar al-Assad's ascent to the presidency in 2000. In that year Syrians – including the opposition – largely accepted the son taking his deceased father's place (which established a new precedent in the Arab republics) because they were afraid of destabilizing the country and dragging Syria into conflict. Many, too, feared the possibility of another wave of mass repression similar to that of the 1970s and 1980s – most notoriously the 1982 events in Hama, which were formative for Syrians' relationship with the regime. More importantly, by 2000, many Syrians were ready to accept any form of change and wanted to believe that Bashar al-Assad could be its emissary. And after 'the young heir'[1] took the opportunity granted by his inaugural speech on 17 July 2000[2] to promise reform, they hoped that he would modernize the regime and the state.

Syrians thus grudgingly accepted the younger Assad's accession to the presidency. His father had been Syria's autocrat for three decades, and there was hope that his departure would mean important changes regardless of who replaced him. The rumour mill soon ascribed all sorts of positive qualities to the young president-in-waiting: his modern mentality, his brief period living in the West, his relationship with the business class and his efforts to promote IT infrastructure in Syria since his designation as heir apparent. This was almost enough to distract from the state's flagrant violation of the constitution and the mechanisms by which the succession was guaranteed – even when the 'popular referendum' confirming his accession on 10 July 2000, in which an unlikely 97.3 per cent of the votes were cast in his favour, was described in frankly medieval terms as a *mubaya'a*, or 'oath of allegiance'.[3]

At any rate, the generation that rebelled in 2011 was a generation born after the Hama massacre of 1982 and after the dismantling of the bipolar international system of the Cold War. This generation had come of age under the younger Assad and was not captive to the ideological credos of his father's era – credos that by now were little more than a particularly tedious part of the school curriculum. They also had access to media outlets other than official state television. They were not as easily intimidated by

---

[1] In early 1994, when Bassil al-Assad, the eldest son of Hafez al-Assad, died in a car accident, his brother Bashar was twenty-eight years old and leading a fairly normal life. Within less than a year, he had been transformed into a volunteer first lieutenant, and within three he had been promoted to colonel (despite the legal requirement that any prospective colonel have at least fifteen years of service). In the hours following his father's death, Colonel Assad was promoted yet again, this time to general; he was also made commander-in-chief of the armed forces and president of the republic who won 97.3 per cent of the vote.

[2] See the full speech at: *Al-Bab*, 17 July 2000, at: https://bit.ly/33LRDTd (accessed 26 December 2021).

[3] Note that not only are the numbers usually exaggerated and referendums in Syria are not free elections, but also that the real rate of voter turnout is never announced. Figures from the top echelons of the regime complained to me about low voter participation rates (around 20 per cent) in spite of the known methods of persuasion and intimidation. In this light, a return of 97.35 per cent for 'yes' votes may be realistic since it would be safer to refrain from participating in the referendum than voting 'no'.

the horrors of Hama, which to them were a story told by the older generation rather than a living memory.

The young president's promises of reform triggered an immediate shift in the political environment. Elitist civil political forums began to spread in which current issues were discussed and demands for reform raised – the so-called 'Damascus Spring'. This movement was led by the opposition and mainly represented by figures from the National Democratic Rally (NDR)[4] and a number of Syrian leftists, Arab nationalist and liberal intellectuals. It aspired to become a national democratic partner that could help the regime reform. And to the dismay of the security apparatus, it regularly justified its activities with reference to ethical maxims in the young president's speeches, seeking to legitimize these activities in the eyes of the state.

Many saw the Damascus Spring as heralding democratic change in Syria. For the first time, critical subjects were up for public debate.[5] On 16 November 2000, the government released 600 political prisoners. In 2001, the first privately owned newspaper in four decades was authorized (suspended in 2003).[6] There were discussions on an end to the state of emergency,[7] political freedoms, a national dialogue conference for all political forces in Syria and the abolition of Article 8 of the Syrian constitution (which makes the Baʿth Party the leader of the state and society),[8] as well as a modern political party law that would allow for political pluralism, competitive presidential elections permitting the peaceful rotation of power and the imposition of presidential term limits.

---

[4] Founded in 1979, the National Democratic Rally (NDR), or the National Democratic Gathering, later became the core of the Damascus Declaration (DD) coalition. The NDR continued to operate as an umbrella organization until the founding of the National Coordination Body for Democratic Change (NCB) in Syria. The NDR was a political coalition representing the major opposition parties. It was established in 1979 during the confrontation with the Muslim Brotherhood, and includes the Democratic Arab Socialist Union, the Revolutionary Arab Workers' Party, the Democratic People's Party (formerly the Syrian Communist Party – Politburo), the Arab Socialist Movement and the Democratic Arab Socialist Baʿth Party (although no representative has attended a meeting in twenty years). Its leadership committee consists of ten members, two for each member party.

[5] Najib Ghadbian, 'The New Asad: Dynamics of Continuity and Change in Syria', *Middle East Journal* 55, no. 4 (Autumn 2001), 624–41.

[6] Ibid.

[7] In September 2000, some ninety-nine Syrian intellectuals signed a statement calling on the Syrian authorities to end the state of emergency and abolish martial law, which had been in place in Syria since 1963. See: 'Syria's Intellectuals Call for an End to the State of Emergency and the Release of Detainees', in *The Damascus Spring: Issues, Currents and Endings* [Arabic], ed. Radwan Ziadeh, Reform Issues Series 17 (Cairo: Cairo Institute for Human Rights Studies, 2007), 293–7.

[8] Article 8 of the Syrian constitution of 1973 (which was adopted on 13 March 1973 and remained in force until 27 February 2012) states: 'The leading party in the society and the state is the Socialist Arab Baʿth Party. It leads a patriotic and progressive front seeking to unify the resources of the popular masses and to place them at the service of the Arab nation's goals.' See: 'The Syrian Constitution – 1973–2012', Carnegie Middle East Centre, at: https://bit.ly/3qqv9Pp (accessed 26 December 2021).

The regime's tolerance for these demands, however, was short-lived. Promises of real reform soon dissipated: reform was reduced to neoliberal economic reforms in alignment with new business networks and modernization was understood by the president as empowering young technocrats close to him against the party bureaucracy.[9] Repression by the security forces resumed its well-established role as the main mechanism for sustaining power and controlling society. Commentators who did not want to give up hope excused the young new president, accusing the so-called 'old guard' of blocking his reforms. Others claimed that as a newcomer he was too weak for the presidency, comparing him unfavourably to his father. But, as I will later show, neither claim was true.[10] He inherited a presidency which was much stronger than the one his father seized and it took him time and effort to consolidate it. His father consulted the party leadership – people of his own age who travelled much of the road with him. In contrast, Bashar, especially after breaking Syria's international isolation in 2007, viewed such consultation as a sign of weakness, although he often changed his mind after listening to the latest report from an official whom he did not intend to consult.

As the crackdown on pro-reform voices began, the Syrian regime began to promote quite a different political discourse from the one it had so recently adopted in the run-up to the new president's inauguration.[11] Justifying the obstruction of political liberalization, this discourse was built around three main points.

The first and most dangerous argument was that a strong authoritarian state was crucial to maintaining political and economic stability and protecting society from social turmoil.

The second argument was that reform was not an urgent priority given the foreign pressures and 'imperialist conspiracies' facing Syria, particularly after the Iraq war of 2003 and the assassination of Hariri in 2005.[12] This

---

[9] In late January 2001, then Information Minister Adnan Umran blasted the 'proponents of civil society' as the 'new colonialism'. See: 'Imran Criticizes the Proponents of Civil Society: Part of a New Form of Colonialism', in *The Damascus Spring*, 367–9. On 18 February of the same year, six months after the inaugural speech, then Vice-President Abd al-Halim Khaddam condemned intellectuals and insisted that the regime 'will not allow Syria to become another Algeria or another Yugoslavia'. His later claims notwithstanding, in 2001 Khaddam represented the conservative and anti-reformist faction within the regime.

[10] See a critique of this trend in: Ghadbian. See also the introduction to the Arabic translation of: Steven Heydemann, *Authoritarianism in Syria: Institutions and Social Conflict* [Arabic], trans. Abbas Abbas (Beirut: Riad el-Rayyes, 2011 [1999]), 15.

[11] Hazem Nahar, *Trajectories of the Regime and the Opposition in Syria 2000–2008: A Critique of Visions and Practices* [Arabic], Reform Issues Series (Cairo: Cairo Institute for Human Rights Studies, 2009), 17.

[12] While the neoconservatives were in office, many Arab and Syrian democrats (including the author) were convinced that it was necessary to ignore the regime's repressive domestic policy, at least in public, and stand with Syria in the face of the external challenges presented by US policy. Once the neocons were safely out of office in 2007, many of these democrats (myself included) resumed their public disagreements with the regime. Before that, these criticisms were made privately through backchannels.

rhetoric made domestic debates secondary to the battle against external conspiracies and subordinated social and political demands to foreign policy and the conflict with Israel. It also entailed accusing dissidents of being collaborators and agents of foreign conspiracies.

The third argument was an appeal to what the regime called Syria's *khususiyya* or 'particularity' – its unique characteristics and circumstances.[13] Although this rhetoric heightened fears about social fissures, it was by no means a sociological reading of a complex and diverse society. It boiled down to the condescending idea that Syrian society was not ready for democratization and required long preparation before political reform could begin.

Bashar al-Assad was not a political reformer. He knew that substantial reforms would endanger the regime, while his main concern was to sustain it and modernize the economy, which, for him, meant opening it up to private investment. This idea had been present in Assad's thinking since he took power. In fact, he had alluded to it in his much-feted inaugural speech. 'We cannot apply the democracy of others on ourselves,' he told the People's Assembly, already assuming the patronizing rhetoric of a lecturing schoolmaster, which was to become the standard mode in all his speeches of this kind. He continued:

> Western democracy, for example, is the outcome of a long history that resulted in customs and traditions which distinguish the current culture of Western societies. In order to apply what they have, we must live their history with all its social signification. As this is obviously impossible, we must have our own particular democratic experience, which stems from our history, culture, civilization and which is a response to the needs of our society and the requirements of our reality.[14]

This is, of course, the same argument made by essentialists of all kinds, among them Islamists and orientalists. What this argument fails to recognize is that if there are no general features of a democratic system, then the term 'democracy' is meaningless. Needless to say, Bashar did not brood over the nature of a particular Syrian democracy; this was merely another expression of the regime's demagoguery in justification of authoritarianism.

Assad expanded on this theme in a 2001 interview with *Asharq al-Awsat*:

> My intention is to work as hard as I can, but I cannot promise progress. Progress does not depend on the president alone, but on all sectors of society. And since

---

[13] Suhair Atassi, 'The Damascus Spring: The Experience of Jamal al-Atasi's Forum for National Dialogue' [Arabic], in *Democratic Transition in Syria and the Spanish Experience*, ed. George Ayrani and Radwan Ziadeh, Reform Issues Series 23 (Cairo: Cairo Institute for Human Rights Studies, 2009), 65.

[14] *Al-Bab*, 17 July 2000, at: https://bit.ly/33LRDTd (accessed 26 December 2021).

every individual in society is needed to make progress [...] there must be a promise of progress from society itself. The president can issue decrees and laws but this is not sufficient to say that progress has been made [...] social development must proceed in parallel with development in other fields.[15]

Society must promise the president that it will evolve, and in turn the president will decide whether it deserves to be rewarded with reform. It is difficult to imagine more arrogant or presumptuous rhetoric. Few primary school teachers would address their pupils in this manner – never mind a newly inaugurated president with no proven organizational skills, whose sole qualification is being the son of the previous incumbent. The younger Assad's attitude was that of the entitled scion writ large, whose sense of personal prerogative completely outstrips his intellectual and practical ability.[16]

In this sense he was exactly like the 'young wolves' who surrounded him and were to drive the economic liberalization (and corruption) characteristic of his tenure. Their policies had dramatic consequences for the social base of the regime, and if they entailed a shift in the regime's foreign alliance, this clique had no objection to that either. In short, Bashar was just another inept son of an older generation of officials, some of them born rich, others made rich by their relationship with the president.

II. The Damascus Declaration

Despite harsh security repression and systematic arrests of Syrian opposition figures during these years, Syrian Democratic Forces (SDF)

---

[15] Interview on 2 February 2001, in *The Damascus Spring*, 515.
[16] This idea continued to dominate the thinking of both Assad and those around him after the popular protests against his regime began, and in fact only became more entrenched. For example, Farouq Abu al-Shamat, the chair of the committee drafting a new political parties law, explained in June 2011 that the process was taking so long because 'the Syrian people do not have a political culture, and there is no citizen participation in political life'. The work of the committee was thus to 'overhaul' parties and make them capable of 'mobilizing' the different parts of society in order to confront 'internal and external challenges'. The final law would have to guarantee the formation of 'patriotic parties that will reinforce reform and strengthen the edifice of democracy and political pluralism'. See: *al-Quds al-Arabi*, 14 June 2011, at: https://bit.ly/3szQ9FV (accessed 26 December 2021). From a semiotic perspective, we can see the concrete expression of this position in the images and videos broadcast by the media in the early period of the revolution, which showed Syrian officers addressing detained citizens who were arrested during the peaceful protests as they were seated in buses or in school classrooms turned into temporary detention centres. Officers asked the detainees to repeat slogans of loyalty to the president, in a scene reminiscent of a primitive primary schoolroom. Those who refused or who did not shout loud enough were beaten. In another scene, a soldier brutally beats an older man, asking him in the tone of a brutal disciplinarian: 'What is it that you want? You want freedom, no? Do you want freedom? Is this the freedom that you want?' This was the regime's response to the protest chant 'Syria wants freedom'.

persisted in their demands for political reform and refused to back down. The shared visions that emerged between the political forces and a number of the figures who participated in the Damascus Spring resulted in the establishment of a national opposition coalition named after the Damascus Declaration (DD), a statement of unity published in October 2005. The declaration brought together most of the opposition and bore signatures from parties of various intellectual orientations (leftists, socialists, liberals, nationalists) as well as activists with civil society committees. Significantly, the document was also signed by the Muslim Brotherhood – defying the infamous Law 49, which since 1980 had made membership in the Brotherhood or involvement in its activities a criminal offence. Putting their names alongside those of Brotherhood representatives was itself a daring move on the part of the intellectuals who signed the petition.[17]

On paper, the DD was the largest political grouping of opposition forces since the Baʿth took power in 1963. Its signatories exploited the narrow margin of action and expression permitted in the early days of the younger Assad's tenure to protest the regime's failure to keep his reformist promises and its refusal to change its ways, especially after the Syrian Baʿth Party conference in June 2005. But the subsequent crackdown on opposition activists by the security agencies eradicated all hope of reform. Opposition figures were detained or banned from travel, and the security forces were given carte blanche in suppressing political activity, including civil society organizations that promoted civil liberties or human rights.

The events surrounding the DD showed how weak the opposition parties' social base had become after decades of authoritarian rule and highlighted the rise of a new breed of activists. They also demonstrated the ideological disarray of the forces of the left after the collapse of the socialist bloc, with some of those forces now pinning their hopes on the intensifying pressure on the regime exerted by the direct US presence in the region and even the threat of military intervention on the model of the US invasion of Iraq.[18] Those parts of the Syrian opposition that held such opinions were not disillusioned by the American-Syrian rapprochement after 2007 or the colossal failure in Iraq, carrying the same deluded hopes at revolution's beginning in 2011. In fact, the target of US pressure on the regime was its

---

[17] From discussions with the Syrian opposition figure Hazem Nahar, it appears that the agreement with the Muslim Brotherhood was made before the publication of the declaration. However, the domestic opposition asked the Brotherhood to announce that it was joining a day later, so as not to give the impression that there were pre-existing links between the groups.

[18] ACRPS, 'The Positions of the Syrian Opposition toward the Central Arab Causes', 16 February 2012, at: https://bit.ly/3HgYlPL (accessed 26 December 2021).

regional policy and its support for Hamas and Hezbollah, not internal issues in Syria.[19]

In an interview with the Lebanese newspaper *An-Nahar* in 2003, Riyad al-Turk, a veteran opposition figure and secretary-general of a faction of the Syrian Communist Party, had already argued that in invading Iraq, the US had rid that country of an 'internal occupation',[20] reversing years of regression under the Ba'thists[21]: from 'fifty degrees below zero', the invasion had returned Iraq to the absolute 'zero' of the colonial era, which it would be easier to fight against. Iraqis and Syrians freed themselves from foreign occupation, 'but both peoples despaired of throwing off internal occupation after a third of a century'.[22]

It is hard to gauge how widespread these sorts of views were – they varied considerably in intensity[23] and major sections of the opposition did not agree with this analysis. However, enough left-wingers had abandoned all their previous ideas and were now hoping for US intervention that the term 'former left' was coined to describe them. In any case, even the most 'confused' wings within the opposition cannot really be blamed for their confusion. They were in part reacting against a leftist and nationalist rhetoric that trumpeted Arab unity and anti-imperialism while largely disregarding questions of civil and human rights. Even so, this rhetoric alienated them from Syrian public opinion.

This faith in foreign intervention was to be a consistent problem for Syria's beleaguered democrats. While no one publicly supported the US invasion of Iraq, largely due to the prevailing mood in the region, they seemed to see it as a legitimate model for bringing down dictatorships and

---

[19] Joshua Landis and Joe Pace summarized the dilemma of the Syrian opposition in this regard: 'Despite the Bush administration's rhetoric on supporting freedom in the Middle East, its Syria policy has been focused almost uniquely on changing Asad's foreign policy, which Syrians overwhelmingly support, and not on changing Asad's domestic polices or improving conditions inside Syria, which is what Syrians want. This focus makes it very difficult for the Syrian opposition to support U.S. pro-democracy rhetoric and policies, which are widely seen as pretexts for destabilizing regimes that oppose U.S. interests in the region.' Joshua M. Landis and Joe Pace, 'The Syrian Opposition', *Washington Quarterly* 30, no. 1 (Winter 2006–7), 62.

[20] This term was used by Burhan Ghalioun in his *Manifesto for Democracy*, first published in 1976. See: Burhan Ghalioun, *A Manifesto for Democracy* [Arabic], 5th edn (Casablanca, Morocco: Arab Cultural Centre, 2006), 115.

[21] *al-Hiwar al-Mutamaddin*, 14 February 2007, at: https://bit.ly/3ptfTSy (accessed 26 December 2021).

[22] *Middle East Transparent*, 1 June 2005. Archived copy available online: https://bit.ly/32zClR9 (accessed 26 December 2021).

[23] Various intellectuals of the Iraqi left held similar positions and came up with similar theoretical justifications for intervention. Some even helped promote the lie that the Hussein regime had weapons of mass destruction and that Iraqis would welcome foreign forces with flowers. By the end of the twentieth century, many former Arab leftists had essentially become neoliberals supportive of neoconservative policy. This is not only an Arab phenomenon: many leftist intellectuals in the West had made the same transition decades before, on the eve of and after the collapse of the socialist camp.

advancing the struggle for civil rights and freedoms. A year later, following the Hariri assassination and widespread Lebanese outrage at the Syrian regime,[24] some of the opposition again pinned their hopes on a foreign intervention.[25] On that occasion they found themselves completely out of step with Syrian popular opinion, which united behind the regime during the crisis and especially after the Lebanon war of 2006. And when Syrians finally did come out to protest *en masse* in 2011, they were faced with an unsympathetic Obama administration unwilling to export democracy and repeat the mistake of military intervention in Iraq. Intervention was once again a non-starter.

The image of the opposition was further sullied by the establishment of new organizations in the US such as the Reform Party of Syria (RPS) led by Fareed al-Ghadiri, which was established in 2003, and the National Democratic Renaissance Party headed by Abdulaziz Meslat.[26] These parties enjoyed the support of the George W. Bush administration at a time when popular antipathy to the invasion of Iraq and American unconditional support for Israel was at its peak in all Arab countries, Syria included. This made it easy to equate even the domestic parties with the Iraqi opposition, which was used to advance the American invasion and the destruction of Iraq.

III. Rebranding the regime and the consolidation of power

The Assad regime, meanwhile, continued its steady move away from the promises of reform that had originally served as a main source of legitimacy for Bashar al-Assad, given that a bequest is not a legitimate way of achieving power in republics. Along with reform, Bashar's pledge to combat corruption had been foundational to legitimate his claim to the presidency.

---

[24] Rafiq al-Hariri had served as the prime minister of Lebanon twice, with his most recent term ending in 2004. His assassination ignited outrage both in Lebanon and internationally, and the Syrian regime (via its local client Hezbollah) was widely held to be responsible. The subsequent protests in Lebanon (the 'Cedar Revolution') forced Damascus to bring an end to more than twenty-five years of occupation, which had begun with an intervention in the Lebanese Civil War (1975–90). The incident also seriously damaged Syria's reputation internationally.

[25] Some of those involved in the DD fell into this camp, but by no means all; there were others who wanted to begin any statement with a condemnation of US policy in the region before discussing democracy. The disagreement was so fierce that the Arab Socialist Union Party (ASU), the Communist Action Party (CAP) (also known as the Communist Labour Party), and a handful of other small opposition parties opposed to intervention walked out of the meeting of the DD National Council on 2 December 2007. During the revolution, the parties and figures of the NDR would become part of the NCB. See: ACRPS, 'The Positions of the Syrian Opposition toward the Central Arab Causes'.

[26] Kamal Deeb, *The Contemporary History of Syria: From the French Mandate to the Summer of 2011* [Arabic] (Beirut: Dar al-Nahar, 2011), 744–5.

But instead of combatting corruption, his regime allowed it to climb to unprecedented heights: the web of relationships connecting the president's family, the security forces and the business classes grew ever denser, the number of compulsory partnerships (i.e. legalized kickbacks to regime-loyal 'silent partners') rose ever higher, and public displays of wealth became more brazen than ever before. People were arrested simply for expressing a view. While efforts were made, with French support, to reform the government bureaucracy, political reform was smothered in its cradle.

The regime argued that economic reform along market lines was crucial for 'the current historical phase' while delaying political reform indefinitely. Ignoring the huge difference in size between the Chinese and Syrian economies, dismissing the fact that in the absence of a strong manufacturing sector Syrian liberalization would simply drive people into the service and tourism sectors, and – most disastrously – disregarding Syria's predominantly agricultural character, the regime decided to import the Chinese model, which seemed to offer the best combination of market economy and authoritarianism. It thus removed itself from the management of the production process and began to gradually lift the subsidies on staple goods. New laws licensed the establishment of commercial banks and private communications companies, set up a stock market and investment funds, and facilitated an influx of foreign investment, mainly from the Gulf. The new 'social market economy' – a term that was chosen to imply the preservation of the social progress achieved by the Syrian state – meant liberalization with an eye to maintaining political loyalty. The public sector was neither privatized nor reformed but left to slowly suffocate under the pressure of imported goods and vibrant private sector competitors.

In order to attract investments, corporate bodies like the peasants' and workers' union, which had incorporated huge social segments within the Ba'th regime since the 1960s, were debilitated. In parallel, the economic liberalization process created a complex, cross-sectarian web of interests and coalitions, joining the new capitalist class with the sons of the ruling political and security elite. The new capitalist class comprised the sons of the families of the old economic elite (such as the Shallah, Attar, Kuzbari, and Ghreiwati families) in alliance with the new economic-political elite through investment consortiums such as the Syrian Holding Company and Sham Holding Company. Under such conditions, liberalization becomes self-contradictory: it translates into the creation of monopolies controlled by those close to the regime – in short, crony capitalism. The country thus gets the worst of both worlds: it loses the benefits of the public sector without gaining those of economic competition.

This economic transformation contributed to a broad process of impoverishment in the countryside and the cities, in addition to harming the middle class and rolling back the subsidies and services provided by the state. Such measures had a decisive impact on the early development of the protest movement in Syria. Broadly speaking, this was a popular movement against political repression and against a structural corruption that combined economic neoliberalism with political authoritarianism. In this sense, the Syrian experience of economic liberalization resembled its Tunisian and Egyptian predecessors. The difference is that in Syria the security forces had a tighter grip. Moreover, the direct involvement in business by multiple security agencies allowed for extremely arbitrary practices, forcing every businessman to seek the protection of at least one security agency. And an ideological political party, though marginalized by economic liberalization, remained present in the background. The ship of state was brought firmly under the control of a coalition made up of the ruling family, the new businessmen and the security forces,[27] which reaped substantial financial rewards as a result.

In the 2000s the idea that Syria was under colonial attack gained considerable traction among the Syrian public, especially after 2005, when the Hariri assassination led to the withdrawal of Syrian troops from Lebanon and ushered in two years of international isolation. The period of international isolation came to an end thanks to successful regime manoeuvring: by supporting resistance in Iraq and Lebanon, it extorted renewed international recognition of Syria's role in Lebanon after the failed Israeli attack in 2006 and proved the need for coordination with Syria in Iraq. The Syrian-Turkish-Qatari cooperation followed by a reconciliation with France broke the isolation. The regime had no more excuses to justify postponing the reforms promised when Assad took over the presidency. But in fact, the regime became much more rigid and brutal. As Raymond Hinnebusch put it, Asad 'might have invested his nationalist legitimacy in an opening to the opposition, but instead the regime appears to have seen this as an opportunity to move against dissent.'[28] It became increasingly obvious to Syrians and non-Syrians alike that these promises had been no more than a ruse intended to ease the transition between the older Assad and his son and that the young president lacked any real desire or will to carry out the modernizing reforms that Syrians craved.

But the regime had ridden out the wave of international hostility and felt more powerful than ever. Washington's ambassador had returned to the embassy in 2009, relations with Saudi Arabia had begun to improve and

---

[27] ACRPS, 'The General and the Particular in the Ongoing Syrian Popular Uprising', 15 May 2011, at: https://bit.ly/3evkkpv (accessed 26 December 2021).
[28] Raymond Hinnebusch, 'Syria: From "Authoritarian Upgrading" to Revolution?' *International Affairs* 88, no. 1 (2012), 103. See also: *Open Democracy*, 4 October 2011, at: https://bit.ly/3LFo9qK (accessed 28 April 2022).

the regime was recapturing some of its lost influence in Lebanon. Representatives of countries across the world were lining up to visit Damascus and 'gain Syria's favour', as official media put it, portraying Assad as a figure of great international significance. The regime saw no need to carry out any reforms.

Then 2011 brought revolutions in Egypt and Tunisia, and protests in Daraa – the Syrian counterpart to Sidi Bouzid, the provincial city where Tunisia's revolution began.[29] Despite the violent response of the security forces, protesters did not call for the fall of the regime, but preferred to make specific demands. Many believed that this time the regime would have to make changes – willingly or unwillingly – especially since it had been unable to immediately break up the protests. And the regime seemed to agree. Senior figures close to Assad told the press that they could expect a reform agenda to be set out by the president in his next speech.[30] But when the much-anticipated speech was finally given on 30 March 2011, it dashed these hopes completely. Not only did Assad refuse to recognize that the protests were demanding reform, he accused those participating of sedition. He talked bluntly of a conspiracy against the nation and told protestors they were 'either with me or against me', dismissing the possibility even of a grey area between the two:

> Crushing *fitna* [sedition or civil strife] is a national, ethical and religious duty, and anyone who is able to help crush it but does not is himself guilty of strife [...] As the Holy Qur'an tells us, 'Strife is graver than murder.' Anyone who plays a part in it, intentionally or unintentionally, is working to murder his nation. There can thus be no place for those who sit on the fence [...] This is not a question of the state, but of the nation [...] The conspiracy is broad, and we are not seeking a fight... Syrians are a peaceful and amicable people, but we have never hesitated to defend our causes, our interests, our principles. If we are forced to fight today, then we welcome it.[31]

---

[29] Regarding this comparison between Sidi Bouzid and Daraa, see: Azmi Bishara, *The Glorious Tunisian Revolution: The Structure of a Revolution and its Evolution through Its Daily Chronicles* [Arabic] (Beirut: ACRPS, 2012), 204. An English version of this book was subsequently published. See: Bishara, *Understanding Revolutions*, 66.

[30] On 22 March 2011, Vice-President Farouq al-Sharaa held a press conference about the ongoing protests in Daraa and the political reforms that the leadership was expected to enact. See: *Sham FM* (Syria), 22 March 2011, at: https://bit.ly/3JkNK8g (accessed 26 December 2021). In a meeting with the Chinese special envoy to the Middle East, Sharaa announced, 'President Bashar al-Assad will make an important speech in the coming two days that will reassure the people.' See: *Annahar*, 29 March 2011. Archived copy available online: https://bit.ly/3yWGaMa (accessed 26 December 2021). Presidential adviser Buthayna Shaaban likewise told Agence France-Presse news agency on 27 March 2011, 'President Assad will address his people very soon to explain the situation and clarify and elaborate on the reforms that have already been decided.' See: *BBC* (international), 27 March 2011, at: https://bbc.in/3DfWxWl (accessed 26 January 2022).

[31] *SANA*, 30 March 2011. Archived copy available online: https://bit.ly/3EsUD3E (accessed 26 December 2021).

Assad had chosen the rhetoric of confrontation, setting off on a path of escalation from which he would be unable to escape. Some observers speculated that hardliners within decision-making circles in Syria (or perhaps in Syria and Iran) were afraid that a less inflexible speech might set off a chain reaction of retreats and concessions. This was, after all, exactly what had happened when Ben Ali and Mubarak had adopted more conciliatory rhetoric in their addresses to their respective nations. We have no evidence to confirm these speculations. I know that he did not like the idea of being a 'pushover' and that he personally wrote that speech. In dictatorships like Syria, the regime does not split between hardliners and moderates, because no-one is powerful enough to split the regime. Regime insiders can advise, but there is one decision-maker. Some security officers did not like the idea of experimenting with openness at the beginning of Assad's term. But Assad alone reached his conclusions and became harder than the rest. Similarly, some high-ranking security officers thought that weakening the party was a bad idea because it was the most important cover for the regime. But Assad did not listen, and his policies and the new coalition between the ruling family, the security apparatus and business networks continued to marginalize the party.

We also know that the pro-regime demonstrations were organized in such a way that millions of people throughout Syria (in every city except Daraa, which was mourning the victims who fell in demonstrations) came out to cheer for Assad the day before the speech was to be broadcast. This can only have encouraged him to stay the course. It was hardly going to convince him that he needed to pursue real reform.

This was, of course, an exercise in self-delusion. There were certainly genuine regime supporters in Syria, as well as many people who, while not pro-regime, were worried about the possible ramifications of a revolution. But the numbers that came out on 29 March could only be mustered by shepherding public servants and employees of politically sympathetic companies out of their workplaces to participate. How much spontaneous support the regime could count on can be measured by its inability to drum up demonstrators on weekends, when state sector workers could not be so easily corralled. But the president was blind to all this. He had seen people chanting his name, and it had had the desired effect.

IV. Precursors of protest

Since the 1980s, Syrians had had no experience of organized protest, whether political or demand-oriented. Fresh from its victory against the Islamist uprising (1976–1982), the regime had reorganized itself, turning

Syria into a police state. The security forces had become the main element in the relationship between state and society. Under the pretext of the state of emergency – which soon became little more than a fig leaf disguising contempt for the rule of law – they had been granted broad powers allowing them to interfere in the daily lives of citizens. The bloody suppression of the Hama uprising in 1982, with the brutality and the casualties left to rumours amid a media blackout, served as a brutal lesson in what would happen to those who rebelled. When a new generation came of age that did not remember this lesson, the regime would try and reproduce it. But this time it would apply the Hama model throughout Syria and in full view of the cameras, ultimately turning city after city into a new Grozny.[32]

After Hama, political life in Syria became a desert. Political activism of any kind was seen as suspect; even pro-regime activities that did not originate with the regime itself were treated with suspicion. Unlike other Arab dictatorships like Egypt and Tunisia – where NGOs and unions continued to enjoy a margin of freedom – protest movements were completely non-existent. This did not change after the younger Assad took power: the security services continued to permeate every aspect of political and public life.

As a result, naturally enough, Syria under Bashar al-Assad saw only one significant protest movement, the 2004 Kurdish uprising. Although there were many historical and social tensions behind the uprising, it cannot be understood without considering the overthrow of Saddam Hussein in 2003 and the emergence of an autonomous Kurdish region in Iraq. The immediate spark was a local dispute: a clash between Arab tribesmen from Deir ez-Zor and Kurds after a football match. The dispute rapidly took on a political colouring, however, because of Kurdish-Arab disagreements over the US invasion of Iraq. Since the Syrian public generally felt great sympathy with the plight of Iraqis, they looked askance at the uprising by Syrian Kurds. In contrast, the Muslim Brotherhood and many of the left considered it part of the democratic struggle for Syrian Kurdish political and cultural rights.[33] After the incident Mashaal Temu, spokesman of the recently founded Kurdish Future Trend, observed, 'The Iraq war liberated us from the culture of fear...[P]eople saw a Kurd become president of Iraq and began demanding their culture and political rights in Syria.' Joshua Landis and Joe Pace, who quoted Temu, added, 'Even nervous Arab activists

---

[32] The regime pursued a military strategy very similar to the Russian approach in Chechnya (1994–6 and 1999–2002): the all-out, indiscriminate bombardment of cities; extensive use of tanks and armoured vehicles; and the cutting of supply lines between different areas under the control of armed groups. President Putin was the architect of both the wars in Chechnya.

[33] Azmi Bishara et al., *The Question of Syria's Kurds: Reality, History and Mythology* [Arabic] (Beirut and Doha: ACRPS, 2013), 95.

once sympathetic to the Kurdish plight hesitated to support a movement, many of whose leaders affectionately referred to President George W. Bush as Abu Azaadi (Father of Freedom).'[34]

The renewal of President Bashar al-Assad's mandate for a second term in 2007 was a critical juncture, the starting point for new and unprecedented social dynamics. As noted above, he had managed to weather the storm of international isolation following the Hariri assassination in 2005, thanks to the failure of US policy in Iraq and the success of the Lebanese resistance against Israeli aggression in 2006. Once again, however, he refused to fulfil the popular demands for reform and change, this time capitalizing on Western and Arab overtures to his regime and the recognition of its central role in Iraq and Lebanon.

Bashar al-Assad, like his father, was good at shoring up his regime with an effective, active foreign policy that made him 'indispensable' and cast him as a pillar of regional stability. Typically, the need for Syria's stabilizing influence resulted from the regime's concerted effort to create instability – a method of extortion used by the regime to help others better 'understand' its 'vital regional role'. The regime conceived this strategy as self-defence against powers that threatened it or plans to impose conditions on it.

The young president thus worked to undermine the US project in Iraq by providing support to the resistance against occupation, including safe passage for radical Salafi jihadis. The Syrian regime had a vested interest in maintaining instability in Iraq. This was not a principled stance against foreign intervention – indeed, the regime had formerly supported the coalition forces during the Second Gulf War in Kuwait, thereby improving its bargaining position in Washington. This time, the Syrian regime supported the resistance to deny the US the regional success that would allow it to dictate terms to the Syrian regime. As the US project in Iraq floundered and Iranian influence began to grow, and as sectarian divisions escalated to near-civil war in Iraq, the neoconservative policy failure in the region became apparent.

Assad's refusal to follow through with reforms stoked increasing popular resentment against the regime. Most of this can be traced to the disastrous consequences of the regime's economic policies. By 2007, economic liberalization and the rapid transition from a command to a market economy had produced stark inequality. The Damascene and Aleppan bourgeoisie who had taken advantage of their links to key regime figures and the security forces to secure franchises, privileges and import licenses for Chinese goods (which flooded local markets and quickly drove domestic

---

[34] Landis and Pace, 'The Syrian Opposition', 53.

competitors out of business) had prospered. The poor, meanwhile, suffered, with the state's withdrawal from production sending unemployment skyrocketing to 34 per cent of the workforce.[35] At the same time, the cost of living increased, hurting poor Syrians and the middle class, especially after subsidies on staple goods were gradually phased out. And these policies had serious social and psychological ramifications. It is difficult to imagine how degrading it is to stand in queues for hours, only to have to bribe a civil servant to secure enough fuel to sustain the household, especially for heating. But this is exactly what Syrians on low incomes were reduced to when the regime abolished the general fuel subsidy in April 2008 – its price soared by 42 per cent – and replaced it with means-tested coupons that it was completely unequipped to distribute in an efficient or timely manner.

Although agriculture made up between 25 to 27 per cent of the Gross Domestic Production (GDP) in 2001, according to the World Bank and UN Food and Agriculture Organization's (FAO) estimation respectively, and accounted for around 31 per cent of the workforce,[36] the new economic strategy paid very little attention to this sector. After a difficult cold snap in 2005, between 2006 and 2009 agriculture endured the worst drought in fifty years. During the eight months from October 2007 to May 2008, the worst of the crisis, rainfall ranged between just 25 per cent and 85 per cent of the cumulative average.[37] According to the FAO, the wheat and barley harvest in 2007 and 2008 shrank by 47 per cent and 67 per cent respectively.[38] Under the combined pressure of the catastrophic drought and the termination of fuel subsidies in 2009 (including for the diesel fuel needed for irrigation pumps), tens of thousands of families who had been farmworkers relocated from the eastern region to makeshift camps around Damascus. The United Nations (UN) Office for the Coordination of Humanitarian Affairs (OCHA) estimated in 2008 that the loss threatened over a million Syrians with malnutrition and unemployment.[39] And as the new business networks close to the regime thrived and the wealth gap widened, poverty and food prices rose. The price of the average food basket of Syrians increased by about 20 per cent in 2010.[40]

But the government failed to address this humanitarian crisis. The result was tens of thousands of unemployed young men who began to gather in

---

[35] This subject is discussed at length in: Barout, *The Last Decade in the History of Syria*.
[36] FAO, 'Counting the Cost: Agriculture in Syria after Six Years of Crisis', 2017, at: https://bit.ly/3MUGEb8 (accessed 13 June 2022); World Bank, at: https://bit.ly/3tBLIu7 (accessed 13 June 2022); World Bank, at: https://bit.ly/3OczbFi (accessed 13 June 2022).
[37] Barout, *The Last Decade in the History of Syria*, 126–7.
[38] Ibid., 127.
[39] *BBC Arabic*, 2 October 2008, at: https://bbc.in/3EpCpjr (accessed 26 December 2021).
[40] Landis, 'The Syrian Uprising of 2011', 79–80.

the squares of the capital looking for day-to-day employment in agriculture, construction or sanitation, further fuelling resentment against the regime.

The reformist technocrats and business people around Assad wanted to turn Syria into a bigger version of Lebanon by investing in services, real estate, banking and tourism. Only the latter's income reached in 2010 an unprecedented level of 12 per cent of the GDP. These were also the fields of interest for Gulf investors. As Hinnebusch wrote, 'The absence of rule of law deterred long-term productive investment in industry and agriculture and the return of much of Syria's enormous expatriate capital. Only 13 per cent of investment after 2000 was in manufacturing', while cheap imports left small manufacturers without markets.[41]

The general economic outlook was not helped by the regime's decision to subordinate everything to foreign policy. During the period of isolation between 2005 and 2007, investments from the Gulf increased as did trade with Iran, China and Turkey. Ankara, for reasons of its own national security, took advantage of Syria's isolation to end animosities with its neighbour and open a market for Turkish goods and investments and a transit to the Gulf states; it had stood by Damascus, but this came at a price. Agreements were signed that largely favoured Turkey,[42] facilitating an influx of Turkish goods into the local market. Local manufacturing, notably the furniture industry in Damascus's satellite towns (Saqba, Zamalka and Darayya), was driven out of business by cheaper, more attractive Turkish alternatives. The same applied to many other factories producing food, toys, clothing and shoes. Tens of thousands of families lost their sole source of income, and the Strategic Cooperation Agreement of 2010 was to accelerate the process.[43] The regions worst affected by these developments would actively participate in the revolution.

When the government did seek to intervene locally, it often did so unjustly and offered exemptions to any set of regulations it introduced, thus creating opportunities for corruption. Legislative Decree 49/2008, for example, required anyone who sought to make any changes to property rights in real estate in border regions to obtain advance permission from 'the competent administrative authorities in Damascus'. This meant that

---

[41] Hinnebusch, 'Syria', 101.
[42] In 2004, Syria and Turkey signed a major trade agreement which came into force two years later. In 2006, they concluded the Investment Encouragement and Protection pact, which raised Turkish investment in Syria to over $700 million. The same year a Free Trade Zone agreement was signed, entering into effect in 2007; that agreement was suspended in late 2011. See: Munir al-Hamash, 'An Arab Perspective on the Reality of Arab-Turkish Economic Relations' [Arabic], in *Arabs and Turkey: The Challenges of the Present and the Wagers of the Future*, pref. Muhammad Nureddine (Beirut and Doha: ACRPS, 2012), 238.
[43] Ibid., 299; Barout, *The Last Decade in the History of Syria*, 321. It is not likely that the agreement itself was behind the March 2011 protests, since it was signed at the end of 2010.

any project in these areas – digging a well, renting or selling land, building a house or a commercial building – would henceforth require a license from the security establishment. The decree was particularly hard on Syrians in Daraa, the rural areas northwest of Homs and north of Aleppo, parts of Deir ez-Zor and al-Hasakeh, most of which are either agricultural areas or trade hubs with neighbouring states. Resentment towards this law was undoubtedly a major driver of protests in these areas.[44]

While it denied those on the borders the right to dispose freely of their property, the regime was busy expropriating others' lands *tout court*, generally without fair compensation. These lands were typically incorporated into ambitious plans for urban development, facilitating corruption. In 2005, as part of the 'New Damascus' plan, owners of large tracts of land in the leafy Western Ghouta area (such as Madamiyet Elsham, Kafr Sousah and Mazzeh) were compelled to hand over their property at modest prices not exceeding SYP 100,000 ($2,000) per hectare. Three years later, the government began selling that same land off to investors – this time at more than SYP 1 billion ($20 million) per hectare[45] – who were supposed to use it to build vast malls and luxurious accommodation for upper-class Syrians. It is no surprise, then, that the people of the Western Ghouta led the popular protests in Damascus itself. Some of them later took up arms.

At around the same time, work was beginning on 'Dream of Homs', a joint project with the Qatari Diyar Company which envisioned a redevelopment of the historical city centre.[46] The residents of this area feared that they would be driven out of their homes, and events took a sectarian turn when it was rumoured that the project sought to replace the primarily Sunni population of Old Homs with Alawi migrants from the countryside.[47] In fact, the traditional Homsi bourgeoisie stood to lose out from the development primarily because they had no stake in the malls and commercial centres that were to be built, which obviously has nothing

---

[44] European Centre for Kurdish Studies, 'Decree 49: A Tool for Confiscating the Property of the Kurds? Observations on the Political and Economic Repercussions of the Decree', Report 6, August 2010, 4.
[45] *Kassioun*, 12 April 2011, at: https://bit.ly/3poT9TM (accessed 26 December 2021).
[46] *Syria News*, 5 November 2007. Archived copy available online: https://bit.ly/32DFIqd (accessed 26 December 2021).
[47] A distinction should be made between popular beliefs, which to believers seem to be true and are influential in practice, and actual facts. In recent decades Syria's cities have seen extensive in-migration from all parts of the countryside, driven by agricultural crisis. Naturally enough given the respective sizes of their communities, there has been far more migration to Homs from nearby Sunni areas than from Alawi areas. But the Alawi migrants took up residence in specific neighbourhoods which then took on a specific demographic character – neighbourhoods which were also economically distinct from the areas around them insofar as most of their inhabitants worked in the state sector. The areas around Hadara Street and Ekrima in Homs are relatively prosperous examples. Poorer Alawis, meanwhile, congregated in Zahraa and Nuzha, which have provided many recruits for the so-called popular committees and the National Defence Army (the regime militias known colloquially as the *shabbiha*).

to do with sectarian affiliation. Nonetheless, resistance to the project took on a sectarian character. These developments also explain why Homsis specifically called for the fall of the then-governor, Mohammad Eyad Ghazal, during the earliest protests in their city: he was the driving force behind the Dream of Homs project.[48]

The poor and middle classes adversely affected by the government's economic policies, the impoverishment and 'proletarianization' of the middle classes, agricultural devastation in much of the countryside and subsequent rural migration all coalesced into a rising tide of anger and resentment. In 2008, this tide finally began to translate into small acts of protest. These had limited impact – they were embers foreshadowing the revolution – but it is no small thing for people to break through the wall of fear like that created by the Syrian regime.

V. Protest in the run-up to the revolution

Perhaps the most significant trigger of protest was the abolition of fuel subsidies in early 2008. This triggered a wildcat strike by minibus drivers. Minibuses, known locally as *servis*, are a crucial and omnipresent part of public transport infrastructure in Damascus. When the subsidy cut went into effect, tripling the cost of diesel and doubling that of petrol overnight, drivers announced that they would not be working the following day. Traffic in the capital was brought to a grinding halt. Although on that occasion the security forces seized many minibuses and detained drivers, this did not deter them from going on strike again in late 2010 after the Damascus governorate granted local investors licenses to operate large buses along the capital's major arterial roads. The 2010 strike was again dealt with using security measures, which were followed by attempts to contain the affair through dialogue with the strikers. As a result, the Transportation Ministry formulated a new plan that allowed small buses to operate on routes linking Damascus with its satellite towns, but without permitting them to enter the city.[49] Notably, the security establishment attempted to contain social outrage at the neoliberal economic policies coming out of the president's office.

Farmers who were hit by rising fuel prices also showed some resistance. In Syria, the producers of so-called 'strategic crops' are only allowed to sell their

---

[48] An interview with Najati Tayyara, conducted by Hamzeh al-Moustafa, ACRPS researcher, on 3 August 2012.
[49] Hamzeh al-Moustafa, *The Virtual Public Sphere in the Syrian Revolution: Characteristics, Currents, Mechanisms for Shaping Public Opinion* [Arabic] (Doha and Beirut: ACRPS, 2012), 98.

goods to the state, at prices set centrally. But in the aftermath of the subsidy cut, wheat, cotton and sugar beet farmers refused to sell their products until they were offered more money. Although the state did eventually agree to pay a higher rate, it remained below the level demanded by the farmers.

Another event that met with serious resistance was a July 2010 decision by Ghiyath Barakat, the minister of higher education, to ban the *niqab* from university campuses on the grounds that it was incompatible with 'academic traditions and the ethics of the campus'.[50] Coming just weeks after a similar ban had been imposed on schoolteachers 'to preserve the secular character of the state', the decision caused an uproar, and a silent sit-in was held outside the Damascus University Liberal Arts Faculty to protest it. This was the first student mobilization against a government decision, and notably attracted many students who wore neither the *niqab* or the more typical headscarf; many saw the decision as either a violation of personal freedom or a pretext for a broader protest. In fact, the ministry's efforts came in for harsh criticism from no less a pro-regime figure than the conservative religious scholar and TV preacher Sheikh Muhammad Said Ramadan al-Buti. Known for his knowledge of hadith, Qur'anic exegesis and occasional criticisms of literary and artistic freedom, Buti took advantage of his Friday sermon on 1 December to link 'God's wrath' (i.e. the ongoing drought) to these 'provocative decisions'.[51] Buti played the traditional role of the cleric as protector of tradition, an 'independent' mediator between the ruler and the believers and between the ruler and the 'word of God'; he was consistently supportive of the regime until his assassination at the Iman Mosque in Mazraʿa on 21 March 2013.[52] But he took advantage of times of crisis, when the regime needed clerics' support, to present demands that were broadly opposed to the secularization of the social and personal spheres.[53]

These two significant incidents, small as they were, had had no precedent in Syrian society for decades. The mere fact that they happened reflected a broader and deeper anger simmering just beneath the surface, even if it did

---

[50] Ibid.
[51] Ibid., 99.
[52] State TV claimed that eighty-four were wounded in a suicide bombing killing Muhammad Said Ramadan al-Buti along with at least forty-one others. The death toll reported rose later to almost fifty. See: *The Guardian*, 21 March 2013, at: https://bit.ly/36Qc6YP (accessed 27 March 2022); *DW*, 23 March 2013, at: https://bit.ly/3IL37Fg (accessed 27 March 2022). It later transpired that story published in official Syrian media was not correct: Buti was killed by a small explosion near his table. A number of people, including Buti's grandson, were killed in the attack, but the number of the dead did not even approach that given in the media. See: *BBC* (international), 9 April 2013, at: https://bbc.in/3JLgh6G (accessed 27 March 2022). For video footage of the bombing of the mosque, see: YouTube, 9 April 2013. Archived copy available online: https://bit.ly/3NX42WP (accessed 15 June 2022).
[53] For a comprehensive survey and analysis of the relations between the Syrian clergy and the regime in Syria, see: Thomas Pierret, *Religion and State in Syria: The Sunni Ulama from Coup to Revolution* (New York: Cambridge University Press, 2013).

not produce any political slogans or a leadership that was capable of framing these demands and politicizing them. As the Arab Spring began to unfold across the region, however, Syria started to see protests of quite a different sort.

Protests began in Tunisia on 18 December 2010. By the time that Ben Ali fled the country on 14 January 2011, the revolutionary wave had reached Egypt, where a vast mass of demonstrators would soon take to Tahrir Square seeking to oust the regime. Syrians were watching these developments closely, and within days, a small group of Syrian activists abroad had published a press release calling on 'Syrian youth' to assemble peacefully in front of the parliament in Damascus and on Saadallah al-Jabri Square in Aleppo on 4 and 5 February to 'demand freedom' (not, as yet, to bring down the regime).[54] Soon enough, Facebook pages with names like 'The Syrian Revolution against Bashar al-Assad' were being set up by digitally savvy activists, most of them outside Syria, especially in Europe.[55] These activists took up the call, recasting it as a 'Syrian Day of Rage' mirroring the 28 January Day of Rage protests in Cairo weeks before.

The regime was aware of these calls for protest and managed to contain them. Regime figures even reached out to members of the Arab and Kurdish opposition to ensure that the opposition parties would not turn out. The calls for demonstrations on 4 February 2011 by activists abroad resulted in empty squares.[56] Encouraged, the regime decided to end its long-standing block on Facebook, YouTube and Twitter as a show of strength. (Days earlier Assad had assured the *The Wall Street Journal* that Syria was 'stable' thanks to its 'close link to the beliefs of the people'. He did not mean religious beliefs but the public mood supportive of Syrian foreign policy.) This decision would subsequently have very serious consequences, as social media was to play an important role in escalating protests after they began and reaching out to foreign press. Pages like 'The Syrian Revolution against Bashar al-Assad', Sham Network, Flash, Ugarit News, and 'We are all Hamza al-Khatib' were to be very influential during the revolution, and Facebook and Skype would allow local networks around the country to connect with one another and circumvent the security forces. Coordination committees were formed to organize young revolutionaries in Syria and abroad. These

---

[54] *Souryioun Net*, 1 February 2011. Archived copy available online: https://bit.ly/3JkRG92 (accessed 26 December 2021).

[55] This page (which was founded on 18 January 2011 and was later known as the 'Syrian Revolution Network') regularly exhorted Syrians to go out and demonstrate against the regime. It also shared news and video content about the revolution from Syrian and international websites. At the beginning of the revolution, it had around 2,000 subscribers; at the time of writing the Arabic version of this book, it had nearly 700,000. See: al-Moustafa, *The Virtual Public Sphere in the Syrian Revolution*, 39. Eleven years after the revolution, the page had almost two million 'likes', and a similar number of followers (as of March 2022). See their page on: Facebook, at: https://bit.ly/3uAfM92 (accessed 27 March 2022).

[56] Barout, *The Last Decade in the History of Syria*, 174.

civic groups – the local coordination committees (LCCs), the Syrian Revolution Coordinators Union (SYRCU) and the General Commission of the Syrian Revolution (GCSR) – were composed largely of young people and played a major role in organizing protest activities both locally and nationally in Syria.

The Hariqa Market incident of 17 February 2011 in the old city of Damascus, however, was not organized over Facebook. In fact, it was barely organized at all. After the sons of some local merchants were insulted and then given a beating by police, locals gathered spontaneously at the market to protest. It was here that the first anti-regime slogans were heard: 'the Syrian people will not be humiliated', 'the fox is guarding the henhouse'.[57] The impromptu gathering and the chanting of these two spontaneous slogans (one protesting corruption and the other security repression) brought together, in a single act, the many facets of the Syrian revolution as it appeared in its first year.

The regime's response was swift. Given the prevailing atmosphere in the Arab region, it was on the alert, keen to contain the rage before it escalated. The interior minister appeared personally at the location and promised that the policemen involved would be brought before a disciplinary tribunal the following day. This most probably did not happen – throughout the revolution, not a single soldier, officer or security official was tried or held accountable for a violation, or even a crime, committed against Syrian citizens. If such a thing had occurred, the regime would certainly have publicized it as widely as possible. Members of the security forces were completely unaccountable, which is often the case when tenacious police action is the only thing standing between a regime and defeat. The threat of punishment might make a security officer think twice in exactly the moment that the regime needs him to act without hesitation.

The relationship between authoritarian regimes and the repressive security apparatus they depend on to control society is not one of master and servant, even if relations with individual officers may take this shape. As institutions, however, they are part of the regime. Accordingly, they can occasionally present rulers with a *fait accompli* which must be accepted because the ruler needs these organs to be content and loyal and cannot reinvent them at will in any given moment.

The Hariqa Market incident was the smoke billowing from the volcano: a sign of what was to come. The distinctive features of the revolution were already present: a spontaneous eruption of pent-up anger, communal solidarity with victims of injustice, and resentment of systematic

---

[57] For footage of the chants during the Hariqa protest, see: YouTube, 17 February 2011, at: https://bit.ly/32tY8tj (accessed 26 December 2021).

humiliation and corruption. And the regime was aware of the symbolic significance of the Hariqa Market incident. The pro-regime *al-Watan* ran an interview with one of the young men who had been beaten, Imad Naseeb. In the newspaper's account, Naseeb not only denied being the 'Syrian Bouazizi', but he also claimed never to have heard of him. The young man seemed to feel that being like Mohamed Bouazizi was an accusation – a stain on him and not the police – and so he had to deny it. The tone of the article suggested that a phantom revolution loomed, waiting for something to set it off.

VI. Solidarity with the Libyan people as a political message

On 22 February 2011, civil society activists held a sit-in in front of the Libyan embassy in solidarity with the Libyan revolution and to protest the regime's use of violence against the protesters in Benghazi.[58] This was interpreted as veiled criticism of the Syrian regime – unsurprisingly, since attendees chanted slogans which were hardly subtle: 'Killing your people makes you a traitor'; 'O freedom where are thee? Muammar's rule is standing between you and me'; and 'Qaddafi out'.

On 23 February 2011, the activists having refused to go home voluntarily, the sit-in was broken up by the security forces as participants shouted 'Peaceful protest! Peaceful protest!' and 'Beating your people makes you a traitor'.[59]

Unlike the Hariqa Market incident, the Libyan embassy sit-in was an organized political event carrying political significance. Activists sent out a public call for participation via Facebook, just like their counterparts elsewhere. During the event, they chanted political slogans that were directed at the regime, an unprecedented move. Moreover, the sit-in lasted over two days, 22 and 23 February, and attracted activists from across Damascus and nearby towns. This explains why the security forces used force to break up the sit-in, instead of attempting to contain it as they had the Hariqa gathering. After the Libyan embassy sit-in, political graffiti began appearing on city walls, including the slogan 'the people want to bring down the regime'. Within a few weeks, this graffiti campaign would result in the arrest of a group of teenagers in the provincial city of Daraa.

---

[58] For footage of the Libyan embassy sit-in, see: YouTube, 23 February 2011, at: https://bit.ly/3ExuCQG (accessed 26 December 2021).

[59] An interview with Marwa al-Ghamian, conducted by Nerouz Satik, ACRPS researcher, on 13 September 2011. Ghamian is a political activist who took part in the sit-in in front of the Libyan embassy.

2

From spark to fire

The Daraa uprising that spread in the Houran Plain region had a great impact on the other Syrian provinces, especially the city of Homs and those in the Damascus rural periphery (Rif Dimashq). Two events were central to the revolution: the Clocktower Square protest in Homs on 18 April 2011 and the Good Friday protest in Damascus and its countryside on 22 April 2011. With these two demonstrations, protest began to shift from the local to the national level.

I. The Daraa uprising

After the flight of Tunisia's Ben Ali on 14 January and the collapse of the Mubarak regime in Egypt on 11 February, anti-regime graffiti began to appear on walls and buildings across Syria. Slogans like 'you're next, doctor!' – Assad is a trained ophthalmologist – 'God, Syria and freedom!' and 'the people want to bring down the regime' were suddenly everywhere.[1] In late February, the security forces responded by rounding up those suspected of being responsible.[2] Among the detainees were about twenty individuals

---

[1] A local activist arrested during the first days of the uprising, Raed Abazeed, attests to the presence of graffiti on school walls in Daraa (an interview with Raed Abazeed, conducted by the ACRPS research team on 13 September 2011). As well as in Daraa, our interviewees tell us that activists (some of them members of the Syrian Socialist Nationalist Party (SSNP), the Socialist Union and CAP) wrote anti-regime graffiti on walls in Damascus and the nearby town of at-Tall (an interview with Fayez Sara, conducted by the ACRPS research team on 13 September 2011).

[2] Political graffiti is not a new phenomenon in Syria, where alternative outlets for anti-regime sentiment are limited. Graffiti artists attacked the government over Syria's controversial participation in Operation Desert Storm (1991) and during the confrontation with the Brotherhood in the 1980s. Around the time of the Assad succession, slogans like 'the country was ruined when they gave it to a child' appeared on university campus walls.

from Daraa, most of whom were children under the age of fifteen.³ There had been earlier incidents of this kind in the city: a doctor, Aisha al-Msalma, had been detained after telling a colleague she hoped 'the same happens here' after the fall of Ben Ali.⁴ But it was the arrest of the children of Daraa and their subsequent mistreatment at the hands of the security forces that was to set Syria alight.

It goes without saying that the Arab Spring was the trigger for these incidents. People had been tortured and humiliated, even killed, by the security forces before. And Daraawis had plenty of economic and social grievances: the region was marginalized and impoverished, ignored in development plans and rife with corruption,⁵ a situation exacerbated by the ongoing rivalry between Governor Faysal Kalthum (backed by the president's brother, Maher al-Assad)⁶ and the regional Chief of Political Security Atif Najib, who competed to squeeze the most money possible out of the region. But neither economic marginalization nor abuse by the security forces had led to popular outcry before. Events in Tunisia and Egypt were changing the way Syrians reacted. In Daraa as elsewhere, the Egyptian revolution in particular had got people talking. What would reform or democracy look like in Syria? What were the chances of a popular revolution happening here? Members of the opposition parties (the Arab

---

[3] There is no clear evidence that the children arrested were behind the graffiti. In fact, most testimonies collected suggests that it was the work of party activists. Wael Abu Rshaidat, the uncle of one of the children, told us, 'The children were arrested because of a security report filed by a Daraa al-Balad police officer who they used to throw stones at during his shift at a police checkpoint. The policeman complained to the Political Security Directorate and told them that the kids had been throwing Molotov cocktails at him. They were only accused of being behind the graffiti once they were in PSD custody. Some locals say that the kids' names were found written next to graffiti saying "the people want to bring down the regime"' (A face-to-face interview with Wael Abu Rshaidat, conducted by the ACRPS research team in Doha on 25 February 2012). The number of the detainees was confirmed by Mithqal Abazed, the lawyer who took over the case and one of the members of the delegation that met with regime officials during the incident (virtual interview via Skype with Mithqal Abazed, conducted by Ahmad Abazed, member of the ACRPS Syrian Revolution Documentation Project, on 9 September 2019). It is worth noting that when the Arabic version of this book was published in 2013, the author was sceptical about the Daraa children's case from the beginning, as noted above. This was criticized by some activists, but as became clearer with time, this scepticism was warranted.

[4] There are several narratives about the fate of Aisha al-Msalma. One common version is that the security forces tortured and humiliated her, and shaved her hair off before her release, and that the family tried to keep the incident quiet to avoid further persecution. We have not been able to establish the veracity of these narratives. A face-to-face interview with Nasr, *nom de guerre* Abu Anas al-Shami, conducted by the ACRPS research team in Doha on 13 March 2013. Abu Anas contacted Aisha's brother on her release.

[5] Additionally, Decree 49, enacted on 10 September 2008, which restricts the ability of people living in certain border areas of Syria to sell or purchase property without prior approval from the authorities, exacerbated the situation. Its repeal was thus among the demonstrators' first demands. To read the decree in Arabic, see: Syrian Parliament, at: https://bit.ly/3tMPEZm (accessed 13 June 2022).

[6] Colonel Louay al-Ali, head of the Daraa Military Security Branch, who raided the school and arrested the children, also supported Faysal Kalthum.

Socialist Union (ASU), the Communist Action Party (CAP) and Brotherhood supporters) worked together to plan small demonstrations. On 15 March, a disparate group of party activists, lawyers, engineers, doctors and politically engaged young people called for a gathering in front of the Daraa courthouse to demand reform, freedom and the release of political detainees.[7]

The suspects rounded up in late March were mostly teenagers. They were taken from Daraa to the central Political Security office in the neighbouring As-Sweida governorate, where they were tortured.[8] Representatives of Daraa's major families sent a delegation to Atif Najib to try and secure their release, but they were humiliated and sent away empty-handed. It was rumoured that their ʿuqul – their traditional headdresses, which they would have placed in front of Najib in an act of supplication – had been thrown in the rubbish bin. It was also rumoured that Najib had taken the opportunity to insult their female relatives at length. This may have been an exaggeration, but it is clear that the delegation felt humiliated, and that many others who had not been present felt that the treatment they had received was unjustifiable.[9]

---

[7] A face-to-face interview with Nizar al-Haraki, conducted by the ACRPS research team in Doha on 13 March 2013; a face-to-face interview with Wael Abu Rshaidat, conducted by the ACRPS research team in Doha on 25 February 2012. It is worth noting that the activists did call for this gathering, especially those from the ASU of Syria, but when the demonstrators approached the courthouse, they found the security forces gathered in front of the building, so they decided to disperse. Demonstrations took place later in Daraa al-Balad, where the locals supported the activists and the regime had a tenuous security grip.

[8] It was rumoured at the time that the children had been branded or had their fingernails pulled out. Based on the matching testimony of Wael Rshaidat, Raed Abazeed and Nizar al-Haraki, these rumours seem to be exaggerations; the children were certainly tortured at As-Sweida security branch but were not subjected to such extreme violence. Nonetheless, they proved useful for political mobilization and gave the incident a moral significance similar to the self-immolation of Mohamed Bouazizi in Tunisia or the murder of Khaled Saeed in Egypt. This demonstrates the clear impact of the Arab Spring, including the exaggeration of the event and its dissemination in a manner that incentivizes people to protest.

[9] A face-to-face interview with Wael Abu Rshaidat, conducted by the ACRPS research team in Doha on 25 February 2012. It is worth noting that my original scepticism of this story was warranted. It turned out that the delegation met with Kalthum and Louay al-Ali, who were the ones who told them that the children were transferred to the central Political Security office in As-Sweida. As for blaming Najib and spreading rumours about him, this was mostly due to his relationship with the president (he is the cousin of Bashar al-Assad). This version of events is based on interviews with some members of the delegation sent to Atif Najib by representatives of Daraa's major families, conducted by Ahmad Abazed, member of the ACRPS Syrian Revolution Documentation Project; as well as with a virtual interview via Skype with Mithqal Abazed, conducted by Ahmad Abazed, member of the ACRPS Syrian Revolution Documentation Project, on 9 September 2019; a virtual interview via Facebook Messenger with Jihad Mahameed, conducted by Ahmad Abazed, member of the ACRPS Syrian Revolution Documentation Project, on 26 June 2019; and a virtual interview via Skype with Sheikh Muhammad Abdulaziz Abazed, conducted by the ACRPS Syrian Revolution Documentation team on 19 May 2019. Sheikh Muhammad Abdulaziz Abazed participated in the meetings with regime officials demanding the release of the children and was also among the delegation that met Bashar al-Assad.

The initial reaction came on 15 March, when demonstrators gathered in the Hamidiyeh Market chanting for freedom (although regime supporters also seem to have joined the crowd and chanted pro-regime slogans). The security forces responded by arresting everyone they could, including some of the infiltrators. On 18 March, a Friday, huge numbers came out to protest the treatment of the children and the parents who had sought to use traditional mediation to secure their children's release. Although this coincided with the call for a Friday of 'rage' published on the Facebook pages mentioned in Chapter One, what happened in Daraa had very little to do with the plans made there. The protesters chose the name 'Friday of Dignity'[10] to encapsulate their message. Nonetheless, the security forces fired on protesters, killing two men, Husam Ayyash and Mahmoud al-Jawabra.

When funeral proceedings were held for Ayyash and Jawabra the following day (19 March), it seemed like all Daraa had come out to see them off.[11] The funeral procession quickly turned into a protest march. Chants like 'killing your people makes you a traitor' (first heard during the Syrian youth protest in front of the Libyan embassy on 22 February 2011) and 'the Syrian people will not be humiliated' (debuted at the Hariqa Market incident) were heard from the crowd. Other chants circulated during this occasion, including the famous chant 'the people want to bring down the regime', which was first heard in this protest, but it was not received well by the demonstrators so it was dropped.

The regime had resolved to deal with the events in Daraa by mobilizing its 'rapid response' and 'counterterrorism units'[12] to suppress them.[13] It too had been paying attention to events in Egypt and Tunisia. Its strategy from the very beginning was thus to try to crush protests quickly enough that they would not escalate into fully-fledged revolution. But its attempts to do so had precisely the opposite effect. The violence meted out by the security

---

[10] In my essay on theories of revolution, titled 'On Revolution and Susceptibility to Revolution', I assigned a central role to the issue of humiliation and dignity. The essay is available in English as the first chapter in: Bishara, *Understanding Revolutions*.

[11] An interview with Raed Abazeed, conducted by the ACRPS research team on 13 September 2011.

[12] There are no such forces with these names; the forces mobilized were part of General Intelligence Branch 234, known among the Syrians as Branch NAJAH, after its location. But since these forces are involved in rapid response and anti-terrorist activities, some Syrians call them 'anti-terrorist forces'.

[13] Within hours of the protest on 18 March the regime had redeployed its forces by helicopter to Daraa Stadium. These units are relatively unfamiliar to Syrians; since, they had only been used domestically during a handful of police raids and during the anti-smuggling campaign of late 2010. Their black uniforms immediately distinguish them from the army, security forces and police. When they first appeared in Daraa in 2011, locals assumed they were Hezbollah fighters – hence the chant 'no to Iran and no to Hezbollah!' A face-to-face interview with Nasr, *nom de guerre* Abu Anas al-Shami, conducted by the ACRPS research team in Doha on 13 March 2013; A face-to-face interview with Bilal Turkiya, conducted by the ACRPS research team in Doha on 13 March 2013.

forces during the Friday of Dignity and thereafter – recorded on mobiles and uploaded to social media – outraged Daraawis and then Syrians across the country, transforming the protests first into a tenacious local uprising and ultimately a national revolution. The regime thus achieved precisely what it was trying to avoid. Of course, it is not at all clear that protesters in Daraa were aiming for a national mobilization. But this is what they were ultimately to achieve – in conjunction, of course, with the nascent regional movements that had begun to develop independently in each governorate and which would eventually become the revolution's distinctive coordination committees.[14]

The following day (20 March), according to Nizar al-Haraki, senior regime figures descended on Daraa to try and calm tensions. Brigadier Rustum al-Ghazali had spent much of the previous day talking to the victims' families[15] and trying to ensure that they would not encourage escalation. Now a delegation led by Deputy Foreign Minister Faisal Mekdad (who is originally from the Daraa governorate) and Usama Adi, a member of the Regional Command Council (RCC) (the party politburo) arrived to attend the wakes. The response was probably not what they were hoping for. One young man present told Mekdad to 'run back to your master and tell him that killing your people makes you a traitor'.[16] Meanwhile, Hisham al-Ikhtiyar – the head of the National Security Bureau, making him the highest-ranking intelligence official in the country – was addressing a gathering of local notables. Prior to the meeting, protests broke out in the city, leading to the fall of a third martyr from Daraa, Ra'id Akrad. Ikhtiyar openly threatened attendees at the gathering: 'You are liars, yesterday you were two hundred people, and today you're two thousand! You use children as a pretext to demonstrate ... You have twenty-four hours to resolve the matter. If not, we know how to do it ourselves.' Upon hearing that protesters had set fire to the front gate of the courthouse and broken windows at a government hospital, he went further: 'I'll make the Houran rue the day it did this. By the time I'm finished with you, you'll be dreaming of the days you had a courthouse and a hospital! I'll bring Daraa down on top of you if this isn't resolved!' An elderly man stood up and told Ikhtiyar, 'We'd sacrifice ourselves for President Bashar, but your rhetoric is unacceptable!' Usama Adi intervened and attempted to defuse the tensions, asking the

---

[14] Activist Omar Edlbi says that after the 15 March protests, activists had already agreed to organize local demonstrations in their own governorates for the following Friday (18 March), before they were aware of the children's arrest. Serial interviews with Omar Edlbi, conducted by Hamzeh al-Moustafa, ACRPS researcher, on 3 August 2012, 5 August 2012 and 1 April 2013.

[15] The families of Husam Ayyash and Mahmoud al-Jawabra, who were killed on 18 March.

[16] A face-to-face interview with Nizar al-Haraki, conducted by the ACRPS research team in Doha on 13 March 2013. Nizar al-Haraki was present at the meeting as a representative of the local community.

notables to help calm the situation in Daraa. But when the notables made their way to the sit-in to try and convince demonstrators to go home, they were met with chants of 'liars, liars!' Protesters then announced a general strike across Daraa for the following day.[17] Much like the party branches and the peasant and workers unions, notables and clerics were important mediators between the regime and local communities, but this network was incapacitated in the first decade of Bashar's rule.

On 21 March, the general strike came into effect, and workplaces across Daraa were left completely empty. At the same time, engineers, doctors and professionals gathered in front of the local Ba'th Party branch office to demand freedom, dignity, the release of detainees, an end to the state of emergency and recognition of civil liberties. The following day, a field hospital was set up to treat those injured or struggling to breathe after clashes with the security forces, and a civil committee was established to lead the protest movement.

Initially, those protesting in Daraa wanted nothing more than the release of the detainees and redress for the humiliating treatment that they had experienced. It was only after the security forces' violent response that they began to make explicitly political demands. This process was driven by the formation of local organizing committees comprising students, civil society activists and representatives of political parties. These committees took charge of leading the protests and made them part of an organized political movement.

At this point, the regime changed tack. The local security response had proven insufficient, and its usual trick of alternately cajoling and intimidating the city's notables had had no effect on the protesters.[18]

On 22 March, the army was deployed to Daraa. Military checkpoints were set up on all the main roads into the city and at major intersections. Seven activists with known political affiliations were arrested.[19] The regime had assumed that this would cow the protesters, but in fact, it only served to make them more radical. And it now made the fateful decision to escalate.

Since the very beginning of the protests in Daraa, the Umari Mosque in the Old City – close to the local party branch office where the sit-ins had begun – had served as a rallying point for participants. By the evening of

---

[17] Ibid.
[18] I subsequently learned that Sharaa was one of the state officials visiting Daraa on 21 March. An interview with Major General Mohammad al-Haj Ali, director of the Syrian National Defence College from 2008 until the date of his defection from the Syrian army on 2 August 2012, conducted by Maen Talaa, member of the ACRPS Syrian Revolution Documentation Project, in Doha on 25 May 2019.
[19] These were Nizar al-Haraki, Muhammad Ammar, Shukri al-Mahameed, Isam al-Mahameed, Issa Masalma, Bassam al-Masri and Abd al-Rahman Masalma. The detainees had quite different political backgrounds: three from the Socialist Union, one from the CAP and three Islamists.

22 March, it was hosting dozens of demonstrators. 'Initially the security forces stayed away from the mosque because of its symbolism,' one activist, Bilal Turkiya,[20] said:

> But on the evening of 22 March, they started to take up positions in the neighbourhoods around it. People started to feel uneasy – they knew something was going to happen. At around 4 in the morning, the electricity was cut off from the whole of the Old City, and then the rapid response and counterterrorism forces came out of the Ba'th Party branch office and stormed the mosque. The protesters used the speakers [for the call to prayer] to call for help. Some young men raced down to help them, but they shot at them with live ammunition. Six people were killed – one of them, Dr Muhammad al-Masri's brother,[21] was executed on the spot. That was the first summary execution. Then the regime sent cars out announcing a curfew.

During the attack on the mosque, the security forces were filmed desecrating copies of the Qur'an. Few had forgotten the regime's attempts to whip up public outrage at similar scenes in Guantanamo Bay or around the Danish cartoon controversy.

The popular reaction was immediate. According to Turkiya:

> Young men from all the villages around Daraa, especially Hrak, Kherbeh, Mseifra and Sura, headed for the city on foot. Thousands of them managed to get past the military checkpoints. The army didn't try and stop them or prevent them from protesting. And the security forces let them get all the way to Tishreen Square, which is right by the governorate buildings. But when they got close to the branch office [and the Umari Mosque], they started shooting at them. Dozens were killed.

The morgue at the national hospital received twenty-five bodies that day, Turkiya said.

The first days of the Daraa uprising are a microcosm of the Syrian revolution. The regime ignored people's basic demands, refused to think about why they might be protesting and focused exclusively on how to smother the movement in its crib – whether that meant containment or

---

[20] A face-to-face interview with Bilal Turkiya, conducted by the ACRPS research team in Doha on 13 March 2013.
[21] Update for the English edition: The victim's name was Ashraf al-Masry, an engineer. The Umari Mosque storming saw the first killing of a doctor (Ali Ghisab al-Mahameed, who was shot in the ambulance on his way to help the demonstrators), the first field execution (Ashraf al-Masry), and the first death of a child (Ibtisam Masalma) in the revolution. A virtual interview via Skype with Ibrahim al-Masri (known during the revolution as Omar al-Hourani), conducted by Ahmad Abazed, member of the ACRPS Syrian Revolution Documentation Project, on 29 September 2019.

brute force. It invoked imaginary terrorist gangs and foreign conspiracies to justify crushing the protests. All the propaganda still current today was born in the first days of the revolution. Syrian state TV showed wads of cash and caches of weapons supposedly discovered inside the Umari Mosque as evidence for its fabricated version of events. But this phase of what would become a revolution was still a community-based, civic, unarmed uprising with no clear aims and no international dimension. Even in this early period, the regime was invoking a terrorist conspiracy to explain away what was happening.

Despite the regime's brutal response and its readiness to commit murder, the Syrian revolution in its first months remained entirely peaceful. In this it was no exception to the general rule of Arab revolutions. The protest movement in Syria followed more or less the same path as the Tunisian revolution, with Daraa playing the role of Sidi Bouzid. It began as a local popular reaction to a specific violation of human rights against the backdrop of general political and social injustice, a reaction that the regime could not contain. As in Tunisia, this reaction then spread to other provincial regions – the towns around Damascus, Homs, Latakia, Hama, Deir ez-Zor – where it took on a new and more radical dimension, becoming a popular uprising demanding freedom, reform and change (without, as yet, targeting the regime as a whole). The difference, however, was that the revolutionaries in Syria were confronting a different sort of regime, in a different sort of society, against a different geopolitical backdrop.

The widening popular uprisings stopped at the gates of Damascus and Aleppo. Resentment against the regime was no less common in these cities than elsewhere. But the security forces had a tighter grip here, and the classes that benefited most from the regime were concentrated within their limits, influencing broad swathes of local society. These classes were hesitant. They feared losing what they had gained in the last decade, but they also feared the possible repercussions of a revolution for a multi-sectarian society like Syria's. They were haunted by the examples of Iraq and Lebanon, a point we will return to below. But the lack of broad popular participation in these two urban centres during the early days of the protests does not mean that the Syrian revolution was a rural uprising or an uprising of the poor.

Poverty, as we have seen, can be a driver of protest. It can rage and roar. But this does not necessarily produce a political revolution. In fact, protests rooted in poverty tend to be disorganized, depoliticized and easily suppressed. Other than promises and the inevitable recommendations of investigative committees, they leave little trace. Protests of the poor endure only if there are politically aware groups among the poor classes who can use the energy of social protest to mobilize them around identity or class, forming the basis of persistent political action.[22] Otherwise, poverty in the absence of development is antithetical to political participation. It keeps much of the population out of public affairs and denies them political influence, encouraging apathy, cultural emptiness and acquiescence to the existing regime due to their preoccupation with satisfying daily needs.[23]

Poverty and marginalization were not the main motive for the Syrian revolution. Nor did it start in the countryside. Of course, economic and social marginalization did help mobilize the masses around political demands at a very early stage. The revolution did begin in the urban centres of the marginalized and impoverished periphery (the medium-sized cities and large towns). But this is precisely the point. The revolution became political in the capital cities of the governorates – places where there was a middle class, where there were educated and politically engaged professionals inspired by Tunisia and Egypt and desperate for change. These cities were mostly the social base of the Ba'th. Some participants had prior experience as human rights defenders or members of the opposition. These groups took charge of leading and organizing the protest movement before the countryside and the poverty belts surrounding the urban centres joined in large numbers. The revolution's main constituency was made up of those who had lost out as a result of the regime's neoliberal policies, many of them constituencies of the ruling party. But it was not a rural revolution and it was not limited to the countryside.

I noted above that the Syrian revolution initially followed a similar path to its counterpart in Tunisia, with the city of Daraa standing in for Tunisia's Sidi Bouzid, but there were many contextual differences that influenced how it developed and spread, related to the nature of despotism in Syria and the structure of Syrian society. There were also crucial differences in the political and organizational experience of the opposition forces in each country. In Tunisia there was a certain margin of freedom for union and political activity. This meant that there was an established body of activists with experience in labour and student activism and political parties, both clandestine and semi-public.[24] In Syria, meanwhile, the totalitarian character of the authoritarian regime precluded any form of political activity, including labour or community activism. Syrians were in effect trained in the arts of struggle and organization *during* the revolution. The younger members of political parties and the existing opposition forces did contribute to that process. But the main body of the revolutionaries, who

---

[22] Bishara, *Understanding Revolutions*, 121.
[23] Ibid.
[24] Bishara, *The Glorious Tunisian Revolution*, 155.

had no previous political experience, received their training in political activism under the shadow of repression as the revolution was raging.

The core of activists produced by the early days of the revolution included many young members of the opposition parties, but it was predominantly made up of unaffiliated, politically and socially aware newcomers from all religious and regional backgrounds (including Aleppo and Damascus). The regime was to kill and imprison thousands of these activists and drive many more into hiding or exile. One of the most significant of the regime's many crimes, was the demolition of the civic dimension of the Syrian revolution. Many activists who survived continued to work in the aid sector or in the media, a kind of activism which demands great sacrifices and which cuts across sects and communities. Very few of them took up arms. The majority of this generation of activists was either murdered, imprisoned, or exiled. The fate of thousands of them is still unknown – or as the Syrian phrase has it, 'nobody's heard anything since they were arrested'. These were the first heroes of the Syrian revolution: civic and community activists. And the regime treated them as enemies.

II. A peaceful popular revolution

The popular uprising unfolding in Syria presented the regime with an essential dilemma. On one hand, the security apparatus was at the heart of the dissatisfaction driving protest. On the other hand, it was the regime's only familiar means of dealing with dissent. And as the protests expanded, the security forces, and later the army itself, were to become its main agent in the governorates.

Over the last two decades, the security forces had developed into a sort of parallel state operating behind the façade of party and government. The security forces were present at every moment of Syrians' lives. They were the main link between the president and the regime and society. In addition to routine control, intimidation, and repression of dissent, they provided regular reports on the popular mood and the extent of economic and social discontent as well as political activity. But their role was not codified in law, and they were entirely absent from public discussion or debate.

The steady infiltration of every domain of life by the security forces allowed them to become the primary actor within the state, marginalizing the party. Representative bodies (the People's Assembly and the local councils) had lost any meaningful function. Ministers and prime ministers had become no more than senior bureaucrats, unwilling to exercise their full legal powers for fear of offending the security establishment – a mistake that could be fatal to one's career, or even life. Senior security officials could call senior employees and give them instructions that contradicted their minister's directives. It was the security forces that really governed, in the sense of managing the state. A security officer unofficially outranked all other public servants. Directors of government departments and institutions often complained that junior security officers on their staff could make or break policy and wielded influence far beyond their own.

The security establishment had two solutions to the daily challenges faced by Syrian citizens: surveillance and violence, occasionally supplemented by alliances with local notables (the self-described 'progressive' Syrian regime treated the Syrian people as a mere collection of local confessional and clan communities). This fed resentment towards regime policy among the poor and the immiserated middle classes. But it also kept Syrians living in fear. When the protests of 2011 saw the population suddenly overcome this fear – the main source of the security establishment's power – the security forces' response was to escalate, to be unprecedently brutal, in the hope of regaining their lost power of deterrence. Violence was the solution. If violence had so far failed to stymie protest, it was not because it was the wrong medicine but because the dose had been too low.[25] The logic underpinning the security mentality was that if force did not work, more force would.

This is not at all to say that what happened can be blamed on the security forces rather than the regime. The regime *is* the security establishment, and vice-versa. The security establishment did not mislead the regime. Assad was the ultimate decision-maker, and he opted – out of the various proposals made by the different agencies – for the most extreme strategy. He took pains to emphasize unity of purpose at the top levels of government in his 30 March speech: 'They want to be reassured that the president is a reformist but that those around him are holding him back. To the contrary, those around me are constantly pushing me forward [towards reform].'[26]

The spread of the Daraa uprising beyond the confines of the governorate came on 25 March, when protests were held in several towns and cities across Syria. One significant protest took place in Sheikh Dahir Square in the coastal city of Latakia, on the other side of the country from Daraa. After initial demonstrations were broken up by the security forces, the Latakian movement shifted to a model of continuous sit-ins in historical neighbourhoods like

---

[25] An International Crisis Group report quoted a security official in this connection: 'Officers reacted aggressively whenever pressed about the shortcomings of the security solution. They repeat that they can finish all this within two days, if only they were given a free hand. They complain that they are still operating with too many constraints. True, the orders have been to avoid large-scale operations that could provide the West with an excuse to intervene.' See: International Crisis Group, 'Syria's Mutating Conflict', Middle East Report, no. 128, 1 August 2012, 5, at: https://bit.ly/3IUoGED (accessed 21 December 2021).

[26] To watch Assad's full speech, see: *C-SPAN*, 30 March 2011, at: https://bit.ly/3EhwNrB (accessed 21 December 2021).

Sleibeh. But the dispersal of the Albi Square sit-in on 8 April and the crushing of Independence Day demonstrations on 17 April served to isolate the movement within the peripheral slum district of South Raml, an area largely inhabited by Palestinian refugees and rural migrants from the governorate's countryside and from neighbouring Idleb. Protests continued to be held here until mid-August.[27] The movement was more successful in nearby Jablah, Latakia's sister city, and Banyas, which sits just over the border from Jablah in the Tartous governorate. Here protests continued unabated from 25 March throughout April. In some cases, unorganized young men were seen carrying weapons. Damascus's satellite towns (Duma, at-Tall, Harasta) and Homs also began to witness protests around the same time.

Greater use of violence had failed to end the protests. In fact, the security forces' response had produced an entirely unanticipated popular reaction, one that was increasingly beyond their control. Their supposedly encyclopaedic knowledge of Syrian society developed over decades of surveillance and control counted for nothing.

During the first month of the Syrian revolution the balance seemed to be shifting against the regime. New zones of protest were constantly emerging and the security forces were on the back foot.[28] Incidents like the Clocktower Square sit-in in Homs (18 April) and the Good Friday protests in Damascus (22 April) exposed the double bind in which the regime now found itself. We will focus on these incidents because they represent important turning points for the revolution. When the regime fired on protesters with live ammunition, more protesters came out to join them. When they tried *not* firing on protesters, new groups joined the protest movement. At the Friday of Determination protests of 15 April, for example, the regime's decision not to use firearms on the protesters encouraged thousands of others to join demonstrations in most of Damascus's satellite towns, as well as in Daraa, Homs and Latakia.[29] Moreover, the Kurdish regions and the city of Deir ez-Zor saw the first stirrings of local protest, warning of a possible future explosion there too.

Why did the regime decide not to fire on 15 April?[30] In part it was because of how the protests were developing. Attempts to violently suppress

---

[27] Interviews with a group of intellectuals and political figures including Thaer Deeb, Shams al-Deen al-Kilani, Ali Rahmoun and Bassam Yousef, conducted by Nerouz Satik, ACRPS researcher, at different locations and on various dates.

[28] International Crisis Group, 'Syria's Mutating Conflict'.

[29] It was clear that the decision to abstain from shooting was taken following communications between the security services and some activists and local notables in the governorates, in addition to internal assessments by the regime. The decision also coincided with the president's meetings with notables from rebellious cities and some of the martyrs' families, and the formation of a new government.

[30] With the exception of a speech made by Buthayna Shaaban on 13 May, the regime at no time promised that it would not fire on protesters. However, all the testimony collected by the ACRPS and contemporary media coverage confirms that the security forces did not use live ammunition from the Friday of Resilience on 8 April through to 16 April, the day of Assad's speech to the new cabinet.

the Friday of Resilience protests the previous week (8 April), which had left more than twenty people dead and dozens more injured, had in fact been the trigger for fresh protests and vigils in public squares throughout the Daraa governorate (Jasim, Ankhal, Hrak, Daʿel, Nawa, as-Sanamayn, Tassil, and Kafr Shams). The rhythm of protest accelerated: in place of impulsive expressions of solidarity, demonstrations were now being held in those towns on a daily basis, with demonstrators insisting that they would stay in the streets until their demands were met.[31] Moreover, as I have noted, cities outside the Daraa governorate – in Homs, Latakia, Jablah, Banyas and the Damascus periphery – were now seeing protests – peaceful protests that looked like weddings or popular gatherings, with crowds clapping and chanting popular ballads, patriotic songs and slogans.

At the same time, the regime was struggling to maintain its narrative. From the very beginning of the protests, regime figures had invoked 'infiltrators' and 'third parties' involved in a conspiracy intended to undermine Syria's 'resistance'. This line had been taken up by regime allies, particularly Iran and Hezbollah. On 12 April the spokesman of the Iranian Foreign Ministry described the protests – protests which, it must be stressed, were still entirely peaceful, and which by this point had left over 200 people dead – as 'the product of foreign intervention', an 'evil deed committed by the Westerners and the Americans and especially by the Zionists'. Calling them an attempt to 'exaggerate the demands of a small group and present them as the demands and the will of the majority', he warned of falling for 'this game being played by the Americans'.[32] On a speech on 25 May, Hezbollah Secretary-General Hassan Nasrallah called on Syrians to 'preserve their regime and allow the Syrian leadership the space to put the necessary reforms in place', stressing that 'the fall of the Syrian regime is in the interest of America and of Israel',[33] although he did not go so far as to brand the popular movement a conspiracy.[34]

---

[31] At this point these demands were still limited to replacing the governor, disciplining Najib and offering an apology to the families of those killed. Some political demands had also been made by local activists, who wanted greater public freedoms, an end to the state of emergency and the repeal of Article 8 of the constitution, which gives the Baʿth Party a privileged position as leader of the state and society.

[32] Al Jazeera, 12 April 2011, at: https://bit.ly/30KA8BB (accessed 21 December 2021).

[33] For Hassan Nasrallah's speech on 25 May 2011, see: Moqawama, 25 May 2011, at: https://bit.ly/3qhWrrd (accessed 21 December 2021).

[34] Hezbollah subsequently adopted a position closer to that of the regime, emphasizing the role of Islamist groups and 'the American-Zionist-Gulf conspiracy'. In a speech on 25 May 2013, Nasrallah was to announce the party's full engagement in the regime's war against the Syrian people, securing its place as an active part of a sectarian axis that included Iran, the Nouri al-Maliki government in Iraq and the Assad regime. See: Moqawama, 25 May 2013, at: https://bit.ly/3yLdkhL (accessed 21 December 2021).

The official explanation for the protesters killed by gunfire was that infiltrators (*mundassin*) were firing at both protesters and the security forces. This was hardly going to convince the public, but 'infiltrators' continued to be a regular fixture of Interior Ministry statements right up until the end of April, when their place was taken by 'Takfiri groups'. The president himself regularly characterized the alleged conspiracy as 'germs' infesting the Syrian body – a constant and indisputable presence that had to be fought by 'immunity', i.e. by Syrians resisting their seditious messages: 'Germs exist everywhere on the skin and in the internal organs. Throughout the history of medicine, scientists have not sought ways to exterminate these germs, but ways to strengthen the immunity of our bodies. This is what we should consider, and it is more important than analysing the conspiracy.'[35]

There had been more deaths on the Friday of Resilience than at any previous protest to date. The next day, the Interior Ministry issued a statement accusing infiltrators of the killings. It seems unlikely that they expected any prominent public figure to dispute this. But popular anger was such that a member of the People's Assembly, Nasr al-Hariri, appeared on Al Jazeera to condemn the security forces and call on the president to stop the bloodshed; he then tendered his resignation. On the same day, Samira Masalma, editor-in-chief of the state-owned *Tishreen* newspaper, expressed scepticism about the presence of a 'third party' and demanded that senior security officers be investigated and punished for their negligence if infiltrators really had been present. Samira Masalma was immediately fired, while Nasr al-Hariri was forced to retract his resignation and placed under house arrest, where he remained until fleeing Syria on 23 August 2012.[36]

Assad's failure to outline any credible reform measures in his speech to parliament on 30 March had outraged protesters. The regime was aware of this, and it was quickly put about that a reform agenda would be set out in his speech to the new cabinet on 16 April. This speech was in fact a didactic one and showed Assad at his most condescending. To complete the farce, the attentive ministers scribbled down every word he uttered, as he set out in schoolmasterly fashion the duties of government and the need to respond to every complaint. The point was clear: Assad could not be held responsible for the failings of his ministers. He avoided terms like 'sedition' and 'conspiracy', returning to his old theme of reform and emphasizing the legitimacy of popular protests and demands. And he set a date for the promised end to the state of emergency and the enactment of a law regulating peaceful assemblies and demonstrations.

---

[35] To watch Assad's full speech at Damascus University, see: *C-SPAN*, 20 June 2011, at: https://bit.ly/3pbyYsh (accessed 21 December 2021).

[36] *Ammon News*, 24 August 2012, at: https://bit.ly/3qbISJW (accessed 21 December 2021).

In an attempt to calm the situation and defuse popular anger in the run-up to the speech, the security forces were ordered to stop firing on protesters, and 'significant political concessions' were offered.[37] The governors of Daraa and Homs were dismissed, the governor of Daraa and the head of its Political Security branch were prosecuted, and an official inquiry was launched into events in Daraa. Committees were established to discuss lifting the state of emergency and to draft new laws regulating political parties, the media and assembly. The families of those killed in Daraa and Banyas were invited to the presidential palace. Moreover, in an attempt to appeal to the conservative Damascus bourgeoisie and to the religious establishment, it was announced that a theological institute was to be set up in Damascus, that hundreds of teachers dismissed for wearing the *niqab* would be reinstated and that the newly opened Damascus Casino would be shut down.[38] Although the regime was closely connected to large

---

[37] On 31 March, pursuant to a presidential decree, the Regional Command Council (RCC) of the Baʿth Party formed two committees: one to draft legislation allowing for the lifting of the state of emergency, which was to complete its work by 25 April, and one to address the 'problem of the 1962 census in al-Hasakeh governorate', which was to complete its work by 15 April. The Supreme Judicial Council likewise assembled special commissions to investigate all deaths (civilian and military) in the governorates of Daraa and Latakia. The Daraa commission held its inaugural session on 5 April, when it cross-examined Atif Najib. On 13 July, two and a half months late, it ruled that Najib and former Governor Faysal Kalthum should be barred from leaving the country. Other than the travel bans, no other punishment was handed down. See: *Asharq Al-Awsat*, 14 June 2011, at: https://bit.ly/3Eev2vi (accessed 21 December 2021).

On 4 April, Assad issued a decree establishing the Sham Higher Institute for Religious Studies in Damascus. The following day, 5 April, he ordered the reinstatement of the 1,200 teachers dismissed for wearing the *niqab* and the closure of Syria's only casino. See: *The Guardian*, 6 April 2011, at: https://bit.ly/314nygn (accessed 21 December 2021).

On 19 April, the cabinet ratified a decree bringing an end to the state of emergency throughout Syria and another abolishing the Higher State Security Court set up in 1968. It also approved a draft decree 'regulating citizens' right of free protest, one of the basic human rights guaranteed by the constitution of the Syrian Arab Republic', although under this decree, protests required a permit from the Interior Ministry, whose staff either laughed applicants out of the building or arrested them on the spot. See: *Al-Akhbar* (Lebanon), 20 April 2011, at: https://bit.ly/3J4UDuf (accessed 21 December 2021).

[38] This last measure is among the conditions set by Muhammad Said Ramadan al-Buti to secure his support for the regime. Buti did not attend the prayer for rain, which on 5 December 2010, the president himself had asked to be performed throughout Syria's mosques after the noon prayer on Friday, 10 December 2010. Buti criticized the way the rain prayers were carried out in Syria. He had attributed the lack of rain to three factors: a Syrian TV series, broadcasted in Ramadan 2010, that he had warned would 'spread misfortune' in the country given its supposed criticism of the Qurʾan; a directive issued by Bashar al-Assad banning the wearing of a *niqab* in teaching, study, and exam halls (not because Buti disagreed with the ban, but because he believed that the minister of education used it to dismiss some 1,200 *niqab*-wearing teachers who were 'mad enough to stand and teach with the *niqab* on [their] face'); and, thirdly, the warnings given by Buti to the Syrian Islamic 'private schools' regarding their religiosity saying, 'We put our children there to raise them with a religious upbringing. What is the matter with you? [...] Why this hostility to manifestations of religion?' However, Buti expressed his hope that the drought could be turned around if these three causes were addressed. He warned that if they were not then water depletion would be imminent. See *Syria News*, 5 November 2010. Archived copy available at: https://bit.ly/3v7eUZY (accessed 11 April 2022); *Syria News*, 13 December 2010. Archived copy available at: https://bit.ly/3LXjfp8 (accessed 11 April 2022).

constituencies within these groups, it did not want the revolution to turn their heads. And the regime also made a play for Kurdish support. A presidential decree granted full citizenship to the many al-Hasakeh Kurds who were registered as foreigners; Kurdish New Year (*Neyrouz*) was made a national holiday; and Law 49, which denied those living in border regions the right to freely dispose of their land, was revoked.[39]

Syrians, who had little faith in regime figures and institutions, saw no reason to stop their peaceful protest. If anything, the regime's apparent openness to reform encouraged them to keep going. Syrians knew that legal changes meant little so long as the regime governed not through law but through the security services. Even if the opposition parties did not feel the same way, for most Syrians, changes to the law were not news.

In an era of revolutionary change, the regime was also struggling with the time factor. Steps towards reform were taken retroactively – that is, the concessions offered in advance of the Friday of Determination corresponded to demands made in the earliest days of the Daraa uprising. If these concessions had been made then, they would have been enough to change the course of events. But as it was, the regime's concessions lagged behind the protesters' demands. By 19 April, when the state of emergency was lifted by presidential decree, the constant protests had already made it a dead letter. Whether the state said it was legal or not, people were assembling and demonstrating. And they no longer wanted to reform the regime – they wanted to change it. They wanted the privileges of the Baʻth Party and the president to be abolished as a preamble to a new constitution, a national unity government headed by a politically neutral figure and ultimately a democratic transition.

III. The Homs Clocktower Square sit-in

It is not difficult to see why Homs was one of the first cities to join the protests that had begun in Daraa. As well as the potent cocktail of social and political resentment present throughout Syria, there were a number of local factors at work which made Homsis particularly willing to protest. These factors were to sustain the city's revolution through long months in which it seemed to be standing alone against the regime. At the same time, they were to produce some of the first sectarian clashes in the country. Similar clashes were later seen in other cities that, like Homs, had witnessed waves of immigration from the countryside and the emergence of new

---

[39] Bishara et al., *The Question of Syria's Kurds*, 102-3.

neighbourhoods with an Alawi majority, and where the Alawi presence in the security apparatus and other government positions was dominant.[40]

The governor of Homs, Mohammad Eyad Ghazal, was exemplary of the authoritarian security state's alliance with business interests. I have already had cause to discuss the Dream of Homs redevelopment of the Old City, a project cut short by the revolution. But Ghazal had been involved in many other similar projects, including the appropriation of agricultural land in al-Basateen[41] and Mimas[42] and the Tadmur City project. Individually and cumulatively, these projects had hit locals hard. It was thus no surprise that the first political demand articulated by the people of Homs was the removal of the governor.

Homs also boasted one of the earliest symbols of the revolution, the blogger Tal al-Mallouhi. The then nineteen-year-old Mallouhi, a member of one of Homs's oldest families, had been arrested on 27 December 2009 for criticizing the regime online. To add insult to injury, she was accused of being recruited as a spy for the US by her lover, an Austrian officer in the UN peacekeeping forces deployed along the separation line in the Golan Heights. Mallouhi served as a rallying cry for protesters in Homs from the very beginning of the demonstrations, and her honour became a stand-in for the honour of the city.[43] After the local activist Suhair Atassi was beaten

---

[40] An interview with Najati Tayyara, conducted by Hamzeh al-Moustafa, ACRPS researcher, on 3 August 2012. An interview with Omar Edlbi, conducted by Hamzeh al-Moustafa, ACRPS researcher, on 5 August 2012.

 Rapid migration from the countryside to the cities picked up after independence and intensified during Ba'th rule. This 'increased the percentage of Alawites in Latakia from the single digits on the eve of independence in 1945 to around 50 per cent in the first decade of this century; in Homs from near zero to about 25 per cent; in Tartus from about 30 per cent to 80 per cent; and in Banyas from less than 10 per cent to around 60 per cent during the same period'. See: Heiko Wimmen, 'The Sectarianization of the Syrian War', in *Beyond Sunni and Shia: The Roots of Sectarianism in a Changing Middle East*, ed. Frederic Wehrey (London: Hurst, 2017), 67. This, coupled with Alawi officers' domination of the security forces and their employment of relatives from the villages in local state organs, created tensions with the largely Sunni and Christian urban population. These cities were also the site of the first sectarian skirmishes. See also: Fabrice Balanche, '"Go to Damascus, My Son": Alawi Demographic Shifts under Ba'th Party Rule', in *The Alawis of Syria: War, Faith and Politics in the Levant*, ed. Michael Kerr and Craig Larkin (Oxford: Oxford University Press, 2015); Kheder Khaddour, 'The Alawite Dilemma (Homs 2013)', in *Playing the Sectarian Card: Identities and Affiliations of Local Communities in Syria*, ed. Friederike Stolleis (Beirut: Friedrich Ebert Stiftung, 2015), 11. While the massive influx turned the Alawi quarters of the coastal cities into integral parts of enlarged urban areas, migration to Damascus was accommodated to a significant extent at the periphery of the city. For a portrayal of one of these new neighbourhoods erected for security personnel, see: Kheder Khaddour, 'Assad's Officer Ghetto: Why the Syrian Army Remains Loyal', Carnegie Middle East Centre, 4 November 2015, at: https://bit.ly/3qYNnZe (accessed 13 June 2022).

[41] In the Gardenia district, part of the appropriated land, flats in the two residential towers erected under the redevelopment plan went for SYP 100 million ($2 million).

[42] The governorate drew up a plan for development along the Homs–Tripoli Road based on the appropriation of agricultural land on both sides of the road in the Mimas region, which was to be turned into luxury residences.

[43] Barout, *The Last Decade in the History of Syria*, 233.

and detained during the Interior Ministry protest in Damascus on 16 March, a new chant developed: 'Suheir, go tell Tall: the Syrian people still stand tall'.[44] The dignity of these two victims of injustice became symbolic of the dignity of Homs as a whole.

During the last quarter of 2010, the government had launched a campaign against 'economic crime', in particular diesel smuggling. Thousands of families in poor neighbourhoods on the outskirts of the city depended on smuggling for their livelihoods, and this campaign hit them hard. Once protests got underway in Homs, the people of these neighbourhoods – most of them of Bedouin origin – were to be the most energetic participants. They were also the first to take up arms against the regime. Gun ownership is very common in areas of this kind and in the border areas through which smuggling routes run, as are complex relationships with the security forces (in the form of kickbacks and bribes but also in the occasional political uses made of these networks, for example to smuggle weapons over the borders). These factors undoubtedly influenced the trajectory of the revolution in many places, in particular as regards the move towards unorganized, local armed action.

Homs joined the protests on the Friday of Dignity (18 March), when around two hundred individuals gathered in front of the Khalid Bin al-Waleed Mosque to demand freedom and the dismissal of the governor. On the Friday of Honour the following week (25 March), the security forces surrounded the mosque in anticipation of further protests, forcing locals to gather at several other locations (mainly mosques in Khalidiyeh, Bayyada and Deir Baalba). The security forces were completely unprepared for multiple protests in different neighbourhoods and were unable to prevent their rapid coalescence around a single demonstration that ended up at Clocktower Square.[45] 'I heard that the protest had reached central Homs,' one opposition figure, Najati Tayyara,[46] tells us:

> I went out to see for myself and found the security forces spread out along Abdulhamid al-Durubi Street. I managed to get to a street corner overlooking the square, and from there I saw this enormous protest. There wasn't a single placard with the president's face on it, and that really threw me. We'd never had a big gathering without pictures of the president. There were around 7,000 young people there, led by a young woman who they were carrying on their shoulders, chanting

---

[44] In addition to the chants, a 'We Are All Tal al-Mallouhi' Facebook page was set up in the first days of the revolution.
[45] To watch the Clocktower Square protest during the Friday of Honour, see: YouTube, 1 April 2011, at: https://bit.ly/328TNMv (accessed 21 December 2021).
[46] An interview with Najati Tayyara, conducted by Hamzeh al-Moustafa, ACRPS researcher, on 3 August 2012.

'Suheir, go tell Tall: the Syrian people still stand tall' and 'the people want to end the state of emergency!' It filled me with joy to see it.

The protesters' arrival in Clocktower Square marked a turning point. Although they were not yet calling for the fall of the regime, some of them did tear down pictures of Assad and his father hanging at the entrance to the Officers' Club on the square.[47] This was the first time that the protest movement had taken explicit aim at the head of state, revealing in this burst of vindictiveness[48] just how tense things were in the city.

At first, the security forces were highly disciplined. They avoided scuffles with protesters and made no attempt to disperse the protest by force. Some officers attempted to convince attendees to bring the protest to an end peacefully. But they failed.[49] Najati Tayyara relates the scene on the Friday of Honour:

> As the protest was going on, a pro-regime demonstration made up of people from Ekrima, Zahraa and Nuzha [Alawi neighbourhoods] arrived at the square. There were Political Security men with them and carloads of *shabbiha* carrying sticks. As soon as they reached the square, the *shabbiha* attacked the anti-regime protesters and the security forces started firing tear gas into the crowd. Hundreds of protesters were arrested [...]. After that, checkpoints were put up everywhere, especially around the clocktower, so it was very difficult for protesters to get back into the square. They only managed to do it three weeks later, for the 18 April protest.[50]

During the weeks between the Friday of Honour (25 March) and the Clocktower Square sit-in, demonstrations were organized on a daily basis. Every time the security forces shot someone dead, the next day their funeral processions would develop into a fresh protest, where more people would be killed, leading to more protests the next day. The Friday of Martyrs (1 April) saw a dramatic acceleration in this process. The death of

---

[47] For the pictures of the two Assads being torn up during the Friday of Honour, see: YouTube, 26 March 2011, at: https://bit.ly/3GWbxJq (accessed 21 December 2021).

[48] There was a carnival-like quality to the tearing up of the pictures at the Officers' Club. The same scene repeated itself in other cities, where it became something of a ritual: a young man would clamber up the front of the building, kick down the photo and then tear it up before throwing the shreds to the crowd.

[49] The Friday of Honour and the mutilation of the Assads' photos led to sharp sectarian polarization between Sunni and Alawi neighbourhoods in Homs, which manifested in incidents like the *shabbiha*'s assault on the Nur Mosque in Khalidiyeh and in protest chants like 'let's say what we mean/we don't want to see Alawis!' A string of assassinations would later target senior military figures, including Major Eyad Harfoush (Alawi), Colonel Mueen Mahla (Alawi) and Colonel Abdo Khodr al-Tellawi (Sunni).

[50] Serial interviews with Najati Tayyara, conducted by Hamzeh al-Moustafa, ACRPS researcher, on 3 August 2012 and 7 November 2011; An interview with Omar Edlbi, conducted by Hamzeh al-Moustafa, ACRPS researcher, on 3 August 2012.

twenty-three-year-old Tahani al-Khalidi,[51] a young woman from Bayyada who was shot while filming a protest that began at the Khalid Bin al-Waleed Mosque, released a surge of popular anger in Teir Ma'la and Baba Amr, and the protests quickly spread into Khalidiyeh.[52]

This dynamic – deaths leading to funerals becoming protests leading to more deaths – was ultimately to lead to the Clocktower Square sit-in on 18 April. Although the media paid little attention to the developments in Homs, the days leading up to 18 April were full of protest. On the Friday of Determination (15 April), Homsis came out in force, particularly in Bab al-Siba', Deir Baalba and Khalidiyeh. On that occasion, in advance of Assad's speech, the security forces did not fire on the crowds. However, when the speech was broadcast the following day, it failed to satisfy the protesters, and they came out in large numbers yet again to say as much. This time the security forces responded brutally, leaving more than fifteen young men dead. The day of 17 April saw another major protest, now against a regime that had turned extremely violent.

On 18 April, the funerals of seven young men from Hamidiyeh, Bab al-Dreib and Tall al-Nasr quickly developed into a major protest.[53] But unlike previous funerals, demonstrators headed for Clocktower Square, where they quickly overwhelmed the security checkpoints set up weeks earlier.[54] As soon as the protesters arrived, other Homsis began to join them, and the ultimately tragic Clocktower Square sit-in began. With Tahrir Square still fresh in Syrians' minds, a mass sit-in in a public square had an almost magical quality in the minds of young protesters at that time.

This symbolism was not lost on the regime, which had taken great pains to avoid such sit-ins across Syria. But those in charge of the security response in Homs had not anticipated that so many people would turn out for the funerals. Nor had they anticipated that many of their officers would be busy in the neighbourhood of Ashira,[55] where locals clashed with the security forces after the body of Sheikh Badr Abu Musa, a senior member of the Fawaara clan, was released to his relatives with clear

---

[51] Tahani al-Khalidi was the first woman to die during the protests in Homs. For footage of the funeral, dated 5 April 2011, see: YouTube, 5 April 2011, at: https://bit.ly/32j1gZb (accessed 21 December 2021). The first woman to die during the revolution was Sabta Akrad, a seventeen-year-old killed during the Friday of Honour protests in Daraa on 25 March.

[52] The security forces were ordered by then governor Mohammed Eyad Ghazal to hold a wake for the young woman and to pay her parents blood money (*diya*) in compensation for her death. But the notables of the Bayyada neighbourhood lowered their traditional headbands ('*uqul*), signifying their rejection of this overture. See: Barout, *The Last Decade in the History of Syria*, 235.

[53] For footage of the funeral, see: YouTube, 18 April 2011, at: https://bit.ly/3yKLRwL (accessed 21 December 2021).

[54] To see the protesting crowds in Hamidiyeh district before they reached Clocktower Square, see: YouTube, 18 April 2011, at: https://bit.ly/3H0YLJL (accessed 21 December 2021).

[55] During the clashes, the residents of Ashira used stones, sticks and Molotov cocktails.

signs that he had died under torture.⁵⁶ These clashes escalated into a veritable tribal uprising, with most of the Bedouin residents of Deir Baalba and Baba Amr joining spontaneous protests which cascaded into the square.

The Clocktower Square sit-in was only the second city centre protest of the Syrian revolution, after the Umari Mosque sit-in in Daraa. What was more, it was held in a central square and brought together more than 70,000 people, making it much bigger than its predecessor. The Homs sit-in had no specific demands. It was purely political, an attempt at reproducing Egypt's Tahrir Square in Syria. Tents were quickly put up and civic committees formed that disarmed anyone entering the square. A leadership committee was formed by a group of notables, prominent public figures and clergymen, and the protesters agreed to stick to the committee's line.⁵⁷ And for the first time in the Syrian revolution, despite the misgivings of some of those involved, people were heard to chant 'the people want to bring down the regime' and 'the people want to bring down the president'.⁵⁸

IV. The end of the Clocktower Square sit-in

For the regime, the Homs sit-in marked an unacceptable failure of its strategy to prevent the occupation of central squares in large and mid-sized cities. A protest with such remarkable levels of popular participation could not be allowed to continue.⁵⁹ It thus decided to bring it to an end by any means necessary. At first it tried a relatively gentle approach: an official representative met with the leaders in the middle of the night and requested

---

[56] Barout, *The Last Decade in the History of Syria*, 237.

[57] There were various reasons for the haste with which the protesters assembled a leadership committee made up of local notables, rather than allowing leaders to emerge organically from the dynamics of the protest, as in Egypt. The main concern was to assuage sectarian tensions: prior to the sit-in some protesters had wanted to march on the Alawi-majority district of Zahraa to avenge the pro-regime popular committees' attack on the Nur Mosque in Khalidiyeh, and leaders were needed to keep these impulses in check. An interview with Muhammad Saleh, conducted by the ACRPS research team on 30 November 2011.

[58] In his testimony on the Clocktower Square sit-in, activist Najati Tayyara said, 'In their speeches, the clergymen and the intellectuals had emphasized that before we chanted "the people want to bring down the regime" we should think about what that would mean. But the mass of the protesters was not interested. In fact, they tore down a large picture of President Assad from in front of the police station in the square. They also pulled down the Ba'th Party flag.'

[59] The National Unity Tent set up on Clocktower Square hosted delegations from all over the city, which came to express solidarity with protesters and make speeches. Representatives of the merchants and artisans of Homs attended, as did a delegation from the Christian neighbourhoods, which expressed their solidarity with protesters' demands and stressed the need to prevent sectarian unrest. Some young Alawis also made speeches attempting to alleviate sectarian tensions. The political parties, particularly CAP and SSNP, and civil society committees were also represented.

that they end the sit-in because the demands made – the lifting of the state of emergency and the release of detainees – were to be met the following day. The representative also hinted at the possibility of violence, warning his interlocutors that the authorities would not allow the sit-in to carry on until the following morning.

When this failed, the regime began to make explicit threats of violence, culminating in a phone call from a senior security officer to a local cleric at 1.30 am to tell him that if the sit-in did not end within half an hour, it would be dispersed by force and without concern for deaths and injuries. This was not an idle threat. The activist Najati Tayyara, who was present in the last hours of the sit-in, recounts:

> There wasn't enough time to dismantle the sit-in. We were only given half an hour. We tried to convince people to go home, but they started shooting even before the ultimatum had expired. At 1.50 am we were fired on from the direction of the police station, then from Abd al-Hameed al-Durubi Street and everyone started running in random directions. Nobody knew what was going to happen.[60]

The number of deaths and injuries remains unclear even today.

Although the regime managed to break up the Clocktower Square sit-in, it was not able to prevent protests elsewhere in the city. Demonstrations were now decentralized, moving to densely populated neighbourhoods such as Khalidiyeh and Baba Amr. Over the next eleven months, all the way through to March 2012, Freedom Square in Khalidiyeh became the hub of protest in Homs, hosting huge gatherings every Friday. In a particularly symbolic gesture, locals built a wooden model of the city's clocktower in the middle of the square.[61]

The Clocktower Square sit-in was a turning point. We have already seen how it broke the taboo against targeting the regime and the president specifically. But the regime's response also had other effects. Images of *shabbiha* from Alawi quarters dancing with the security forces in the ruins of the sit-in ramped up sectarian tensions and opened the door to all sorts of incidents which will be discussed in more detail in the relevant chapter below. In the neighbourhoods around the city's outskirts (particularly Baba Amr, Ashira and Deir Baalba) and some of the satellite towns to its north (Ar-Rastan and Talbiseh) and west (Houla, Taldu and Tall Kalakh), locals had started to take up arms in communal self-defence. And shortly after

---

[60] To see the moment that the security forces fired on protesters in Clocktower Square, see: YouTube, 19 April 2011, at: https://bit.ly/3mmWdxO (accessed 21 December 2021).

[61] To see the model of the clocktower during the Khalidiyeh protests, see: YouTube, 30 December 2011, at: https://bit.ly/3ecvzDf (accessed 21 December 2021).

the sit-in, the army was deployed for the first time in the revolution, ostensibly against Salafi groups seeking to establish 'Islamic emirates' in Bab al-Siba' and Hamidiyeh in Homs. This vocabulary was to dominate the official discourse for months to come.

Events in Homs were early indications of what was to come in the Syrian revolution. Crackdowns on urban protest had simply led to its redirection through other channels – towns and peripheral neighbourhoods – and to a gradual transition from peaceful protest at great cost to armed action. This transition was the natural result of the course taken by the protests. Although this course was similar to that of other Arab revolutions, nobody in Egypt or Tunisia had dared to fire on a mass sit-in.[62] The Clocktower Square sit-in belonged to a model of protest generated by urban centres and by the middle classes. But the regime's response sent protest off in a very different direction, towards armed action and sectarianism. This was hardly surprising, given that some of those killed during the protests happened to be from tribal communities where gun ownership was widespread.[63] But a question must be asked here. Was it the revolution that led to sectarian polarization in Homs?

The answer is a definitive 'no'. The sectarian rift can be traced back to the 1960s and the side-effects of rural migration to the city. Alawi neighbourhoods, as previously noted, have long existed in isolation from the rest of urban society. They have their own economies, their own markets and (unofficially) their own schools.[64] Moreover, there were various instances of raids against the Zahraa neighbourhood to avenge the death of Bedouins killed by that neighbourhood's residents, although usually the clergy were eventually able to calm the situation. In 2006, for example, three men slit the throat of an Alawi Political Security officer in a mosque in Bab al-Dreib before fleeing to Saudi Arabia. Alawi men were sometimes beaten up in conservative Sunni-majority neighbourhoods.[65]

---

[62] This was true until Abdel Fattah El-Sisi's military coup in July 2013 and the attack on the Rab'a al-'Adawiyya Square sit-in in Cairo, which, in my opinion cannot be understood without the, by then, many precedents committed by the Syrian regime.

[63] In these parts of Homs, gun ownership is a local tradition imposed by socioeconomic reality: many residents are involved in smuggling. Sources close to the armed movement say that weapons began to be smuggled in from Lebanon in late April 2011, residents were not using them to attack the army unless the latter decided to storm a town, as in Tall Kalakh (14 May) and ar-Rastan and Talbiseh (30 May). Guns were usually used for kidnapping or individual assassinations. For example, on a single day in July, around thirty people were kidnapped or killed. It was only in August that guns began to be commonplace in public and in October that the first armed battalions were formed. Saad al-Hariri apparently financed the smuggling of weapons from Lebanon; some battalions were ultimately named after him and his father.

[64] Interviews with a number of Homs locals including Omar Abdallatef, Fathi Bayoud and others, conducted by Hamzeh al-Moustafa, ACRPS researcher.

[65] Interviews with a number of Homs locals who witnessed these events, conducted by the ACRPS research team in Latakia between 5–30 November 2011.

When Hafez al-Assad died on 10 June 2000, young men from Alawi neighbourhoods came out onto the streets *en masse* armed with batons and chains, particularly in areas bordering on Sunni-majority districts. It is still unclear whether these men anticipated Sunni attacks on their neighbourhoods or were hoping to deter any Sunni protesters from taking advantage of a moment of regime weakness. Regardless of their intentions, their presence led to clashes that left one man dead and ten injured.[66] Such incidents were to occur again during the revolution.

In fact, the events of June 2000 reflect a broader dynamic of relevance to the revolution. The president's death meant a journey into the unknown: Would Syria return to the pre-Assad era? Would the persecution so central to their communal historical memory resume? Would they lose the privileges that they had acquired under the Ba'thist state? These concerns were a major driver of violent minoritarian behaviour in these neighbourhoods and among many poor Alawis with little education, as well as those working in the Syrian security agencies. Bequeathing the presidency to Hafez al-Assad's son allayed these fears, but they were to resurface a decade later.

V. Good Friday: The uprising of the cities of the Damascus countryside

In Damascus there was a brave attempt to organize a sit-in in the Abbasiyeen Square on Good Friday, 22 April. It is impossible to understand this protest without understanding the role of the satellite towns and cities of the Damascus periphery. It was an attempt to bring revolution to the capital by having the periphery march on the centre, a model successfully pioneered by revolutionaries in Tunis and Cairo. The crushing of this sit-in was to have dramatic consequences for those peripheral areas, which were now to join the revolution wholeheartedly.

The towns and cities surrounding Damascus fall administratively under the Damascus Rural governorate, but demographically and economically they are an inseparable part of the capital itself. Before the revolution they were home to hundreds of thousands of people: the largest, Duma, with over 134,000 residents, represented the urban and economic centre of Eastern Ghouta,[67] while nearby Harasta boasted another 107,000.[68] They also have a

---

[66] An interview with Najati Tayyara, conducted by Hamzeh al-Moustafa, ACRPS researcher, on 7 November 2011.
[67] Barout, *The Last Decade in the History of Syria*, 226.
[68] The most important cities in Eastern Ghouta are Harasta (107,000 residents), Arbin (54,000 residents), Jawbar (61,000 residents) and Zamalka (54,000 residents).

long history of political engagement. The area around the capital bore most of the weight of the struggle against the French occupiers in the capital and provided many of its heroes, such as Hasan al-Kharrat, a prominent commander in the Great Syrian Revolt (1920–5). After independence, Duma was a bastion of Nasserism and one of the strongholds of popular resistance to Syrian secession from the United Arab Republic (UAR) in 1961.[69] Since the 1980s, under the influence of Brotherhood figures from the Damascus group[70] and moderate Salafis, they have shifted towards Islamism, but without losing the deep concern for pan-Arab causes. Some Salafi groups were also active in the area, although with limited influence.[71]

The first protests in these towns and cities took place on the Friday of Honour, 25 March. The largest, in Duma[72] and at-Tall,[73] both mustered around 1,000 people. The chants invoked the familiar themes of freedom and dignity ('the Syrian people will not be humiliated', 'God, Syria and freedom') as well as expressing solidarity with the children of Daraa. On the same day, the first of many nightly sit-ins was held in front of the Grand Mosque in Duma, with more than 5,000 participants who chanted 'peaceful protest!' 'national unity, Muslims and Christians!'[74] and 'we will not tire, we will not go home!' Afterward, and for the first time in the protest movement, a popular committee was formed made up of local notables, with the opposition activist Adnan Wehbe[75] as its chairman. A popular youth committee was set up under its aegis to organize activists on the ground. The Duma protests soon began to draw in people from across Eastern Ghouta.

In the days following 25 March, the regime put together its own 'popular committees' to quell any further demonstrations, and the security forces, including snipers, took up permanent positions around the Grand Mosque. The next Friday – the Friday of Martyrs, 1 April[76] – protests originating at

---

[69] The United Arab Republic (UAR) was a federation between Egypt and Syria established in 1958. Three years later, following a military coup in Damascus, Syria withdrew from the federation.

[70] The Damascus Brotherhood, centred around Sheikh Isam al-Attar and his students, was more moderate than the hard-line Aleppan-Hamawi current that led the armed struggle against the regime.

[71] A face-to-face interview with Raja al-Nasser, conducted by the ACRPS research team in Doha on 13 September 2011. Nasir is a member of the NCB and the secretary of the ASU Party.

[72] For footage of the Duma protest during Friday of Honour, see: YouTube, 26 March 2011, at: https://bit.ly/3sknBAl (accessed 21 December 2021).

[73] For footage of the at-Tall protest during the Friday of Honour, see: YouTube, 12 January 2011, at: https://bit.ly/3EezBFN (accessed 21 December 2021).

[74] This affirmation of national unity was a response to individuals chanting 'neither Iran nor Hezbollah/ we want a government that recognizes the one God' the previous week. Official media used this chant to tar the protesters with accusations of sectarianism. For footage of the evening sit-in in Duma, see: YouTube, 26 March 2011, at: https://bit.ly/32q13TW (accessed 21 December 2021).

[75] Dr Adnan Wehbe was a leading member of the ASU. He was shot dead at his practice by security forces on 2 June 2012.

[76] The name 'Friday of Martyrs' was chosen in response to Assad's use of the term 'victims' to refer to those killed during earlier protests.

mosques across the city tried to force their way back into the square, but the snipers fired on the crowds, killing six people and preventing protesters from reaching their goal.[77] This was the first time that live ammunition had been used against protesters in the Damascus periphery and marked a turning point for events there. The majority of the local population now rose up against the regime. The funerals of those killed, held two days later on 3 April, brought some 60,000 people out onto the streets.[78] Violence did not discourage other towns from joining the protest movement and because they had political leadership, the funeral demonstrations had a civic and patriotic character. The sectarian slogans that were occasionally heard at protests were notably absent.[79] In their place, patriotic chants – including, for the first time, the famous 'one, one, one, the Syrian people are one!' – dominated the scene.

As we have already seen, the failure of its strategy led the regime to try a different approach. The families of those killed in Duma on 1 April were invited to the presidential palace in Damascus, and Assad ordered the release of 191 detainees from the city[80] and promised that the security forces would no longer intervene in protests there. Similar meetings were held with notables from other cities. Ultimately, the president's promises were to produce nothing of substance – whether in regime policy or in terms of accountability for officials responsible for killing protesters – and those who remained recalcitrant even after meeting the president were to be brought into line by violent measures. This was quickly to rob this approach of any effectiveness. But on the Friday of Determination (15 April), at least, the security forces did not to fire on demonstrators.

The Friday of Determination was to see another significant first. As a result of the promise not to fire, there were demonstrations organized in various towns around the capital (Jawbar, Duma, Harasta, Madamiyet Elsham, Darayya, Arbin, Kisweh). The demonstrators at each numbered in the thousands. The Duma march made its way to Harasta, where local protesters joined those from their neighbouring town. The fateful decision was then made to march on Abbasiyeen Square in the heart of the capital

---

[77] Of those killed, we know the names of six only: Ibrahim Mubayed, Ahmad Rajab, Fuad Ballah, Mohammed Alaya, in addition to two others, one from Khouli family, and the other from the Eissa family. See: *Al Jazeera*, 1 April 2011, at: https://bit.ly/3Ei3l4K (accessed 21 December 2021).
[78] For footage of the massed protestors in Duma, see: YouTube, 3 April 2011, at: https://bit.ly/3GVYGXM (accessed 21 December 2021).
[79] Variations on 'no to Iran and no to Hezbollah/we want a president who fears God', which were occasionally heard at protests in Duma and the villages of Daraa governorate. The leaders of the Duma protests were able to contain these sorts of chants, replacing them with patriotic alternatives like 'Muslims and Christians/we all want freedom!', 'national unity!' and 'no Salafism and no terrorism/this is a youth revolution!'
[80] *Al-Thawra*, 11 April 2011, at: https://bit.ly/3ees7Ic (accessed 21 December 2021).

itself.[81] 'Nobody anticipated this,' Wael Salam,[82] who was present, explains. 'The people in Arbin, Zamalka and Ein Terma heard that the Duma and Harasta protests were heading for Abbasiyeen Square. People came in cars and on motorbikes to join in. The closer the protest got to Damascus, the bigger it got. By the time we arrived in Jawbar, there were around 5,000 people.' Although the protesters were ultimately dispersed by the security forces using batons and tear gas, they were able to get within 100 meters of the square.[83]

This attempt to launch a sit-in marked a change in the dynamic of the local protest movement. It fed the belief that the uprising needed to be brought from the periphery to the centre in order to pressure the regime. It also served as an opportunity for leaders and organizers from the capital's different satellite towns to meet and coordinate. The day after the Friday of Determination, the organizers began making preparations for a new march on the square, a permanent sit-in that would allow the revolution to put down roots in Damascus:

> They obtained tents and some first aid equipment and medicine so they could set up a field hospital, and they handed out fliers and shared posts on Facebook telling people how to deal with tear gas. It was agreed that the protests shouldn't be clumped together along a single route but should follow three different routes [Zabaltani, Jawbar and Tijara] in order to force the security forces to spread themselves thin.[84]

The development of this strategy for bringing the revolution to Damascus marked a shift from spontaneity to organization, aided by the formation of leadership committees that were able to supervise the protests and influence the choice of chants and the slogans painted on banners.

The new sit-in was planned for the following Friday, 22 April, which, to demonstrate the revolution's inclusivity and national character, was dubbed Good Friday for the Christian holiday with which it coincided. On that day, protesters from Duma once again marched to Harasta (only 6 km from Abbasiyeen Square) in preparation, with many participants taking buses to

---

[81] For footage of the two protests joining together, see: YouTube, 15 April 2011, at: https://bit.ly/3yNh2Y9 (accessed 21 December 2021).
[82] Wael Salam (alias Khalid al-Umar) is one of the most prominent activists of Eastern Ghouta. He was a member of the coordination committees before joining the General Commission for the Syrian Revolution, and was later a member of the Revolutionary Military Council in the Damascus periphery. ACRPS researchers conducted several interviews with him.
[83] *BBC Arabic*, 15 April 2011, at: https://bbc.in/3yMgstD (accessed 21 December 2021).
[84] A virtual interview via Skype with Wael Salam (alias Khalid al-Umar), conducted by the ACRPS research team.

the area close to the square. At the same time, more than 10,000 protesters from Arbin, Zamalka, Saqba, Jawbar and Kafr Batna converged on Zabaltani Street and began marching on the square from that direction.

If demonstrators had reached the square, this would have shown the failure of attempts to isolate the capital from the protest movement elsewhere. It might have led to a Habib Bourguiba Street or a Tahrir Square in Syria: a mass sit-in attracting such broad popular participation that it would have been impossible to break up without massive casualties. The marchers were very aware of how real a threat this was. The regime had shown that it was willing to inflict such casualties in Clocktower Square four days earlier. But they were nonetheless determined to push through.

The two demonstrations marched over a kilometre before encountering any resistance. But when they arrived in Zabaltani, the security forces opened fire, killing more than fifty people and dispersing the protesters, thereby foiling – albeit temporarily – their attempt to bring revolution to the capital. Events elsewhere make it clear that the senior leadership had given orders to fire to security chiefs across the country. Massacres also took place in Daraa (Hrak) and Homs, with around 100 people killed in total during the Good Friday protests.[85] For so many people to be killed at a peaceful protest is staggering (although these numbers would pale to insignificance compared to the violence the regime was to unleash in 2012). After 15 April, the regime had concluded that holding fire meant allowing the revolution to grow. It had thus reverted to its previous policy. But as April rolled on, local popular uprisings were beginning to transform into a fully-fledged national revolution – a revolution that aimed to bring down the regime.

The attempt to reach the Abbasiyeen Square had failed, and with it the strategy to bring revolution to the capital. But once again, the security forces' response provoked a popular reaction that made it into a turning point. Good Friday had set the outskirts of Damascus alight – Qaboun, Qadam, Assali, Hajar Aswad – as well as the poor neighbourhood of Midan in the heart of the capital. These districts began to participate in protests on a daily basis. The revolutionary movement also spread for the first time to the University of Damascus, specifically the science, arts and law faculties. More and more people came out to protest, with more and more ambitious demands. And most fatefully, after Good Friday demonstrators across Syria began to chant for the fall of the regime, a demand that cut across geography and united revolutionaries throughout the country. With mounting popular

---

[85] *Arraee*, 23 April 2011, at: https://bit.ly/3mjNgW8 (accessed 21 December 2021).

momentum, the revolution was now to make the transition to mass popular mobilizations in city after city. But these mobilizations would ultimately be crushed after the regime deployed the army in the cities in August 2011. The large-scale military operations would drive protesters back into the claustrophobic alleyways of old cities and out into the countryside, paving the way for the armed uprising.

3

Protests in the main squares

Between June and early August 2011, the revolution took another turn with the spread of large demonstrations to Syria's central squares and public spaces, when hundreds of thousands came out to protest in Hama, Deir ez-Zor and other major cities. At the same time, the protest movement developed in the Idleb governorate, especially the cities of Ma'arrat An-Nu'man, Saraqab, and Jisr ash-Shughur, and the centre of Idleb City itself, where tens of thousands of protesters gathered on a daily basis until the regime assault on the city in March 2012.

I. Hama, memories revisited

Hama is among the largest cities in Syria after Damascus, Aleppo and Homs. The population of the entire governorate, as of January 2011, according to Central Bureau of Statistics (CBS) report, was 2,113,000; the city alone had a population of 925,000 in 2010.[1] Hama became synonymous with the ruthless determination of the Assad family to stay in power. During the 1982 massacre, when Hafez al-Assad's troops unleashed a bloody 27-day assault on the city from which the Fighting Vanguard group (which split from the Muslim Brotherhood) declared jihad on the regime, thousands of Syrians were killed. The number of casualties remains uncertain. Initial reports estimated the number at 5,000, while critics, researchers and human rights reports put the number between 20,000 and 40,000. Up to 1,000 individuals were reported missing. Syrians in general, including the Brotherhood, did not follow the call of the Vanguard and condemned its methods, but this did not spare them collective punishment.[2]

---

[1] This dropped to 844,000 in 2014. OCHA, 'Syrian Arab Republic – Population Statistics', at: https://bit.ly/3NAzHgV (accessed 31 March 2022); Macrotrends, at: https://bit.ly/3qQuJ5U (accessed 31 March 2022).

[2] For a relatively new account of the Islamist uprising see: Brynjar Lia, 'The Islamist Uprising in Syria, 1976–82: The History and Legacy of a Failed Revolt', *British Journal of Middle Eastern Studies* 43, no. 4 (2016).

Three decades later, similar tactics were reportedly employed by Hafez's son, Bashar, as he attempted to end the revolution. Hama saw some of the largest protests, as well as some of the bloodiest crackdowns.³

The first significant protest in Hama took place on 25 March, when somewhere between 500 and 1,000 protesters – many of them from areas that had borne the brunt of the 1982 massacre – met at the Umar bin al-Khattab Mosque to voice their anger at the storming of the Umari Mosque in Daraa. But with this limited exception, the nascent protest movement led by a group of young Hamawis initially failed to muster much support. Hama was both geographically and psychologically distant from Daraa, a city known for its strong support for the regime and for providing disproportionate numbers of security officers and party apparatchiks (Daraa was known as a 'reservoir of the Baʿth'). Hamawis' sense of solidarity with the people of Daraa was thus limited. It was only when protests arrived in nearby Homs (47 km away) that Hama set off along its inexorable path towards popular revolution.

The brutal response to the protests in Homs and the use of 'popular committees' recruited from the Alawi neighbourhoods there brought Hamawi demonstrators out onto the streets with increasing regularity from early April onwards, and in increasing numbers. Nonetheless, even the Friday demonstrations of 8 April (the Friday of Resilience) and 15 April (the Friday of Determination) remained small-scale, attracting 2,500–3,000 people. During the latter protest, the largest so far, the attendees gathered in front of the civil registry building (the Personal Status Administration) in the city centre and almost managed to push through to al-Assi Square.

Al-Assi Square held a special significance for activists and organizers. Like other central squares it was an obvious venue for a large revolutionary gathering of the kind that had been so successful in Egypt and in Yemen. It also had its own symbolic value as a historically important place.⁴ With this in mind, activists made plans for a huge protest on Good Friday (22 April), hoping that they would be able to overwhelm the security forces and make it to the square. And when the day came, the protests that marched on the

---

³ *Time*, 8 March 1982. Archived copy available online: https://bit.ly/3J1zos8 (accessed 31 March 2022); Immigration and Refugee Board of Canada, *Syria: Destruction of Hama and Hums in Syria*, 1 October 1989, SYR2294, at: https://bit.ly/3IOv27q (accessed 31 March 2022); *BBC* (international), 27 April 2012, at: https://bbc.in/3JWBVVG (accessed 31 March 2022).

⁴ Al-Assi Square sits at the heart of Hama, right next to the old city. It is the city's only major open space and the location not only of government buildings, but of other important institutions (major banks and companies). When the forces of the Arab Revolt entered the city in 1918, they raised the flag in al-Assi Square, and in the early years of the mandate period the city's rebels clashed with French forces in the area. The square also hosted major protests against the Baʿth Party in 1963.

city centre from various mosques across the city were able to push through to al-Assi Square. The security forces broke up the protest with live ammunition, leading to the first death in Hama: Suhaib Sotal.[5]

The inherited and reproduced collective memory of Hamawis is a part of their political identity.[6] There was no need for fresh repression, or social and economic grievances, as a catalyst to stoke their disaffection with the regime. But Hama had long lived in fear of a repeat of the 1980s. Some of the city's inhabitants were old enough to remember how the security forces had crushed the protests of 1964, and many more had been alive during the events of the 1980s. Even for those who had not, these incidents were mythologized and charged with emotion, as is so often the case with oral histories.[7] The main obstacle was thus the worry that, as in the 1980s, Hama would find itself abandoned by Aleppo and Damascus, left to stand against the regime alone.[8] The punishment meted out to the city's inhabitants on that occasion had been catastrophic – not only untold numbers of dead, but thousands of residents displaced and dispossessed of their property due to their alleged sympathies with the Muslim Brotherhood, the systematic collective punishment long endured by Hamawis in the aftermath of the uprising. There was also the notorious massacre of

---

[5] For footage of the Hama protest on Good Friday, see: YouTube, 22 April 2011, at: https://bit.ly/3EwmqAp (accessed 22 December 2021).

[6] During the 2011 protests, a public inquiry was launched into the 1982 Hama massacre, led by Hisham al-Ikhtiyar (head of the National Security Bureau), Osama Udai (head of the Agricultural Bureau) and Ahmad Khaled Abdel Aziz (the governor of Hama). On 12 June, after the inquiry submitted its report, the regime published an official acknowledgement of the deaths and injuries during the massacre and also of the unjust expropriation of property in the aftermath, which was to be returned to its rightful owners 'within a month'. Death certificates were also to be issued for 15,000 people killed, allowing the families to finally move forward with inheritance and other legal procedures. See: *Aksalser*, 12 June 2011, at: https://bit.ly/3ubW8lc (accessed 17 January 2022).

[7] The events of 1982 must be approached critically, and a distinction must be made between the beginning of the protest movement and the responsibility of extremists on both sides for the catastrophic events that followed. The massacre has acquired a symbolic value independent of the actual events: historical, psychological and behavioural factors coalesce here, most obviously in attempts to minimize or massively exaggerate the number of victims. See the interview with Adnan Saad al-Din about the era of the Muslim Brothers in Syria on *Witness to the Age* [TV programme], on: *Al Jazeera*, 11 November 2012, at: https://bit.ly/3JawmTG (accessed 22 December 2021).

[8] The armed confrontation between the state and the Brotherhood began in Aleppo in 1980. That year the regime summarily executed dozens of people who it claimed were Brotherhood members. It soon became clear, however, that many innocent people had been killed, giving the impression that random executions had been carried out solely to intimidate citizens. Hama came out to protest in solidarity with Aleppo, beginning a peaceful uprising that the Fighting Vanguard transformed into an armed campaign.

prisoners in the Tadmor Prison on 26 June 1980 in the aftermath of the attempt to assassinate Hafez al-Assad.[9]

As the protests grew, however, these fears began to dissipate. By May, despite the deployment of the army, the regime had been unable to crush demonstrations in Daraa, the Damascus periphery, Homs or Latakia, and the revolution was now spreading into Deir ez-Zor, the Kurdish regions, the Aleppo governorate and even parts of Damascus. It was clear that a massive popular revolution was under way all over Syria. And demonstrations in nearby towns and villages that had remained quiescent in the 1980s – in particular the villages to the north of the city – provided an additional fillip to protests in Hama itself.

From 'Azadi Friday' (20 May 2011),[10] protests in the city began to grow in scale and intensity. Graffiti calling for the authorities to disband the 'traitor army' and replace it with a 'national army' – a new demand – appeared scribbled on a wall in Shamaliyyah, close to the Umar bin al-Khattab Mosque.[11] Dozens of children had been killed in Shamaliyyah and the surrounding neighbourhoods during the 1982 massacre, and the damage still visible on many buildings there[12] was now to play a central part in motivating protesters.

During the Azadi Friday protests, the security forces beat a protester who was hurling stones, Umran Dweik, so badly that he was paralyzed and later died;[13] the scene was caught on camera and was later broadcast on TV. In people's minds, these scenes became associated with the image of Hamza

---

[9] How many people were killed during the massacres carried out in the early 1980s in Aleppo, Idleb, Tadmor and Hama remains controversial, and the question is doubly controversial in Hama, where neither the regime nor the Brotherhood has provided a figure. The popular narrative in Hama itself says that 40,000 people were killed, 20,000 detained and 100,000 forcibly displaced. These figures are exaggerated, but they give a sense of the terror that engulfed the city during the three weeks between 2 February and 20 February 1982. The French daily *Le Matin* claimed shortly after the massacre that 10,000 people had been killed, 20,000 detained and 600,000 blacklisted, while the *Economist* cited a figure of 30,000 deaths (including military casualties) from a Brotherhood source and 9,000 from local hospitals. See: Khalid al-Ahmad, 'The Great Hama Massacre (1982)' [Arabic], Arab Orient Centre for Strategic Civilization Studies, 6 February 2006, at: https://bit.ly/3mpJri3 (accessed 22 December 2021). Robert Fisk, a journalist who entered Hama shortly after the massacre, gave a contemporary estimate of around 10,000 dead. See: *Independent*, 10 February 2007, at: https://bit.ly/3Ews05P (accessed 22 December 2021). Patrick Seale, who drew much of his information from the regime itself, estimated that most likely 5,000–10,000 people had been killed. See: Patrick Seale, *Asad of Syria: The Struggle for the Middle East* (Berkeley: University of California Press, 1988), 334.
[10] Friday 20 May was dubbed 'Azadi Friday', using the Kurdish word for freedom.
[11] A face-to-face interview with a protest organizer in Hama who wishes to remain anonymous, conducted by Hamzeh al-Moustafa, ACRPS researcher, in Doha on 10 September 2011.
[12] Bullet and shell markings are still visible on buildings in the Shamaliyyah district, and there are signs of house demolitions in the area between Hareen, Baroudiyeh and Hamidiyeh.
[13] For footage of the beating of Umran Dweik, which was broadcast by regional and international media, see: YouTube, 24 May 2011, at: https://bit.ly/3piDoO3 (accessed 22 December 2021).

al-Khatib,[14] a thirteen-year-old from Daraa who was tortured to death while in the custody of the security forces (he died on 25 May). After this, popular participation began to climb to unprecedented heights.

On 3 June, dubbed 'Friday of the Children of Freedom', two enormous demonstrations were held simultaneously in Hama, one beginning in Hadir and the other in the market district (Nazlet al-Jizdan). Between them they brought more than 150,000 people out onto the streets, and both marched on al-Assi Square. To prevent the first demonstration from reaching the square, the security forces fired into the crowd, leaving around 150 people dead. This provoked massive popular outrage across the city, and by the evening of the following day, the security forces had withdrawn from Hama entirely.

Al-Assi Square would host massive demonstrations on every subsequent Friday until the army entered Hama in early August. Opposition activist Khuzama Udai describes one such demonstration on Get Out Friday (1 July) as 'the largest demonstration the city had ever witnessed':

> Every part of local society took part: the poor, the middle class and those well-off people that weren't regime allies. It wasn't just men. Women and children were there as well, in such numbers that I can confidently say nobody stayed at home that day. And there were people from nearby areas, too, especially the towns north of the city. In fact, some people even came from the villages of the western countryside, especially Masyaf.

On that occasion, protesters formed a massive Syrian flag, challenging the 'Biggest Flag' march organized by regime supporters on the Mazzeh highway in Damascus.[15] They sang the national anthem and chanted for

---

[14] On 20 May, Hamza al-Khatib's body was released to his family bearing the clear signs of torture. A picture of the body soon began circulating as evidence of the regime's sadistic practices (the fact that some of the damage could be attributed to natural bloating notwithstanding). At the time I described this as a 'hate crime', warning that the picture could be used for sectarian purposes, and argued that it must represent an extreme case. Since then, however, thousands of videos and images have been published attesting to unimaginably horrific kinds of murder carried out by the security forces. See my interview about the Arab Spring and the movement for change on *Talk of the Revolution*, [TV programme], on: *Al Jazeera*, 21 August 2011, at: https://bit.ly/3yQxy9V (accessed 22 December 2021).

[15] Like its counterpart in Yemen, the regime quickly responded to protests by organizing its own demonstrations. The first and largest such demonstrations took place on 29 March in Damascus, Aleppo, Deir ez-Zor and Latakia, in advance of Assad's speech on 30 March.

Pro-regime demonstrations continued to be organized even as the participation in the anti-regime protests expanded, with the security forces attempting to mobilize their own popular base. After the Clocktower Square sit-in in Homs, 'popular and economic forces' called for demonstrations to express support for the president, and similar calls were heard in Latakia and Banyas after the arrival of the army in late April 2011. During the first months of the protests in Deir ez-Zor, too, the clans organized major pro-regime protests, although after June 2011, most of them changed their position. Similar attempts to organize pro-regime demonstrations in Hama, however, failed, and an attempt to march from the villages west of the city to al-Assi Square was blocked by demonstrators within the city itself. As-Sweida, Tartous, Aleppo and al-Hasakeh also saw weekly pro-regime demonstrations.

the fall of the regime and the ouster of Assad. Prominent local figures gave speeches calling for detainees to be released.[16] Similar scenes recurred every Friday.

The months after 4 June marked the longest period of civil disobedience in Syria's history (fifty-nine days). The state was totally absent, even in terms of basic service provision. It fell to the popular committees to manage the city's affairs, a mission they undertook with great energy. Hama stood defiant until the army 'reoccupied' it in early August. And while the military intervention brought an end to civil disobedience, the city had enjoyed a long spell of liberation and of self-government, demonstrating the strength of its citizens.

II. Deir ez-Zor: The effectiveness of youth groups

Geographically and culturally, Deir ez-Zor has far more in common with western Iraq (Anbar, Ramadi) than with the rest of Syria, from which it is relatively remote.[17] State policy only exacerbated this sense of isolation: as of 2011, the region still lacked modern transport infrastructure and was poorly connected to the capital and to other governorates. Local graduates resented that jobs in oil or in education were typically taken by outsiders from other parts of the country (a problem with a distinct sectarian colouring). Events in Daraa thus had little resonance for Deiris. The first small local protests had less to do with solidarity than the desire of young activists to demonstrate against the regime for broader political reasons.[18]

There were obvious socioeconomic grievances in the eastern region. The drought of 2006–10 had deprived thousands of families of their main source of income and produced widespread youth unemployment, forcing many people to relocate to poverty-stricken slums in the western cities or join the wave of seasonal migration for work in Lebanon. Moreover, although the governorate produces oil, the profits were not spent locally, and the region remained underdeveloped. Close family and cultural ties with the tribal communities of neighbouring Iraq meant that many Deiris also had strong feelings about the regime's recent rapprochement with the Nouri al-Maliki government in Baghdad, which was felt to be hostile to those communities.

---

[16] An interview with Khuzama Udai, conducted by Hamzeh al-Moustafa, ACRPS researcher, in Doha on 3 August 2012.
[17] The city of Deir ez-Zor is located 432 km from Damascus, 378 km from Homs, 533 km from Daraa, 538 km from Latakia and 320 km from Aleppo.
[18] For footage of the Deir ez-Zor protest during the Friday of Resilience on 8 April 2011, see: YouTube, 8 April 2011, at: https://bit.ly/3J7TQsp (accessed 22 December 2021); YouTube, 15 April 2011, at: https://bit.ly/3d35y8P (accessed 22 December 2021).

The tribal factor, not present in Hama, was also significant in terms of its repercussions for domestic politics. From before Hafez al-Assad's palace coup of 1970 – the so-called 'Corrective Movement' – local clans like the Baqqara[19] and Uqaidat[20] had been closely allied with the Baʿth Party. By 2005, however, this dynamic had shifted, and Nawaf al-Bashir of the Baqqara (whose father had been a close supporter of the leading Baʿthist Jalal al-Sayyid) was a signatory to the DD. Senior tribal figures like Bashir and members of the Dandal family were to add a popular dimension to the protests in the city and drive their expansion. The tribal factor was also to produce the first defection from the regime on 11 July 2012, when the Syrian ambassador to Iraq, Nawaf Fares, a member of the Uqaidat clan, resigned and fled to Qatar.

The first protests in Deir ez-Zor took place on 25 March, the Friday of Honour, when a few dozen young people came out to express their solidarity with the people of Daraa.[21] For the first month of the uprising popular participation remained limited. Less than fifty people took part in the protests on the Friday of Martyrs (1 April)[22] and the Friday of Resilience (8 April), while the pro-regime demonstrations organized by state officials and held around the same time were much larger by comparison.[23] Certainly, this is understandable knowing that the officials ordered civil servants, school students, etc. to take part in the pro-regime rallies.

---

[19] The Baqqara clan is among the largest in Deir ez-Zor. Its traditional home is on the left bank of the Euphrates, in the area around the city of Deir ez-Zor itself. It has been sedentary since at least the 1940s. Its leader Raghib al-Bashir secured a parliamentary seat after independence, and this seat was inherited by his son Nawaf. See: Ahmad Wasfi Zakaria, *The Clans of Syria: A Treatise on the Geography, History, Settlements, Ethics, and Customs of the Syrian Desert* [Arabic], vol. 2, 3rd edn (Beirut: Dar al-Fikr al-Muʿasir; Damascus: Dar al-Fikr al-ʿArabi, 1997), 566–7.

Like all clans, urbanization dealt a serious blow to the Baqqara's internal cohesion, but a certain tribal solidarity has remained thanks to political and other interests – not least the desire to maintain representation *vis-à-vis* the government. Many urban notables, including the Aiesh, Ayyash and Abboud families, have claimed Baqqara affiliation in order to win votes in Deir ez-Zor itself.

[20] The Uqaidat are one of Syria's largest sedentarized clans. They are a confederation made up of several local branches (*uqaidat* itself means 'alliances' or 'pledges'). Although spread across multiple governorates, they are concentrated in Deir ez-Zor, which the Bou Saraya branch call home. Most rural migrants to the city were Uqaidat, and the clan also makes up the majority of the population in Abu Kamal and Mayadin (Abu Kamal, in fact, is named for an Uqaidat branch). Due to its large size, it held two parliamentary seats before the Baʿth took power. Until the 1950s the Uqaidat were led and represented by the Hafl family. Since the rise of the Baʿth, however, this position has been contested by the Dandals – one of whom, Dahham al-Dandal, stood on the Baʿth list in the 1954 elections. Both the Dandals and Nawaf Fares, the ambassador to Iraq who defected early on in the revolution, belong to the Bou Hassoun branch, who are based in Abu Kamal. On the Uqaidat and their origins and settlements, see: Zakaria, 568–86.

[21] For footage of the protest, see: YouTube, 25 March 2011, at: https://bit.ly/3pl5zfa (accessed 22 December 2021).

[22] For footage of the protest, see: YouTube, 6 April 2011, at: https://bit.ly/3J9JAjg (accessed 22 December 2021).

[23] *Alriyadh*, 30 March 2011, at: https://bit.ly/3LU32kI (accessed 20 June 2022).

Several factors contributed to explain the slow start to the protest movement in Deir ez-Zor. The tribal factor played a key role. The Syrian state has never been able to create a state-national identity capable of absorbing the country's various pre-national constituent communities. In Deir ez-Zor, it instead sought to guarantee the population's loyalty by showering tribal leaders with largesse. After the 2003 Iraq War, the 'ruling family' established marital ties with clans in the eastern region.[24] Moreover, under Bashar, the settled Bedouins of the eastern region (the *shawaya*) became a major source of recruits for the army and the security forces, institutions which offered them a means of social advancement and escape from the inferior status they had suffered from in the city itself since its establishment in 1864[25] – a dynamic not unlike that at work in impoverished Alawi areas.

Finally, the security forces took a relatively relaxed view of protests in Deir ez-Zor, an approach quite at odds with their behaviour elsewhere. Aware that in a city where tribal custom remained very important any deaths would lead to a major reaction, they held back from using serious violence against demonstrators. This largely succeeded in keeping tribal leaders on side and thus containing further demonstrations. They were to persist with this approach despite the gradual growth of the protests until 1 May, when Deir ez-Zor saw its first death, Ujail Ahmad al-Ujail.[26]

Despite all these factors, and despite the opposition of tribal leaders, on 15 April (the Friday of Determination) some 500–1,000 people marched through Deir ez-Zor, the biggest protest in the city so far.[27] Even such relatively limited numbers attest to the hard work and determination of the youth groups active in the city. Those driving the uprising at this point were politically engaged, educated young people who had grown up outside the traditional tribal framework. But after 15 April, popular participation began to grow. Protests were held on a daily basis in the Qusur, Jbeileh and Hamidiyeh neighbourhoods. Young clan members and even some tribal leaders began to join in. From 22 April (Good Friday)

---

[24] Perhaps the most notable example is Maher al-Assad, the president's brother, whose wife Manal Jadaan is the daughter of an Uqaidat sheikh.
[25] The term *shawaya* refers to Bedouins who have given up nomadic pastoralism in favour of settled agriculture. It is widely used in the east of the country and by extension in the areas around Aleppo. According to Ahmed Wasfi Zakaria, a historian who has studied Syrian tribes, some members of this group consider the term offensive, saying it connotes weakness and reflects urban notables' contempt for them. In Deir ez-Zor itself it is commonly said that *shawaya* 'need a passport to enter the city'. The urban notables have a similar relationship with other farmers. See: Zakaria, 562.
[26] Ujail al-Ujail was the first civilian killed in Deir ez-Zor, although a soldier, Amir al-Hunait, had been shot earlier for refusing to fire on civilians. See the database of the martyrs of the Syrian revolution: *Syrian Shuhada*, 22 June 2012. Archived copy available online: https://bit.ly/33UzhzL (accessed 22 December 2021).
[27] For footage of the Friday of Determination in Deir ez-Zor on 15 April 2011, see: YouTube, 22 April 2011, at: https://bit.ly/3eebtZc (accessed 22 December 2021).

onwards, the protests spread to nearby cities, in particular Abu Kamal[28] and al-Mayadin.[29]

The regime now found itself facing a major security dilemma. Avoiding violence and relying on tribal leaders to contain opposition activity was not working. In fact, more and more people were joining the protests, and the sheikhs were facing growing criticism within their tribes for standing by a regime that was shooting people.[30] But firing on protesters would provoke tribal solidarity. As is so often the case, the proximal cause of great events was a mixture of chance, individual psychology and blunder. The tribal shift from loyalty to the regime to solidarity with its children is the opposite of the traditional historical causality. There is no necessary cause that explains the events that led to the transformation. We cannot neglect the complex role of psychological factors among those who felt that the regime was repaying them for their loyalty by killing their relatives, nor can we neglect sentiments of local solidarity.

The events of the Friday of Defiance, 6 May, show how a security crackdown became the regime's only option. On that day, the attendees of various smaller protests that had begun at mosques across the city attempted to organize an open sit-in in a public square outside the Uthman bin Affan Mosque, close to the old airport.[31] Just three days earlier, local leaders had met with Assad and returned to Deir ez-Zor with promises that protesters' demands would be met and that there would be no further deaths.[32] By this point, however, preventing sit-ins had become central to regime strategy. The security forces opened fire, killing four people.[33]

A red line had been crossed. The tribal factor, previously an obstacle to the protest movement, was now to become a major asset. Those leaders who had remained allied with the regime were now marginalized by those who opposed it, in particular Nawaf al-Bashir and the Dandal family. And the results were spectacular. From Azadi Friday (20 May) onwards,[34]

---

[28] For footage of the Abu Kamal protests during Good Friday on 22 April 2011, see: YouTube, 22 April 2011, at: https://bit.ly/3mLCDM3 (accessed 22 December 2021).

[29] During Good Friday, the people of al-Mayadin gathered in front of the party branch office and called for the overthrow of the regime. The security forces did not use violence to disperse the protest. For footage of this protest, see: YouTube, 23 April 2011, at: https://bit.ly/32pz2vM (accessed 22 December 2021).

[30] A virtual interview via Skype with an activist from Deir ez-Zor who wishes to remain anonymous, conducted by Hamzeh al-Moustafa, ACRPS researcher.

[31] For footage of the beginning of the sit-in at the Uthman bin Affan Mosque on 6 May 2011, see: YouTube, 7 May 2011, at: https://bit.ly/3svAcAH (accessed 22 December 2021).

[32] Not all tribal leaders met with the president. The delegation comprised a small group of longstanding regime loyalists: Raghid al-Qadduri, Ahmad al-Abboud, and Abd al-Fattah Fteih. See: *Syria News*, 3 May 2011. Archived copy available online: https://bit.ly/3Eoi6D0 (accessed 22 December 2021).

[33] *Al Jazeera*, 6 May 2011, at: https://bit.ly/3snyl0Q (accessed 22 December 2021).

[34] For footage of the Azadi protest on 20 May 2011, see: YouTube, 20 May 2011, at: https://bit.ly/3qaX05S (22 December 2021).

protesters numbered not in the hundreds but the tens of thousands. On the Friday of the Clans (10 June 2011) – a name promoted by 'the Syrian revolution against Bashar al-Assad' Facebook page[35] – more than 50,000 people from across the city converged on Freedom Square.[36] Faced with such numbers, the security forces largely withdrew from the city, retreating to their headquarters. The vast and peaceful protest that followed made the city's support for the revolution clear. And over the following days, with the security forces gone, the demonstrations grew ever larger. On 22 July (the Friday of the Sons of Khalid bin al-Waleed), some 150,000 people came out to protest.[37]

In the event, the 22 July protest was to be the last to take place in a public square. The following Thursday, 28 July, the security forces launched a major operation in the Huwaiqa neighbourhood, arresting hundreds and leaving six people dead. This was an attempt to dissuade locals from taking part in protests planned for the next day ('Your Silence Is Killing Us' Friday – 29 July 2011). The regime could not tolerate hundreds of thousands of people calling for its ouster. As elsewhere, it had failed to understand the significance of the moment or to recognize what was needed. Instead, it was desperately trying to turn back the clock of history.

On 1 August, 200 tanks and military vehicles surrounded the city of Deir ez-Zor. The regime announced that a military operation had begun against 'terrorist gangs that have been terrorizing civilians'. Much akin to Hama, this operation was to successfully put an end to the Deir ez-Zor protests. Nonetheless, these protests had had a significant psychological, political and media impact and had provided irrefutable proof that the regime narrative of limited popular participation was a lie. It was now clear that there were Syrian cities opposed to the regime and willing to rise up against it as soon as they were sure that they would not be shot at.

This reality was also visible in the governorate of Idleb, where the protesting masses re-enacted the scene of Hama's al-Assi Square, mobilizing much of the city, though the turnout was naturally smaller given Idleb's size.

---

[35] Various voices active in the virtual public sphere argued that the name 'Friday of the Clans' was antithetical to the civic and pan-national character of the revolution. Clan chiefs were not reliable over the long run and the politicization of clans did not serve any democratic cause.
[36] For footage of the Friday of the Clans protests on 10 June 2011, see: YouTube, 10 June 2011, at: https://bit.ly/3FmAvkP (accessed 22 December 2021).
[37] The Syrian Observatory for Human Rights has estimated the number of protesters at 300,000, while the local coordination committees (LCCs) said that there were as many as 400,000. An examination of the crowds in Freedom Square, however, suggests a more conservative figure of 150,000. For footage of this protest, see: YouTube, 22 July 2011, at: https://bit.ly/3edEm7R (22 December 2021).

III. Idleb

Situated in the far north of the country, Idleb is Syria's gateway to Turkey and Europe. For centuries it was a meeting point for European and Anatolian caravans making their way along the Silk Road. Today it is the link between the coastal and central regions on the one hand and the northern and eastern regions on the other, serving as a bridge between the agrarian Jazeera and the Port of Latakia. The governorate itself, which boasts 1.5 million people, is a relatively new creation, brought into being out of parts of the Aleppo, Hama and Latakia governorates under the UAR (1958–61). Its mountainous geography, particularly towards its north-western end (Jisr ash-Shughur and Jabal az-Zawiya), has given the region great strategic importance ever since the Middle Ages. Under the French (1920–46), the villages of Jabal az-Zawiya were a major rallying point for nationalist forces. The same dynamic was to apply during the Syrian revolution.

There were many reasons to protest in Idleb. The socioeconomic problems were present: the governorate was systematically neglected by the state, and the governorate's 'forgotten cities' were not only called by this name because of their archaeological treasures. Some towns, moreover, had suffered during the confrontation with the Muslim Brotherhood in the 1980s: Jisr ash-Shughur[38] and to a lesser extent the cities of Maʿarrat An-Nuʿman and Khan Shaykhun.

One of the first towns of the governorate to see protests was Saraqab, where dozens of young men came out after Friday prayers on 25 March to chant 'after today no one is afraid' and 'killing your people makes you a traitor'. Throughout the revolution, Saraqab was to remain unusually engaged. It was to become famous for its civic (and pithy) chants, its revolutionary murals, its vocal rejection of sectarianism and its emphasis on a civil-democratic state. Many analysts are inclined to explain the early protests in Saraqab through a tribal lens. Since some of the locals are decedents of Bedouin clans with historical connections to the western communities in Iraq, including the Beijat (Saddam Hussein's clan), and along with socioeconomic connections, the area became a consistent bastion of opposition to the Syrian regime, particularly during the long period of enmity between the Syrian and Iraqi regimes in the 1980s.

---

[38] In March 1980, Jisr ash-Shughur was encircled and bombarded by Special Forces units led by Ali Haydar. After they entered the city on 10 March, Haidar's units carried out some fifty summary executions and set fire to around thirty houses. This massacre was witnessed by Tawfiq Salha, a member of the RCC. See: Khalid al-Ahmad, 'The Massacre of Jisr ash-Shughur' [Arabic], Arab Orient Centre for Strategic and Civilization Studies, 27 October 2005, at: https://bit.ly/3yNvbo8 (accessed 22 December 2021).

Dozens of Saraqabis joined the Iraqi resistance following the US invasion in 2003. However, these factors, as important as they are, cannot on their own explain Saraqab's participation in the revolution. It is important to bring other dimensions rooted in the political development of the town, which historically (or since the 1960s) had hosted a left-wing presence and a number of active leftists, including members of the Salah Jadid Ba'th Party, Nasserists, and the Communist Party Political Bureau (Riyad al-Turk section).[39] In fact, the initial protests were led by young activists (Nasserists, communists and Islamists) and students, whose influence was clearly visible in the political engagement of the local revolutionary movement, the chants and slogans used, and the methods of protest adopted.[40]

It is only once these activists began to organize roving protests every Friday that popular participation really took off. And after the regime lost military control of Saraqab, the leadership committees that the young activists had founded would confront the Islamist battalions' attempts to impose religious diktats on the town. They would elect a local council to oversee public institutions and services. Saraqab was only one example of a pattern seen elsewhere in Syria: progressive forces would initiate and lead the first protests. But when the protests gathered momentum and were joined by vast sectors of the population, the Islamists would try to marginalize them, either by appealing to the public's religious sentiments or by force.

Ma'arrat An-Nu'man also saw protests on 25 March, albeit small ones in backstreets and residential neighbourhoods. It was not easy to protest in Ma'arrat An-Nu'man: the city is strategically located on the Damascus-Aleppo highway that connects northern and southern Syria, and as a result the regime was particularly anxious to maintain control here. Local activists were to adopt a tactic of 'roving protests' beginning in the villages on the outskirts. On 15 April (the Friday of Determination) this tactic allowed 2,000 protesters to reach the city centre before being dispersed by the security forces.[41] A week later, during Good Friday, tens of thousands of

---

[39] It is worth mentioning that several activists, including communists and Islamists, were arrested during the 1970s and 1980s.
[40] Among the manifestations of the enlightened political character of the protest movement was the fact that Saraqab rejected the religious dictates of the extremist movements that controlled the city at later stages of the revolution. During the month of May 2013, for instance, the city witnessed clashes between the locals and these groups. These incidents fall outside the purview of this book, but they nonetheless affirm my analysis of the nature of the political movement in the city.
[41] For footage of protesters from the surrounding villages entering the city centre on the Friday of Determination, on 15 April 2011, see: YouTube, 16 April 2011, at: https://bit.ly/3JlnY3M (accessed 22 December 2021).

protesters marched on the city from east, west and southeast.⁴² The resulting demonstration was the largest nationwide on that day and was able to block the highway.⁴³ The same thing happened on the Friday of Rage (29 April), when protesters set tires on fire and built barricades on the highway, blocking traffic for a whole day before government vehicles were used to clear the road. After this the army was deployed all along the highway from Khan Shaykhun through Ma'arrat An-Nu'man to Saraqab,⁴⁴ and protesters were forced back into the smaller squares of the city. Nonetheless, Ma'arrat An-Nu'man continued to see regular protests of 50,000–75,000 people until 16 June, when the army occupied the city. The subsequent clashes with the newly organized armed battalions ultimately led to the displacement of most of Ma'arrat An-Nu'man's population to refugee camps on the Turkish border and the destruction of much of its housing and infrastructure.

The towns and villages of Idleb (Kafr Oweid, Jisr ash-Shughur, Bennsh and Kafr Nobol) saw their first protests on the Friday of Martyrs (1 April). In Kafr Nobol, more than 1,000 people turned out to chant for 'God, Syria and freedom'. Like Saraqab, Kafr Nobol was to become known for its caricatures and witty chants, which reflected the high degree of political awareness among the town's organizers and again proved that humour does not mix with fanaticism and religious pedantry. Local activists, many of whom were former detainees with the CAP, had a long history of opposing the regime: natives of Kafr Nobol had participated in the Damascus Spring and featured prominently among the signatories of the Statement of the Ninety-nine and the Statement of the 1,000, two democratic open letters published at the turn of the millennium.⁴⁵ The work of these experienced and capable activists and intellectuals meant that Kafr Nobol continued to protest peacefully even as the revolution became an armed conflict. They also prevented the development of an Islamist hegemony there of the kind that eventually took over neighbouring Bennsh, where paintings and civic chants eventually gave way to black flags and calls for an Islamic state after the city was taken over by the Nusra Front in late 2012.

---

42 An interview via telephone with Omar Shaheen, conducted by Hamzeh al-Moustafa, ACRPS researcher, on 22 April 2011. Omar Shaheen was a protest organizer in Ma'arrat An-Nu'man who was killed on 13 September 2011.
43 For footage of the Good Friday protests in Ma'arrat An-Nu'man, see: YouTube, 23 April 2011, at: https://bit.ly/3mpQnLU (accessed 22 December 2021).
44 An interview via telephone with Omar Shaheen, conducted by Hamzeh al-Moustafa, ACRPS researcher, on 2 May 2011.
45 Among these prominent figures were the novelist Abdulaziz al-Mousa.

The town of Jisr ash-Shughur deserves special consideration here. In the media and among politicians, Jisr ash-Shughur is synonymous with the transition to armed struggle. It was here that the first organized attacks on the security forces' headquarters took place on 6 June and here that Hussein Harmoush, the first major army defector, announced his defection and the formation of the Free Officers' Brigade (FOB). The displacement of so many people by the violence in the city has also contributed to this impression. This underrates the significance of the peaceful protest movement here. Jisr ash-Shughur was no different from the other towns and villages of the Idleb governorate in this respect. However, the bitter memory of the massacre carried out by the regime in the 1980s, in conjunction with the regime's violent response to protest in the present, was ultimately to take the protest movement in a very different direction – one feared by many.

The first protests in Jisr ash-Shughur were held on 1 April, the Friday of Martyrs. On this occasion, a few dozen protesters gathered near the central square to express their solidarity with Daraa and chant for 'God, Syria and freedom'. The numbers were similarly small on 8 April (the Friday of Resilience) and 15 April (the Friday of Determination).[46] Nonetheless, several people were detained by the security forces. On 17 April, security informed the family of one of the protesters who had been detained, Muhammad Kuwais,[47] that he had died in custody. When his body was released, it showed signs of torture.[48] More than 1,000 people turned out for his funeral procession the following day.[49] After the burial, attendees blocked the Aleppo Road, demanding that other detainees be released and that the security forces reveal the fate of various other people who had disappeared, some of them as far back as the 1980s.

During the Good Friday protests (22 April), more than 1,500 people marched in Jisr ash-Shughur.[50] The following week (the Friday of Rage), it was 5,000 people, and they were now calling for the fall of the regime.[51]

---

[46] For footage of the demonstrations, see: YouTube, 16 April 2011, at: https://bit.ly/317VMAb (accessed 22 December 2021).

[47] Muhammad Kuwais was a van driver on the Beirut–Jisr ash-Shughur line, and not a protester. He was tortured and killed by the *shabbiha*, along with two of his passengers. An interview with Tariq Abdel Hai, an activist from Jisr ash-Shughur, conducted by Manhal Barish, member of the ACRPS Syrian Revolution Documentation Project, in Antakya on 18 July 2019.

[48] YouTube, 25 November 2011, at: https://bit.ly/2Zwej8p (accessed 22 December 2021).

[49] For footage of Kuwais's funeral procession on 18 April 2011, see: YouTube, 19 April 2011, at: https://bit.ly/3piYv2X (accessed 22 December 2021).

[50] For footage of the Good Friday protests in Jisr ash-Shughur on 22 April 2011, see: YouTube, 23 April 2011, at: https://bit.ly/3JejFau (accessed 22 December 2021).

[51] For footage of the Jisr ash-Shughur protests on the Friday of Rage on 29 April 2011, see: YouTube, 30 April 2011, at: https://bit.ly/3svfNM6 (accessed 22 December 2021).

Peaceful protests of a similar size continued to be held throughout May.[52] But a series of incidents also took place that month that drove a turn towards armed action. On 7 May, ten people were reported killed and three wounded in an attack on a passenger bus near Homs, an incident widely blamed on the *shabbiha*.[53] Regular police and army raids on the villages around the city spurred young men there to start carrying weapons. Finally, after the security forces fired on protesters on Azadi Friday (20 May), leaving several people dead, angry crowds stormed government buildings, including the post office and the local Baʿth Party branch office. At the same time, the regime was deploying army units around the town, ostensibly at the request of locals who had begged for help. In response to this claim, on 3 June (the Friday of the Children of Freedom), protesters in Jisr ash-Shughur came out carrying olive branches, denying that armed groups were present or that they had requested military intervention.[54]

Since 18 April, the security forces – aware of how far they were from the centre of the governorate and thus from reinforcements – had tried to avoid provoking demonstrators in the town. But on 3 June they fired on protesters, leaving several people dead and injured, including a young man named Basil al-Masri who was actually killed when he attacked a police station along with two of his companions. The next day, 4 June, the city came out *en masse* for the funerals,[55] and the security forces again used live ammunition against them. In response, some locals took up weapons, and on 5 June, twenty-seven people were killed in clashes, including five security officers.[56] On the following day, 6 June, a crowd of armed men from the city and surrounding villages stormed the security branch office in the city and killed everyone inside. More than 100 soldiers were killed,

---

[52] On the Friday of Defiance (6 May), more than 5,000 people gathered in the main square to call for the overthrow of the regime and reaffirm the peaceful and pan-national character of the revolution. See: YouTube, 7 May 2011, at: https://bit.ly/32iw0JY (accessed 22 December 2021). On the Friday of Syria's Women (13 May), another protest carried the independence flag for the first time; held in the newly rebranded Freedom Square, it was broken up using live ammunition. See: YouTube, 13 May 2011, at: https://bit.ly/3yPsORL (accessed 22 December 2021). On Azadi Friday (20 May), members of the Baʿth Party presented their resignations in front of protesters, who demanded that the army remain outside the city. See the video with the same date: YouTube, 20 May 2011, at: https://bit.ly/38kgEqN (accessed 25 April 2022). And on the Friday of the Protectors of the Homeland (27 May 2011), around 8,000 people came out to protest – the largest crowd ever seen in Jisr ash-Shughur. See: YouTube, 31 May 2011, at: https://bit.ly/33QVmz2 (accessed 22 December 2021).
[53] *CNN* (international), 9 May 2011, at: https://cnn.it/3Ekd1LV (accessed 22 December 2021).
[54] For footage of the statement given on 6 June 2011, see: YouTube, 7 June 2011, at: https://bit.ly/33PFs86 (accessed 22 December 2021).
[55] After Basil al-Masri's funeral, protestors attacked the police stations and burned the post office building, where a small military security detachment was stationed. In the afternoon of that day, 4 June, the protestors managed to enter the building and killed all the security personnel present. Many of the attackers, who were throwing stones and burning tires towards the building, were shot to death. *BBC* (international), 22 June 2011, at: https://bbc.in/3k4VYWz (accessed 31 March 2022).
[56] *BBC Arabic*, 5 June 2011, at: https://bbc.in/30SNlIO (accessed 22 December 2021).

some say as many as 120. But instead of condemning the attack, the Syrian opposition claimed that the soldiers were killed by the regime because they defected.

Some saw the attack on the security office as fundamentally sectarian, largely because the government employees and their family members who appeared on state TV pleading for military intervention were largely from Ein Jorjin, Deir Samman and Ashtabraq – all Alawi villages.[57] Proponents of this view held that the army's preparations to enter Jisr ash-Shughur in response to these demands fuelled sectarian tensions within its ranks, ultimately leading to the defection of Harmoush and other officers, who then led the attack on the branch office. This version of events is given more credence by the evening protests that took place on the same day, when demonstrators carried olive branches and reiterated that the city rejected military intervention and that those calling for it were not locals.[58] In any case, on 10 June the army occupied the town, displacing 10,000 people, mostly to Turkey. Over the following year Jisr ash-Shughur was to be transformed into a military base.

The protest movement in the city of Idleb itself followed a similar trajectory to those elsewhere in the governorate. The first small protests in Idleb city took place in early April 2011. But huge protests in public squares only began to appear after the transition to armed action had begun: the first protests in the main square were held 'under the protection' of armed men whose stated purpose was to prevent the security forces from intervening. This argument for the use of weapons was to spread quickly to other regions, although it is fairly obviously an *ex post facto* justification rather than an actual motivation insofar as taking weapons to a protest endangers the protest itself. The real reason for the proliferation of weapons at protests was the intensification of regime violence, which produced a reaction among the clans and in rural and border regions.

Idleb's central square continued to see regular large protests until early March 2012, when the army took over the city and the armed battalions withdrew. Even as the pace of armed action accelerated, there were around 150–175 peaceful protests in the towns of Idleb governorate, according to statistics compiled by various organizational committees – more than any other governorate.

---

[57] An interview via telephone with Omar Shaheen, conducted by Hamzeh al-Moustafa, ACRPS researcher, on 12 June 2011.
[58] For footage of the evening protest in Jisr ash-Shughur on 6 June 2011, see: YouTube, 7 June 2011, at: https://bit.ly/3Ejmq6y (accessed 22 December 2021).

4

Masses in the cities: The revolutionary movement in Damascus and Aleppo

From the outset, the regime sought to tighten its grip on Syria's two largest cities, Damascus and Aleppo, and ensure that they did not succumb to the revolution. Rejecting any political solution to the crisis, the Syrian regime now turned increasingly to the army. At first military operations were limited – Daraa on 25 April, Homs on 28 April, Jisr ash-Shughur on 10 and 11 June – but gradually the army became the main bulwark against revolution. The regime believed that its army was coup-proof, its officer corps loyal enough and cohesive enough that it would not turn against its master as the Tunisian and Egyptian armies had. From the beginning of this military campaign, the regime fought hard to keep the revolution out of Damascus and Aleppo; as early as 22 April (Good Friday) it showed its willingness to use extreme force to this end. Its long-standing alliance with the urban bourgeoisie initially made its task easier. But the atrocities that it committed elsewhere angered many people in both cities and gradually began to turn many formerly ambivalent or even pro-regime citizens against it.

Damascus

It would not be fair to say that Damascus only joined the revolution in the aftermath of massacres elsewhere in the country. The poverty-stricken neighbourhoods on the outskirts of Damascus were involved in the protest movement from the very beginning. These were areas hit hard by both broader social polarization and the more specific land appropriations discussed in Chapter One, and thus fit the general pattern seen elsewhere. No shared interests bound residents here to the regime, and their general disaffection with the regime primed them for revolt. Moreover, central Damascus itself was the scene of the Hamidiyeh Market protest (15 March), the opening salvo of the revolution, and the sit-in in front of the Interior

Ministry the following day. But given the security forces' tight grip on the capital, the huge corps of state employees and the presence of extensive interest groups dependent on the regime, protesters struggled to develop the momentum necessary for a fully-fledged popular uprising.

Marwa al-Ghamian,[1] who took part in the earliest protests in Damascus, gives us an idea of the difficulties that new activists faced:

> After the successful revolutions in Egypt and Tunisia, I talked to people about what we should do. All I got was rejection and disapproval. They weren't against the idea, but they were terrified of the brutal regime response and convinced that revolution in Syria was impossible. But after being slapped by a security guard in front of the Libyan embassy on 22 February and insulted by him in my own homeland, I decided to reach out to other people to do something. I created a Facebook account under a fake name, 'the Free Damascene', and I joined a page called 'Isn't it time for the Damask rose to flower?' There was a protest planned for 1.00 pm on 12 March in front of the Umayyad Mosque. I tried to get my friends to come but they refused, so I decided to go on my own around noon. I waited for ages and nothing happened. [...] I went into an internet café and logged into the account. It turned out that everyone was there in the marketplace but they'd been too scared to chant!

Although few people turned out on 15 March and their small group began to chant 'killing your people makes you a traitor' in the middle of the Hamidiyeh Market, the protest was immediately broken up by the security forces. A similar attempt in front of the Umayyad Mosque was equally unsuccessful.

Nevertheless, these remarkable street scenes set off shockwaves among Syrians, suggesting that Syrians, too, might ride the Arab revolutionary wave. Such optimism was reinforced by the sit-in held by activists, academics, intellectuals and the families of political prisoners in front of the Interior Ministry on 16 March to demand the release of political prisoners and civil liberties.

Activist Deiaa Dughmoch,[2] who participated in the Interior Ministry sit-in and was arrested, told us that while in custody, he and the other detainees were beaten, mocked and humiliated by the security forces. One protester turned out to be an Alawi from Tartous.

Their rapid and violent dispersal notwithstanding, these early protests encouraged others. Throughout the following weeks, young members of the middle classes, university students and intellectuals from all sectarian

---

[1] An interview with Marwa al-Ghamian, conducted by Nerouz Satik, ACRPS researcher, on 13 September 2011.
[2] A face-to-face interview with Deiaa Dughmoch, conducted by Nerouz Satik, ACRPS researcher, in Doha on 13 September 2011.

backgrounds made repeated attempts to organize demonstrations in the major squares of the capital. Some were successful in organizing short-lived sit-ins: more than 1,000 protesters gathered in Marjeh Square on the Friday of Honour (25 March),[3] and both that Friday and the Friday of Determination (15 April) there were protests at the Kafr Sousah roundabout.[4] But gathering in these prominent public locations proved to be near-impossible because of the heavy presence of the security forces and of the so-called popular committees (the regime militias popularly known as the *shabbiha*).

Activists thus redirected their efforts towards neighbourhoods with a long history of opposition to the regime, such as Midan, and to the neighbourhoods on the outskirts of the city that were more difficult for the security forces to enter. Nonetheless, the difficult security situation continued to be a major problem for the revolutionaries; although the embers of protest did not die out, neither did they set the capital alight. The protest movement was to come in fits and starts, with major spikes often corresponding to massacres or developments elsewhere.

One such spike took place on 27 August 2011, which coincided with Laylat al-Qadr, the holiest night of Ramadan. After military operations in Hama, Deir ez-Zor and the Damascus periphery earlier that month, thousands of worshipers who had gathered at the Rifai Mosque for evening prayers stuck around afterwards to protest. In response, the security forces stormed the mosque, beating those present, including the elderly sheikh Osama al-Rifai.[5] This triggered a wave of solidarity protests across the capital, and many Damascenes attempted to gather in public squares. But the army was deployed in Damascus for the first time, preventing the protests from gaining momentum. The brothers Sariya and Osama al-Rifai were prevented from preaching from the pulpit.

Some of the traditional Sunni clergy that were close to the regime, exemplified by Sheikh Muhammad Said Ramadan al-Buti, condemned the protests as a Western conspiracy but seized the opportunity to make demands of the president, like allowing female teachers to wear the *niqab* while teaching, closing the Damascus Casino and allowing the broadcast of a religious satellite television station. Other traditional but oppositional clerics, like the Rifais, were well connected with the Damascene merchants. They joined the protests after hesitation only in June, and the mosques they headed, especially the Zaid Mosque, became departure points for Friday

---

[3] For footage of the Friday of Honour protest in the Marjeh Square in Damascus on 25 March 2011, see: YouTube, 26 March 2011, at: https://bit.ly/3mF4vRH (accessed 28 December 2021).
[4] For footage of the Kafr Sousah roundabout sit-in on 25 March 2011, see: YouTube, 25 March 2011, at: https://bit.ly/3z3iWnN (accessed 28 December 2021).
[5] *Al-Habib Ali al-Jifri*, 29 August 2011, at: https://bit.ly/3rbuuDw (accessed 28 December 2021).

protests. But they were not democrats; they supported the economic neoliberal reforms, and their criticism of the regime was directed against its secularism (and in the 1960s, its socialism). During the period of its international isolation following the invasion of Iraq and the assassination of Hariri, the regime appeased them with various measure, but relations deteriorated after 2007 once the regime regained its self-confidence and took several steps that again alienated them: banning the *niqab* in universities and schools, opening a casino in Damascus and ignoring their fury with what they considered the dissoluteness of Syrian drama productions. In contrast, reformist moderate sheikhs who demanded democratic reform, like Ahmad Mouaz al-Khatib, joined the protests from the beginning.

In February 2012, another major wave of protest swept Mazzeh and the less poor parts of Kafr Sousah, two areas on the outskirts of the capital that had become bastions of opposition activity. This time the trigger was increasing violence by the security forces and military operations, particularly in Baba Amr, in Homs, earlier that month. On Saturday 18 February, more than 10,000 people came out for the funerals of three people shot by the security forces, where they chanted 'why are we afraid? God is with us!' and 'one, one, one, the Syrian people are one!', expressed their support for the Free Syrian Army (FSA), and waved the independence flag, which had become the symbol of the revolution. This was Damascus's largest protest so far, and the numbers on the street were bolstered by many others chanting along from their balconies. Although the security forces and *shabbiha* from Mazzeh 86 (a suburb with an Alawi majority where originally families of low-ranking officers and security cadres lived) used live ammunition and tear gas to try and disperse it, the protest only really broke up when it began to snow and people went home.[6]

The sight of so many people demonstrating in the capital disturbed the regime, but it provided some welcome relief for pro-revolutionary opinion after Russia and China's second veto of a draft United Nations Security Council (UNSC) resolution earlier that month. It showed the failure of the *cordon sanitaire* around the capital and set in motion new dynamics of protest there, especially in Kafr Sousah, which would subsequently host many similar protests.[7]

A major turning point came in mid-2012. On 25 May of that year, 108 people, including 34 women and 49 children, were massacred in Houla

---

[6] For footage of the Mazzeh protest on 18 February 2012, see: YouTube, 18 February 2021. Archived copy available online: https://bit.ly/3mFQUcT (accessed 28 December 2021); YouTube, 18 February 2012, at: https://bit.ly/3mAXDok (accessed 28 December 2021).
[7] For footage of the funeral procession in Kafr Sousah on 31 March 2012, see: YouTube, 31 March 2012, at: https://bit.ly/3sBT559 (accessed 28 December 2021).

district north of Homs. For the Damascene merchants, who until now had remained impassive in the face of regime atrocities, a line had been crossed. On 1 June, the historic markets of the capital (Hariqa, Hamidiyeh, Midhat Pasha and Bab Sreija) went on strike. The strike lasted three days and was only broken when the security forces began destroying stock and vandalizing buildings to force merchants to reopen.

Days later, on 7 June, the markets were shuttered again to protest the army's assault on Duma. The alliance between the merchants and the regime was beginning to falter, and it looked like the capital was headed towards a mass uprising. The regime thus changed its strategy. It deployed armoured vehicles and military personnel to checkpoints across the city and redoubled its efforts to crush the protests in the satellite towns and root out the armed insurgency that was quickly developing there.

Popular civic protest nonetheless grew steadily within Damascus through to 17 July 2012, when pro-revolution media outlets, in collaboration with opposition figures and military commanders in Istanbul, announced a campaign to liberate the capital militarily. In the event, the 'Battle for Damascus' amounted to no more than a handful of clashes between regime soldiers and opposition fighters, many of whom had taken refuge in the capital after the army offensives in the satellite towns (Zamalka and Duma) and quickly withdrew once it became obvious that their host neighbourhoods were not equipped for a lengthy struggle.[8]

Aleppo: Hesitation and apprehension

Keeping the revolution out of Aleppo was almost as important as keeping it out of Damascus. The Aleppo governorate was home to 6 million people, around a quarter of the total Syrian population. The city itself was the economic capital of the country and played host to much of Syria's industry and commercial activity. Indeed, Aleppo narrowly missed out on becoming the capital of an independent Syria during the 1940s, and throughout the 1950s was a major political centre that rivalled Damascus in its parliamentary importance.

The French researcher Fabrice Balanche, who is known for his interpretation of modern Syrian history through the lens of demography

---

[8] This was neither the first nor the last time that the revolutionary media and military commanders were to mislead the public. Such exaggerated claims bolstered the credibility of the regime's (totally untrustworthy) media, undermined revolutionaries' morale and disrupted armed action, not to mention adding to a general sense of information overload. Citing non-existent plans not only raised hopes that were subsequently dashed, resulting in disillusionment, it also discouraged the development of *actual* plans or of a credible media discourse.

and sectarianism, explains the reluctance of Aleppans to join the revolution by pointing to the distrust between the urban and rural population and the presence of large Christian (especially Armenian) and Kurdish communities in the city.[9] The first factor may have played a role, but the second does not explain the city's quiescence. In fact, in other times of crisis Aleppo's diversity has pushed it in the opposite direction. Demographic composition, then, does not explain everything. Economic and political factors played a more important role. The Sunni majority did not behave like a sect, and the revolution did not turn it into one, although the sectarian propaganda resonated with many Sunnis. Even so, different segments of the Sunni majority behaved differently; though the majority belonged to single confession, it was not one political community.

Economic factors have been central to Aleppan politics since independence. After Syria joined the UAR in 1958, nationalization did much to undermine the Aleppan bourgeoisie and triggered massive capital flight to neighbouring countries, especially Lebanon. The bourgeoisie thus threw their weight behind the separatist coup that brought Syria out of the UAR in 1961, leading to the polarization of local politics between pro- and anti-UAR forces. After the Baʿth Party took power in 1963 and embarked on another ambitious nationalization programme under Jadid, the bourgeoisie found themselves in the political wilderness again, and were only reconciled with the regime after Hafez al-Assad purged the left wing of the party in 1970. Assad's policy in Aleppo as in other industrial cities was to encourage the consolidation of local identity at the expense of national identity and to allow loyal local elites to monopolize municipal government while reserving key positions in the army and security forces for his own placemen, particularly people linked to the regime by sectarian or other loyalty ties. The grant of the city to loyal businessmen and party apparatchiks as a quasi-fiefdom (under the slogan 'Aleppo for the Aleppans, Damascus for the Damascenes') cultivated a class of what Ibn Khaldoun referred to as 'people of the state' – people who understood, as he put it, that statecraft and commerce ply the same road, that hypocrisy can move one closer to political status and political status can bring wealth.

This intersection of interests, however, did not last long. The rise of the new businessmen under the Assad regime was a direct threat to the traditional Aleppan bourgeoisie, who were now forced to compete for rents, import and export licenses, and public contracts. At the same time the regime was making a concerted attempt to crush the Brotherhood – which had many sympathizers in Aleppo – which entailed a six-month

---

[9] Fabrice Balanche, 'Géographie de la révolte syrienne', *Outre-Terre* 29, no. 3 (December 2011), 437–58; Hokayem, 46.

security crackdown in the city that left hundreds of assumed Brotherhood supporters dead[10] and a campaign of harassment against local capitalists suspected of funding the organization, many of whom went into exile. In the popular imagination, Aleppo became associated with resistance to the regime.

Throughout Hafez al-Assad's tenure a heavy security presence kept Aleppo under control, and tense relations with Turkey cut Aleppo off from its old economic milieu. When Bashar took power, however, things changed. Hoping that it would be able to rally support around the succession, the regime offered extensive economic reforms (essentially a vehicle for enriching loyal elites) and made regenerating Aleppo a key priority. The local chambers of commerce and industry developed much stronger connections with the central government, and many Aleppan capitalists became part of the second generation of 'new businessmen' providing profitable outlets for the Gulf and the expatriate capital that flooded Syria. Assad granted these businessmen most investment contracts for state institutions in tourist areas as well as other municipal investment and services projects.

State policy in Aleppo worked in parallel with the expansion of trade between Syria and Turkey, which allowed Aleppo to regain some of its long-lost presence in the Turkish market and to become a marketplace for nearby Turkish towns. Turkish and Aleppan businessmen and investors found ways to work together.[11] In many ways Aleppo was thus the main beneficiary of the regime's new economic policy, and this goes a long way towards explaining the city's limited engagement with the revolution in its early days, the enthusiasm of its youth groups notwithstanding.

In fact, the displacement of around 300,000 people from Hama, Idleb and Homs following military operations in those cities made the city something of a boom town in late 2011, with the new arrivals (dubbed 'the new tourists' by locals after tourism to Syria declined in 2011) stimulating retail, services, construction and the rental market. Of course, this was not to last. But for the time being, residents of the slums and other poor neighbourhoods used Fridays not to protest but to erect new unlicensed buildings, taking advantage of the security forces' newfound preoccupation with mosques and public squares. While other Syrians were filling the streets on the Friday of Dignity or the Friday of Resilience, Aleppans were

---

[10] On Eid al-Adha (11 August 1980), the security forces killed dozens of people in the Masharqa neighbourhood. The following day, raids were carried out at properties linked to Brotherhood militants across the poor areas of the city. This information comes from Aleppans' own accounts, but for corroboration, see: *Syrianoor*, 31 July 2012, at: https://bit.ly/3euDz2Q (accessed 28 December 2021).

[11] Barout, *The Last Decade in the History of Syria*, 374.

facetiously celebrating 'Concrete-pouring Friday' and 'the Friday of Construction'.

The youth groups' failure to galvanize protest in the city of Aleppo itself meant that the people of the hinterland were forced to take up the slack. One of the most notable attempts to bring the revolution into the city, 'Aleppo Volcano' (30 June), saw young people from various nearby towns hold simultaneous protests in a number of Aleppan neighbourhoods. But locals refused to join them, and the protest was quickly dispersed by the security forces. The resulting blow to the revolutionaries' morale was effectively exploited by the regime, which organized several major demonstrations of its own to show that Aleppo remained overwhelmingly loyal.

What the regime had failed to take into account, however, were the close demographic ties between the rebellious areas nearby and the poor neighbourhoods in the city itself. The major military operations that began in the governorate in August 2011 left many people dead, and in response, Aleppans from poor or rural backgrounds began to hold solidarity protests. These protests, in poor neighbourhoods like Salahuddin, al-Sukkari, Bustan Elbash, Halaq and Sakhour, began to mobilize large crowds in the first months of 2012. By mid-year as many as 200,000 people were attending protests in these areas: during the Friday of Merchants and Revolutionaries... Hand in hand towards Victory (8 June 2012), for example, nearly 50,000 people turned out in Salahuddin alone. This was the largest protest Aleppo had seen since the beginning of the revolution, and the chants adopted by protesters affirmed that the city had overcome its apathy.[12] After the Salahuddin march met up with another demonstration originating in A'zamiyyah and attempted to push through to the centre of the city,[13] the security forces opened fire, leaving eleven people dead. On the same day, some 10,000 people came out to protest in Bustan al-Qasr.[14]

Alongside the growing protest movement in these neighbourhoods, students at the University of Aleppo began to demonstrate in larger and larger numbers. The student body, whose members come from all over Syria, became a measure of the middle classes' participation in the revolution. And the university protests encouraged others to participate, including many professional associations. The Bar Association was particularly active, holding repeated sit-ins in the city's courthouse. On 27

---

[12] Major chants included 'Aleppo, rebel, rebel! Shake the presidential palace'. For footage of the Salahuddin protest on the Friday of Merchants and Revolutionaries... Hand in hand towards Victory, see: YouTube, 8 June 2012, at: https://bit.ly/3JlcblP (accessed 28 December 2021).
[13] For footage of the meeting of the two protests, see: YouTube, 8 June 2011, at: https://bit.ly/3EAqgbE (accessed 28 December 2021).
[14] For footage of the Bustan al-Qasr protest, see: YouTube, 8 June 2012, at: https://bit.ly/3pyoX8X (accessed 28 December 2021).

July 2011,[15] some 100 lawyers held a sit-in to demand the release of detainees and an end to violence against protesters; on this occasion the *shabbiha* stormed the courthouse, attacking the lawyers and arresting some of them. Two more sit-ins were held on 5 March[16] and 4 April[17] to protest the domestic use of the army, attracting around 50 and 100 lawyers respectively.

Aleppo was prepared for a peaceful protest movement like the one in Damascus. The demonstrations were growing gradually, just as they had in Hama, where they had eventually developed into a fully-fledged popular revolution. But events were to take a different turn in Aleppo. Fighting had begun in the nearby countryside quite early on. And in late July 2012, fighters brought it into the city itself, beginning the Battle for Aleppo.

This was a disastrous decision for the city and for the revolution. The regime responded with predictable brutality, turning large parts of the city into battlefields and then reducing them to ruins. Entrenching in cities did not deter the regime, which surrendered nothing but piles of rubble. The staggering cost and limited gains of the military option lost the armed rebels a large part of their popular support. They were not professional military planners, and it showed. The liberation of Aleppo started to look like an occupation of the city by the countryside. And when neighbourhoods were 'liberated', the regime had no scruples about turning the full might of its air force and artillery on them. Moreover, the fighters were an inexperienced and disparate group operating under many different names. This gave cover to parties willing to commit crimes and violations in the liberated city. There were only two options for struggle against such a regime: peaceful demonstration or guerrilla warfare. Occupying cities was a disaster.

By late 2011, the regime, its brutality notwithstanding, had been unable to stop peaceful and civic protest. Nor did the rapid militarization of the revolution. Although limited, protests remained a constant phenomenon throughout. Moreover, the peaceful revolution had successfully delegitimized a regime that maintained a complex web of foreign ties and had long convinced the world to overlook its repression due to its purportedly stabilizing role in the region. The revolution proved its own legitimacy in the Arab world and more broadly, spurring the Arab League on 10 September 2011 to call for an end to the violence and the withdrawal

---

[15] For footage of this sit-in, see: YouTube, 27 July 2011, at: https://bit.ly/3ethelU (accessed 28 December 2021).
[16] For footage of this sit-in, see: YouTube, 5 March 2012, at: https://bit.ly/3esC8BV (accessed 28 December 2021).
[17] For footage of this sit-in, see: YouTube, 5 March 2012, at: https://bit.ly/3pxI8iX (accessed 28 December 2021).

of heavy weaponry from urban areas, guarantees for the right of peaceful protest and a national dialogue between the regime and the opposition as a prelude to a democratic transition.[18]

But the regime dug in. With its steady escalation – shooting, arresting and torturing demonstrators and bombarding Syrian cities – it shifted the course of the revolution. As more revolutionaries took up arms for the legitimate reason of self-defence, the more religious the discourse became. New extremist religious elements, which were not committed to the goals and spirit of the civil revolution, attracted ever more unpoliticized segments of the oppressed population to their ranks. The same population that for four decades had never dared to challenge the regime came to besiege it everywhere. But the great sacrifices and struggles of the Syrian people did not bring down the regime with a resounding crash. Instead, the underpinnings of the regime were gradually eroded. The price, however, would be the gradual disintegration of the Syrian state and society.

---

[18] *Al-Hayat* newspaper leaked the text of the initiative on 6 September 2011, two days before Arab League Secretary-General Nabil el-Araby visited Damascus, but it was not officially unveiled until 10 September 2011, which is the date I use here. The regime initially refused to engage with the initiative but subsequently formally accepted it, though it continued to use live ammunition against protestors. As a result, the Arab League proposed the second Arab initiative (22 January 2012), which called for the transfer of President Assad's authorities to his vice-president and the formation of a national unity government. These diplomatic efforts towards a political solution will be discussed in detail below.

5

An armed revolution

This chapter tracks the shift from peaceful revolution to armed rebellion. In the first months of the revolution, some people began carrying arms, primarily in self-defence. The attack on the security headquarters in Jisr ash-Shughur in June 2011 was a critical juncture in the turn to offensive armed struggle. By February 2012, after the 'liberation' of az-Zabdani and the army assault on Baba Amr, the Syrian revolution had become a fully-fledged armed revolution – a path that could only lead to an internal war. This chapter details the failure of the FSA to devise a coordinated military strategy. It also examines the Battle for Aleppo and the surprising fall of ar-Raqqa into the fighters' hands.

Prelude to armament

Even in the face of lethal violence, Syria's revolutionaries persisted with the peaceful tactics of their Egyptian and Tunisian counterparts for many months. From the very beginning of the revolution, however, there were those who argued that Syria was much more like Libya[1] than either of these countries – that because of the iron grip of the security forces and the prohibition on mass gatherings, armed struggle, leading ultimately to foreign intervention, was the only way to topple the regime. As time went on, the brutal treatment consistently meted out to peaceful protesters was to make this argument seem more and more compelling.[2]

The more it relied on excessive force, the more the regime's legitimacy was eroded. The crisis had shown the Syrian state for what it was: a cluster of

---

[1] The military units (named after Muammar al-Qaddafi's sons) that took over the functions of the army were a negation of the state, which became no more than a regime and the various units and militias it relied on. Having seen the success of the uprisings in Tunisia and Egypt, the Libyan regime pursued a strategy similar to that of the Syrian regime: it opened fire on any public gathering in order to prevent it gaining momentum.

[2] This is not to say that the Syrian revolution copied the Libyan model. Syria's path was unique, as I argue throughout this book.

security agencies, military entities and unofficial militias, an entity that had long ago been appropriated by a corrupt regime reliant on a complex network of interlocking interests from which it could no longer be distinguished. By 2012, the regime was effectively waging all-out war against its own people. Even the army, which prior to the revolution had enjoyed a measure of independent legitimacy – despite Syrians' awareness of army corruption and the humiliating experience of military service – was gradually absorbed into the regime and its doctrine of repression at all costs. Those regime figures who attempted to maintain the army's traditional role of defending the country from external threats, first among them Defence Minister Ali Habib,[3] a hero of the 1982 Lebanon War, were at best marginalized or placed under house arrest.[4]

For many revolutionaries, then, the regime had become an occupying army.

During August 2011, the month in which the army was directly deployed in various cities, hundreds of thousands of people still demonstrated in spite of the killings of peaceful demonstrators. In September, however, the number of protestors dropped to thousands each day.[5] Demonstrations cannot withstand an army that is willing to shoot.

Other than giving in, the only option was to organize to face the regime with arms. Once we understand this attitude, the development of the armed struggle in Syria becomes much more comprehensible. Not only was there no advance planning – let alone a conspiracy[6] – the spontaneity and gradual evolution of the armed rebellion to meet generally local needs were to be its greatest weakness. The absence of any unified plan or organized political force behind the fighters meant that those taking up arms were left without any sort of political education. The only forces whose mindset was inclined to armed action were the jihadi Salafis who had fought in Afghanistan or in Iraq, and organized groups like al-Qaeda.

---

[3] Ali Habib was one of the heroes of the Battle of Marj al-Sultan during the 1982 Israeli invasion of Lebanon, a major victory in which almost an entire enemy brigade was annihilated and an Israeli plan to cut off the Damascus–Beirut highway was foiled. For the regime, Marj al-Sultan is a glorious page in the history of the Syrian army and of Arab militaries more generally.

[4] On 8 August 2011, Habib was replaced as minister of defence by Daud Rajiha. Official sources claimed that he had been dismissed for health reasons, but false rumours were spread that he was killed by the regime. Habeeb's replacement coincided with major military operations in Hama and Deir ez-Zor. According to an officer stationed at the presidential palace, who wished to remain anonymous, figures within the military establishment had launched a smear campaign against Habeeb months before his removal, claiming that he was incompetent and was preventing the army from acting decisively to eliminate the armed groups. The officer adds that Habeeb was placed under house arrest immediately afterwards.

[5] Raymond Hinnebusch estimated that 25,000–30,000 people were involved in daily demonstrations in September. I do not know how he, or his source the International Crisis Group, reached this number, but the numbers did drop substantially during September. Hinnebusch, 'Syria': 109.

[6] This refutation of the conspiratorial interpretation of armed action does not preclude later intervention by regional and other foreign states to support or even exploit it in some cases.

Militarization begins

Weapons initially began to appear during the first months of the revolution. At first, their presence was largely a matter of tradition – gun ownership is a customary practice, especially in Syria's tribal communities and in the countryside, and this extended to many peripheral neighbourhoods with large tribal populations, especially near to the borders. It was a legitimate form of self-defence in the face of the violence used by the *shabbiha* militias and the security forces, who enjoyed complete unaccountability. At this point, bearing arms was an individual and local 'communal' matter. But as the revolution drew on, these same towns and districts would become bastions of the armed opposition.

There were various early examples of this pattern. After the storming of the Umari Mosque in Daraa on 23 March 2011, young men enraged by the behaviour of the security forces armed themselves and took up positions around the old city to prevent any further raids.[7] In Banyas, Mohammad Ali Bayasi – an associate of Abd al-Halim Khaddam, a former deputy prime minister who had defected in 2005 – led efforts to arm protesters in the city throughout April, procuring weapons through oft-plied smuggling routes into Lebanon.[8] These efforts resulted in several limited clashes with the security forces and the army in and around Banyas.[9]

In the predominantly Bedouin Baba Amr neighbourhood of Homs, the killing of Sheikh Badr Abu Musa in April 2011 led to an all-out firefight between young tribesmen and the security forces, killing fourteen people and injuring fifty. That same month in Talbiseh and ar-Rastan, where angry protesters had set fire to a statue of Hafez al-Assad on the Homs-Hama expressway,[10] locals fought back against security officers involved in a major operation in those areas. Similar processes were at work in the Damascus periphery, the Houran and in the countryside around Hama and Idleb, although every area had a different religious, tribal and organizational profile driving the taking up of arms.

---

[7] According to an activist from Daraa, the week after the assault on the Umari Mosque, young men armed themselves with hunting rifles and a handful of AK-47s and set up positions around the old city (Daraa al-Balad) to prevent a second attack. Before the army entered Daraa on 25 April, however, these young men only clashed with the security forces on one occasion. A face-to-face interview with Khalid al-Jawabra, conducted by Hamzeh al-Moustafa, ACRPS researcher, in Doha on 19 March 2012.

[8] According to a member of the Bayasi family involved in the arms smuggling operation, Bayasi was able to get around thirty weapons into Banyas (twenty Russian rifles, two machine guns, two rocket-propelled grenade launchers and six pump-action rifles).

[9] An interview with an activist involved in the Ma'an movement in Banyas who wishes to remain anonymous, conducted by the ACRPS research team in Cairo on 7 May 2013.

[10] Barout, *The Last Decade in the History of Syria*, 237–8.

At the same time as civilians were beginning to arm themselves, defections from the army – both officers and enlisted members – were gathering steam. A great deal was made of these defections by the revolutionary media, which used them as cover for the carrying of weapons by civilians: any armed men seen on the streets were defectors who refused to shoot at their own people and not, as the regime narrative claimed, extremist insurgents. However understandable this line may have been, the one constant truth observable throughout the revolution is that the majority of the revolutionaries were always untrained civilians. Those defectors who did join the revolutionaries were predominantly enlisted men. While defecting officers did join the revolution or return later once organized armed action began, at first the majority fled abroad with their families, fearing regime reprisals; they knew that it was standard practice to harass or even detain the families of political fugitives, using parents or other relatives as leverage to force them to hand themselves in.

Jisr ash-Shughur: A turning point

The attack on the headquarters of the security forces in Jisr ash-Shughur in early June 2011 did not change the largely peaceful character of the revolution seen in mass protests, but marked a turning point toward armed struggle, which became the main mode of the revolution between early and mid-2012. Although weapons had appeared before, until then they had always been used in self-defence. Now, however, they were being used for retaliation. In revenge for thirty-eight people killed during clashes the previous day, the attackers killed 120 security employees. This was a vendetta. It was a new type of incident, a new dynamic that had not been present in the civic protests. But it would soon become a central part of the revolutionary movement, pushing it ever closer towards the pit of intercommunal strife.

In Jisr ash-Shughur the revolutionary media attempted to gloss over what had happened: the public line was that the army had killed its own soldiers.[11] Rather than considering what the response should be to these events, they questioned the events themselves, making it impossible to

---

[11] In an interview conducted by the ACRPS research team with a police officer who wishes to remain anonymous, and who survived the Jisr al-Shughur massacre, he stated that the Syrian authorities could have rescued those besieged in the security headquarters, but instead left them to die. The officer believes that the authorities made that choice to prove the veracity of their claims about armed terrorist gangs murdering the members of the security forces and the army. This, of course, is his personal reading of the situation, and it is nearly impossible to ascertain the intentions of actors in such situations or to construct arguments based on assumptions.

conduct a serious, objective discussion. This both undermined their credibility and ruled out any possibility of accountability or of learning from events. This pattern was to repeat itself every time the rebels committed a crime: the revolutionary media accused the regime of responsibility and avoided taking a strong stance against such actions. The broader pro-revolution Arab media colluded in this by publishing opposition narratives as received, without proper verification. But ultimately these accusations were believable because the regime was *known* to have already committed far more brutal crimes.

The Jisr ash-Shughur attack coincided with another momentous event: on 9 June, Major Harmoush had announced the formation of the FOB in Jisr ash-Shughur, which was supposed to stand up to the regular army and defend the city.[12] Now, as defections from the army stepped up, similar groups began springing up across the country, most of them claiming affiliation with the FOB. Some opposition figures began to call for all the revolutionaries to arm themselves and for defectors to protect peaceful protests. While statements like this one were not uncommon, taking weapons to a peaceful protest to protect protesters is a contradiction in terms: going to a protest armed necessarily makes it an armed protest. In such cases, arms will provide no protection because security forces will respond much more brutally to an armed protest than an unarmed one. This line of argument was no more than a dubious pretext for the ongoing militarization of the revolution. Organizational committees and Facebook pages that had denied or played down the role of armed actors now began to report on their operations as revolutionary acts.[13]

At a time when the regime was systematically responding to every peaceful protest with overwhelming brutality, many political figures had pinned their hopes on an international intervention, à la Libya. It is impossible to believe that anyone was seriously convinced that self-defence – or the sort of communal armed action that had developed in the countryside and some provincial towns and cities – was capable of defeating the regime militarily.

The revolution, or at least those parts of it that had previously denied the presence of weapons on the ground, now clearly needed a front. It found such a body on 27 July, when Colonel Riad al-Asaad announced the formation of the FSA. The latter was to operate as an umbrella organization encompassing all kinds of armed action – individual and communal – against the government forces that were attacking protesters. In what was

---

[12] For Harmoush's announcement of his defection, see: YouTube, 9 June 2011, at: https://bit.ly/32OWAKB (accessed 3 January 2022).
[13] Mustapha, *The Virtual Public Sphere in the Syrian Revolution*, 139.

becoming the conventional line on armed action, its battalions were to 'protect peaceful demonstrations and counter security raids and military operations'.[14] While the number of people willing to take up arms and the frequency of armed clashes rose steadily, the civic side of the revolution remained dominant throughout this period. Protests, organizing and the flurry of long-suppressed political debate between intellectuals and ideological groupings continued apace. The transition to armed revolution came only at the beginning of 2012, as the regime's ever-escalating violence against protesters made peaceful demonstrations increasingly untenable.

Another turning point came in mid-January, when tenacious fighters in az-Zabdani, near Damascus, managed to secure an agreement that the army would not enter the town so long as opposition fighters did not attack government positions. This limited success led many to the premature conclusion that armed struggle really could work. Opposition figures now began to demand weapons for the FSA – 13 January was celebrated as 'Support the FSA Friday'. Limited arms shipments encouraged the shift from resistance to ending regime control over whole areas of the country. Soon enough armed groups were announcing the 'liberation' of areas like Baba Amr in Homs and Duma in the Damascus periphery.[15] While governorate capitals generally stayed under regime control, the countryside and the small towns were becoming bastions of opposition activity.

A month later another blow was dealt to those who were still desperately hoping for foreign intervention. A proposed political solution put together by the Arab League and presented to the UNSC for adoption as a resolution was vetoed by Russia and China in early February.[16] This was the second time a draft resolution on Syria had been torpedoed by those powers, and for those within the opposition who were still struggling to grasp the difference between Syria and Libya, the Russian and Chinese veto was a rude awakening. It was now obvious that there was little hope for the Libyan model or any of the variations that the opposition had envisaged (military intervention, significant material support). Nevertheless, many people clung to the illusion, while others abandoned it and started making demands for safe zones and arms. Even an attempt to impose a political solution through international pressure seemed unlikely now that the Arab League initiative had failed. With or without UNSC resolution, the US was

---

[14] For the FSA announcement, see: YouTube, 29 July 2011, at: https://bit.ly/3FRfNKa (accessed 3 January 2022).

[15] ACRPS, 'Is the Syrian Revolution Entering a New Stage?', 6 January 2013, at: https://bit.ly/3E7yPdS (accessed 3 January 2022).

[16] *UN News*, 4 February 2012, at: https://bit.ly/3zhXHia (accessed 3 January 2022).

unwilling to repeat the experience of Iraq or Afghanistan or to directly confront Russia and Iran, and there was little concern for the ongoing destruction of Syria. The military option was never really on the table. The Russian veto was only an alibi. In fact, Western powers were wary even of indirectly backing the armed revolt, providing only very limited media, logistical and humanitarian support.

Poor coordination, poor organization

Fighters operating under the FSA name showed great courage defending their fellow Syrians against brutal regime violence. But the FSA has never been an army in the sense of a unified body with a chain of command and organizational hierarchy. It has always been a loose umbrella organization, a political front for disparate armed actors. The initial transition from local, communal armed action towards armed revolution took place in name only: armed actors were still fighting a communal, local revolution. Although their adoption of the FSA banner encouraged assumptions to the contrary – the press chased FSA commanders in Istanbul for statements on events they themselves were learning about from the media, and videos recorded by local fighters were broadcast as though they were the official line of a coherent organization – the armed battalions remained operationally entirely independent of the high command in Turkey.

This was not for want of trying. Many of those involved really did want to create a centralized and well-organized revolutionary army that would prefigure an equally well-organized state, and it was widely believed that disorganized action would lack popular legitimacy. But no actual hierarchical structure or effective political-military vehicle was established.

When individuals or groups announced that they were joining the FSA, all that they meant was that they were joining the armed revolution. There was no attendant organizational commitment. Contacts were made mostly in order to receive support once Arab and Western countries started offering financial backing and limited arms deliveries. With time, relatively organized brigades were created, some boasting thousands of committed fighters who obeyed their commanders. But these continued to operate independently.

The FSA commanders were not subordinated to a political leadership, and in the absence of a military chain of command and of regular supplies, they had no systematic military strategy, the heroism the battalions in the field often showed notwithstanding.

But there was no blueprint for the revolution to follow and no obvious alternative in the face of brutal regime violence. For those on the ground and for the commanders, the move to armed action was irreversible. They were convinced that it was the only way to topple the regime.

With no grand plan, no centralized command structure and no organized army, the armed movement remained overwhelmingly local in scope. Its objectives became the liberation of this or that town, objectives that could only be achieved with great sacrifice but that meant very little without a broader strategic vision.[17] Larger armed groups began to emerge, and the armed revolution proved to be even more disorganized and disunited than the opposition in exile, which at least managed to create enduring organizational frameworks.

The military councils that were set up in February 2012 to coordinate efforts at the governorate or regional level seemed to offer the most obvious route to a solution. On 5 February 2012, Brigadier-General Mustafa al-Sheikh established the Supreme Military Council (SMC – the highest military leadership of the FSA) to coordinate efforts between the different councils, the first of several attempts to bring the dozens of FSA brigades and battalions on the ground under a unified command structure.

During the first five months of their existence, the regional military councils were the main representatives of the armed movement. Their leaders became legitimate and authoritative spokesmen for the FSA. At least at the regional level, divisions between battalions seemed to have been overcome. But in fact, various groups – particularly those with Salafi inclinations – remained outside the councils. And even among affiliated groups the councils' record was uneven. Mustafa al-Sheikh, Riad al-Asaad and Colonel Qassem Saadeddine all tried to establish themselves as the main spokesman of the SMC, and there were regular public disagreements with the political opposition. The creation of a Joint Staff led by General Salim Idriss in December 2012 failed to solve these problems.[18]

The general sense of disunity was exacerbated by the constant creation of new brigades on the ground, most of them entirely outside the councils' ambit. Weapons and money were readily available from a diverse range of international backers, many of them making up a private support network, especially in the Gulf region. These states did not trust one another and had diverging assessments of the situation on the ground, the effectiveness of specific groups and the political identity of those groups. While Qatar and Turkey acted with a degree of coordination, Saudi Arabia was suspicious of both, and neighbouring Jordan – more wary of supporting a revolution on

---

[17] The regime also had a strategy, albeit a very simple one. It maintained army positions and airfields outside the cities that it had lost, cut them off from the outside world and bombarded them with artillery, mortars and airstrikes.
[18] *Youm7*, 10 December 2012, at: https://bit.ly/3D32HY1 (accessed 3 January 2022).

its doorstep and more influenced by the US position – had an entirely different attitude from all three. The same countries that called again and again for the unification of the armed opposition thus helped to fragment it by maintaining their own funding channels and their own lists of favoured groups – while circumventing, of course, the central command.

Fragmentation, rejection of higher authority and struggles over leadership dogged both the political and the military aspects of the Syrian revolution. The spontaneity of the initial demonstrations meant that many revolutionaries were unwilling to recognize an institutionalized leadership as a higher frame of reference. This was also true of the Tunisian and Egyptian revolutions. But in those cases, the revolution did not last long enough for this to be a problem (although it had serious repercussions for the transitional period in Egypt). The Syrian case differed in two important respects. On the one hand, the authoritarian nature of the regime meant that there was no base level of political organization in the public sphere that the revolution could build on. On the other, the Syrian uprising went on much longer, under much more complex circumstances, and ultimately made the transition to military action – all characteristics demanding a high level of organization if success is to be achieved.

There were exceptions to this general trend, particularly at the local level. The work of the coordination committees – arranging protests, aid work, their media strategy – was highly organized and coherent. At its best, local military action could also be highly coordinated.

But this never translated into a broader, unified military strategy. Outside ar-Raqqa, the rebels never took control of a whole governorate or any other large contiguous area of the country: the security forces and the army retained bases and checkpoints in every region. The rebels' approach, moreover, was something of a double-edged sword. Whenever the armed rebels entered an area, the regime would subject it to such brutal bombardment that the civilian population would flee *en masse*. Liberated areas were thus quickly 'liberated' of their inhabitants.

Aleppo provides a stark example of this dynamic. As soon as the Tawhid Brigade[19] moved into the city, a mass civilian exodus began before any

---

[19] Aron Lund writes, 'The Tawhid Division has fought alongside Islamists from non-FSA factions such as Jabhat al-Nosra, Ahrar al-Sham, and Fajr el-Islam. According to some sources, it is funded by exiled Islamists, including the Muslim Brotherhood.' However, the Tawhid Brigade was not a religious movement. 'While some members and leaders appear to be convinced Islamists, others are not. Abdul Qadir al-Saleh on the one hand refers to the jihadi group Jabhat el-Nosra as "our brothers", saying he will cooperate with anyone fighting the regime; but, on the other hand, he strikes a decidedly un-salafi note by insisting on the equal rights of Christians and other religious minorities.' Aron Lund, 'Syrian Jihadism', UI Brief, no. 13, Swedish Institute of International Affairs, 14 September 2012, 17.

clashes had even taken place. The neighbourhood where fighters initially took up positions, Salahuddin, lost around 90 per cent of its population before being levelled as soon as serious fighting began. The FSA then decamped to nearby Saif al-Dawla and al-Iza'a, both densely populated, setting off a second massive wave of internal displacement and filling parks and schools in other parts of the city with refugees. Within a few weeks the rebels were announcing 'tactical withdrawals' from these areas, but not before they had suffered great material and human destruction. The important point here is that this bizarre 'strategy' did not change the military balance with the regime. In the struggle against a regime without scruples that was ready to bombard its own cities, occupying neighbourhoods – as opposed to military bases or airfields – damaged the social base of the revolution and had no strategic effect.

As militarization proceeded apace, the revolutionaries established control over broad swathes of the country, eventually arriving at the gates of the capital. The armed struggle allowed the revolution to continue despite the regime's brutal response. But it was also a much longer and more costly route to take. The transition to armed action started spontaneously and under massive regime pressure – that is, it was more the regime's choice than the revolution.

The Battle for Aleppo: A city in revolt or the attack of the countryside?

By 19 July, the rebels had liberated a substantial area to the north and east of Aleppo, and there was a heavy concentration of FSA forces in A'zaz, al-Bab, Andan, Haritan and Daret Azza.[20] These successes may have had some strategic importance, but they did not shift the balance. The regime's strategy had always been to maintain a *cordon sanitaire* around the main cities and prevent any revolutionary mobilizations inside them; it could afford to lose small towns and sections of the marginalized countryside. The FSA battalions thus began to seriously consider an attack on Aleppo itself, in coordination with the Aleppo Military Council headquartered in Salahuddin. If they could take control of the city, they might be able to tip the balance against the regime.

---

[20] After their defeat in A'zaz, near Aleppo – where rebels destroyed more than eleven tanks – the regime withdrew almost entirely from the areas to the north and west of Aleppo City, concentrating its forces in As-Safira complex, the Nayreb and Kuwyres airfields, the barracks of the 46th Regiment (seized by the rebels in November 2012) and the Infantry School (lost in December 2012).

On 20 July, the Tawhid and Fateh Brigade moved into the neighbourhoods of Salahuddin, Sukkari and Sakhour. Two days later, Colonel Abduljabbar al-Uqaidi, leader of the local military council, announced the beginning of the 'battle to liberate Aleppo', calling on all nearby forces to lend their support to the struggle. The battalions of rural Aleppo answered the call, and within days some 7,000 rebel fighters had taken control of large portions of the city – including Salahuddin, Saif al-Dawla, Sakhour, Masakin Hanano, Qadi Askar and Bustan Elbasha – and had almost reached the centre.

These developments put the regime on the back foot. In response, it declared a 'full mobilization' for what the pro-regime *al-Watan* called – echoing Saddam Hussein – the 'mother of all battles', the 'last battle to be fought by the Syrian Arab Army', after which 'Syria will be extricated from its crisis and the Islamist-Turkish-Qatari project to control the Middle East will be officially declared a failure'.[21] To prevent the rebels from reaching Sa'dallah al-Jabiri Square, the regime deployed fighter jets for the first time (the rebels did not have – and would never be allowed to obtain – anti-aircraft weapons). Airstrikes against rebel-held neighbourhoods produced a massive wave of displacement towards refugee camps in Turkey and rural villages outside regime control. Almost all the Syrian army forces in Jabal az-Zawiya, in Idleb, were redeployed to Aleppo to reinforce the failing garrison. As a result, the regime was able to check the rebel advance. But it did not succeed in ousting them from the neighbourhoods they had already taken.

Aleppo is a case study in the shortcomings of both the revolution and the armed struggle – not as a revolution against injustice and dictatorship (which the revolution was) or a natural reaction to extreme violence (which the armed struggle was), but in the sense that both brought to the surface all the existing contradictions and shortcomings of Syrian society. An offensive made up of thousands of fighters from the countryside could not help but look like an attack on the urban by the rural. This deepened an existing sense of alienation and mistrust *vis-à-vis* the revolution and produced friction between the revolutionaries and the locals – friction that in its turn allowed for abuses because of a lack of organization and discipline.

The sea change towards engagement with the peaceful revolution that had been on the horizon in the weeks leading up to the offensive dissipated. In June it had seemed that massacres in Homs and Hama had turned even the business community against the regime. But the behaviour of the armed

---

[21] *Iraqibeacon*, 26 July 2012, at: https://bit.ly/3A1SJrB (accessed 7 August 2022).

groups operating under the banner of the revolution – protection rackets, kidnappings of wealthy businessmen and their families, thefts, and even some assassination attempts – reversed this shift entirely.[22] Although the *shabbiha* of the region, particularly the mafiosi of the Berri clan, had pioneered such tactics themselves under the regime, the businessmen opted for the devil they knew.

Events in Aleppo also revealed a new dynamic that had not been present in the revolution up to this point. Salafi groups, including the al-Qaeda-linked Nusra Front, played a significant role in the battle for the city – many of them fielding scores of Arab fighters from outside Syria. These groups rejected the values of citizenship, equality and democracy that had driven the revolution from the outset. The Nusra Front, for example, distinguished clearly between 'Muslims' (i.e. Sunnis), *dhimmis* (non-Muslims enjoying protected but inferior status) and apostates (who must be killed), and considered democracy a heretic, godless system. But unlike some other brigades, it was disciplined. It had learned from its experience in Iraq and the revolt of the Sunni Arab tribes against it (the Sahwa alliance of 2007–8). The Nusra Front thus tried to polish its reputation, so did not steal from or assault civilians, and after taking over grain silos and petrol stations, the group took pains to distribute goods to locals. As a result, it developed a much better reputation.[23]

Overall, the Battle for Aleppo did not help the revolution and did little to enhance its image. The opposition behaved unusually badly, and the willingness of commanders to abandon the battlefield and prey on the civilian population was unmatched elsewhere.[24] The rebels' decision to take the city rather than the bases around it – and the regime's willingness to use

---

[22] Even before the FSA entered the city, armed men were already carrying out kidnappings of businessmen and their families, stealing private cars and demanding protection money for factories located in the hinterland. Some members of the bourgeoisie were also assassinated for pro-regime sympathies or their funding the *shabbiha* – most prominently Sariya Hassoun, son of the grand mufti.

[23] After numerous thefts and armed burglaries, the Legal Committee (recognized by all the battalions active in Aleppo) invited those living in opposition-controlled areas to file any complaints against fighters with them. In a subsequent statement, the committee announced that the majority of complaints submitted concerned Ghuraba al-Sham and demanded that the movement hand over its commander Hassan Jazra and five other named individuals by noon on 14 May. Ghuraba al-Sham refused to comply, and shortly after the ultimatum expired, hundreds of fighters stormed their headquarters, leading to clashes that ended with Jazra's fighters fleeing into Inzarat and the industrial district. The committee impounded the stolen property found at Ghuraba al-Sham's headquarters and returned it to its rightful owners. Although Ghuraba al-Sham appealed to the Tawhid Brigade, the latter issued a statement affirming its 'full support for the Legal Committee'. See: *Sawt al-Kurd*, 16 May 2014, at: https://bit.ly/3eI41G7 (accessed 3 January 2022).

[24] This phenomenon was so extreme that on 15 May 2013, the head of the Revolutionary Military Council (RMC) in Aleppo issued a statement calling on commanders to leave their bases and return to battle. YouTube, 14 May 2013, at: https://bit.ly/3eGuu77 (accessed 3 January 2022).

even the most advanced and destructive weaponry against neighbourhoods outside its control – meant that much of Aleppo was reduced to ruins. According to Minister of Health Saad Abdelsalam al-Nayef, by January 2012 more than 48 hospitals and 400 ambulances had been seriously damaged during the fighting, with some 27 hospitals and 200 ambulances put completely out of operation.[25] At the same time, all but five of the local pharmaceutical factories had totally halted production, with those that remained operating at chronic low capacity due to the lack of fuel and electricity. But all this destruction, while alienating Aleppans, failed to bring a decisive end to the battle. And like Homs before it, Aleppo had brought the tensions underlying Syrian society to the surface. It was an ominous warning of what was to happen elsewhere as the revolution drew on.

The Battle for the Damascus periphery

The Damascus periphery had long been a destination for migrants from elsewhere in the country. Duma, Harasta, Darayya, Qaboun, Kafr Batna and Zamalka – where the population was concentrated – acted as dormitory towns for the capital, offering cheaper rents at a manageable distance; many inhabitants here were originally Damascenes driven out of the city over the early 2000s by the rising cost of living. Jaramana, Qatana, al-Qutayfah, Qudsiya, and Tishreen, meanwhile, played host to generations of migrants from poorer areas of the country, while various other areas had absorbed a huge wave of migration from the Golan following the Israeli occupation in 1967.[26] The government had failed to ensure that development kept pace with this exploding population, and as a result, neither the original population nor the more recent arrivals enjoyed a dignified life.

During the first months of the revolution, the Damascus periphery had been a bastion of peaceful protest. But the extreme violence used by the regime meant that these same areas – specifically Duma and az-Zabdani – became the first in the country to embrace armed struggle as the path to ousting the regime (with the exception of some neighbourhoods of Homs), especially as peaceful protests proved unable to achieve that objective.

---

[25] *Assafir* (Lebanon), 22 January 2013, at: https://bit.ly/3Qrf48c (accessed 3 January 2022).
[26] An estimated 137,000 people were displaced by the Israeli occupation of the Golan Heights. Today, if we include their families, the displaced number more than 500,000, although no precise statistics are available. In 2011, the majority were living in Damascus and its periphery, with others resident in camps set up in Daraa, Homs and Quneitra.

From a very early point in the revolution, armed locals and army defectors began to take over parts of Duma and neighbouring Harasta, launching regular night-time attacks on checkpoints and on military buses.

Although it was concerned that they might become a gathering-point for the armed opposition – as Benghazi had in Libya – at first the regime decided not to risk entering Duma or Harasta. The towns were densely populated and close to Damascus and it was clear that the fighters enjoyed substantial local support. But as the power of the armed groups grew, and particularly after regime forces were stopped at the outskirts of az-Zabdani by armed men there in January 2012, this position began to change. By the end of the month the army had launched a full-on assault against the two cities, supported for the first time in the revolution by the Republican Guard.

The attack on Duma and Harasta cost those cities dearly. But at the same time, new armed groups were popping up in Duma and all over Eastern Ghouta. The early fighting saw the formation of the Duma Martyrs Battalion and Zahran Alloush's nascent Islam Brigade, an outfit rooted in the local Salafi movement. By March these groups were launching regular operations and countering those of the army.[27] At around the same time, a group of defectors joined the Furqan Brigade to set up the military council in Damascus and its periphery.[28] The council was to claim responsibility, in conjunction with other groups, for two massive bombings at the General Staff HQ in September of that year.[29]

The June–July 2012 assault on Duma was more destructive, and displaced more people, than any before it. On 15 July, fighters from the city relocated to a number of poor neighbourhoods around Damascus, including Tadamun, Hajar Aswad and Midan. Two days later they announced the 'Battle for Damascus'. But although a spectacular bombing at the National Security Bureau wiped out the regime's Crisis Cell – an attack whose details remain unclear[30] – the clashes in the capital lasted only a few days and were confined to the neighbourhoods that the fighters had fled to. It quickly became clear that there was little prospect of maintaining a serious military presence in those neighbourhoods.

---

[27] International Crisis Group, 'Tentative Jihad: Syria's Fundamentalist Opposition', 12 October 2012, 17–18, at: https://bit.ly/3EePzzQ (accessed 3 January 2022).
[28] For the announcement of the formation of the RMC, see: YouTube, 22 March 2013, at: https://bit.ly/3JyCDIR (accessed 3 January 2022).
[29] FSA (Damascus), 2 September 2012. Archived copy available online: https://bit.ly/3HuPxG1 (accessed 4 January 2022); FSA (Damascus), 26 September 2012. Archived copy available online: https://bit.ly/3JBz5Wk (accessed 3 January 2022).
[30] The Islam Brigade claimed responsibility for the attack but provided no evidence.

In the following days, the battalion commanders held a series of meetings over Skype and on the ground to assess these developments and agree on their next move. They attributed the defeat to a lack of coordination between battalions and to equipment shortages.

To solve the first problem, two new military coalitions were formed in the Damascus periphery. The first, the Brigades and Battalions for the Purification of Syria, brought together the Free Men of Houran, Ahfad al-Rasul, Duma Martyrs, and Ummahat al-Mu'mineen Brigades and the al-Bara' Battalion.[31] The second, Ansar al-Islam, was composed of the Islam, Furqan, al-Habib al-Mustafa and al-Haqq Brigades and the Sahaba Battalions. Uniting the two coalitions proved difficult because of the stark ideological divide between them: Ansar al-Islam rejected relations with the West and maintained that Syria had to be an Islamic state.[32]

By the end of October 2012, however, almost all of these groups had fallen in behind the newly set up Revolutionary Military Council (RMC) headed by General Ziad Fahd,[33] which oversaw five local RMCs in different areas around the capital. This was made possible by strong personal relationships between commanders and agreements to put aside ideological differences until a later date.[34] Only the al-Habib al-Mustafa Brigade and the al-Bara' Battalion remained outside the RMC – for political and ideological reasons, but also because of their commanders' personal ambitions.[35] The RMC also agreed to cooperate with the existing military council for Damascus and the periphery.[36]

By the last months of 2012, the armed opposition around Damascus were following a single unified plan and drawing on a common supply of equipment. Alongside the accelerating pace of armed action elsewhere in the country, this allowed them to launch an assault against the Air Defence Battalions. Airbases in Marj al-Sultan, Aqraba and Harran al-Awameed all fell under opposition control, and the Damascus airport was besieged, much reducing traffic. These achievements were even more significant than taking control of strategic areas in Eastern Ghouta.

---

[31] These were very loose coalitions that were frequently made, undone and remade. Other sources name different factions here.
[32] A face-to-face interview with Nasr, *nom de guerre* Abu Anas al-Shami, conducted by the ACRPS research team in Doha on 20 March 2013.
[33] For the announcement of formation of the RMC in Damascus and its periphery, see: YouTube, 27 October 2012, at: https://bit.ly/31f1S1p (accessed 3 January 2022).
[34] Members of Hizb al-Tahrir helped convince battalion commanders to join the RMC. A face-to-face interview with Nasr, *nom de guerre* Abu Anas al-Shami, conducted by the ACRPS research team in Doha on 20 March 2013.
[35] Ibid.
[36] FSA (Damascus), 29 October 2012. Archived copy available online: https://bit.ly/3mRNDar (accessed 3 January 2022).

In the end, however, the armed opposition was unable to maintain momentum, and as in Aleppo, the military situation around the capital eventually settled into an unshakeable status quo. The areas south and east of the southern Damascus bypass – Nahr Eisheh, Yarmuk Camp, Zamalka, Darayya – continued to see regular clashes from July 2012 through to the original writing of this book. The bypass itself came to mark an immovable border between regime- and opposition-controlled areas. But even if the FSA had managed to cross this line, it would not have changed much. The only real way of shifting the balance was to establish control over a continuous area between Eastern and Western Ghouta (Darayya and Madamiyet Elsham).[37] This was the aim of the battle for Darayya that began in early November 2012. Between 9 and 11 February 2013, the opposition succeeded in pushing beyond the bypass and taking control of the Haramla, al-Adnan and Zamalka Bridge checkpoints, giving them access to Jawbar and bringing them within a hundred meters of Abbasiyeen Square. The regime's constant counteroffensives against Darayya attest to the significance of these areas.

The destruction inflicted on the Damascus periphery was immense by any standard. Harasta was left completely unfit for human habitation: some 80 per cent of buildings were seriously damaged or destroyed by the regime raids, and after the civilian exodus those who remained were left with nowhere to buy food or basic supplies. In Duma, two neighbourhoods were completely destroyed, and others suffered catastrophic damage. In Darayya, the vast majority of locals fled and all four approaches to the city were destroyed, turning it into a depopulated urban battlefield.[38]

It is notable that despite the massive destruction, popular support for the revolution in the Damascus periphery showed no sign of wavering. In other words, the high cost of the armed confrontation – paid, in the final analysis, by the general population – was not the primary determiner of attitudes towards the revolution. The decisive factor was the behaviour of opposition fighters towards the locals and the respect they showed for their rights and personal freedoms. Unlike in Idleb and Aleppo, many of the rebels in the Damascus periphery were local to the districts they fought in.[39] And of course, the region had a long history of political engagement,

---

[37] Darayya, a district characterized by moderate religiosity, played an important role in the peaceful protests, but it was relatively late to join the armed struggle compared to other towns in the Damascus periphery.

[38] Virtual Interviews via Skype with a number of political activists and locals, conducted by Nerouz Satik and Hamza Mustapha, ACRPS researchers.

[39] After Jaysh al-Islam became the major power in Ghouta, there were incidents of kidnapping and executions, most notoriously the disappearance of human rights activists Razan Zaitouneh, Samira Khalil and Wael Hmadeh in late 2013, a few months after the Arabic edition of this book was published.

which meant it had more experience with organization and was more resilient in the face of regime violence.

Ar-Raqqa Blitzkrieg

The city of ar-Raqqa, some 370 km away from Damascus, is the capital of one of the most neglected governorates of Syria. Part of the broader eastern region, it is seriously underdeveloped and has been a major source of migration both within and beyond Syria's borders. It has the highest levels of poverty and illiteracy and the highest school dropout rate of any governorate in the country. Despite hosting Lake Assad, the Ba'th and Euphrates Dams, extensive oil fields and much of Syria's wheat and cotton production, it was excluded from development plans under Hafez al-Assad, and was ignored entirely by the regime until the invasion of neighbouring Iraq in 2003 made it significant to national security. From 2003 onward, the regime made efforts to cultivate the loyalty of tribal sheikhs in ar-Raqqa, showering them with largesse and in some cases even allowing them to carry weapons; members of loyal tribes were rewarded with jobs in the army, security forces and the party apparatus. As a result, ar-Raqqa largely remained quiet throughout the first year of the revolution, and those demonstrations that were organized were broken up with the help of tribesmen deployed by pro-regime sheikhs. It was in ar-Raqqa, in fact, that Assad chose to perform Eid al-Adha prayers on 6 November 2011.

On 15 March 2012, the first anniversary of the revolution, several small protests were organized in ar-Raqqa City. The regime responded by firing on protesters, killing three people. In what by now had become a familiar pattern, on 17 March the funeral processions of those killed developed into an enormous demonstration, with more than 100,000 protesters marching through the Mansour district – the largest demonstration of that year in Syria.[40] It was not ar-Raqqawis' loyalty to the regime that had been preventing them from joining the revolution but the role played by traditional social forces. As in neighbouring Deir ez-Zor, which is sociologically similar to ar-Raqqa, the tribes had nipped small protests in the bud and prevented them from evolving into something larger.

Ar-Raqqa did not take up arms against the regime until late 2012. Pro-regime tribes continued to check both peaceful and armed action in the

---

[40] For footage of protests in ar-Raqqa, see: YouTube, 17 March 2012, at: https://bit.ly/346tQO0 (accessed 3 January 2022).

governorate. Moreover, the city had become a sort of safe haven hosting hundreds of thousands of Syrians from elsewhere in the country. It was thus in everyone's interest to avoid the spread of fighting to ar-Raqqa, and within the city itself there was a sort of unwritten agreement to this effect. When clashes began, they came from outside.

The first military confrontations took place in mid-September as part of the 'Battle of the Border Crossings'. On 20 September, the revolutionaries managed to secure the Tell Abiad crossing on the Turkish border, and shortly thereafter they took over the town of Tell Abiad itself. The army then withdrew from most of ar-Raqqa governorate, concentrating its forces in Tabaqah (50 km to the west of ar-Raqqa City) close to the dams and the oil wells. Encouraged by this development, some of the armed opposition factions, especially those of the Syrian Islamic Front (SIF) – established in December 2012, it was then led by the major jihadi Salafi organization Ahrar al-Sham – mounted a lightning offensive against regime bases across the region. The Ba'th Dam fell on 4 February 2013, Tabaqah and the Euphrates Dam on 11 February and the governorate prison on 3 March. On 4 March, rebel forces took control of the Political Security, Air Force Intelligence and State Security Directorates, the party branch office, and the governor's residence in ar-Raqqa itself, and with the fall of the Military Security Directorate on 7 March, the whole of the city was in rebel hands.[41]

The rebel takeover of ar-Raqqa was made easier by the broader military situation. The regime had completely lost control over the northern and eastern parts of the neighbouring Aleppo governorate: for battalions operating in these areas, the oilfields and dams on the other side of the governorate border were an obvious next target. The decision to redeploy Syrian troops to Deir ez-Zor to check the rebel advance there meant that resistance in ar-Raqqa was weaker than it might otherwise have been. Moreover, the creeping advance of opposition forces in the Damascus periphery (Jawbar, Qaboun, Barzah) and the requirements of a major offensive against the old city of Homs prevented the regime from sending reinforcements.

These favourable circumstances notwithstanding, the most important factor in ar-Raqqa's rapid fall – fighting lasted less than three days – was close coordination between fighters inside the city and rebel battalions outside it, facilitated by Turkey and Qatar, which also helped arm the rebels. Among the thousands of Syrians who had taken refuge in ar-Raqqa were many young men who were now determined to take up arms against the regime, particularly those from rural Deir ez-Zor and Aleppo. These

---

[41] They subsequently lost control of the city to the Nusra Front, which lost it to ISIS.

fighters played an active part in the taking of the city, storming government buildings in coordination with the beginning of the offensive from outside and taking regime forces totally by surprise.

With the fall of ar-Raqqa City, the regime lost control of almost the entire governorate – that is, some 10.6 per cent of Syria's total area and around 5 per cent of its population. Only the Tabaqah airfield and the headquarters of the 17th division held out against the rebel offensive.[42] For the first time the rebels had managed to capture the governor, the party chairman and the heads of the local security and military directorates. And they had taken control over a contiguous area connecting the liberated regions in the north and east, which until this point had remained isolated islands surrounded by regime forces. They could now move fighters and weapons freely between Aleppo and the east. This was to have major consequences for the Battle for Deir ez-Zor and the border crossings with Iraq.

---

[42] Which the regime continued to use as a base for air raids against the cities of the governorate, in keeping with its broader strategy at that time.

6

The regime's strategy

This chapter discusses the regime's strategy for crushing the protests. It dissects Bashar al-Assad's key speeches, including his defiant speech to the People's Assembly on 30 March 2011 and other speeches in which he adopted a more conciliatory tone. It argues that on the ground, Assad pursued a consistent policy of brute force. It then discusses the role of state media and its claims that peaceful protests were a 'conspiracy' against the regime and protesters 'infiltrators' or 'armed gangs' (and later 'Takfiris' or 'terrorists'). Finally, it explores the role of the *shabbiha* militias in suppressing the protests, providing historical insight into their origins.

The official discourse

As we have already seen in Chapter One, on 30 March 2011 – after weeks of protests – Assad delivered a much-anticipated speech to the People's Assembly. The president was expected to strike a reformist tone to contain the escalating revolution. Instead, calling the Arab revolutions 'virtual waves' and externally motivated 'conflicts', he presented Syrians with two choices: either stand with the regime, or stand against it. The latter would then be a stance taken by who he described as those following 'virtual waves' and 'fads' serving foreign powers determined to end Syrian resistance to imperialism. Hoping to capitalize on fears of instability, particularly among Syria's religious and confessional minorities, Assad used the word *fitna* (civil strife or sedition) no less than seventeen times,[1] invoking the spectre of sectarian unrest and foreign conspiracy. The regime, he maintained, was unshakeable and would not give way under pressure, and he was its most intransigent element. He would force the unnamed 'others' behind the recent disturbances to back down, but under such circumstances any concessions to the protesters would 'be a sign of weakness'. The

---

[1] *Al-Akhbar* (Lebanon), 31 March 2011, at: https://bit.ly/3Jvhtvj (accessed 3 January 2022).

relationship between state and society is 'not a matter of each putting pressure on the other'; it is built on citizens' loyalty to the regime in exchange for the regime meeting 'society's needs'. By trying to force the regime to meet those needs, Syria's citizens were 'getting their state into the habit of submitting to internal pressure' – a habit that would inevitably lead to it 'submitting to foreign pressure' as well.[2] In short, they were committing treason.

This identification of popular pressure to meet popular demands with foreign pressure was not new. This allegation had been made so often that it had become a stock trope, that does not need any justification or additional explanation, save a few words about the alleged beneficiaries of the conspiracy and the dissenters plotting it. The regime's counterespionage and external intelligence forces have always been deployed primarily against the domestic opposition. It was this mentality that led the regime to treat its own people as an enemy, as a hostile foreign population, to subject densely populated areas to artillery bombardments and airstrikes, and ultimately to pursue a fully-fledged war at home. 'The people' are acknowledged only insofar as they are loyal and docile. Maintaining this docility requires constant vigilance on the part of the security forces, who work day and night throughout the year to suppress any dissident or sceptical voice. Even before the revolution, the regime not only arrested, tortured and assassinated individuals deemed a threat; it also tacitly viewed the people as a whole as a potential enemy. When the protests began, this covert attitude became overt and the rising people became the enemy.

The attitude is palpable in many of Assad's speeches. 'This is not a revolution!' he exclaimed to staff and students at Damascus University on 10 January 2012. 'Does a revolutionary further the enemy's aims, making him both revolutionary and traitor? Of course not. Is [a revolutionary] completely lacking in honour, ethics and religion? If we had real revolutionaries, in the established sense of the word, then you, I and the entire people would be marching behind them today – and that's the truth.' Those opposed to his regime were not revolutionaries but enemies, and foreign enemies at that: 'We are no longer in the field of domestic politics. We are facing a real war, and war requires a different approach from a domestic dispute where all parties are Syrian.' In his address to the Riad Hijab cabinet[3] on 20 June 2012, he reiterated that Syria was facing 'a real state of war in every respect', and asked the government to mobilize all available resources in pursuit of 'victory in this war'.[4]

---

[2] *C-SPAN*, 30 March 2011, at: https://bit.ly/3EhwNrB (accessed 21 December 2021).
[3] Riad Hijab's cabinet lasted from 23 June 2012 until Hijab defected on 6 August 2012.
[4] Syrian Ministry of Local Administration and Environment, 27 June 2012, at: https://bit.ly/3zDLxlV (accessed 16 June 2022).

From the outset, the regime insisted on depicting the revolution as a foreign conspiracy targeting Syria because of its stances against Western policies in the region. Implicit in this is the complete denial of the spontaneous, popular character of the revolution, its authentic social and political motives, and its revolutionary political content. In every protracted conflict with its political opponents – in Hama against the Muslim Brotherhood or in its conflict with the PLO – the regime organizes media campaigns, seminars, public disavowals and TV debates to 'prove' that they are in league with outsiders. The security forces come up with a fictitious story and this is disseminated by the pro-regime media, including friendly journalists from Jordan and Lebanon. The immediate victim of these campaigns is, of course, the target. But in the long run, it is the causes that the regime exploits that truly suffer as a result of this policy, as they are tarred by fabrication and deception. Indeed, the regime has instrumentalized the plight of Palestine so thoroughly that many doubt how hostile it really is to Israel.

In a speech to the People's Assembly on 3 June 2012, Assad divided Syrians into two camps. The 'vast majority', he said, supported him and his reformist programme. Only a small minority, servants of foreign powers who feed off blood and destruction, continued to oppose him.

On occasion Assad struck a more conciliatory tone. At the inauguration of the Adil Safar government on 16 April 2011 – during a flurry of 'goodwill' gestures – he described all those who had died during the protests as 'martyrs', apparently responding to criticism of the language used in his previous speech. He also promised to put an end to violence against protesters.

The regime had begun to take precautions against revolution as early as mid-February 2011, as the Tunisian and Egyptian presidents were overthrown and protests began in Libya, Bahrain and Yemen. It put the security forces on an emergency footing, ordering them to exercise extra vigilance to prevent large protests developing anywhere in the country. At the same time, it launched a PR offensive at home and abroad, explaining that Mubarak and Ben Ali were deposed because they were agents of imperialism[5] and hoping to demonstrate that – unlike his recently deposed counterparts – Assad was much loved by his citizens. Some researchers believed that Assad did enjoy a degree of popularity, due mostly to what seemed like regional successes and people's fear of instability, and that this popularity enabled him to launch real reform.[6] But this was not his

---

[5] See for example: Sami Moubayed, 'Lesson from Egypt: West Is Not Best', *Forward Magazine*, no. 48, (February 2011), 4; Bouthaina Shaaban, 'The Real Evils Plaguing the Region', *Forward Magazine*, no. 48 (February 2011), 16.
[6] Wieland, 184.

intention. He knew better than we did that his regime would not withstand – probably could not withstand – substantial political reforms. He had inherited a plantation that might need some upgrades to make it more productive, presentable and modern – perhaps even to provide his subjects with better services – as long as his ownership of the plantation was obvious to all and unquestioned, with loyalty to his own person being the sole criterion determining who belonged to the plantation, i.e. who is a Syrian.

On 8 February, it announced that the long-standing block on four social media sites (YouTube, Facebook, Blogger and Maktoob Blog) was being lifted, a gesture of confidence after the failure of the protests planned for 5 February.[7] On 15 February, Assad made a carefully choreographed public appearance at the Umayyad Mosque in central Damascus during *mawlid*, the anniversary of the Prophet's birth.[8] Meanwhile, the security forces were warning prominent opposition figures (Arif Dalila, Michel Kilo, Mazin Uday, Akram al-Bunni, and Hazem Nahar) that they had traced the Facebook posts calling for protests to Israel and that anyone who came out to demonstrate would be treated as a 'collaborator'.[9] This was a direct threat and an early indicator of the regime's intention to smear any popular movement as a foreign conspiracy.

The regime was, of course, fully aware that revolutions are not the result of individual decisions but of rising tension and discontent, and it sought to address this problem as well. Ministers were told to pay more attention to complaints, and local officials showed an uncharacteristic interest in citizens' needs. Moreover, areas that seemed particularly susceptible to revolution because of poor economic conditions and strong local solidarities were singled out for special treatment. In the southern district of Houran, party officials made unprecedented visits to remote villages, where they promised improvements to public services.[10] On 7 March, Assad personally inaugurated a project to redirect water from the Tigris to the village of Ein Diwar in al-Hasakeh.[11] A week later, he and the first lady visited impoverished villages in As-Sweida to announce plans for local development.[12] Plans to introduce a VAT and end fuel subsidies were frozen, and the 2011–15 Five-Year Plan was suppressed for fear that its

---

[7] *Shahb News*, 9 February 2011, at: https://bit.ly/3G7yadN (accessed 3 January 2022).
[8] YouTube, 15 February 2011, at: https://bit.ly/3ddLvEF (accessed 3 January 2022).
[9] A face-to-face interview with Hazem Nahar, conducted by Hamzeh al-Moustafa and Nerouz Satik, ACRPS researchers, in Doha on 15 August 2011.
[10] International Crisis Group, 'Popular Protest in North Africa and the Middle East (VI): The Syrian People's Slow Motion Revolution', 6 July 2011, 5, at: https://bit.ly/3pbbSBY (accessed 3 January 2022).
[11] *Alrai Media*, 8 March 2011, at: https://bit.ly/3dcl4PG (accessed 3 January 2022).
[12] *Alanba*, 19 March 2011, at: https://bit.ly/3xH129v (accessed 3 January 2022).

content – which included further liberalization measures – would stoke popular discontent.¹³

Hijab, who was governor of Latakia when protests began and was subsequently appointed minister for agriculture in the Safar government, summed up the situation as follows:

> After the Egyptian revolution, the regime was worried. It told government officials that they needed to respond to citizens' demands. The security agencies were optimistic because they believed that the army had played the deciding role in regime change in both Egypt and Tunisia and that the president was popular among the general population. The Regional Command Council [...] decided to accelerate the reform process and to implement the resolutions made at the Tenth [Party] Congress in 2005. This included drafting a law regulating political parties, changing the government, communicating more broadly with citizens and investigating the harmful effects of economic policies and of the free-trade agreements – especially with Turkey. But they did not have enough time to review policy, because this happened less than two months before the revolution.¹⁴

In the political sphere, however, the regime made no concessions. Although on 7 March a decree was issued pardoning all political detainees, it was withdrawn shortly thereafter, and the state news agency (Syrian Arab New Agency 'SANA') removed the item from its website only three hours after it had been published.¹⁵ A subsequent decree restricted the pardon to those who had committed minor crimes and were over the age of seventy – a much smaller group, although one prominent detainee, Haytham al-Malih, was released due to his advanced age.¹⁶ Remarkably, SANA claimed that its original report had been put on the website by hackers and that the image of the report had been photoshopped.¹⁷

At times the regime took a relatively relaxed attitude towards small protests that showed little sign of developing into large gatherings. On rare occasions it even allowed large demonstrations to go ahead. But this did not mean that it was willing to tolerate them in principle or had any intention of listening to their demands. It was part of a broader containment strategy. And when this containment strategy failed, the regime fell back on

---

[13] International Crisis Group, 'Popular Protest in North Africa and the Middle East (VI)', 6.
[14] A face-to-face interview with Riad Hijab, conducted by the ACRPS research team in Doha on 12 March 2013.
[15] SANA also published a statement from the interior minister saying that the decree would be implemented immediately and that detainees at the Sednayah and Adra prisons would be released to their families on 12 March.
[16] *BBC Arabic*, 8 March 2011, at: https://bbc.in/3EhhgJ1 (accessed 3 January 2022).
[17] *Sham FM*, 10 March 2011, at: https://bit.ly/3JMvDs6 (accessed 3 January 2022).

brute force. The president issued directives ordering the security forces not to fire on protesters, but these had little effect on the ground, and the security forces were not held accountable. Either nobody paid attention to his orders or he himself told the security forces to disregard them. Assad claimed to have been 'convinced' by his meetings with local delegations that citizens' greatest concern was the extensive powers of the security services and the violation of their dignity. But his decrees curbing their authority were never actually implemented.

Moreover, it soon became clear that all the regime's other concessions were mere rhetoric. The inner circle of the regime has always been aware that the real problem for the Syrian people is the political-security complex – that is, the regime itself. Although in the media they denounced the revolution as a foreign conspiracy, among themselves they recognized the need to meet some of the people's demands (in the regime lexicon this is known as 'reform', although the real motivation is always simply to contain discontent without making any real changes). But force remained their primary strategy because they were always convinced that the ultimate aim was to bring down the regime, even before any such demands were made by protesters. This was a self-fulfilling prophecy. As the number of those killed rose, the protests that had begun in Daraa spread wider and wider and grew more and more ambitious, eventually demanding thoroughgoing, systemic change. And when this happened, the regime was triumphant: all its suspicions had been vindicated. But what ultimately led to the spread of the popular movement and the radicalization of its demands was the unprecedented crackdown. The brutal force unleashed by the regime left the people no choice but to disperse and go back to their previous life, or to fight.

When protesters did begin calling for its ouster, the regime responded by declaring war. And once that threshold had been crossed, its sole objective was to win – or at least to ensure it had the upper hand in a future political settlement. Alongside its use of violence, it launched a campaign to brand the revolutionaries 'Islamist terrorists' and then 'Takfiris', hoping that this would forestall international support and alienate their potential domestic audience. Of course, the revolutionaries that they faced were civic revolutionaries, and even when organized Islamists joined their ranks, they remained a small minority for a long time.[18] Both Takfiri and non-Takfiri Islamists likely became a more organized and active minority, but they were never a majority. Nonetheless, the regime used every means at its

---

[18] Even after the beginning of armed struggle, it was generally believed that organized Islamist groups of all sorts were a small minority until the end of 2012. See for example: *Le Figaro*, 31 July 2012, at: https://bit.ly/3NVYcp2 (accessed 13 June 2022); Lund, 'Syrian Jihadism', 10.

disposal to transform the Syrian revolution into an Algerian-style civil war, the results of which are well documented.

The media strategy

The regime recognized that there were economic, political and social factors that were all likely to drive protest. Nonetheless, despite the fact that its strategic objective at the time was to come to an understanding with the US over Syria's role in the region – and although Bashar al-Assad was negotiating with Israel through Turkish mediation just before the Israeli war on Gaza 2008–9 broke out,[19] and the Gulf states were a vital source for correcting the trade balance, remittances and financial aid[20] – regime propaganda intended for Arab consumption consistently claimed that Syria was the target of a foreign conspiracy intended to undermine its anti-imperialist position. Addressing the West, on the other hand, it sought to win itself a place in the 'anti-terror' club by focusing on the Nusra Front and exaggerating the role of Salafis in the revolution when their role was still marginal.[21]

From the very beginning, the regime sought to discredit the protesters, taking advantage of the lack of neutral media capable of reporting events accurately. The first revolutionary protest – the sit-in outside the Interior Ministry on 16 March 2011 – was reported in the official newspaper *al-Thawra* as follows: 'While some families came to submit written requests regarding family members arrested for various crimes, infiltrators attempted to exploit the situation and call for protests by inciting [people] in the Marjeh area. Local shop owners and citizens responded spontaneously, shouting patriotic slogans and making clear that they reject any attempt to sow chaos or to undermine national security.' This is of course completely at odds with reality. More often than not, those confronting citizens

---

[19] There were many indications that Assad and his foreign minister at the time were keen to reach a peace agreement with Israel with a modification of his father's position on drawing the line of the 4 June borders with Israel. Recep Tayyip Erdoğan and his foreign minister Ahmad Dawood Oglu were more than happy to act as mediators.

[20] Sylvia Poelling, 'Syria's Private Sector: Economic Liberalization and the Challenges of the 1990s', in *Political and Economic Liberalization: Dynamics and Linkages in Comparative Perspective*, ed. Gerd Nonneman (Boulder: Lynne Rienner, 1996), 170–1.

[21] On 15 May 2013, as this book was being written – and as the role of the Salafi factions became more dominant – Bashar al-Jaafari, the Syrian ambassador to the UN, gave a speech to the General Assembly in which he maintained that his government was doing no more than fighting terrorism. Among other stories cited to prove his case, he claimed that revolutionaries had looted and then torched a historic synagogue near Damascus.

mid-protest will be plainclothes security officers or otherwise on the regime's payroll. But it was characteristic of the line the regime would take.

At first foreign media organizations were prevented from entering Syria. When images of the security forces brutalizing protesters leaked out, the regime accused the international and Arab media of fabricating them, attributing these actions to the 'global conspiracy' against Syria. In reality, of course, it was the Syrian official media, directed by the security agencies, that were the real experts in fabrication. On 26 March 2011, state TV broadcast an interview with an Egyptian citizen who confessed to being a US national who was paid to provide Israel with photos and footage from inside Syria; months later, he appeared on Egyptian TV to explain how he was forced to make these confessions after being caught up in a wave of arrests following the 25 March protests in Damascus.[22] On 8 April, official media shared a video of armed men firing at an unknown target, claiming that they were armed militants shooting at the security forces in Daraa.[23]

The regime's objective behind these claims was not to convince Syrians of its version of events. The real aim was to make it difficult for people to tell truth from lies amidst all the stories and rumours that were perpetually being spread by the pro-regime outlets, while stoking debate about the revolution and its potentially catastrophic outcome. In parallel, the regime continued to deploy terms like 'sectarian strife' and 'Salafism' to cement the idea of a divided Syrian society in the minds of the populace.

In early November 2011, with the first Arab League initiative in the works, the regime agreed to permit some pro-regime or neutral organizations to operate inside Syria. Even then, however, it continued to take great pains to discredit unfavourable coverage of the revolution's progress. 'Eyewitnesses' were conjured up to lionize the president and dismiss alternative accounts as tendentious or fake. Individuals reported dead by Facebook pages or by Arab media were interviewed on state TV. These interviews may have been the product of careful staging by the security agencies. Equally, opposition activists may have misreported the deaths. The consistent campaign to confuse facts started to bear fruits in the international media, too.

The regime's claims were often obvious, even amateurish, fabrications. When the popular uprising broke out in Daraa, for example, the official media claimed that 'infiltrators' had been 'going to the offices of the security forces and other authorities, pretending to be high-ranking security personnel, and claiming to have been given strict orders for the police to

---

[22] See the interview with Muhammad Radwan on ONTV at: YouTube, 1 August 2011, at: https://bit.ly/331bLk8 (accessed 3 January 2022).
[23] *Shahb News*, 9 April 2011, at: https://bit.ly/3mTGx5l (accessed 3 January 2022).

use violence and live ammunition against any suspicious crowd'.[24] This is of course absurd and unimaginable for any Syrian, but there is a certain logic to the dissemination of lies of this kind. Firstly, *pretending* to believe lies, acting 'as if' they were plausible (to borrow Lisa Wedeen's phrase), is a sign of loyalty – or at least of fear, which for the regime is the same thing. The regime does not care whether loyalty stems from love or fear, and actually prefers fear because it is more credible and certain. It seems that the human psyche can develop mechanisms that can transform fear into love, or a combination of awe and love, especially when the feared subject is seen as 'almighty' and omnipotent. Secondly, publishing outright falsehoods serves to conflate truth and untruth, cultivating a sense that both are narratives of equal value but that one is patriotic and the other treasonous. Thirdly, the point of the official media narrative in general is not so much to persuade listeners of its own veracity but to make them doubt other narratives.

Some non-Syrians may well have bought into the regime's propaganda, whether because they believed the regime's claims that Syria was the last bulwark of resistance to Israel or because they were part of a developing bloc driven more by sectarian solidarity than by credibility and trust. Domestically, however, the regime was less interested in whether people believed its propaganda than whether they *pretended* to believe it. Cultivating a state of general dissimulation where people act as if the regime is popular – reminiscent of Caligula's 'let them hate me, so long as they obey me' – is a practice dating back to the 1980s. Under Hafez al-Assad, the regime drew heavily on the cultural practices of totalitarian regimes, erecting statues of the Father-Leader, organizing massive rallies, and demanding spectacular displays of loyalty, sometimes backed up with 'theory'.[25] It was obvious to everyone that Syrian totalitarianism was a cheap copy. The 'bronze' statues put up in public squares were quite literally made of plaster. But the regime learned that if it could not establish broad cultural hegemony, enforced hypocrisy was a reasonable stand-in.[26] Citizens pretending to love the leader are in some ways more valuable than them actually loving the leader, because it is based on, and encourages, fear. As Wedeen puts it, 'The regime produces compliance through enforced participation in rituals of obeisance that are transparently phony both to those who orchestrate them and to those who consume them.'[27]

---

[24] *Al-Thawra*, 21 March 2011. Archived copy available online: https://bit.ly/3mMYkLu (accessed 3 January 2022).
[25] Loyalists wrote and published many propaganda books about Assad's 'thought' and character.
[26] Lisa Wedeen, *Ambiguities of Domination: Politics, Rhetoric, and Symbols in Contemporary Syria* (London: University of Chicago Press, 1999).
[27] Ibid., 6.

The unlimited power with which the regime, particularly the president, was endowed meant only that people did not count. They were humiliated, powerless people who feared the regime so much they worshipped it. The mere idea of revolt is apostasy, inviting unlimited rage, charges of treason and collaboration with foreign conspiracies, and other secular synonyms for apostasy.

The regime line was pushed tirelessly by various Lebanese channels and newspapers – NBN, al-Manar, OTV, and *al-Diyar* – as well as their Syrian counterparts, al-Dunia TV and *al-Watan*. These outlets churned out endless rumours and conspiracy theories and often published stories fed to them by the security agencies or by journalists close to Syrian or Iranian intelligence. And alongside its traditional propaganda machine, the regime was quick to find ways of countering the 'new media' of the digital public sphere on their own turf. A 'Syrian Electronic Army' was soon conducting an extensive campaign of its own on social media to fight what it described as the 'bias' of Arab and Western media,[28] regularly hacking pro-revolutionary websites[29] and launching smear campaigns against members of the opposition. Countless new websites were set up by regime agencies and their affiliates, including al-Wihda (created by the Syrian ambassador to Jordan, Bahjat Sulayman), Syriana, Sham Press, Aksalser ('against the current') and Damas Post; the economic, political and social content of their arguments all boiled down to blind repetition of the regime line.

The exact content of this line changed repeatedly in accordance with the regime's external and domestic propaganda needs before eventually settling on the spectre of Takfirism and terrorist groups, terms that were clearly geared towards stoking the fears of Western audiences. From February through to March 2011 – when the Arab revolutions were at the height of their popularity – regime journalists were rolled out to make bizarre definitional arguments about what would constitute a 'real' revolution. Through to the end of April 2011, 'infiltrators' were supposedly shooting at protesters and the security forces alike, increasingly joined by 'armed gangs'. With the prominent involvement of the cleric Anas Airut in the Banyas protests and calls by some Homsi protesters for a 'jihad' after the brutal regime response to demonstrations, from April onwards, 'Salafi militants' became the new bogeyman; 'armed Salafi groups' were blamed by the Interior Ministry for a string of deaths in Homs. (Although local sources maintain that these were the work of the *shabbiha*,[30] it is beyond doubt that

---

[28] See: *Syrian Electronic Army*, at: https://bit.ly/3tAnqAv (accessed 16 June 2022).
[29] *Aksalser*, 27 March 2012, at: https://bit.ly/3De5P3v (accessed 3 January 2022).
[30] Human Rights Watch, 9 August 2011, at: https://bit.ly/3o6Jz7j (accessed 3 January 2022).

April 2011 witnessed mutual acts of sectarian retribution in both Homs and Banyas. The various opposition outlets denied such acts instead of acknowledging and condemning them.) 'Takfiris' followed close on their heels, particularly after the Jisr ash-Shughur attack in June. From December 2011, after the first suicide bombings, it was 'terrorist organizations'. Finally, in May 2012, the regime settled on 'the Nusra Front' and 'al-Qaeda' as their go-to villains. Throughout the whole process, the (belated) support provided to the revolutionaries by Gulf states was held up as evidence of a Qatari-Saudi-Turkish conspiracy against Syria. For some audiences, the US and Israel were included in this conspiracy – despite both countries' lack of enthusiasm, to say the least, for the revolution.

Meanwhile, the regime treated Syrians as distinct constituencies with their own particular demands, rather than as a people striving for freedom, democracy and social justice. So, for example, Assad received delegations from Duma, Daraa and Hama to discuss specific demands in their local communities. Even political reforms and calls for dialogue often assumed a sectional dimension. On 7 April 2011, for example, Assad issued a decree granting Syrian citizenship to people registered in al-Hasakeh as foreigners,[31] and on 6 April 2011, the leaders of the Kurdish parties were invited to meet with the president,[32] an invitation also extended to the former general overseer of the Muslim Brotherhood, Ali Sadr al-Din al-Bayanuni, on 4 June 2011.[33]

All this amounted to a strategy whose goal was the total elimination of a political adversary. From day one the regime's purpose was to preserve the entire authoritarian apparatus. This meant destroying its enemies not only physically but morally, through character assassination. For the domestic audience, revolutionaries were portrayed as 'infiltrators' and 'foreign agents', part of a conspiracy to undermine Syria's anti-imperialism; for the West they were 'terrorists' and 'extremists', another front in the global war on terror. The regime did not care about the obvious contradiction. What mattered was not to maintain a consistent line but to undermine the image of the revolution in East and West, making it easier to win the real battle – a battle that would be decided on the ground, militarily. This meant fomenting and then managing chaos. And that was a game the regime knew only too well.

---

[31] *Al Akhbar* (Lebanon), 8 April 2011, at: https://bit.ly/3E2igkW (accessed 20 June 2022).
[32] *D-Press*, 6 April 2011. Archived copy available online: https://bit.ly/3Qphh48 (accessed 16 June 2022).
[33] A face-to-face interview with Ali Sadr al-Din al-Bayanuni, conducted by the ACRPS research team in Doha on 7 October 2012. The Brotherhood could only hope for such an invitation before the revolution and would have readily accepted it.

Diagnosis and strategy

When the protests first began, there were two main schools of thought on how to deal with them within the regime. Calling these 'factions' or 'camps' is difficult in a regime where the decision lay with a single individual who received all reports and information from the security forces. In fact, since this book argues that the regime always wanted to crush the uprising, it may be more accurate to describe the disagreements that emerged as a sort of double-facedness in the regime's discourse (and not its actual actions) – occasional differences of opinion, without a genuine split. This double-facedness manifested itself in different ways and at different points.

During the earliest protests, for instance, it was security officials – in alliance with the new businessmen and their private militias – who took on the main task of suppressing the protests.[34] But some security chiefs, including relatives of the president, were summarily dismissed (although not punished or prosecuted, of course) after giving orders to fire on demonstrators.[35] The regime also sent mixed messages at other times. In the run-up to each of Assad's speeches, the security forces adopted a relatively light touch in order to avoid escalating tensions. On the Friday of Determination, the day before Assad's speech to the new cabinet, there were no deaths at any of the many protests across the country, despite an attempt by demonstrators from the Damascus periphery to storm Abbasiyeen Square.[36] But when the speech failed to stop protesters assembling in Latakia and Homs in the next few days, the regime responded with typical brutality. Although on 21 April, Assad announced that he was lifting the state of emergency, disbanding the State Security Court and promulgating a law permitting peaceful protest,[37] more than a hundred people were killed during the demonstrations of the following day (Good Friday).[38] All this took place *before* the regime had declared outright and perpetual war against its own people.

Differences of opinion within the regime appeared at other times as well, but they were generally accompanied by a singularity of purpose when it came to actual action. Some figures within the regime praised the

---

[34] An interview with a contracted private militiaman who wishes to remain anonymous, conducted by the ACRPS research team in Damascus on 10 November 2011.

[35] See the details of discussions between Assad and Anas Suwaid, a sheikh from Bab al-Siba', as reported by Suwaid, 13 January 2012, at: https://bit.ly/3d5I03l (accessed 3 January 2022). Assad also dismissed the head of the Banyas Political Security branch office, Amjad Abbas, after he appeared in a video stamping on protesters: *Al Arabiya*, 20 April 2011, at: https://bit.ly/3I7fMmZ (accessed 3 January 2022).

[36] *BBC Arabic*, 15 April 2011, at: https://bbc.in/3yMgstD (accessed 3 January 2022).

[37] *Zaman al-Wasl*, 21 April 2011, at: https://bit.ly/3paCS3i (accessed 3 January 2022).

[38] *BBC Arabic*, 23 April 2011, at: https://bbc.in/3mREmPM (accessed 3 January 2022).

Samiramis Hotel conference held in late June 2011 in Damascus by members of the opposition and other prominent personalities, which was supposed to come up with recommendations that would help bring the crisis to an end.[39] Nonetheless, the organizers were not certain that the authorities would allow them to go ahead with the conference until the early hours of the first day.[40] Moreover, after the National Dialogue Conference (NDC) of 11 and 12 July – which was organized on Assad's own orders[41] – the security forces refused to implement the NDC's resolutions, which included the freedom to demonstrate.[42] Some figures from the Baʿth Party even appeared in the media to incite opposition to the conference, which in any case the opposition did not take seriously.

In the first stage of the revolution, Assad tried to combine the security solution – which he never entirely turned away from – with limited political measures. He promulgated several new laws to regulate political parties, the media and elections and ordered the drafting of a new constitution.[43] But this new legislation did not extend to the powers or structure of the security apparatus. Its purpose was to give the *impression* that he was open to reform. Its actual content served only to extend the life of the regime. The parties' law, for instance, gave the power to license new parties to a committee headed by the interior minister; the decision to permit or prevent the formation of a party remained with the government.[44] The new

---

[39] The conference was titled 'A Syria for All under a Civil-Democratic State'. Among the most notable participants were Michel Kilo, Luai Husain, Mundhir Khaddam and Fayez Sara. See: *Al Jazeera*, 6 February 2014, at: https://bit.ly/3xGTxiY (accessed 3 January 2022).

[40] *Al-Akhbar* (Lebanon), 28 June 2011, at: https://bit.ly/3sSNV4U (accessed 3 January 2022).

[41] *Al-Thawra*, 2 June 2011. Archived copy available online: https://bit.ly/3t7xu4X (accessed 3 January 2022). The committee was made up of the Vice-President Farouq al-Sharaa, Safwan al-Qudsi, Haitham Sataihi, Yasir Huriya, Hanin Nimr, Abdallah al-Khani, Walid Ikhlasi, Munir al-Hamsh and Ibrahim Daraji. It concluded that dialogue was the only way to end the crisis; that there was a 'higher national need' for stability in order to pursue further reforms; that 'forgiveness' would be key to moving past the difficulties of the current situation; that 'sovereignty' was an overriding principle that must be protected at all costs and that no foreign intervention should be permitted; that any assault or willingness to condone assaults on citizens and public or private property should be rejected; that political prisoners and those detained during the recent events should be released; and that public freedoms, human rights, anti-corruption and the rule of law were all major priorities.

[42] *Al-Tharwa*, 13 July 2011. Archived copy available online: https://bit.ly/3oPcIDx (accessed 3 August 2022).

[43] A committee was set up to draft a law regulating political parties on 5 June, and the law was promulgated by presidential decree two months later. See: *Al-Akhbar* (Lebanon), 22 June 2011, at: https://bit.ly/3pfAZme (accessed 3 June 2022); *Sham FM*, 4 August 2011, at: https://bit.ly/3obuvFr (accessed 3 January 2022). The elections law was promulgated in its final form on 26 July. The main change was the transfer of responsibility for supervising elections from the executive to the judiciary. See: *Albayan*, 28 July 2011, at: https://bit.ly/3rrg4PU (accessed 3 January 2022).

Assad first announced his intention to amend or replace the constitution on 20 June. The new constitution only passed into law, however, on 27 February 2012, following a referendum. See: *France 24*, 20 June 2011, at: https://bit.ly/3DKn78u (accessed 3 January 2022); *France 24*, 27 February 2012, at: https://bit.ly/3rQakPK (accessed 3 January 2022).

[44] *Al-Thawra*, 6 August 2011. Archived copy available online: https://bit.ly/3Hpwxsm (accessed 3 January 2022).

constitution, meanwhile, imposed a two-term limit on presidential candidates. But since this provision only applied going forward and terms were set at seven years, this gave Assad the right to stay in power until at least 2028.[45]

In any case, once Assad had settled on the extreme approach, regime figures who favoured reforms, like those who headed the NDC, were sidelined. As we have already seen, Defence Minister Ali Habib was dismissed. Vice-President Farouq al-Sharaa was gradually marginalized, along with other prominent party figures.[46] It was the grouping at the heart of a vast web of connections in the business and security sectors that now held the president's ear. It is for this reason that two years of extreme bloodshed failed to produce a major split within the regime. As a system by which wealth and power are distributed, it managed to operate as a single bloc focused on one man: Bashar al-Assad.

This kind of regime tolerates corruption among insiders not only as a bribe, but also as a tool of control. Leading figures live in constant fear of their corruption being made public. When it becomes notorious, the president can always cashier them and gain a reputation as a crusader against corruption.

Three days after Syrians first chanted 'the people want to bring down the regime' on Good Friday, Assad sent the army into Daraa. This was an attempt to shift the problem away from the person of the president and onto the military by implicating them in the conflict very early on, long before the revolutionaries stepped onto the path of armed struggle. The aim was to provoke clashes with protesters so as to conflate defence of the regime with a defence of the army – a popular institution – and strengthen the regime's claim that the issue at hand was the defence of the Syrian state rather than a struggle for democracy.

Initially, it was the leaders of the security agencies around Assad and his family who controlled the situation on the ground. As the regime moved

---

[45] Regarding the cabinet's role in the reforms, Hijab in his testimony said, 'The new government had no role in "resolving the crisis". Adil Safar maintained that under the constitution, the government was a purely executive body with no relation to other issues. All he was concerned with was his personal interests. The entire "reform package" ratified by the government was drawn up on the direct orders of President Assad. The government's role was simply to approve it.'

[46] According to Hijab's testimony, Sharaa was against using the security agencies to deal with the crisis: 'He demanded real reforms and said that priority should be given to dialogue sponsored by the president. [In response] Assad cut him out for about a year and refused to speak to him. He even hinted to me that he was planning to replace him as vice-president with [Foreign Minister] Walid al-Muallim and appoint [Muallim's deputy] Faisal Mekdad as foreign minister. Eventually he did meet with him alone, during the RCC meeting after the bombing of the National Security building [...] After that, Sharaa scheduled a meeting with the president and the rest of the leadership, where he expressed in the strongest terms his personal loyalty to Bashar al-Assad.' See Sharaa's interview with *Al-Akhbar* (Lebanon), where he emphasized the need to put an end to the violence and called for a settlement, 17 December 2012, at: https://bit.ly/3JDxGP6 (accessed 3 January 2022).

steadily towards fully-fledged warfare with its own people, however, Assad became a central part of the army's command structure, and the military commanders in charge of operations became the real decision-makers on the ground. They were loyal to the president and obeyed his orders, implementing them in light of their evaluation of the situation in the field. The security agencies were brutal, and when the army was deployed it was clear that it was being sent to war, but this was a war against Syria's own citizens. The fact that no officer or soldier was brought to account for atrocities is indicative of Assad's strategy and the mood in the army. According to Hijab:

> While I was governor of Latakia [in the first months of 2011], we received repeated directives from the Crisis Cell – and specifically from its head, Muhammad Saeed Bekheitan – telling us that there should be no bloodshed, that anyone who killed anyone should be held accountable, that nobody should fire on protesters. When I spoke to him, Bekheitan maintained that these were orders from the president himself. But the behaviour of the security forces on the ground was completely different, especially when they detained or imprisoned people. They were also instructed that the chief of the security branch office had to be out on the streets with his officers in order to keep things under control and limit the chances of accidents – because sometimes shots were fired by an unknown party, and people would be killed or injured without us knowing who the perpetrator was.

I believe that Assad was in charge, but he sent ambiguous messages and used two different languages, one with civil officials, ministers, and governors, and the other with officers and security agencies, telling them to do whatever it took to suppress the rebellion. He may have informed his ministers of one thing and then changed his mind, giving his security apparatus opposite instructions without informing the ministers of the change. There may also have been some initial tactical confusion about the most effective tools for containing protests in different regions. But Assad's 'reforms' were either not taken seriously or not accepted by the constituencies of the uprising, and with time the strategy and the tactics melted into one in the crucible of violent confrontation. Even if Assad gave orders to try to peacefully contain demonstrations in some areas due to foreign or local factors (tribal considerations for example), these orders were vague, and both the security agencies and the army quickly reported the failure of this tactic, noting that it encouraged the protestors to continue and others to join.

With regard to the military bombardment of Deir ez-Zor, the confusion in the issuing of orders and the role of the security agencies in decision-making, Hijab says:

I asked the president not to allow the army to shell Deir ez-Zor. He assured me that they would do no such thing and that he, as president, would not allow them to. He asked me to communicate this to the minister of defence and the chief of staff, who passed the orders on to the military units [around the city]. They both reassured me that there would be no shelling of Deir ez-Zor and that they had replaced the local division commander. But the real orders came from the intelligence services, the security agencies, and people close to Assad, and their orders contradicted the president's. My sister's house was gutted by fire and my own house was damaged in the shelling.

Hijab maintains that Assad became the prisoner of his security strategy and of the security chiefs:

> It was not the air force command but the chief of Air Force Intelligence, Jamil Hassan, who gave fighter pilots their orders. There were military operations carried out that not even the chief of staff and his deputy knew about. On one occasion, Dhu al-Himma Shalish [Assad's cousin and head of presidential security] told me that the director of protocol, Muhieddine Misilmaniya, had tried to intervene on behalf of his brother-in-law, who'd been arrested by Air Force Intelligence. The president gave orders for him to be let go, but Jamil Hassan refused. Shalish called Jamil Hassan to try and mediate and told him that it wasn't right to ignore a directive from the president. Jamil Hassan agreed, but only 'as a favour to you, and not to Bashar al-Assad'.[47]

This story spread quickly within the political elite as proof of the arbitrary power of the security forces. But it may be, of course, that it was a fabrication by Dhu al-Himma Shalish intended to support the myth of the 'good president' versus the 'corrupt entourage'.

Old guard figures like Jamil Hassan use this tone in private conversations to demonstrate their own importance, and while the president could fire him at will, Assad nevertheless needed his officers around him as his regime came under threat. Security officials understood that rallying around the president meant regime continuity and he understood that he had to rely on them, believe their reports and tolerate their conduct (given his insensitivity to human suffering, this was likely not difficult). They were sent to suppress the uprising unbound by any law or convention. The president was in charge, and he was therefore responsible.

Part of the regime's strategy was to push protesters into taking up arms by *shabbiha* to provoke violent clashes, thus justifying savage repression

---

[47] A face-to-face interview with Riad Hijab, conducted by the ACRPS research team in Doha on 12 March 2013.

by the security forces[48]; a similar tactic had been employed by the Syrian regime several times in the previous decade. The aim was to create a military confrontation that would marginalize the uprising and consolidate local popular and international support for the regime against terrorism. Here we can distinguish between two different cases: Homs and Latakia.

In Homs, after clashes with organized groups of armed local rebels in August 2011, the security forces stopped firing on protesters unless they tried to gather in one of the major squares. Armed clashes were limited for the most part to confrontations between the security forces and gunmen. In Latakia, protests were concentrated in the southern Raml neighbourhood, whose layout meant that the security forces struggled to prevent public gatherings. Although locals had access to weapons, they did not use them against army or security checkpoints, using primitive explosives (dynamite) to see off regime incursions into their district itself. When protesters began calling for the 'execution of the president', however, regime forces massed heavy weaponry near the neighbourhood and subjected it to shelling from turret-mounted guns.[49]

The regime offered its people a choice: halt the protests and accept the 'reforms' declared by the president or face a military confrontation. On 28 September 2011, Assad told former Lebanese Prime Minister Salim al-Hoss that the 'difficult days' were over and that security problems were limited to Homs.[50] What he meant was that since the army's intervention, the security forces had been able to break up the protests in every urban centre (in particular Hama, Deir ez-Zor, Latakia and Daraa) except Homs, and that in Homs itself protesters had armed themselves and would be easily crushed by the army.

As the revolution began to make the transition from peaceful protest to armed action in early 2012, and as fighters began to mass in specific areas of the countryside and the urban periphery, the regime doubled down on the use of military force regardless of the cost. The Battle for Baba Amr in February 2012 saw extensive use of heavy weaponry – the Hama or Grozny strategy. Entire residential neighbourhoods of Harasta and Duma were levelled. The only reservation the regime seemed to have – or rather, the only apparent international check on its behaviour – concerned the air force, which was not deployed against the revolution during its early stages.

---

[48] An interview with a contracted private militiaman who wishes to remain anonymous, conducted by the ACRPS research team in Damascus on 10 November 2011.
[49] Interviews with Latakian opposition figures, including Shams al-Deen al-Kilani, conducted by the ACRPS research team.
[50] *Elnashra* (Lebanon), 28 September 2011. Archived copy available online: https://bit.ly/3sT8AWA (accessed 3 January 2022).

But it later became clear that there was no such check preventing the regime from using even this extreme level of force. As the regime experimented with the deployment of heavy weaponry, it smashed barrier after barrier, until it discovered that there were no real barriers beyond the international community's verbal condemnations.

The sharp distinction between the urban and the rural gave opposition fighters a kind of parity with the army, although the balance of forces skewed strongly in the latter's favour so long as it controlled the cities and the opposition remained scattered across the countryside. The regime tried its utmost to keep the conflict limited to the countryside and to set up a *cordon sanitaire* around the cities, making it easier to crush the armed uprising.[51]

On 18 July 2012, several members of the Crisis Cell, including the chair, Deputy Vice-President Hasan Turkmani, were killed in the bombing of the National Security Bureau building in Damascus. The Crisis Cell was a working group of the most senior security and military officers. Its objective was to smother the revolution. But its task was not to make decisions in its own right but to come up with 'recommendations' as to how to 'resolve' the crisis.[52] The cell also established an operations room bringing together the security agencies and the military, planned the regime's response to the crisis, gave orders to those involved in events on the ground, and mobilized volunteers from the unions and the political organizations (especially Ba'thist activists) in order to support efforts to confront the revolutionaries, whether actively on the ground or through the media.

The cell was originally chaired by the assistant secretary of the RCC, Mohammed Saeed Bekheitan. After Bekheitan proved incapable of solving or managing the crisis to the satisfaction of senior security officials, he was replaced as chair by Deputy Vice-President General Turkmani. Habib, the ill-fated defence minister, was also removed from the cell after repeated objections to the regime's policy.[53] The eventual list of members included Turkmani; Bekheitan; Generals Daud Rajiha, Asef Shawkat and Mohammad Ibrahim al-Shaar (the new defence minister, his deputy and the interior minister); Brigadiers Ali Mamluk, Muhammad Dib Zaytun, Jamil Hassan and Abd al-Fattah Qudsiyyah (the heads of the General Intelligence, Political Security, Air Force Intelligence and Military Intelligence directorates respectively); Hisham al-Ikhtiyar (head of the National Security Bureau); and the retired brigadier Salih al-Naeemi as secretary.

---

[51] ACRPS, 'Is the Syrian Revolution Entering a New Stage?'.

[52] This seems to be strong evidence against the hypothesis that Assad was a hostage of the security agencies, except in the sense that he relied on their reports and recommendations.

[53] A face-to-face interview with Riad Hijab, conducted by the ACRPS research team in Doha on 12 March 2013.

In the aftermath of the attack, General Fahd al-Furayj was appointed as defence minister and deputy commander-in-chief, Mamluk, was made director of the National Security Bureau, Brigadier Rustum al-Ghazali (formerly director of the Military Security Directorate branch office in Damascus) became chief of Political Security and Muhammad Dib Zaytun (formerly of Political Security) took over the State Security Directorate.

Rumours spread that the regime itself was behind the bombing, based on the speculation that the only people who could carry out a coup had been gathered in that room. Whatever the truth, the incident was a low point for the regime, and people who believed in armed struggle become more confident about advocating it. It was at this point that the air force began to conduct regular strikes, though it is hard to determine whether the trigger for this shift was the bombing itself or the Battle of Aleppo.

The Battle of Aleppo, which began on 20 July 2012, marked the failure of the regime's attempts to confine the revolution to the countryside and upended the pre-existing balance of forces. At the same time, rebels from the Damascus periphery began moving into the outskirts of Damascus following military operations in Eastern Ghouta.[54] Meanwhile, on the international stage, Russia and China used their UNSC veto to prevent the activation of Chapter 7 provisions for conflict management, which would have empowered the UN to deploy peacekeepers.[55]

The combination of these three developments – the bombing, the rebel assault on Aleppo and the protection provided by the Russian-Chinese veto – may have facilitated the move towards air power. Helicopters were first used in the fighting in Damascus and Aleppo on and immediately after 22 July:[56] the rebels' advance towards the centre of Aleppo on 24 July was checked by machine guns fired from helicopters.[57] The next day, fighter jets were deployed for the first time, subjecting rebel-held neighbourhoods to a systematic campaign of destruction.[58] The air force was soon taking part in operations across the country, turning all of Syria into one battlefield.

In order to meet the regular army's need for additional manpower, in summer 2012 security officers and representatives of the military founded the National Defence Army (NDA) or Popular Army. On 18 January 2013, a Syrian source told Russia Today that the NDA was intended to act as 'a support force for the regular armed forces, who are focusing on combat

---

[54] ACRPS, 'Is the Syrian Revolution Entering a New Stage?'.
[55] Al-Thawra, 20 July 2012. Archived copy available online: https://bit.ly/3eIuy6j (accessed 3 January 2022).
[56] Ammon News, 22 July 2012, at: https://bit.ly/3zkaaBS (accessed 3 January 2022).
[57] BBC Arabic, 24 July 2012, at: https://bbc.in/3sWIUYX (accessed 3 January 2022).
[58] BBC Arabic, 25 July 2012, at: https://bbc.in/34ivLPJ (accessed 3 January 2022).

operations' – a force numbering at that time between 8,000 and 10,000 men. Several low-ranking Iranian officials boasted that it was their idea, but in fact, the Syrian regime had its own experience in recruiting and using militias. In return for a monthly salary, these men – and women[59] – were expected to protect neighbourhoods from attacks by rebels.[60] Recruitment focused mainly on areas that had not participated in the revolution so far. Most recruits were civilians completing their military service or members of the so-called popular committees (the *shabbiha*). As the fighting escalated, the regime also began to use recruits from abroad, particularly Iranians, and in areas along the Syrian-Lebanese border, it relied on Hezbollah fighters,[61] and later Shi'i militias from other countries organized by Iranian Revolutionary Guards, especially the Quds Brigade headed by Qassim Suleimani.

The Syrian regime's desperate desire to guarantee its survival and the complex network of economic and political interests on which it relied are not enough to explain why it chose such a destructive path. It confronted the armed opposition with the most extreme violence and showed itself willing to destroy whole neighbourhoods by aerial bombardment if necessary. The only option that it ruled out entirely was negotiations, which might have resulted in, although gradual, regime change. Instead, it offered Syrians a single alternative to violence: ending the revolution and joining a non-committal dialogue with no guaranteed results. Nor could its mission of 'resistance' to imperialism explain its behaviour: if it were concerned for its military position *vis-à-vis* Israel, it could have accepted a compromise solution that would have left the armed forces intact while putting an end to the abuses of the security forces and to corruption. The only possible explanation, in fact, is a vindictive rage towards those who dared to rebel against it. The regime believed either it would have Syria's cities or no one would.

In the meantime, against this backdrop of ultra-violent repression of protest, corruption continued to thrive. During peacetime, the regime's security and administrative apparatus had turned everything – from tenders for state projects to customs duties to traffic tickets and food vouchers – into a source of graft. Wartime opened up new vistas of

---

[59] *Russia Today Arabic*, 23 January 2013, at: https://bit.ly/3sTStIa (accessed 3 January 2022). Regardless of whether the reports of a female unit were true, it was, at heart, a message reminding the West that the Syrian regime was a secular one, at a time when the number of Islamist extremists was increasing in Syria.
[60] Syrian Observatory for Human Rights, 8 January 2013. Archived copy available online: https://bit.ly/34iwf8v (accessed 3 January 2022).
[61] A face-to-face interview with Riad Hijab, conducted by the ACRPS research team in Doha on 12 March 2013.

corruption, as money was demanded for everything from arrests (officers demanded huge sums to free people arrested on minimal charges or even kidnapped) to the release of bodies (families were asked to pay to receive the corpses of relatives) to soldiers' applications for military leave.

The s*habbiha*

One of the main tools in the regime's arsenal was violence perpetrated by actors who were not formally part of state institutions. From the earliest days of the protest movement, hired men from outside the security forces were used to break up demonstrations. This phenomenon is not unique to Syria. The Egyptian *baltagiyya*, the Yemeni *balatija* and the Libyan *murtazqa* were all cut from the same cloth. But their Syrian counterparts are by far the most organized example. They also enjoy an unmatched degree of state endorsement, often operating alongside the security forces.

Although these units officially operate under the respectable name of 'popular committees', and later NDA (among others), they are known universally as *shabbiha* (singular *shabbih*). Originally a local dialect word referring primarily to thugs and smugglers in the Latakia governorate with ties to the Assad family – a phenomenon with a long history in that region[62] – during the Latakia protests in early 2011 *shabbiha* began to be used to refer to civilians recruited by the regime.[63] The term then spread throughout Syria, and today the *shabbiha* themselves wear this name with pride, to the extent that '*shabbiha* forever!' is a common chant at their rallies.

Shabbiha are largely recruited from the urban periphery – from areas inhabited by migrants from the countryside who have never adopted an urban lifestyle. They have lost the positive values of solidarity that exist in

---

[62] In the 1980s and 1990s, the *shabbiha* were the 'bodyguards' of Hafez al-Assad's relatives in their native Latakia. These men were famously violent thugs and subjected the inhabitants of Latakia to extreme and humiliating treatment, operating above the law thanks to their connections to the ruling family and to the regime. Recruited from the countryside, many of them took up residence in Ziraa neighbourhood and became involved in smuggling through the port of Latakia or over the Lebanese and Turkish borders. Over time other prominent figures from the coastal region acquired their own 'bodyguards' and smuggling rackets. The *shabbiha* reached the height of their power in the early 1990s, when they clashed regularly with the army, most famously during a confrontation with the Republican Guard on the Hama–Latakia Road. A regime crackdown in the mid-1990s, however, drove them back into the countryside, and as of the early 2000s their presence was largely restricted to the countryside around Jablah and Qardaha (the Assads' ancestral town). Fawaz Haddad, a Syrian author, gives a good description of the *shabbiha* of the 1990s in his novel *A Fleeting Scene*.

[63] Figures like Ali Martakoush, president of the Farmers' Union in Latakia, recruited *shabbiha* to provoke clashes with the protesters, leading to many injuries. Martakoush is known to be deeply corrupt. He was dismissed by the RCC on 1 July 2011. Interviews with cultural figures, conducted by the ACRPS research team in Latakia on various dates.

the countryside while retaining their backwardness. Many of them are convicted felons of ill repute even in their home regions. They are notorious for using knives, batons and chains to attack their victims.

The *shabbiha* are partly financed by the Bustan Elbasha Association, which was run by Assad's cousin Rami Makhlouf, who seemed to be quite content with using a charity for this aim.[64] They played a key part in the repression of protest in most Syrian cities. They had become fascistic death squads in the full sense of the word, receiving monthly salaries and showing themselves willing to carry out all sorts of atrocities.

Many protesters interpreted the mobilization of the *shabbiha* through a sectarian lens, because many *shabbiha*, like the Assad family, are Alawis. The Alawi community as a whole has been blamed for their actions. Although the Arab media have often encouraged this misconception, it is neither fair nor factual. The *shabbiha* are far from exclusively Alawi, and include mercenaries, felons[65] and party members of all religious and ethnic backgrounds. In Aleppo, Deir ez-Zor and ar-Raqqa, it was pro-regime tribesmen who were deployed against protesters, while in the Kurdish regions the regime was able to rely on the fighters of the Democratic Union Party (Partiya Yekîtiya Demokrat or PYD). And in the refugee camps of Adra and Yarmuk, Ahmed Jibril's Popular Front for the Liberation of Palestine (PFLP) splinter group took on the task of suppressing anti-regime demonstrations, leading to numerous intra-Palestinian clashes.[66]

The *shabbiha* phenomenon is therefore driven not by sectarian background but a thuggish form of loyalty to the regime, a willingness to commit crimes and cash incentives. Nonetheless, social frictions have often meant that it has been *interpreted* in a sectarian fashion, particularly in religiously diverse areas. In Latakia, where *shabbiha* were generally recruited from nearby Alawi villages, it led to sharp sectarian polarization (although moderate clerics and local notables were initially able to contain sectarian tensions in the city). The same happened in Homs, where the

---

[64] In fact, this practice has a long history. Jamil al-Assad's *shabbiha* of the early 1980s were organized through the Imam Murtada Association.
[65] Many *shabbiha* were recruited among prisoners released under general pardons issued early in the revolution. Some of these formed gangs for the purposes of kidnapping or theft, sometimes in the name of the regime and sometimes the revolution. Criminals released by presidential pardon were among the first people to take up arms against the regime during the peaceful protests, most notably the Homsi Bilal al-Kin.
[66] This culminated in the storming of the Popular Front for the Liberation of Palestine (PFLP) headquarters by Palestinian protesters in May 2011, after the regime allowed young Palestinians to cross the border into the occupied Golan Heights on the anniversary of the Nakba. Many of the Palestinians were subsequently shot by the Israel Defence Forces (IDF). This was seen as a flagrant attempt to exploit the Palestinian cause for political gain by diverting attention away from demonstrations within Syria.

recruitment of young men from (majority Alawi) Zahraa and Ekrima to break up protests in (majority Sunni) Khalidiyeh, Bayyada and Karm az-Zaytoun produced sharp divisions comparable to those in Beirut during the Lebanese Civil War. This spawned a series of tit-for-tat sectarian incidents that laid the groundwork for a fully-fledged armed confrontation.

During the first year of the revolution, the regime used the *shabbiha* to break up protests and to humiliate and intimidate the population, hoping to dissuade them from joining in. On occasion it leaked video recordings showing members of the *shabbiha* killing or torturing people as a warning of the fate that awaited anyone who took part in demonstrations. But this strategy backfired. The *shabbiha*'s behaviour was a stark reminder of the nature of the regime that Syrians were rebelling against – and that they were no longer willing to endure.

From mid-2012 onwards, however, the function of the *shabbiha* began to shift. With the revolution quickly becoming an armed uprising, defections and desertions from the army accelerated, and draft dodging became increasingly common among those who were eligible for military service. To meet its need for military manpower, the regime thus turned to the popular committees, which it now reorganized into a new institution, the NDA. The latter was used primarily for the purposes of urban warfare – some of its commanders were trained specifically in this by Iranian advisors. It was at the forefront of the failed assault on Old Homs in March 2013 (where its inexperience was a major cause of the defeat).

Unlike other Arab regimes facing revolutions, the Syrian government has never condemned the crimes of the *shabbiha*. In fact, it has praised their 'patriotic actions' in defence of the homeland. They are the 'popular response' to the 'foreign conspiracy'. This is an extension of an old Ba'thist tactic. Just as, at one time, any criticism of the regime voiced at a public event would be met with a chorus of boos from trained members of the 'popular organizations' in the audience (student, worker and peasant unions) and other gatherings were attacked by these 'patriotic' citizens, the *shabbiha* give the impression that it is the Syrian people and not the regime that is hostile to the revolution. The regime turned a blind eye to their flagrant criminality, which sometimes had a pronounced sectarian character (the *shabbiha* of Homs sold items looted during the suppression of the revolution there at a so-called 'Sunni market'). It even allowed them to establish private prisons in more than one region, most notably in the village of Deir Shmil close to Hama, and to detain kidnapped individuals held to ransom. These practices increased sectarian tensions in mixed cities and regions.

The revolution, too, produced its own *shabbiha*, who beat civilians and those who disagreed with them or used sectarian and populist rhetoric to discredit other opposition figures. They also had their media *shabbiha*, who could be seen on TV programmes assaulting their opponents physically or using the foulest of language to insult even opposition figures who disagreed with them. It is clear that the corruption, violence and ethical degradation of the regime infected not only its own constituency.

7

Ruralization of the party and sectarianization of the army: The origins of sectarian discourse and violence

This chapter reviews the manifestation of sectarianism and sectarian violence in the Syrian revolution. It delves into the roots and background of sectarianism, examining its intersection with the political regime and Syria's social structure. The aim is not to discuss in detail the history of confessions and confessional communities and sectarianism in Greater Syria, nor is it to expose the myths of sectarian ideology. Instead, it casts a critical eye at sectarianism, as a societal and ideological phenomenon that affects and is affected by the behavioural patterns of the political regime and Syrian society more generally.

Syrian society is ethnically and religiously diverse. Although Arab nationalist sentiments have run deep among the population since independence and Arab nationalist parties enjoyed decades of genuine broad popularity, the dictatorship failed to create an inclusive national framework capable of absorbing or assimilating this diversity. Its top-down secular nationalist ideology has failed to unite society or to cultivate a common secular civic culture. Nationalist slogans have become just another weapon in the regime's arsenal, used to cultivate loyalty among specific social groups, alongside a range of regionalist, sectarian, religious and traditional strategies by which the regime treats Syrians not as equal citizens within a single society but as its subjects, who are easier to deal with when approached as members of distinct communities. With the passing of time, a political and cultural perception has arisen among many Syrians that the secular ideology of the regime is no more than a fig leaf for the rule of a confessional minority. I believe, and hope to demonstrate, that the regime is not the regime of the Alawi community, but rather that the militarization of the ruling party entailed turning the Alawi community into the community of the regime. It is true that the leadership of the security apparatus (including the military) comes mostly from one confessional community, but this does not mean that the regime is the regime of that community.

The biggest threat to the Syrian revolution was always the potential for the struggle for democracy against dictatorship to morph into a sectarian struggle. Change in Syria – as elsewhere in the Levant – should have taken place through gradual peaceful reform. But the regime not only decided against this route, it also actively laboured to present itself as a victim of sectarian extremist Islamism and a representative and protector of confessional minorities in Syria, framing its atrocities as part of the war on terrorism.

I. The roots of the sectarianization of the army and the militarization of sectarianism

Sectarianism in Syria is a relatively new phenomenon that can be traced back to the Ottoman Empire. The Ottoman state sought to monopolize Muslim orthodoxy by branding dissident Muslim sects as heretics and forcing them to practice in secret; Christians and Jews were considered *dhimmis* who were treated differently in different historical phases, creating a lasting sense of historical injustice among some minority groups. The colonial powers, meanwhile, used the protection of minorities as a pretext for interference in the empire's domestic affairs. And over the course of the nineteenth century, the Tanzimat reforms and Syria's integration into the world market produced a backlash that sometimes took on a sectarian character. In some cases, the repercussions of foreign trade, the change in the status of traditional classes and conservatives' objection to the Tanzimat in Greater Syria took the form of attacks against Christian communities, who, by dint of the reforms, had become citizens instead of *dhimmis* and gained some privileges due to their favoured status with foreign consulates.[1]

Riots in Aleppo in 1850 and Damascus in 1860 demonstrate the point. The Aleppo incident began as a revolt against taxation and conscription that targeted the houses of Muslim notables as well as wealthy Christian neighbourhoods; it took on a sectarian dimension only after Bedouin stormed the city from outside. Nonetheless, foreign public opinion deemed the whole uprising to have been sectarian in character and called immediately for protection for Syria's Christians.[2]

The Damascus riots ten years later were an extension of sectarian violence taking place in nearby Mount Lebanon, which left 20,000

---

[1] Long after the appearance of this book, my book on sectarianism was published, which includes chapters dedicated to Lebanon and Syria.
[2] Muhammad Jamal Barout, *The Arab Enlightenment Movement in the Nineteenth Century: The Aleppo Circle, a Study and Selections* [Arabic], Issues and Debates of the Arab Nahda, 17 (Damascus: Ministry of Culture, 1994), 30–1.

Christians dead across the region and hundreds of villages, churches and monasteries in ruins (in addition to the damage and deaths suffered by Muslims).[3] Mobs were encouraged by the local religious establishment, which was closely linked to the traditional merchant class. This class had sustained serious losses with Syria's integration into world markets and as the centre of gravity of trade shifted from caravan centres like Damascus and Aleppo, controlled by old Muslim merchant families, to seaports, where Christian and Jewish merchant families were on the rise. The traditional merchant families in these cities were also the main reservoir for religious scholars, who had shown great hostility to recent Ottoman reforms introducing equal citizenship in place of the traditional Sunni-*dhimmi* distinction. On this occasion, the state responded quickly, handing down severe punishments to perpetrators in order to forestall European intervention.

The process of building a modern state saw Syria move steadily away from this sectarian legacy. The Great Arab Revolt against Ottoman rule laid the foundations of a Syrian political entity. The revolt was led by Tanzimat Arab officers, who played an important role in the mandate period and in the founding years of the Iraqi and Syrian states (though not without tension with local notables). With the rise of a middle class and a new class of professionals who had received a secular education, ideas of Arab nationalism were formulated by thinkers of various religious backgrounds. The founders and leaders of these currents were urban Muslims and Christians, but it is only natural that the middle classes of religious minorities had a special interest in Arab nationalism, since it conceived of them as belonging to an Arab majority.

Syrians resisted French attempts to divide their country into sectarian statelets, rising up against the mandatory authorities in 1925 and ultimately forcing the French government to recognize Syrian unity (minus Lebanon) in 1936. Attempts to distinguish Alawis as a distinct non-Muslim community by creating separate courts[4] and a separate category in a new personal status law were rejected not only by Alawi clerics but by the Conference of Sunni Ulama as well.[5] The religious establishment – a bulwark of conservatism under the French mandate – was keen to rise above sectarian differences in the name of patriotism and anti-colonialism.

---

[3] Sayyar al-Jameel, *The Modern History of the Arabs* [Arabic] (Amman: Al-Shuruq Publishing, 1997), 433.
[4] Yusif Hakeem, *Syria and the French Mandate* [Arabic] (Beirut: Al-Nahar Publishing, 1983), 41, 68.
[5] Stephen Hemsley Longrigg, *Syria and Lebanon under the French Mandate* (London: Octagon Books, 1972), 295; Muhammad Jamal Barout, 'Sectarianism: Its Manufacturing and False Consciousness', paper presented at a conference titled 'The Arab Revolution and Democracy: The Roots of Sectarian Conflicts and How to Combat Them', ACRPS, Doha, 28 January 2012.

Hostility to colonialism united Syrians and helped bring into being a new national identity. But at a time when different regions were poorly connected, the urban and the rural were sharply distinguished and the country underdeveloped – and when Syria was governed by a colonial power whose policy was to deal with people through their sectarian identity – it could not bring about full national integration. Regional grievances were voiced and bemoaned in the struggle for leadership under the French mandate. After independence, as state-building continued based on civic principles, Syrians were taught the same national school curriculum, a national army was established and inclusive national organizations emerged representing all sectors of society. Members of religious minorities were well-represented on the electoral lists of nationalist and leftist parties such as the Syrian Socialist Nationalist Party (SSNP), the communists and the Ba'th, as well as on the independent and tribal lists. Radical secular parties used the liberal era between independence and the Ba'th coup in 1963 to organize, and were active in schools and the university, in the army and among peasants against landowners. They attracted parts of the middle classes from all confessions, as well as religious minorities. This period saw few signs of sectarian tension except under Adib al-Shishakli in the 1950s.[6]

Monopolization of rule by the Ba'th Party, which ascended to power after a military coup on 8 March 1963, led to the gradual militarization of the party. Promotion from 'supporter' to 'active member' was made conditional on completion of a military training course and a period of active service at the front. This trend receded during the 1970s but returned in the 1980s during and after the struggle against the Muslim Brothers, with the creation of armed factions within the party and its organizations and the militarization of the youth wing along the lines of traditional fascist parties. Power was given to social and political elites that saw the army as their main route to social mobility, a view widespread in the poor and marginalized peripheries and among religious minorities. The historian Hanna Batatu estimated that already by the mid-1950s, about 65 per cent of all non-commissioned officers in the Syrian military were Alawis.[7] I would include the Druze and the Ismaili officers among them.

---

[6] One flash of sectarian unrest took place during clashes between the army and the people of the Druze-majority Jabal al-Arab in 1954, which left hundreds of Syrian Druze dead. Adib al-Shishakli had attempted to have Sultan al-Atrash, one of the leaders of the Great Syrian Revolt of 1925, arrested because of his open opposition to the policy of abolishing privileges granted by law to tribal sheikhs and community figures; the purpose of this policy was to forcibly assimilate minorities. Atrash was a towering figure in Syrian society, and his support was often sought by politicians. See: Deeb, 131.

[7] Hanna Batatu, 'Some Observations on the Social Roots of Syria's Ruling Military Group and the Causes for its Dominance', *Middle East Journal* 35 (Summer 1981), 341. Landis, 'The Syrian Uprising of 2011', 72.

As John Devlin put it:

> During the 1940s and 1950s, the Baath message of pan-Arabism appealed to many levels of Syrian society, but its socialist or social justice message was most attractive to those who believed that they were not receiving a fair share of the state's resources. In Syria, a state that lacked an industrial proletariat of any size, that meant rural people [...] 'Alawi boys who could get to secondary school often chose the military academy as a promising start for social advancement. Once in power, Asad naturally selected trusted men—brothers, cousins, clansmen in the first instance—for sensitive posts, and 'Alawis have been prominent in the military and security services since the mid-1960s. That Syria is ruled by a man from a village in the 'Alawi hill country and that the rural areas of Syria have for more than twenty years obtained a respectable share of the state's resources are striking consequences, though surely not intended ones, of the Baath movement 'Aflaq and Bitar started a half-century ago.[8]

The army was one of the few means of attaining employment and social advancement for young men from these regions, who were welcomed into the army in large numbers under the French mandate and thereafter. We should not forget that overrepresentation of these social groups did not change the fact that the army was the strongest and most modern institution of the post-independence state. The Ba'th Party's monopoly on power and the restriction of public freedoms, including freedom of expression and political organization, eventually led it to rely on the security agencies and the social groups that ran them, curtailing the ability of other social groups to win political influence. The most important factor, however, was the army's control over the Ba'th Party and then over government, following a string of critical battles that were decided within the army and the party. The sectarianization and then Ba'thification of the Syrian military took place over four major stages.

1. French occupation and the mandate in Syria until independence (1920–46)

The sectarianization of the army began under the French, who recruited local troops to serve in their colonial army (originally called the Légion syrienne). Although according to a recent study, the common claim that these forces were recruited primarily from minorities is an

---

[8] John F. Devlin, 'The Baath Party: Rise and Metamorphosis', *American Historical Review* 96, no. 5 (December 1991), 1404.

oversimplification, the French did '[favour] some minorities over others'.⁹ They also created several units with a specific ethnic or religious character: two Assyrian regiments in the Jazira, a Druze unit in As-Sweida, and mounted Circassian and Alawi units. This army was inherited by the newly independent states that came into being on 17 April 1946, with the majority of its troops – 17,000 of 25,000 – taken by Syria and the rest by Lebanon.¹⁰ The Ministry of Defence, however, immediately moved to reduce this number, in the name of breaking up 'ethnic blocs' that had developed within the army, and by 1948 had reduced it to less than 7,000 soldiers.¹¹

In the years after 1946, the old guard of so-called 'French officers' who had served under the mandate was supplemented by a new crop of Syrian officers trained at the Homs Military College, whose first cohort graduated in 1945. This latter group were more open to the left-wing and pan-Arab ideas becoming popular in the country at the time. They were more likely to join ideological movements, in part because of the frustrations of the Palestine war of 1948. These frustrations produced a coup and the short-lived military dictatorship of Husni al-Zaim (April–August 1949), the first of its kind in the Arab world.

More significant in its implications for the future of Syria, however, was Shishakli's countercoup later the same year (replacing Sami al-Hinnawi who had in turn overthrown Zaim). Shishakli, whose official tenure lasted from 1953 to 1954, was a 'French officer' who held progressive views, adopted radical secularism and respected the Mustafa Kemal Atatürk model of modernization. He was close to the younger generation and to Akram al-Hawrani, a political strongman from a notable family in Hama and a radical socialist who would later become one of the founding fathers of the Arab Socialist Ba'th Party. This alliance produced the first secret ideological organization within the army, setting a precedent for the Ba'thist 'Military Committee' that took power fourteen years later (some of its members were in fact veterans of the Shishakli-era organization). Shishakli, himself of Kurdish origin, also tried to 'Sunnify' and 'Arabize' the army, but succeeded only in reducing the number of Christians.

---

⁹ N. E. Bou-Nacklie, 'Les Troupes Speciales: Religious and Ethnic Recruitment, 1916–46', *International Journal of Middle East Studies* 25, no. 4 (November 1993), 645–60.

¹⁰ Nizar al-Kayyali, *A Study in the Contemporary Political History of Syria, 1920–1950* [Arabic] (Damascus: Tlas Publishing, 1997), 195.

¹¹ Arif al-Arif, *The Nakba: The Nakba of Jerusalem and the Lost Paradise, 1947–1952* [Arabic], vol. 2 (Saida: al-Maktaba al-Asriya, 1956), 349, 358; Ahmad al-Sharabati (defence minister), the second session of 28 August 1948, in *The Official Gazette* (Damascus), 4 November 1948.

2. Competing military, ideological, and regional blocs (1954–63)

With the coups of 1949, the army left the barracks for good. As the Cold War intensified and the Middle East became an important part of the global competition between the US and Union of Soviet Socialist Republics (USSR), partisan politics within the ranks only increased. Between Shishakli's fall in 1954 and the coup of 8 March 1963, the organization he had set up within the military split into two large blocs: the 'Liberationists', named after Shishakli's Arab Liberation Party, and the Socialists, associated with Hourani's new Arab Socialist Party. Alongside smaller groupings associated with the SSNP, led by Colonel Ghassan Jadid, and with the left, these two blocs were to dominate the army throughout the later 1950s. A third large group – the Damascene Bloc, which attracted conservatives and independents and placed greater emphasis on military professionalism – briefly competed with the Socialists and Liberationists, but collapsed after the assassination of its leader Colonel Adnan al-Malki in April 1955 and the subsequent Suez crisis and the rise of Nasserism. As the Syrian political elite became fragmented in the mid-1950s, the escalating competition between the two blocs threatened to split the army in two. So not only was the political landscape fractured, but the ground was prepared for the army to float a military coup as the solution to the political polarization. A delegation of Arab nationalist officers visited Cairo in January 1958, supported by the Ba'th, and tried to convince Gamal Abdel Nasser of unity with Syria. Arab nationalists rallied masses in Syria in support of the idea.

Union with Egypt in 1958 seemed to offer a way out of political chaos. Both blocs agreed to Nasser's stipulation that the army should be depoliticized and parties kept out of the military. But this did not last. As soon as Nasser began to dismantle officer networks by transferring members to civilian posts or to commands in Egypt, new blocs began to form. The most important of these was the Military Committee set up by Ba'thist officers, most of them Alawis or Ismailis, which was formed in Egypt after Nasser tried to neutralize active officers by transferring them from Syria to Egypt. This sectarian character should be pointed out, although sectarian considerations were of little relevance to the creation of the committee, which owed much more to the realities of Cold War power politics. The officers themselves were secular Arab nationalists. Most of them did not back the decision by the Ba'th Party's historical leadership to dissolve the party based on Egypt's conditions.

The members of the Damascene Bloc had largely survived the Nasserist purges of the army because of their professionalism, their perceived non-partisanship and their non-involvement in the plots and coups of recent years. As a result, the officers that led the coup against the union on 28 September 1961 came from that bloc. This set off a power struggle within the army. The Damascenes tried and failed to purge the remaining Ba'thist officers. The Military Committee, meanwhile, built a shaky alliance with other unionist and Nasserist organizations within the army that had coalesced around Colonel Jasim Alwan (shaky insofar as every constituent part was looking for an opportunity to get rid of the others).

This struggle culminated in the events of 28 March–1 April 1962, in which the Damascenes overthrew the civilian government they had put in place six months earlier, and unionist forces in Aleppo led by Alwan (and including Ba'thists) launched an abortive countercoup. Although this latter attempt, along with others that year, was quickly suppressed, the Ba'thists were now one of the three most important forces within the army alongside the Nasserists and the Damascenes. Their importance was confirmed at the Homs Conference, a military event which redistributed command posts within the army. As the Damascene faction declined between April 1962 and March 1963 – especially after a failed January coup in which Damascene officers allied themselves with members of the Muslim Brotherhood – the Ba'thists and the Nasserists emerged as the kingmakers.

Partly for social and class reasons and partly for partisan reasons, Alawi, Ismaili and Druze officers were very well-represented on the Military Committee, while the majority of the Damascene Bloc (and of the unionists and Nasserists) were Sunni. Many Christian officers were in quasi-alliance with the Damascenes, while independents leaned one way or the other according to political necessity. Nonetheless, none of the leaders of these blocs presented themselves or their groupings in sectarian terms. Their self-conception was political-ideological or professional. Although familial, local and regional links combined with a sense of being 'brothers in arms' to determine alignments and alliances, they were fraternal, not sectarian, factions.

As the secessionists' power dwindled, the Ba'thists and the Nasserists were working ever more closely together, and on 8 March 1963, these two forces seized power in a coup. Although cooperation had proved fruitful – a joint Ba'thist-Nasserist grouping had been formed within the army, and Ba'thist-Nasserist influence had spread throughout politics and society – it did not long survive their taking power. The failure of a project to build a new Arab union (this time including Syria, Egypt and Iraq) the following month triggered a breakdown in relations between the two parties, and on 18 July the Ba'th purged the Nasserists. They were now on a very dangerous path indeed: the path of monopoly rule.

Between July 1963 and February 1966, with the Ba'th now firmly in control, the struggle shifted to within the party itself. Here it often took on a sectarian colouring. The civilian wing, represented by the National

Command Council (NCC),[12] accused the Military Committee of building 'sectarian blocs' and using them to mobilize supporters and undermine the party's legitimacy. The members of the Military Committee themselves also exchanged accusations of 'overlapping' sectarian loyalties, leading to the exile of the committee's leader, Brigadier Muhammad Umran, in 1964. By 1965, accusations of sectarianism were overt and sectarian discourse within the army a matter of public knowledge. Everyone agreed that it was a bad thing, which is why the accusation was so serious. New officers recruited because of their Ba'thist background and cashiered officers now recalled to active duty came overwhelmingly from the 'minorities' or from the Daraa governorate (Houran). And a great struggle for the army was now taking place between Brigadier-General Amin al-Hafiz, a Sunni, and Brigadier Salah Jadid, an Alawi. The struggle was finally decided on 23 February 1966, when the NCC (including the historical leader Michel Aflaq) was essentially exiled to Iraq – splitting the pan-Arab party irrevocably – and the army purged of its supporters.

Since the majority of the Nasserist, independent and unionist officers purged over the course of 1963 and 1964 were Sunnis – as were the majority of the Ba'thist officers loyal to the NCC – officers from other minorities, particularly Alawis, Ismailis and Druze, became grossly overrepresented in the army. Although the purge of 1966 was cast as a dispute between the left and right wings of the party, above all it gave expression to a growing polarization between a rural Alawi-Ismaili-Druze grouping (as well as cadres from rural Daraa) and a more urban grouping. This was a complex struggle. It cannot be reduced to class, regional, sectarian or political differences alone; all these factors were acting together.

The Ba'thists who struggled among themselves for power used every means possible to guarantee loyalty. When young men left their villages and moved to the city, they looked for a relative who had already 'made it' as a ministry employee or army officer, to help them find employment; this and similar sorts of ties became loyalty networks. Officers could be certain of the loyalty of other officers if they were relatives or had come from the same village or region. Nevertheless, cross-sectarian, cross-regional ideological, and fraternal loyalties in a secular party like the Ba'th should not be underestimated. Without them people like Hafez Assad would never have been able to seize power.

---

[12] In Ba'th terminology, the parties operating in specific Arab countries are regional branches of the pan-Arab party, whose supreme organ is in theory the National Command Council (NCC). The top committee of the Syrian branch is the RCC. After the 1966 coup, the Syrian and Iraqi Ba'th split and established their own NCCs, which are largely symbolic. The RCC in Syria serves as the party politburo.

But the enemies of the Februarists (the radical leftists who ousted the NCC) nonetheless condemned them as sectarians, referring to them as the 'adas (lentil) coalition' – 'adas serving as an acronym for Alawi, Druze and Ismaili. The marginalized Sunni cities also came under the influence of this movement as part of a broader process by which the rural was coming to dominate the urban.

The cities themselves were politically divided as well. All Syrian communities, rural and urban, were influenced by leftist discourse and a string of socioeconomic transformations – the emergence of a public sector, the growth of a proletariat, and, even more significantly, the creation of a class of small and middling farmers as a result of land redistribution, which reached its peak between 1966 and 1969.[13]

3. First phase of a doctrinaire army

The notion of the 'doctrinaire army' first appeared in Yassin al-Hafiz's *Some Theoretical Premises*, which was adopted as official doctrine at the Sixth National Conference of the Ba'th Party after the defeat of the Nasserists. What it meant in practice was the Ba'thification of the army. Professional officers who refused to take up party membership were labelled 'comrades in arms' (as opposed to 'comrades in doctrine' or ideological comrades) and gradually removed or reappointed to unimportant desk jobs or training posts. By the first half of the 1980s there were few of these officers left in the army.

Between 1966 and 1970 there were further conflicts within the Ba'thist military leadership. The purge of Salim Hatoum's supporters after an abortive mutiny in As-Sweida in September 1966 reduced the number of Druze officers considerably. The struggles after the 1967 Six Day War also saw Ismailis increasingly side-lined, a trajectory that culminated in the suicide of the security chief Abd al-Karim al-Jundi in 1969. As a result, factions coalesced around three leading Alawi officers. The first of these, Jadid, was the architect of the Ba'thification of the army; he had been chief of staff since 1963 as well as assistant regional secretary to the RCC. The second, Muhammad Umran, was already ejected in 1966. He had created an effective secret military organization made up of junior and mid-ranking officers recruited between 1964 and 1966 to 'protect the revolution', but was imprisoned after the Februarist coup; his organization was later

---

[13] Land reform began in 1958 under the UAR. Gamal Abdel Nasser had already implemented an extensive land reform programme in Egypt, and hoped to break up large estates and make agrarian policy a key part of politics in Syria as well. The programme was accelerated under Salah Jadid. From 1974, however, Hafez al-Assad halted agrarian reform as part of a rightward shift towards revitalizing the private sector.

given official form as the Defence Battalions. The only leading Alawi officer who remained to face Jadid, Hafez al-Assad, was initially the least significant. But after Umran was arrested, Assad was able to secure the support of Sunni, Christian and independent officers and of Umran's orphaned organization, many of whom were hostile to Jadid's radical platform and his efforts to sap the cities' remaining economic and social power to the benefit of the countryside – not to mention his formidable intelligence apparatus, which terrified even its original architect, Jundi.

Unlike the Jadid and Assad factions, which were religiously mixed and had civilian supporters, the Umran group was almost exclusively composed of Alawi officers and built on personal loyalty to the leader. But it was nonetheless influential because it controlled so much of the military. Umran aligned himself with Salah al-Din Bitar, one of the two intellectuals who founded the party, and who left the Ba'th in early 1966, accusing the Februarists of fascism and founding the Arab Unionist Movement to replace it.

The doctrinaire army camouflaged all these divisions, since all the officers involved were Ba'thists. The conflict between Jadid and Assad in the aftermath of the Six Day War was multifaceted and complex. It concerned the relationship between state and society, how to deal with Israel, Arab and international relations, socioeconomic policy towards Syrian cities in the interior and the approach to the nascent Palestinian resistance. Hafez al-Assad was committed to Arab nationalism and the Palestinian cause, but he was also a pragmatist who did not accept Jadid's radical socialism. He also disliked the isolation a radical regime in the Arab world would bring. believing that Arab solidarity was needed if Syria were to wage a war to liberate the Golan lost in 1967. In addition to all this, it was a struggle over power. On 16 November 1970, Assad, then defence minister, was easily able to take power in what he called a 'Corrective Movement' against the 'slippery mentality' of his predecessors (a term which subsequently entered the Ba'thist lexicon as the counterpart of the 'perfidious right', as Assad's opponents referred to him and his supporters).

4. The rebuilding of the Syrian army (1970–83)

This stage can be subdivided into two parts. The first, 1970–3, was spent preparing for the October (Yom Kippur) War. This period saw the army greatly strengthened and laid the groundwork for Syria to become a regional power with its intervention in Lebanon in 1976. During this phase recruitment focused on Alawis. But there was now a degree of discrimination between Alawis from different backgrounds. This was not because of any sectarian antipathy towards different subgroups of Alawis. It was a matter of loyalty. The traditional Alawi clan leadership was being replaced by senior officers.

Those from the Haddadeen and, to a lesser extent, the Khayyateen clans – Jadid and Umran's clans respectively – had to prove their loyalty before being accepted into the army, while the Haydaris, who had provided a great deal of support to Jadid, were almost totally excluded from the military establishment. Loyalist Nimeilatis and Kalbis (Assad's clan) were recruited in large numbers. Murshidi Alawis, meanwhile – a small sect that deifies its leader, the Murshidis had been consistently persecuted under the Ba'thist governments of the 1960s and were legally unable to practice their faith under the Penal Code until 1969 – were now recruited in large numbers into the private army of Rifaat al-Assad, Hafez's younger brother. These Defence Battalions, originally set up by Muhammad Umran to 'protect the revolution', were essentially granted freedom of religion in exchange for loyalty to Hafez al-Assad.

In the second phase a presidential decree was issued setting up a Republican Guard, but its provisions were not meaningfully implemented. Instead, Rifaat al-Assad built up a private army of his own within the military establishment. This private army came from diverse backgrounds, but its commanders were chosen for their absolute loyalty to Rifaat, and its backbone was sectarian and clannish. Its members reserved the title of 'leader' for Rifaat himself (and called Bassil al-Assad, who later rose to prominence, 'the boss'); Hafez al-Assad was referred to only as 'the president'. These titles invite a semiotic analysis of the relationship between families, politics and power in Syria.[14]

As part of building the doctrinaire army, Rifaat al-Assad adopted a leftist rhetoric that, superficially at least, represented a break with the ideas and policies of his brother. This made him popular with the Communist Party (subordinated to the Ba'th within the multi-party National Progressive Front 'NPF'), who referred to him as Syria's Fidel Castro, and he had repeated meetings with a member of the Soviet Politburo, Heydar Aliyev – although it seems that Aliyev was actually trying to bring Rifaat into line and prevent him from moving against the president.[15] Over the course of

---

[14] An analysis of this kind was attempted by Wedeen in *Ambiguities of Domination*, but she focused exclusively on ritual and sloganeering – topics well-known to any Syrian. Another important topic that she did not address is the internal semiotics.

[15] Heydar Aliyev's visit to Damascus came at the height of the crisis between Rifaat and Hafez and brought an end to the former's attempts to take power. Rifaat was close to the Union of Soviet Socialist Republics (USSR), and by the time of the visit seems to have come to the conclusion that his coup had failed; Aliyev offered him a way out in the form of the settlement that made him one of three vice-presidents (alongside Zuhayr al-Masharqa and Abd al-Halim Khaddam). The officers involved in the crisis were sent to Moscow accompanied by foreign minister Farouq al-Sharaa. The ACRPS archive has testimony given to Muhammad Jamal Barout by some of the main figures involved in the visit. Also see: *al-Hayat* (London), 15 June 2000. Archived copy available online: https://bit.ly/3b1bphe (accessed 16 June 2022).

the 1970s, Rifaat managed to make himself into the main representative of the 'left' Ba'thists, adopting Jadid's radical rhetoric in order to lend an ideological character to rural and sectarian loyalties. In reality, Rifaat's most significant allies were Saudi princes, one of whom – Abdullah Abdulaziz, who was to become the king – married an Alawi woman during this period. In short, the Saudis and Soviets thought of him as their man. But he had no qualms about changing his language and tone to suit the circumstances: in exile, in Spain and France, he became a 'democrat'.

In the second half of the 1970s, the Fighting Vanguard organization – an offshoot of the Muslim Brotherhood – launched a campaign of assassinations against Alawi officers, culminating in a massacre of Alawi cadets at the Homs Artillery School in June 1979 (Sunnis were allowed to leave unscathed). The Vanguard considered the regime to be 'Nusayri' (Alawi) and declared a jihad against its heterodox rule. Adopting a wholly sectarian language, the Vanguard assassinated party officials, judges, university professors and even Sunni clerics accused of collaborating with the 'Nusayri regime'.[16] The Artillery School massacre served as the basis for a whole campaign of sectarian incitement. The Brotherhood itself, which disavowed the methods of the Fighting Vanguard, subsequently became involved in armed action after being prosecuted alongside the organization. During this period, new military recruitment policies were put in place. In exchange for accepting training at university camps, students were granted a six-month reduction in their military service. Military training became a compulsory part of the curriculum, and even though the grade did not go towards their GPA, students had to pass in order to graduate. This was a purely authoritarian move. But its effect was to create a dumping ground for unwanted officers. The university camps were staffed largely by Sunnis, Christians, Armenians, leftists, independents and non-Ba'thists, as well as time-servers who were happy with this type of work. These officers were felt to be untrustworthy and putting them in charge of the camps was a sort of coup-proofing.

In April 1983, the Defence Battalions were dismantled following a failed coup attempt, along with the broader network of Rifaat's supporters in the party and security forces. Rifaat loyalists had dominated the RCC appointed by the seventh party conference in 1980. But the party leadership stood by Hafez al-Assad at this crucial juncture, ushering in a new period in the development of Syria's military institutions.

[16] They killed Sheikh Muhammad al-Shami (1980), Rashid al-Khatib (1981) and preacher of the Umayyad Mosque Salah Uqla (1985). See: Pierret, *Religion and State in Syria*, 65. These facts should be remembered when we mention the assassination of Sheikh Muhammad Said Ramadan al-Buti (21 March 2013), as the armed revolution turned to a civil war.

5. 'Our leader forever' (1983–2000)

With Rifaat's coup defeated, Defence Minister Mustafa Tlas personally visited each military unit to receive pledges of allegiance to Hafez al-Assad from officers and enlisted men both. The famous chant 'our leader forever, Hafez al-Assad!' dates from this period. Some of the pledges of allegiance were written in blood to signify a willingness to sacrifice – and perhaps as a symbolic affirmation of a blood tie between the president and his supporters, replacing the actual blood tie with his brother Rifaat. The regime became more and more patrimonial, and the president's position was consolidated to the level of personal cult. (This was the status that Bashar al-Assad inherited: the presidency had become an *a priori* strong position regardless of who occupied it.) The decree creating a Republican Guard was finally implemented through restructuring of other divisions. The Defence Battalions had been replaced by a new private army.[17]

Sectarian practices continued. Ali Duba, head of Military Security between 1983 and 2000, granted his officers varying degrees of influence in accordance with their clan affiliations, seeking to maintain balance between them. Similar power-sharing arrangements became common elsewhere in Alawi life: in the distribution of parliamentary seats and party positions, for example. This development was largely a Latakian phenomenon and did not extend to the large Alawi population of Tartous. But the parcelling out of influence and offices became increasingly common in state institutions, from the cabinet down to town councils, among all ethnic and religious groups. Security officers were mainly recruited from the rural areas of Latakia (Jabal al-Alawiyyin) and from Bedouin tribes, alongside loyalists from elsewhere. The main force, meanwhile, was drawn from areas like Idleb.

By 1986 Syria was entering a new 'Brezhnevian' phase characterized by monotonous party rituals that nobody believed in, coupled with attempts to transform the uninspiring Hafez into a charismatic ruler.[18] The army also ballooned to some 500,000 men.

This made the army the country's largest employer, absorbing tens of thousands of young men into its ranks. The security forces also grew enormously during this time. The majority of recruits came from rural areas felt to be pro-regime – the Alawi countryside and the Bedouin communities of the desert (largely the Homs governorate). In these regions partible inheritance had left many farmers with tiny plots of land, and

---

[17] Mustafa Tlas, *Three Months that Shook Syria* [Arabic] ([n.p]: [n.p], [n.d]), 25–7.
[18] Absolute autocracy coupled with scarce public appearances gave Hafez al-Assad a sort of 'charismatic ambiguity'. This ambiguity was the result of power and absence more than the president's enchanting presence or qualities; at any rate, he never achieved real popularity.

drought and the collapse of the traditional agricultural-pastoral system in the desert had done serious damage to the economy, making a career in the police or military particularly attractive. The budget for recruiting informers was also dramatically expanded, and each of the security agencies – their notional jurisdictions and specialties notwithstanding – acquired offices focusing on education, higher education, the economy and even individual religions.

The military presence in Lebanon, meanwhile, exacerbated army corruption. Smuggling networks operating with the connivance of officers (or under their control) regularly used the 'military lane' at checkpoints and border crossings to transport illegal goods. Conscripts completing their military service were able to secure quasi-official leave by bribing their commanding officer. Moreover, the elite was no longer reproducing itself. No party conference was held between 1974 and 2000, and the membership of the RCC, the cabinet and the military command remained more or less the same from 1987 to 2000, reflecting a state of bureaucratic paralysis. The regime had perfected its clientelist structure.

Throughout this phase there was great rural in-migration to the cities. Thousands of those rural migrants were Alawis joining the army and the security forces: many graduating cohorts at the military academies had a clear Alawi majority. From a security perspective, loyalty took on a sectarian character, and this process of sectarianization expanded to encompass appointments to all state institutions. Since all economic life in Syria was by this point a prisoner of clientelist relations with the regime, corruption networks cut across all religious groups, but the strongest party was always the security apparatus, whose sectarian character was well known. Criticisms of the security agencies thus began to take on a sectarian edge, even among the capitalists and merchants who benefited from relationships with the security forces but resented having to share their profits.

By the end of this period a new generation had appeared made up of the children of Alawi officers and politicians. This new generation consisted of officials' progeny born and raised in the city who, like Bashar and the other sons of Hafez, attended the same schools as the children of rich Sunni and Christian families. They treated the security forces instrumentally as the real base of the state, business as the proper foundation of the economy, technocrats as the right people to manage ministries, and the party as an object of contempt. And they were to provide the social base for Bashar al-Assad's new regime.

The leaders of this new base were the 'young wolves': the children of security and political officials, the descendants of the old Sunni wealthy families who were ready to join the business networks and the *nouveaux riches*.

II. The social base of the Baʻthist regime and the process of ruralization

Much has been written on sectarianism in the Ottoman period and under French rule. Much has also been written about efforts made after independence to move past this legacy. This book will not try to assess the success of these efforts. It will only note that the Baʻthist period has introduced a new element into the equation: the ruralization of the administrative apparatus as a result of massive rural in-migration and recruitment into state institutions. In a strong, developed, modern state capable of absorbing migration of this kind, this would not have posed a problem. But in an ideological, one-party, military state too backward to do so, it could not but cause difficulties. In this section we will consider the social base of the regime, drawing on Batatu's classic work on the Syrian peasantry to do so.

The 1963 Baʻth coup was the work of a military elite dominated by men from the countryside who preferred the rural to the urban. As Table 7.1 shows, although the officers of the Military Committee came from all over Syria and represented many religious groups, the majority were from rural backgrounds.[19] Most were small or middling peasants, with only a few representatives of the merchant or industrial classes – men from those strata tended to prefer foreign or diplomatic careers.[20]

The rural origins of the Military Committee had significant repercussions for Syrian society. Its policies primarily benefited the countryside. The peasantry gained unprecedented political and economic influence, allowing it to compete with and later to dominate the urban classes. Thanks to land reform, in 1970-1 small and medium landowners (owners of 10–100 hectares of land) accounted for some 58.7 per cent of the agricultural sector – up from a mere 36 per cent in 1955, and about 33 per cent in 1944.[21]

Moreover, the dramatic expansion of the state bureaucracy and the nationalization of companies threw the doors open wide before a huge influx of country people into the cities lasting throughout the 1960s: the population of Damascus rose a staggering 46.7 per cent between 1960 and 1970.[22] It is worth noting that by 1968 state-sector employees made up the

---

[19] Hanna Batatu, *Syria's Peasantry, the Descendants of its Lesser Rural Notables, and their Politics* (Princeton, NJ: Princeton University Press, 1999), 146–9.
[20] Ibid.
[21] Ibid., 156.
[22] Ibid., 160.

Table 7.1 The Origins of Military Committee Members

Name	Sect	Origin	Class
Mazyad Hunaydi	Druze	Rural As-Sweida	Farmer (small landowners)
Muhammad Umran	Alawi	Rural Homs	Farmer (small landowners, religious notability)
Bashir Sadeq	Sunni	Damascus, Midan quarter	Middling merchant
Abdulghani Ayyash	Sunni	Hama City	Middling industrial
Salah Jadid	Alawi	Rural Latakia	Middle peasantry (notables)
Ahmad al-Mir	Isma'ili	Masyaf (a small town), Hama	Feudal origins (religious notability)
Hafez al-Assad	Alawi	Rural Latakia	Small peasantry
Abd al-Karim al-Jundi	Ismaili	As-Salamiyeh (a small town), Hama	Peasantry (middling landowners, notables)
Uthman Kanaan	Sunni	Rural Alexandretta (now in Turkey)	Peasantry (small landowners)
Munir al-Jirudi	Sunni	Damascus periphery	Peasantry (small landowners)
Husain Milhim	Sunni	Rural Idleb	Peasantry (small landowners)
Hamad Ubayd	Druze	As-Sweida City	Peasantry (middling landowners, notables)
Salim Hatoum	Druze	Rural As-Sweida	Peasantry (middling landowners)
Muhammad Rabah al-Tawil	Sunni	Latakia City	Urban middle class (religious notability)
Mustafa al-Hajj Ali	Sunni	Rural Daraa	Peasantry (small landowners)
Ahmad al-Suwaydani	Sunni	Rural Daraa	Peasantry (middling landowners)
Musa al-Zubi	Sunni	Rural Daraa	Peasantry (middling landowners)
Mustafa Tlas	Sunni	Ar-Rastan (a small town), Homs	Peasantry (middling landowners)
Amin al-Hafiz	Sunni	Aleppo City	Urban middle class

Source: Hanna Batatu, *Syria's Peasantry, the Descendants of its Lesser Rural Notables, and their Politics* (Princeton, NJ: Princeton University Press, 1999), 146–9.

largest single group within the party, accounting for some 32 per cent of 'active' or 'full members'.[23]

The predominance of rural elements and rural interests on the party agenda explains why the merchants of Aleppo and Damascus supported the Corrective Movement in 1970 – to the extent that one merchant procession marched through the streets carrying signs reading 'We implored God for Aid—*al-Madad*. He sent us Hafez al-Assad'.[24] The merchants had been hit hard by the nationalizations and resented dealing with administrators of rural origin who lacked an 'understanding of the

---

[23] Ibid., 161.
[24] Ibid., 175.

intricacies of trade and thus wittingly or unwittingly raised all sorts of impediments in its path'.[25] Assad promised a new focus on the private sphere and an end to the 'vindictive' anti-urban policies of his predecessor. But although he may have been more open to urban concerns, the new president failed to break the ruralizing pattern. True, there was less rural migration in the 1970s than in the 1960s, but the state and party apparatus continued to grow and so, too, did the rural population in Damascus.

Until the 1980s, the party – still dominated by rural interests – remained the main instrument by which the regime retained control over society. Absent civilian institutions or social accountability, the combination of a security state, a swollen public sector and an increasingly prosperous private sector (fed in large by Gulf investment after 1973) gave rise to a parasitic 'new bourgeoisie' whose members made their money from smuggling, graft and corruption. This class was drawn from the Ba'thist commanders and apparatchiks of the 1960s, who had become the state officials of the 1970s. It coexisted with the merchant 'old bourgeoisie' of Damascus and Aleppo, whose interests were protected in exchange for political loyalty. It soon became a central plank of the regime's social base, and alongside other developments like the break-up of the USSR led to a diminution in the role of the party, which became increasingly a matter of constitutional formality.[26] The regime adapted to this new reality, granting greater leeway and 'independent' parliamentary seats to business owners, clergymen and tribal leaders, who have accounted for 33.2 per cent of the Popular Assembly since 1994.[27] Of course, this representation is not political in nature.

Syria is, then, a state of one-party rule, but the politicized military and security dominate the party. However, it is not a rule by a military junta, but a dictatorship. The first circle around the autocrat is composed of the security and army commanders; the second, the so-called regional leadership of the party; and the third, the government and all manner of unions and corporative arms of and within the regime. Historically, it was first the party, which produced the organization in the military, and then the president. The structure of the regime since the 1970s is thus the exact inverse of the historical process that generated it.

Hinnebusch eloquently summed up the few attempts to diagnose the nature of the regime before the revolution as follows:

---

[25] Ibid., 160.
[26] The 1973 constitution required presidential candidates to be party members and to be presented by the RCC before approval by popular referendum.
[27] Ibid., 277.

The Baʿth came to power by a military coup and the army is a central pillar of the regime, but it is an "army-party symbiosis," not mere military rule. The Alawi minority sect has dominated it, but it is not simply a minority regime and incorporates a cross-sectarian coalition. At its centre is the personal dictatorship of Hafiz al-Asad, but his power rests on complex institutions. It has been described as a regime of the state bourgeoisie, but it also rose out of and incorporates a significant village base. Thus, no single one of the typical explanations of the regime—army, sect, class—adequately captures its complex multi-sided nature.[28]

This was to change under Bashar.

Bashar al-Assad inherited from his father a social base shifting towards a festering parasitic class that operated within the state itself and in the space between state and business. As we saw in Chapter One, he oversaw the completion of this shift towards alliances built on corruption and autocracy. The party was almost completely side-lined as neoliberal policy and drought (2005–9) destroyed the social base that had supported the regime when it took power in 1963. These disasters drove a new wave of ruralization, with more than a million people, largely from the east and northeast, taking up residence in urban slum neighbourhoods and 'poverty belts'.[29] Migration placed additional pressure on the already ruralized cities, driving up the crime rate and increasing extremist religiosity. But at the same time, it provided them with a population more willing to engage in protest. This wave of migration was quite different from that of earlier decades. The spread of education, especially higher education, and the exposure to satellite TV since the 1990s, had given these migrants greater political and cultural awareness and stoked their frustration and a desire for change. It was this segment of society that first took up the banner of the Arab Spring and came out into the streets to call for reform – and who later, once the regime had shown itself unwilling, began to demand comprehensive change.

Bashar al-Assad's relationship with the army began under his father, who hoped to use it to ease the succession. During his early years in power, he left the military establishment alone, allowing the existing balance of power to continue. From 2005 onwards, however, he changed tack. He

---

[28] Raymond Hinnebusch, *Syria: Revolution from Above* (London and New York: Routledge, 2002), 1. See also Volker Perthes, *The Political Economy of Syria Under Asad* (New York: I.B. Tauris, 1995); Itamar Rabinovich, *Syria under the Baʿth, 1963–66: The Army-Party Symbiosis* (Abingdon: Routledge, 1972); Nikoalos Van Dam, *Struggle for Power in Syria: Sectarianism, Regionalism and Tribalism in Politics, 1961-80* (London: Croom Helm, 1981); Michael H. Van Dusen, 'Syria: Downfall of a Traditional Elite', in *Political Elites and Political Decelopment in the Middle East*, ed. Frank Tachau (Cambridge, Mass.: Schenkman Pub. Co, 1975).

[29] *BBC Arabic*, 2 October 2008, at: https://bbc.in/3EpCpjr (accessed 4 January 2022).

purged the commanders left over from the Hafez era,[30] replacing them with officers he had grown up with and leaning heavily on the fiercely loyal Republican Guard. The army was encouraged to see itself as serving first and foremost the president's family. Pictures of Bashar were pinned to every soldier's uniform, and many military vehicles began to sport images of the three Assads – Hafez, Bashar and his brother Maher – under them the caption 'this is how the lions gaze'.

At the same time, Maher – a colonel who was also directly involved in the business sector – acquired greater influence within the elite Fourth Division and began to create an independent power base for himself across the military institution. Despite the similarities, however, circumstances prevented Maher from becoming another Rif'at. Although there were sometimes tensions between the two brothers, they could not compare with the relationship between their father and their uncle. Moreover, Bashar was in a much stronger position than his father had been in the 1970s. Although many people cast doubt on his ability to govern at this time, Bashar inherited the full authority of a presidency his father had consolidated through a long struggle inside and outside the military establishment.

Assad's main achievement during this period was the purge of the old guard within the army, who had believed themselves to be beyond his reach. He also marginalized the party entirely. Bashar al-Assad also hastened the process of economic liberalization, which dangerously undermined the alliances of the Ba'thist regime, along with the social bases that were traditionally loyal to Ba'thist rule. The upshot of all this was that the elite surrounding the president grew more powerful while state institutions were greatly weakened (with the exception of the security establishment).

The president showed his unlimited power at the party conference of 2005. Rather than announcing tangible steps towards gradual reform as anticipated, he imitated his Egyptian and Tunisian counterparts by delaying all political measures indefinitely and doubling down on economic liberalization and integration into the international market using Gulf, expat and foreign investment. The plan for an associations law, for example, was consigned to a secret drafting process behind closed doors, where it would remain unpromulgated on the pretext of unspecified legal technicalities that needed to be overcome; the law was still being drafted when the revolution broke out years later. Far from a great reformer, Assad had proved himself to be an obstacle to any reform efforts. His liberalization

---

[30] In the introduction to the Arabic translation of his book *Syria: Revolution from Above* (Beirut: Riad el-Rayyes, 2007), Hinnebusch estimates that Bashar had already changed 60 per cent of the army officers.

process weakened the corporate dimension of the Syrian regime, drained its populism of any meaning while preserving the populist discourse, and widened the income gap.

The result of all this was that in 2011 the traditional social base of the regime revolted against it. The fiercest opposition to the regime came from the same parts of society that had once produced the Ba'th Party's staunchest supporters. Tens of thousands of workers, farmers and former Ba'thist intellectuals participated in the revolution, which started in Daraa, one of the historical reservoirs of party cadres. Syrians joked that it was the 'active members' of the Idleb branch office who were behind events. And this was not entirely farfetched. The sometime enemies of the Ba'th – businessmen, those in favour of better relationships with the Gulf, those who wanted peace with Israel – were now the regime's allies. The mass membership of the party, on the other hand, were at the receiving end of neoliberal policy. By the time the revolution began, all that remained of the broad base was a specifically sectarian constituency.

In this period, Alawis were not officially recognized as a separate religious group. In order to control the majority, the regime took pains to avoid presenting them as a sectarian community – a minority. The Alawi community, as an entity beyond the state, was slowly ground down, and Alawis were pushed towards full dependence on and identification with the regime; traditional livelihoods were undermined and replaced by state employment. Any political opposition among Alawis was violently suppressed. Critical Alawis were driven gradually into the cultural and artistic sphere, where they constituted no threat to the regime.

III. The nature of the regime and the rise of the 'young wolves'

Some commentators are keen to make comparisons between the Syrian Ba'thist regime and its Iraqi counterpart under Saddam Hussein. The Syrian regime, however, is something quite unique. True, both these regimes were autocratic security states. But the 'sectarianization' of the Syrian state has no cognate in Iraq. Moreover, Saddam's Iraq was a rentier state that used oil revenue and did not rely on society for its fiscal needs. As Table 7.2 shows, the Syrian regime received revenues from its dwindling oil resources and foreign aid (especially from the Gulf region), but has no oil wealth comparable to Iraq. It must therefore extract income directly from society, whether through taxation – which comprises a relatively low share of state revenues, and due to tax evasion is collected mainly by deduction from wages – or the unofficial taxes of corruption levied on businesses and

Table 7.2 Syrian State Revenue Pre-2011

	2000	2001	2002	2003	2004	2005	2006	2007	2008	2009	2010
General government gross debt (% of GDP)[31]	152.1	144.5	132.4	133.4	113.0	50.7	45.0	42.7	37.3	31.2	30.0 projected
Oil production (barrels per day)[32]	548,000 540,000[33]	581,000	548,000	527,000	495,000 431,000[34]	450,000 400,000[35]	435,000	415,000	398,000	375,000	385,000
Oil revenue (minus production cost of oil) (% of GDP)[36]	25.18	17.44	16.93	19.25	21.32	26.51	25.75	21.32	–	–	–
Oil exports (% of GDP)	–	–	–	–	–	14.2[37]	–	–	11.3[38]	–	–
Non-oil tax revenue	36[39]	–	–	–	–	–	–	48[40]	–	–	–

[31] IMF, 'World Economic Outlook Database: Syria', October 2019, at: https://bit.ly/3nti1rS (accessed 25 July 2022).
[32] BP, 'Statistical Review of World Energy', June 2011, 8, at: https://bit.ly/3J5ly9r (accessed 25 July 2022).
[33] Syria's Tenth Five Year Development Plan 2005–2010, 488.
[34] IMF, 'Syrian Arab Republic: 2009 Article IV Consultation', Country Report, no. 10/86, March 2010, 17, at: https://bit.ly/3PPy3s3 (accessed 25 July 2022).
[35] Ibid.
[36] *The Global Economy*, at: https://bit.ly/3b32hch (accessed 25 July 2022).

According to the Tenth Five-Year Plan 2005–2010, export revenues from oil and oil derivatives constituted 70% of foreign exchange returns and financed 45% of the state budget. The oil and gas sector alone constituted one-fifth of the Syrian GDP, according to the Tenth Five-Year Plan, and the revenues from the export of crude oil and its derivatives represented nearly three-quarters of export revenues, contributing to financing nearly half of the state's general budget (*The Tenth Five-Year Plan 2005–2010*, 'Chapter Twelve, Energy Sector Oil, Gas, Electricity and Mineral Resources', 486–487).

[37] Taysir al-Radawi, 'Shedding Light on the Eleventh Five-Year Plan', Symposium, Syrian Economic Society, 5 January 2011, 11, at: https://bit.ly/3b7nTEA (accessed 25 July 2022).
[38] Ibid., 12.
[39] Ibid., 8.
[40] Ibid.

(% of total revenue)				
Tax revenue (% of GDP)	8.8[41]	—	14[42]	—
Non-tax revenue (% of GDP)	14.5[43]	—	—	—
Indirect taxes (% of GDP)	—	13[45]	—	8.8[44]
Direct taxes (% of GDP)	—	69[47]	—	6.5[46]
Direct taxes (% of total taxes)	—	53[48]	48.2[49]	42[50]
Income tax (% of total tax)	30.8[51]	—	24.4[52]	—
Foreign grants (% of GDP)	0.21[53]	—	—	—

[41] As the average period of the Ninth Plan 2000–2005, see: *Tenth Five-Year Plan 2005–2010*.
[42] This percentage was much lower than the Tenth Five-Year Plan had anticipated, and much lower than it should have been, as tax revenues were expected to constitute 17% of GDP (al-Radawi, 8.).
[43] According to the Tenth Five-Year Plan 2005–2010.
[44] Barout, *The Last Decade in the History of Syria*, 101.
[45] Ibid.
[46] Ibid.
[47] Ibid.
[48] Al-Radawi, 8.
[49] Ibid.
[50] Barout, 101.
[51] Al-Radawi, 8.
[52] Ibid.
[53] According to the Tenth Five-Year Plan 2005–2010.

citizens trying to manage their daily lives, in the form of bribes, protection money and 'silent partnerships' in major enterprises. Needless to say, corruption 'taxes' do not benefit state institutions but rather regime strongmen and other state employees. Even poorly paid civil servants supplement their income with bribes.

This means that the Syrian regime, especially in its degenerate phase when it combined despotism with neoliberalism, does not even spare its allies. Its major figures covet the wealth of the business class. It is a kleptocracy – or, to use the colloquial Syrian term, a *tashlih* order, a system of 'taking 'em for everything they've got'. This in turn produces unofficial networks of violence outside the state apparatus, the *shabbiha*, whose practices are known as *tashbih*. This *tashlih*-and-*tashbih* attitude of the security state towards its citizens is an exceptional case and an unusual form of governance.

These relatively late phenomena are the result of an authoritarianism that relies on a decayed public sector and pursues economic liberalization under conditions of blurred borders between politics, security and the economy and amidst overlapping networks of officers and businessmen. But, as discussed above, this is not how the Ba'th regime began. It was invested in top-down modernization, agricultural reforms and the redistribution of wealth through taxation and state services. It maintained vertical and horizontal corporatist links between regime and society through the party and unions of peasants, workers, women and students. Lastly, it held what some considered a populist commitment to satisfying social needs,[54] a commitment that created deficits that oil sales could not compensate for. Volker Perthes considered its power structure to be a system of 'authoritarian corporatist group representation'.[55]

Syria's economy is based on value added by agriculture, services and manufacturing. Historically, the state has survived on the income brought in by the public sector, but this has barely sufficed to finance its massive bureaucracy. As a result, state employees are paid very badly at every level. Petty corruption supplements the income of junior civil servants, and grand corruption serves as a means of capital accumulation for members of the so-called 'bureaucratic bourgeoisie'. Bribes often well exceed official salaries. One form of corruption, abetting tax evasion, is so common that the state brings in very little revenue from taxes. The irony is that corruption is itself a sort of taxation – a kind of redistribution of wealth not through

---

[54] Heydemann, *Authoritarianism in Syria*, 208–9.
[55] Perthes, *The Political Economy of Syria Under Asad*, 134. For the concept of corporatism, see: Howard Wiarda, *Corporatism and Comparative Politics: The Other Great "Ism"* (Armonk, NY: M. E. Sharpe, 1997).

the state, but directly to its employees, first and foremost the powerful. In flagrant contradiction to the law and to the idea of the public good, citizens, poor and rich alike, pay junior officials simply to secure what they are legally entitled to, while businessmen pay senior civil servants to help them secure contracts or find ways around the law. In state agencies that regularly levy fees and fines (customs, border control, the police), bureaucratic-feudal or bureaucratic-security networks distribute the money raised: the border guard who imposes a fine at the border will kick back a substantial cut to the officer who gave him the post. Senior officials are 'granted' bureaucratic fiefdoms providing a guaranteed income.

Corruption is so pervasive in Syria that it has become a structural feature of the Syrian state. Even routine procedures are almost impossible without recourse to bribery. This has produced its own value system in which cunning and the ability to find ways around the law are the most important traits. This value system gives those with access to senior officials ('keys') authority and power and makes such access a point of pride. At the same time, the liberalization programmes have allowed senior members of the security agencies and bureaucracy to enter the market as businessmen; it is difficult to find a restaurant on Mount Qasioun that does not belong to someone from this background.[56] When fresh capital began to flow into the Syrian market, these strongmen quickly found places for their children or sons-in-law in the new holding companies set up by the capitalist class, foremost among them Sham Holding and the Syrian Holding Company.

The regime's attempts to create an economically liberalized authoritarianism included efforts to reconstruct the business class by attracting foreign capital. Limited economic liberalization started in the mid-1980s with the drop in oil prices and the pressing need for the private sector as a source of growth. A new business elite emerged in Syria to become the new economic network, which was further consolidated in the 1990s due to the surge in non-productive private-sector investments. The continued amalgamation between capitalists and bureaucrats had a direct influence on Syrian economic institutions, especially in shaping the parameters of the reform process, which in return redounded to the benefit of the business networks.[57]

---

[56] The head of appropriation projects in the Damascus governorate, Muhammad Malo, said in a press statement in November 2010: 'There are no licensed restaurants in Qassion except for three (Domiana, La Montana, Ahla Talla); as for the unlicensed establishments, they were closed down.' These restaurants all belong to businessmen who are influential within the state. See: *DP News*, 21 November 2010. Archived copy available online: https://bit.ly/3EOJ8DH (accessed 4 January 2022).

[57] Bassam Haddad, *Business Networks in Syria: The Political Economy of Authoritarian Resilience* (Stanford, CA: Stanford University Press, 2012), 170.

Syria's existing business class had made their money by providing investment opportunities for Gulf and expat capital at a time when huge surpluses were accumulating in the Arab petrostates. But the accelerated liberalization measures of 2005 and 2006 – during which around eighty new decrees and laws on the investment climate and the structure of the economy were promulgated[58] – were part of a new drive to attract foreign capital, which was directed towards a 'new' business class.

Just as in Tunisia and Egypt, this class was to serve as the engine of growth built on investments in areas historically dominated by the (now shrinking) state.[59]

These investments were carried out in close cooperation with the government, which provided licenses and go-aheads. They were often facilitated by corrupt deals or involved members of the security or political elite directly. They focused on real estate and on services, moving into the space left behind by state companies. The new economic networks 'were able to sway the pattern of state intervention in the economy according to their [...] interests, which invariably superseded those of the state and the business community as a whole [...] By empowering its private partners with whom it shared temporary interests, and by alienating the remaining social forces, the regime shuffled social alliances through existing or new institutions'.[60]

Very little money found its way into manufacturing or into agriculture, the traditional mainstay of the Syrian economy and of crucial importance to its traditional base. Indeed, the pact with the new business class further undermined the implicit socio-political contract between the regime and its traditional supporters: agrarian and public sector workers.

Not every stockholder in the main investment companies can be blamed. While some enriched themselves happily though corrupt practices and tax evasion, others were forced to do so because without powerful friends it is impossible to invest in Syria. Equally, the fact that some businessmen came out in support of the revolution does not, in itself, mean that they are paragons of virtue. The point here is not to put stockholders on trial but to explain the structure of the Syrian business sector and its links to the security forces and to politics.

In 2010, the magazine *Economy and Transport* published a list of the hundred wealthiest businessmen in Syria. While business families close to the regime are

---

[58] Muhammad Jamal Barout, *The First Basic National Report for the Syrian 2025 Project, the Axis of the Economy and Productivity: Surveying and Analysing Macroeconomic Trends in Syria (1970–2005)* [Arabic] (Syrian Arab Republic, State Planning Commission and the UNDP), 265.
[59] On Tunisia, see: Bishara, *The Glorious Tunisian Revolution*, 15–35.
[60] Haddad, *Business Networks in Syria*, 171.

conspicuously absent (the Makhloufs, the Shaleeshes, the Khaddams, Tlases, Shehabis, Suleimans and so on), the list otherwise seems to be a fairly accurate reflection of reality. Some 23 per cent of those listed are the sons, business partners or known fronts of officials, and 22 per cent come from traditional merchant families who lost out in the nationalizations of the 1960s and have regained their wealth through partnerships with senior regime figures. Another 48 per cent are 'new businessmen' who also largely made their money in this way. It is worth noting that only 7 per cent conducted their affairs primarily outside Syria, which implies that the interests of the vast majority of the Syrian business class are concentrated within the country.

The businessmen on the list are concentrated geographically in Damascus, Aleppo, Latakia and – to a lesser degree – Homs and Hama, with only one group from the entire eastern region (ar-Raqqa, Deir ez-Zor and al-Hasakeh). Of those on the list, only 16 per cent were Alawi (compared to 69 per cent who were Sunni and 14 per cent Christian), but they tended to be much wealthier – that is, despite representing a minority of businessmen, they control most of the money. The classic example is the Makhloufs, who are related by marriage to the Assads. The Makhloufs hold monopolies in mobile communications, duty-free markets and oil. They also hold major stakes in various private banks, insurance and construction companies, import consortiums and commercial agencies.[61] Other parts of the bourgeoisie excluded from these favourable relationships with the regime have been quite willing to use this skewed distribution of wealth as part of sectarian agitation.

The structure of the private sector is based on what Mahmoud Abdel-Fadil has called 'competitive monopolies'.[62] These are a relatively recent development. In 2000, for example, the state sold the rights to set up a mobile phone network to the Makhloufs and their Lebanese partners, the Miqatis. Although the Makhloufs had no prior experience in the communications sector, all other applications for licenses were denied. At first the roll-out was shared between the Makhloufs' Syriatel and the Egyptian conglomerate Orascom (Mobinil), which belongs to Naguib Sawiris. But once the infrastructure was in place, Sawiris was cut out entirely. The MP Riad Seif, who spoke out against the deal, was arrested along with several other opposition figures, showing the extent of collusion between the state and its favoured businessmen.[63]

---

[61] Samir Seifan, 'Income Distribution Policies and Their Role in the Social Eruption in Syria' [Arabic], research paper presented to the ACRPS, to be published in a forthcoming book on Syria.
[62] Mahmud Abd al-Fadeel, *Arabs and the Asian Experience: Lessons Learned* [Arabic] (Beirut: Centre for Arab Unity Studies, 2000), 195.
[63] Seifan, 'Income Distribution Policies'. For more details, see: *The Experience of Riad Seif: Issues in Industry and Politics* [Arabic] (Damascus: n.p., 1999).

Another common practice is to force successful businessmen to take on partners from officials' families, either in exchange for smoothing out bureaucratic problems or taxes or simply as protection money. Powerful families often end up taking over these companies and removing the original owners.

This socioeconomic group constitutes, along with its direct beneficiaries, the hard core of the regime. It has promoted good relations with the Gulf states, the West and Turkey. It has also supported the 'peace process' – its members have little interest in anti-imperialism or the Palestinian cause. For them the regime does not represent 'resistance' or 'rejectionism' or even sectarian interests; it is a source and protector of money and power, pure and simple. They favour a liberal Western lifestyle but have no desire to extend it beyond their homes, hotels and establishments – a privilege that the regime, led by a man who is one of their own far more than he is a Ba'thist, has been happy to give them. Of course, there are other components to the regime, often with different priorities. But it is this new class of businessmen, and in particular the 'young wolves' around Bashar al-Assad, who hold the greatest sway over the regime.

The views and lifestyle of Bashar al-Assad have little in common with Iran or Hezbollah; rather, he is a part of the social group described above. But the rhetoric and geostrategic interests of the regime, and the internal conflict keeps the regime in the so-called 'axis of resistance'. While Hafez al-Assad and his companions exploited Arab nationalism and the Palestinian cause in regional disputes, they also sincerely believed in them.

8

Sectarian violence unleashed

The Syrian revolution began as a civic revolution in every sense of the word. There were organizers, participants, aid workers and journalists from all religious backgrounds. The revolution's 'political wing' formed outside Syria, also had a diverse ideological and confessional makeup, and maintained a democratic discourse based on the idea of citizenship. It was rare for a Syrian politician to voice sectarian sentiments, even as a matter of individual opinion. There were a handful of exceptions – clerics outside the political opposition and the occasional sectarian demagogues in the media – but none of these individuals held a position of political responsibility.

As time went on, however, a sharper sectarian rhetoric began to emerge, especially among the armed factions and their admirers on social media, although this rhetoric failed to dominate the revolution's core demands and political programmes or to transform it into a civil war, despite the pressure to move things in that direction. That can be attributed to three main developments.

Firstly, the violent repression of civic activists during the first stages of the revolution – often culminating in murder, imprisonment, and exile – shifted the centre of the revolution to new parts of society less interested in political programmes and public responsibility than their day-to-day experience, who tended to see the security regime as an Alawi regime. Secondly, the regime persistently portrayed the revolution as an Islamist one, supported by foreign conspiracy. Thirdly, a regional alliance of a sectarian character, particularly the Iran-Iraq-Hezbollah coalition of dogmatic political Shi'ism, emerged to provide political and military backing to the Syrian regime.

I. Channels of sectarianism during the revolution

The sectarian argument was part of a political discourse adopted by the regime during the earliest protests. As early as Assad's speech of 30 March

2011, when he branded the protest movement 'sectarian sedition', it was clear that the regime was planning on fomenting anxiety about sectarian unrest, implying that only the authoritarian state could preserve the unity of state and society in Syria and that responding to demands for democracy would lead to sedition and division. It is quite possible, too, that the regime – fully aware that its policies had made Alawis its backbone – had concluded that the revolution must be a reaction to the concentration of wealth and power in the country and that any such reaction must carry a sectarian charge.

With the weight of tyranny lifted, and the excessive level of the regime's violence, polarization between regime loyalists and the opposition increased sectarian tensions in the popular consciousness in mixed areas. At first, these tensions did not express themselves violently. But protests were concentrated in Sunni-majority population centres, while most other groups balked at joining protests.

The regime line was used to justify firing on peaceful protests because 'armed infiltrators' were present. This encouraged sectarian tensions, and fuel was added to the fire by some political figures associated with the revolution. Maamun al-Homsi, for example, openly branded the regime 'sectarian' and 'Alawi',[1] as did Yusuf al-Qaradawi, an influential religious scholar and popular preacher. In a Friday sermon given on 25 March 2011, Qaradawi called the Syrian president a 'prisoner of his sect', adding that 'the Syrian people treated him as a Sunni'[2] – a strange way of saying that Syrians tolerated the confessional affiliation of their president.[3]

Sectarian tensions were also stoked by TV channels broadcast from the Gulf. Adnan al-Aroor, another popular preacher whose speeches were broadcast on the Saudi-funded Safa and Wisal TV,[4] gave expression to a dangerous populism that hoped to galvanize sectarian and communitarian

---

[1] Maamun al-Homsi's sectarian rhetoric was on full display in a video he uploaded to YouTube on 18 December 2011: 'A salute to the heroes of Syria, the Sunnis of Syria … After today, you despicable Alawis will either have to abandon Assad, or Syria will be your graveyard. [...] Enough silence [...] Stop the killing of the Sunnis! [...] An eye for an eye and a tooth for a tooth! [...] There will be no minorities and no sectarianism [...] If you do not abandon Assad after today, we will erase you from Syria [...] We will make Syria into a graveyard for the Alawis [...] You will know, after today, who the Sunnis really are.' See: YouTube, 19 December 2011, at: https://bit.ly/3aW88zW (accessed 12 June 2022).

[2] *Youm7*, 25 March 2011, at: https://bit.ly/335n76E (accessed 5 January 2022).

[3] In 2013, Yusuf al-Qaradawi ruled that Alawis were unbelievers and not to be treated as Muslims. Speaking at a conference held by the International Federation of Muslim Clerics in Doha to support the Syrian people, he said, 'The late Syrian President Hafez al-Assad belonged to a sect that is even more unbelieving than the Christians and the Jews, since its adherents perform none of the Islamic rituals.' See: *Al Jazeera*, 1 June 2013, at: https://bit.ly/3sV61TT (accessed 5 January 2022).

[4] Adnan al-Aroor is a native of Jarajimah neighbourhood of Hama. After graduating from the University of Damascus, he moved to Saudi Arabia, where he began to develop a demagogic rhetoric combining Wahhabi Salafism and Brotherhood thought. Many of his writings have a sectarian bent and are fiercely critical of Shi'a and Sufis in particular, occasionally accusing them of apostasy. See: Mustapha, *The Virtual Public Sphere in the Syrian Revolution*, 95.

feeling by presuming to express 'what many think but are not willing to say'. While often claiming that they want to coexist with the Alawis and other religious groups, in the same breath people like Aroor made it clear that the 'sectarian majority' should rule. In effect, of course, this means that the self-appointed spokesmen of the sectarian majority should rule, i.e. those who incited sectarian passions in the first place. In authoritarian regimes minorities always rule, whether the incumbents belong to an ethnic minority or majority.

Syria provides an important example of how sectarian political consciousness is manufactured, as social norms governing acceptable speech are broken and sectarianism becomes the basis of a new demagoguery which justifies incitement against other religious groups by reference to alleged historical injustices. This perspective divides society along sectarian lines and identifies the *sectarian* majority as a *democratic* majority on whose behalf it speaks, as if it were the 'party of a confessional community'. In fact, the Sunni majority was not a sect and did not come to behave like a single political community, in spite of the attempts to mobilize Sunni sectarianism against the regime

These attempts paralleled the sectarian loyalties that were crystalizing around the regime and disguising their sectarianism with secular language, by arguing that criticism of the regime itself was automatically sectarian – even democratic critique of sectarian tendencies that actually existed within the regime – and that any defence of the regime was automatically secular, even when motivated by sectarian or minoritarian calculations.

As in many of the Arab revolutions, the mosque was initially the main (though not exclusive) rallying point for assemblies and protests, especially on Fridays, which are the first day of the weekend in Syria and the day on which weekly communal prayers are held. As protests became a daily event, however – and as people realized that the regime had no reservations about attacking holy places and that mosques offered them no protection whatsoever – mosques ceased to play this role. Nevertheless, in order to justify their immoral neutrality, which in effect meant supporting the regime, some intellectuals criticized the centrality of mosques in popular protests in a multi-confessional society and cast aspersions on the motivations of protesters.

In the early days of the revolution, protests seemed to be coming from a specific part of the population (Sunnis). As events escalated and protests spread into new and religiously diverse areas, there were fears that sectarian violence would break out. These fears became a reality with a scattering of incidents that prefigured large massacres carried out by militias and regime forces like those in Houla, Qubayr, and Treismeh.[5]

---

[5] During the writing of this book, horrendous sectarian massacres took place in Jdidet al-Fadl, Beida, and Banyas.

The first of these incidents took place in the largely Sunni city of Latakia, which on 25 March 2011 became one of the first Syrian cities to rise up in support of Daraa.[6] In districts bordering Alawi neighbourhoods, such as Hursh and Qnainis, protests morphed into clashes between residents of different religious backgrounds. These clashes quickly evolved into tit-for-tat attacks between Sunni and Alawi neighbourhoods and sectarian brawls between students at Tishreen University, aggravated by unidentified cars that drove through residential areas warning locals of imminent attacks from their neighbours. Perhaps the most dramatic moment came on 25 March itself, when Alawis from nearby villages attempted to enter the city *en masse* to avenge members of the security forces who had supposedly been stabbed to death by Sunni protesters.[7] A serious sectarian confrontation was prevented by the army and security forces, which turned the villagers back near the Tishreen University roundabout. Religious and community leaders then made a huge collective effort to calm sectarian tensions in the city, which allowed Latakia to avoid uncontrollable sectarian violence.[8]

Other incidents took place around Banyas. This part of the Syrian coastline is religiously diverse, with significant populations of Alawis, Sunnis and Christians. In Banyas itself, sectarian tensions first developed after Sunni neighbourhoods joined the protests and gave vocal support to the revolution, and by April 2011, the city had become sharply polarized. Violence began on the morning of 10 April, when *shabbiha* from nearby Alawi villages fired on a mosque during the dawn prayer, leaving a local man called Usama al-Shaikha dead. In response, the Sunni neighbourhoods took to the streets, with some protesters wearing funeral shrouds to symbolize their willingness to die for the revolution.[9]

Tensions rose even further when nine soldiers were killed in an attack on an army bus the following day,[10] as well as an Alawi citizen called Nidal

---

[6] Hijab, the Syrian prime minister who defected in mid-2012, said in a personal interview that the sectarian element was paramount in the Latakian protests. During his brief tenure as governor of Latakia in 2011, he discovered that no more than 20 per cent of civil servants were Sunnis, while Alawis enjoyed privileged access to state employment, and in many cases benefited from 'masked unemployment', or jobs with a salary but no responsibilities. Hijab added that when he met with the residents of Sleiba and Saknatori districts after the beginning of the protests, promising them 1,000 government jobs, more than 12,000 people from these neighbourhoods applied. He also mentioned that the Sunni-majority neighbourhoods in Latakia, such as Sleiba, Saknatori, Qnainis, and al-Raml (a Palestinian camp), largely lacked state services, especially sanitation and health services.

[7] This narrative was common in the Alawi neighbourhoods of Latakia, but no-one was able to give proof or name the individuals who were allegedly killed. Nor did the official media publish a story at the time, suggesting that this story may be part of the sectarian mobilization that overtook the region at this time, whose origins are unclear.

[8] Interviews with a number of residents of Sunni and Alawi neighbourhoods, conducted by the ACRPS research team at the beginning of the revolution.

[9] For footage, see: YouTube, 11 April 2011, at: https://bit.ly/3FVNY3C (accessed 5 January 2022).

[10] *Russia Today Arabic*, 11 April 2011, at: https://bit.ly/3mXAoFw (accessed 5 January 2022).

Jannoud, whose body was mutilated. Opposition supporters in Banyas maintain that Jannoud was a member of the *shabbiha*, that he was involved in the mosque shootings and that his body was not mutilated.[11]

One particularly significant incident took place in the nearby village of Beida. Members of the security forces and the *shabbiha* rounded up villagers in the central square, where they forced them to lie on the floor and filmed themselves beating, stamping and treading on them.[12] The footage was soon broadcast around the world. This incident had a clear sectarian symbolism: the officers had the marked coastal accent characteristic of Alawi villagers and used Alawi-sounding nicknames. Such acts contributed to a sense that the security forces were all criminals, feeding hatred of the *shabbiha* and a desire for revenge. They paved the way for sectarian clashes, albeit limited, in Jablah and Tall Kalakh later that month.

The other major theatre of sectarian tension during this early period was Homs, where the regime's violent response to protests polarized the city along similar lines to Banyas. From April 2011 onwards, the city saw intermittent kidnappings and assassinations in Sunni and Alawi neighbourhoods. These accelerated in late 2011 and became a regular occurrence in neighbourhoods on the border between Sunni and Alawi areas, particularly Khalidiyeh (Sunni), Zahraa (Alawi) and Ekrima (Alawi), before developing into large-scale sectarian atrocities in March 2012. We will discuss these clashes in more detail below.

The regime's strategy produced an armed reaction that ultimately resulted in the complete disappearance of state authority from many regions. In a country where national identity and civil society were weak and the regime was widely perceived as an Alawi one, this was dangerous. Furthermore, regime violence and the expansion of public political action brought a new pattern of popular religiosity into the foreground quite distinct from traditional popular religiosity, characterized by diversity and tolerance.

This new form of religiosity drew heavily on a Salafi vocabulary popularized by religious media, charitable and religious organizations, and long stays in the Gulf, particularly in Saudi Arabia for work, although it was not linked to any particular Salafi movement or institution. It spread quickly in rural regions, which scored precipitously low on every marker of development, poverty, education, health, deprivation and human security.

---

[11] An interview with Bassam Yousef, conducted by the ACRPS research team in Latakia, 21 November 2011.

[12] See: YouTube, 14 April 2011. Archived copy available online: https://bit.ly/3JLuv7O (accessed 5 January 2022).

This turn to religion can be understood in some cases as a reaction to deteriorating living conditions, or a way of emphasizing identity as an expression of pride and as recompensing for lost dignity in the context of the political reality in Syria. It cannot, however, account for the protests in themselves; it explains only the form of consciousness that underpinned the confrontation. The great contradiction in Syria is social and political, but in a complex, multi-confessional society where populist Salafism mixes with social sectarianism – entrenching the social divisions and polarizations that emerge in any great crisis – it gave rise to a sectarian confrontation.[13]

The rhetoric of this new form of popular religiosity helped to create a different understanding of the Syrian struggle in some regions, leading to the emergence of an exclusionary approach whose objectives differed markedly from the general civic and democratic character of the revolution. In Homs, as previously noted, sectarian polarization well predated the revolution. The policies of the governor Mohammed Eyad Ghazal (discussed above) had intensified these feelings, creating a constituency receptive to sectarian rhetoric.

The first incidents of sectarian collective punishment in Homs took place in November 2011. On 1 November, opposition gunmen attacked a passenger bus on the line between Homs City and the Alawi village of Jeb Abbas, killing all aboard.[14] The next day, pro-regime gunmen attacked a factory in Kafr Laha village in Houla, killing eleven workers.[15] On 19 November, opposition gunmen targeted another bus carrying workers near Masharfah village in eastern Homs, leaving eleven people dead and three wounded.[16]

From January 2012, the pattern of sectarian violence shifted from targeting buses and individuals to attacks on families. For the first time, women and children were killed and bodies mutilated. The most horrific attack took place in Karm az-Zaytoun in March 2012. There were similar scenes in Rifai on 11 March, when *shabbiha* militiamen killed thirty-nine locals after opposition fighters withdrew ahead of the army's entry into the district. In both cases bodies were maimed and some victims were burned alive.

---

[13] ACRPS, 'The Recent Bombings in Syria: Do They Change Reality on the Ground?', June 2012, at: https://bit.ly/3GTaYA4 (accessed 5 January 2022).
[14] The exact number of deaths ranged from nine to eleven depending on the source. See: *Reuters Arabic*, 2 November 2011, at: https://reut.rs/32OXCqk (accessed 5 January 2022).
[15] Syrian Observatory for Human Rights, 2 November 2011, at: https://bit.ly/3qMJJAR (accessed 5 January 2022).
[16] *Almadenah News*, 19 November 2011, at: https://bit.ly/3r8jWn9 (accessed 5 January 2022).

II. Crimes by the regime and its henchmen against civilians

On 25 March 2012, the regime gave its assent to the Kofi Annan plan, and a ceasefire came into effect on 12 April. There was an immediate reduction in the number of military operations and armed confrontations and in the level of societal and sectarian violence. Kidnappings and murders declined and there were no new pictures of mutilated bodies. With relative calm restored, community leaders launched fresh efforts to reconcile different parts of society and to secure the release of kidnap victims. But this atmosphere of reconciliation was short-lived. On 25 May, more than 100 people – most of them women and children – were brutally murdered in Taldu (Houla district) by Alawi militiamen. The massacre came on the heels of sectarian incidents against nearby Alawi villages, including an attack on a taxi that left five people dead. It also took place at a time when the army was planning to move into the town, raising suspicions of military involvement. In any case, on 26 May opposition gunmen retaliated, murdering an Alawi family in the nearby village of Shumariya. The authorities blamed al-Qaeda.[17]

The Houla massacre and other such incidents included acts of unusual savagery. The particularly brutal violence of the 'nearby other', which takes place in times of social breakdown and division, reared its ugly head. It justifies collective punishment based on the identity of the victims. In such cases it means little to wax poetic over good neighbourly relations and long histories of coexistence. Histories of coexistence are certainly longer – they are the rule – but the exception is nonetheless atrocious. Physical violence is intimately linked to physical proximity – to the sense of betrayal that accompanies the 'realization' that the denizens of a neighbouring village or city quarter are in fact an enemy.[18]

The Syrian state sheltered the perpetrators of the Houla massacre and refused to blame the army or the local *shabbiha*. This only increased the sense that this was a sectarian struggle, and that the state – so quick to accuse al-Qaeda of murdering a Shiʻi family but unwilling to 'leap to conclusions' when a massacre was committed against an entire town – was itself a sectarian state.

---

[17] Ministry of Interior (Syria), 26 May 2012, at: https://bit.ly/3eRVGQh (accessed 5 January 2022).
[18] It seems to me that there is no solution to this except to forcibly put down sectarian violence in the first instance and then to work on developing a shared identity, equal citizenship and the feeling of participating in a unified national project – not to mention eliminating state-sponsored identity politics. Attempts to deny sectarian violence notwithstanding, the trajectory of the Syrian revolution shows clearly that this is the greatest hurdle to democracy in Syria.

Manifestations of human evil: Echoes of the Lebanese Civil War

The sectarian massacres carried out by *shabbiha* militiamen supported by the army (and vice-versa) during the revolution resemble those seen elsewhere wherever the perpetrators fall under the control of a minoritarian mentality (even if the political group that this mentality represents is not a numerical minority, as in the case of the Shi'i political parties in Iraq) and paramilitary structures have emerged within and outside the state apparatus. Minoritarian militias rely on intimidation and physical violence in order to see off what they see as a 'threatening' majority. (The majority can win the battle if it is not deterred by cruel, collective retaliation.) They tend to respond to any act committed by a member of the opposing camp – the killing of a soldier or the assassination of a leader – with an arbitrary massacre in a location associated with the perpetrators. Those targeted are targeted simply because they belong to a 'rival identity'. A calculated political objective may sometimes lurk behind the apparently unthinking lust for vengeance: population displacement in order to achieve demographic homogeneity, for example, in the Balkans. Fears of ethnic cleansing and the displacement of Sunnis from the coastal region and from Homs, with the purpose of establishing an Alawi state, haunted the popular consciousness in these regions throughout the revolution.

What we are discussing here is something quite out of the ordinary. It is a manifestation of human evil. Massacres do not generally take place 'organically' or unprovoked. They are usually preceded by the murder of one or more individuals from the ruling or strong 'minority', although they are occasionally a spontaneous part of military operations or of the simple build-up of hatred. Of course, survivors have a right to remember the massacre in a way that imagines that there was no reason whatsoever, since they themselves committed no fault, and criminals targeted them solely because of their identity or location. Scholarly research on such phenomena tends to come to quite different conclusions from the victims and the murderers both. The closest analogue in the region, both geographically and culturally, is the Lebanese Civil War, where the Lebanese Forces carried out massacres against Palestinians and Lebanese Muslims.

On 6 December 1975, the militias of Bachir Gemayel's Lebanese Phalange kidnapped some 300 people in Beirut (largely Muslim Lebanese and Palestinians) and murdered no less than seventy others, an event that came to be known as 'Black Saturday'. The attackers targeted Muslim Lebanese workers in the port of Beirut as well as random pedestrians in Muslim neighbourhoods like Bashoura. The Phalange acknowledged responsibility, blaming 'rogue elements' who had 'reacted irresponsibly' to the killing of four of Gemayel's bodyguards.[19] Samir Kassir has noted that Christians did not face similar collective punishments since the Palestinian and leftist parties prevented similar reactions.[20] And while it is true that the national movement and the PLO did not commit massacres, with one exception, the Damour massacre of 1976, the Druze militias also carried out pogroms in Christian villages. In much the same way, Shi'i and Alawi villages in Syria were not subjected to counter-massacres during the Syrian revolution, except the Aqrab massacre in December 2012. Of course, ISIS and the Nusra Front committed mass crimes against Druze and Alawis; this was not, however, an expression of intercommunal sectarianism, but political Salafi jihadism.

Another massacre took place in August 1976 in the Tal al-Zaatar Palestinian refugee camp. Despite a truce between the Lebanese Forces and the PLO, on 13 July 1976, a young Palestinian from the camp killed the Phalangist military commander William Hawi. In response, Gemayel's Lebanese Forces and Camille Chamooun's militias joined forces to launch a decisive attack on the camp.

In the run-up to the massacre, the camp was besieged and subjected to heavy bombardment by the Lebanese Front, particularly the Phalangists. It was denied all supplies, including food, in an attempt to starve out the defenders. The Syrian military saw off all attempts by the national movement and the Palestinians to break the siege,[21] including a counter-siege on Zahle. The camp was left to the mercy of the militias until it fell on 12 August. Phalangist militiamen then poured into the camp and carried out a horrifying massacre – the first massacre of Palestinians by other Arabs. Although the Phalangists had promised the camp's defenders safe passage and guaranteed the safety of its civilian inhabitants, more than 3,000 Palestinians were killed, most of them in on-the-spot shootings that targeted whole families.[22] The Tal al-Zaatar massacre established a Lebanese 'model': siege and bombardment, assault, and atrocities against civilians.

Finally, the events of Sabra and Shatila represent perhaps the most horrendous, most cowardly of massacres. On this occasion, there were no military confrontations: the PLO had withdrawn from Beirut two weeks earlier, and there were only a few individual fighters left to protect the

---

[19] Yezid Sayigh, *Armed Struggle and the Search for State: The Palestinian National Movement, 1949–1993* (Oxford: Institute for Palestine Studies, 1997), 371–2.
[20] Samir Kassir, *The Lebanon War: From National Strife to Regional Struggle, 1975–1982* [Arabic], trans. Salim Anturi (Beirut: Al-Nahar Publishing, 2007), 134.
[21] Although Tall az-Zaatar was militarily indefensible, the Syrians facilitated the taking of the camp by keeping Palestinian Liberation Organization (PLO) forces busy defending positions along a long line of engagement.
[22] Sayigh, 571–2.

civilians. Nonetheless, after a bomb explosion at the Phalange headquarters left Bashir Gemayel and thirty others dead, Elie Hobeika (the Lebanese Forces' head of political security) and Ariel Sharon (the Israeli defence minister) agreed that the best response would be to carry out a pre-arranged plan to enter the Palestinian camps and wipe out the 'saboteurs'. The massacre began on 16 September 1982 and lasted for three days. According to the most comprehensive study on the massacre,[23] it left 3,500 Palestinians dead, including women – some of them pregnant – and children. Many were executed and their bodies mutilated in scenes reminiscent of Tal al-Zaatar.[24]

III. Sectarian massacres committed in Syria from the beginning of the revolution until 2013

Throughout 2012 and through to the publication of this book, the regime pounded villages and cities from the ground and from the air, leaving thousands of civilians dead. But what we are interested in here is the question of 'up-close' massacres carried out against civilians in their own neighbourhoods, in the course of militia incursions or after those neighbourhoods fell to the army. I have already discussed some of these tragic incidents, but in the rest of this section we will consider other examples in more detail.

Karm az-Zaytoun (9–11 March 2012): In early September 2011, a wave of sectarian crimes swept over the city of Homs: families were driven out of their homes, buses were attacked and individuals were kidnapped or assassinated. These crimes opened the door to even more serious atrocities, with the first taking place in Karm az-Zaytoun in March 2012. Several sectarian incidents had taken place in the run-up to the massacre. On 26 January, following shelling of Sunni-majority areas, opposition gunmen attacked the Alawi-majority neighbourhoods of Naziheen, Wadi al-Dhahab and Zahraa with RPG rounds, leaving four people dead (including two women) and around twenty injured.[25] On the same day, fourteen people –

---

[23] Bayan Nwaihed al-Hut, *Sabra and Shatila, September 1982* [Arabic] (Beirut: Institute for Palestine Studies, 2003), 557. Bayan Nwaihed Al-Hut drew on statistics, documentary evidence, recordings, interviews, and other methods to put together a comprehensive study of the massacre. It is our hope that future researchers will conduct similar studies on the events in Syria. We have attempted to be as accurate as possible here, but we have not been able to give each individual case the time and space it deserves.

[24] Deeb, 589.

[25] A virtual interview via Skype with a resident of the Zahraa (one of the three Alawi-majority neighbourhoods attacked) who wishes to remain anonymous, conducted by the ACRPS research team, 27 January 2012.

including eight children – were killed in a retaliation attack on Karm az-Zaytoun by gunmen from the Alawi-majority neighbourhoods.[26] Opposition fighters responded by murdering two men, five women and five children from a Shi'i family (the Bahadils) in the same area.[27] These incidents fomented hatred and a desire to get revenge on the 'nearby other' whenever the opportunity presented itself – as it did, to one side, when the army launched a successful offensive on the neighbourhood between 9 and 11 March 2012, leading to the withdrawal of opposition fighters. With the operation over, the neighbourhood was attacked by militiamen, most of them belonging to the Halloul family (residents of Alawi-majority Ekrima). The attackers killed at least forty-seven people, most of them women and children, and desecrated the bodies. The Syrian Network for Human Rights (SNHR) recorded at least 224 deaths during the military operation in the neighbourhood.

These killings were not part of an armed confrontation or a specific act of vengeance. There were no immediate reasons for the attack. The mutilation of corpses and the use of bladed weapons (knives and machetes) added a criminal dimension to the sectarian massacre. Although the locals knew the names of the perpetrators, the government refused to even question them, thus indicating that they would turn a blind eye to such actions, if not encourage them actively. Indeed, the persistence of such sectarian incidents can be attributed in part to the regime's media policy. Media outlets close to the regime consistently attributed them to 'terrorist groups' or other similar bogeymen. In the case of Karm az-Zaytoun it blamed 'Takfiris' from the Qarabees neighbourhood, who it claimed had killed the victims for being religiously moderate and refusing to confront the security forces.

Rifai (21 March 2012): The day after the Karm az-Zaytoun massacre, opposition gunmen responded by targeting Alawi families in Karm al-Lawz, killing fifteen people (including children).[28] In response, militiamen took the opportunity presented by the army offensive on the Rifai neighbourhood to carry out a repeat of Karm az-Zaytoun, flooding into the neighbourhood in the army's wake to carry out atrocities similar to those seen elsewhere. The General Commission of the Syrian Revolution counted thirty-nine bodies in Rifai with mutilated faces or torsos and accused *shabbiha* from the Alawi neighbourhoods of responsibility.

---

[26] *Al Ahram*, 27 January 2012, at: https://bit.ly/3HC1ppL (accessed 5 January 2022).
[27] An interview with Muhammad Saleh, conducted by the ACRPS research team in Latakia, 30 November 2011.
[28] Ibid.

Qubayr/Maarzaf (6 June 2012): This massacre took place alongside a large military operation in the areas to the north and west of Hama. The regular units leading this operation were accompanied by Alawi *shabbiha* militiamen from the nearby village of Aslieh. On 6 June, these militiamen killed 88 people in the village of Qubayr in Maarzaf district, including 22 children and around 22 women. Victims were shot or stabbed or set on fire, with the charred remains of at least eight people found in the area. As in other cases, the massacre was a reaction to other sectarian incidents. In March, five Alawis from Aslieh had been killed by opposition gunmen, and a teacher was kidnapped on the charge that her villager had been part of army operations in the neighbouring village of Halfaya. Several other sectarian clashes had followed involving gunmen from Maarzaf. The violent behaviour of the Aslieh residents was part of a broader context of tit-for-tat attacks.

Treismeh (12 July 2012): In July 2012 the army occupied the village of Treismeh, Hama governorate, after days of shelling. Soldiers and members of the *shabbiha* (most of them from nearby Sefsaf) went on to kill more than a hundred locals, including sixty-seven non-combatants. This time there was no obvious immediate reason for the massacre: the military operation was directed against a meeting of FSA commanders.

Shammas: Shammas in Homs suffered two massacres. The first took place on 13 May 2012, when Alawi gunmen killed twenty-five locals (including the imam of a mosque) despite the fact that there had been no military or security operations in the area. This attack was likely a reaction to the dumping of bodies on roads and in nearby woodlands as well as occasionally in Homs itself. The second massacre took place on 11 August 2012, after the army and *shabbiha* assaulted the neighbourhood, clashing with rebels. Regime forces rounded up 350 locals and abused them in the central square. According to SNHR, twenty-two were then killed extra judicially.

Thiyabiyeh (26 September 2012): In September 2012 the Damascus periphery town of Thiyabiyehwas subjected to heavy artillery fire coupled with raids on homes and killings carried out by Shi'i and Alawi militias around Sayyeda Zeinab. As clashes edged closer to the Sayyeda Zeinab shrine – a site of great religious significance to Shi'is in particular – Syrian and non-Syrian Shi'i militiamen descended on nearby Thiyabiyeh to support the army's offensive against the village, where they executed around seventy people according to the SNHR account. Another massacre took place on 18 February 2013, after a mortar shell fell on the shrine. On that occasion over 100 people were killed, most of them women and children.

Jdidet al-Fadl (15 April 2013):[29] On 15 April 2013, clashes took place between regime forces and the armed opposition near one of the checkpoints around the town of Jdidet al-Fadl in the Damascus Rural governorate. The next day, soldiers surrounded the town on all sides and prevented anyone from entering or exiting, cutting off electricity and communications as the army often does during operations. Snipers were also deployed to tighten the siege. After the army entered the village later that day, they were joined by *shabbiha* militiamen from Sumariya and Masakin al-Shirkah, who, according to SNHR, killed at least 191 people (17 armed men and 174 civilians), with dozens of others unaccounted for.

Beida and Ras al-Naba' (2–4 May 2013): In early May 2013 regime forces in Banyas captured a wanted individual who told them that his comrades

---

[29] The massacres carried out in the Damascus periphery are too numerous to be fully documented in a single book and are best investigated by legal specialists. I have not discussed these massacres here. Nor have I looked at massacres that took place after, or during, combat operations, although combat operations emphatically do not justify shelling civilians. Killing civilians is a war crime. After the first 'liberated cities' were declared in az-Zabdani and Duma, the army launched major operations in many parts of the Damascus Rural governorate, especially in the Eastern Ghouta. During these operations, the regime carried out several massacres, with varying numbers of victims.

Hammouriyah massacre: On 20 February 2013, military aircrafts bombed Hammouriyah, killing 52 people, including five children and two women, and injuring 75 people, according to the Syrian Network for Human Rights (SNHR), at: https://bit.ly/3aQGhRv (accessed 14 June 2022). Following the attack, activists documented the scenes of dead victims and others who had been burned. See: YouTube, 21 February 2013, at: https://bit.ly/3MKeG1v (accessed 14 June 2022).

Zamalka massacre: On 30 June 2012, the Syrian security forces and the *shabbiha* entered Zamalka, killing Abd al-Hadi al-Halabi. On the same day, 4,000 local residents joined his funeral procession. During the procession, a missile that the locals believe was fired from a helicopter landed in the midst of the crowd, causing a large explosion. Within seconds, 72 of the attendees were dead, while 400 others were wounded according to the documentation of the SNHR. To see the moment that the missile hit, see: YouTube, 30 June 2012. Archived copy available online: https://bit.ly/3MJ60sg (accessed 12 June 2022).

Madamiyet Elsham: The military carried out massacres and arbitrary executions in the aftermath of every military operation in this area. On 28 July 2012, the security forces executed the entire Rajab family and members of the Jibb and Mansour families. See: YouTube, 29 July 2012, at: https://bit.ly/3eX5s3q (accessed 5 January 2022). Also, on 6 August 2012, the *shabbiha* executed seven young men from Mu'adamiyah and disfigured their bodies. See: YouTube, 6 August 2012, at: https://bit.ly/3pW2JxH (accessed 5 January 2022).

Artuz al-Balad: The army raided Artuz al-Balad on 1 August 2012. According to the Federation of Coordination Committees, activists subsequently documented 47 deaths, while locals estimate that 72 people were killed, some shot, others stabbed or hacked to death by the *shabbiha*.

Darayya: The most horrific of all the massacres around Damascus. On 25 August, after a ground assault had failed to retake the town due to fierce local resistance, regime forces at Mazzeh Airfield and other positions around Damascus sent hundreds of missiles raining down on Darayya; 300 people were killed, most of them women and children.

were hiding in Beida. The army sent soldiers into the village to arrest them, resulting in a firefight. Reinforcements were sent in and the village cleared of armed opposition. The army then withdrew, leaving Beida and neighbouring Ras al-Naba' at the mercy of sectarian militiamen. These militiamen then proceeded to murder 459 people, including 92 children and 71 women, the majority of them cut down with bladed weapons or burned alive.

Kherbet Elsawda (15 May 2013): In mid-May 2013, during clashes in Houla district, Homs governorate, the army and the *shabbiha* entered the village of Kherbet Elsawda and stabbed or shot eighteen people.

Basateen al-Wa'r (18 May 2013): The Basateen al-Wa'r neighbourhood in Homs housed more than 500,000 displaced Syrians who had fled Old Homs and nearby villages. On 18 May, following clashes with opposition fighters, regime forces at the military academy began shelling the neighbourhood. Shortly thereafter, sectarian militiamen entered and murdered seventeen people with knives and machetes. Homs locals interviewed by the ACRPS team maintained that this 'Alawi attack' was intended to drive out the people of the neighbourhood and take it over.

9

Between revolutionary violence and remnants from previous eras

This chapter make distinctions between different manifestations of violence in Syria. It differentiates political from social violence and looks at instances where they mix. It also distinguishes between violence employed during the revolution and before it, when patterns of violence became embedded in Syria's social fabric (for example, *the shabbiha*). Indeed, the years preceding the revolution saw a sharp rise in crime. This chapter examines as well the different groups employing violence in Syria, including global jihadis,[1] Salafis that were not global jihadis, and other groups of indeterminate ideology that were created following the militarization of the revolution (al-Farouq Battalions, for example). Lastly, I look at the spike in crime on the edges of the revolution, which came with the breakdown of public order and a weakened civil society.

Although societal and political violence are distinct phenomena, in times of instability and crises, such as revolutions, they overlap. Some forms of political violence seem to draw on the dynamics of societal violence, especially when propelled by social divisions or social loyalties. Similarly, societal violence may be cloaked in political objectives. In Syria's case one must thus distinguish between the violence of an armed revolution and the societal and political violence that intersected with it, creating the impression that the revolution entailed more serious excesses than those that resulted from it directly. It should also be noted that most of the rebels who took up arms had no training in the responsibility that comes with carrying weapons. The majority of these fighters came from constituencies that felt direct harm from despotism, and they joined the revolution with

---

[1] ISIS was not yet active in Syria as this book was sent to publication in 2013. The dispute between what was revealed to be the mother organization and its branch in Syria (Nusra Front) was just beginning: ISIS decided to act directly in Syria and the two organizations became enemies. I subsequently wrote a book on ISIS, published in 2018. See Azmi Bishara, *The Islamic State Organization 'ISIL': A General Framework and Practical Contribution to Understanding the Phenomenon* [Arabic] (Beirut and Doha: ACRPS, 2018).

the aim of self-defence or liberation – often both. Among the revolutionaries was also an ideologically motivated minority with political objectives unrelated to the goals of the revolution, in addition to another, criminal minority, or people who found in the revolution an opportunity to take up arms – a kind of legitimized criminal activity.

By the beginning of 2012, violence began to increase markedly, attracting much attention in the public sphere and in the media. Certain forms of criminal violence, of course, had been commonplace even before the revolution, often with the connivance of state organs that made use of criminal bands in protection rackets or in smuggling. The *shabbiha* were engaged in constant criminality, with the security agencies either turning a blind eye or getting directly involved. The authorities also encouraged communal antagonisms as a means of controlling society: rivalries between Bedouins and Druze in As-Sweida, Ismailis and Alawis in Qadmous and Masyaf, and Kurds and Arabs in Quamishli and al-Hasakeh, for example, not to mention the regular clashes between crime families in Aleppo (Berri-Hamideh, Ghasasneh-Baqara, Mardil-Arab, Batoush-Uqaidat).[2] But with the check imposed by the state gone, old social dynamics were also beginning to find new expression, alongside other, new dynamics, of the kind that typically emerge in revolutionary times, and which could no longer be ignored.

The regime and the opposition differed both in their attitude to violence and how they exploited incidents of violence politically. Regime media (state-owned and private) consistently tried to link the popular revolution to any act of violence, whatever its background (criminal, jihadi or sectarian). The opposition, on the other hand, always blamed the regime for any violent act, even when this meant adopting conspiracy theories. They were unwilling or unable to address these challenges directly by establishing a genuine political leadership or designing a clear national strategy to confront them. And the unprecedented violence meted out by the regime made it easier to accuse it of responsibility for violent acts even on those occasions when it was not involved.

No analysis of the violence intrinsic to the Syrian revolution can ignore the basic truth of the regime's violence against its own people. Let there be no doubt that this violence was all-encompassing and restricted neither by laws nor norms. The struggle in Syria became an armed conflict because the regime pursued a strategy of armed repression of civil protests during the first year. It is not unusual for violent tendencies to develop on the periphery of armed conflicts, especially when the people as a whole arm

---

[2] Aziz Tabsi, 'The *Shabbiha* Phenomenon: Early Indices of the Decline of the Military Clique' [Arabic], *Damascus Journal* (London), no. 1 (March 2013), 59.

themselves (including the most marginalized sections of society). But the situation was made even more complex by the rebels' failure, except in few cases, to set up a joint security apparatus capable of maintaining public order in the face of abuses. In fact, the rebels were barely able to organize their own self-defence, while the armed factions that appeared later did not turn into a liberation army capable of maintaining order, even those of them that thought in terms of liberation. The factions had contradictory understandings of order. Some of them maintained public order in their regions fairly well; others did the same but in addition used violence to impose their ideology, while still others bred warlords that were embroiled in criminal acts themselves.

In the very first months of the revolution the security forces' dogged pursuit of a policy of violent repression against peaceful demonstrations and protests engendered new forms of violence in response, most of them defensive: young people fighting back against humiliation and brutalization. Eventually some of these young people took up arms and formed armed battalions made up of civilian volunteers and defecting soldiers, whose purpose was to protect themselves and their communities. Thus, as previously discussed, 'self-defence' became the justification for taking up arms – a transition that was aided by the defection of soldiers and officers from the army to the ranks of the revolution.

As the confrontation with the regime escalated, organized armed factions emerged and state authority collapsed across large parts of the country. This led to the emergence of various other forms of violence, aggravated by the weakness of civil society and feeble mechanisms of social control: crimes, sectarian incidents, and abuses carried out by armed men claiming affiliation with the FSA. Other violent phenomena were the work of jihadis who fought in Iraq and Afghanistan and already established jihadi groups that pursued their war against the regime. They did not join the revolution, but rather took advantage of it.

I. Jihadi violence

Jihadi violence in Syria predates the revolution and is not specific to it. It inserted itself into the trajectory of a peaceful, civil revolution that met with violent repression. The first indicators of its presence came with the suicide and car bombings of late December 2011 in Damascus, which continued sporadically thereafter. Armed struggle began to spread rapidly across the country, however, in the second half of 2012.

The Syrian revolution was a quest for freedom and dignity. From its earliest days it was inclusive and patriotic. It was not a protest against the regime's ideology or its foreign policy – it was a civic popular uprising giving voice to popular anger. It was this that was at the heart of the protests' geographic expansion and its ability to draw in ever broader sections of society. On the periphery of the protest movement, however, a kind of extremist religious thought – which well predated the revolution – found a niche for itself. This extremist thought came with its own set of ideological tenets and intellectual frames of reference. And in the white heat of revolution, during the phase of militarization and mobilization, they evolved.

Many factors explain the emergence of Salafi popular religiosity in marginalized areas of Syria: labour migration to Saudi Arabia; susceptibility to the sectarian tone of Salafi preachers; the specifically non-political form of Salafi religiosity, which emphasizes identity difference and implies a sense of chosenness and supremacy, making it easy and cost-free for the marginalized to adopt (non-political Salafism was easily politicized by jihadi Salafi groups during the revolution); and the spread of religious institutes, originally intended to produce obedient religious civil servants that would act as the instruments of authoritarianism within the religious sphere. But the regime could not control them.

The clerical establishment's relationship with the regime had its ups and downs, but it did not rely on the regime financially. Instead, it was financed by society, especially merchants, and was also allowed to receive contributions for its charities from the Gulf states. The 'independent' clergy benefited from economic liberalization twice over: once because the merchants who contributed to religious charity flourished, and again because these charities were encouraged to expand their activity due to the growing social need as state services were curtailed.

There were clergymen who were just another of the Ba'th Party's 'popular organizations', whose role was to regulate the religious domain just as the Workers' Federation did with respect to labour and the Farmers' Federation with respect to agriculture. However, this was not true for the mainstream clergy.[3] The state could not control the mood and the discourse neither in the Shari'a institutes nor in the Qur'an circles in the mosques. Known as 'institutes for the memorization of the Qur'an', these circles carried the name of al-Assad to associate it with the Qur'an after the confrontation with the Muslim Brotherhood, but were not run by the state.[4]

---

[3] Due to ideological reasons and historical circumstances that cannot be analysed here, the Ba'th regime did not turn the religious establishment into a state institution, unlike other Arab countries and unlike the Turkish secular model. For more details, see: Pierret, *Religion and State in Syria*, 17–22.

[4] Ibid., 71–2.

The graduates of these institutes, however – most of whom came from rural backgrounds and impoverished villages – found that the clerical establishment was a world of competing power centres in which jobs were a matter of patronage. Many were simply shut out of the upper reaches and consigned to poorly paid local jobs as preachers or officiants. The great inequalities within the establishment thus produced a widespread class of 'junior sheikhs' who flocked to the revolutionary banner. Some of these clerics quickly took up the task of providing religious guidance to the armed factions, forming the backbone of the religious courts that sprouted up in the 'liberated regions'.

Some graduates of the institutes showed extremist proclivities long before the revolution, particularly in the aftermath of the 2003 US invasion of Iraq. They avoided confronting the regime in part because it tolerated their religious and organizational activities so long as they were directed at the US occupation. In fact, the Syrian authorities actively helped Salafi fighters from groups like Suqur al-Qaʿqaʿ to cross the Iraqi border, as well as acting as a transit hub for Salafi jihadis from other Arab countries. But within Syria itself, the extremist phenomenon remained limited to a handful of marginalized rural towns. And after the government reached an understanding with the US regarding Iraq in 2007, it began a crackdown on Salafi jihadi organizations within its borders. These currents considered the revolution just a revolt against a common enemy: the regime. But their methods and their goals differed from the bulk of the revolutionary movement, especially regarding their vision of an Islamic state in Syria. They were early advocates of armed action, maintaining that peaceful demonstrations would not bring down the regime.

The main public face of the Salafi jihadis in Syria has been the Nusra Front. There were already similar groups in the country before the revolution, largely veterans of the jihad in Iraq, as well as a spectrum of Palestinian and other Arab jihadis. Salafis were involved in the earliest protests in Jabal az-Zawiya and the countryside around Aleppo (particularly Andan, Tall Refaat and to a lesser extent Mareʿ). But in part because of the anti-revolutionary media's interest in this particular group and in part because of a widespread belief, at the beginning of the revolution, that it was a regime puppet,[5] the Nusra Front attracted the most attention. Later it attracted the admiration of youth because of its daring and consistent armed actions. Moreover, the Nusra Front claimed responsibility for the

---

[5] Some commentators believe that the Nusra Front was an unintended product of the regime's support for jihadis in Iraq. Elizabeth O'Bagy, 'Jihad in Syria', *Middle East Security Report*, no. 6, Institute for the Study of War, September 2012, 33. However, the political opposition, both the SNC and SOC, found it easier (at least in the beginning) to shed doubt on the Nusra Front by considering it a part of a plot by the regime to associate the revolution with terrorism. Aron Lund, 'Syrian Jihadism', 29–30. The regime of course claimed that the Nusra Front (and ISIS) were US creations.

majority of suicide bombings and car bombings during the revolution, a tactic it seems to have adopted because of a lack of sufficient fighters to confront the regime directly during its earliest days, before it attracted fighters from abroad and all over Syria.[6] The group was also responsible for the execution of some thirteen security officers in Deir ez-Zor on 4 June 2012 after they were captured, echoing the systematic violence meted out by the regime.[7]

Other jihadi battalions also emerged. Some fought under the banner of the FSA while maintaining their own hierarchies, names, and political and ideological frames of reference. The rulings of religious courts affiliated with these factions drove a rise in the number of field executions like the killing of the Berri family *shabbiha* on 1 August 2012 and of twenty soldiers captured during the takeover of the Hananu army base on 10 September 2012. This fed a growing fear of the unregulated spread of weapons and paramilitary groups and a sense that the armed groups' behaviour was beginning to resemble that of the regime.

Nusra-style jihadi violence was one of the main threats to both the civic and the armed revolution, especially with the use of car and suicide bombings. For those affiliated with such groups, bombing the headquarters of the security agencies has moral and symbolic value: it shows their ability to target the very heart of the regime. But the concrete outcome of these operations was the death of dozens of civilians who happened to be in the wrong place at the wrong time. The suicide bombing in As-Salamiyeh on 21 January 2013, for which the Nusra Front claimed responsibility,[8] shows the grave material and moral consequences of this type of attack. Although the bombing targeted the party branch office, it left some twenty-five civilians dead. Moreover, since As-Salamiyeh is a largely Ismaili city – one

---

[6] A number of suicide bombings occurred in 2011-2012: at the State Security HQ in Kafr Sousa and the Regional Security branch office near al-Baramika (23 December 2011); in the Midan neighborhood (6 Januar 2021); at the Air Force Intelligence and Criminal Security Directorate HQ in Damascus (17 March 2012); at the Political Security Directorate in Aleppo (18 March 2012); in the Qazzaz district (10 May 2012); and in a residential area of Ghazi neighborhood, Deir ez-Zor (19 May 2012).

[7] The statement issued at the time read: 'God has permitted the lions of the eastern region in Deir ez-Zor to capture a group of vermin belonging to the security agencies and the *shabbiha*. [The detainees] were interrogated and a description of their crimes and a list of their shameful acts were extracted from them, and their just punishment [execution] was carried out.' See: *Alriyadh*, 5 June 2012, at: https://bit.ly/3ISUSHN (accessed 1 February 2022).

[8] Statement 507 from the Nusra Front: 'At precisely 7.28 on the evening of Monday, 21 January 2013, the martyr and hero Abu Abdallah al-Jabbar al-Najdi, one of the heroes of the Nusra Front in Homs, detonated an Isuzu truck laden with 3.5 tonnes of explosives in one of the most heavily fortified security compounds of As-Salamiyeh region. The hero managed to reach his target, relying on God, and propelled by a desire for revenge against those infidels who have persecuted our people in Homs and committed the most horrendous massacres against the Muslims of Homs. See: *Moheb Jabhat al-Nusra*, 30 March 2013, at: https://bit.ly/34splNO (accessed 1 February 2022).

which had been closely involved in the revolution from the very beginning, contributing to its inclusive character – the regime and its supporters were able to use it as evidence that the revolution was a sectarian uprising representing only the Sunni population. Suicide and car bombings in Mazra'a (21 February 2013) and al-Sab' Bahrat Square (8 April 2013) in Damascus had similarly high civilian death tolls.

The jihadi groups consider civilian deaths, whether in Damascus, Aleppo, Deir ez-Zor, or As-Salamiyeh, as a trifling matter when compared to the 'greater end', which in some cases is little more than a sacrifice if they are Sunnis or retribution if they belong to other confessional communities. Just as the regime subordinates all concerns to the goal of remaining in power, at any cost, these groups subordinate them to their understanding of religion. In both case ideology and/or power are substitutes for moral judgement. In their willingness to sacrifice civilians, they resemble the regime, although we must not forget that the sheer scale of the regime's violence and the number of its victims dwarf those of jihadi movements. Their behaviour brought terror to the daily lives of citizens: on public transportation, at large gatherings, even when visiting government buildings. This general state of fear was reminiscent of bombings in post-occupation Iraq, whose spectre had done much to quiet the Syrian political mood after 2003 and make Syrians willing to prioritize stability over all else, including public probity and democracy. Moreover, it made it possible for the regime to present the revolution as the work of Takfiri groups, doing untold damage to the revolution's international and domestic image and to its actual and potential social base.

Nonetheless, despite initial popular hostility to these groups, they gradually won acceptance in many pro-revolutionary circles. This shift did not take place in a vacuum. It was the result of a number of important factors.[9] The apparent failure of peaceful struggle to achieve the revolution's aims gave credence to jihadi claims that it had always been futile and that armed struggle was the only answer. Equally, as foreign military intervention (the Libyan option) seemed increasingly unlikely and the civil uprising ebbed, the jihadis continued to exhaust the regime. Extremist groups had their own weapons and their own financial support networks (rarely and only indirectly states or official bodies that can be regulated or made accountable internationally). Finally, the spread of sectarian discourse within much of the opposition, in reaction to repeated sectarian massacres

---

[9] International Crisis Group, 'Tentative Jihad'.

carried out by the regime and its militias, meant that reservations about jihadi rhetoric began to fade somewhat.

As the revolution drew on, a political mood began to emerge that framed hostility to dictatorship in distinctly non-democratic language. Even secular businessmen who felt that they had been harmed by the security regime's control over the economy expressed their grievances in sectarian terms.

The Salafi jihadi presence grew stronger. Citizens who had taken up arms as individuals or as part of popular battalions were drawn into these groups, whose regular funding and sophisticated armament were the envy of other FSA groups.

It would not be possible here to make an exhaustive list of all jihadi battalions and factions in Syria, but they can be subdivided into a few groups.

1. al-Qaeda-inspired global jihadi salafis (Nusra Front)

The most notable of these groups was the Nusra Front, which appeared in late January 2012 and claimed responsibility for a string of suicide bombings. The Nusra Front established several 'emirates' in Syria, each headed by a commander ('emir') and overseeing several religious courts. At first it avoided mixing with FSA battalions; it believed that overthrowing the regime was only half the battle and the ultimate aim was to establish an Islamic state rooted in the Sunna and the practice of the 'righteous forebears' (*al-salaf al-salih*). The Nusra Front was one of the best organized jihadi groups, benefiting from a solid leadership and organizational hierarchy that coordinated its activities nationwide. Led by Abu Muhammad al-Julani, known by his followers as 'the conqueror', it set out its ideological vision in a manifesto, *Strategy for the Regional War in Syria*,[10] written by al-Qaeda member Abdallah Bin Muhammad. This vision has three main aspects.

The first of these is flexibility in positioning and movement. For the Nusra Front, Syria represents a 'long-term theatre of combat with far-reaching influence', requiring the use of autonomous forces capable of adapting to the circumstances of the battle. The success of this approach is demonstrated by the Nusra Front's expansion in Syria. It began with a small number of individuals who examined local environments where the

---

[10] Interviews with fighters and activists in Idleb, conducted by the ACRPS research team, claimed that 'this manifesto is distributed to all members of the Nusra Front in the region. It sums up the strategy and beliefs of the Nusra Front and is available on the internet'.

organization could set up shop. Spots near the Iraqi border like Deir ez-Zor and areas north of Aleppo and in nearby areas of Idleb were selected for their poverty and the popularity of modes of Salafi religiosity, as well as their proximity to the Turkish border. It then began to introduce a limited number of fighters, who were immediately deployed to the most dangerous parts of the front, where they won the acceptance and even the support of the revolutionaries because of their obvious courage.

As the flow of Arab and foreign fighters increased, the Nusra Front reproduced this model in other cities that it identified as receptive to or unlikely to oppose a jihadi organization. Before the revolution, Syria had been a staging ground for jihadi movements. During the revolution, it became a theatre of the 'global' Islamist jihad. This transformation did not happen overnight but was rather a gradual evolution. Eventually, in a manner akin to the international brigades of the Spanish Civil War, al-Qaeda supporters began joining the fight in significant numbers. Syrians were also allowed to join and flocked to the Nusra Front banner in their dozens – some because of ideological sympathies and others because of the group's ready access to weapons.

Another important part of the 'flexibility' strategy was to avoid concentrating forces in densely populated civilian neighbourhoods that could easily be besieged by regime forces.[11] This allowed the Nusra Front to avoid clashes with civilians and FSA battalions, who it suspected would turn on it as soon as they were able to strike a deal with foreign backers.[12] Once it had sufficient boots on the ground, the Nusra Front laid siege to the regime's fortified military bases: the 46th Regiment Barracks, the Sheikh Salman base and the Infantry School in Aleppo. In seizing these bases, it acquired large quantities of ammunition and equipment without recourse to foreign funding. It also took over several border crossings, giving it control over supply lines; reports suggest that it distributed weapons to various battalions with different ideological or political programmes. The combination of all these factors won the Nusra Front significant sympathy and even support. Not a single military organization on the ground expressed its support for the US decision, in December 2012, to designate it a terrorist organization. Even though the Nusra Front denounced the National Coalition for Syrian Revolutionary and Opposition Forces (SOC) (which became the major, internationally recognized political organization of the opposition) as a 'conspiratorial

---

[11] As it is obvious in the Idleb district, the Nusra Front did not abide by this strategic principle.
[12] *al-Hayat*, 8 January 2013. Archived copy available online: https://bit.ly/3ueM5vR (accessed 1 February 2022).

project', the coalition itself unilaterally condemned the Nusra Front's blacklisting.

The second major principle of the Nusra Front's strategy is to have a clear and specific functional role. In the first instance, this role should be military, because 'he who holds power on the ground will, consequently, hold all other forms of power'. This is a lesson learned from al-Qaeda's failed state-building experiment in Iraq of the early 2000s, which saw it prematurely setting up ministries and appointing officials before being crushed militarily. Although the Nusra Front established control over certain neighbourhoods in Aleppo, necessitating some kind of administration, this administration remained extremely limited because the front feared clashes with locals over the implementation of Shari'a.[13]

The third major principle is the 'continuation of the struggle', which is to say that there are many secondary goals preceding the establishment of an Islamic state that require persistent jihad. The Nusra Front had a long list of targets in Syria, from the 'Nusairi' (Alawi) regime through to the 'Zionist enemy' and ultimately any alternative regime incompatible with the beliefs of al-Qaeda. Julani himself said as much in public, calling on 'the people of Syria' not to replace the existing regime with a 'Western' alternative.

Members of the Nusra Front first entered Syria from Iraq in late 2011. Its founding statement, read out by Julani in a video clip, is dated 24 January 2012, although it was only published on the al-Qaeda-affiliated al-Manara website on 25 May.[14] Julani called on Syrians to gather around the banner of 'there is no God but God', which represents 'real change'. Moreover, he condemned calls for foreign intervention by the 'Western enemy', the Turkish government ('a cudgel in America's hand') or even the Arab League (a doomed project). According to Julani, the Nusra Front was created so that Syrians would not have to rely on 'foreigners' (despite its own international flavour). And while he was quick to add that the jihad in Syria was a kind of resistance against the Iranian 'Safavid' project, he did not mention the Nusra Front's affiliation with al-Qaeda.

In its early days, according to a list published on al-Manara, the organization had only a few dozen fighters distributed across a number of fronts, all of them brought in from Iraq. In 2012 a number of Syrian fighters joined the group, but there were steep requirements for membership. Those wishing to join had to undergo multiple examinations and a religious instruction course prior to their induction. Fighters also had to pass a rigorous set of hurdles in order to be trained and prepared before being sent

---

[13] Ibid. This strategy was opposed to the ISIS strategy, but the Nusra Front ended up establishing an emirate in Idleb when the area became its last redoubt.
[14] For this statement, see: Daily Motion, at: https://bit.ly/3Hn9G14 (accessed 2 February 2022).

to the frontlines. The Nusra Front was distinguished by its iron discipline: a regional commander distributed local fighters into smaller groups whose leaders were accountable for their performance. This left only a small margin for improvisation or arbitrary actions.[15]

As much as possible, the Nusra Front avoided 'camping' on the front lines, preferring to return to camps on the outskirts of towns and cities and avoid contact with locals (even during aid work and service provision), although it was willing to take part in long sieges when the target location contained weapons depots or significant spoils, as was the case with Khan Tuman in Aleppo.[16] In Aleppo City itself, the Nusra Front kept its distance from local military formations (the Tawhid and Haqq Brigades, for example, and the RMC). It took control of oil fields in Deir ez-Zor, fighting off FSA competitors, particularly al-Farouq Battalion, in order to secure its grip.

Hassan Abu Haniyeh estimated the number of Nusra Front fighters in Syria, as of early 2013, at 4,000, including 1,500 Syrians.[17] Table 9.1, based on various sources, demonstrates the number of Syrian Nusra Front Fighters comprising more than a third of the total number of fighters from other nationalities as of early 2013. At any rate, our estimates and those of researchers focusing on Islamist movements suggest that the numbers given in the media at time were highly exaggerated.

Table 9.1 Nusra Front Fighters by Nationality

Nationality	Number	Nationality	Number
Syrian	1200	Chechen	40
Saudi Arabian	380	Turkish	40
Jordanian	350	Afghan	35
Iraqi	330	Moroccan	30
Lebanese	250	Sudanese	25
Yemeni	180	Uzbek	25
Palestinian	150	American	20
Egyptian	100	Tajik	20
Tunisian	90	European	20
Algerian	45	Rest of the World	20

Source: The numbers in the table are from early 2013, based on various sources, including testimonies, media sources and US government estimates.

---

[15] Interviews with a number of frontline fighters in the Nusra Front, including Abd al-Rahman al-Mustafa in Eastern Ghouta, Samir Ahmad in the Yarmuk Camp, Abd al-Rahman Bakkar in Aleppo, Mohammad Hajj Bakri in the Hama countryside, and Abu al-Baraa in Ma'arrat An-Nu'man, conducted by the ACRPS research team.

[16] For scenes of the weapons obtained by the fighters on Khan Tuman, see: YouTube, 16 December 2012, at: https://bit.ly/3L368mY (accessed 1 February 2022).

[17] Al Jazeera, 11 March 2013, at: https://bit.ly/3HqQtM8 (accessed 1 February 2022).

Splits within the Nusra Front

The Nusra Front was affiliated with al-Qaeda. However, throughout 2012 the organization consistently avoided acknowledging this fact in any of its published statements. It only recognized this fact in 2013, after a major split within its ranks.

On 9 April 2013, Abu Bakr al-Baghdadi, the self-proclaimed emir of the Islamic State of Iraq (ISI), released a video in which he announced the merger of the Nusra Front with his organization to create an 'Islamic State in Iraq and Syria'. Baghdadi called on 'fighting' jihadis in both movements to band together, arguing that 'the supreme religious necessity in this moment is to join a more developed and complete [organization]'.[18]

He dedicated much of his speech to the Nusra Front, saying that it was he who had sent Julani to fight in Syria and supported him with men and equipment. The following day, Julani responded with a speech published on al-Manara. Having begun pointedly with a set of Qur'anic verses on the subject of sedition, he denied any knowledge of the merger. He admitted that he had been part of ISI, that Baghdadi had sent him to Syria, and that ISI had provided funding and manpower to the Nusra Front, and he said that the front had learned things from its experience in Iraq that had 'pleased the hearts of the Muslims in Syria'. But he suggested that Baghdadi rise to a 'loftier' level, swearing direct allegiance to Ayman al-Zawahiri, the leader of al-Qaeda as a whole. And he made it clear that the Nusra Front would not change its symbols or name.[19] This was a struggle over leadership, but also strategy: the Nusra Front claimed that it wanted to avoid the mistakes of ISI in Iraq.

According to testimony collected by the ACRPS research team, this dispute triggered a major split within the Nusra Front. Some commanders, particularly in Deir ez-Zor, ar-Raqqa and the areas east of Aleppo, swore fealty to Baghdadi. Others, particularly in Daraa, Ghouta, and the areas around Hama and Idleb, remained loyal to Julani. Many of the Syrian fighters simply withdrew entirely, joining Ahrar al-Sham, the largest faction of the Islamic Front in Syria. Video recordings began to appear under the ISIS name, as in ar-Raqqa, where an ISIS-linked jihadi group publicly executed three officers on 14 May 2013.[20] This was only the beginning.

---

[18] *Wattan* (Palestine), 10 April 2013, at: https://bit.ly/3HwCX9L (accessed 6 February 2022).
[19] For Julani's speech, see: *Al Manara Al Bayda'*, 10 April 2013. Archived copy available online: https://bit.ly/34EXXwb (accessed 6 February 2022); *Al Jumhuriya*, 23 July 2013, at: https://bit.ly/3LgmsRt (accessed 6 February 2022).
[20] *Syria Noor*, 14 May 2013, at: https://bit.ly/3guU9k1 (accessed 6 February 2022).

2. Other Salafi groups

This category consists of Salafi groups whose objectives are limited to Syria, whose sole goal is to bring down the regime and to establish an Islamic state in its place. This ensemble of movements is larger and broader than the Nusra Front. Their Salafi values are reflected in their names, their discourse and their symbols, but they coordinate and cooperate with the military councils of the FSA in the governorates. They also differ in their practices: they do not impose Islamic laws and punishments and they do not possess their own religious courts, preferring instead to submit to common religious courts set up jointly by multiple Islamist groups. The most notable of these organizations are Ahrar al-Sham (established in November 2011), Suqur al-Sham in Idleb (established in November 2011), Jaysh al-Islam in Duma (established in June 2012), Ansar al-Islam in Damascus (established in August 2012), the Ansar Battalions in Homs, the Syrian Revolutionaries Front (whose establishment was announced in Istanbul in June 2012), the Tawhid Brigade (established in July 2012 and considered the largest fighting force in Aleppo), and the al-Mustapha Brigade in Eastern Ghouta.

Starting in late 2012, the Salafi battalions that once cooperated closely with the Nusra Front – Ahrar al-Sham and Suqur al-Sham, for example – began to distance themselves from that organization by raising their own banners, establishing unified dress codes and adjusting their rhetoric to make it more amenable to the Syrian public. One Suqur al-Sham commander said in an interview that 'Suqur al-Sham is an Islamic movement that believes in the Islamic state'. When pressed on the differences between his movement and other jihadis, he responded, 'What we have on offer is clear. We propose to the people rather than impose on them, and it is the people – once the regime has fallen – who will decide the form of the state.'[21]

When our research team interviewed a local from Menbij, an area under Ahrar al-Sham control, he told us, 'The Ahrar flag is everywhere, but so is the revolutionary flag. They've set up a religious court for people to use, but there's no enforcement of Islamic [corporal] punishment. Rulings are limited to either prison or fines.' According to the source, the group's fighters were concentrated in centres outside the city, except a handful who acted as a sort of civil police. The state administration and private companies were operating as usual, and violations were rare.[22]

---

[21] *Al Jazeera International*, 15 May 2013.
[22] An interview with Ibrahim Abd al-Kareem, conducted by the ACRPS research team on 10 May 2013, after the book manuscript was drafted and before it was finalized and printed.

Many of the Syrian Salafi groups joined the SIF, whose creation was announced on 22 December 2012. Led by the commander of Ahrar al-Sham, whose *nom de guerre* is Abu Abdullah al-Suri (real name, Hassab Aboud), it was often described as the most effective fighting force in the country despite not being the largest. Aron Lund considered it the largest of the jihad movements.[23] It certainly played a decisive role militarily but was weakened by conflicts with the Nusra Front and ISIS; though it avoided fighting them, they did not do the same.

3. Groups established after the militarization of the revolution

These are groups that were not necessarily religious but that flirted with Salafism either because they wanted funding, due to the hegemony of the discourse of Salafi factions or because the experience of war tends to make people more religious. There are numerous such groups operating in Syria. One good example is the Farouq Battalions, which at their founding were very much within the model of defensive communitarian militarization but quickly shifted towards jihadism, establishing a religious committee and special religious courts. The circumstances under which the Farouq Battalions emerged differ markedly from those of the jihadi groups described above.

The Farouq Battalions were first established in mid-2011 as part of the rising wave of militarization. The organization had no specific ideological or doctrinal character, although it reflected the popular religious culture of the city of Homs. Most of its members were young men who had begun their revolution in the peaceful protest movement before making the transition to armed struggle, although some were recent defectors, including the then commander, Lieutenant Abdul Razzaq Tlas. The Farouq Battalions were the only militarized group that won popular approval in the city, particularly in Old Homs and the peripheral neighbourhoods; its command centre was in Baba Amr until its takeover by the army in late February 2012. In addition to its base in Homs, the group was also active in Idleb, around Hama and in the rural Damascus periphery.

The reputation of the battalions won them many new recruits, including Salafi groups with access to Gulf funding. This funding gave the Salafis an outsized voice in the organization and drove disagreements among the leadership, ultimately leading to Abdul Razzaq Tlas's removal due to a 'shameful act' contravening the Shari'a, which increasingly became the battalions' ideological touchstone. Political committees and other bodies were established in line with the Shari'a, and religious courts were set up to regulate fighters' behaviour.

---

[23] Lund, 'Syrian Jihadism', 31.

Most of the many groups of this kind that emerged over the course of the revolution joined the FSA-affiliated Syrian Islamic Liberation Front (SILF). The SILF[24] saw itself as broadly 'Islamic' without having any specific ideological character and brought together many different battalions. By mid-2012, numerically it made up the backbone of FSA strength on the ground.

Although some jihadi groups were part of the FSA,[25] their presence was alarming because it was accompanied by practices antithetical to the goals of the revolution: the spread of black banners, the appearance of religious courts and the declaration of an Islamic state in northern Syria (11 November 2012, in response to the formation of the SOC). This had a negative impact on the revolution. Moreover, it helped the regime by providing ready evidence for the line it had been pushing since the very beginning – that this was an Islamist uprising.

II. Criminal forms of violence

The social instability resulting from the breakdown of public order and the weakness of civil society led to a spike in criminality around the edges of the revolution. The revolutionary events provided a ready justification for any criminal act: 'I did it for the president/the revolution!' Crimes were committed on both sides.

Such developments are to be expected in protracted revolutions in which the state loses its ability to maintain order but has not been replaced by alternative institutions. They are even more dangerous in marginalized peripheries and complex societies.

Even in the years preceding the revolution, Syria had seen a sharp uptick in criminality, driven in large part by widespread poverty, agricultural breakdown and the attendant population displacement, and the flow of refugees from Iraq. At the same time, corruption was putting down ever deeper roots, spreading ever further within the state apparatus and providing protection to the armed smugglers who operated in the border regions. The presence of these social problems could clearly be discerned even through the media blackout. Certain parts of the country had become

---

[24] At its founding, the SILF brought together more than twenty groups of different ideological inclinations, including revolutionary and military councils, Islamist battalions close to the Brotherhood and Salafi organizations (most notably Suqur al-Sham, al-Farouq Battalions and the Islam Brigade). The Tawhid Brigade joined in early 2013.

[25] It is worth noting that during the revolution it was difficult to classify the groups, given the fluidity of the situation and the many transformations of the factions. The ideological jihadis never considered themselves part of the FSA.

veritable no-go zones: travelling on the ar-Raqqa–Damascus highway carried a constant risk of theft, armed robbery and rape over the decade preceding the revolution; the mountainous Hama–Latakia road was completely under the control of criminal gangs, who extorted night-time travellers; and the backroads have never been entirely safe, especially in remote parts of the country.

This situation was exacerbated by the transformation of the police force (which is not considered part of the security apparatus) into no more than a source of state salaries, which had long abandoned its function to maintain order. In many cases policemen were actively complicit: it was common for thieves and smugglers to offer a share of the profits for safe passage.

By 2011, there were no less than 64,000 wanted criminals at large in Syria,[26] who remained free largely thanks to the collusion of the police and security agencies. Public faith in and respect for the police fell precipitously. Even decrees as simple as the ban on smoking on public transport or mandating the wearing of seatbelts went unenforced except in as much as they provided the opportunity to secure bribes. The state was not, in any case, too concerned with building a strong police force. It is a well-known fact in Syria that the Interior Security Directorate (i.e. the police) is the least well-manned and the weakest of all the security institutions.

The number of crimes reported increased markedly and consistently between 2001 and 2006. Table 9.2 shows that crimes and misdemeanours increased by 52 per cent in that five-year period, while the year 2007 alone saw a 20 per cent increase in crime rates. These figures show that criminality

Table 9.2 Crime Statistics in Syria 2001–6

Year	2001	2002	2003	2004	2005	2006
Felonies	4455	5156	5996	6204	6847	6812
Misdemeanours	41564	44663	47212	56768	70661	77521
Crimes against public morality and ethics	918	955	830	992	1127	1001
Property crime/ financial crime	2149	2619	2875	3143	3888	4147
Narcotics cases	1100	1550	1934	2132	2982	3833

Source: See the data from the Interior Ministry's Criminal Security Department cited in: Muhammad Jamal Barout (ed.), *The State of Syria's Population, the First National Report, 2008* [Arabic] (Damascus: Syrian Commission for Family Affairs/UN Population Fund, 2008).

[26] On 20 June 2011, Assad issued a general pardon for all crimes committed before that date. In a speech at the University of Damascus, he said that there were some 64,000 people wanted by the police, but he did not make it clear whether they were included in the pardon. See: *Al Jazeera*, 21 June 2011, at: https://bit.ly/3GjFBOo (accessed 1 February 2022).

was spreading more and more within Syria. Regime claims that Syria was stable and secure until the revolution notwithstanding, data shows that Syria was the least safe it had ever been and was only getting less so.

It is worth noting that many convicts were included in the pardons issued by Assad in the early days of the revolution. Some were even paid by the security agencies to help break up protests, while others took advantage of the chaos to return to theft, looting or kidnapping. The sheer length of the Syrian revolution and the appearance of 'grey areas' where the state held no power encouraged the proliferation of armed criminal violence. Combating crime was never a priority for the regime or the security forces, and criminal acts acquired a new legitimacy, since they could be cast as rebellious acts against the regime or, in the case of the *shabbiha*, as patriotic zeal in response to the revolution. The pro-regime militias also murdered, looted and kidnapped for 'a bit of extra cash', and this form of violence must be seen within that context. Human rights organizations in Syria[27] have documented dozens of these incidents, attributing them to 'unknown criminals'.

Kidnappings were a particularly prominent phenomenon during the revolution. This type of crime targets the rich, merchants, businessmen and their families with the aim of obtaining a ransom. Families are usually quick to pay for fear of the consequences for their loved ones. Most kidnappings have taken place in the major cities, particularly Aleppo and Damascus.

Meanwhile, theft and armed robbery began to spread along the main highways, with unknown gunmen intercepting cars and holding their passengers hostage to demand money 'for the revolution' or 'the FSA'. Robberies became common along the Damascus–Aleppo highway and around Homs, Hama and Idleb – pro-revolutionary areas that suffered particularly badly.

In Aleppo, kidnappings and other criminal acts became much more common after clashes between the army and the armed opposition, which controlled parts of the city. Several FSA battalions attempted to limit the infractions and to hold perpetrators responsible. In many cases, however, opposition groups resorted to kidnapping themselves, targeting merchants and tribal notables in order to finance weapons purchases and claiming that the victims were 'pro-regime'. Many such incidents took place in

---

[27] A joint daily report is issued documenting incidents considered to be the responsibility of neither the regime nor the opposition by the Committees for Defence of Democratic Freedoms and Human Rights in Syria (CDF), the Kurdish Committee for Human Rights – Observer, the Arab Organization for Human Rights in Syria (AOHRS), the Human Rights Organization in Syria – MAF, the National Organization for Human Rights in Syria, and the Kurdish Organization for the Defence of Human Rights and Public Freedoms in Syria (DAD). These reports are published on the website of the Arabic Network for Human Rights. See: ANHRI, at: https://bit.ly/3J037C9 (accessed 1 February 2022).

Maskaneh, near Aleppo,[28] and in other parts of Syria, including the areas around Damascus. In other cases, crimes were part of the sectarian violence that swept across several multi-confessional regions, particularly Homs, the areas to the west of Hama, and the neighbourhoods of Tishreen and Qaboun in Damascus.[29] On several occasions the victims were released in exchange for a ransom or for hostages taken by the other side.

Certain 'Robin Hood'-style gangs were also active during the revolution, particularly during military operations, when they would take advantage of the general chaos to steal from the rich and redistribute their loot to those who had lost business as a result of those operations. At the same time, the state extorted businessmen and forced them to pay to fund the *shabbiha* militias.

---

[28] In Maskanah there were clashes between pro-regime clans and FSA battalions from outside the city, who kidnapped a senior member of the pro-regime Khafajiyyin tribe (locally known as al-Ahnaf bin Qais after a famous mediator from Arab history). The battalions demanded a ransom of SYP 15 million, but the tribe refused and clashes escalated into a fully-fledged armed conflict. Most of the tribe were displaced from Maskanah but then gradually returned.

[29] Locals from Tishreen and Qaboun (which have a mixed population), interviewed by the ACRPS research team, claimed that there were checkpoints almost on every street. Some of these were run by the army, others by the FSA, while others still were manned by local Sunni and Alawi families that kidnapped people from both sides in the hope of securing ransom payments.

10

The opposition

Opposition parties did not have a mass presence in Syria prior to the Syrian revolution. In fact, most protesters only came to know their leaders during the revolution thanks to media coverage of the events. But this does not mean that the opposition was non-existent. Opposition parties and political forces like the NDR long operated under difficult circumstances and were the spearhead of the well-known political movement known as the Damascus Spring. But the regime maintained a tight grip over political life and had co-opted many of the pre-existing parties through the NPF of leftist and socialist parties that accept the Ba'th Party's role as 'leader of state and society' as set out in Article 8 of the constitution.

In the 1980s, the political scene in Syria teemed with opposition parties and movements with elite support, many of them affiliated with the NDR. Many of these refused to join the NPF because of their objections to Article 8. There were also many Kurdish parties – the Kurdish Democratic Party (KDP), the Yekiti and the Azadi being the most significant – although their platform was not Syrian-national but Kurdish nationalist.

In the wake of the confrontation with the Muslim Brotherhood, during which the Brotherhood itself was criminalized and its members imprisoned or expelled from the country, similar treatment was meted out to the parties of the left, whose cadres were regularly abused and tortured in regime jails (although as abundant prison literature shows, the Brotherhood came in for the greatest share of the brutality; just being a member of the Brotherhood was a capital offence under Law 49/1980).

I. Syrian opposition activism pre-revolution

1. The Damascus Spring (2000–2001)

When Bashar al-Assad took power in 2000 promising reform, a wave of democratic energy shot across the country, the so-called Damascus Spring. Suddenly, all sorts of taboos were broken. For the first time, the emergency law, Article 8 and proper elections were all discussed openly. A raft of political forums and civil society organizations were set up by intellectuals to work towards political reform. It was a political efflorescence of a kind not seen in Syrian political life since the Ba'th coup in 1963, a bottom-up movement driven by individual and collective effort in a range of cultural, economic and social circles.

It would be fair to say that the Damascus Spring reflected the activism of a cultural elite more than party attitudes. Those involved were more intellectuals and civil activists than politicians in the strict sense of the word, although many of them had links with the opposition parties. And as has often been the case elsewhere in the world, these intellectuals seemed to be more involved in demanding change. But this also made it much easier for new actors beyond the confines of the traditional opposition to join the movement and prevented its monopolization by any specific party or group.[1]

Political forums

Studies on Syria typically link the Damascus Spring to Assad's ascent to power. This may be true in terms of the timing, but elite socio-political activism critiquing government policy and demanding reform and democracy was already present in the last years of Hafez al-Assad's tenure. In fact, this period saw the emergence of several public discussion forums, and some even received official acknowledgement. The Syrian Economics Association, for example, met regularly before 2000 to debate government economic policy and was emboldened by Bashar al-Assad's decision to attend (before becoming president), which led attendees to believe that they enjoyed his protection – that they were 'covered', as the Syrian term has it. Other unofficial forums – the Abu Zlam Forum for Civilizational Studies and the Dummar Cultural Forum, for example – also saw daring debate on political issues between large numbers of intellectuals. The authorities turned a blind eye to the activities of these forums and their growing popularity.[2]

The parliamentary elections of 1998 produced a new crop of opposition figures willing to make more audacious demands. Arif Dalila ran expressly as a reform and change candidate, although he failed to win a seat. Businessman and MP Riad Seif, who likewise demanded changes to the electoral law and urged parliament to carry out its constitutional role of holding the government to account, also ran and was re-elected. In the

---

[1] *The Damascus Spring*, 10.
[2] Ibid., 11.

same year, Hafez al-Assad made a speech that differed markedly from his normal rhetoric: at the opening of the Sixth Legislative Convention, he slammed state corruption, accused the bureaucracy of inefficiency, and called for new administrative measures and broader modernization.

There was a reason for all this. Hafez's health was deteriorating and he was keen to ensure that his son succeeded him. The price to be paid to legitimize this transition was limited doses of anti-corruption, modernization and economic liberalization. These steps were not part of a real change, of course, so much as an attempt to improve the regime's international image ahead of the handover, especially in the West. Western writers and journalists waxed lyrical on the beginning of a far-reaching process of change within the regime that would be completed on the ascension of the heir apparent, a process that would apparently transform the regime's attitude to both the Western countries and Israel. Many believed in the coming change.

Hafez al-Assad died on 10 June 2000. The People's Assembly immediately convened an emergency session, which was broadcast live – a rare occurrence in Syrian parliamentary history. The parliament took some time to eulogize the deceased president before announcing the formation of a committee to discuss Article 83 of the constitution, which required any presidential candidate to be at least forty years of age. The committee met for half an hour and decided unanimously to recommend that the article be amended to reduce the minimum age to thirty-four years – Bashar's age at the time. Its recommendation was then unanimously approved by the People's Assembly.

With these constitutional niceties out of the way, the next day Vice-President Abd al-Halim Khaddam issued two legislative decrees promoting Bashar to the rank of general and making him commander-in-chief of the armed forces. Within a week a party congress had been held (the ninth) to select a new RCC, which elected Bashar secretary-general. This in turn automatically made him head of the NPF. The RCC then presented him to the People's Assembly as a candidate for the presidency, where his candidature was approved – again unanimously. All that remained was the popular referendum to confirm his inauguration, held on 10 July.

All of this was expected, and even self-evident, as if Syria were an absolute monarchy. While Syrians were not surprised, in private they mocked the process, especially the attempt to render it constitutional by changing the constitution.

The succession took place entirely within the institutions of the regime itself. No organized dialogue took place with any of the opposition parties or with cultural and social figures to secure their agreement or even to neutralize opposition. Instead, the regime took immediate action to contain the opposition by traditional methods. Over the course of the succession the security agencies contacted dozens, perhaps hundreds, of opposition figures, intellectuals and activists to make it clear that they should not make a scene.

Bashar al-Assad's first speech on 17 July 2000 struck a tone of respect for different opinions and called once again for change. Practical steps followed: 600 political detainees were released, Mazzeh Prison was closed down and there was a marked fall in legal harassment of opposition figures (summonses for interrogation, travel bans, etc.). These steps, however small, were enough to usher in a wave of activity in the public sphere. Activists set up forums and discussion groups in almost every governorate.[3] The rate at which they were set up and the unprecedented candour of their debates seemed to herald change, an end to more than forty years of dictatorship. Moreover, attempts were made to unite the opposition. The most notable of these was a statement issued by ninety-nine intellectuals calling for an end to the state of emergency and martial law, a general pardon for political detainees and the establishment of a state of law that permitted civil liberties, acknowledged political and intellectual pluralism and the freedom of assembly, press and expression, and allowed citizens to express their different interests in a framework of social cohesion, peaceful competition and institution-building, in a manner that would allow everybody to participate in the development and the flourishing of the nation.[4]

The statement was a response to those within the regime who wanted to postpone political reform and to focus, instead, on implementing economic and administrative changes to modernize the state and 'prepare the ground' for political change. The signatories to the statement argued that 'any type of reform [...] will not bring tranquillity and stability to the country unless it is coupled [...] with the long-awaited political reform, for it is the only measure capable of bringing Syrian society, slowly but surely, towards safety, and of bringing the state back to society and society back into politics'.[5] This was the most 'revolutionary' aspect of the statement, since it moved beyond specific demands to a general call for regime reform.

The 'statement of the ninety-nine' was followed by the 'statement of the 1,000', formally titled the Founding Document of the Civil Society Revival

---

[3] The most significant of these were the Jamal al-Atasi Forum for Democratic Dialogue (held at Atasi's home in Mazzeh), the National Dialogue Forum (held in Damascus by the MP Riad Seif), the Cultural Forum for Human Rights (Damascus, Khalil Maatouq), the Homs Dialogue Forum (Najati Tayyara), and the Rayyis Forum (led by the Ba'thist MP Suheir al-Rayyis, who received an official government permit).

[4] 'Syria's Intellectuals Call for an End to the State of Emergency and the Release of the Detainees', in *The Damascus Spring*, 293–5.

[5] Radwan Ziadeh, 'The Forum Phenomenon in Syria: Between the Labyrinth of Law and the Utility of Politics', in *The Damascus Spring*, 290–1.

Committees. This document repeated the demands of its predecessor (end to the state of emergency, political pluralism, civil liberties), but also added new demands, most notably:

- The enforcement of the publications law, which guaranteed press freedom but was suspended under martial law.
- The issuance of a new, democratic electoral law to regulate elections at all levels and guarantee the effective representation of all Syrians, oversight of the electoral process by an independent judiciary and the operation of parliament as a genuine legislature that exercises executive oversight.
- Guarantees for judicial independence and transparency and the equality of rulers and ruled before the law.
- Recognition of citizens' economic rights (most of which were provided for by the constitution), most importantly their right to a fair share of national wealth, to suitable employment, and to a dignified life, and the rights of future generations to the national wealth.
- A reconsideration of the relationship between the National Defence Forces (NDF) and the state, and the Ba'th Party and the state (Article 8's provision that the Ba'th is the 'leader of state and society'), and any other principle that excludes the people from political life.

At this point the regime began to sense that the forums were going too far. They had galvanized political and social activity among a much broader section of Syrian society, and it worried that they were only the tip of the iceberg, concealing a broad desire for freedom and democracy.

The forum debates had begun to touch on sensitive topics such as the regime's past and the legacy of Hafez al-Assad, which was the sole source of legitimacy for a president who inherited the presidency from his father. The authorities thus began to crack down on the forums' activities in early 2001, when Information Minister Adnan Umran publicly branded civil society activists part of the 'new colonialism' – a colonialism that relied not on armies but 'organizations and institutions'.[6] This was quickly followed by draconian requirements on forum organizers. The state had to be informed of speakers' names and titles fifteen days in advance and be given a list of attendees. Forum organizers were also instructed to provide the security agencies with a transcript of any talk to ensure compliance with the constitution and the law.

These conditions constricted the activities of the smaller forums, but larger forums like the National Dialogue Forum and the Jamal al-Atasi

---

[6] 'Umran Criticizes the Promoters of Civil Society: Part of a New Colonialism', in *The Damascus Spring*, 367–8.

Forum continued to operate without regard for the newly imposed measures.[7] The government then introduced additional conditions requiring forums to be licensed by the Ministry of Social Affairs. The majority of forums applied for a license, but only the Atasi Forum was granted one, on the strict condition that it operate as a 'cultural' and not a political forum. This essentially made all other forums illegal and most of them were wound down, with only two significant examples remaining. The first, the Rayyis Forum, sought to bring the state's opinion closer to that of the opposition bodies; since it was led by a Ba'thist and had already been given a license, it enjoyed a measure of protection. The second, the Atasi Forum,[8] continued to hold monthly sessions until May 2005, when a paper was presented on behalf of the Muslim Brotherhood, leading to the arrest of the forum committee. Those detained included Suhair Atassi, Hussein al-Aoudat, Hazem Nahar and Ali al-Abdallah. They were all released a week later except for Ali al-Abdallah, and the forum was permanently shut down.

2. The Damascus Declaration (2005–2008): Opposition party activism

The opposition parties' expectations that the new president would undertake political reform that would end decades of Ba'th Party rule were dashed. Their hopes were revived after the fall of the Iraqi regime in 2003, when some thought that the risk that democracy would be used as a pretext for colonial intervention (as it had been in Iraq) might prod the regime into taking the initiative and launching a national dialogue. But in fact, the opposite happened. The regime decided to use a heavier hand, imprisoning several opposition figures and citing the international situation to justify delaying any reform measures.

Assad's approach became even more radical after the assassination of former Lebanese Prime Minister Rafiq al-Hariri, partially on the pretext of a US 'conspiracy' to impose political conditions.[9] The opposition expected the regime to use the tenth party conference held in June of that year to announce measures for reform, development and modernization. But, in

---

[7] 'Forum Activities Frozen after Authorities Demand "Prior Approval"', in *The Damascus Spring*, 507.
[8] ACRPS, 'The General and the Particular in the Ongoing Syrian Popular Uprising'.
[9] US Secretary of State Colin Powell did in fact visit Syria in May 2003 to present Assad with a list of semi-public political demands. The regime used this to present itself as a pillar of resistance to the neoconservatives, whose invasion of Iraq had been deeply unpopular. For coverage of Powell's visit, see: *The Guardian*, 5 May 2003, at: https://bit.ly/3HoGKpw (accessed 2 February 2022). American pressure on Syria had nothing to do with human rights or democratic reforms but rather was concentrated on Syria's regional policy and was more concerned with defending Israel than the Syrian people.

fact, none of these expectations proved true. In response, the parties of the NDR and the civil society committees held a series of dialogue sessions and debates, eventually leading to the formulation of the DD for Democratic Change, published on 16 October 2005.[10]

In unprecedented language, the declaration described the regime as 'the only hurdle to the process of democratic change in Syria; it is unwilling, or unable, to undertake any serious reform or change'. This marked a shift in the opposition's rhetoric. It was no longer petitioning the regime for reform – it now envisioned democratic change independent of the regime, since it was increasingly clear that there would be no top-down democratization.

The alliance of parties that coalesced around the DD quickly became the largest opposition grouping in Syria, particularly after it was joined by the Muslim Brotherhood (in exile). But in addition to the persecution and prosecution of its members by the state, the declaration was unable to escape factional infighting and intellectual and political disagreements (not to mention differences in foreign alignments). There were significant differences over the priority to be given to pan-Arab causes: one camp maintained that the declaration should focus exclusively on democracy in Syria and avoid taking a position on issues like Arab unity, Palestine or Iraq, while the second camp argued that these issues should be placed on an equal footing with the democracy question, not least to avoid conceding ground to the regime. The close links that were established between the Brotherhood (a significant party to the declaration) and former Vice-President Khaddam, after his defection, also undermined the declaration's image, since the deeply unpopular Khaddam was seen as a symbol of corruption and dictatorship.

In May 2006, the regime launched a wide-ranging campaign of arrests. The immediate trigger was the Beirut-Damascus Declaration of May 2006, a joint statement by Syrian and Lebanese intellectuals calling for an end to Syria's involvement in Lebanon.[11] This was an unpopular move, and the authorities were able to exploit it to crack down on the DD more broadly. Michel Kilo, a well-known writer and member of both the Civil Society Revival Committees and the DD's Provisional Committee, was detained for the familiar crimes of undermining national feeling, inciting racial and

---

[10] Nahar, *Trajectories of the Regime and the Opposition in Syria*, 105.
[11] Syrian troops had withdrawn from Lebanon in April 2005 following the Hariri assassination, but pro-Syrian forces, including Hezbollah, continued to agitate against the government of Fouad Siniora that had formed in the aftermath. The Beirut-Damascus Declaration, signed by more than 272 Syrian and Lebanese intellectuals, insisted that relations between Lebanon and Syria should be equal and healthy. It was interpreted by some as an endorsement of the 14 March alliance that had led protests against the occupation, which was unpopular in Syria.

sectarian hatred, publishing false or exaggerated information that harms the image of the state and libelling the president and the national courts – the same charges levelled against many former and future detainees. Kilo was soon joined in detention by many other intellectuals, politicians and human rights activists who had signed the Beirut-Damascus Declaration.[12] Others were repeatedly interrogated or had their property vandalized by the security forces.

Nonetheless, the DD National Council held its first meeting on 1 December 2007. It elected a leadership committee and issued a statement demanding a democratic system and a return to popular sovereignty and the peaceful transfer of power. In response, the security agencies arrested many of the declaration's key figures.

II. The opposition during the revolution

1. Ad-hoc initiatives and conferences

The protests in 2011 came as no surprise to the opposition. Its members were involved in organizing some of the earliest protests while the regime was on high alert in the aftermath of the revolutions in Egypt and Tunisia. But it could not have expected a popular uprising to begin in Daraa and spread to other cities and governorates. It had imagined, for a range of political and security reasons, that Syria would be well behind the revolutionary curve due to the highly repressive character of the regime and the social sectors tied to it. Long and bitter experience of regime repression meant that some opposition forces, such as the Kurdish parties, even told their supporters not to participate in the protests organized in the run-up to the revolution.[13] The Brotherhood, too, kept its distance – since 2009 it had suspended active opposition to the regime because of its support for Hamas and had been in sporadic communication with

---

[12] Among the most prominent were Sulaiman al-Shummar, a senior figure in the Workers' Party and a member of the Provisional Committee; Mahmoud Marei, secretary of the AOHRS; Anwar al-Bunni, a human rights activist; Ghalib Amir, a leading figure in the Arab Democratic Socialist Union; Nidal Darwish, a member of the Committees for the Defence of Human Rights in Syria; Mahmud Issa, a translator and senior member of the CAP; Khalil Hussain of the Kurdish Future Current in Syria; Muhammad Mahfuz, a member of the board of directors of the Jamal al-Atasi Forum; and Safwan Tayfur, an activist from Homs.

[13] The Kurdish Democratic Alliance, for example, issued a statement on 2 February 2011 that asked Assad to 'take practical steps to reduce tensions on the ground in Syria through various measures to further the construction of a democratic state' while telling Kurds to retain 'self-control', vigilance and prudence and 'preserve civic peace'. See: Bishara et al., *The Question of Syria's Kurds*, 99.

Damascus through Turkish and Hamas mediation; it had also dropped its association with Khaddam.[14]

From the very beginning of the revolution, a stark distinction emerged between the domestic opposition – which operated directly under the regime yoke – and the opposition in exile. The former crafted far more cautious slogans and demands, while the latter were quick to take up the slogans of full regime change, with many pinning their hopes on foreign intervention (the Libyan model). The opposition in exile were also far more intransigent, rejecting any dialogue with the regime.

In the first months of the revolution, the opposition failed to establish a unified leadership capable of bringing together all its different factions and currents. The first attempt to do so was domestic: the National Coordination Body for Democratic Change (NCB) was formally inaugurated on 30 June 2011, after three months of meetings with representatives of all opposition parties (Arab, Kurdish and Assyrian).[15] Although it initially succeeded in uniting many of the leftist and Kurdish nationalist parties,[16] the different factions did not communicate with one another or coordinate on the ground and their own administrative structures were sclerotic. Moreover, some were willing to jump into bed with anyone that offered them support – including the US, which was completely at odds with the popular mood at that time.

The opposition in exile, meanwhile, began by holding a series of improvised meetings better described as 'solidarity activities' than genuine organizational initiatives. Meetings in Istanbul (26 April) and Antalya (1–2 June), which included representatives of several major opposition parties, including the Brotherhood,[17] produced a statement calling for the

---

[14] Ali Sadr al-Din al-Bayanuni, the Brotherhood's former general guide, told our research team in a face-to-face interview, 'After the beginning of the [Arab] Spring, the Brotherhood sent a message to the regime via mediators, including Khaled Meshaal, head of the Hamas political bureau. [We] asked them to begin a process of comprehensive political reform and gradual historical reconciliation, because Syria – according to the Brotherhood – was ready to revolt against the system of government'. Bayanuni says that the message included the following statement: 'The Brotherhood will not start the revolution, but if it happens, it will not stand idly by. It will support it.' A face-to-face interview with Ali Sadr al-Din al-Bayanuni, conducted by the ACRPS research team in Doha on 7 October 2012.

[15] The members of the NCB included Arif Dalila, Hussein al-Aoudat, Burhan Ghalioun, Michel Kilo, Hazem Nahar, Abdul Aziz al-Khair, and Habib Issa.

[16] At its inception, the NCB included all the parties of the NDR, the Together for a Free Syria Movement and a handful of minor Marxist parties and local organizations. It also included four Kurdish parties, with the most significant the Kurdish Democratic Party (KDP) in Syria and the PYD. See: 'National Coordination Body for Democratic Change', Carnegie Middle East Centre, 15 January 2012, at: https://bit.ly/35IOMLY (accessed 2 February 2022).

[17] The Brotherhood was initially wary of participating in the Antalya conference as it did not want to be at the forefront of opposition to the regime – especially given that the regime had consistently claimed that the revolution was an Islamist conspiracy. Moreover, it did not want to undermine ongoing attempts by the Arab League and other international actors to convince the regime to negotiate via national dialogue. Nonetheless, its leadership (the Shura Council) ultimately decided to send a delegation to the conference with observer status.

president to resign and transfer his powers to the vice-president. It was not until a subsequent meeting in Brussels (4 June) that a National Coalition to Support the Syrian Revolution was set up. This meeting made clear the Brotherhood's desire to play a bigger role in opposition groupings, whether overtly or covertly.[18]

Back on the domestic front, on 27 June a consultative meeting of 'independents' from the local opposition was organized at the Samiramis Hotel in Damascus. Attendees called for the overthrow of the despotic regime and a democratic transition, and for the end of the 'security option' as a precondition for national dialogue.[19]

As the protests and their demands escalated, the Islamist politicians Haytham al-Malih and Imad al-Din Rashid called for a 'national salvation' conference, to be held in Istanbul and Damascus on 16 July. The conference was dominated by Islamists and clerics, with the Brotherhood particularly well represented, and ended with a public spat between the two organizers.

The Islamist political opposition started to appear. Before the eruption of the revolution, it was confined to Brotherhood activities abroad and covert work in mosques inside Syria. Some Islamists even maintained relations with the people in power due to their jobs; others were clerics or taught Shariʿa in universities, but they were not politically active, even during the Damascus Spring. They knew all too well that the regime's limited tolerance did not include them. But the real reservoir of the Islamist opposition appeared later when the revolution began to morph into an armed rebellion.

The initiatives continued to pile up without an inclusive national formula being reached. Young Syrians in Ankara representing the coordination committees active in the field in the first months of the revolution announced the formation of a Transitional National Council (TNC) on 29 August.[20] Although the composition of the council reflected Syria's diverse political, religious and ethnic makeup, most of the ninety-five prospective members were not aware of their membership prior to the announcement. It was simply a hurried attempt to do something, illustrative of young activists' restlessness with the belated formation of a unified political representation for the popular uprising.

---

[18] Some 200 figures, most of them Islamists, took part in the conference, which resulted in the formation of three committees to support the revolution. These committees later joined the SNC after its establishment in October 2011. See: *Foreign Policy*, 13 March 2013, at: https://bit.ly/30Jp6g5 (accessed 2 February 2022).

[19] The NCB was formed before, not after a consultation that followed this meeting; some serious journalists got the wrong impression. Kristin Helberg, *Brennpunkt Syrian: Enblick in ein Vershclossenes Land* (Freiberg, Basel, Wien: Heder, 2012), 94.

[20] *Asharq Al-Awsat*, 30 August 2011. Archived copy available online: https://bit.ly/3L5zK2U (accessed 2 February 2022).

The Independent Islamic Current (IIC) and the National Action Group (NAG)[21] immediately rejected the initiative, since they had called for a consultative meeting of Islamist and technocratic figures in Istanbul with the intention of forming their own TNC, the establishment of which was duly announced on 15 September.

Although the TNC was not representative of the opposition, it was distinguished by the presence of a new category of relatively young activists whose stated aim was to assemble a group of technocrats and qualified figures to represent Syrian society. The choice of 'Transitional National Council' was a clear allusion to the Libyan body of the same name; the activists hoped that like the Libyan council, they would be able to secure international recognition and from there a military intervention.

The Doha meeting

The Doha Meeting, held between 4 and 8 September 2011, was a far-reaching effort to unite the opposition. It was larger than previous conferences, bringing together all parts of the traditional opposition without exception (the Istanbul Group that had formed the TNC, the NCB from inside Syria, the DD, the Brotherhood,[22] the IIC and the independents). Although it laid the groundwork for the establishment of the Syrian National Council (SNC) a month later, this was not the organizers' original intention. Opposition figures attending an academic conference on the Syrian revolution at the Arab Centre for Research and Policy Studies (ACRPS) asked the center's administration to host a political gathering for activists in Syria and in exile to discuss the future of the opposition. Although this began as a theoretical discussion, during the first and second sessions activists insisted that practical steps be taken to unite the opposition parties under a single banner, which they said had become an urgent popular demand.[23]

A committee was formed to draft a statement setting out the points on which all the groups present could agree, with every group represented. The statement was then presented to the mass of attendees, who indicated agreement on the broad vision: the need to overthrow the regime, reject

---

[21] Several organizations calling themselves the National Action Group (NAG) emerged during the revolution. This NAG was a group of opposition figures led by Abdulbasit Sieda, Wael Mirza, Basma Qudmani, Ahmad Ramadan and others.

[22] There was no Brotherhood delegation present on the first day of the conference, but attendees agreed to set up a committee whose purpose was to try and get them on board, and on 8 September, Brotherhood representatives attended and agreed to join the Coalition.

[23] This was a spontaneous initiative. The original conference was supposed to be a forum for intellectual discussion and not to unify the opposition. The ACRPS is able to act with complete freedom in activities of this kind and does not require permission or licensing from the Qatari authorities.

dialogue and side fully with the revolution, and to create a national coalition open to all opposition forces

This coalition, the largest in Syria's history, would be tasked with setting up a national council made up of independents, activists and representatives of pre-existing initiatives and bodies.

The Istanbul Group (Abdulbasit Sieda, Ubaidah Nahhas, Ahmad Ramadan, and Wael Mirza) refused to join the new coalition[24] (even after agreement on its political identity) because it preferred the idea of a national council. Some members agreed to join on the condition that they held a specific percentage of seats on the board,[25] raising the spectre of the power-sharing deals that dogged the opposition in subsequent years. There were also disagreements between the Istanbul Group and the NCB[26] regarding the political tone to be set and the NCB's insistence that leaders should be chosen from the domestic opposition. Burhan Ghalioun and Hazem Nahar worked hard to try and reconcile the two groups but did not succeed.

Nonetheless, the conference was able to produce a statement that enjoyed the provisional agreement of the NCB, the Muslim Brotherhood, the DD, the independents and a group of youth activists, all of whom had also consented to the creation of a coalition to be led by twenty-five people (sixteen in Syria and nine living abroad). But delegates decided to postpone the announcement of the coalition until 11 September, giving them time to secure the final stamp of approval from their superiors. And although they had signed the Doha document, they did not implement it, for various reasons.

The NCB, for instance, merely 'welcomed' the new coalition when it was announced, implying that it was not a party to the agreement made in Qatar and demanding the addition of the 'Three Nos' (no to violence, sectarianism and foreign intervention). Under pressure from representatives of the PYD on its board, it also requested the addition of an annex on the rights of Syrian Kurds. Its leadership seems to have been very uncomfortable putting their names on any explicit call for 'bringing down the regime and every part and symbol [of the regime]' or outright rejection of 'all dialogue' and was likely looking for an escape route. Leaders were planning to hold their first convention later in September, and were very aware of the

---

[24] This was the name ultimately adopted by the opposition a year and half after the Doha meeting.
[25] See the testimony of Hazem Nahar on the Doha meeting (4–6 September 2011): *Saaa 25*, 7 August 2018, at: https://bit.ly/3ARjBJE (accessed 2 February 2022).
[26] The Istanbul Group accused the meeting's organizers of being responsible for the Arab League initiative (details of which were published by *al-Hayat* on the day of the conference), which demanded that the regime establish dialogue with the 'Coordination Committee and the other opposition forces'.

sensitivity of the situation. They may also have been holding out hope for a settlement. In any case, this incident showed how unwilling the opposition in exile was to understand the political language and the general conditions that their domestic counterparts had to navigate.

In the immediate aftermath, the DD and the Istanbul Group began holding direct talks with the intention of cutting out the domestic opposition entirely.

The fact that the Doha Statement coincided with the announcement of the first Arab League initiative – which called for an end to violence, withdrawal of troops from the cities and national dialogue as a prelude to democratic transition – was taken as evidence of a dastardly plot to undermine the revolution. In an attempt to one-up their political rivals, these same parties condemned the initiative as a 'lifeline' for the regime, disregarding its actual content, which would clearly have facilitated the dismantling of the regime, especially its provisions for the withdrawal of troops from the cities – it was because of this article, in fact, that the regime rejected it out of hand.

Events have shown that these circles had wildly unrealistic expectations and grossly misread the political situation both in Syria and the wider region.

The manoeuvres surrounding the statement point to another serious problem for the opposition: a lack of trust between the various parties, rooted in dynamics long predating the revolution. Although the Brotherhood delegates in Doha signed the statement, they made it clear that they would only table it in their Consultative Council once the NCB had announced its endorsement. The representatives of the DD, meanwhile – piqued by the recognition of the NCB in the Arab League initiative[27] – insisted that they would only sign it once the Brotherhood had approved it. The IIC, even more bizarrely, accused the signatories from the traditional opposition of plotting to co-opt the revolution. All this at a gathering hosted by a neutral party with the simple objective of creating a space for dialogue, not even uniting the opposition.

All these factors came together to render the Doha Statement a dead letter. Nonetheless, it was an important step forward and paved the way for the creation of the SNC on 2 October. The SNC's founding statement comprised the same issues and demands as the Doha Statement, and it had the same signatories, with the exception of the NCB, which did not join the

---

[27] As noted in the footnotes above, the text of the initiative called for dialogue between the regime and 'the Coordination Council', because the NCB had managed to create an organized framework for itself and was well-known.

SNC. The Doha gathering was the broadest opposition meeting, in terms of representation, to take place during the revolution.

Having followed these events closely, it is my opinion that the Syrian opposition never had any intention of uniting. This was not simply a matter of competition, ambition, and historical rivalry – although these elements were certainly at play. The main reason was that one part of the opposition had pinned its hopes on foreign intervention, while the other still believed there was a chance of a negotiated settlement with the regime and a national dialogue to which it would have been a party. Events have shown that they were both wrong, and therein lies the tragedy of the Syrian opposition: both of its strategic options turned to dust, and it lost its chance to become the political compass guiding the revolution.

Instead, the revolution took a third, different path, imposed by circumstances on the ground. This led the opposition towards a sort of media activism (some may call it journalism, but I prefer this term). Under such conditions it was no surprise that it adopted slogans like 'the street leads', 'revolutionary spontaneity', 'the free army', and – most curious of all – 'we are not leaders, we are the political arm of the revolution', an assertion that was repeated ad nauseam. 'Leadership' itself became a dirty word for the political opposition, and a general mood of insubordination prevailed. Any leader who managed to secure consensual appointment faced objections as soon as they took charge, without having an opportunity to prove themselves amid complicated circumstances. This was a political opposition opposed only to political opposition. By the time it had matured enough to work together, the opposition had already been made obsolete by military developments on the ground – and many opposition members had become beholden to their foreign sponsors.

The creation of the SNC

This flurry of conferences without any obvious effect caused great frustration among protesters on the ground, who dubbed the protests of 23 September 'the Friday of Opposition Unity'. Syrians active on social media began to warn that the opposition had 'one last chance' to get their act together or risk facing calls for the 'overthrow of the opposition' as well as that of the regime.[28] In response, opposition figures held intensive meetings in Istanbul, and on 2 October they announced the establishment of the SNC. The founding statement called for 'bringing down the regime and every part and symbol [of the regime], including the head of state'. The

---

[28] ACRPS, 'The Reality of the Syrian Opposition and Current and Future Challenges', October 2011, 3, at: https://bit.ly/3e7aMRJ (accessed 13 March 2022).

SNC also named a political leadership and a general secretariat, which described itself as the 'central pillar of the Syrian revolution at home and abroad'; SNC members followed this up with similar statements describing it as the 'legitimate representative' of the revolution. The first chairman chosen was Burhan Ghalioun. An unusual feature of its structure, reflecting the balance of power between the different entities operating under its umbrella, was that the term of the chairman was only three months, which undermined Ghalioun's position despite the respect he enjoyed among much of the opposition.

The SNC brought together a broad swathe of the partisan and organized opposition, including the Brotherhood, the DD, the IIC, the NAG, and various independent and party-linked figures involved in an individual capacity. It also incorporated several of the new activist organizations, such as the LCCs and revolutionary command councils. Although from early 2012 onwards, its members began to organize into blocs – the Change Current, the Free Clans, the Turkmen Bloc, the Independent Democrats and so on – all these groups continued to operate under the SNC banner. The only significant bodies that refused to join were the NCB and the recently founded Kurdish National Council (KNC).[29]

The council was accused of representing the Muslim Brotherhood disproportionately and struggle for control of the body began even before it was created. It would be dogged by the same personal and political animosities – most of them long predating the revolution and totally unrelated to the current critical stage – as other such initiatives.

It took a long time for the opposition to organize. The SNC played an important role in carrying the political message of the revolution, but it did not develop a stable structure. Its members competed in giving statements to the press.[30] An attempt by its president, Ghalioun, to renew his term for an additional three months was considered by members to be indicative of a dictatorial tendency, demonstrating members' childish understanding of democracy, as well as the high degree of mistrust and competition among them.

Although the SNC managed to unite much of the opposition within an inclusive political framework, it was unable to forge its various constituent parts into a unified leadership able to act decisively without waiting for a consensus – able, that is, to guide the revolution and design policies. This is despite its liaising with international actors, who, with Syria high on the international agenda, looked for an organized political representative of the revolution.

---

[29] Bishara et al., *The Question of Syria's Kurds*, 129–30.
[30] An early impression was made by Helberg, 96.

Representation on the SNC was split between the Brotherhood (five seats), the DD (four seats), the Kurds (four seats), the NAG (five seats), and the independents (nine seats), with the Brotherhood being the most organized faction. This distribution encouraged the creation of blocs with the aim of controlling the council's decisions. Moreover, the constituent parties continued to operate independently, often conducting independent correspondence with regional and international powers as served their own interests and undermining the SNC's foreign relations. In addition, the SNC's founding charter made consensus – rather than majority voting – the basic principle of decision-making within the executive office and the general secretariat. The need for unanimous approval from all factions often brought the SNC's activities to a grinding halt, especially with regard to contentious issues like major political initiatives, coordination with other opposition bodies or the selection of officeholders.

To be fair to the SNC, external factors also did much to hamper its work. Although the US government welcomed its creation and formally acknowledged it as 'a legitimate representative of the Syrian people' during the second Friends of Syria Conference held in Istanbul on 2 April 2012, it always harboured reservations about its role. It justified these reservations on different grounds at different times – sometimes the alleged dominance of Islamists,[31] sometimes its inability to unite the opposition. More than once, it tried to circumvent the SNC entirely. The then US ambassador to Syria, Robert Ford – who along with his French counterpart Éric Chevalier regularly and ham-fistedly interfered with the work of the opposition – was central to attempts to replace the SNC with a 'liaison and communication committee' after the opposition's Cairo Conference (2–3 July 2012)[32] – attempts that met with failure.

---

[31] The US accusations were intended to justify Washington's perceived inaction and its attempts to replace the SNC with a more pliant body. Nonetheless, starting in 2012 the Brotherhood made attempts to dominate the council. This was clear from the great number of new Brotherhood-linked committees and organizations that sought representation on the SNC, including the National Union of Free Students (Hassan Darwish), the Association of Syrian Clerics (Muhammad Farooq al-Batal), the Independent Islamic Current (IIC) (Ghassan al-Najjar), the Federation of Civil Society Organizations, the Syrian Arab Tribal Council (Salem Abdulaziz al-Meslet and Abd al-Ilah al-Milhem), the Civilian Defence Committee (Nazir al-Hakeem), the National Action Front (Ahmad Ramadan and Ubaidah Nahhas), the National Action Front for Syria's Kurds (Hussein Abdelhadi), the National Coalition for the Protection of Syrians (Haitham Rahmeh) and the Syrian Aid Association (Hamdi Othman). Other groups close to the Brotherhood include the Syrian Revolution Facebook page, which has generally chosen the names under which Friday protests are held, the Revolutionary Council of Aleppo and Surroundings (Ahmad Ramadan), the Hama Revolution Group, and the Syrian Committee for Human Rights. This last group was led by Walid Saffour, who later became the Coalition's ambassador to the UK. See: *Foreign Policy*, 13 March 2013, at: https://bit.ly/30Jp6g5 (accessed 2 February 2022).

[32] This conference was organized by the Brookings Institution.

The council received limited financial backing,[33] support for the armed factions being channelled through other avenues. Saudi Arabia and the United Arab Emirates (UAE) claimed it was too influenced by the Brotherhood, and US criticism intensified in the following months and subsequently prompted another proposal for a (more US-friendly) replacement body, this time from the former MP Riad Seif. Only the expansion of the SNC into the coalition in late 2012 quieted these criticisms, although Western governments continued to periodically attack the coalition. Not every criticism directed at the opposition by a Western official was innocent or in the opposition's best interests.

The establishment of the SOC

The SOC – generally known simply as the Coalition – was established on 11 November 2012. It was a product of discussions that had begun at a conference in Cairo several months earlier (2–3 July), and was yet another attempt to move past the fragmentation that by now had become a serious burden on the opposition. It also reflected a US desire to side-line the SNC and to replace it with a body more amenable to US policy, although in the event the SNC won significant representation on the Coalition and an SNC figure, Mouaz al-Khatib, became its leader.

In the months leading up to the founding of the Coalition, a number of new initiatives were launched to bring the opposition together. The most notable of these was Ghalioun's proposal for a National Initiative Commission, which would have been made up of consensus figures and appointed a provisional government to fill the political vacuum. This idea was soon bogged down in an interminable debate over how to select the cabinet, with some proposing that the whole process simply be handed over to the SNC. Former MP Riad Seif also came up with a proposal for a stripped-down 'National Initiative Commission' representing the SNC parties as well as other opposition groups, which would have broken the deadlock over the SNC's attempts to be the sole voice of the revolution. The Seif initiative, which was accompanied by Western promises of immediate recognition and extensive funding, soon became the central plank of Qatari, Turkish and Arab efforts to unite the opposition. In the course of

---

[33] Armed factions, wounded people, refugees and political activists all turned to the council for help. According to the second president of the SNC, Abdulbasit Sieda, the council suffered from lack of resources: 'Billions were spent in Iraq and Afghanistan, but we only received some 15 million dollars from Qatar and Saudi Arabia during these past six months.' In his view, the mainstream political opposition was too underfunded to effectively support the revolutionary movement inside Syria, and so gain its trust and loyalty. Interview with Abdulbasit Sieda, SNC president, Uppsala, Sweden, 13 August 2012. See also: Lund, 'Syrian Jihadism', 19–20.

negotiations held in Qatar in the run-up to the official meetings scheduled for 8–11 November, however, the nature of the proposed commission changed dramatically, and by the time that it was put to delegates it looked a lot more like a parliamentary body, empowered to form a provisional government, a judicial commission and a unified military council. It was this vision that formed the basis of the Coalition.

These initiatives came at a time when both popular opinion in Syria and international and Arab powers were calling for opposition unity. Developments on the ground had made this issue more important than ever: the FSA's liberation of swathes of territory, the uptick in army defections and the need for a political alternative to the regime. If the regime fell, those Western countries interested in Syrian affairs wanted to make sure that there was a provisional government ready to take its place and check the unregulated flow of arms and the growth of fundamentalist, extremist movements. The opposition figures behind the proposals – as well as some Arab governments and Turkey – knew this, and hoped that by establishing the Coalition, they would secure more effective US engagement, especially after Obama won his second term in November 2012. These hopes remained unrealized, however. The US consistently showed itself to be the Western power most reluctant to support the Syrian revolution and most hesitant to abandon the regime.

The Coalition's birth was not an easy one. The SNC, in particular, was suspicious of what it felt was an attempt to circumvent it and to downplay its 'success' in establishing itself as the legitimate representative of the Syrian people, at least for states that supported the opposition. In the plans to set up an 'Initiative Commission' it heard echoes of US calls for it to be replaced. Negotiations thus settled on a compromise: a coalition. As the name implies, the Coalition was not a single integrated force but rather an alliance between the SNC (with its various constituent parts) – which received 40 per cent of seats, the largest single share – and the other opposition forces. Naturally, this had serious ramifications for its effective functioning. It proved unable to leave behind the factional squabbles and backroom deals that so undermined the SNC – a fact that was made particularly clear during the elections to appoint the chair of the provisional government on 19 March 2013.[34]

The provisional government

The main objective behind the creation of the Coalition was to make it possible to appoint a government capable of administrating the regions

---

[34] ACRPS, 'The Syrian National Coalition: Motivations for its Formation and Building Blocks of Success', 11 December 2012, at: https://bit.ly/3mko95c (accessed 2 February 2022).

outside regime control, in order to prevent the chaos of a power vacuum. But this was easier said than done. Disagreements within the coalition and between the foreign governments that supported the revolution meant that it was only able to elect a chair of the provisional government at its meeting in Istanbul on 18 March 2013, when it finally appointed Ghassan Hitto, an SNC member, to that role. Several previous meetings had been scheduled and then postponed, with the most recent originally set for 12 March, because of an inability to agree on the nature of the provisional government more generally.

There were two basic orientations on this question within the Coalition. The first was represented by the SNC bloc, especially the Brotherhood, in alliance with the secretary-general Mustafa al-Sabbagh. This group sought to form a provisional government as soon as possible in line with the 6 March resolution passed by the Arab League's Council of Foreign Ministers, which promised the Coalition Syria's seat at the Arab League (and thus a place in the coming Doha Summit) so long as it formed an executive. They argued that this would help undermine the regime's standing in the Arab world and might pave the way to international recognition as the legitimate government of Syria. They had no desire to await the outcome of the ongoing Russian American negotiations, especially since the talks – which had been underway since 30 June the previous year – had made no significant progress towards implementing the Geneva Accords (in particular Article 9, which provides for the formation of a transitional government).

The second orientation was led by the chairman, Mouaz al-Khatib, and comprised mostly liberals and independents. This group was wary of the provisional government idea, preferring an 'Executive Commission' under the supervision of the Coalition's political leadership. Before forming this commission, it wanted to increase the representation of various groups (women, young people, revolutionary activists and minorities) and of military commanders on the ground, in particular Salim Idris's unified SMC. It maintained that the first priority for any executive or national authority should be preventing chaos in the 'liberated regions' and the prevention of 'unconscionable acts, the most dangerous of which is the partitioning of Syria'. Khatib argued that while it would certainly be politically useful to have a government capable of taking up Syria's seat at the Arab League, this was not an end in itself and could be postponed indefinitely. While Khatib and his supporters did not reject the idea of an executive body on principle, they had serious reservations as to the form, name and composition of this body as well as the timing of its formation.

These differences played an important part in the debates over who was to head the provisional government and thus delayed the selection of the government's other members. The first name to be put forward was Riad

Hijab, who had served briefly as the regime's prime minister between June and August before defecting. But the SNC objected to this on the grounds that the opposition's first cabinet could not be led by someone who had served in the same capacity under Bashar al-Assad – an argument reflecting the often-unhelpful attitude to defectors among certain parts of the opposition, which regularly excluded or derided them even as it passionately called on officers and officials to abandon the regime and join the opposition.

Over the following weeks, some twelve candidates were discussed and dismissed before Hitto was finally elected by a majority vote of 35 to 13 in mid-March.

Hitto was a relatively unknown businessman who had lived in the US for many years and was known to be close to the Brotherhood. His appointment did nothing to mend divisions. The atmosphere surrounding the election process (rather than the choice of Hitto per se) was one of the main reasons for Mouaz al-Khatib's abrupt resignation of the chair just days before the Arab League summit in Doha. Hitto faced problems in forming a cabinet because of hostility from Saudi Arabia, whose affiliates within the opposition boycotted the process from the beginning.

This episode put the fragmentation of the opposition and its subsequent dependence on foreign powers on full display: if the opposition had been united, foreign powers would have been forced to accept it on its own terms. Along with Saudi Arabia, who claimed Hitto was a Brotherhood figure, the US had deep reservations regarding the formation of the cabinet and the US was quick to downplay Hitto's significance. (US pressure led the Coalition to postpone meetings to agree on the nature of the government on more than one occasion.) In testimony to the House Foreign Affairs Committee, Ambassador Ford maintained that the provisional government was an 'interim' body whose sole responsibility was management of the liberated areas and would immediately be superseded by the 'transitional government' at the heart of negotiations with Russia. European countries, particularly France and the UK, largely followed the US lead. They welcomed the formation of a provisional government but treated it as little more than another means of forcing Assad to the negotiating table as a first step towards implementation of the Geneva Accords. Anglo-French attempts to reverse the European Union (EU) ban on arming the opposition were also part of this strategy.

Alongside these obstacles to the formation of a provisional government, however, there were also incentives to bring it forward. The most notable of these was the aforementioned Arab League resolution on Syria's seat in the League, which offered it to the Coalition conditional on the formation of an executive arm. Despite US objections, the league did in fact transfer the seat to the Coalition during its twenty-fourth session in late March 2013, where the Coalition's delegate represented Syria as a whole. It would not be an exaggeration to say that Arab League pressure was the decisive factor in the opposition overcoming its differences on this particular issue.

The league's decision to hand Syria's seat over to the Coalition came as a surprise to many observers and marked a new kind of collective Arab action. It was the first time the Arab League had done anything of the sort since its founding in 1945. Even during the 17 February revolution, it had refused to give Libya's seat to the National Transitional Council until the fall of Tripoli and the unambiguous collapse of the Muammar al-Qaddafi regime. Now, however, it had not only stripped the regime of all legitimacy but given official recognition to the Coalition, opening the door to recognition at the UN as well. The closing statement at the summit included an article urging international and regional organizations to recognize it as the sole legitimate representative of the Syrian people. In other words, it had been given an enormous responsibility that it now had to live up to. But the Arab League itself did not live up to its responsibility by following up its decision.

The establishment of the Coalition was a turning point for the revolution, as it went some way towards offsetting the fragmentation of the opposition. A full investigation into these issues is beyond the scope of this study, but we can sketch out some of the major challenges facing the Coalition here.

The real test of any national coalition born out of an agreement between various opposition parties is its ability to become an institutional framework that rises above the narrow visions and specific interests of its constituent parts. The success of the Coalition must be judged solely on its performance on the ground and its ability to determine a strategy for overthrowing the regime and transitioning to democracy and for managing Syrian society in the meantime. Here it clearly failed, perhaps largely because it conceived of itself as an executive body rather than a quasi-parliament bringing together numerous political forces to prefigure a pluralistic Syria. But like all parliaments, it seemed more interested in its own debates rather than in action elsewhere. This revolution required a political council that was recognized even by those who disagreed with it and which could rise above internecine conflicts. It needed a council that would spend all its time on obtaining backing for its own political, military and media strategy and convincing supporting countries to channel their support to the armed groups as the revolution's centre of gravity shifted towards a poorly organized armed struggle against an extremely powerful enemy.

Thanks to intersecting geopolitical interests in Syria, this enemy received a carte blanche to deploy an unprecedented level of violence, including a scorched earth policy, while the opposition's access to arms was severely limited. The leaders of the political and military revolution in Syria faced a set of key tasks – the formulation of a unified military strategy, institution-building in the liberated zones and in exile, the crafting of a sophisticated diplomatic and media offensive capable of countering the regime's rhetoric about Islamic terrorism – that were essential if the regime was to be overthrown. But the coalition did not have real authority over the FSA, to say nothing of the factionalized jihadi groups and warlords. And the further the revolution slid into a civil war, the more marginalized the political opposition became. This factor alone was enough to undermine its international status.

However, this was not the only factor. The US and other Western allies continued to justify their unwillingness to support the revolution by blaming the opposition, exaggerating its deficiencies and demanding it become ever more inclusive, as if it were an elected parliament in a democracy rather than an opposition body in a revolution, which needed a minimal degree of homogeneity in order to be able to lead. At times it looked as if the main issue was the opposition and not the regime. The polarization between Arab countries that were wary of the entire revolutionary wave in the region on one hand, and Qatar and Turkey, on the other, also had a negative impact on the revolution.

11

New actors

The early stages of the revolution saw a great deal of new activism at the grassroots level, whether in organizing demonstrations or in aid or media. This phenomenon spread quickly among politically aware youth and intellectuals and involved tens of thousands of activists, including coordination among hundreds, perhaps thousands, of their representatives across the country. Despite the brutal repression by the regime that annihilated a whole generation of civil activists (by targeted killings, imprisonment and exile) and the marginalization of these organizations by armed action, many of them have continued to be active in relief and media work. Neither the media nor academic research has paid enough attention to the relief and volunteer networks that spread in Syria itself and in the countries hosting refugees. Their activities included organizing secret schools for children and opening clinics and hospitals in bombarded and liberated areas and refugee camps. Most importantly, they exemplify the original promise of the Syrian revolution – and for this reason alone they deserve more academic attention.

This chapter first describes the coordination groups and organizational structures that emerged during the revolution, including the LCCs, the GCSR, and the SYRCU. It then assesses the role of satellite TV in the revolution, looking in particular at the impact of the coverage of Arab news networks.

I. Coordination groups

Coordination groups emerged as a new actor on the opposition scene, reflecting youth activism, Syrians' diversity and the nature of the elites in different regions. They were a unique expression of the revolution's civic nature and its indefatigable capacity for self-government. From the first weeks of the protests, protesters began to organize themselves and articulate their slogans and demands. This form of organization evolved into groups coordinating protest, social media activism, media coverage and first aid in different localities across Syria. Although various types of coordination committees emerged, these groups were not necessarily ideological – they often brought together people of many ideological persuasions. Rather, they were built around opposition to dictatorship, aspirations for freedom and dignity, and a sense of local identity.

LCCs[1]

The LCCs were some of the first organizations to emerge. At their peak in 2012 there were some 130 of them across the country, but this number fell to about 70 as a result of the militarization of the revolution, when many LCCs, particularly in conflict regions, ceased to operate.[2] Omar Edlbi, an LCC founder, explains the background:

> In the first week of the protests, there was a need for the groups that had taken to the streets to communicate and coordinate among themselves, to escalate their activities. A 'media office' – a Skype room, effectively – was set up to allow the regions to communicate with one another and exchange news. After discussions, we decided to turn these groups, referred to as 'coordination groups', into a revolutionary bloc made up of field and media groups. We started, cautiously, to network with other coordination groups until we agreed on 19 April 2011 to form a bloc called the Media Office for the Syrian Revolution.[3]

On 22 April 2011, the coordination groups issued their first statement in the name of the LCCs, which called on the president to end the Ba'th Party's monopoly on power and to implement the calls for freedom and dignity by means of peaceful democratic change. The statement called for 'the release of all prisoners of conscience, the dismantling of the current security apparatus and its replacement with another with legally defined powers that operates according to the law'.[4] These were all reformist demands, but in Syria they meant a revolution against a regime that did not accept reform. The LCCs comprised three main offices: the locally active coordinating groups in each region, a media office handling news coverage, and an advisory body.[5]

---

[1] The LCC Facebook page had some 30,000 followers as of February 2013. As of March 2022, it had over 360,000 followers. Facebook, at: https://bit.ly/34oA4Jz (accessed 4 May 2022). The LLCs used to maintain a website (http://www.lccsyria.org) in English and Arabic that documented daily developments on the ground with YouTube clips. An archived copy is available online, at: https://bit.ly/3JhJ8zg (accessed 16 March 2022).
[2] An interview with Omar Edlbi, conducted by Hamzeh al-Moustafa, ACRPS researcher, on 1 April 2013.
[3] Ibid.
[4] Al Jazeera, 22 April 2011, at: https://bit.ly/34cm3yH (accessed 2 February 2022).
[5] An interview with Omar Edlbi, conducted by Hamzeh al-Moustafa, ACRPS researcher, on 1 April 2013.

On 11 June 2011, the LCCs issued a statement setting out their vision for the political future of Syria and proposing solutions to the crisis. This statement affirmed that 'the central issue and first objective of the revolution is to change the political system, as a precursor to ending the mandate of the current president, who is politically and legally responsible for his regime's crimes against Syria and the Syrian people'. It also called for a national conference to formulate a roadmap. The conference would determine a transitional period of no more than six months, during which time the government would be in the hands of a transitional council composed of civilians and military personnel.[6]

Edlbi explains the role of the committees:

> The committees carried out social and documentary work, monitoring and training in cooperation with European organizations. They readied communication equipment and high-resolution cameras, took care of computer security, and engaged in relief work. They also formed [branches of] the National Unity Committee in conflict zones, which were multi-confessional – in fact, most of the members were from 'minorities communities' – although they played less of a role later because most of the members were arrested. The committees did not tend towards militarization, although they cooperated with the FSA on relief work, media, and legal support.

Most of the membership, with a few exceptions,[7] were secular and civil-democratic. The LCCs were a founding bloc of the SNC and had a representative in the Coalition.[8]

SYRCU

The formation of SYRCU was first announced on 1 June 2011 by activists representing the coordination committees in Homs, Deir ez-Zor, Daraa, and urban and rural Damascus. It defined its mission as 'representing civil action on the ground politically and in the media, coordinating and unifying action in the field, and laying the ground work for a council of youth and revolutionary activists to defend and realize the aims of the revolution'.[9] The SYRCU comprised the Sham Network, the Flash Network, and the Syrian Revolution Against Bashar al-Assad Facebook page, which

---

[6] LCC Facebook page, 13 June 2011, at: https://bit.ly/3oiEvN4 (accessed 2 February 2022).
[7] An interview with Omar Edlbi, conducted by Hamzeh al-Moustafa, ACRPS researcher, on 1 April 2013.
[8] Ibid.
[9] The founding statement is available at: SYRCU, 1 June 2011, at: https://bit.ly/34EYC0U (accessed 6 February 2022).

accounted for one-third of SYRCU. Later, at the beginning of 2012, it had about eighty affiliated committees across the country. SYRCU joined the GCSR and made up about 80 per cent of its structure. The SYRCU had a populist and Islamist-tinged ideological character.[10]

GCSR

The GCSR was established on 18 August 2011 as an attempt to unite the revolutionary grassroots. The idea was to bring all the local and online coordination groups under one umbrella, but at its establishment only three LCCs and a large part of SYRCU signed up.[11] Personal factors and disputes over whether the GCSR should be an alliance or a merger prevented the articulation of a unified vision, and although some coordination groups were happy to work closely with others on the ground, disagreements continued.[12] The LCCs largely insisted on retaining their separate identity, and some of those active in SYRCU concurred.[13]

'The General Commission undertook consultations with the coordinators across Syria to draft statements and take decisions,' explains Nidal Darwish, a GCSR leader. 'We had people demanding amendments [to the statements like] "civil state" instead of "democratic state." But the leaders of the committee, who represent different social and ideological groups, worked hard to make the statements consensual – not leftist or rightist, but patriotic.'[14]

The GCSR wanted to reproduce the experience of Egypt's Revolutionary Youth Coalition by creating a broad front of revolutionary forces outside the traditional opposition – especially given the latter's weakness and fragmentation – in order to influence Syria's future, attempting to create an alternative political framework to both the regime and the opposition. In the beginning, it was an effective organization and became a go-to source for Arab news media. After the militarization of the revolution, it was also involved in armed action as part of the FSA, which it endorsed in its

---

[10] A face-to-face interview with Nidal Darwish, activist and founding member of the General Commission of the Syrian Revolution (GCSR), conducted by Hamzeh al-Moustafa and Nerouz Satik, ACRPS researchers, in Doha on 24 February 2012.
[11] Ibid.
[12] Ibid.
[13] Our research has also found that it was generally difficult for individuals to fully integrate into these organizations. No new political parties emerged in the early period of the revolution – the tendency was always towards alliances, not mergers, and even the smallest organizations were intent on preserving their unique 'identity' within any larger partnership (even when the unitary body has no power or resources).
[14] For the GCSR founding statement, see: GCSR, 16 November 2011. Archived copy available online: https://bit.ly/3BU0Lo7 (accessed 3 August 2022).

statements. The GCSR did not maintain its own online presence – it expressed itself online through its affiliates, in particular the Syrian Revolution Facebook page – although it was sometimes involved in the naming of Friday protests. Its work was conducted through daily Skype meetings, with activists dividing up tasks and roles.[15] Like the LCCs, this organization was weakened and gradually disappeared after the arrest of some of its members and the transition of others to exile.

II. Satellite television

The revolutions of 2011 took place against the backdrop of a global communications revolution that has made our world more interconnected than ever before. This revolution greatly undermined authoritarian regimes' control over the media through the proliferation of satellite TV channels, which quickly became an important player in shaping and influencing attitudes (even with the rapid spread of social media). Arab satellite TV does not just broadcast news from other Arab countries. It offers an alternative to censored local media, giving citizens access to news that they otherwise would not see.

The first Arabic-language satellite channels were established in 1995, all of them funded by Saudi capital: MBC (broadcast from London), ART, and Orbit. The really ground-breaking development, however, came with the founding of Al Jazeera in 1997, which was the first satellite channel to take on political taboos and did not hesitate to interview oppositional figures from different Arab countries. Since then, many other channels have been launched, some Arab and others Arabic-language arms of international broadcasters (al-Hurra, al-Alam, BBC, CNN, France 24, DW, Russia Today, Sky). Competition between the different channels, the endless search for scoops and their relentless efforts to attract audiences hungry for knowledge during international crises produced an ever-greater flow of information, which bypassed both national boundaries and government restrictions. As a result, authoritarian regimes are no longer able to cover up crises and keep them entirely out of the media. Satellite news channels can amplify and highlight particular events, giving them more airtime than other events of comparable importance. They can formulate a story from a certain point of view by carefully coining words and altering the tone when

---

[15] For more details on GCSR, see: al-Mustapha, *The Virtual Public Sphere in the Syrian Revolution*, 155–60; and the GCSR website. Archived copy available online: https://bit.ly/3rsyb7y (accessed 6 February 2022).

presenting it. They may try to convince the public of incorrect facts, but while this might have some immediate success, it backfires at the cost of their credibility.

According to the results of the ACRPS Arab Opinion Index survey for 2011 (the year of the Arab revolutions), conducted in twelve Arab countries, television was the number one source of political news for Arab citizens (67 per cent).[16] Al Jazeera and Al Arabiya were the channels most watched by Arabs during the Arab revolutions. Of the 67.3 per cent who watched satellite TV, Al Jazeera was the one number source of political news in 2011, with 31.6 per cent, followed by Al Arabiya with 9.8 per cent.[17] The remaining 50 per cent were distributed among the other Arab satellite channels, including official and non-official channels.[18]

In the decade leading to the revolutions, Al Jazeera became the most popular news channel among the Arab public. In 2001, for instance, during the war in Afghanistan, it was unique among global channels in its ability to access Taliban leaders. Its angle was also different from the dominant American line, bringing it closer to Arab audiences, who viewed US military intervention on the pretext of combating terrorism with suspicion. The same was true during the second Palestinian Intifada and the 2006 Israeli invasion of Lebanon. It was most clear, however, during the 2003 US-led invasion of Iraq, when Al Jazeera focused on the devastation inflicted on the country and on refuting US claims about weapons of mass destruction and bringing democracy to the country. To counter Al Jazeera's coverage, the US ultimately launched its own Arabic-language channels, most notably al-Hurra and al-Hurra Iraq.

Despite the proliferation of new channels, Al Jazeera remained one of the most popular among Arabs, primarily because it was willing to take sides on pan-Arab issues like the Arab Israeli conflict. On ordinary news days, it provided an unprecedented platform for discussing domestic issues that the censors kept out of the national media, even hosting representatives of Arab opposition movements banned in their own countries. It sided with the popular movement against Arab dictatorships and took a supportive position on all the revolutions, despite several regimes shutting down its offices and jamming its broadcasts. It continued to operate this way even after the emergence and spread of social media.

---

[16] ACRPS, 'The Arab Opinion Project: Arab Opinion Index 2011', March 2012, 84, at: https://bit.ly/3wYJuY7 (accessed 6 February 2022). In 2011, ACRPS conducted the survey in twelve Arab states through face-to-face interviews with a total of 16,173 respondents. For more information and latest findings, see: *Arab Index*, at: https://bit.ly/3uReZkm (accessed 6 February 2022).
[17] These numbers have dropped dramatically since then.
[18] Ibid., 85.

When the protests in Syria began in Daraa in March 2011, they were forced to compete for airtime with several other significant developments in the Arab world: the UNSC resolution of 18 March imposing a no-fly zone in Libya and the NATO military intervention of 27 March; the ongoing Yemeni revolution, which escalated quickly after President Ali Abdullah Saleh's attempts to break up the protests; and the turmoil of the transitional periods in Tunisia and Egypt. As a result, news from Syria slid down the list of priorities. The situation was exacerbated by the difficulty of obtaining information from professional sources, as well as political sensitivities around state relations with Syria (friendly Qatari relations with the Syrian regime in the case of Al Jazeera). In any case, the limited demands being made at this early stage were not as exciting as the calls to overthrow regimes heard elsewhere. Syrian news received no more than a minute or two of bulletin coverage in a given news hour, without reports or analysis, and no political or opposition figures were given airtime. Moreover, most satellite channels were not particularly friendly towards the revolution. BBC Arabic seemed the most inclined towards positive coverage, but this changed early on.

Al Jazeera and Al Arabiya covered the Daraa protests from day one, although they did not necessarily use reliable sources (eyewitnesses). But they provided no coverage of events in other governorates, such as the Damascus periphery or Latakia, except on the Friday of Honour (25 March). They were fiercely criticized for this by pro-revolutionary circles in Syria, many of whom saw an obvious link between Al Jazeera's lack of interest and Qatar's close ties to the regime (although Al Jazeera Mubasher, the live channel, broadcast some events from Syria even when its parent channel was not paying much attention). Al Jazeera was believed to have enormous audience during the revolutions: the first question asked after any demonstration was whether it had made it onto Al Jazeera's news reporting.

The regime shared this belief, but drew the opposite conclusion – that satellite TV was a source of unrest and chaos. In a political culture like Syria's, anything that is not broadcast has not really happened. For regime supporters, for example, simply reporting that there had been a protest in Syria – or that people had been shot by the security forces – was a political and media taboo. Al Jazeera and Al Arabiya were accused of manufacturing, amplifying and fabricating the protests. Pro-regime voices quickly became hostile to Al Jazeera. On 25 March, dozens of young Assad supporters gathered in front of the channel's office on the Mazzeh road to protest its 'lack of credibility' and 'exaggeration of events',[19] even though at that point

---

[19] YouTube, 27 March 2011, at: https://bit.ly/3AQ24BE (accessed 2 February 2022).

Al Jazeera's coverage had, if anything, downplayed their significance. Pro-regime rallies often featured slogans attacking Al Jazeera and Al Arabiya, with protesters at a march in Damascus on 29 March chanting 'Al Jazeera, you dirty lot/come and see *our* protest!' and 'Arabiya, are you in Hebrew?/Come and see the fuss we're making!' It is worth mentioning that all this came after Al Jazeera's first video report on the Daraa protests and the storming of the Umari Mosque on 23 March. Although the network's reporters were careful on this occasion to present both sides' narratives even-handedly, this was not enough for the regime and its supporters. Indeed, it seems likely that the anti-Al Jazeera demonstrations were the work of the security forces and were organized pre-emptively to deter the satellite channels from covering events.[20]

Al Arabiya broadcast its first report on the protests in Syria on 25 March 2011, focusing on the mobilization in Latakia. The regime did not deal with Al Arabiya in the same way as Al Jazeera – it knew that the channel only had a limited audience in Syria and did not support the revolutions in other countries, so it did not expect it to support it in Syria. In fact, Al Arabiya's viewership had fallen after the Egyptian revolution because it was felt to have shown an implicit bias towards the Mubarak regime, putting it out of step with the Syrian popular mood. But its coverage of events in Syria subsequently won it much popularity there as well as the enmity of the regime.

Between 15 March and 16 April, neither Al Jazeera proper nor Al Arabiya was the main source of news for supporters of the protest movement in Syria. They preferred other channels that gave the protests more airtime and offered them ample space in their discussion programmes, most prominently the Arabic-language arms of the BBC and France 24. Syrian opposition channels such as Orient TV and Barada also had a good following at the beginning of the revolution because they suspended all other programming and devoted all their airtime to the protests in Syria. But after Assad's 16 April speech, Al Jazeera increased its coverage dramatically, especially when the protests expanded to new areas (Homs, Damascus periphery, Latakia, Banyas, Jablah, Hama, etc.) and began calling openly for the overthrow of the regime.

---

[20] Other satellite channels were not harassed by the regime and its supporters in the same way. Based on discussions with officials early on in the revolution, the special treatment meted out to *Al Jazeera* was not so much a matter of trying to pressure the channel into not covering events as it was a sense of betrayal – an unmet expectation that *Al Jazeera* would provide favourable coverage just as it had to other 'resistance' groups in Lebanon and Gaza. This means not only that there was no conspiracy against the regime, but also that the regime itself hoped that Qatar, the owner of *Al Jazeera*, would support the regime. See *Al Jazeera* report on Syria: YouTube, 23 March 2011, at: https://bit.ly/3IRzToK (accessed 2 February 2022).

Syria moved rapidly up its news agenda and was soon second only to the Libyan revolution. With the fall of Qaddafi on 20 October, it became the lead story, with a full twenty minutes in every news hour dedicated to Syrian news.

The shift in Al Jazeera's coverage was inaugurated by a long report on 16 April, which was exceptionally strident in tone and openly attacked – even mocked – the regime's version of events. The report focused on the demand for regime change and the expansion of the protests, especially in the Damascus periphery, and the 15 April attempt by protesters to force their way through to Abbasiyeen Square.[21] On the same day, another report was broadcast challenging Assad's speech to the new cabinet and pointing out its contradictions. The report attacked Assad for ignoring protesters, who, it pointed out, were no longer calling just for reform but for thoroughgoing regime change.[22] With this, it was clear that the Qatari ban on attacking the regime had been lifted. One month after the beginning of the revolution, Al Jazeera's journalists had received the green light from its managers, implying that, before this moment, someone had been holding them back.

In early May 2011, the channel dispensed with its eyewitness format and provided activists with satellite internet, allowing them to circumvent the regime's communications blackouts on Fridays or during military operations. On 20 May, it carried its first live broadcast of the revolution – protests in Hama. From then on, live coverage gradually replaced the YouTube clips that activists had been sending in since the beginning of the revolution, showing the beginning and end of demonstrations and their violent suppression by the security forces. This trend was also visible on Al Arabiya and Orient. Al Jazeera also began a new chapter in its history by enabling revolutionaries to become correspondents under fire (some of whom were shot by the army or the security forces, including Muhammad al-Masalma, *nom de plume* Muhammad al-Hourani, who was killed in Daraa on 18 January 2013, and Abu Yazen al-Hamawi, who was killed alongside an Al Jazeera team in Maʻarrat An-Nuʻman in 2012).

Events began to be choreographed for maximum impact on satellite news. Placards were made and demonstrations held for the media's benefit. Political messages from one town to another were often relayed by the media: 'People of Damascus, people of Damascus/here in Hama we've brought down the regime'; 'From Quamishli to Houran/the Syrian people will not be betrayed'; or 'O Aleppo, revolt, revolt/make the Republican

---

[21] For Majed Abdulhadi's report, see: *Al Jazeera*, 16 April 2011, at: https://bit.ly/3Lg3mKC (accessed 25 April 2022).

[22] For Fawzi Bushra's report, see: YouTube, 17 April 2011, at: https://bit.ly/34pUP7E (accessed 6 February 2022).

Palace shake.' Revolutionary songs were also composed for demonstrations covered by the media: 'Come on Bashar, just go' or 'Heaven, heaven ... by God my country.' Activists also made use of live broadcasts to send messages to the political opposition or to other states and humanitarian organizations. Almost any event or political act in the revolution took place with cameras present. Flying demonstrations often lasting no more than fifteen minutes were organized in particularly dangerous areas, such as Damascus, so that news of protests in Damascus could be broadcast. This was important for morale – but anyone who went looking for the protest would not find it, because it had already dispersed long before it hit the screen.

During the armed struggle, the media stopped being simply a transmitter of events and began to actively participate in them, with TV channels hosting political and military analysts who offered advice to the revolutionaries on how best to confront regime forces. Media had a greater presence during this period than it had had during the peaceful protests. The collapse of regime control in many areas made it easier for journalists to work from inside Syria and report on confrontations from the front line. TV channels had a large network of correspondents in Syria, some of them full-time employees (the main team) and some of them activists contracted by the network.

The Syrian revolution highlighted the critical role played by the media during crises and the great impact it can have on the trajectory of events. The revolution could not have maintained such momentum and such a political presence amid regime repression and a media blackout. Satellite channels mobilized the public against the regime and helped expose its crimes. But as the months drew on, the media increasingly made the revolution its cause, in the partisan sense of the word. Opposition news was published without fact-checking and some of it subsequently proved to be false. Activists themselves may have misled journalists by providing them with unverified or exaggerated information because they believed it served the revolution. The regime may have done the same, laying a trap for the media that allowed it to discredit hostile coverage. For example, in the immediate aftermath of the Jisr ash-Shughur massacre, pro-revolutionary channels such as Al Jazeera and Al Arabiya reported that the 120 soldiers killed had been shot for attempted desertion, when in reality they were killed by armed rebels, some of whom were deserters themselves, in an attack on the headquarters of the security forces, before the armed struggle began. The same outlets also accused the regime of killing several leading academics in Homs, citing activists as the source,[23] when in fact it was the work of opposition

---

[23] *Albawaba*, 28 September 2011, at: https://bit.ly/3rsUolJ (accessed 6 February 2022).

gunmen;[24] they did the same when the French journalist Gilles Jacquier died in an RPG attack on a pro-regime demonstration in the city in January 2012 (which also left six Syrian residents of the Zahraa neighbourhood dead).[25] The pro-revolution media also ignored the frequent assassinations of pro-regime government employees in Homs and Idleb, including school principals and the heads of peasant associations and other government bodies, and the daily attacks on security and military checkpoints.

The pro-revolutionary media thus allowed many things that warranted criticism to go unchallenged, except insofar as they interviewed pro-regime figures. This category includes some truly horrific acts. These media outlets did not fully live up to their responsibility as journalists. It is true that they were always willing to host regime representatives, giving them a platform to spread their propaganda and to attack the governments of the countries that host the channels. And needless to say, they were much more objective than the regime's own media, which was no more than a propaganda tool where lies were the rule. But they did help guide and inform the revolution itself, since they proved willing to act as its uncritical spokesmen in the service of regime change. They were also undiscriminating with respect to the opposition itself, often seeming to favour the loudest and most intransigent irrespective of how much support they enjoyed on the ground.

Nonetheless, in spite of their failings, the satellite TV channels provided all the Arab revolutions with invaluable services, and the Syrian revolution would not have been able to persist without them. The regime recognized this: after 25 March 2011 – the Friday of Honour protests in Daraa – satellite channels were banned from operating outside Damascus, where they were expected to relay only the official information provided by the government.[26] Nevertheless, the whole world came to depend on the information that they provided in cooperation with the local media networks set up by the revolutionaries, from individuals working alone to organized coordination groups and networks. All this was extremely dangerous and left many media activists dead or injured.

---

[24] The figures included Dr Hassan Eid (24 August 2011), head of thoracic surgery at the National Hospital in Homs, who was murdered by opposition gunmen who claimed he had been killing patients linked with the opposition; Nael Dakhil, deputy director of the Faculty of Chemistry at Homs University (26 September 2011), a Christian who was killed for unclear reasons; and Mohammad Ali Aqil, the Shiʻi deputy dean of the Faculty of Architecture (also 26 September 2011), who had been accused of being a Hezbollah representative and organizing Shiʻi militias to attack demonstrators. According to Muhammad Saleh, these were all figures who had participated in national dialogue, expressed opposition to regime policies and demanded real democratic measures. Eid had been involved in the effort to calm tensions when two Alawi men were killed on 16 July. On 28 September 2011, Aws Abdulkarim Khalil – an Alawi nuclear engineer – was also assassinated by unknown attackers. See: *Albawaba*, 28 September 2011, at: https://bit.ly/34sPyMe (accessed 2 February 2022).

[25] *AlKhalij*, 12 January 2012, at: https://bit.ly/3y1Gc50 (accessed 2 February 2022); *Le Figaro*, 20 January 2012, at: https://bit.ly/3rHz1xR (accessed 2 February 2022).

[26] *Al Jazeera*, 25 March 2011, at: https://bit.ly/3utcIx6 (accessed 6 February 2022).

12

Political solutions and international positions

This chapter presents and analyses the various failed attempts to arrive at a political solution up until March 2013. It considers the positions of international and regional powers and explains how the revolution came to be caught up in geostrategic struggles. Despite widespread condemnation of the Assad regime, it enjoyed the solid support of its allies; the revolution, in contrast, lacked any significant international backing. As with other Arab revolutions, the regime consistently played on the fear of Islamist movements taking power, which would ostensibly lead to chaos and civil war, while also doing everything it could to direct events in that direction. And all this took place against the backdrop of a changing US regional strategy and Russia's resumption of a global role.

I. Proposed political solutions

No international body proposed a political solution to the Syrian crisis until some six months after the revolution began on 25 March 2011. Although the diplomatic tone became steadily more strident during this period, and Nabil el-Araby, the secretary-general of the Arab League, did make an official visit to Syria in July, foreign governments continued to call only for an end to the violence and accelerated reform. It was not until August – five months into the revolution – that Obama suggested that Assad should step down,[1] but this was more wishful thinking than a political goal coupled with a plan, or at least the will to achieve it.

After the deployment of the army in urban areas, concerned parties pushed for a second Arab League visit. On 10 September, Araby returned to Damascus and presented Assad with the first initiative suggested by the Arab League's Council of Foreign Ministers.

---

[1] *Reuters Arabic*, 18 August 2011, at: https://reut.rs/3m69ydL (accessed 3 February 2022).

Under the initiative, the regime was expected to immediately end violence against civilians and withdraw its troops from the cities, release all political prisoners and demonstrators, and provide compensation. Moreover, it was expected to commit publicly to a transition towards a democratic and pluralist system of government, with free and fair parliamentary elections to be held before the end of the year and presidential elections to follow in 2014 (the end of Assad's constitutional term). All willing opposition groups would have been invited to participate in a national dialogue forum, which would have worked with the regime to choose a consensus prime minister to head a temporary national unity government and oversee the electoral arrangements. Once elections had been held, the largest parliamentary bloc would form a new government, and the parliament would create a committee to draft a new democratic constitution, which would then have been put to a referendum; the regime was expected to put in place and stick to a specific timetable for the whole process.

This was a gradual reform programme leading to a democratic transition. The initiative took as its starting point the importance of Syria as a state, and its position in the Arab regional order and in the Arab-Israeli conflict – the aim was to solve the crisis through reform and avoid creating a pretext for foreign intervention.[2] The text of the initiative made it clear that the Arab countries wanted to avoid the collapse of Syrian sovereignty and a repeat of the disastrous experiences of Iraq and Libya. Such scenarios were particularly pressing at a time when defections were accelerating and armed action expanding. It is worth noting that subsequent proposals put forward by Kofi Annan and Lakhdar Brahimi were actually derived from this detailed initiative. It was the most thorough and most realistic programme to be floated at this point.

In any case, the regime refused to commit to the initiative. Various opposition groups also rejected it out of hand because the NCB (the only organized political entity at the time) and 'others' were named explicitly as examples of parties that the regime should be engaging with; many of them also believed sudden, comprehensive regime change was still possible, likely following from foreign intervention. In response, on 16 October the Arab League's Council of Foreign Ministers established a committee to 'induce the Syrian leadership to cease all violent action, withdraw its military, and initiate dialogue [...] with opposition elements in order to implement political reforms meeting the aspirations of the Syrian people'.[3]

---

[2] I was closely involved in drafting the initiative.
[3] *Al Jazeera*, 17 October 2011, at: https://bit.ly/3HtdKNi (accessed 3 February 2022).

Although the regime objected to Qatari chairmanship of this committee,[4] the Arab countries' united front forced it to engage with the committee, and on 26 October its members met with Assad in Damascus to discuss implementation of the initiative. On 30 October, Syrian Foreign Minister Walid al-Muallim made an official visit to Doha, where he agreed to a preliminary implementation plan, the Arab Action Plan. This plan, ratified by the Council of Arab Foreign Ministers on 2 November, provided for the release of those detained during the revolution and for free movement within Syria for Arab League and international observers, as well as the media. It also stipulated that all acts of violence and all armed action in the cities must cease. Assuming that the regime made good progress, it anticipated that a national dialogue process would begin 'within two weeks'.[5]

When it became clear that the regime had no intention of halting military operations or of responding to the league's concerns, however, an extraordinary meeting of the ministerial council held on 12 November resolved to suspend Syria's membership and to call on Arab countries to recall their ambassadors and impose political and economic sanctions. The resolution was adopted with the approval of eighteen states; Lebanon and Yemen (still led by Ali Abdullah Saleh at this point) voted against, while Iraq abstained. Nonetheless, the league held out hope for a political solution. At the ministerial council meeting of 16 November, the regime was given another opportunity to implement the plan and league observers were dispatched to oversee it. The observers arrived in Syria in early January 2012. Two weeks later, they left, citing the ongoing violence and the regime's failure to comply with the Action Plan.

On 22 January 2012, the ministerial council ratified an amended version of the plan. The first initiative had provided for dialogue with the president and asked him to head the reform process personally. The second Arab initiative retained the general provisions of the first – a national unity government with full powers, expedited elections – and stipulated that Assad should hand over power to his vice-president, who would work with the national unity government to implement a detailed transitional roadmap. It offered a new opportunity to save Syria as a state and a nation and to avoid an international tug of war while also bringing about regime change independent of the struggle for power between the regime and the opposition. Had it been implemented, it would have prevented a great deal

---

[4] *SANA*, 17 October 2011. Archived copy available online: https://bit.ly/3L4HSkg (accessed 3 February 2022).
[5] Arab League, 'Syrian Revolution and Action Plan' [Arabic], at: https://bit.ly/3IYA8i2 (accessed 3 February 2022).

of tragedy – tragedy that those who believed in the impending victory of the revolution had not even considered.

Since the league lacked the ability to enforce its decisions, a majority of delegates voted to submit the resolution to the UNSC.[6] These moves came at a complex juncture internationally. In the aftermath of the Libyan crisis, a Western bloc was now facing down another led by Russia and China. On 4 November, these states – arguing that they had been duped into supporting the resolution for a no-fly zone in Libya to protect civilians, which was then exploited to justify intervention for regime change[7] – had used their veto to block a UNSC resolution condemning the regime's violent response to the popular revolution. On 4 February, they used their veto again, this time to block a resolution supporting the Arab League initiative (the other thirteen states on the council voted in favour). This was a major setback for diplomatic efforts to stop the violence and bring about a peaceful transition. A struggle against a dictatorial regime had become an international crisis tied up with the interests of various international and regional powers. And in the absence of the US, Russia was to be the most effective and influential international player, preventing any serious international action to protect civilians and stop the regime from crushing the revolution.

The next significant proposal was a six-point plan put forward by the joint Arab-international envoy Annan in March,[8] which was followed in June by a meeting of the Action Group for Syria.[9] Both Annan's plan and the final statement of the Action Group took several provisions verbatim from the Arab initiatives, including its vision for the creation of a 'transitional governing body' formed by 'mutual consent' and exercising 'full powers' in order to oversee the transition (i.e. a national unity

---

[6] ACRPS, 'Is the Arab League Capable of Saving Syria?', 21 November 2011, at: https://bit.ly/33i2AvY (accessed 14 February 2022).

[7] The resolution was a point of contention between then President Dmitry Medvedev and Prime Minister Putin, who did not want to repeat the same mistake as president. Putin considered regime change under the pretext of democracy or the protection of civilians to be an expansion of the sphere of US influence.

[8] The six-point plan called on the Syrian government to 1) commit to an inclusive, Syrian-led political process to address Syrians' legitimate aspirations and concerns; 2) commit to a cessation of fighting and armed violence in all its forms by all parties to protect civilians and stabilize the country; 3) ensure the timely provision of humanitarian assistance to all areas affected by the fighting and immediately implement a daily two-hour humanitarian pause; 4) intensify the pace and scale of release of arbitrarily detained persons; 5) ensure freedom of movement throughout the country for journalists; and 6) respect freedom of association and the right to demonstrate peacefully.

[9] The Action Group included the permanent members of the UN Security Council (UNSC), plus Turkey as chair of the Organization of Islamic Cooperation, Qatar as chair of the Arab Ministerial Committee, Kuwait as chair of the Council of Arab Foreign Ministers and Iraq as chair of the 2012 Arab Summit, as well as the European Commission and the UN.

government).[10] But important issues were left open to interpretation – would Assad be a part of the interim government? Would he lead the transition process, as Russia was to contend? – allowing the US to claim that the agreement provided for an Assad exit and for Russia to say the exact opposite. This was almost certainly by design.

As a result, the plan gained the formal approval of the Western powers, Russia, China, Turkey, Iran and the Arab countries, as well as many parties on the ground. But the differences in interpretation made it effectively unenforceable. And when the UK tabled a resolution to place sections of Annan's plan under Chapter 7 of the UN Charter – which provides for collective interventions to maintain the peace – Russia and China vetoed it again.

This put an end to any possibility of Annan's plan producing a settlement in Syria, making it clear that Syria would be the first state to pay the price of Russia's return to global significance and that Moscow saw the tragedy unfolding in the country in purely geostrategic terms. The veto ruled out a political solution capable of putting an end to the destruction, social polarization, sectarian and communal unrest, and economic breakdown already visible on the ground (driven by falling investment and US-European sanctions), and left the parties within Syria no realistic alternative to military confrontation.

After Annan's resignation on 2 August 2012, Brahimi was appointed joint UN-Arab League envoy. Brahimi failed to put forward a new vision or plan for a political solution in Syria. His starting point was the points of agreement ostensibly reached at Geneva, and he faced the same problems as his predecessor: without US-Russian agreement on the purpose of his mission, he could not move forward. And all the US and Russia could agree on is that the mission should exist.[11]

II. Geostrategic calculations and international positions

The Syrian revolution began against a complex geostrategic backdrop. The regime, which consistently used foreign policy as a source of popular legitimacy, had sought a rapprochement with the West and the US to cool tensions, finding common interests in various geopolitical areas – particularly Iraq before the US withdrawal. At the same time, it had

---

[10] UN Office at Geneva, 'Action Group for Syria – Final Communiqué – 30 June 2012'. Archived copy available online: https://bit.ly/3NQrDZ6 (accessed 3 February 2022).

[11] There was no movement until the US and Russian foreign ministers agreed to hold a second Geneva Conference. The only point of agreement was that there should be an open dialogue, without a time frame or clear goals.

maintained a strategic alliance with Iran, particularly in security issues. It had also hoped to form a new alliance with Turkey, concluding a series of agreements which – although favourable to Turkey – served to break its international isolation. The effects of this had begun to be felt in July 2008, when Assad was invited to participate in the Mediterranean Summit in Paris. With Obama's election at the end of that year, Syria's isolation came to an end.

During the first few months of the revolution, foreign powers remained circumspect, calling only for an end to violence and for a 'reform process'. There were fears of a second Iraq and anxieties about Syria's specific regional role – most significantly the border with Israel and the regime's part in 'fighting terror'. Moreover, until October 2011, the NATO powers were preoccupied with the ongoing intervention in Libya, and even their criticism of the regime's violent tactics was relatively restrained. As such, the revolution's move towards armed action was largely spontaneous. The only foreign support available was financial, and that was largely from other Arab countries. Western states not only declined to arm the revolutionaries, but actively sought to prevent them from acquiring the sort of weaponry that might have shifted the balance.

As the regime doubled down on the military solution and Syrians showed their determination to continue with the revolution, however, there was a more significant international reaction. This reaction brought with it new international divisions. On one hand, broad public sympathy for the revolutionaries in Arab countries prompted the Arab League to step in as a 'mediator' to encourage reform. Western discourse then began to take a sharper tone, calling on Assad to step down. Turkey terminated its six-year alliance with Damascus. On the other hand, Iran maintained its support, and Iraqi Prime Minister Nouri al-Maliki – who had accused Assad of supporting terrorists, holding him responsible for major bombings in the Green Zone in Baghdad – also sided with the regime, intensifying the sectarian character of the pro-Assad bloc. For Arab public opinion, Maliki was the child of foreign intervention, of overlapping Iranian and US interests, and a product of political sectarianism.

An analysis of international actors' role in the revolution is crucial. The regime's campaign to crush the revolution received significant support from Russia and China. Since the communications revolution made it possible for the atrocities of authoritarian regimes to be broadcast worldwide, Syria has become the only regime to get away with the sort of crimes it has visited on its own people. Finally, no civil revolution could continue under fire, and no armed revolution could last without funding and arms.

It would be impossible to cover every government's stated positions here. I will focus on main actors: the US, Russia, Turkey, Iran, Saudi Arabia and Qatar. These were the most active and influential international players in the revolution, particularly after the slide towards armed action.[12]

1. The US

The American position on Syria is part of its overall strategy in the Middle East. Since the collapse of the USSR, this strategy has been defined by three main factors: Israeli security, securing oil supplies and preventing disruption to the global economy, and combatting terrorism (as the US defines it). For the US, Syria is the 'enemy' of Israel, but other interests have prompted it to maintain permanent open channels with Damascus. There have, however, been a few periods when relations have been seriously strained.

In the early 2000s, when the neoconservatives were advocating regime change, the US placed a great deal of pressure on the regime to modify its foreign policy: to end its support for Hezbollah and Hamas, reduce its presence in Lebanon and break with Iran. In 2003, shortly after the invasion of Iraq, Colin Powell visited Damascus with a series of semi-public demands; and in 2004, the Bush administration classified Syria as a rogue state, and Congress passed the Syria Accountability Act in response to testimony given and lobbying by Lebanese leaders (most notably Michel Aoun, now a Syrian regime and Hezbollah ally).[13]

Following the assassination of Rafiq al-Hariri, US-Syrian relations reached their lowest point ever. Syria was accused of responsibility, and Detlev Mehlis, head of the Commission of Inquiry, claimed that there was sufficient evidence to indict Syrian officials, which was not true. The incitement against Syria in that case was political, and it seems that Mehlis was part of the campaign. The incident provided a pretext for greater Western pressure on Syria, especially after UNSC Resolution 1559, which demanded the withdrawal of Syrian troops from Lebanon. Resolution 1559 was the product of a Franco-American rapprochement after a period of chilly relations rooted in France's opposition to the invasion of Iraq. US political discourse began to focus on delegitimizing the Syrian regime, citing its 'support for terrorism' (i.e. Hamas and Hezbollah), its decision to allow anti-US 'insurgents' to enter Iraq and a campaign of political assassinations it was alleged to have carried out in Lebanon. Syria found

---

[12] Like the rest of the book (with the exception of a new introduction and conclusion for the English edition), this chapter was written in 2013.
[13] The Syria Accountability Act banned US investments and exports to Syria (except food and pharmaceuticals), restricted the movement of Syrian diplomats and downgraded diplomatic relations between the two countries.

itself increasingly isolated internationally. It is important to note, however, that the aim of all this was not to bring about regime change but to force the existing regime to adapt to the neoconservatives' policy in the Middle East.

In any case, as resistance to the US occupation intensified, the Bush administration was forced to reconsider its attitude. The highly contested 2005 Iraqi parliamentary elections had cast a pall over the 'nation-building' exercise there, and the disastrous Israeli invasion of Lebanon in 2006 had allowed Syria to resume a prominent role in Lebanese politics. The neoconservatives were also suffering closer to home: in March 2006, the Baker-Hamilton Commission advocated dialogue with all concerned parties in Iraq, opening the door to a rapprochement with Damascus and prompting Donald Rumsfeld's resignation as secretary of defence. The US resumed security coordination with Syria around the Iraqi border the same year, and Mehlis resigned from the Commission of Inquiry, which was then restructured under UNSC Resolution 1644.

By the end of the year Syria had deployed an additional 7,000 troops to the eastern region to prevent fighters crossing into Iraq. It recognized the Iraqi government and restored diplomatic relations with Baghdad (frozen since the 1990s). It also agreed to attend the 2007 Annapolis peace conference alongside Israeli PM Ehud Olmert, providing the Republicans with much-needed electoral capital ahead of the 2008 presidential election. This last move was the culmination of a series of similar gestures from Assad: at the 2005 funeral of Pope John Paul II in Rome, he had publicly shaken hands with Israeli President Moshe Katsav, indicating a willingness to soften the stance on Israel if Syria's international isolation came to an end. In spring 2008, indirect Syrian-Israeli negotiations began with Turkish mediation.

After Obama took office in early 2009, Syrian-American relations saw something of a thaw. There was hope that the Syria Accountability Act would be repealed and that greater economic cooperation and bilateral trade would follow. Syria itself came once more to count on a proactive US, particularly in the ongoing negotiations with Israel. And there was a dramatic change in language on the US side. In April 2010 John Kerry, the chairman of the Senate Foreign Affairs Committee, made the first of four official visits to Damascus. Even Syria's decision to withdraw its backing from the victorious Iraqi List after the 2009 Iraqi parliamentary elections and instead support a renewed term for Maliki – a decision taken under Iranian pressure and representing an end to a long-standing division over Iraq policy between Damascus and Tehran – had little effect on this new US warmth: Maliki's premiership was also agreed upon by the US. Washington's main aim in Iraq was now to effect a rapid withdrawal of its troops. There was a tense moment when Syria's allies in Lebanon attempted to overthrow Saad al-Hariri's government with the encouragement of Damascus. But the US decision had been taken, and the ambassador returned to Damascus in 2010. The internal policies of the authoritarian regime played no role whatsoever.

The Syrian revolution thus began at a time when Syrian-American relations were improving. The US position hardened only gradually, and was then reversed. From March to May 2011, it limited itself to verbal condemnation of regime violence and calls for regime-led reform. From mid-May 2011 to mid-August 2011, as the Syrian army became involved in suppressing the protests, the US began to impose economic sanctions on regime figures and moved towards calling for Assad's resignation. After October 2011, its attitude was characterized by a sterner diplomatic tone with the regime, a more open approach to the opposition and support for the Arab initiatives.[14]

Of the Western powers the US was the most reluctant to support the revolution – a reluctance that had a major impact on the European position, which we do not consider here because it has been so affected by the US. With the failure of a political solution, the direct US role in the crisis shrank considerably. Nonetheless, it tried to exert influence over the opposition. This point is worth examining in depth. In all its communications

---

[14] It is worth looking chronologically at the most prominent US statements throughout 2011. On March 16, State Department spokesman Mark Toner asked the Syrian government to recognize citizens' right to demonstrate freely and to recognize legitimate demands. On March 23, a State Department spokesman accused the Syrian government of using 'violence, intimidation, and arbitrary arrests to hinder the ability of its people to freely exercise their universal rights.' On March 27, Secretary of State Hillary Clinton ruled out any military intervention by the US in Syria, and said that the majority of members of Congress considered Assad a 'man of reform.' On April 28, Republican Senator John McCain called on Assad to step down, saying he had 'lost legitimacy' by resorting to the military solution. On May 18, the US administration imposed direct sanctions on Assad and various political and security officials. On June 15, the White House called on Assad 'to implement reforms or step down.' On June 24, White House spokesman Jay Carney announced US-Turkish coordination on Syria. On July 1, the US welcomed the domestic opposition conference and demanded that Damascus stop military operations and begin a 'real process' for the democratic transition in Syria. On July 12, Obama announced that Assad had 'lost his legitimacy because of his inability to implement the democratic transition,' but Obama refrained from calling for him to step down. On August 12, the US administration imposed sanctions on the Syrian oil sector, and Clinton reiterated that 'President Assad has lost the legitimacy to lead.' On August 18, Obama called on Assad to step down. See: *BBC Arabic*, 16 March 2011, at: https://bbc.in/31Z27OD (accessed 4 August 2022); *BBC Arabic*, 24 March 2011, at: https://bbc.in/3d52bBM (accessed 4 August 2022); *Al Jazeera*, 27 March 2011, at: https://bit.ly/3yspsUE (accessed 4 August 2022); *BBC Arabic*, 18 May 2011, at: https://bbc.in/3oVzs5C (accessed 4 August 2022); *Al-Hayat* (London), 16 June 2011. Archived Copy Available Online: https://bit.ly/3oREajZ (accessed 4 August 2022); *BBC Arabic*, 20 June 2011, at: https://bbc.in/3INftOJ (accessed 4 August 2022); *BBC Arabic*, 1 July 2011, at: https://bbc.in/3Jslp06 (accessed 4 August 2022); *Al Jazeera*, 13 July 2011, at: https://bit.ly/3Q1SXVe (accessed 4 August 2022); *Al Jazeera*, 12 August 2011, at: https://bit.ly/3EXFrMN (accessed 4 August 2022); *Reuters Arabic*, 18 August 2011, at: https://reut.rs/3m69ydL (accessed 3 February 2022).

with opposition figures, the US attempted to determine their positions on issues like Islamist movements, chemical weapons, and Israel. It even tried to coerce the opposition into taking public positions on these issues, which it considered central to its policy in Syria.

Robert Ford, the US ambassador to Syria, told a congressional committee in April 2013 that there were 'four key things that we're working towards. First and foremost, we do not want Syria's large stock of chemical weapons to be used or to fall into the hands of terrorist groups. Second, we do not want Syria to become a base for terrorist operations. In addition, it needs to be a source of stability in the region more broadly. [...] And we do not think that these things can be achieved without a political transition, a negotiated political transition'.[15] The fourth point was merely an assessment, meaning that if it were possible to achieve the 'key things' without a political transition, so be it.

The evolution of the US stance

The Arab revolutions exposed the shift in US policy away from direct intervention under Obama. They also forced the US to reconsider its foreign policy instruments in the Middle East and move towards a 'soft power' strategy. In an attempt to break with the policies of the Bush era, the Obama administration spent three years trying to re-establish trust with authoritarian Arab allies. Yet, Washington found that its position now risked alienating Arab public opinion. It was thus obliged to respond positively to the Arab revolutions while trying to limit their effects on Israel, oil supplies and counterterrorism without recourse to military intervention. At the same time, the Obama administration still needed Syria's assistance in resolving the problems inherited from its predecessor in Iraq and Afghanistan; it was concentrated on achieving a nuclear deal with Iran and unwilling to take a particularly strident position against Assad. It settled on the self-delusion of encouraging the regime to reform itself and to end the violence, a safer option than regime change.

The widespread image of a young, reformist president, who spent some time in the West[16] – and with a record on economic liberalization, one of the cornerstones of reform as far as Western governments were concerned – reinforced this position, as did the relatively limited demands of the protests in the early weeks of the revolution. The escalation of the popular

---

[15] Jeremy M. Sharp and Christopher M. Blanchard, 'Armed Conflict in Syria: U.S. and International Response', Congressional Research Service, 22 April 2013, 17, at: https://bit.ly/3shSghL (accessed 3 February 2022).

[16] In the rosy image painted by many Western media outlets, Assad and his wife Asma had strong Western values, as evidenced by the fact that they wore jeans, mixed with the people and drove their own cars.

uprising and the calls to overthrow the regime did nothing to change the American position per se.

The US position can also be attributed to other factors. As Hillary Clinton said explicitly, the absence of extensive trade or economic links meant that Washington lacked leverage in Syria. Since the administration was unwilling to provide the revolution with money and weapons, it was confined to the position of observer – unlike, for example, in Egypt, where the US enjoyed very good relations with the military. There, the US had asked the military not to take part suppressing the protests and within two weeks of the start of the protests had told Mubarak he should step down. Syria's ethnoreligious complexity and its relevance to the broader regional order also made the US wary, as did the weakness of the organized opposition and its lack of connections to the protesters; the opposition was also unable to exercise serious influence over international public opinion. Moreover, US policymakers misread the situation. Many journalists, analysts and thinktanks were convinced that there was a struggle going on between a reformist wing led by Assad himself and hardliners linked to the security forces, who were supposedly leading the charge against demonstrators.[17] Finally, the US was concerned about the repercussions for Israel. The regime took advantage of this by allowing Syrian and Palestinian demonstrators to cross the armistice line in the Golan, signalling that it was the only thing standing between Israel and chaos. As Makhlouf, Assad's cousin, told the *New York Times* in May 2011, 'If there is no stability here, there's no way there will be stability in Israel.'[18]

The limitations of US influence in Syria made it necessary to send messages via an allied regional power, Turkey. Turkey had become an influential player after June 2011, when around 10,000 people fled across its borders in the aftermath of the Jisr ash-Shughur events. Its geopolitical position, its strong relations with Damascus and its real influence on the opposition – perhaps to the point of being able to secure its participation in a regime-led political process – also recommended it as an intermediary.

But this was a two-way street. As the revolution gained pace, Turkey's (as well as that of Saudi Arabia, the other key US ally in the region) increasing frustration with Damascus finally prompted Washington to demand Assad step aside in August.

---

[17] The names of Maher al-Assad and Asef Shawkat were mentioned specifically. This was, in fact, simply a new version of the 'evil advisors' myth. Shawkat had been excluded from positions of influence since 2009 and held only a ceremonial position as deputy chief of staff; he was called to take a part in the consultations only after the eruption of the revolution. And Assad was not a reformist fighting hardliners within the regime.

[18] *The New York Times*, 10 May 2011, at: https://nyti.ms/3omcJPr (accessed 3 February 2022).

Nonetheless, other than sanctions, no practical measures were put in place against the regime. The US preferred to engage with the Arab League's efforts to reach a political solution rather than get more involved on its own account, a decision effectively exploited by Russia. And when Russia's use of its veto torpedoed these efforts and the revolution moved inexorably towards armed action, the US failed to limit the regime's use of heavy weapons while imposing restrictions on the rebels. Not only did it refuse to supply the opposition with arms, it prevented others from doing so as well, even after recognizing the SNC as the legitimate representative of the Syrian people.

There were other reasons for the relative weakness of the US position. The Islamist bent of many of the groups fighting on the ground alarmed Washington, which was afraid of fostering an extremist regime hostile to its interests (as had happened with the Taliban in Afghanistan). The killing of the US ambassador in Benghazi and the takeover of northern Mali by jihadi movements made this concern more pressing. Policymakers preferred to reach a settlement with Russia, no matter how long it took. Although more sympathetic to the revolution than Russia and less friendly to the regime, the US shared Russia's fear of radical Islamists and of an unstable Syria, particularly given the possible repercussions for Israel. As Kerry put it, 'Coordination with Russia […] is the lesser evil.'[19] This same consideration led Obama to reject a proposal from Clinton and the former CIA chief David Petraeus for arming and training opposition fighters.[20]

The US, in short, failed to support the revolution before it turned into a civil war and before Islamist factions spread throughout the country. There was a yawning gap between the secretary of state's pro-revolutionary statements, made to mollify Arab opinion, and the actions of the US administration. This, more than anything else, shows that the 'American conspiracy' beloved of pro-regime propagandists never actually existed. The Syrian leadership itself clearly knew this – there were no official Syrian statements against the US throughout the revolution. That was left to hired pens, either unknown or known not to be serious, and propagandistic websites that spun the revolution as an American or American-Turkish-Gulf conspiracy.

2. Russia

From the very beginning of the protests, Russia has stood determinedly with the regime. The Kremlin showed little enthusiasm for Arab revolutions,

---

[19] *Russia Today Arabic*, 24 January 2012, at: https://bit.ly/3GMWWQe (accessed 14 February 2022).
[20] *The New York Times*, 2 February 2013, at: https://nyti.ms/3AWLznj (accessed 3 February 2022).

whether in Syria, Tunisia, or Egypt. It consistently warned of the threat of Islamist governments – and in Egypt and Tunisia, it demonstrated that it would prefer a non-allied regime than a democracy that might put Islamists in power. Moreover, the revolution came at a time when Russia was making its comeback as a superpower. Having proved itself in Georgia, it now hoped that the US presence would gradually decrease in the Middle East, bruised by Iraq and Afghanistan, producing far more oil domestically than previously and less interested than it had been in the region.

Russia demonstrated a consistent disdain for the revolution and encouraged the regime to crush it by force. It provided an uninterrupted and unconditional supply of weapons to the Syrian armed forces. It has also used its UNSC veto to stymie moves towards a political solution. On 4 October 2011, it vetoed a draft resolution (proposed by European states) to condemn 'grave and systematic human rights violations' in Syria, which also hinted at the prospect of sanctions if the regime did not change course.[21] On 4 February 2012, it again used its veto to block UN adoption of the Arab Action Plan.[22] And although it backpedalled and endorsed the Annan plan, on 19 July, its interpretation of the plan prevented the UNSC from placing it under Chapter 7 of the UN Charter, which would have allowed the imposition of non-military sanctions on the regime in the event of non-compliance.

The Russian Foreign Ministry was the loudest voice speaking against the revolution internationally. It even held talks with the opposition in an attempt to persuade them to accept Assad and to engage in dialogue with the regime without preconditions. Those opposition figures who met with Russian representatives said that the latter informed them that they were personally uncomfortable with Assad's policies, stressed that the Kremlin was not committed to his rule, and asserted that the Syrian people should decide his fate; but they were against regime change although it was obvious that maintaining the regime meant keeping Assad. The Iranians reached the same conclusion. Russia's actual policy was clearly to stick by the regime, not even pressuring Damascus to implement reforms.

A reading of the Russian position

Attempts to interpret Russia's support for the Syrian regime as a continuation of their Cold War relationship or as a product of strong trade relations[23] or

---

[21] *Assafir*, 5 October 2011.
[22] *BBC Arabic*, 4 February 2012, at: https://bbc.in/3sbTMQO (accessed 3 February 2022).
[23] Trade between Russia and Syria in 2012 was worth some $2 billion, up 58 per cent from $1.3 billion in 2009. See: *Shahb News*, 24 May 2012, at: https://bit.ly/3HJMFpc (accessed 14 February 2022).

even military cooperation and Russian arms sales[24] all fall short of the mark. These factors are all significant, but they are not the main strategic motivation. To understand the Russian position, we must look to the Kremlin's attempt to reassert itself on the global stage, particularly in Asia, be it the Middle East or Central Asia. Russia chose this region as the main theatre for its return to prominence because US influence there was declining and the failure of US interventions created a potent local partner willing to cooperate with Moscow: Iran.

In reasserting its international position, one of Russia's strategies has been to stem Western influence by emphasizing the sovereignty of states as sovereignty of authoritarian regimes against democratization, blocking NATO expansion and ensuring that former Soviet states that have not joined NATO are firmly within Russia's sphere of influence. The closest vision for the restoration of Russia's superpower status may be the idea of a 'New Eurasia', sketched out by Aleksandr Dugin in his 1999 book *The Foundations of Geopolitics: The Geopolitical Future of Russia*.

Like other works on geopolitics without a socioeconomic dimension, Dugin's book is superficial, but it is popular for political reasons. It gives expression to Russian policy under Vladimir Putin – the policy of a former superpower trying to reclaim its old role by force and strategic manoeuvre, having dispensed with ideological illusions. Communism has been supplanted by a pragmatism grounded in power politics, nationalism and superpower nostalgia. Humanitarian discourse, even sensitivity to humanitarian issues or to human rights, is completely absent from this approach.[25]

Dugin's book resembled a 'presentation'; it need not be accepted by the decisionmaker, but it speaks to his political mood and ends up popularizing it. It identifies Iran as Russia's most strategically important Islamic ally, the gateway to the Arab world, Central Asia and warm-water ports. He also argues that Arab states hostile to Atlanticism – first and foremost Iraq and Libya, and then Syria, whose attitude to the West he says is inconsistent – are Russia's natural allies.[26] The events of 2003 removed Iraq from the

---

[24] In the first decade of the 2000s, Russian arms sales to Syria were relatively limited: more weapons were sold to India, China, Algeria, Iran, Venezuela, Malaysia, North Korea, Vietnam, Hungary, Greece, and the United Arab Emirates (UAE). After the revolution, however, sales increased dramatically, and by the end of 2013 were expected to reach $1.6 billion, putting Syria in fifth place on the list of customers. See: *Assafir*, 15 February 2013, at: https://bit.ly/3xoDWF0 (accessed 15 June 2022).

[25] China is similar to Russia in this respect. Its approaches other countries with the aim of benefiting politically and economically, but unlike the USSR or the US, it holds to no universal discourse or socio-political system it seeks to export. China is completely uninterested in the nature of the regimes with which it cooperates. It similarly works tirelessly in international institutions to prevent any restrictions on states' use of weapons.

[26] Alexsandr Dugin, *The Foundations of Geopolitics: The Geopolitical Future of Russia* [Arabic], trans. Emad Hatem (Beirut and Tripoli, Libya: Dar Al-Kitab Al-Jadidah Al-Muttahidah, 2004), 286–94.

'Eurasian equation', and the 2011 NATO intervention did the same for Libya. While Russia did not give up on those countries, Syria was, for the moment, the only country in the region beyond Western control, and a country in alliance with Iran to boot.

Russian attempts to draw Syria into the Eurasian project or cooperation with its customs union began with the start of the Syrian revolution, taking advantage of the regime's need for international support to counter Western pressure and sanctions.[27]

Dugin's vision also revives old Russia's antipathy to Turkey. The Eurasian project has reinstated Russia's Orthodox character, but this has strengthened non-Russian forms of national consciousness as well.[28] In particular, since many citizens of the Central Asian states – and indeed many citizens of Russia itself – are of Turkic or Muslim origin, there is a vast reservoir of power that Turkey, a NATO member, could use to expand into the Russian sphere once it has secured its position in the Middle East. This would mean the transfer of the cultural problem to the Russian interior and its ethnic isolation,[29] by cutting it off from citizens of Russian nationality in the Eurasian states. If Atlanticist Turkey clashes with a Eurasian Russia rooted in Orthodox Russian nationalism, Chechnya, Dagestan and Abkhazia would burst into flames.[30] In this analysis, Turkey is Russia's main adversary in the Caucasus and Central Asia. But Dugin and his like are not politicians. Pragmatism, the will to avoid conflict with Turkey that might destabilize Central Asian countries, Recep Tayyip Erdoğan's will to distinguish Turkey's position within NATO, US-Turkish differences over the Kurdish question and economic relations between Russia and Turkey – all of this prevented differences between Turkey and Russia in Syria from awakening historical disputes.

Russia's approach to the revolution in Syria was geostrategic. The Middle East is less important for its national interest and security than its immediate Central Asian neighbours. But Syria has a different significance. It is Russia's foothold on the Mediterranean, providing its Black Sea fleet with a warm-water outpost. Moreover, Moscow knew that the US had grown wary of direct intervention and it was keen to take advantage of this development

---

[27] See, for example, the Syrian government's July 2011 bid to join the customs union between Russia, Kazakhstan, and Belarus: *Russia Today Arabic*, 16 July 2011, at: https://bit.ly/3zymW1L (accessed 1 March 2013); or the 2012 negotiations between the Syrian government and the Eurasian Economic Commission on the establishment of a free trade area between Syria and the states of the Customs Union. See: *Anba Moscow*, 25 May 2012. Archived copy available online: https://bit.ly/3NW4OOW (accessed 15 June 2022).

[28] Henry Laurens, *The Empire and Its Enemies* [Arabic], trans. Bashir al-Sibai (Cairo: National Centre for Translation, 2010), 64.

[29] Dugin, 211.

[30] Ibid., 290–1; 302–3.

in order to block the further expansion of NATO and the US sphere of influence. Washington was unwilling to see a repeat of the Libyan intervention – which Russia sees as an Anglo-French scheme (facilitated by Qatar) based on a deliberate misinterpretation of the resolution on a no-fly zone, a trick it could have scotched with its UNSC veto if it had known what was going to happen in advance.

So long as the Syrian regime survives, even in a weakened state, Russia believes it will retain geostrategic influence. Putin has thus resurrected a far-reaching, international superpower policy. Most elements of the new discourse of a mighty Russia are not inherited from the Soviet era but from the Czarist era, including the emphasis on the Orthodox Church and the 'protection of minorities' in the case of the Middle East.

But Russia's tone during the Syrian revolution and the Arab revolutions more generally revealed something deeper than just cold, rational calculation. The generation to which Putin and his foreign minister belong has something of a complex about the war in Afghanistan, which they see as a great humiliation at the hands of Islamist forces, the beginning of the end for the Soviet empire. Putin's actions in Chechnya showed his desire to restore Russian prestige in a battle against Islamists. Afghanistan, Chechnya and Syria are easy to conflate for a generation still reeling from a politico-cultural crisis of this kind.

Russia has succeeded in setting the pace of international policy towards Syria. With Turkey and the West unwilling to intervene directly and/or to arm the revolutionaries, it managed to set itself up as the most significant geostrategic player. Its support, alongside that of Iran and Iraq, is the main reason the Syrian regime has been able to survive so long.

3. Turkey

Turkey, a neighbour of Syria, a large regional state, and a member of NATO, played an influential part in the Syrian revolution. The protests began at a time when Syrian-Turkish relations were improving. Nonetheless, Ankara was critical of the regime's response to the protests and called on it to lead a reform process before settling into a more active role. Turkey was the only one of Syria's neighbours to support the revolution – Iraq and Lebanon supported the regime and helped it to circumvent sanctions, while Jordan followed the Arab majority, providing only very limited support at a much later stage and preventing official action by Syrian dissidents within its borders (although it opened its borders to refugees, including army defectors).

The thaw in Syrian-Turkish relations dates back to the victory of the Justice and Development Party (Adalet ve Kalkınma Partisi or AKP) in the

2002 elections. Only four years previously, Syrian support for Kurdish militants and water disputes had brought the two countries to the brink of war. But 2002 onwards saw unprecedented levels of coordination and economic exchange. Aside from the new ideological orientation of Turkey's government, the regional state environment – geographical, ethnic and historical – has played a prominent role in its foreign policy. Turkish diplomacy takes place along three axes: the Western sphere from the Atlantic to the Urals (including Russia, Georgia, Armenia and Israel); the Turkic sphere in Central Asia, comprising the post-Soviet republics there; and the Islamic sphere, which extends from the Middle East and Iran through to Pakistan.

The effectiveness of the Turkish role in each of these spheres has been influenced by its own domestic politics as well as the international order in which it operates. Historically, the Turkish state was a secularist republic and a member of NATO whose mission in international relations was to orient Turkey towards the West.

During the Cold War, its geostrategic concerns were confined to the Western sphere, where, as the second largest ground force in NATO, it played a pivotal role in the containment of communism. When the USSR collapsed, however, the rules of the game changed, and Turkey was forced to reconsider its priorities. The independence of five new Turkic Muslim republics – Azerbaijan, Turkmenistan, Kazakhstan, Uzbekistan and Kyrgyzstan – allowed it to develop an active foreign policy in Central Asia under the pretext of pan-Turkic feeling.[31] Although hopes for Turkic political unity were thwarted by the new republics' unwillingness to replace one imperial power with another and by the intervention of the US and Russia, Turkey managed to establish strong connections with the new republics. However, the pan-Turkic project was not a real option.

Turkey soon shifted its focus back to the Western sphere. On 31 December 1995, Turkey established a customs union with the EU; on 12 December 1999, it was accepted as a candidate for full membership. Since then, however, objections from various EU countries, particularly France, have prevented any further progress. The reasons are partly demographic and religious: Turkey has a population of 80 million, large relative to the European population of 500 million, and its accession would make Muslims 20 per cent of the EU total. There were also political pretexts,

---

[31] Muhammad Nur al-Din, *Turkey in Changing Times: Concerns of Identity and the Conflict of Options* [Arabic] (London: Riad el-Rayyes, 1997), 42.

most notably the Cyprus issue, the dispute with Greece, the Kurdish question and the role of the military.[32]

The book *Strategic Depth*, published by the future AKP member and Foreign Minister Ahmet Davutoglu in 1999, argued that confining Turkey's strategic priorities to a single geographic sphere risked placing it (as a peripheral country) at the mercy of changes at the centre. Instead, its foreign policy should take advantage of its unique geographical position to make it the meeting-point of a multiplicity of axes: the Western sphere, Central Asia, the Balkans, the Middle East and the Islamic belt. It should be based on the principles of domestic cohesion and peace, regional legitimacy and close cooperation with Europe and the US. The main aim in practice was to accomplish a 'reset' with its neighbours by pulling back from a number of ongoing disputes.

Although this strategy was not uniquely Davutoglu's invention – Turkish foreign policy had been evolving in this direction since the premiership of Turgut Özal – it was adopted enthusiastically by the AKP government when it came to power in 2002. Turkey maintained good relations with the US and greatly strengthened its economic ties to the EU. It also sought to forge new and stronger links in Central Asia, leaving behind the paternalism of the 1990s in favour of equal relations between sovereign states. It tried to turn the page on historical problems with Greece and Armenia,[33] notably signing a provisional normalization of relations agreement with the latter country in 2009. Its GDP began to grow rapidly, with its economy becoming the seventeenth largest worldwide.

At the same time, Turkey began to pay much more attention to the Middle East. Here its policy diverged from that of the US. The communist threat was gone, and since the Özal years, Turkey had steadily increased its economic engagement with the Islamic world. Moreover, the neocons' war on terror, which began shortly before the AKP took power, did not accord with Turkish priorities: it destabilized the region while also reducing the role played by local allies (like Turkey) in favour of direct intervention. Intellectually and culturally, too, the mobilization of Western opinion against Islam and the policy of regime change did not sit well with the AKP. This strategic divergence was exposed by the invasion of Iraq, when Turkey made great efforts to avoid war and ultimately refused the US's request to use Turkish territory and airspace for the invasion.

---

[32] Alexander Abi Younis, 'Confused Relations between Turkey and the European Union' [Arabic], *National Defence* (Beirut), no. 331 (January 2011), at: https://bit.ly/3s61iy2 (accessed 3 February 2022).

[33] Turkish nationalism is on the rise again after Erdoğan's policies led him to an alliance with the conservative nationalists.

One reason that Turkey was so keen to avoid a war in Iraq was that the status quo was very much in its interests with respect to the Kurdish question. This issue has had a major impact on Turkey's relations with neighbouring Arab states. During the Iraq embargo, for example, Ankara was willing to cooperate with Baghdad so long as the Turkish army was permitted to pursue fighters with the Turkish Kurdistan Workers' Party (PKK) over the border.[34] Syria's support for the PKK, conversely, was the main cause of animosity between the two countries in the 1990s, and the resolution of this issue with the Adana Agreement of 20 October 1998 made possible a major thaw in relations.[35] The US occupation had the opposite effect.[36] A fully-fledged and officially recognized Kurdish entity was set up within the new federal structure, an entity that facilitated the concentration of PKK fighters on its territory,[37] attempted to annex oil-rich Kirkuk and strengthened ties with Kurdish political movements in Turkey.

The fragmentation of Iraq after the occupation drove further rapprochement between Turkey and Syria. Syria, too, had suffered from the invasion – more so than any other Arab country except Iraq. The US was using the threat of regime change to pressure Damascus to change its foreign policy. Moreover, developments in Iraq were influencing Syria's domestic politics, particularly in Kurdish areas. In 2004, a football match touched off a Kurdish uprising in Quamishli, which soon spread across northern Syria. As a result, Damascus moved closer to Ankara on security issues, and this served as a gateway to greater economic, political and military cooperation. Turkey mediated indirect negotiations between Syria and Israel in 2008, and in 2009 the two countries set up a common strategic cooperation council and held joint military exercises.

In short, Turkey had no interest in regime change in Syria, never mind plotting to bring it about.

The Turkish position on the revolution can be divided into two phases, each of them discussed in some detail below.

The first phase lasted from the beginning of the protests in Daraa through to the Turkish foreign minister's visit to Damascus (18 March 18–9 August 2011). The events in Daraa coincided with the adoption of UNSC Resolution 1973, which established a no-fly zone over Libya and sanctioned the use of 'all necessary measures [...] to protect civilians and

---

[34] Mostafa Al-Labbad, 'The Kurdish Question in the Turkish Politics' [Arabic], *al-Siyasa al-Dawliya* 42, no. 169 (July 2007), 190.
[35] Ibid.
[36] Ibid., 193.
[37] Subsequent differences between the Kurdish leadership of Iraq (the Barzanis) and the Kurdistan Workers' Party (Partiya Karkerên Kurdistan or PKK) led to the improvement of the relations with Turkey.

civilian populated areas under threat of attack' in the country, including airstrikes.[38] Unlike many Western and Arab countries, Turkey was opposed to the no-fly zone, branding it 'unhelpful' and 'fraught with risk' and saying that any military intervention would be counterproductive.[39] This was a point of disagreement with Qatar. Ankara had more reservations about the Libyan revolution than its counterparts in Tunisia and Egypt, where it quickly made its position clear. At first it tried to keep its options open, perhaps because of its extensive trade with Libya ($9.8 billion in 2010, with $100 billion in investment promised over the next three years).[40] But Qaddafi's violent response to the protests, NATO ownership of the intervention, unfavourable public opinion and the regime's deteriorating position eventually pushed the AKP to support the revolutionaries. Moreover, once Qaddafi's defeat was inevitable, Turkey was unwilling to miss out on the prospects for cooperation with the new Libya.

Having lost one Arab ally, Turkey did not want to lose another. Syria was its economic gateway to the Arabian Peninsula and allowed it to play a political role in the Arab-Israeli conflict. It also had serious economic interests in Syria itself. As such, its initial aim was to persuade the regime to pursue serious reforms and thereby contain the protests. It did this along two major axes. On one hand, it offered the regime extensive advice and support so long as it carried out the necessary reforms, which it also saw as a convenient way of promoting the 'Turkish model' and bolstering its regional legitimacy.[41] On the other, it sought to ensure it had the necessary means to pressure the regime to follow through. The AKP government was

---

[38] A copy of the resolution is available at: UN Official Document System, 17 March 2011, at: https://bit.ly/3mFEWzs (accessed 13 June 2022).

[39] ACRPS, 'Turkey's Position on the Libyan Revolution', 21 March 2011, at: https://bit.ly/3Hqebbc (accessed 3 February 2022).

[40] Ibid.

[41] The most significant Turkish statement made between 15 March and May 2011 came from President Erdogan himself, who warned Assad that the popular revolutions taking place across the Middle East might inspire opposition demonstrations in Syria and encouraged him to pursue democratic reforms in the country. After Assad's speech on 30 March, he added that he expected the Syrian government to 'lift the state of emergency, release political detainees and draft a new constitution', and that he would be speaking to Assad himself to encourage him to follow this path. On 6 April, Turkish foreign minister Ahmet Davutoglu met with Assad in Damascus, where he expressed his country's support for the preliminary reform measures and said that Turkey was willing to provide any help necessary to accelerate these reforms. On 27 April, a Turkish delegation met Assad to discuss 'possible reforms', and the Turkish parliament called for 'serious measures to promote social peace and stability, put an end to violence and protect basic rights and freedoms in Syria'. On 1 May, Davutoglu said that Turkey rejected 'any foreign intervention in Syria', calling for a domestic solution to the crisis. See: *Al Arabiya*, 23 March 2011, at: https://bit.ly/33qMZKd (accessed 8 August 2022); *Syrian Safahat*, 13 May 2011, at: https://bit.ly/3p1wCLL (accessed 8 August 2022); *Al Jazeera*, 6 April 2011, at: https://bit.ly/31UagnE (accessed 8 August 2022); *Youm7*, 29 April 2011, at: https://bit.ly/3deiXOB (accessed 8 August 2022); *Al Jazeera*, 1 May 2011, at: https://bit.ly/3QboFzy (accessed 8 August 2022).

convinced that strong Syrian-Turkish relations[42] gave it the moral and political clout needed to persuade Assad.

But all its efforts in this direction failed. The regime was convinced that its international connections and the guaranteed loyalty of the army and the security establishment meant that it would be able to crush the protests. It thus categorically rejected reform. A Turkish proposal for mediated dialogue with the Muslim Brotherhood, whose emigre leaders had been resident in Istanbul since 2009, was dismissed outright.[43]

Turkey thus tried to ramp up the pressure by taking a more strident diplomatic tone, allowing the opposition to meet on Turkish soil and offering refuge to Syrians fleeing across the border – including army defectors. It did this even before anything that warranted fleeing the country had taken place: on 3 April 2011, less than a month into the revolution, it announced that it was housing some 250 Syrians from Turkoman villages in Latakia and Idleb in a newly built refugee camp in Yayladagi, designed to be expanded.[44]

Turkey's sway with the regime was weakened by the US's reservations about the revolution, its muted diplomatic tone and its willingness to back regime-led reform. The ongoing support of Russia and Iran also strengthened the regime's hand against Ankara. Tehran had taken a pro-regime position at a very early point, and had made it clear that it would defend Syria against any prospective military intervention. Turkey, meanwhile, had no desire to damage its strong economic ties with Iran. Moreover, the leadership of the Turkish armed forces was not convinced that the deteriorating situation in Syria really constituted a threat to Turkish national security. Even as the government was blasting the storming of Hama, the Turkish defence minister announced that Turkey had no intention to establish a buffer zone along the border. The army tacks closer to NATO's position than to the government's on issues of this kind. Although eventually it was to change its mind on intervention, it was initially wary of unilateral confrontation because NATO was against it. And despite a diminution in their political influence over a decade of AKP rule, the armed forces still played a major part in determining military policy then.

---

[42] Ties between the two countries extended to friendships between the Assad and Erdoğan families. The same applied to the relationship between Assad and the Qatari emir.

[43] In his interview with ACRPS researchers in September 2012, former Supreme Guide of the Brotherhood Ali Sadr al-Din al-Bayanuni described a series of attempts to reconcile the regime and the Brotherhood both before and after the revolution began. Mediators included Turkey, Qatar and the Hamas political bureau chief Khaled Meshaal. Hijab, who briefly served as PM under Assad, confirmed in his testimony that Ankara attempted to convince Assad to hold a dialogue with the Brotherhood. The regime rejected all these overtures.

[44] Barout, *The Last Decade in the History of Syria*, 274.

Other domestic factors were also at play. Although most Turks supported the revolution, a Marshall Foundation survey conducted in September 2012 found that 76 per cent were opposed to military action against the Syrian regime and only 18 per cent were in favour.[45] There were also complicated concerns to do with the Kurdish issue. Turkey's support for the revolution was a major factor in determining the position of Kurdish parties within Syria, especially the PKK-linked PYD, which found that its hostility to Turkey produced a new convergence of interests with its old allies in Damascus. Finally, many of Turkey's Alawis – who comprise around one-third of the country's population and include Turks, Kurds and Arabs[46] – were opposed to intervention.

The combination of all these factors helped prevent the AKP government from playing a greater role against the Syrian regime and changing the course of the revolution. This gave the regime the ability to dodge Turkish government initiatives for more than six months before the total breakdown of relations between the two states. That only came on 22 September 2011, when Erdoğan announced that Assad had to step down to resolve the crisis in Syria, marking the beginning of phase two of Turkish-Syrian relations.

Turkey seems to have miscalculated. It overestimated its influence in Damascus and was drawn into making forceful statements it could not follow through on. It did not consider many important factors – or else did not imagine that the Syrian dictatorship would be so stubborn and so willing to use violence against its own people, or that Russia would support it to the bitter end.

The change in Turkey's position embarrassed Assad. Turkish support had helped break Syria's political isolation. Since 2005, state media had been heaping praise on the AKP government and the Turkish PM, even going so far as to describe Turkey as a 'sister country' – a term usually reserved for other Arab states. The Ministry of Education had modified the history curriculum to give a far more positive account of the Ottoman Empire and its history in the Levant,[47] abandoning the traditional account of backward foreign occupation. Syrian and Turkish TV companies had co-produced period dramas (*Fall of the Caliphate*, *Magnificent Century*) that cast the Ottoman period in a very positive light.[48] Now the Syrian

---

[45] *Assafir*, 14 September 2012.
[46] Yousef Ibrahim Al-Jahmani, *The Alawis in Turkey* [Arabic] (Beirut: Dar Al-Kunouz Al-Adabiyah, 2003), 75.
[47] Those familiar with the old and new curricula will note the obvious softening of tone towards the Ottoman period, which is taught in both middle and high school. The phrase 'Ottoman occupation' now appears only in chapter titles and subheadings, with less loaded phrases ('Ottoman period', 'Ottoman Empire', 'Ottoman presence') replacing it in the body of the text. The narrative of injustice and backwardness imposed on Arab countries is notably absent.
[48] *Al Jazeera*, 4 May 2010, at: https://bit.ly/3gnzeiN (accessed 3 February 2022).

media was forced to change tack. It began to warn of the AKP's 'neo-Ottomanism' and accuse it of seeking to put the Brotherhood in power in order to further its agenda.[49]

But the broader geostrategic context meant that in real terms, the new Turkish attitude was of little significance to the regime. On one hand, both Iran and Russia were suspicious of growing Turkish influence in the region. On the other, the US's withdrawal from the area meant that Turkey's hard-line policy had little support from Washington. Ankara was thus forced to reassess its earlier calculations. Since it was unable to intervene militarily, it played the cards it had been dealt: supporting the opposition and providing refuge.

With respect to the opposition, Turkey played a key role. It helped the opposition to develop and coordinate, providing both financial and logistical support, and became the rallying point of the opposition, particularly after the formation of the SNC in October 2011. Turkish diplomacy also helped secure international recognition for opposition bodies: at the second Friends of Syria Conference, held in Istanbul on 2 April 2012, the parties were persuaded to describe the SNC as 'a legitimate representative of the Syrian people'. Turkey also allowed the SNC and various non-SNC opposition parties to open political offices in Istanbul, Ankara, Antakya and Gaziantep. All this meant that Turkey had a great deal of influence over the opposition and its political choices. The Turkish-Syrian border also became the main venue for meetings between army defectors and rebel commanders. The majority of FSA command structures – the Joint Command established in February 2012 and the Supreme Command created in December of the same year – were set up on Turkish territory, with the aim of bringing all FSA units under a united structure paralleling the SNC in the political realm.

Ankara was unable to supply the revolutionaries with weapons directly because that would have required the approval of the National Security Council and of parliament, where there was strong opposition to AKP policy on Syria. The government circumvented this obstacle by facilitating the flow of arms (and later foreign fighters) to the opposition through its territory. The Turkish border was also open to various relief organizations, and the assistance provided by the Turkish government made it one of the main centres of aid work.

As the violence escalated, the number of Syrians seeking to cross the border grew steadily. According to Davutoglu, as of 13 February 2013, there

---

[49] The ease with which Syria accused former 'strategic allies' of betrayal and conspiracy further exposed the hollowness of its ideological rhetoric. It also yoked it to conspiracy theory, since nothing but a 'global conspiracy' could explain why so many allies and friends had abandoned it.

were 182,000 Syrian refugees in Turkey.[50] The Turkish state assumed responsibility for the refugees, without the UN supervision put in place in Iraq, Lebanon and Jordan. Official Turkish discourse rejected the label 'refugee', insisting on 'guests' instead, and Syrian refugees in Turkey live in better conditions than those in other neighbouring countries. The number of refugees allowed Ankara to put additional political and moral pressure on pro-regime countries, particularly Russia. Turkish officials regularly accused Russia of responsibility for the displacement of Syrians – to the point that Russian Foreign Minister Sergei Lavrov accused 'one of Syria's neighbours' of trying to exploit the refugee issue to justify military measures.[51]

Turkey played an active role in supporting and influencing the opposition, and without its decision to open the border the revolution could not have continued. The revolution also showed that 'neo-Ottomanism' is no more than a propaganda strategy underpinning economic expansion. It is rather a delusion among Arab Islamist movements that are seeking a return to ottoman era. The AKP may play to this illusion when addressing Arab public opinion, but it does not make much of it at home – the Turkish electorate is committed to the Turkish nation state – or in official foreign policy. Those who expected Turkish policy to be dictated by this neo-Ottomanism instead discovered that Turkey is a modern nation-state with a strong military establishment and a ruling party separate from the state that must take into account Turkish public opinion and Turkish national interests, as well as domestic issues (particularly the Kurdish issue).

4. Iran

It is impossible to understand how the Syrian regime persisted so long without considering Iran, which has supported Damascus politically, financially and militarily. Even if Iran did not encourage the regime to adopt its hard-line stance (although it seems likely that it did), the regime could never have survived or been so violent without Iran's belief that '[i]f we lose Syria, we cannot keep Tehran', as Mehdi Tayeb, the head of the Ammar Foundation, put it in February 2013.[52] In March 2013, Chief of Staff Fayrouz Abadi committed Iran to 'defend[ing] Syria with our very existence'.[53]

---

[50] *Atlas News*, 16 February 2013, at: https://bit.ly/3rm14C5 (accessed 3 February 2022).
[51] *Russia Today Arabic*, 18 August 2012. Archived copy available online: https://bit.ly/3I762bc (accessed 13 March 2022).
[52] *Al Arabiya*, 15 February 2013, at: https://bit.ly/3Gir3il (accessed 3 February 2022); *Al Jazeera*, 24 February 2013, at: https://bit.ly/3ggIi98 (accessed 3 February 2022).
[53] *Almadenah News*, 10 March 2013, at: https://bit.ly/3oLWfjM (accessed 14 February 2022).

Iran's foreign policy is built around five fundamental principles[54]: the Iranian national interest; strengthening regional influence; control of the Gulf waterways; political Shiʻism as state ideology and means of influencing neighbouring Shiʻi communities; and the sense of being a major regional state.[55] Its hostility to US policy – which in the immediate aftermath of the Islamic Revolution was rooted in antipathy to an 'arrogant' global power – is now based on a desire for respect for its sovereignty, system, decisions and regional position. These principles have played a major role in shaping relations between Iran and the Arab states. Its attempts to win the political loyalty of Shiʻis and to control the shipping lanes, coupled with Iraq and Saudi Arabia's fears of its support for political Shiʻism (the 'export' of the Islamic Revolution) and its potential influence on their Shiʻi citizens, has been a source of constant tension with Iraq and the Gulf states and, between 1980 and 1988, outright warfare (the Iran-Iraq War). Its anti-US and anti-Israeli positions and support for the Palestinian cause, on the other hand, have allowed it to cultivate several Arab allies, from the PLO to Syria.[56]

From the moment that Tehran expelled the Israeli ambassador and handed over the embassy to the PLO, Syria began to consider Iran as a potential ally in the struggle against Israel – a replacement for Egypt, which after the Camp David Agreement (1978) had dropped out of the equation. During the Iran-Iraq War, it sided with Tehran, in part because of long-standing disagreements with Baghdad and in part because of anxieties about Saddam Hussein's Arab and Gulf ambitions. After the war, relations continued to grow stronger, despite the ideological gulf between the two regimes.

Even after the decision to begin US-led peace negotiations with Israel in the early 1990s, relations remained close, since Damascus refused to link the peace process to ending the Iranian alliance. Iran was similarly pragmatic on the issue, even though the future of Syrian support for the Lebanese resistance remained unclear in the event that Israel agreed to return the Golan and lay the foundations for a lasting peace.

Syria's relations with Iran were thus oriented towards maintaining a 'geostrategic balance', strengthening its military capabilities and its negotiating position vis-à-vis Israel,[57] and checking Iraqi ambition. In return, Syria provided Iran with a way of exercising influence in the Arab-

---

[54] Azmi Bishara, 'The Arabs and Iran: General Remarks' [Arabic], in *The Arabs and Iran: A Review of History and Politics*, ed. Azmi Bishara and Mahjoob Zweiri (Beirut and Doha: ACRPS, 2012), 10–11.
[55] The sense of cultural superiority over the Arabs is a feeling that contradicts the constant emphasis on the concept of the Islamic *umma*, or nation. Turkey may also hold a comparable sense, but Turkey does not talk about an Islamic nation, and it is not its state ideology.
[56] Bishara, 'The Arabs and Iran', 24.
[57] Ahmed Khalidi and Hussein J. Agha, *Syria and Iran: Rivalry and Cooperation* [Arabic], trans. Adnan Hassan (Beirut: Dar Al-Kunouz Al-Adabiyah, 1997), 114.

Israeli conflict and supporting the resistance in Palestine and Lebanon, shoring up Iran's regional role and popular legitimacy, and forcing major international actors to take it seriously, thereby ending its isolation.[58] Syria was also seen as an Arab partner that would reduce the chances of polarization along Arab-Persian lines and could act as an intermediary in Iran's dealings with Arab Gulf states.

The US occupation of Iraq in 2003 gave Iran an opportunity to expand its influence. It quickly established links with Shiʻi Islamists in the country, particularly the Supreme Council of the Islamic Revolution in Iraq (SCIRI), the Sadrists, and the various forms taken by the Daʻwa Party, including the Rule of Law alliance led by then-PM Nouri al-Maliki. Considering the Shi'i demographic majority a political majority, Iran believed that Iraq should be ruled by Shiʻi political parties. During Maliki's tenure, it threw its weight behind a sectarian government that pursued vindictive policies against non-Shiʻis.

Syria, meanwhile, sought alliances with pan-Arab and nationalist parties, including Ayad Allawi's Iraqi List, which was highly critical of Iranian involvement in Iraq. Initially, Iran benefited from the American occupation of Iraq, especially the US cooperation with political Shiʻis in Iraq, but Syria considered the US presence a threat from the beginning. It also cultivated other forces capable of disrupting the US occupation, including jihadi forces. This meant that – temporarily at least – Syrian and Iranian interests in Iraq were in opposition. But after the Iraqi List beat the Rule of Law alliance at the 2009 parliamentary elections, Iran pressured the Syrian leadership to withdraw its support for Allawi and back a second term for Maliki in exchange for extensive economic concessions, most importantly the reopening of the Baghdad-Banyas pipeline. In this stage, the Americans were also ready to drop their secular ally (Allawi) and support Maliki for the sake of stability, which could only be guaranteed through temporary understandings with Iran.

With this obstacle overcome, differences over Iraq rapidly faded into the background, and relations with the Iraqi government itself also warmed considerably after years of hostility. Since 2010, Syria's foreign policy has followed the Iranian line in many areas, despite the tensions that this has caused in its relations with other allies such as Turkey and Qatar. Just as in Iraq, Syria's alignment with Iran led it to change its approach in Lebanon, where Damascus had convinced its allies to join Saad al-Hariri's new government after an understanding reached with Saudi Arabia and Qatar around the Doha Agreement (2008); in early 2011 – at a time when

---

[58] Ibid., 199–200.

Hezbollah was accused of involvement in the Hariri assassination – Syria's allies withdrew from the Saad al-Hariri government, causing it to collapse.

At the beginning of the Arab revolutions, Iran did not have a consistent position. The Tunisian protests took it by surprise, particularly given its excellent relations with the Ben Ali regime. It supported the revolution in Egypt and, for a while, in Yemen, where it soon threw its weight behind the Houthis and separatist movements in the south. It welcomed the popular revolution against Qaddafi in Libya but expressed serious reservations about the NATO intervention. But it supported the uprising in Bahrain with enthusiasm. According to Supreme Leader Ali Khamenei, the Arab revolutions were 'signs of an Islamic awakening' inspired by the Iranian Islamic Revolution,[59] part of a shift that 'has continued thanks to the steadfastness and efforts of the Iranian people since the Islamic Revolution', and would hopefully end with an Iranian-style 'popular regime based on religion'.[60] The Iranian line was that the revolutions were uprisings against rulers that had bowed down to the West and abandoned the Palestinian cause. There was an element of truth to this, but it was not the main dimension in the Arab revolutions. Iran simply wanted to cast the revolutions as a defeat for its enemies. And this also meant rejecting the possibility that the Syrian protests were a revolution, because the Syrian regime was not subordinate to the West.

At first, then, Iran praised most Arab revolutions. But as the winds of change began to blow across Syria, Iran embraced the regime line on the protests and endorsing its response. Despite being the only theocracy in the region, it allied itself with counterrevolutionary forces on the grounds that the revolutions were being exploited by Islamists. Its approach has been determined by its national interests and regional alliances. The Iranian regime places great importance on foreign policy, and, unlike Turkey, its approach is not checked by any complex democratic politics at home. This is of course short-sighted – domestic politics will ultimately be decisive, even in Iran.

Iran followed a sectarian policy with respect to the Arab revolutions. It presented itself as the defender of Arab Shiʻis, seeking to transform

---

[59] Firas Abu Hilal, 'Iran and the Arab Revolutions: Positions and Repercussions', ACRPS, September 2011, 3, at: https://bit.ly/3spFNbW (accessed 3 February 2022).

[60] Ali Khamenei maintained that current events in North Africa, in Egypt, Tunisia, and some other states, were an 'Islamic awakening' of the kind anticipated during the Islamic Revolution: 'Other peoples are watching us. For them, the most important thing that the [Islamic Revolution] has achieved is our political independence and our resistance to the enemies.' Khamenei called on the Egyptian people 'not to retreat until the establishment of a popular system based on religion. Clerics must play an exemplary role. When the people are outside the mosques chanting slogans, they must support them. God willing, part of the army will join the people'. He also noted that 'the main enemy of the Egyptian army is the Zionist regime and not the Egyptian people'. See: *Alwatan Voice*, 4 February 2011, at: https://bit.ly/34U3EH1 (accessed 14 February 2022).

religious identities into political loyalty. It became obsessed with alliances based on shared confessional identity, especially in Iraq, where power is concentrated in the hands of a sectarian civilian-security alliance. These alliances explain Nouri al-Maliki's staunch support for the Syrian regime despite a long history of political differences, particularly with respect to Syria's support for jihadi movements in Iraq, before it began coordinating with the US and the latter dropped its conditions.[61]

During the first few months of the revolution, Iran's position was that the revolution was a 'Western conspiracy' against anti-imperialism comparable to its own Green Movement (which the Iranian regime had described in similar terms when it faced protests in 2009).[62] On 12 April 2011, the spokesman for the Iranian Foreign Ministry described the protests of the previous three weeks as 'the malicious work of Westerners, particularly Americans and Zionists'.[63] At this point, the US had not even expressed support for the protesters.

It was not long, however, before the mounting death toll and the unfavourable international climate led Iran to moderate its tone. On 27 August, Foreign Minister Ali Akbar Salehi gave a statement saying, 'Governments should respond to the legitimate demands of their people, be it Syria, Yemen or other countries. The people of these nations have legitimate demands, and the governments should respond to these demands as soon as possible.'[64] So that this position did not appear to contradict previous statements, Iran continued to brand the Syrian protests an 'American game', quite unrelated to the just demands of the people.

Iran also criticized regional countries (Turkey, Saudi Arabia, Qatar) for their support of the revolution. Differences over Syria caused a serious decline in Iranian-Turkish relations, with the first signs of tension appearing after Turkey hosted the second Friends of Syria Conference on 2 April

---

[61] Syrian-Iraqi economic cooperation developed after the revolution. In June 2011, Iraqi Finance Minister Rafi al-Issawi met with a Syrian delegation to discuss lifting customs duties on Syrian goods entering Iraq. Economic estimates indicate that Iran forced Nouri al-Maliki to provide support to the tune of $9 billion, including extensive trade and investment agreements. In July Iran, Iraq and Syria signed a $10 billion natural gas agreement. Naturally, Maliki denied any Iranian pressure, claiming that Syria protects Iraq from terrorist infiltration. See: ACRPS, 'Effects of Sanctions on Syria's Macroeconomy in 2012', 22 January 2012, at: https://bit.ly/3zPNxHZ (accessed 13 Jun 2022).

[62] The reformist movement in Iran criticized the official position on Syria. Reformist Mohammad Sadr said that 'what Iran should be doing is advising President Assad to listen to his people and carry out real reforms'. On 23 April 2011, the website of opposition figure Mir-Hossein Mousavi, *kaleme.net*, criticized the official Iranian media for its coverage of events and for talking of a 'quiet Friday in Syria' despite the killing of some 100 Syrians that day. Mousavi pointed out that even the official Syrian media had admitted that several civilians had been killed. See: Abu Hilal, 'Iran and the Arab Revolutions', 9.

[63] *Al Jazeera*, 12 April 2011, at: https://bit.ly/30KA8BB (accessed 3 February 2022).

[64] *Al Jazeera*, 27 August 2011, at: https://bit.ly/3GtH8S5 (accessed 3 February 2022).

2011; the criticism levelled against Turkey by Iran was sharp enough that the Iranian ambassador was summoned to hear a protest from the Turkish government.

Iran then chose Baghdad to host international crisis talks over its nuclear programme in July the same year, a calculated snub to Ankara. In an official statement, Salehi said, 'If we were made to choose between Turkey and Syria, we would certainly choose Syria.' Although Turkey and Iran have different confessional associations, there was no sectarian dimension to their disagreement. But the same cannot be said for the dispute that developed between Iran and Saudi Arabia, which belatedly threw its weight behind the Syrian revolution – the first Arab revolution for which it expressed support – in order to prevent Iranian expansion in the Gulf and the Levant, where Iran worked to turn Shi'i confessional affiliation into loyalty to Iran.[65]

Over the course of 2012, there were repeated attempts to find a political solution to the Syrian crisis, most notably the second Arab League plan (ultimately scotched by the Russian-Chinese veto), the Annan plan and the Geneva communique, which served as the basis for Brahimi's subsequent efforts. Iran's position on each plan was primarily determined by whether it provided for Assad's abdication, a demand that Tehran rejected outright. It refused to engage with the second Arab League plan because it envisaged the president delegating his powers to the senior vice-president.[66] It was much more open to Annan's efforts, which featured no such stipulation and were the work of a man who had openly said that Iran would have to be a major party to any political solution, despite the opposition of the Western states and many Arab countries.

Although the Annan plan failed, the US and Russia agreed that the Geneva communique issued by the Action Group for Syria would form the basis of a future political settlement. This was an alarming development for Iran, because the US and Russia seemed to be moving towards an agreement that would exclude it. On 16 December 2012, Iran thus launched its own political initiative[67] comprised of six fundamental points: an immediate end to all military operations, under UN oversight; humanitarian assistance and the lifting of sanctions; national dialogue to prepare the ground for a consensus transitional government, whose main responsibility would be to arrange legislative elections in order to move ahead with drafting a new constitution; the release of all those imprisoned for peaceful political

---

[65] The turning point was King Abdullah's statement on Syria on 7 August 2011. See: *Al Arabiya*, 8 August 2011, at: https://bit.ly/3zLPyoa (accessed 15 June 2022).
[66] *Al-Thawra*, 8 February 2012, at: https://bit.ly/3HqkOKC (accessed 3 February 2022).
[67] *Mehr* (Iran), 16 December 2012, at: https://bit.ly/34wWvvL (accessed 3 February 2022).

activity; an immediate halt to misinformation campaigns; and the formation of a reconstruction committee to assess the damage and work out how to move forward.

This initiative was as far as Iran was willing to go. Ignoring the fact of the popular revolution against dictatorship, it limited the duties of the transitional government to holding parliamentary elections and allowed Assad to stay, with full powers, until the presidential elections scheduled for July 2014. Anything beyond this was dismissed out of hand. Salehi made this clear on 27 December 2012 when he said, 'Iran will not allow foreign solutions to be imposed on Syria from afar.'[68] Naturally, Iran did not consider its own solution to be 'foreign' or 'imposed from afar': it was the Syrian revolution that was the real impostor. In a speech given a week later at the Damascus Opera House, Assad set out a proposed solution that was almost identical to the Iranian initiative.

The Syrian-Iranian relationship is no longer simply an alliance, it is becoming a relationship of subordination. The Syrian regime's survival now depends on Iranian military and economic support. Iran, in turn, treated the Syrian revolution as a domestic national security crisis.

It is important to emphasize Iran's national interest in order to counteract the exclusive focus placed by much analysis on the sectarian element in Iran's decision-making. Although sectarianism is an important determinant of Iranian foreign policy, Tehran's position on Syria is not simply a matter of exporting the Islamic Revolution or religious solidarity with the Shi'i-linked Alawis. It is also about Iranian nationalism. Iran is not only concerned with religion and confession but with its own supreme national interests, although this is not to say that the religious ideology of the Iranian regime can be ignored. The Syrian revolution was a threat to its regional position.

Despite its presumed commitments to the values of the Islamic Revolution, including championing the oppressed peoples of the world, Iran entirely ignored the ethical dimensions of the events in Syria. It is only possible to understand the Iranian position if we recognize the complex web of international relations that surrounds it. A country like Iran, with a regional agenda and national security interests in many neighbouring states did not hitch its wagon to a collapsing dictatorship with no regional or international legitimacy for nothing. Above all else, it feared what might replace Assad[69] and worried that the future regime would be closer to Turkey and the 'moderate' Arab states, thereby breaking its crescent of

---

[68] *CNN Arabic*, 27 December 2012, at: https://cnn.it/3GtK4y5 (accessed 3 February 2022).
[69] Talal Atrissi, 'Iranian Goals and Interests in the Arab Order after the Revolutions' [Arabic], paper presented at 'Geostrategic Transformations in the Context of the Arab Revolutions', a conference organized by the ACRPS, Doha, 15–17 December 2012.

influence that stretches from Tehran to the Mediterranean (Iraq, Syria, Lebanon).

The Iranian focus on resistance to Israel does not justify its position on the Syrian revolution. Its opposition to Syrians' legitimate demands and its refusal to condemn the regime's killing and torture of protesters – condemnations it was willing to issue in every other Arab revolution – encouraged sectarian propaganda against it and left Syrians disillusioned with Iranian rhetoric on Palestine, which began to come across as instrumental. It took the killing and displacement of huge numbers of people to even slightly change Tehran's. Iran not only provided political, moral and financial support for the regime, it gave it equipment, expert advisors and officers (as well as Hezbollah fighters and Iraqi militiamen), a fact that the head of the Revolutionary Guards openly admitted.[70] If he was willing to say this much in public, there is no telling what else was going on behind closed doors.

The Arab revolutions shook Iran's view of its role in the region. The main divide in the Arab world is no longer between different blocs but between regimes and their peoples. Iran has made a desperate attempt to map the new division onto old alignments. This was one aspect of the struggle against sectarianism and the polarization of pro-revolution public opinion into religious and secular camps. There were other contradictions, too, that Iran was unwise to ignore. The most important of these was Iran's identity as a theocracy – the only state in the region whose system of government gives a constitutional role to the clergy.

We began this section by saying that Iran treats Syria as though it were an Iranian province. In fact, regime change in Syria would be a blow to Iran that would have real repercussions for domestic politics, especially as there is strong civil opposition to the regime. It would not be surprising if a successful revolution in Syria were followed by serious change in Iran. No wonder, then, that Iran sees developments there as a matter of domestic national security.

5. Saudi Arabia

Saudi-Syrian relations have experienced periods of cooperation and at times rivalry and rupture. For our purposes here, I will focus on relations during Bashar al-Assad's tenure, from 2000 through to the beginning of the Syrian revolution in 2011.

During the first two years of Assad's presidency, the Saudi position was cautious. Riyadh had no issue with Hafez al-Assad being succeeded by his

---

[70] *BBC Arabic*, 16 September 2012, at: https://bbc.in/3gpNPtO (accessed 3 February 2022).

son, but it wanted to test the new balance of power within the regime and gauge the new president's ability to lead such a complex regime. The older Assad's relations with the Saudi regime had been generally cooperative. Public tensions were avoided even in the 1970s and 1980s, when, for example, Assad denounced Prince Fahd bin Abdulaziz Al Saud's peace initiative (1981) for a solution to the Arab-Israeli conflict and the Palestinian issue, in the name of 'militant Arab solidarity'. Moreover, he had sided with the Gulf states against Iraq in 1991, and despite the alliance with Iran had always tried to strike a balance between Iranian and Saudi interests.

Several factors contributed to the warming of relations in 2002. In March of that year Syria supported Crown Prince Abdullah's initiative for peace with Israel at the Arab Summit in Beirut, which also saw the first face-to-face meeting between Abdullah bin Abdulaziz Al Saud and Assad. The summit provided an opportunity to settle various contentious issues, particularly the two countries' respective spheres of influence in Lebanon. As a result, Syria endorsed the Saudi-backed Rafiq al-Hariri's bid to remain prime minister despite his sharp disagreements with its own man, Lebanese President Émile Lahoud. The covert understanding reached in 2002 also explains why Saudi-Syrian relations did not immediately deteriorate in 2003 after stark differences emerged regarding the US invasion of Iraq.

But this did not last, and the invasion of Iraq proved to be a turning point. In 2004, as the Syrian regime grew increasingly alarmed by the US direct military presence in Iraq, it tightened its grip on the opposition in Syria and Lebanon, and used coercion and threats to secure the renewal of Lahoud's mandate. This was a return to its old strategy of monopolizing power in Lebanon via reliable allies. The following year, a string of Lebanese politicians with anti-Syrian views were assassinated, most notably Hariri himself. Riyadh nonetheless threw its weight behind the Lebanese 14 March alliance, which won the 2005 parliamentary elections on an openly anti-Syrian ticket. It also supported international efforts to place pressure on the Syrian regime, most notably UNSC Resolution 1559, which called for the withdrawal of Syrian troops from Lebanon.

Although Syria's influence in Lebanon was reduced by the victory of the 14 March alliance, it was given an enormous boost by the 2006 Israeli invasion. The alliance and Saudi Arabia blamed Hezbollah for the invasion, placing themselves at odds with Arab public opinion, which considered the Israeli invasion an aggression. The Syrian regime, meanwhile, gained considerable popular and Arab capital from its support for the resistance. Damascus was able to capitalize on this to regain momentum in Lebanon and undermine the Saudi position. On 15 August 2006, Assad announced the formation of the 'axis of resistance', an alliance comprising Syria, Hezbollah, Iran and Palestinian forces. He stated that the purpose of this new alliance was to counteract the 'axis of Arab moderation' allied with the neoconservatives, and gloated that the failed Israeli intervention had 'sunk the half-men and their half-positions'. This statement was perceived as a direct attack on and insult to the Saudi leadership.

Despite the setback of the July war, however, the struggle was not over. Saudi Arabia retained significant influence in Lebanon through the 14 March alliance, which was still in power. Syria's allies, meanwhile, were only able to disrupt the government's functioning, whether by use of Lahoud's presidential prerogative or (in the case of the political parties) by withdrawing from government or parliament. This dynamic continued until May 2008, when the government attempted to dismantle Hezbollah's communications network and break its control of airport security. In response, Hezbollah decided to resolve the political dispute with violence, seizing control of much of Beirut.

Hezbollah's action brought Lebanon once again to the brink of civil war. On this occasion, however, regional actors were quick to seek a political solution, which came in the form of the Doha Agreement. Michel Sleiman was chosen as a consensus president and a national unity government was formed, with sixteen ministries going to the majority (the 14 March alliance), eleven to the opposition (the pro-Syrian 8 March alliance) and three earmarked as presidential appointments. All parties agreed not to withdraw from the government or obstruct its functioning.[71] The agreement also indirectly delimited the Syrian and Saudi roles in Lebanon and encouraged them to resolve their differences. The results of the 2009 elections – where Syria's allies won the 'blocking third' of seats they needed to veto new legislation – made such a resolution possible.

The 2009 results were not so different from those of 2005. But the regional and international context had changed. Syria had emerged from its international isolation, and Western states – including the US – had begun to warm to the Syrian leadership, recognizing its significance for regional stability. After Assad visited Jeddah on 23 September 2009, King Abdullah made an official visit to Damascus on 7 October 2009, turning a page on the years of hostility. A new understanding was established between Riyadh and Damascus on several issues, including Iraq and Lebanon. On 30–31 July 2010, King Abdullah touched down in Damascus before accompanying Assad to a trilateral summit with Sleiman in Beirut. At the summit, Syria agreed to support Saad al-Hariri's government. In September, after making an implicit apology for earlier statements hostile to Syria,

---

[71] *Al-Riyadh*, 22 May 2008, at: https://bit.ly/3ohA1pK (accessed 3 February 2022).

Saad al-Hariri visited Damascus,[72] the seat of the country he had accused of assassinating his father in cooperation with Hezbollah.

By the time protests began in Syria in March 2011, Syrian-Saudi relations were positive. Riyadh had accepted that Syria should play some role in Lebanon, despite Syrian attempts to expand that role. On 26 November 2010, an attempt to undermine Hezbollah's efforts to remove the Lebanese PM by intensifying investigations into its role in the Hariri assassination forced Syria to close ranks with its ally. But although this led to disagreements with Saudi Arabia (as well as Turkey and Qatar), the newly solid relations between Damascus and Riyadh meant that there was no return to animosity.

Many factors shaped the Saudi position on the Syrian revolution, but Iran's role in Iraq and anxieties about its involvement in the Gulf states – particularly given its attempts to cultivate constituencies in Bahrain and Saudi's own Eastern province – were particularly important. Saudi Arabia is a conservative monarchy, with no margin for democracy and freedom of expression. It is a rich rentier state with the resources to simultaneously fund its state apparatus and social services, support other conservative states in the region, monopolize Arab transnational media (before the emergence of non-Saudi cable channels such as Al Jazeera) and contain large numbers of intellectuals and possible forces for change. Riyadh has been hostile to all the revolutions. It has opposed popular protest as a path to change even where that protest is directed against its enemies (in Libya, for example), identifying its conservative position with stability through the existence of authoritarian governments. Its position on Syria did not deviate fundamentally from this attitude.

At the beginning of the revolution, Saudi Arabia appeared to support the Syrian government. On 27 March 2011, Assad received a telephone call from King Abdullah in which he expressed Saudi support for Syria in the face of a 'conspiracy' targeting its security and stability, stressing that Saudi Arabia stood alongside the Syrian leadership and people in their attempts to foil this plot, according to the official Syrian account.[73] Moreover, Riyadh provided direct financial assistance. On 7 April, the governor of the Saudi Monetary Authority announced that the kingdom was providing $140 million in development loans to Syria and was looking into providing more. In exchange, Syria backed the Saudi-led Peninsula Shield intervention in support of the Bahraini monarch, with Foreign Minister Walid al-Muallim emphasizing that the Peninsula Shield troops were 'not occupation

---

[72] *Al-Ayam* (Bahrain), 9 September 2010, at: https://bit.ly/3GpZDXR (accessed 3 February 2022).
[73] *Syria News*, 28 March 2011. Archived copy available online: https://bit.ly/3gkAP9a (accessed 3 February 2022).

forces. They are there as part of a legitimate framework'.[74] Syria and Saudi Arabia thus shared an inter-sectarian, anti-revolutionary position.

For many months, Syria worked hard to keep Saudi Arabia happy. It is difficult to find a single official statement criticizing Saudi Arabia before 3 March 2013 – some two years into the revolution. Although pro-regime media (Dunya TV) did accuse Saudi figures of involvement in the 'conspiracy' earlier on, they targeted Bandar bin Sultan bin Abdulaziz Al Saud, who at the time was something of a political outcast and could be attacked freely. Saudi Arabia, for its part, also tried to maintain a positive relationship with the regime. It wanted Syria to rein in its allies in the Lebanese opposition, who were seeking to remove Saad al-Hariri as PM, and hoped to secure this in exchange for its support against the protests. At this point the sectarian factor was marginal to its calculations and to the calculations of other states.

But as the revolution drew on, the kingdom changed tack. On 7 August 2011, six months into the revolution, King Abdullah issued an official statement blasting the 'shedding of innocent blood' as inimical to 'religion and morality', describing events in Syria as 'unacceptable to the Kingdom of Saudi Arabia', and warning the Syrian leadership that it had two choices: either it would 'carry out its historic role' by implementing 'rapid, comprehensive reforms' or else it would 'slide into chaos'.[75] Nonetheless, the statement was meant as a warning, not as a complete break with the regime. It called only for an end to the security solution and for a government-led reform process. It did not suggest that the president should step down or that the regime should be overthrown. And the only real action taken by Riyadh was to recall its ambassador 'for consultations' – it did not close its embassy or break diplomatic ties.

Various factors explain the change in the Saudi position. The first is the impact of public opinion. The massacres carried out by the regime produced an unprecedented sense of popular solidarity with the revolutionaries. The assault on Hama on 7 August, which left at least 400 people dead and took place immediately before the king's statement, led many to indirectly accuse the leadership of allowing the Syrian regime to carry out atrocities unchallenged. There was a sectarian dimension to this – inevitable in a country in which Salafi ideology and modes of religiosity are so widespread. Clerics and religious institutions branded the Syrian government the 'Nusairi regime'. Iran and Hezbollah's support for the regime also contributed to this sectarian quality.

---

[74] *Asharq Al-Awsat*, 20 March 2011, at: https://bit.ly/3unft2V (accessed 3 February 2022).
[75] *Al Arabiya*, 8 August 2011, at: https://bit.ly/3HtEgWQ (accessed 3 February 2022).

The international climate had also changed. Western powers had begun to adopt a sharper diplomatic tone on the Syrian crisis, arguing that Assad had lost his legitimacy to govern, and both the US and EU were imposing sanctions on the president and other regime figures. Even long-standing regime ally Turkey was moving towards a more strident position. There were suggestions that Turkey was threatening the kingdom's leadership of Sunni opinion (all new concepts superimposed onto regional politics by propaganda in the Arab media). The new Saudi line thus accorded with the changing international position on Assad.

Moreover, the Saudi-Syrian understanding on Lebanon had broken down. On 30 June 2011, the Special Tribunal for Lebanon delivered indictments of four members of Hezbollah who were accused of planning and executing Hariri's assassination.[76] The Syrian regime anticipated a fresh round of pressure in Lebanon and decided to remove Saad al-Hariri as PM to prevent the government from cooperating. Its allies resigned from Saad al-Hariri's government *en masse*, and it then pressured Najib Mikati to form an alternative ministry, using its influence to secure the necessary vote of confidence in parliament. In effect, Syria was opting for an exclusive alliance with Hezbollah, even if that came at the expense of relations with Saudi Arabia. According to our sources, Saudi Foreign Minister Saud bin Faisal bin Abdulaziz Al Saud and a broader grouping within the Saudi administration had never been happy with the concessions made to Syrian influence in Lebanon. Syria's actions seemed to vindicate this position. This grouping consistently pressed for a clearer, more strident Saudi position against the Syrian regime.

Between the official statement in August and the beginning of February 2012, Saudi action against Syria took place entirely within the confines of the Arab League. On 25 November 2011, Saud bin Faisal asserted that the Gulf states were ready to come up with a plan similar to the Gulf Initiative for Yemen.[77] He emphasized the need for an Arab solution along the lines of the first Arab League plan put forward in September, arguing that if the Arab states did not reach an agreement with Syria, it would invite foreign intervention and UN involvement.[78] On 9 December, the Saudi intelligence chief confirmed that Assad had rejected Arab offers to find a solution, and said that it was difficult to know how to deal with Assad because 'he denies

---

[76] *The Guardian*, 30 June 2011, at: https://bit.ly/3mLvSsV (accessed 5 May 2022).
[77] The Gulf Initiative provided for the formation of an opposition-led government and immunity for Yemeni President Ali Abdullah Saleh after his resignation. See: *Asharq Al-Awsat*, 24 November 2011. Archived copy available online: https://bit.ly/3HwPbPK (accessed 3 February 2022).
[78] *Russia Today Arabic*, 25 November 2011. Archived copy available online: https://bit.ly/34x6Wzr (accessed 3 February 2022).

that his commanders have given any orders to fire on demonstrators'; he also said that Assad would not step down voluntarily.[79]

By January 2012, with Iranian and Russian support making diplomatic and economic measures increasingly useless, the kingdom was beginning to lose patience. On 22 January, it withdrew its observers from the Arab League monitoring mission on the grounds that it was not willing to be used as a 'false witness' to justify 'crimes against our Syrian brothers'. This coincided with the mooting of the second Arab League plan, which as we have noted called for Assad to delegate his powers to a vice-president and looked to the UNSC for enforcement. After Russia and China vetoed the plan on 4 February, however, Riyadh definitively concluded that there could be no diplomatic solution to the crisis and that the only way of changing the balance of power on the ground was to arm the Syrian opposition.

At the Friends of Syria conference held in Tunis in late February, Riyadh broke decisively with the regime and rejected any possibility of Assad staying on. Saud bin Faisal told attendees that the Syrian government was 'more like an occupation force' and that the only way to resolve the crisis was to bring about a 'transfer of power – whether voluntarily or by force'.[80]

Saudi Arabia now moved to demand openly that the Syrian people be given weapons to defend themselves (in my assessment, they had already been open to arming the opposition for a month beforehand). Saud bin Faisal made this point explicitly on 11 March 2012 during a meeting with the German foreign minister, where he maintained that 'the Syrian people must be allowed to defend themselves against the regime'.[81] From that moment, it became one of the few states providing weapons to the rebels. This position put it at odds with the US, which continued to seek a political solution via talks with Russia. But Riyadh was now convinced that the only feasible solution was a military one, and that the various plans put forward were vague and lacking in enforcement mechanisms. On 22 January 2013, Saud bin Faisal reiterated, 'It is impossible to imagine a negotiated settlement with a regime that does this to its own country, history and people.'[82]

It is difficult to gauge the full extent of Saudi involvement in the revolution. Riyadh had a liaison office in Amman (headed by Prince Faisal bin Sultan) overseeing military coordination and another in Istanbul (headed by a close assistant of Hariri, the Lebanese MP Okab Sakr). We do

---

[79] *Russia Today Arabic*, 10 December 2011, at: https://bit.ly/3olrbHM (accessed 3 February 2022).
[80] *Syria News*, 24 February 2012. Archived copy available online: https://bit.ly/3grlWS9 (accessed 3 February 2022).
[81] *Syria News*, 11 March 2012. Archived copy available online: https://bit.ly/3oipbj9 (accessed 3 February 2022).
[82] *Al Jazeera*, 22 January 2013, at: https://bit.ly/34eVA3l (accessed 3 February 2022).

not know much about the activities of the Saudi intelligence taskforce headed by Bandar bin Sultan. We do know that cooperation between Saudi Arabia and Turkey was far less significant than that between Turkey and Qatar, and that the office in Amman has been forced to scale down its activity because of Jordan's hesitant position on the revolution. But Saudi activity had also included the broader society, including religious associations, businessmen and Islamic relief organizations, which worked alongside their counterparts in Syria. Private money flowed directly to humanitarian aid groups and armed factions until it was stopped by the Saudi government in May 2012; thereafter all financial aid had to be channelled through official agencies.[83] Overall, Saudi Arabia – working through Bandar bin Sultan – expressed strong opinions on the political leadership of the opposition, pressuring it to accept Saudi views. It seemed that its well-worn approach in Lebanon served as a model for its approach to its allies elsewhere in the Levant.

6. Qatar

Qatar has a citizen population of around 300,000, who in 2012 made up only 18 per cent of a population composed largely of expats and migrant workers. It is a state that relies on gas revenues and is trying to diversify its sources of income. Its per capita income is the highest in the world. Citizens of Qatar do not pay taxes and receive privileges which non-citizens do not. Loyalty to the ruling family is based on strong communal ties and a welfare state. These sources of legitimacy have allowed the Qatari regime to remain intact despite rapid economic, demographic, and urban growth and a steady rise in living standards, without the need for much pressure on society. In this respect, it is similar to other states such as the UAE and (at one point) Kuwait, with a margin of freedom wider than the UAE and narrower than Kuwait. There are no proposals to democratize Qatar and given these factors it seems unlikely that there will be any time soon.

This introduction is necessary because of the apparent contradiction between Qatar's system of government and its support for change in the Arab world. Not being a democratic state itself, Qatar seems unqualified to advocate for democracy in the region. But unlike, say, Saudi Arabia – whose citizens make up a large majority of a population with many social issues, not least poverty – Qatar does not feel threatened by the spread of democracy. Other monarchies more vulnerable to democratic demands (Bahrain, Saudi Arabia, Jordan) may see this as Qatari selfishness.

---

[83] *The Guardian*, 14 August 2012, at: https://bit.ly/3NWzIvC (accessed 14 June 2022).

Nonetheless, this has been the reality of Qatar's political vision and action in dealing with Arab public opinion for more than a decade. The UAE, with a similar system of rule, is also not threatened by democracy in the region, but nevertheless pursues a strident, consistent anti-democratic course.

Qatar strikes a balance between its Western alliances, especially with the US (motivated by inter-Arab conflicts and Qatar's need for recognition as an international player, especially during Emir Hamad bin Khalifa Al Thani's early years), its relations with Iran for geostrategic reasons (it has borders only with Iran and Saudi Arabia, which is a major, if not the major factor in defining its foreign policy, including its alliance with the US), and action on issues popular with Arab public opinion.

Qatar's position on Syria is important because, on the face of it, it was one of the most consistent and enthusiastic supporters of the revolution. At first, as critical moments came and went, Qatar seemed to be the *only* state actively and consistently supporting the revolution, and it became the focus of much pro-regime propaganda as a result. At some points, it was the most influential player in the revolution. But the Qatari position was also very complex, for several reasons. Prior to the revolution, Syrian-Qatari relations had reached unprecedented levels of cooperation and coordination, especially in economic matters. The two countries supported the resistance during the war in Lebanon in 2006. Qatar had sided with Syria during its dispute with Saudi Arabia and had helped break Damascus's diplomatic isolation after the Hariri assassination, taking advantage of its excellent relations with the Nicolas Sarkozy administration.

When the Arab revolutions began, the emirate decided to throw its weight behind change. It did not initiate the protests or encourage them – Qatar is not a revolutionary country. Arab regimes have generally blamed the Qatari-owned Al Jazeera for popular protest because it discusses issues never broached in state media. There has also been a tendency to accuse political opponents, especially Islamists, of being Qatari puppets, both during and after the revolutions. In reality, the Islamists' strength – and others' ambivalence about a democracy that might bring Islamists to power – well predates the Arab Spring and cannot be attributed to Qatari support. And in fact, the novelty of the revolutions was that for the first time in years civil, *non*-Islamist forces were in the spotlight. But Qatar's flexibility, its break with familiar coalitions and alliances – often for Qatari motives that had nothing to do with democracy – and its refusal to play the established role of a small or Gulf state made it a scapegoat for events elsewhere.

Syrian-Qatari relations before the revolution

When Bashar al-Assad came to power, Syrian-Qatari relations were tense. After Emir Hamad overthrew his father and began to chart a foreign policy course independent of Riyadh (which the latter never accepted), Syria had come down firmly on the side of Saudi Arabia. (This difficult relationship with Saudi Arabia was one of Qatar's most important motivations for closer alliance with the US.) But the emirate saw the inauguration of the new president as a chance to open a new chapter in its relationship with Damascus, and an opportunity to do so came in 2003, when Riyadh and Damascus fell out over Iraq. A Syrian state visit to Doha opened the door to economic cooperation, and thirteen agreements were soon signed between the two countries.

By 2007, Qatar was the leading Arab investor in Syria, overtaking Saudi Arabia. Among the most significant Qatari-backed projects were the International Islamic Bank, founded in 2005 with capital of $100 million, and the Syrian-Qatari Holding Company (SQHC) and Syrian Credit Company (SCC), both set up in 2007 with an estimated capital of $5 billion each.[84] The SQHC intended to invest some $8 billion in the Diyar Dimashq project in the centre of the capital,[85] and Qatar's own Diyar company launched additional tourist projects in Ras ibn Hani ($350 million)[86] and Tamdor ($5 billion).[87]

In the political sphere, the occupation of Iraq in 2003 produced two competing blocs: the 'Axis of Resistance' (Syria, Iran and Hezbollah) and the 'moderates' (Saudi Arabia, Egypt and other US allies). Qatar was not keen to join either one. Qatar is a monarchy with strong ties to the US, which maintains a large military base in the country. These ties meant that it could not be part of the same bloc as Iran, which openly denounced the US and its regional policy. At the same time, its poor relations with Saudi Arabia and Egypt meant that it was unwilling to be drawn into an alliance led by Riyadh, which could make it subordinate to Saudi Arabia.

To this end, the emirate has maintained links with Islamist and resistance groups outside the political consensus – Hezbollah and Hamas, for example. Although in some cases the emir's personal sympathies play a significant role, this is first and foremost a political investment, a proven source of political and diplomatic capital. Whenever the West needs to communicate with these forces, it has sought Qatari mediation. Among other diplomatic coups, Qatar has helped secure the release of abductees across the world and hosted negotiations between the US and the Taliban.

---

[84] *Syria News*, 22 April 2010. Archived copy available online: https://bit.ly/35LNDDo (accessed 3 February 2022).
[85] *Elaph*, 24 November 2008, at: https://bit.ly/34X2g6s (accessed 14 February 2022).
[86] *Asharq Al-Awsat*, 28 February 2008, at: https://bit.ly/3oHZoS3 (accessed 3 February 2022).
[87] *Syria News*, 5 November 2007. Archived copy available online: https://bit.ly/3IYZsUX (accessed 3 February 2022).

More broadly, Qatari foreign policy has focused on mediation and conflict resolution in its own region and in the Arab world. Examples of this include the Lebanese reconciliation conference held in Doha in 2008, Qatari mediation between the Sudanese government and the Darfuri rebels, the Palestinian talks between Fatah and Hamas, and the Taliban negotiations. All this has put Qatar firmly on the global political map.

Its avoidance of political blocs has given Qatar considerable freedom to manoeuvre in foreign policy compared to other US allies in the Gulf. It was able to establish warm relations with Syria at a time when there was substantial US and Western pressure on the regime, and ultimately to break its diplomatic isolation. Moreover, it has been able to pursue a popular policy on the Arab-Israeli conflict, standing by Hezbollah during the Israeli invasion of Lebanon in 2006. It was likewise highly critical of the Israeli attack on Gaza in 2008–9, calling for an emergency Arab summit to support Hamas and closing the Israeli Trade Office in Doha.

The hostile response of the 'moderate' powers to the 2009 emergency summit – Saudi Arabia and Egypt refused to attend, with the Saudi government pressuring other Arab countries to follow suit and ensure that the summit was inquorate – pushed Qatar closer to Syria, and the two countries continued to enjoy very close relations through to 2011. Syria's toppling of the Saad al-Hariri government in Lebanon on 16 January 2011 violated the Qatar-brokered reconciliation agreement and was a blow to the Qatari position in that country. Nonetheless, relations remained strong right up to the revolution.

Qatar's stance post-revolution

At the beginning of the Arab Spring, Qatar demonstrated sympathy to all the Arab revolutions through its media. Other than the role played by Al Jazeera, however, for the most part it did not have the chance to offer material support for the Tunisian and Egyptian revolutions given their relatively short duration. In Libya it provided rebels training and weapons, and in Yemen it gave some political forces financial subsidies. In Egypt and Tunisia, however, its role was exclusively diplomatic (although the post-revolutionary government in Cairo did benefit from $500 million in Qatari grant money). And when revolution spread to Bahrain, Qatar was more circumspect, despite its good links with the moderate opposition there. The Gulf states had agreed to support the king and deploy the joint Peninsula Shield force to help suppress the popular uprising. Moreover, Qatar had reservations about Iranian enthusiasm, especially given the sectarian dimension to the protests. Nonetheless, Bahraini state media regularly attacked Qatar because of Al Jazeera's coverage of the uprising, Qatar's failure to publicly support the Bahraini regime, and a Qatari attempt to act as mediator, although the depth of Gulf backing for the regime meant that this attempt was doomed from the start.

When Syrians came out to protest in March, the Qatari leadership faced a dilemma. Staying silent in the face of regime brutality risked undermining the popular approval it had won by supporting the revolutions. But Syria was a long-standing ally, and Qatar did not want to lose its extensive economic interests in the country by demonstrating open hostility to the regime. Doha thus pursued a cautious policy. Al Jazeera was instructed to limit its coverage of events in Syria. At the same time, it sought to persuade the regime to meet protesters' demands in order to prevent protests from escalating. On 27 March, Crown Prince Tamim bin Hamad Al Thani made a visit to Damascus.[88] On the same day, Assad received a phone call from Emir Hamad.

On 2 April, in what was probably a diplomatic protest, the Qatari prime minister (and foreign minister) visited Damascus to deliver a message from the emir. This was the second visit by a senior Qatari official within a week, alongside multiple high-level telephone calls, showing Qatar's concern that the crackdown would lead to an escalation and thus force it to take an anti-regime position. During this period, Qatar's position remained ambiguous. Syrian state discourse maintained that Qatar was 'standing with Syria in the face of attempts to destabilize its security and stability',[89] and the Qatari leadership maintained close contact with the regime throughout the first six months of the revolution. As late as 22 June, Syrian Foreign Minister Muallim told a press conference that all Arab states, without exception, supported Syria, asserting, 'I do not want to disclose the telephone conversations underway between the president and the leaders of these countries, and between me and the foreign ministers of these states, which include the state of Qatar.'[90]

But this last comment reflected the other side of the Qatari position. Al Jazeera, which was very popular in Syria, was permitted to move ahead of the Qatari state in adopting an unapologetically pro-revolutionary line,[91] and the Syrian regime believed that its coverage reflected the undeclared position of the Qatari state. While official Syrian media remained positive, unofficial pro-regime media were thus given the green light for a counteroffensive. Al Jazeera was accused of being a 'Zionist project' set up

---

[88] *DP News*, 28 March 2011. Archived copy available online: https://bit.ly/3rntD2b (accessed 3 February 2022).
[89] *Al Jazeera*, 3 April 2011, at: https://bit.ly/3rnOeDr (accessed 3 February 2022).
[90] *SANA*, 23 June 2011. Archived copy available online: https://bit.ly/3okGwIm (accessed 3 February 2022).
[91] Despite the calls to 'overthrow the regime' heard throughout Syria since mid-April 2011, Qatar continued to hold out hope that Assad would carry out reforms, lead a political process, and undertake political and societal dialogue to contain the crisis. It is noteworthy that this position was not specific to Qatar, but rather represented the consensus of international and regional powers.

to destroy Arab countries. Qatar itself was accused of inciting protest, and outlets like Dunya TV made a patriotic sport of crudely insulting the emir, his wife and family, and the country more broadly.

As if this media offensive were not enough, on 18 July the authorities allowed Syrian demonstrators to attack the Qatari embassy, forcing Doha to withdraw all diplomatic staff. The regime claimed the attack was a spontaneous reaction fuelled by anger at Al Jazeera's 'unprofessional and unobjective' campaign of 'fabrication' against the country.[92]

Alongside the regime's brutal treatment of protesters, these factors all contributed to a growing rift between Qatar and the Syrian leadership. Formal diplomatic relations were suspended after the attack on the embassy, but a full-scale political rupture only became visible in August, when large numbers of troops were deployed to Hama and Deir ez-Zor to suppress the huge popular demonstrations there. Like other international and Arab observers, Qatar made a last-ditch attempt around this time to convince Assad to commit to a political process. On 25 August, Emir Hamad was invited to make a state visit to Tehran,[93] where he tried to secure Iranian support for these efforts. During his meeting with Mahmoud Ahmadinejad, he expressed an unambiguously pro-revolutionary position and warned that the regime would soon collapse if it did not make the necessary changes; the security solution had failed, and Syrians would not back down at any cost.[94]

Despite this newly strident tone, the emir stopped short of demanding Assad's departure. Qatar had not given up on the possibility of a political solution, despite the break with the regime. After becoming chair of the Council of Arab Foreign Ministers in September, it took charge of the Arab League's efforts to solve the crisis. It took the chairmanship of the special ministerial committee set up on 16 October,[95] which reached a preliminary understanding with the regime during a visit to Damascus on 27 October. On 30 October, Muallim visited Doha, where he agreed to a plan for implementation of the first Arab League initiative.[96] During this visit, Muallim tried to convince the emir to make another official visit to Damascus and talk to Assad directly. But relations between the two countries had deteriorated to a point where this was simply impossible.

On 12 November, when the regime failed to comply with the Doha Agreement (as did the opposition, but then the opposition was not an organized entity with control over the revolution), Qatar convened an emergency meeting of the Council of Foreign Ministers, at which Syria's

---

[92] *Al Jazeera*, 19 July 2011, at: https://bit.ly/34vwGfI (accessed 3 February 2022).
[93] Lebanese newspapers close to Syria at the time claimed it was at his insistence, but this was untrue.
[94] *Al Jazeera*, 26 August 2011, at: https://bit.ly/3gh6sQS (accessed 3 February 2022).
[95] *Al Jazeera*, 17 October 2011, at: https://bit.ly/3HtdKNi (accessed 3 February 2022).
[96] *France 24*, 31 October 2011, at: https://bit.ly/3L6P3IU (accessed 3 February 2022).

Arab League membership was suspended.[97] At the next regular meeting of the Council, on 27 November, the ministerial committee proposed a raft of measures, including sanctions. The ratification of these proposals marked the first time that the Arab League had taken action of this kind. Under the sanctions, Syrian officials were banned from Arab countries and their assets frozen, dealings with the Syrian Central Bank were suspended and trade was limited to strategic commodities with a direct impact on normal Syrians' lives.[98] In practice, however, only a small number of Arab states – including Qatar and Saudi Arabia – committed to these sanctions. Jordan and Lebanon announced that they were unable to comply.

Qatar tried to use the new dynamism of the post-revolutionary Arab League, especially after regime change in Cairo, to exert pressure on the Syrian regime. On 14 January 2012, Emir Hamad suggested sending an Arab force to stop what he called the 'Syrian massacre'. He argued that the only way of preventing foreign intervention of the kind witnessed in Iraq in 2003 was to make full use of the existing mechanisms for joint Arab action, which were capable of addressing both internal and external challenges to the Arab countries. He cited the example of the Arab Deterrent Force, which had played an important role in ending the Lebanese Civil War.[99]

Having failed to convince the regime to commit to the Arab League plan, on 22 January the ministerial committee presented an amended initiative to the Council of Foreign Ministers. This moment marked the final break between Qatar and Syria, since the new initiative demanded Assad delegate his powers to a deputy and requested UNSC enforcement. If this initiative had succeeded, Syria might have been saved from the spectre of protracted civil war that was looming over the country, as well as the geostrategic entanglements that were becoming evident around this time. But on 4 February, the Russian-Chinese veto doomed it to failure.

At this point, events began to move in a new direction. With nobody to stop it from taking whatever measures it thought necessary to end the revolution, the regime unleashed the full might of its security apparatus and military forces. While the US prevaricated, Russia became the most influential player simply because it was fully behind the regime.

Qatar was unable to walk back its strident condemnation of the regime. Instead, it changed its tactics. It had already been building connections with the opposition, providing them with the necessary assistance to build a united political entity capable of winning international recognition. In November 2011, it hosted the first General Assembly of the SNC, where it

---

[97] *BBC Arabic*, 6 November 2011, at: https://bbc.in/3unMpZi (accessed 3 February 2022).
[98] *Al Arabiya*, 27 November 2011, at: https://bit.ly/3L7cku3 (accessed 3 February 2022).
[99] *BBC Arabic*, 14 January 2012, at: https://bbc.in/3s8qvX8 (accessed 3 February 2022).

elected its executive bureau. It now accelerated these efforts. It advocated arming Syrians so that they could defend themselves against the regime, and in February 2012 it insisted that this be included in the decisions of the Council of Foreign Ministers. It also provided weapons and other forms of assistance to the FSA and helped it coordinate action on the ground. In March 2013, it played an important role in securing the opposition's control of Syria's Arab League seat, which lasted only for one Arab summit, the one held in Doha.

Qatar's preference was to contain the crisis by pressuring the regime to implement reforms appropriate to popular demands and the revolutionary reality. But Damascus's repressive approach ultimately forced it to look for consensual political solutions that would lead to a regime exit and usher in, gradually and securely, democratic change. It stood by the rebels in a battle against a regime that deployed every weapon in its arsenal against its own people, up to and including ballistic missiles. It was also the revolution's staunchest diplomatic supporter, and helped arm and organize the opposition and provided crucial humanitarian aid. But Qatar, Saudi Arabia and Turkey made many mistakes, whether in inter-state coordination, in their inadequate knowledge of the dynamics of Syrian society and the forces on the ground, or in their competition to support armed groups without going through a Syrian political leadership.

Qatar is not a radical revolutionary force or a superpower with a powerful intelligence apparatus. It is a state allied to the Western camp, which hosts a US base on its territory because of inter-Arab differences and the difficulties of Gulf security. It would not have been logical to expect a state of this kind to support the revolutions. Regardless of its motives, this support came as a surprise. It cannot be understood unless we recognize the political distinctiveness of the leadership, its desire for a truly international economic and political role, and its closeness to Arab public opinion. Nonetheless, its leading role in Syria drew criticism from its Western and Arab allies and its adversaries alike.

7. Israel

Israeli silence during the revolution should not be interpreted as a lack of interest. Developments in Syria are of critical importance to Israel, which has been at war with Damascus ever since it occupied Palestine in 1948. Syria has never been an easy adversary. It has refused to recognize or make peace with Israel, and has supported dissident Palestinian factions opposed to the conciliatory position of the Palestinian Liberation Organization (PLO) leadership. On the other hand, its boundless pragmatism has meant that since 1973 there have been no shots fired on Syria's southern border.

Moreover, since the collapse of the USSR, it has moved towards negotiations, arguing that 'peace is a strategic choice'. In this regard, Syria is an ideal adversary, despite its use of the Lebanese front and other methods developed in Iraq to manage its disagreements with the occupying power. Israel has paid a great deal of attention to Syria's regional role, its influence and status in the Arab world and the Middle East, and the repercussions of change there for Israel's security and regional relations.

Its marked refusal to take a clear position on the involvement of Hezbollah and Iranian forces in Syria is not proof of impotence so much as a desire for the warring parties to exhaust one another in a conflict far from the Israeli front with no clear exit strategy. Israeli press analyses of government positions confirm the view that Israel hopes that Syria will be weakened and that the regime will survive since ultimately it is one with which an understanding is possible.[100]

A policy of ambiguity

From the very beginning of the protests, Benjamin Netanyahu warned his ministers not to make statements about developments in Syria, noting that the less said the better.[101] He himself said little on the subject. In an interview with Al Arabiya in mid-2011, he maintained that any comments on his part would be exploited – not against him, but against genuine reform in Syria. He added that Israel was worried but wanted calm to continue on the Syrian-Israeli border, and expressed his concern about developments in the Arab revolutions in general,[102] especially the prominence of Islamists. This last concern was shared by the Israeli military.[103] Israeli intelligence chief Aharon Zeevi Farkash stated that he refused to call the 'tsunami' in the Middle East an 'Arab Spring' and warned that radical Sunni Islam was growing stronger across the region.[104] The head of the Defence Ministry's political security division, Amos Gilad, meanwhile, predicted that the fall of the Assad regime would lead to the establishment of an Islamic empire in the Levant that would seek to wipe out Israel.[105]

---

[100] In a 31 May 2013 article in *Globes*, Jacky Hugi wrote an account of the positions of Israeli politicians and security officials on two issues: the survival of the Syrian regime and the involvement of Hezbollah in Lebanon. See: *Globes*, 31 May 2013, at: https://bit.ly/39S222G (accessed 3 February 2022).

[101] *The Jerusalem Post*, 29 December 2011, at: https://bit.ly/3wO9GDd (accessed 5 June 2022).

[102] For the full text of the interview with Benjamin Netanyahu with *Al Arabiya*, see: Government of Israel – Prime Minister's Office, 24 July 2011, at: https://bit.ly/3rpaInR (accessed 3 February 2022).

[103] Mahmoud Muharib, 'Israel and the Geostrategic Changes in the Arab World' [Arabic], *Siyasat Arabiya* 1, no. 1 (March 2013), 26.

[104] *Calcalist*, 22 November 2012, at: https://bit.ly/3zryuUE (accessed 8 June 2022).

[105] *Al Arabiya*, 16 November 2011, at: https://bit.ly/3zBx1er (accessed 15 June 2022).

In contrast to its earlier public support for Mubarak in Egypt, during the first year of the Syrian revolution the Israeli government made no statement on the future of the Assad regime. Occasionally it did voice fears that chemical weapons might fall into the wrong hands or that Hezbollah might secure new and sophisticated kinds of armament – fears that then spread to Western states and helped determine their positions on the revolution. The military and the political leadership seemed to express this sentiment in different terms. It is nevertheless unlikely that this reflected an underlying difference in position: in Israel it is the government that makes the decisions, although these decisions are informed by advice from multiple sources, the army chief among them. The military favoured the survival of the Assad regime, which could be relied on to secure the Golan front, and which was certainly better than the alternatives, not least an armed free-for-all just over the border.[106]

Former Mossad chief Efraim Halevy went so far as to declare that the fall of Assad would be a disaster for Israel.[107] Others expressed concern about the possibility of an Islamist government, a concern shared by Russia and, to some extent at least, at odds with the US position in Tunisia and Egypt. Some politicians, meanwhile, hoped for the fall of the regime – or at least said that they would not regret it – because it would weaken the 'axis of extremism' in the region, especially Iran and Hezbollah.

Then-Defence Minister Ehud Barak, for example, said more than once that he hoped for the fall of the Syrian regime and that that this would be 'a blessing for the Middle East'.[108] He predicted that the regime would fall within weeks, arguing that it 'would be a powerful blow to the radical front as a whole, with Iran and Hezbollah in the centre'.[109] Barak later took a more reserved line at a meeting of the Knesset Foreign Affairs Committee, where he warned of possible repercussions for the Golan and perhaps other areas.[110] He nonetheless maintained that 'the Assad family's position

---

[106] *Haaretz*, 19 January 2012, at: https://bit.ly/3GuKMwF (accessed 8 June 2022).
[107] *Mivzakim*, 12 December 2011, at: https://bit.ly/3zCzgy0 (accessed 15 June 2022). Amir Eshel, former commander of the Israeli air force and the director-general of the Israeli Ministry of Defence, expressed concern about the fate of the regime's 'huge stockpile' of chemical and biological weapons if it fell into other hands. *Ynet*, 6 February 2012, at: https://bit.ly/3NNSjcZ (accessed 15 June 2022). General Yair Golan, the commander of the northern region, also expressed his fear of regime collapse and the transfer of advanced weapons to armed organizations, especially Hezbollah. He said that the army would have to change military strategies regarding Syria and Lebanon and the relationship between them, because there were huge changes afoot in Syria, and conditions were similar to those in Libya on the eve of Qaddafi's fall. He added that there was a possibility of the emergence of Syrian 'terrorist organizations'. See: *Globes*, 13 December 2011, at: https://bit.ly/3z4IjHN (accessed 12 June 2022). However, for Amos Yedlin, the former head of Military Intelligence, 'The fall of Assad is a good thing to Israel.' See: *Maariv*, 21 January 2012, at: https://bit.ly/3amoSzP (accessed 15 June 2022).
[108] *NRG*, 11 December 2011, at: https://bit.ly/3LQioX9 (accessed 6 June 2022).
[109] Ibid.
[110] *N12 News*, 2 January 2012, at: https://bit.ly/3MWXTcM (accessed 6 June 2022).

is deteriorating' and that the regime's fall was inevitable.[111] At the Davos summit in early 2012, he told the press that Israel was 'not nervously but cautiously' monitoring events in Syria, particularly the possibility that sophisticated weaponry might find its way to Lebanon.[112] While it is largely correct that Israel is a state built on institutions, it is impossible to ignore the role of the leading politicians, including, for example, Barak's personal antipathy to Syria. (His attempt to walk back initial promises of a full withdrawal to the 1967 borders scuppered peace negotiations with Hafez al-Assad in the 1990s, and he also oversaw the unilateral Israeli withdrawal from southern Lebanon, which Syria cast as a victory for the resistance. These two failures had done a great deal of damage to Barak's political career.)

The Israeli Foreign Ministry issued no official statement on the revolution, but Foreign Minister Avigdor Lieberman criticized Russia for delivering of more advanced weaponry to Syria.[113] Israeli-Russian relations have improved greatly under Putin, who has recognized Israel's regional importance and its influence on Western policy (Israel has always sought good relations with the superpowers, but the USSR severed relations in 1967). There is a cultural and historical commonality between Israel and Russia that should not be overestimated, but it is nevertheless worth noting that some Israeli politicians speak Russian when they meet their Russian counterparts.

Military intelligence proved to have a more realistic idea of the Syrian regime's capabilities than the politicians. Military intelligence has traditionally sympathized with the Syrian regime, at least under Hafez al-Assad, because it was a regime that could be relied on to keep its word and because peace with Syria was always more important – more realistic, even – than peace with the Palestinians. The military intelligence chief in 2011, Aviv Kochavi, stood within this tradition. He maintained that the regime's account of events was true, that gangs had attacked the army and that soldiers made up around one-third of those killed. He stated that there was discomfort within Assad's immediate circles but that 'at this time' it was definitely him who was in charge and not his brother Maher.[114] Despite 'economic collapse', he estimated that the regime would be able to survive for at least a year or two because of the army's 'absolute loyalty'. Similarly, General Amos Yedlin wrote that the Syrian opposition could not win and that the regime had two advantages: a willingness to kill in the name of

---

[111] Ibid.
[112] *The Jerusalem Post*, 29 January 2012, at: https://bit.ly/3q9lqg9 (accessed 3 February 2022).
[113] *Ynet*, 7 December 2011, at: https://bit.ly/3LTLx3r (accessed 6 June 2022).
[114] *Maariv*, 9 July 2011, at: https://bit.ly/3lPfjvZ (accessed 6 June 2022).

self-preservation and Russian support, including the veto against foreign intervention. He predicted that the revolution would degenerate into a protracted civil war, and that the persistence of the Syrian rebels under such circumstances was exceptional.[115]

Despite the policy of ambiguity, it is possible to draw a few conclusions regarding the Israeli position. Israel's ideal scenario was a drawn-out revolution that would drain and weaken Syria as a state. Israel approached Syria – state, regime, and revolution alike – as an enemy. It had an obvious interest in weakening Syria and prolonging the conflict for as long as possible. The two worries were: first, that the regime's authority would collapse and give way to chaos, drawing in armed organizations hostile to Israel, and second, intensification of the Iranian military presence in Syria. These concerns were shared with Jordan, and the revolutionary period saw coordination between Tel Aviv and Amman reach an unprecedented intensity. While meetings between high-level Jordanian and Israeli officials were not publicized, the Jordanians kept other Arab countries apprised of some of their content, and the editor of *Haaretz* wrote an article setting out the development of efforts to create a 'buffer zone' between the Golan and the 'rebel battalions' through Jordanian mediation.[116]

Israel ultimately allowed the regime to use heavy weapons against rebels in the Golan itself, in order to 'prevent chaos'. Anxieties over the regime's chemical and biological weapons falling into the hands of those hostile to Israel also show that Israel saw the regime as a serious and responsible party in this regard. But a year after the revolution began, after it had become clear how serious and inclusive it was and how much staying power and international support it had, the Israeli government changed course.

Conformity with US and European policy

In February 2012, a team of experts from the Ministry of Foreign Affairs recommended ending the policy of ambiguity and calling for Assad's resignation, bringing the Israeli position into line with that of the US, EU and other Israeli allies.[117] Although Lieberman approved the recommendation and submitted it to the cabinet, at this point Netanyahu and Barak opposed any change.[118] But as the revolution gained momentum

---

[115] Amos Yedlin, 'The Arab Spring a Year on', in *One Year of the Arab Spring: Global and Regional Implications* [Hebrew], ed. Yoel Guzansky and Mark Heller (Tel Aviv: Institute for National Security Studies, 2012), 11–21; Saleh Al-Naimi, *The Israeli Strategic Mind: Reading the Arab Revolutions and Predicting their Outcomes* [Arabic] (Doha: Al Jazeera Centre for Studies; Beirut: Arab Scientific Publishers, 2013), 39–44.
[116] *Haaretz*, 15 April 2013, at: https://bit.ly/32V5Vkz (accessed 3 February 2022).
[117] *Haaretz*, 16 February 2012, at: https://bit.ly/3AUkFwm (accessed 3 February 2022).
[118] Ibid.

and the regime became more brutal – and as international revulsion grew – Netanyahu began to cite events in Syria in his speeches to highlight Israel's 'difficult position' in the region. Israel's leaders were aware that people were making comparisons between the Syrian regime's oppressive behaviour and that of Israel, and they wanted to change the narrative. They wanted to show the world that politics in the region was based on force and brutality. In the first week of February, Netanyahu said that 'in recent days we have received reports that have reminded us which region we live in. We have seen the Syrian army slaughtering its people'.[119]

Netanyahu's remarks ushered in a new Israeli line. Statements were now couched in a tone of sympathy for Syrians, condemning the Assad regime's massacres. Attempts were made to link Iran and Hezbollah to the atrocities, undermining their reputation at home and abroad: subsequent Israeli statements almost invariably mentioned their involvement in the conflict. On 27 May, following the Houla massacre, Netanyahu and Barak condemned the massacre and mentioned the support of Iran and Hezbollah.[120] Israeli officials blatantly exploited the blood of Syrians and angry Arab public opinion on Iran and Hezbollah to further their own agenda, which was hostile for reasons quite different from those of the Syrian people. On 10 June, a battery of Israeli officials – Netanyahu, Barak, President Shimon Peres – stepped up their campaign against the regime, accusing Assad of committing more massacres against the Syrian people.[121] But Israel remained opposed to any intervention in favour of the revolution or action to topple the regime. Instead, it tried to align itself with the European and American media position and use it to its own advantage.

Direct military intervention

On 20 March 2013, the newly re-elected Obama met with Netanyahu in Tel Aviv to discuss, among other things, the situation in Syria; according to unverified Israeli intelligence sources, they agreed on a policy of non-intervention.[122] On 28 April, however, the newly formed Security Cabinet (comprising the prime minister and six other important ministers) made it

---

[119] Ibid.
[120] *Haaretz*, 28 May 2012, at: https://bit.ly/3omPrcd (accessed 3 February 2022).
[121] At the opening of the weekly cabinet meeting, Netanyahu said, 'The massacres carried out by the Syrian regime are not being carried out alone. Iran and Hezbollah share responsibility for these massacres and are helping to commit them. The world must see this alliance of the Axis of Evil. Everyone should know what world we are living in.' The head of the Kadima Party, the first deputy PM, joined the condemnation of the Syrian regime and also referred to Iran and Hezbollah's involvement in the massacres. He called on the major states not to be satisfied with words of condemnation, but to intervene against the Syrian regime as they thought appropriate. See: *Haaretz*, 10 June 2012, at: https://bit.ly/3sh8aHg (accessed 3 February 2022).
[122] *Almadenah News*, 22 March 2013, at: https://bit.ly/3AWhLr3 (accessed 3 February 2022).

clear that this policy was not absolute. If Syria transferred weapons to Hezbollah that 'would shift the power balance', Israel would not hesitate to intervene militarily.[123]

Over the course of 2013, Israel carried out airstrikes in Syria on three separate occasions. In January, it hit several targets, including a convoy that it claimed was transporting an advanced SA-17 Russian anti-aircraft missile system to Hezbollah in Lebanon. On 3 May, it struck a shipment of Iranian Fateh-110 surface-to-surface missiles that Israel claimed had arrived at Damascus airport and were due to be sent to Hezbollah. Less than forty-eight hours later, Israeli planes launched an unprecedentedly broad attack on sites around Damascus. Israeli and foreign media outlets reported that this was another strike on Iranian missile shipments and on underground arms dumps and fuel stores on Mount Qasioun, using bunker-busters. Israel expressed satisfaction with the results in multiple leaks to the press. Surprisingly, Syria did not lodge a complaint with the UNSC and made no real response despite threatening to do so. More surprisingly, Russia, Syria's main international ally at this stage, issued no statement condemning the Israeli attack. This suggests that Russia deemed its relations with Israel not less important than those with Syria, and that Russia was an ally of the Syrian regime only on fronts of its own choosing. Israeli air strikes on Syria became routine and the same is true for coordination with Russia. In general, Israel carefully observed the regime's balance between Iranian and Russian support to determine whether a conflict of interest might develop that would benefit Israel.

In early June, the clashes between regime and armed opposition fighters in the Golan intensified, prompting debate over the wisdom of rebels' presence and their efforts to take control of the border crossing. When it became clear that rebels were using the crossing to escape regime forces and not as part of a strategy of confrontation with Israel – which would have left them between two adversaries – Israel began to make contact with them.

Factors influencing the Israeli position

Israeli strategy is based on the concept of constantly shifting 'fronts' that have no necessary connection to geography or recognized borders. Syria's importance to different 'fronts' means that the Israeli position is not only based on its concerns about Syria per se.

---

[123] ACRPS, 'Recurrent Israeli Aggressions against Syria', 18 May 2013, at: https://bit.ly/3FgAi2E (accessed 3 February 2022).

The most directly relevant 'front' is the Golan, occupied by Israel in 1967, where it is keen to maintain the calm that has prevailed since the 1973 war.[124] Of course, events in Syria have a decisive impact on this front[125]: from the Israeli perspective, change here can only be for the worse. Regime change would mean a greater risk of things heating up again.[126] Israel took practical steps against this eventuality: it placed its troops in the region on high alert,[127] bulldozed large areas near the ceasefire line to increase visibility and erected a 'smart fence' around Majdal Shams after protests on Nakba Day and Naksa Day led to attempts to break through the border fence.[128]

Events in Syria are also relevant to other fronts. The most important and active of these is with Iran. There is near unanimity in Israel that regime change in Syria would be a blow to the Iranian-led radical axis in the region.[129] Syria is also important to the Lebanese front, where it is the main source of weapons and political support for Hezbollah (mainly as a channel for Iranian supplies). The results of the internal confrontation in Syria would have a decisive influence on Hezbollah's strength and behaviour,[130] as well as on the political and security situation in Lebanon in general and on Israel's relationship with Lebanon.[131]

Other factors, including peace negotiations,[132] the aforementioned question of the fate of Syria's sophisticated weaponry (especially mobile missiles and chemical and biological weapons), and the impact of Syrian developments on Jordan and on Israeli-Turkish and Israeli-Russian[133] relations, also contributed to the Israeli position.

The differences between Israeli academic, military, media and political analyses largely depended on the relative weight given to all these factors. Those who believed that the most important thing was calm on the Golan front concluded that Israel needed the regime to survive.[134] The same applied to those who feared chaos or the coming to power of a more radical alternative. On the other hand, those who believed that delivering a blow to

---

[124] Edy Cohen, 'Was the Assad Dynasty Good for Israel?' [Hebrew] Begin-Sadat Center for Strategic Studies, 24 May 2017, at: https://bit.ly/3QGCyGL (accessed 22 June 2022).
[125] *N12 News*, 2 January 2012, at: https://bit.ly/3MWXTcM (accessed 6 June 2022).
[126] *Ynet*, 23 December 2011, at: https://bit.ly/3GmWBmX (accessed 3 February 2022).
[127] *Globes*, 13 December 2011, at: https://bit.ly/3z4IjHN (accessed 12 June 2022).
[128] Ibid.
[129] *NRG*, 11 December 2011, at: https://bit.ly/3LQioX9 (accessed 6 June 2022).
[130] *JDN*, 6 December 2011, at: https://bit.ly/3HucjPy (accessed 17 June 2022).
[131] Giora Eiland, 'The Upheavals in the Middle East and Israel's Security', *Strategic Assessment* 14, no. 2 (July 2011), 11, 14.
[132] *The Jerusalem Post*, 29 December 2011, at: https://bit.ly/3wO9GDd (accessed 6 June 2022).
[133] *Ynet*, 7 December 2011, at: https://bit.ly/3LTLx3r (accessed 6 June 2022).
[134] *Haaretz*, 19 January 2012, at: https://bit.ly/3GuKMwF (accessed 8 June 2022).

the radical axis in the confrontation with Iran was the most important thing concluded that it would be best for Israel if the regime collapsed.

There were thus divergent attitudes in Israel towards the revolution and the regime, but overall, there was near consensus on five crucial points. Firstly, on the Golan front, Israel was happy with the regime and worried that its collapse would mean a renewed confrontation. Secondly, Hezbollah's involvement in the conflict was a good thing: it drained its resources and kept it out of the conflict with Israel. Thirdly, any new regime in Syria would be hostile to Israel since it would be in need of domestic legitimacy; the current regime, by contrast, needed international legitimacy and would thus be forced to soften its stance. Fourthly, the defeat of the current regime could provide an opportunity to separate Syria from Iran and Hezbollah, which would be in Israel's interest. Fifthly, events in Syria could lead to the transfer of chemical and biological weapons, surface-to-surface and anti-aircraft missiles to armed groups hostile to Israel, chief among them the Lebanese resistance and Hezbollah. This would be disastrous for Israel. There was thus a consensus that this must be stopped, even if it required direct military intervention.

13

The effect of economic sanctions on Syria's macroeconomy

This chapter examines the impact of economic sanctions on Syria's economy. Limited sanctions were imposed on Syria in the 1980s when Syria was blacklisted as a state sponsor of terrorism. But with the outbreak of the revolution, international powers, including the US, some European states, Turkey and some Arab League states, imposed more comprehensive targeted sanctions, which had a harsher effect on Syria's macroeconomy. This chapter details the sanctions and examines the impact on both Syria's macroeconomic system and the regime's political control.

I. From limited to targeted sanctions

Following the October 1973 war, the Syrian regime pursued a policy of 'no permanent friends, no permanent enemies'. After a long break dating back to late 1962, Henry Kissinger's shuttle diplomacy for the separation of forces, the Geneva Peace Conference and Nixon's visit to Damascus paved the way for enhanced Syrian-US relations to counterbalance Syrian-Soviet relations. US policy in the region at the time allowed for 'positive relations' between the region's states and the USSR, provided those states also maintained comparable relations with the US. As the new Syrian-US relationship evolved after the October 1973 war, USAID, the development arm of US foreign policy, provided both technical and economic assistance. It was in this context that in 1976 the Syrian government for the first time granted oil exploration and exploitation concessions to an American company, which sparked a heated debate between the Syrian Communist Party and its Ba'thist ally within the NPF. All this coincided with closer technical, economic, and military cooperation with the USSR, which was keen not to be left behind.

With the rise of Thatcherism and Reaganism and the subsequent Cold War retrenchment, however, the US moved towards a twofold approach:

pressure and sanctions on one hand and political dialogue on the other. The first set of sanctions was imposed in 1979, after Syria was listed as a state sponsor of terrorism, and made the export of any commodity containing a minimum of 10 per cent US-made components and with a value exceeding $7 million conditional on the approval of a congressional committee. But while the sanctions did hit Syrian imports of medical equipment and other technologies, their effects were limited by access to alternatives, and they did not hamper the ongoing political dialogue, which continued to ebb and flow until the 2005 assassination of Rafiq al-Hariri.

From April 2011, however, there was a shift from limited to targeted sanctions, which was complete by late 2011. The new sanctions differed from previous measures in that they were more comprehensive, with the EU states, Turkey, and some Arab League states signing up. They were also more severe and had greater economic, financial and psychological effects on the macroeconomic capacity of the public economic-social-political system of production and its sources of income and financing. The sanctions applied to individuals, companies, businessmen, investments, credit and the financial, monetary, and banking systems. These sanctions represented a concerted policy package designed, at minimum, to weaken the regime and reduce its political capacities – and, at maximum, to cause the breakdown of its financing and command and control systems.

II. Sanctions against the regime

1. US sanctions

On 29 April 2011, the US imposed sanctions on members of the security and military apparatus, including the commander of the Fourth Armoured Division, Maher al-Assad, and on a unit of the Iranian Revolutionary Guards.[1] The sanctions did not include the president himself until 18 May, when Obama signed an executive order imposing direct sanctions on Bashar al-Assad and six senior officials for their role in crushing the protest movement.[2]

On 29 June, the US expanded its sanctions package, freezing US assets owned by the Syrian security services and prohibiting any US business or

---

[1] *Asharq Al-Awsat*, 24 July 2012. Archived copy available online: https://bit.ly/3gktJRP (accessed 3 February 2022).

[2] The list included Vice-President Farouq al-Sharaa, Prime Minister Adil Safar, Interior Minister Mohammad Ibrahim al-Shaar, Defence Minister Ali Habib, Military Intelligence Chief Abd al-Fattah Qudsiyyah, and Political Security Director Muuhammad Dib Zaytun. See: *BBC Arabic*, 18 May 2011, at: https://bbc.in/3oVzs5C (accessed 3 February 2022).

citizen from doing business with them.³ On 10 August, the US froze the assets of the Syrian Central Bank and imposed sanctions on Syriatel.⁴

Eight days later, on 18 August – the day that he first called for Assad to step down⁵ – Obama issued an executive order imposing further sanctions, including a freeze on all Syrian government assets under US jurisdiction and a ban on any US business dealings with the regime.⁶ As a result, several new companies were blacklisted, including the General Petroleum Company, which dominated Syria's oil and gas industry and was responsible for investment and development in oil and gas exploration in Syria; the Syrian Petroleum Company, which was responsible for oil resources and their development; the Syrian Company for Oil Transport, which managed internal pipelines, transported oil and Syrian oil products, and ran three ports for oil export and import, namely Banyas, Tartous and Latakia; the Syrian Gas Company, which was responsible for transporting and marketing natural gas in Syria; and Sytrol, the State Oil Marketing Company, responsible for the sale of Syrian crude oil to foreign buyers.

On 5 March 2012, the US blacklisted Syrian state radio and television. On 23 April, it extended the sanctions to companies supplying Syria with technology, and to companies and individuals trying to circumvent measures taken in May 2011. Finally, on 18 July, it blacklisted twenty-eight ministers and the governor of the Central Bank.⁷

2. European sanctions

On 10 May 2011, the EU introduced asset freezes and travel bans on thirteen senior regime figures, including Maher al-Assad. On the same day, it imposed an export ban on weapons and equipment that could be used for repression. As with the US, the EU sanctions did not target the president himself until 24 May, when they were extended to include nine more Syrian officials.⁸ On 24 June, the sanctions were expanded to include four military-linked companies and Syrian security officials and businessmen, as well as three Iranian officials accused of complicity with the security crackdown on protesters in Syria.

---

3   *Al Jazeera*, 29 June 2011, at: https://bit.ly/3B2lW4Q (accessed 3 February 2022).
4   *BBC Arabic*, 10 August 2011, at: https://bbc.in/3ujsxXa (accessed 3 February 2022).
5   *Reuters Arabic*, 18 August 2011, at: https://reut.rs/3m69ydL (accessed 3 February 2022).
6   This order froze Syrian government assets in the US and prohibited US citizens from making new investments in or exporting goods to Syria, selling or supplying goods and services to Syria from anywhere in the world, or dealing with the Syrian oil sector in any capacity. See: *Al Jazeera*, 18 August 2011, at: https://bit.ly/32WZttk (accessed 3 February 2022).
7   *Asharq Al-Awsat*, 24 July 2012. Archived copy available online: https://bit.ly/3gktJRP (accessed 3 February 2022).
8   *Al Jazeera*, 24 March 2012, at: https://bit.ly/3om4ClX (accessed 3 February 2022).

The EU only began to impose economic sanctions on 24 September 2011, when it banned any new investment in the Syrian oil sector.[9] On 2 December – after the Arab League had imposed its own sanctions – it went further, banning all dealings with state companies overseeing the petroleum business and exploration projects. The sanctions targeted the General Petroleum Corporation, Sytrol, and the Euphrates Oil Company, as well as requiring European companies to suspend their operations in Syria, starting with Shell[10]; France's Total also ended its operations on 6 December.[11] The sanctions also included various media outlets (*al-Watan*, Dunya TV, Sham Press and the Centre for Scientific Study and Research) and froze the assets of Economy Minister Mohammad Nidal al-Shaar, Finance Minister Mohammad al-Jililati,[12] and ten officials from the army, the Republican and Presidential Guard, the air force, and the Political Security Directorate.[13] On 27 February 2012, the assets of the Central Bank were frozen and precious metal trading was banned, as were charter flights operated by Syrian Air. On 23 April luxury goods exports were also banned. Further sanctions were imposed on the oil and tobacco sectors on 14 May and on new trading companies and the Ministries of Defence and Interior on 25 June.[14]

3. Arab League and Turkey

On 24 November 2011, the Council of Arab Foreign Ministers resolved to impose sanctions on Syria if the Syrian government did not comply with the Arab League's efforts to end the crackdown or failed to stop the killings and release detainees.[15] On 26 November, the league's Economic and Social Council, with the participation of Turkish Economy Minister Ali Babacan, recommended imposing sanctions, and the following day this recommendation was adopted by the Council of Foreign Ministers at its meeting in Cairo,[16] with the Turkish foreign minister also in attendance.[17] Nineteen states voted for the resolution; Lebanon opposed it and Iraq abstained.[18] The sanctions envisioned suspending flights to Syria, stopping

---

[9] *Asharq Al-Awsat*, 24 July 2012. Archived copy available online: https://bit.ly/3gktJRP (accessed 3 February 2022).
[10] *Reuters Arabic*, 2 December 2011, at: https://bit.ly/3AQYlUA (accessed 3 February 2022).
[11] *Al Jaml*, 6 December 2011, at: https://bit.ly/3okZ6Al (accessed 3 February 2022).
[12] *Reuters Arabic*, 2 December 2011, at: https://bit.ly/3AQYlUA (accessed 3 February 2022).
[13] *Al Watan Voice*, 3 December 2011, at: https://bit.ly/3HkuhmC (accessed 3 February 2022).
[14] *Asharq Al-Awsat*, 24 July 2012. Archived copy available online: https://bit.ly/3gktJRP (accessed 3 February 2022).
[15] *BBC Arabic*, 24 November 2011, at: https://bbc.in/346eLwt (accessed 3 February 2022).
[16] *BBC Arabic*, 27 November 2011, at: https://bbc.in/3AVKSLl (accessed 3 February 2022).
[17] *Al Sbah*, 26 November 2011, at: https://bit.ly/3uC3miu (accessed 6 February 2022).
[18] Ibid.

dealings with the Central Bank, ending government trade with the Syrian government (except for strategic commodities that would have affected the lives of everyday Syrians), freezing the government's financial assets, halting financial transactions with the Syrian government, and banning many Syrian officials from travelling to Arab states.[19]

On 4 December, the ministerial committee responsible for liaison with the Syrian government ratified the detailed arrangements for enforcement of sanctions. Nineteen Syrian figures were banned from traveling to Arab countries and their funds and assets frozen. The committee also announced that the Arab states would refrain from selling arms to Syria and halve their commercial flights to the country.[20]

Turkey – Syria's largest trading partner, with trade worth $2.5 billion by 2010 – imposed economic sanctions on Syria on 30 November 2011. These sanctions included a freeze on trade between the two countries, a suspension of dealings between the two central banks, a ban on all types of weapons and military equipment, and suspension of the work of the high-level Syrian-Turkish Strategic Cooperation Council.[21]

According to government statistics, Syria's oil production fell 30–35 per cent at the end of 2011 due to the sanctions.[22] The importation of green diesel also stopped. The Syrian government worked to make up the shortfall from Venezuela.[23] According to official figures, losses to the Syrian economy at the beginning of 2012 resulting from the halt in oil exports came to about $2 billion.[24]

III. The impact of targeted sanctions

Past experience, particularly the harsh, 'targeted' and 'smart' sanctions against Iraq and Iran, shows that regimes are not brought down by sanctions and that it is normally the people who suffer. But the regime's capacity for command and control will be degraded to some extent, and parts of society may turn against it, as seems to have happened in Iran in recent years. Understanding the real impact of sanctions requires a macroeconomic approach drawing on the social and political sciences as well as pure

---

[19] Ibid.
[20] *Al-Akhbar* (Lebanon), 5 December 2011, at: https://bit.ly/3uiR5j7 (accessed 3 February 2022).
[21] *BBC Arabic*, 30 November 2011, at: https://bbc.in/3ugTx9M (accessed 3 February 2022).
[22] *Al-Akhbar* (Lebanon), 26 December 2011. Archived copy available online: https://bit.ly/3HoKaIX (accessed 3 February 2022).
[23] *Al Jaml*, 8 January 2012, at: https://bit.ly/35MfbZ7 (accessed 6 February 2022).
[24] *SANA*, 19 January 2012. Archived copy available online: https://bit.ly/3ASjxtc (accessed 3 February 2022).

economics. What economists call macroeconomic stability is the same thing that social scientists call political and social stability.

All causes of major macroeconomic imbalances have social and political effects. The macroeconomic balance of any country is merely the economic expression of social and economic stability, or lack thereof. The new sanctions imposed on Syria were designed to undermine the macroeconomic balance enjoyed by the Syrian economy between 2005 and 2010 by causing structural imbalances (budget deficits, balance of payments deficits, exchange rate fluctuations, problems with foreign currency reserves, debt, inflation, unemployment, money supply, etc.). These imbalances led directly to the destabilization of the economic-social-political structure and structural crisis.[25]

The effects to which the macroeconomy is exposed are not automatic, direct and immediate in socio-political terms, nor are they uncontrollable. For specific periods, the regime may be able to maintain its regulation of macroeconomic frameworks and indicators even as political and social instability increases. The Egyptian/Tunisian-style authoritarian liberalization pursued intensively between 2005 and 2010 – 'Mexicanization', or policies rooted in the neoliberal belief that trade drives growth – led to major social imbalances, reflected in increased wealth inequality, an increase in the percentage and absolute number of those under the lower and upper poverty lines, an increase in human poverty indicators, the destruction of agriculture, and adverse effects on public and private sector manufacturing and industry, accompanied by an increasing gap in the distribution of power, greater integration between ruling bureaucratic elites, the upper echelons of the business class, and Gulf and Syrian expatriate and foreign capital, and the continuation of the authoritarian relationship between state and society.

Through to the end of the first half of 2011, under the regime of limited sanctions, the Syrian economic-political regime managed to maintain macroeconomic balances and keep the major indicators under control. Even as targeted sanctions were implemented, microeconomic institutions, especially producers, proved very adaptable, taking advantage of experience circumventing sanctions, automatic protection for their products and the decline in foreign imports to open large export markets in Iraq and Iran; this provided new opportunities for growth in production, employment and exports. The manufacturing sector witnessed what many industrialists did not hesitate to call a 'golden age' as a result of markets secured by

---

[25] ACRPS, 'Effects of Sanctions on Syria's Macroeconomy in 2012', 22 January 2012, at: https://bit.ly/3zPNxHZ (accessed 13 Jun 2022).

contracts, since manufacturers who relied on local raw materials made profits of 100 per cent, while those who relied on imported raw materials made profits of 40–60 per cent. Competition from Turkish products also evaporated with the cancellation of Syrian-Turkish agreements.[26]

In fact, the imbalances that did emerge were less a result of the sanctions than of the considerable damage inflicted on transport infrastructure and manufacturing by the military response, which by early 2013 amounted to the almost complete destruction of manufacturing infrastructure. Alongside the more serious short-and medium-term social, economic, political, cultural and human devastation – and the grave damage to the system of development structures in the classical sense of the three underlying indicators of production, income generation, and health and education – this had all sorts of secondary effects.

The irony is that while the conflict disrupted the functioning of the health and education systems, for example, it was their bombardment by the *regular army*, on the pretext that these facilities were under rebel fighters' control, that caused the disruption. After all that, most manufacturing facilities faced ruin.

The effect of targeted sanctions can be seen most clearly in the Syrian banking, financial and energy systems, especially the oil sector and imports of petroleum products. Prior to the revolution, oil was a major contributor to GDP and accounted for around 22 per cent of state revenue. Despite their small scale, oil exports made up the majority of this figure (16–17 per cent of state revenue), thus constituting a vital part of Syria's trade balance.[27] The sanctions thus took aim at the investment and marketing ties of the oil industry, both direct and indirect. Again, however, the greatest damage to this sector was caused not by sanctions but by partial or total destruction and the inability of imports to meet the need for petroleum products due to high consumption by the army. The internal and external inefficiencies of the antiquated Syrian state apparatus also had an impact, since it was bloated, corrupt and overly bureaucratic, with poor distribution and the emergence of mafia-like networks between it and crisis profiteers.

In 2012 after a period of apparent stability, the Syrian macroeconomy entered a critical stage that limited the regime's command and control capacity. The main factor determining the degree of damage to the infrastructure and the erosion of the capacity of the Syrian economy was, in effect, the revolution and the armed confrontations and bombings by the

---

[26] Ibid., 12. Some of this data is based on personal interviews in late December 2011 with several Syrian industrialists.
[27] Nabil Marzuq, 'Economic Sanctions: A Slow Stifling of the Syrian Regime' [Arabic], Al Jazeera Centre for Studies, 19 November 2011, at: https://bit.ly/3glSNI8 (accessed 3 February 2022).

regime, not sanctions. The official state economy was eroded more quickly than the Syrian economy as a whole, but it did not collapse. During the first years of the conflict, it went from being the economy of a state to the economy of one side in a civil war.[28] This type of economy does not collapse precisely because it is no longer a state economy, but rather one form of the struggle for survival, a war economy.

---

[28] The original edition of the book stopped in the year 2013. Later sanctions had a much greater impact on the economy and society, especially after the end of the civil war, when the sources of the war economy dried up while reconstruction that could set in motion a peace economy was and remains obstructed by sanctions. More details and analysis can be found in the supplement to this edition.

Conclusion

The Syrian revolution was an extension of the Arab Spring revolutions, which started in Tunisia. Until its transformation into an armed revolution, it resembled the Tunisian revolution in key aspects of its unfolding. In this book, I have tried to follow the development of the peaceful protests and investigate their structure and transformation into a comprehensive national revolution against tyranny. I have proved the hypothesis that the revolution was spontaneous, civilian and authentic – meaning rooted in Syrian social, economic, and political reality. I have also shown that the revolution occurred in a structurally diverse society and in the face of a security regime in which the army and security bodies are inseparable from the regime and the social structure of the state.

As I discussed in the first chapter of the book, over the last four decades, a two-fold process had been underway in Syria: the integration of the social structure into the security apparatus, and the fusion of both of them with the state apparatus. I have shown the foundations of this in several other chapters, including the long chapter on the relationship between sectarianism and ruralization and the structure of the Syrian army and the regime's security apparatus. In doing so, I aimed to distinguish truth from myth regarding the sectarianism of the regime, or what I call the interpenetration of the regime's social structure and its security structure.

The protest movement in Syria started with demands for political reform made by opposition political forces and civic bodies composed of young people alienated from the ideology and culture of the state, who longed to be free from the security state and were influenced by the revolutionary atmosphere sweeping the Arab region. But the main popular momentum behind the revolution came from the ever-growing social constituencies harmed by the economic and social policies of the regime. When the broader Arab situation showed that change was actually possible, these groups were able, for the first time, to break through the wall of fear that allowed the security regime to exercise power. And as soon as they came out to protest the miserable conditions under which they were living, or in solidarity with relatives or friends who had been killed or abused, the rage that had built up over decades of oppression and humiliation – of violation of property, rights, bodies – exploded. Beneath the layers of repression, fear and self-justification lay a deep well of anger. Once the coping mechanisms ceased to operate, there was only one way that the regime could have placated them: proposing a comprehensive alternative and a new political framework offering rational solutions. But this did not happen.

The regime was prepared to make cosmetic reforms to contain the protests, and even these minimal efforts were contradicted by the attitude of the security forces. It experimented with containment strategies for a short time and soon became firmly convinced that the security-military option was its only way to deal with the protest movement. The atrocities that it committed, having rejected change through reform under its leadership, convinced people of the need to change the regime entirely.

The political reform process was a window of opportunity for Syria's leadership and people to prevent disaster and the vertical splintering of society. But the regime knew that reform meant altering a system based on a foundation of total control, and it feared that ceding any of that control risked bringing the whole edifice tumbling down. It had missed many opportunities for reform and broken its promises repeatedly over the previous decade. This time it underestimated the sheer appetite for change inspired by developments across the Arab world. Rather than containing the protests, understanding the reform demands and holding security commanders who committed crimes against citizens and protesters to account, the regime opted for repression. It gambled that the many sectarian and non-sectarian ties that bound together the security forces, the ruling family, the economic elite and the state bureaucracy would keep the army and the police on its side and prevent another Egypt or Tunisia. It knew that it was this cartel that genuinely ruled Syria – not the Ba'th Party, many of whose members had suffered from regime policy and joined the revolution themselves. The mass membership of the party were just normal Syrians who had been forced to join by necessity.

The Syrian regime considered reform to be an uncertain prospect. It had carried out none of the partial reforms seen between 1985 and 1988 in countries like Egypt, Yemen, Jordan, Bahrain, Algeria or Morocco. It had remained fundamentally unchanged – if anything, it had tightened its grip on the life of its people. The security apparatus and the economic sphere had become so intertwined that corruption became endemic, giving rise to an indispensable parallel economy. The regime's miscalculations meant that the failure to reform and its resort to violence did not quell protest but made people angrier, pushing them into armed confrontation. Society and state apparatuses (such as the army) became polarized, as did society itself.

And as the clash between state and society became entwined with regional and international conflicts, Syria was sent hurtling into the unknown.

Reform would not have guaranteed the regime's survival. But it would have guaranteed a peaceful transition with minimal losses. At a time of revolution, the alternative was never going to be people giving up their demands and surrendering to a repressive regime. The only alternative was armed conflict or even civil war. Both the Syrian people and the regime burned their bridges to their past conditions.

One may be tempted to conclude that this is a distinguishing characteristic of revolution as opposed to protest. Protest action can be suppressed, as people continue to go about their lives in the old ways. But in revolution, if specific modes of protest are suppressed, then people shift to others. However, with a shift to armed struggle, an armed revolution may mutate into a civil war.

The scattered incidents involving weapons before militarization had had a purely local character. It was the regime itself that decided on armed confrontation. There was no central revolutionary leadership capable of considering alternatives. There were only spontaneous reactions by a people that had burned their boats – that is, a people who were willing to do anything but return to the past. These reactions escalated and acquired organized fronts, some of which feared the consequences of taking up arms, while others saw no alternative or were keen to pursue this option. The regime, meanwhile, was fully aware of what it was doing. It planned out its security option in detail and pursued it to the end in alliance with Iran and its puppets and with Russia.

I have traced the dynamics of the popular uprising, the transformation of local uprisings into a civil revolution and finally the transition of civil revolution to community self-defence and then into armament leading to civil war. This was the historical aspect of the book, which delved into a structural analysis of state and society. The use of weapons transformed the revolution structurally, whether in terms of the social sectors involved, the shift of its centre of gravity and social base to the countryside and urban peripheries, and the change in the nature of its leaders in the field as a result of killing, detention, and displacement, or in terms of the relationship between the political front of the revolution and the revolutionaries on the ground and the relevance of regional and international factors to the Syrian revolution.

There were many heroic civilians who took up arms and demonstrated remarkable endurance, sacrifice and determination. But at the same time, the warlord phenomenon began to develop. Armed criminal elements that had existed in the shadow of the security state came out into the open, as well as jihadi elements who did not share the aims of the revolution. The sheer length of the revolution and the growing number of sectarian-tinged massacres and hate crimes polarized Syrian society. The revolution was on the verge of turning into a civil war, and signs of the communal becoming mixed up with the revolutionary had been apparent from the beginning. Because of the fragmentation and diversity of the revolutionary forces on the ground, and despite the duration of the revolution, armed revolutionary citizens received no clear education about the aims of the revolution or the social responsibility involved in taking up arms. They did not become an armed liberation army.

Revolutionaries took control of a number of cities after fierce fighting, without a plan to manage the lives of civilian residents nor address their desperate need for food and medicine under siege conditions. The regime pursued a strategy of ruthless bombardment of the cities it had evacuated, in an effort to put pressure on the environment hosting the revolutionaries. With this strategy, the regime committed one of this century's most violent acts of political terrorism against civilians.

Political initiatives failed to find an exit from the crisis, and as the conflict drew on (and intensified) many new and unpleasant phenomena emerged around the revolution, including sectarian unrest, criminality, jihadism and fundamentalism. At the same time, no political leadership capable of representing the entire revolution emerged, and open disagreements between the most visible revolutionary figures gravely undermined the level of organization needed for a revolution to make decisions about military and political strategies. This is not a question of whether an armed or non-violent strategy should be adopted, or whether the transition should be a political one in which the regime or the president is forced to step down or the regime is defeated by force. The problem was the *absence of a binding framework in which these strategies could be discussed.*

Strategy became the topic of media speculation, not the work of decision-making bodies. I have attempted to explain the structure of the political opposition in Syria and its development during the revolution, pointing out the subjective and objective reasons of this fragmentation. But the biggest danger was in the organizational fragmentation of the armed forces and the emergence of warlords, alongside militant armed brigades and units not subject to a central command, either political or military. The issue here is not the kind of solution, but the future of Syria after any solution. Regardless of the nature of the solution, it is difficult to envisage the unity and reproduction of Syria as a state undertaking its civic functions and with a strong national army. The longer the fighting lasts, the worse the situation will become and the greater this risk.

The geostrategic factor played a great part in the revolution. The regime would not have been able to endure without Russian support and the organic Iranian alliance with Syria.¹ It is clear that Russia's agenda was to restore its role as a global power and not to repeat the experience in Libya after the US retreat from Iraq and Afghanistan. The Arab revolutions threatened Iran's historic achievement of creating a swathe of semi-imperial Iranian influence extending from Iran through Iraq, Syria, and Lebanon to the Mediterranean, and its position as interlocutor with the West as a regional state on the central issues of Western concern, the Arab-Israeli conflict among them. Most significant thing for the future of the region is that Iran, as an official doctrinal religious state, considers it legitimate and natural to use political Shi'ism as a way to achieve influence and is entitled to the loyalty of Arab Shi'a. Turkey, as a regional state supporting the revolution, became involved for other reasons. Western states, meanwhile, have brought agendas of their own into play, such as ensuring that Syrian chemical weapons do not fall into the hands of the rebels or Hezbollah and that Syria does not become a 'base for terrorist operations' but becomes a beacon of stability in the region. This is the language of US diplomacy, which effectively translates into Syria renouncing its positions on Arab affairs and making peace with Israel, which occupies the territory of Syria and Palestine, as well as other issues that have nothing to do with the freedom and dignity of the Syrian people. Hence, during the revolution none of these states were moved by the level of repression used by the regime, and it seems as if the regime was given a green light to commit war crimes against the Syrian people.

If a security regime is able to use any means 'necessary' against its people, it will undoubtedly prolong its life, because regimes typically fall in the face of a popular revolution if the regime splinters and the army abandons it, or if its repression is curbed by some official national (or state) values or by external intervention. If, however, the armed forces do not desert the regime and its orders are carried out by military force against the people, and if the regime uses whatever means of repression it desires in the absence of international controls or moral restraints, and there are also those supplying it with limitless equipment and weapons, then the challenge facing the revolution lies in its ability to wage war against a regime that is

---

1   On 4 May 2013 at a press conference held in the city of Qom, Ali Akbar Velayati, the Iranian supreme leader's advisor for international affairs and at the time a candidate for the upcoming presidential elections, stated that Syria would not have endured for two years without its friends standing by it. Naturally, Velayati said that the danger that Syria's allies had saved Syria, not the Syrian regime, from was Washington, Tel Aviv and the crowd supporting them, not referring to them as the revolution as this did not exist in Iran's calculations: 'Syria is not alone and Iran will not leave it alone in the field.' Velayati added, 'Iran has not revealed all its cards regarding what it is doing and will do for Syria. Without Iran's support, Syria would not have endured in the face of the international conspiracy to topple the regime.' Velayati pointed out that the US and its allies would not be able to overthrow the Syrian regime. See: *Al Jazeera*, 5 May 2013, at: https://bit.ly/3tNC87p (accessed 20 June 2022).

waging a full-scale war against it. Fighting a war requires a high degree of organization and powerful allies, especially when it is against a large and powerful army.

The influence of foreign states that did not actively support the revolution increased because they continued to communicate with political circles and factions of fighters on the ground in accordance with their own agendas. While unceasingly admonishing the opposition about the need for unity, in practice they contributed to the fragmentation of the political opposition and armed factions and the dismantling of their sovereign immunity against foreign intervention in a country that covets control of its strategic position and role. The common denominator between foreign states allied with the regime and those opposed to it that did not directly support the revolution is that the Syrian people, their future and their suffering were not the main concern.

The Syrian revolution is a unique case in the region because of the interplay of factors affecting it, which may lead to catastrophic scenarios unless a political settlement is reached. (I do not say a peaceful settlement, because as a result of the fighting, no settlement can be peaceful.) Such a settlement must ensure the removal of the regime and the survival of the institutions of the state and a gradual transition towards democracy without uprooting these institutions. A political solution seems distant at the time of this writing, more than two years into the revolution. The alternative, it would seem, is the deepening of the conflict and its transformation into sectarian and ethnic conflict, which may produce other potential conflicts in the future.

By detailing the nature of the massacres that have taken place in mixed areas, I have tried to demonstrate local social mechanics in a polarized situation and to examine the aspects of these situations that usually go undiscussed in media coverage. The danger is a prolonged sectarian war, or a failed state after the defeat of the regime. These were not the motives and objectives of the Syrian revolution when it started as a revolt against tyranny. It is not enough to overthrow the regime, as the state may fall with it if there is no political programme around which the revolutionary forces can gather to build the future Syria. It is not enough to point out that 'resistance' for the regime is no more than a hollow slogan. Those who negate all that this slogan represents may be driven to cooperate with states that support Israel against Syria or even with Israel itself. Then we are faced with a failed state under a leadership with no concern for the country's sovereignty and subject to the will of regional and non-regional states.

Sectarianism in the Arab Levant is a calamity not because it is a bogus ideology but because it is rooted in real social and intellectual structures. What is required is the rooting of alternative identities that are more relevant to the modern state, such as citizenship, state nationalism and Arab national culture. This requires the development of a political consciousness. That sectarianism exists in Syria is not a fabrication – it is present in the system of government. We cannot ask those affected by an authoritarian regime based on sectarian and provincial structures to express their feelings spontaneously in non-sectarian language. That is the job of political elites. It is here that the elements of awareness and planning come in; the formulation of demands in sectarian language, even in a struggle against a sectarian system, leads to something akin to civil war. In our era, it does not end with one group eliminating another, but with sectarian-based resolutions that allow for foreign tutelage, as in Lebanon and Iraq. The formulation of the struggle in the language of democracy against tyranny, if the elements needed to win are present, leads to the end of tyranny and the establishment of a society of citizens.

In addition, an entire political axis subordinate to Iran is no longer trying to conceal the doctrinal/sectarian dimension in the mobilization of its popular base and in the justification of its solidarity with the Syrian regime throughout the revolution. Iran is a nation-state like any other, but its official ideology is religious doctrine, and it is the only state in the region, and perhaps the world, ruled by clerics. In my view, this is currently the main factor driving the politicization of confessional communities and the reproduction and reformulation of sectarianism in the contemporary period. The sectarian issue in Syria is thus not based solely on internal factors. Irrespective of the regime's blood-soaked past, its use of violence in the form of detentions and torture, and the indiscriminate use of live ammunition against peaceful protestors to quash the civil revolution are enough to make it illegitimate. This makes overthrowing it a noble mission.

In this book I have shown the degree to which the regime has merged with the organs of state and the extent of the Syrian people's alienation from the regime. This also implies alienation from the organs of the state. At the same time, after two years of revolution and more than a year of armed conflict, during which profound social rifts have deepened and the regime (identical with the state) has shown itself to be the only organized force in Syria, it is no longer permissible to merely work to overthrow the regime without thinking about the future. Because an organized replacement will not be ready immediately after the fall of the current regime, and in fact other conflicts may erupt, there must be a political transition. This is what I mean by a political solution. I believe that Syrian opposition public opinion is ready to accept a transition from one regime to another in the framework of a political solution, but without Bashar al-Assad. Needless to say, his close associates, who were part of the decision-making up until this stage, would have to go with him.

The Syrian revolution is a glorious revolution in every sense of the word. A people took to the streets in defence of their dignity and freedom and showed historic endurance in the face of unprecedented repression that led to the death of thousands under torture and aerial bombardment by their own army. The enormous material and moral energy of this people may be channelled into a great renaissance for Syria, the Levant, and the Arab nation. Equally, it may transform into a toxic energy that destroys itself and its homeland. Everything depends on the awareness and responsibility of political actors (their national responsibility for a revolution that has become a national revolution) and their honesty in representing democratic demands that during the civil revolution have become national demands – demands which for so long in Syria's recent history seemed to be an impossible dream.

Supplement: A critical account of developments since 2013

As I finished this book, which covers the first two years of the revolution (11 March 2011–11 March 2013), I had already concluded that the revolution was heading in an ominous direction. Military action had become the order of the day, carried out by a deeply fragmented armed movement whose members were rapidly turning towards Salafism and pushing aside the dissident officers who had initially led it. The FSA had proved incapable of institutionalizing itself or of establishing a genuine military organization. As the cost of conflict rose, sectarian tendencies spread throughout Syrian society. And the tempo of foreign involvement had steadily increased before running completely out of control. Indeed, over the course of 2013, foreign interventions – whose main pretext was the armed conflict – played a key part in consolidating a state of civil war (and for some parties at least, of proxy war).

With the regime elite and its security forces united behind the decision to put down the peaceful popular uprising by force, continuing peaceful civil gatherings became almost impossible, and the only options were to stay at home or to take up arms. Peaceful demonstrations cannot beat guns unless there are limits on their use. The majority of the activists who had led the first, local demonstrations in the early days of the revolution no longer played a central role, whether because they had been side-lined or because they had been shot, imprisoned and tortured or driven out of the country. Many of them had become aid workers or media figures, while a small number had turned to armed action (most of those who became fighters had not been involved in the peaceful uprising). There were new political and social forces at work.

Armed struggle pushed aside not only the civil revolution but also local armed action, which the new 'battalions' confronted and either crushed or contained with the help of new, largely rural, forces.[1] These latter joined *en masse* as the peaceful demonstrations began to falter and then retreat before the brutal violence unleashed against them. The civil and peaceful forces that had struggled bravely against the regime had been driven back before they had been able to establish a unified leadership of any kind.

With the civil revolution defeated and gatherings, demonstrations and strikes impossible, the rural revolution (not necessarily *peasant* revolution) began – and as far as I am aware, there has never been an unarmed rural revolution. Leadership of the revolution passed from the provincial cities and the satellite towns of the capital to armed movements based in the countryside that occupied urban spaces from the outside: Ar-Raqqa, Idleb, Eastern Aleppo, Deir ez-Zor. And while supporters of the revolution claimed that they were 'liberating' these cities from regime forces, the ways that they governed the areas under their control raised questions about this liberation.

Regime and revolution

The Syrian regime was a regime dominated by a single party – with a number of other allied parties subordinate to it – that had lost its social base and organizational coherence and become another inherited fiefdom (and this applies to the other parties as well). The regime's power rested on the army, the security forces, the corporatist 'popular organizations' and other intermediary bodies. Some academics have described it as authoritarian-populist or even fascist-populist.[2] Hinnebusch, writing in 1996, classified the Syrian regime as a Bonapartist populist-authoritarian regime.[3] At its core, he saw a balance of army, party, and what he called the *jama'a*, or community[4] – that is, the Alawis. The regime used the party and its corporatist mass organizations to maintain connections with society,

---

[1] For a description of Army of Islam (*Jaysh al-Islam*)'s emergence and its defeat of the local FSA group Liwa' Shuhada' Duma, a typical example of this process, see: Kevin Mazur, *Revolution in Syria: Identity, Networks and Repression* (New York: Cambridge University Press, 2021), 203–5; Aron Lund, 'Into the Tunnels: The Rise and Fall of Syria's Rebel Enclave in the Eastern Ghouta', Century Foundation, 21 December 2016, at: https://bit.ly/3MdAVwS (accessed 17 April 2022).

[2] See for example Steven Heydemann, who emphasizes the economic populism of the regime. Heydemann defines economic populism as 'a system in which politically determined distributive commitments exceed available resources' and 'the policies of making and changing distributive commitments, and the politics of institutionalizing these commitments within a system of rule'. Heydemann, *Authoritarianism in Syria*, 5.

[3] Raymond A. Hinnebusch, 'Democratization in the Middle East: The Evidence from the Syrian Case', in *Political and Economic Liberalization: Dynamics and Linkages in Comparative Perspective*, ed. Gerd Nonneman (Boulder: Lynne Rienner, 1996), 153–4.

[4] Ibid., 154.

and sought to build a cross-sectarian alliance supportive of its interests.[5] But by 2010, the party had lost most of its relevance, the cross-sectarian alliance had collapsed, and populist discourse had lost all meaning. Without the fig leaf of the party, the regime's relationship to the *jama'a* was clear for all to see. It was no longer possible to understand the regime without its neo-patrimonial features. Only in a truly neo-patrimonial regime can the presidency of a republic be inherited.

The Syrian regime is authoritarian. It is dominated by the presidency and relies heavily on its security forces. By the early 2000s, the party served as a residual link to its social base without playing any real role in decision making.[6] After the 1973 war – when the liberation of part of the Golan Heights was cast as a victory for the president – the presidency's powers increased. The same thing happened after the clash with the Brotherhood in 1976–1982. After Hafez al-Assad drove his brother Rifaat into exile, it became a veritable presidential monarchy[7] in which it would be possible to pass on power to his son. By the time Bashar al-Assad took over, the presidency had unparalleled power within the regime, far more power than when his father became president. What Hafez had had to struggle long and hard to win, Bashar received ready-made.

This regime does make use of populist rhetoric when it feels it is appropriate. But it is no longer a populist regime. It combines authoritarianism with selectively liberalized economic policy.[8] Even in political decision making, it has been quite willing to pursue unpopular measures like joining the war against Iraq in 1991, fighting the PLO in Lebanon and negotiating with Israel. But it has always been ready to use a populist political discourse to justify its actions, even now that its rhetoric has become so hollow that even those who use it no longer believe it. Today the president is surrounded by a tight circle of senior security and army officers. An elite, active and influential portion of this circle are of coastal Alawi origin. It is also now generally easiest for people from this background to secure government jobs and the associated resources. And in the last decade before the revolution, an alliance between the security forces and capitalists of various sectarian origins steadily displaced the party and its social base.

---

[5] Ibid., 155.
[6] 'The party retains some residual relevance as a link between the regime and its constituency. First, it still functions as a locus of individual "interest articulation", intervening with the bureaucracy to redress constituent grievances, place clients in jobs, and generally to lubricate the creaky workings of the bureaucratic state.' Hinnebusch, *Syria*, 78.
[7] Hinnebusch, 'Syria', 96.
[8] By 'selective', I mean two things: 1) the decision not to liberalize those sectors in which regime control is an indispensable source of strength for the state and 2) cronyism between senior officials and businessmen close to the regime.

It was only to be expected that the regime would try and hide this aspect of its nature by doubling down on its pan-Arabist rhetoric, which has remained substantively the same even when regime policy has openly contradicted it (as when it supported Iran in the Iran-Iraq War). The regime did try to prevent the political contention in Syria from taking on a sectarian quality, making heavy use of traditional leaders and clerics while revitalizing its nationalist bombast. But when major protests began in March 2011, this was no longer enough. The optimism felt in the aftermath of the other Arab revolutions could not be reconciled with a belief, real or pretended, in the regime's cliches. The party's social base had been corroded by a decade of regime policy and undermined the populist elements that had once made it so popular among peasants.[9] And a majority of the population interpreted its behaviour through a sectarian lens, not least because it deployed such excessive violence in regions with a Sunni majority and accused demonstrators of 'inciting sectarian unrest', hinting that they were backed by Islamist groups who sought to form their own 'emirates' within Syria (as well as other elements of the 'foreign conspiracy'). Even at the beginning of the peaceful revolution, the official media published pictures of weapons which it claimed to have discovered in the Umari Mosque in Daraa along with plans for terror attacks. This was an obvious lie, which I was able to confirm during my research for the book.

While the rhetoric that the regime directed at the West raised the spectre of extreme and terroristic Islamists, its rhetoric for domestic consumption branded them Western agents hoping to divide the nation along sectarian lines. At a time when it was calling for national unity even as it accused demonstrators of trying to destroy the country,[10] it was obliged to gather together and unite its core elements. The rhetoric of unity was not enough to consolidate its base, however. From the beginning it was coupled with fear mongering that accused the forces behind the protests of sedition and strife. The regime made a great effort to win over the whole Alawi community by reinvigorating their belief that their collective and individual future was at risk and that their fate was tied to that of the regime. It

---

[9] Barout, *The Last Decade in the History of Syria*, 143–7. See also: Bassam Haddad, *Business Networks in Syria: The Political Economy of Authoritarian Resilience* (Stanford: Stanford University Press, 2012).

[10] The regime's rhetoric and its approach to crushing the revolution has led to its sectarianization and its Islamization, a phenomenon that many commentators have noted. Hassan Hassan and Michael Weiss, for example, interviewed a number of witnesses who maintained that the disrespect for religious symbols shown by regime soldiers and militiamen during beatings or torture was a deliberate attempt to trigger an Islamic-sectarian reaction (as well as the decision to release Islamists from prison). It is not difficult to find similar analyses among those who participated in the early stages of the revolution. See: Michael Weiss and Hassan Hassan, *ISIS: Inside the Army of Terror* (New York: Regan Arts, 2015), 134–5.

dedicated almost as much time to gaining the support of Christians, who had seen what happened to their coreligionists at the hands of ISIS in Iraq (tens of thousands of whom fled to Syria), and with less priority, the Druze and the Ismailis, whose relationship with the regime had always been ambiguous. The only way to achieve this was to scaremonger, whether directly, by claiming that the demonstrations were led by Islamists, or indirectly, by spreading rumours (largely false) that protesters had chanted anti-Alawi or anti-Christian slogans or highlighting the small number of violent incidents in which Alawis were killed for being Alawis during the first year of the revolution.

Parallel to this, during the civil war, the regime started to change its official policy on the legal independence of the Sunni Muslim clergy while interfering to repress dissident sheikhs as necessary or to ensure the support of others, acting to maintain its secular appearance on one hand and its alignment with radical Islamists when needed for foreign policy on the other. It set forth a process of religious reform from above, adopting what it considered moderate Syrian (Levantine) Islam and legally binding the Sunni religious establishment with the regime.[11]

As a rule, the organized demonstrations were civil and secular or local and spontaneous, marked by the character of normal religious and irreligious people and their popular Islam. As in Tunisia and Egypt, Islamists joined the revolution relatively late, with the exception of the emigres, who were active online and in the media. But for the regime, there was no alternative to claiming that Islamist rule was just around the corner. This also served to scare many secular Sunnis away from the protests, as well as those of all backgrounds who feared a new Iraq or Lebanon.

In their 1976–1982 uprising, the Muslim Brotherhood represented the traditional-conservative urban bourgeoisie of the northern cities, Aleppo and Hama in particular. By the 2011 revolution, however, the regime had managed to contain these forces by consolidating common interests, especially during the period of economic liberalization. During the 1976–1982 uprising, the countryside and the urban poor did not support the Brotherhood, because Baʿth policies between 1963 and 1965 had benefited these social strata by bringing land redistribution, new employment opportunities, improved education and medical facilities in the countryside, and road construction; men from poor or rural backgrounds sat at the head of the party ruling over those who had historically dominated them.

---

[11] For more on this subject, see: Rahaf Aldoughli, 'Departing "Secularism": boundary appropriation and extension of the Syrian state in the religious domain since 2011', *British Journal of Middle Eastern Studies* 49, no. 2 (2022), 360–85; Rahaf Aldoughli, 'Securitization as a Tool of Regime Survival: The Deployment of Religious Rhetoric in Bashar al-Asad's Speeches', *The Middle East Journal* 75, no. 1 (2021), 9–32.

These changes had not been forgotten in the intervening fifteen years. The demonstrations of 2011, on the other hand, began not in the big cities but in the provinces, where the new generation had seen only the regime's failures – and were more in touch with the wider world thanks to the spread of satellite TV and then the internet and social media. It was a commonplace in Damascene business and middle-class circles in 2011 to believe that what was happening was a rebellion of the Sunni countryside against the Alawi countryside, of little relevance to them. In reality it was not a rural revolution. It was a revolution of provincial cities and satellite towns that the countryside later joined. And by this point, the Islamists, including the Brotherhood and, to a greater extent, the Salafis, had become much closer to the strata that had once made up the Ba'th base: workers, peasants and the petty bourgeoisie. They were to play a prominent role in, and ultimately to dominate, armed action, as well as aid and media work. But even in these spheres Islamists generally arrived after local forces, made up of both religious and secular people, as demonstrated in the composition of the coordination committees that rapidly proliferated in the early months of the revolution or of the nascent FSA.

The regime accused any popular movement of being a conspiracy and the work of foreign forces. This was not only for propaganda purposes. The regime itself believed it to be true, because it was in its interest to do so. Rather than worrying about how to analyse the drivers of the movement or address its just demands, it could treat protesters as foreign agents and deal with them accordingly at a time when there was general international consensus on the need to maintain stability in Syria in order to avoid the spread of chaos from Iraq to Lebanon.[12] Gulf states like Qatar and Saudi Arabia – who were later accused of conspiring against Syria from the very beginning – continued to support the regime financially for months after the revolution began and praised Syria for not joining the condemnation of the Saudi intervention to crush the revolution in Bahrain. Turkey, too, continued to provide support, hoping that it would be able to convince Assad to pursue reforms.[13] It was in everyone's interest that the regime

---

[12] In the early days of the revolution, the Barack Obama administration expressed a positive view of Bashar al-Assad. On 27 March 2011, Secretary of State Hillary Clinton claimed that '[t]here is a different leader in Syria now, many of the members of Congress of both parties who have gone to Syria in recent months have said they believe he's a reformer'. See Clinton's interview on *Face the Nation* [TV programme]: *CBS News*, 27 March 2011, at: https://cbsn.ws/3vkoeK8 (accessed 14 April 2022).

[13] Marwan Kablan summarizes the regime's foreign positions before the revolution as follows: 'strong relations with Iran, Turkey and Qatar; ongoing improvement in relations with Saudi Arabia, France and the US'. See: Marwan Kablan, 'The Syrian Revolution/the Conflict over Syria: Fallout from an Imbalance of Regional Powers' [Arabic], *Siyasat Arabiya* 18 (January 2016), 66. It is worth noting that between the Hariri assassination and the onset of the revolution, Syrian-Iranian relations had seen unprecedented improvement, in part because both countries were under heavy sanctions and in part because Syrian reliance on Hezbollah increased after its retreat from Lebanon. See: Ibid., 70.

survive in order to preserve stability. Turkey saw the regime as an ally and a gateway to the Arab world. The Gulf believed that it was pragmatic and better than the alternatives, and that it could use that pragmatism to detach it from Iran.[14] In the aftermath of the Hariri assassination, when Riyadh and Damascus were at odds, Qatar had provided generous support to Syria and helped it to secure the rapprochement with France that ultimately allowed it to cast off its isolation. The regime rejected any prospect of reform and insisted that its supporters in the Gulf and Turkey accept it as it was. This continues to be its approach even now. It manoeuvres between Russia and Iran, rejecting even the superficial reforms of the powers of the Popular Assembly suggested by Russia.

The regime's claims that all opposition was a foreign conspiracy and that the demonstrators were terrorists or the puppets of terrorists were not only propaganda. They were also a statement of intent – in much the same way as 'Assad or we destroy the country', graffitied on walls across the country by regime agents at the beginning of the revolution, was more than just rhetoric. The regime maintained this approach so fiercely that it eventually took over the character of the whole revolution: armed action, the reliance on foreign support, sectarian discourse, extremism. The more extreme the armed groups became, the more they depended on foreign states and/or donors and private money from outside. ISIS proclaimed a short-lived caliphate-state on the territory of two other sovereign states. The Nusra Front (al-Qaeda in Syria, founded in early 2012), which has since become Hay'at Tahrir al-Sham (HTS), has likewise founded its own microstate in Idleb. And the SDF, an organization of Syrian Kurds allied with some Arab tribal fighters led largely by Turkish Kurds, has established an 'autonomous region' for Syrian Kurds in the east and northeast of the country, where Kurds do not comprise a majority of the population.

The Syrian revolution has been sectarianized because it was a revolution against a sectarian regime. It is a *sectarian* regime and not the regime *of a particular sect*: most Alawis are not rulers but ruled, just like other communities. The fact that the regime treats them as its own does not mean that they are in charge. The regime's backbone is made up of Alawi officers in both the army and security forces. Similarly, a renewed sense of Alawi solidarity has meant that many of their relatives or fellow clansmen in state employment consider themselves in one sense or another to be 'part' of the

---

[14] This was Saudi Arabia's main concern. Non-jihadi Salafis linked to Riyadh initially rejected the idea of rebellion against the 'head of the community' (*waliy al-amr*) and opposed both civil disobedience and revolution. But as soon as the Saudi position changed, they became the most active peddlers of sectarian incitement against the regime (see, for example Wisal TV, which provided a platform for Sheikh Adnan al-Aroor) and took up arms as readily as the jihadi Salafis they normally condemn. It did not take long for many of them to become fully-fledged jihadis.

ruling regime – justly or unjustly treated, depending on the extent to which they have received a share in power. Some of them have even convinced themselves that they really are the rulers. The attempts to control the traditional Alawi elite by balancing one clan against another, the reinvigorated role played by clan chiefs after their absorption into the regime through bureaucratic appointments, and the rise of a new generation of retired security officers to chief positions (which are hereditary according to Alawi tradition) have not yet been adequately studied. This is quite unlike the 1970s, when Alawis provided some of the fiercest opposition both to the regime and to traditional clan structures and figures, and prisons were as full of Alawis as of members of any other group. In those days, they did not see religious background as a differentiating factor – they were leftists or secular nationalists. But the sect itself has been sectarianized. Thus, the regime is not the regime of a particular 'sect' so much as that particular sect is the sect of the regime and its most solid base.[15] The armed interventions by Hezbollah and Iran heightened the sense that the regime was sectarian, and the revolution itself became sectarian in its rhetoric and its practice. The more it took on the character of an armed revolution, the more religious it became, and the more religious it became the more sectarian and Salafi it became. Armed groups began to consult with so-called 'Shariʻa experts', many of them graduates of the religious colleges and institutes that had sprung up with regime sponsorship over the previous decades. And the more the *conflict* became multiple armed *conflicts*, the more prominent a role foreign forces played in events. Each of these toxic individual factors worked in tandem with the others.

Nor is it possible to understand the fragmentation that has dogged the revolution without understanding the nature of the regime. Under regime rule, Syria has never been an integrated country. The north and south, the different governorates, were only connected through the regime itself. A civil society reproducing itself through interactions in the market was simply never formed. Organization, at the national level, meant the Baʻth Party, its 'popular organizations' and the security forces, not the market. During its half-century of rule, the regime has failed to integrate the Syrian people *as a single people*, whether economically, socially or politically, except via subordination to the Assad family, via the party and the security organs. Assad himself has said this quite explicitly in recent years,

---

[15] I have discussed the issue of sectarianism in a specific work on the subject, published in Arabic several years after this book. It has since been translated into English. Chapter 9 of that book includes a detailed discussion of sectarianism in Syria. See: Azmi Bishara, *Sectarianism without Sects* (Oxford: Oxford University Press, 2021), 261–87.

maintaining that a Syrian is someone who defends the regime, not merely someone who lives in Syria.[16]

Under such conditions, spontaneous action can only take place at the communal level – the neighbourhood, the town, or at best the governorate – in mobilizations that appear at first as though they are revolutions of local communities. The only armed groups that organized at a national level were those that arrived from abroad *already organized* (the Nusra Front and ISIS), but who saw the majority of Syrians simply as Sunnis and the remainder as, at best, outsiders, though they themselves were outsiders from a national perspective. In both form and behaviour, they remained distinct from the indigenous armed groups, even if they managed for a while to dominate their discourse. The initial fragmentation of these latter groups was indicative of the spontaneity with which locals took up arms. Subsequently, factions began to form, merge and split as a result of local balances of power and the exigencies of battle.

Nor did the political opposition manage to form a united front. Even if it had, its 'unity' would have meant little on the ground, since it had no authority whatsoever over the armed factions in the period when the conflict became an armed conflict. The foreign states that supported the armed factions might have helped bolster the opposition's influence over the armed factions, for example by channelling funding through it. But they did not. Instead, they constantly called for unity in the opposition while meddling regularly in its internal affairs, totally undermining its position. Syrians became fonder of the armed groups than of the political opposition. A new warlord populism began to spread throughout the country, encouraging resentment of the political elite and the intellectuals who 'held meetings in hotels' and did not fight – and encouraging as well a willingness to ignore the crimes of those fighting the regime, including those committed against the civilian inhabitants of the 'liberated areas'.

Despite – and perhaps because of – my total moral bias in favour of the Syrian people and their fight against the regime, I have always been openly critical of what I describe here as negative epiphenomena of the revolution, like sectarian unrest, criminal violence, the growing role of jihadi and Salafi groups and the lack of a political leadership that could overcome their divisions.[17] In the original conclusion of this book, I made clear the danger of the rise of warlords and armed factions not subordinate to a central political or military command, warning of a potential slide into civil war,[18]

---

[16] The deeper the conflict has become, the more explicit he has been. See his speech on 26 July 2015 at: *Al Jazeera*, 26 July 2015, at: https://bit.ly/3JuXA68 (accessed 17 April 2022).
[17] For example, see: Bishara, *Syria*, 605. Also see pages 297–8 of this book.
[18] Bishara, *Syria*, 605–6. See page 298 of this book.

particularly given the flagrant and direct involvement of foreign countries in the militarization of the revolution, the exploitation of sectarianism in the clash of regional blocs (particularly since the Iraq war of 2003) and the rise of transnational jihadi organizations. The Kurdish forces, too, operate across borders[19]: the PYD is the Syrian branch of the Turkish PKK, and several commanders in the SDF are PKK members. The SDF are a Syrian/Turkish-Kurdish force that operates according to a PKK agenda.

The political opposition and the armed groups

The revolution had no declared political leadership. Nor was armed action led by a pre-existing armed group whose activities simply expanded over the course of the revolution. The closure of the public sphere and the consistent repression of anyone who raised their voice against the regime succeeded in cutting the opposition off from the majority of the general population, who were haunted at all times by the spectre of the security forces. Some time after the mass protests first began – led by *local* forces – opposition entities did begin to emerge that sought to provide the revolution with a unified public face and voice in dealings with the outside world. The most important of these were the SNC, established on 2 October 2011, and the SOC, established in November 2012. Located outside the country and influenced by the rapid successes of the Arab revolutions in Egypt and Tunisia and the Western intervention against Qaddafi in Libya, their rhetoric was quite different from the more 'realistic' tone struck by the opposition operating inside Syria. The split between the internal and external opposition was one of the defining developments of the first years of the revolution. In both cases, however, the activities of the political opposition were governed by the logic of the various political factions, their disputes, and their jockeying for position in the face of dynamic, spontaneous protests and the aspirations of their participants. These were professional politicians who nonetheless had no experience of politics in a genuinely free environment. As a result, as Burhan Ghalioun, the first president of the SNC, puts it, they did not understand 'the meaning of freedom or the values of citizenship and public responsibility'.[20] Every time one or

---

[19] Phillips concludes that the rise of sectarianism, jihadism and Kurdish nationalism – all three *transnational forces* – was one of the most significant products of the 2003 Iraq war. This took place at the same time as Turkey and Saudi were beginning to play a bigger role in the region in order to check Iranian influence. See: Phillips, 20.

[20] Burhan Ghalioun, *Self-Destruction: The Realities of an Unfinished Revolution, Syria 2011–2012* [Arabic] (Beirut: Arab Network for Research and Studies, 2019), 82. Ghalioun's book was somewhat belated, but late is better than never when it comes to self-criticism. He uses harsher language, but while I agree with his critiques, I do not agree with his tone, which is the product of his personal experience with politics. He makes no allowances for the circumstances under which the opposition was working.

another faction sought to gain an advantage – whether by securing the support of a foreign state or by encouraging groups on the ground to wave placards decrying other factions – the internecine struggles grew fiercer and the opposition's ability to influence events within Syria, public opinion and the actions of foreign states grew weaker.

These institutions were never equipped to lead a spontaneous revolution. Nor did they ever claim to lead it – only to speak on its behalf by presenting themselves as the representatives of the Syrian people abroad. Allied countries (and countries opposed to the regime) supported it in this aim, for various reasons, many of them having little to do with Syrians' suffering or a belief in their liberation. But the whole process was top-down, with no roots among Syrians themselves. Nor did the international community withdraw its recognition of the regime, which continued to represent Syria in international bodies. Even the Arab League's decision to grant the opposition Syria's suspended seat was a purely symbolic gesture.[21] Displaced Syrians, including the vast majority of opposition figures who lacked dual citizenship, were still obliged to renew their passports at regime embassies, whether resident in a pro-revolutionary or a pro-regime country (which the regime, naturally, has transformed into a money-making scheme). UN aid to Syria continued to pass through the regime.

The emigre opposition was unable to establish the sort of unity of purpose that would have allowed it to assert itself against both allies and enemies. The states that supported it did little to help it overcome its internal disagreements and struggles over the leadership – in fact, they used the opportunity to cultivate groups of supporters within opposition institutions. The opposition to this opposition likewise sought competing foreign sponsorship, leading to the emergence of a Cairo opposition and even a Moscow opposition. But the political opposition's main problem was that it was unable to create a popular leadership. The peaceful revolution before the civil war was a social and psychological break with the regime, made up of a series of overlapping local uprisings that burnt out in one area only to break out again in another. Spontaneity was given pride of place. While the masses chanted the names of prominent opposition figures, to them these figures were media personalities. And when they failed to bring instant victory or were unable to convince foreign countries to intervene against the regime – or simply because they lived abroad and were not in prison – the masses quickly turned to mocking them. The constant attempts by the different factions to outflank one another prevented the opposition from seriously cultivating a long-term struggle or political solutions. And the decision to pin all its hopes on foreign intervention à la Libya meant

---

[21] *The Guardian*, 26 March 2013, at: https://bit.ly/3jW7uDC (accessed 21 April 2022).

that anyone who genuinely sought to engage with Arab League or UN initiatives was branded a defeatist and accused of distracting from the plan. During the period of armed struggle, on the other hand, most of the groups on the ground refused to recognize a unified political leadership, and those groups that did recognize it did not listen to it or drew their support from elsewhere. The regional powers that supported the armed groups provided them with funds and weapons directly and individually or via the various regional coordination bureaus and the operations rooms that sprang up in Istanbul and Amman.[22]

The political opposition was made up of forces that had opposed the regime prior to the revolution and suffered the consequences. It also featured many emigre groups operating outside the country: intellectuals, leftists, liberals, nationalists, and Brotherhood members, the new generation of which had grown up almost entirely in exile. These former comrades, who had once stood alone against the regime, did not welcome the new figures who staked their claim to leadership. Nor – with the exception of the Muslim Brotherhood, which had a relatively strong organizational framework that had benefited from an influx of new blood and ideas at the turn of the millennium – did they have the self-confidence to form broad coalitions. To be sure, the friendly foreign states that called for opposition unity, in particular Turkey, Saudi Arabia and Qatar, hosted many meetings to this end. But this achieved very little of positive value, either because of their inexperience and ignorance of Syrian society and its forces, because they had their own preferences and biases or because they were misled by the parts of the opposition closest to them. It is my view that if the united opposition had been capable of putting off the leadership struggles that dogged it from its earliest days, resolving the mutual suspicion left behind by years of difficult

---

[22] Two 'operations rooms' were established. The first, the Military Operations Command (MOC), was founded in Jordan in 2013 and took responsibility for organizing operations and selecting targets in the south of Syria. Its most prominent members were representatives of the US, France, UK, Jordan and Saudi Arabia; only one member was Syrian, although it was in close contact with the leaders of the armed groups. It played a prominent role in the opening of the southern front in February 2014, when opposition fighters almost reached Damascus. The second operations room was the Istanbul-based Joint Operations Centre (Müşterek Operasyon Merkezi or MOM), which also included Turkish representation and was responsible for overseeing operations in the north of the country. The MOM was closely integrated with the CIA programme to train 'moderate fighters' to join the fight against ISIS. But this programme failed, since it was unable to prevent fighters from joining groups that the CIA considered to be extremists or terrorists, and was shut down in 2017. On this programme, see: Youssef Sadak, 'The MOC's Role in the Collapse of the Southern Opposition', Atlantic Council, 23 September 2016, at: https://bit.ly/3xzjlQb (accessed 17 April 2022); Alexey Vasiliev, *Russia's Middle East Policy from Lenin to Putin* (New York: Routledge, 2020), 493; Thomas Pierret, 'States Sponsors and the Syrian Insurgency: The Limits of Foreign Influence', in *Inside Wars: Local Dynamics of Conflicts in Syria and Libya*, eds. Luigi Narbone, Agnès Favier and Virginie Collombier (Florence: European University Institute; Robert Schuman Centre for Advanced Studies; and and Middle East Directions, 2016), 27.

struggle, and if it had had a strong and patriotic belief in Syrian sovereignty, it would have been able to assert itself as an independent national force and to oblige both friends and enemies to deal with it on this basis.

Some countries that supported the opposition subordinated the whole cause to their own changing regional agendas, and it soon became clear that they had never (or no longer) sought to topple the regime. There were states that genuinely sought to bring down the regime for much of the revolution. All these countries made mistakes – their policies did not help to unite the armed groups – but they cannot be blamed for the fragmentation of the armed battalions or for the attendant exacerbation of these problems. Today, however, with the revolution over in practical terms and Syria divided into areas of influence, Turkey, Iran, Russia and the US are fully responsible for what goes on in their individual spheres. The opposition that remains in Turkey (the SNC) no longer has any power and has been reduced more or less entirely to taking orders from the Turkish government. The Cairo Platform and the Moscow Platform,[23] on the other hand, were never real opposition forces.

In the original edition of the book, I concluded that the fragmentation of the armed battalions and the lack of a hierarchy or united command structure – which meant that there was no unified military and political strategy – was far more dangerous than divisions within the political opposition abroad. A united regime in control of its army and security forces and supported by organized foreign forces cannot be successfully confronted by armed groups that sometimes agree and sometimes disagree violently, which defend the areas under their control not only from the regime but also from other opposition groups, which launch raids against one another and which fight the regime itself absent any overarching strategy.

Nor did the armed groups receive the necessary armaments to fight the regime. They were given no anti-aircraft equipment and very little anti-tank equipment. For the most part they had only light weapons, mortars and Katyusha rockets, although they did manage to obtain relatively advanced artillery either from the surplus of the Libyan war or from the regime's own supplies. They also made some of their own equipment, such

---

[23] The Cairo and Moscow 'Platforms' were Syrian political groups formed in 2014 and sponsored by Egypt and Russia respectively. Each was made up of a mixture of former opposition figures and political and cultural figures who had left the regime without making a decisive break with it. They were set up at the same time that the (largely abortive) 'political process' provided for by the 2014 Geneva Conference began, and were given representation on the High Negotiations Committee created by the SNC to represent revolutionary and opposition forces. But they quickly succumbed to internal differences and to disputes with one another and with the SNC, demonstrating the mitotic structure of the Syrian opposition.

as the 'hell cannons', which used gas canisters as bombs, but which, like the regime's barrel bombs, struck at random and caused serious damage wherever they landed. All attempts to convince the US to provide the FSA with more advanced weaponry met with failure. In 2012, the White House blocked a Pentagon-State Department-CIA armament plan on the grounds that there were no guarantees the weapons would not end up in the hands of extremist groups (or that they would change the balance of power on the ground).[24]

At first, there was broad sociocultural harmony between the forces of the civil revolution and the military defectors who formed the FSA in July 2011. But as the FSA's loose organization became even more tenuous, jihadi groups gained increasing influence. These groups, which established hundreds of new battalions and dominated armed action to such an extent that almost every faction was obliged to adopt Islamic or even Islamist rhetoric, were only rarely rooted in the same social groups that had led the coordination committees or organized peaceful demonstrations, and that had demonstrated a high level of civil and patriotic consciousness. Some locals had acquired weapons in response to the security forces' attacks on protesters – or, in the case of some clans or smuggling gangs, had brought their weapons out. In some areas of Daraa, Homs and Duma, this process did eventually result in the formation of local armed groups made up of local strongmen, smugglers and religious people. While these groups could not be described as 'civil', they were at least *communal* in character. But the large Salafi-Islamist battalions that began to emerge towards the end of 2011, some of whom were led by veterans of the wars in Iraq or even Afghanistan, did not develop out of protests or as 'protest protection' forces, as some of them initially falsely claimed with the tacit agreement of the political opposition. (In any case, this is an incoherent claim, since armed action did not protect protesters but made protecting them more dangerous.) Some of these groups – Army of Islam (*Jaysh al-Islam*), Suqur al-Sham, Ahrar al-Sham – retained a distinctly local character tied to particular regions (the Damascus periphery, Idleb, the areas around Aleppo) and continued to recruit locally. Those with a global jihadi agenda, however, like the Nusra Front and ISIS, drew heavily on foreign volunteers from beyond Syria.

---

[24] Then Secretary of State Clinton and CIA Director David Petraeus came up with a plan to arm the Syrian resistance, which was supported by Secretary of Defence Leon Panetta and Martin Dempsey, the chairman of the Joint Chiefs. But Obama, in the middle of his bid for re-election, was worried about the risks and the plan was shelved. See: *The New York Times*, 2 February 2013, at: https://nyti.ms/3MifISH (accessed 21 April 2022); *Foreign Policy*, 7 February 2013, at: https://bit.ly/3xMQmZ4 (accessed 21 April 2022).

At the beginning of the revolution, there were numerous ambushes and armed actions in various parts of the country, most of which were revenge attacks targeting the army and security forces. But at this stage the decision to take up arms was being made *locally* and *communally*, for purposes of self-defence, not as part of a broader plan to pursue the military option. This is a simple fact. The weapons used were simple, for the most part mere hunting rifles. In the second stage of the revolution, armed groups of a local character began to emerge in individual towns or neighbourhoods or across groups of towns, led by civilians or officers who had defected from the army: al-Farouq Battalions in ar-Rastan or the Islam Brigade (*Sariyyat al-Islam*) in Duma, for example, or more significantly Tawhid Brigade (*Liwa' al-Tawhid*), which played a major role in the takeover of eastern Aleppo (and was formed for this purpose from an amalgamation of several factions that was considered a part of the FSA). The Islam that inspired so many of the names of these groups was a popular, traditional Islam. In some cases, it had a Salafi colouring in its emphasis on the 'pure religion' beloved of Salafi preachers and in its semiotics and slogans. But the Islamist-tinged armed groups that emerged during this period retained a strongly local character. This was the case with the Islam Brigade (*Sariyyat al-Islam*) in Duma, which subsequently became the Islam Battalion (*Liwa' al-Islam*) and then the Army of Islam (*Jaysh al-Islam*) under the leadership of a Salafi-Wahhabi tendency that drew heavily on so-called 'scholarly Salafism'.[25] This group's leader, Zahran Alloush, was the son of a sheikh who had worked in Saudi Arabia.

From 2011 onwards, al-Qaeda in Iraq began to send fighters to establish a Syrian arm (the Nusra Front). This group was quickly divided by struggles over leadership and authority, which took a particularly violent form after the establishment of ISIS and the Nusra Front's rejection of the caliphate of Abu Bakr al-Baghdadi. Each of these groups took control of particular areas and established alliances and coalitions with others that changed regularly according to their interests and sources of funding. Unification was often made a precondition of funding, but unity imposed from the outside never lasted very long. On a few occasions, groups formed alliances

---

[25] The term 'scholarly Salafism' (*salafiyya 'ilmiyya*) is a media invention with no basis in Salafi terminology itself. It refers to conservative, non-jihadi Salafism that does not directly intervene in political issues – indeed, is generally obedient to all Muslim leaders – and instead tries to promote pious behaviour in the general population. Scholarly Salafism in this sense is closely associated with Muhammad Nasiruddin al-Albani (1914–1999), one of the leading Salafis of the twentieth century, whose followers can be found in many countries. Politically a conservative, he was opposed to rebellion. But he was made revolutionary by Syrians. For more, see: Azmi Bishara, *On Salafism: Concepts and Contexts* (Stanford: Stanford University Press, 2022).

in order to fight a particular battle. But neither the groups themselves nor the bodies funding them had any overarching military strategy.

The armed groups failed to develop a military plan for how to defeat the regime, never mind form an alternative. They faced constant efforts by the political opposition to outflank them by insisting that the entire regime must fall, including all its institutions and major figures. This was cast as though it were something that the regime itself would do under domestic and international pressure, not as the aim of a practical and integrated plan guaranteeing success. It was as if the only aim was to *bring down* the regime and not to *create an alternative*.[26] It was decided not to discuss the nature of the alternative political system and instead to focus on the aim that united the entire opposition: toppling the regime. It is now clear that this was a mistake. The risk of anarchy and the rise of radical Islamist forces – and their derisory performance as administrators in the areas under their control – became one of the most important elements keeping the regime in power and heightened the reluctance of the 'international community' to overthrow it.

Attempts to integrate the battalions and their influence on national armed groups

From the beginning of the Syrian revolution, many ideologically non-Islamist armed opposition groups made repeated attempts to create a united front against the regime. These attempts all fell victim to internal division. The FSA remained for the most part a collection of autonomous units with tenuous institutional links with one another and, as a result, limited ability to secure support (which initially was limited to local networks of relatives and businessmen). As the struggle against the regime developed and competition for funding intensified, the gulf separating these groups from the jihadi battalions – which were better organized, ideologically coherent, militarily effective and structurally capable of absorbing other groups – grew wider. Generous new sources of funding appeared. Pro-Saudi politicians in Lebanon acted as channels for money from elsewhere, and Syrian expats and Salafi networks in the Gulf succeeded in mobilizing large sums of money and funnelling it to groups fighting on

---

[26] Ghalioun correctly notes that democracy never played a prominent role as a consensus alternative to dictatorship. There were Salafi, Brotherhood and takfiri visions at work as well, and other states involved in the process had their own agendas that had nothing to do with democracy. See: Ghalioun, *Self-Destruction*, 430. But the strongest element in the civilian revolution, before armed action began, was indisputably the force that rallied around democratic demands and called for the replacement of authoritarianism with a democratic system that would guarantee freedoms.

the ground (some of this was directed specifically to groups that did not enjoy state funding, such as the Nusra Front). Non-governmental donations found their way primarily to Islamist groups whose vision accorded with that of the funding bodies, and since these funders had different degrees of Islamist commitment, it led to further divisions between the Islamist groups themselves and between Islamists and the FSA battalions.[27]

In early 2012, the Saudi position on arming the opposition changed. Wahhabi sheikhs began trying to carve out their own niche in the armed revolution and to play a part in the growing Islamization of the struggle. They mobilized their connections, their TV programmes and their social media presence to raise money for Syria. Sheikh Adnan al-Aroor was the most active in this field, fronting programmes on Safa TV and Wisal TV in which he provided commentary on the Syrian revolution. He channelled money from the conservative Gulf audience to Syria, later becoming, albeit for a short time, one of the main funders and controllers of the military landscape in the country as a whole.[28]

The supporting governments tried to pressure the armed groups into overcoming their differences by imposing unity from above. Over the course of the revolution, they forced them to establish a series of 'joint commands' and alliances in order to establish some kind of order, make sure that money was being used efficiently and counteract the tendency towards arms trading and fragmentation into small groups (which hoped, by establishing their own identities, to attract more funding). They also encouraged these factions to set up intermediary commands sympathetic to their own regional agendas.

The foreign funding provided to the FSA battalions was not enough to create an effective organizational framework or to allow them to expand militarily, and many of them ended up joining the larger Islamist groups in pursuit of funding. But the price of this extra funding was abandoning their self-image as unideological groups close to the civil vision of a post-Assad Syria. And the mergers that resulted failed to guarantee political or ideological cohesion.

The Syrian Revolutionary Front, set up in Istanbul on 4 June 2012, provides an instructive and early example of the willingness of armed groups to be absorbed into stronger Islamist battalions. The front included, alongside Islamist groups, many of the local FSA affiliates, in particular the military councils: the Hama Military Council, the Coastal Military Council, the Syrian Tribal Military Council, the Daraa Revolutionary Battalions,

---

[27] Olivier J. Walther and Patrick Steen Pedersen, 'Rebel Fragmentation in Syria's Civil War', *Small Wars & Insurgencies* 31, no. 3 (2 April 2020), 445–74.
[28] *Al-Araby al-Jadeed*, 23 March, 2022, at: https://bit.ly/3JzOZiF (accessed on 17 April 2022).

Ahrar al-Sham, Suqur al-Sham, Baba Amr and the Umayyad Battalions in Damascus and the periphery.[29] Its implicit purpose was to integrate the Islamist forces into the existing political and military cooperation bodies, such as the FSA General Staff, to check their attempts to outflank the FSA battalions on issues like the Shari'a and the future shape of the state, and to separate them from the nascent transnational Salafi-jihadi groups, like the Nusra Front. But it did not last long.

The network of Brothers in Alms, led by Salafi groups of various stripes and centred in the Gulf states, played a major role in shaping the landscape of armed groups. Figures linked to the Ummah Party (banned in several Gulf states) were particularly prominent.[30] Sheikh Muhammad Surur Zayn al-Abidin (1938–2016),[31] whose followers had been involved in previous clashes between the Brotherhood and the regime, once again returned to the political scene thanks to an international network of 'Sururists'; the sheikh himself threw his weight behind the SILF.

Three Islamist factions emerged within the Syrian Revolutionary Front, each of them reflecting, albeit indirectly, different intellectual tendencies which competed for influence but were united by an almost obsessive desire to differentiate themselves from the FSA and the opposition battalions.

The first, Suqur al-Sham, was founded in 2011 as the Suqur al-Sham Brigade (later 'Brigades') by Abu Issa al-Sheikh, who had not particularly well-developed Salafi tendencies. The need for funding, the struggle for influence and the desire to get rid of his main regional rival, Jamal Maarouf, led al-Sheikh to pursue a policy of undermining the FSA battalions in Jabal az-Zawiya. In 2014, he implicitly welcomed the Nusra Front's attempts to penetrate his areas of influence, since he hoped that this would force the other armed groups to submit themselves to his control. Later, however, Suqur al-Sham became a major target of the Nusra Front as it tried to establish control over Jabal az-Zawiya.

The second, Ahrar al-Sham, began as a handful of regional units founded in October 2011; it rebranded itself as a 'movement' in early 2013. Unlike Suqur al-Sham, which was very ambiguous about its ideological position, Ahrar al-Sham always presented itself as a Salafi-jihadi movement, theoretically not different from al-Qaeda, except that it insisted that its aims were strictly Syrian rather than global and it did not implement physical punishments according to Shari'a nor did it impose its doctrine of

---

[29] *Anadolu Agency*, 5 June 2012, at: https://bit.ly/3M9uo6p (accessed 17 April 2022).
[30] Thomas Pierret, 'Brothers in Alms: Salafi Financiers and the Syrian Insurgency', Carnegie Middle East Centre, 18 May 2018, at: https://bit.ly/3uPz1Ng (accessed 17 April 2022).
[31] Resident in Saudi Arabia since the 1980s, he moved to Qatar during the revolution and died there.

Shari'a on the population. Although the group described itself as part of the Syrian revolution, it consistently distinguished itself from the FSA and opposition battalions, constantly undermining the FSA's image by accusing it of theft, chaos, murder and ideological deviations. Along with its military successes and its ability to attract both official and unofficial Gulf support, this propaganda effort meant that other groups saw a constant stream of defections to the Ahrar, which was supported by Qatar. There were various motivations for these defections, but the Ahrar's ability to pay better was certainly one of them.

The third, the Army of Islam, was founded in September 2011 as the Islam Brigade. The majority of its members were ideological activists associated with traditional non-jihadi Salafi groups in Duma, the stronghold of Hanbalism in Syria. Relying at first on primitive guerrilla tactics, the group was initially able to fund itself, perhaps with some support from Salafi networks within Duma. But it was never going to be difficult for Zahran Alloush to secure foreign support. His father had been taught by prominent Wahhabis, including Abdulaziz bin Baz and Muhammad bin Ibrahim al-Sheikh, both of whom had served as grand muftis of Saudi Arabia, and had been at university with leading Wahhabi preachers such as Saleh al-Fawzan and Saleh al-Luhaidan. Alloush himself had received his religious education in Saudi Arabia. As a result, money came pouring in, allowing the Army of Islam to rapidly expand its military activities and develop a more sophisticated organizational structure; many smaller groups active in the region that lacked any means of reaching donors requested incorporation into its military organization.[32] In early 2012, Alloush decided to give the enlarged organization a more appropriate name, calling it first a 'battalion' (*katiba*) and then a 'brigade' (*liwa'*) before finally announcing on 29 September 2013 the founding of the 'army' (*jaysh*) of Islam, which by that point had some 10,000 fighters distributed over 43 different battalions around Damascus.[33] Although earlier mergers had largely been voluntary, from this point onwards Army of Islam sometimes resorted to coercive methods to take over Eastern Ghouta, seeking to exclude various local units including the Army of the Ummah of Duma, the Islamic Union of Levant Fighters (Sufi) and Faylaq al-Rahman (close to the Muslim Brothers). The struggle for influence continued through to April 2018, when all armed groups withdrew from Ghouta to northern Syria under a negotiated agreement with the regime. The Army of Islam itself has a very poor human rights record and is accused of all sorts of

---

[32] Lund, 'Into the Tunnels'.
[33] ACRPS, 'Army of Islam: The Search for a Role in the Future of Syria' [Arabic], July 2015, at: https://bit.ly/37qjcUr (accessed on 17 April 2022).

violations, including kidnapping the civilian activists Razan Zaitouneh, Samira Khalil, Nazem Hamadi and Wael Hmadeh, all of them members of the LCCs and the Violation Documentation Committee, and harassing local media and secular activists.

These three groups – Ahrar, Suqur and the Army of Islam – were not merely local groups. They also competed to absorb other fighting groups at the national level, a project which bore fruit in late 2012 with the creation of two distinct umbrella groups.

The first of these, the SILF,[34] was officially founded on 12 September 2012. At its root it was a political alliance between Suqur al-Sham and the then-Brigade of Islam, alongside twenty other patriotic and non-activist Islamist groups such as the Tawhid Brigade, the Fateh Brigade and al-Farouq Battalions. Its purpose was to secure additional funding by creating a shared Islamic ideological umbrella, as advised by Muhammad Surur Zayn al-Abidin. Although the SILF recognized the FSA General Staff – allowing it to access support from foreign countries participating in the international operations rooms – it represented a first step away from the national-civil and non-Salafi-jihadi image that opposition groups had previously cultivated. In order to secure greater military support, it began to express its support for an Islamic government.

The second project, the SIF,[35] was founded on 22 December 2012. Its main supporter was Ahrar al-Sham, which refused to recognize the FSA General Staff. The SIF comprised ten Salafi Islamist groups, the most prominent of which were the al-Haqq Brigade in Homs, the Islamic Vanguard, the Fajr Islamic Movement and Ansar al-Sham. They stated explicitly that their aim was to establish an Islamic state 'based on the understanding of the righteous forefathers [the *salaf*]'.[36]

The creation of these two organizational bodies made it impossible for many of the national groups to avoid absorption or at the very least alliance and coordination with them in order to maintain their position in an overcrowded theatre. This only became more difficult when the founding groups of the SILF and SIF announced a new alliance, the 'Islamic Front' (IF), in December 2013, bringing more than 60,000 fighters together in one alliance.[37] This regionally-backed 'experiment' was the product of changes in the external political environment after the rise of ISIS and its attempts

---

[34] Syria Islamic Liberation Front (SILF) website. Archived copy at: https://bit.ly/3vAa9bn (accessed 17 April 2022).

[35] 'Charter of the Syrian Islamic Front', Malcolm H. Kerr Carnegie Middle East Centre, 4 February 2013, at: https://bit.ly/3ECjG6c (accessed 17 April 2022).

[36] Ibid.; Lund, 'Syria's Salafi Insurgents'.

[37] Aron Lund, 'The Politics of the Islamic Front, Part 1: Structure and Support', Malcolm H. Kerr Carnegie Middle East Centre, 14 January 2014, at: https://bit.ly/3Mfsu4t (accessed 17 April 2022).

to expand into opposition-controlled areas. It added to the pressure which had already been piling up on the national opposition groups. This was clearly visible in the IF's manifesto, the 'Umma Project', which explicitly rejected democracy, liberalism and secularism and called for the establishment of an Islamic state in Syria, as well as other developments on the ground.[38] Even before the establishment of the IF, thirteen Islamist groups – including those that established the IF – had released a joint statement withdrawing recognition from the SNC, the provisional government and the FSA General Staff.[39]

The presence of jihadi groups like ISIS and the Nusra Front and the increasingly exclusionary character of Islamist discourse were signs of the changing nature of the armed opposition. Its national character was receding, and it was turning from revolutionary-political to jihadi or sectarian violence. The only thing these groups shared with the revolution was the aim of overthrowing the regime. But they opposed all of the revolution's aims and principles: freedom, dignity and the democratic state.

Despite all this, the national groups did not simply give in. Even as the external environment became more difficult and the Islamists grew in strength, they made constant efforts to organize themselves in order to meet the challenges that faced them. Two weeks after the creation of the IF, most of the FSA battalions operating in Idleb and Hama announced the formation of the Syrian Revolutionary Front under Maarouf. Similarly, on 4 January 2014, fifteen national groups operating around Aleppo formed the Army of the Mujahideen. Three weeks later, on 25 January, twelve national and moderate Islamist groups established the Hazm Movement. All these new umbrella movements agreed on the civil character of the Syrian struggle and the need to fight both the regime and the counterrevolutionary jihadi groups.

A few days before the second Geneva Conference (January 2014), these national, non-Salafi-jihadi groups achieved something unprecedented: after a major military campaign, they inflicted a humiliating defeat on ISIS, resulting in its expulsion from much of Syria (Latakia and most of the Idleb, Hama and Aleppo governorates) and isolating it in ar-Raqqa. But despite this success, the US refused to recognize these groups as a 'partner on the ground' in the battle against terrorism or to provide them with meaningful support. The Obama administration insisted that any forces that it trained would only fight ISIS and not the regime. Instead of the national groups, it chose to back the PYD – the Syrian

---

[38] ACRPS, 'The Islamic Front: An Experimental Integration of the Largest Military Groups in Syria' [Arabic], November 2013, at: https://bit.ly/3ElCpm5 (accessed 17 April 2022).
[39] All4Syria, 24 September 2013. Archived copy at: https://bit.ly/3vrhr14 (accessed 17 April 2022).

branch of the PKK, which not only Turkey but also the US lists as a terrorist organization.[40]

The same applies to the Southern Front established in 2014 under the oversight of the Military Operations Command (MOC) to act as an umbrella for all units operating in the south of the country. The Southern Front had a fighting strength of 40,000 men and was promoted as the 'last hope' of the armed opposition and the ideal organized alternative to the Islamist groups – especially after it managed to expel ISIS and impose serious losses on the Nusra Front within its region.[41] But while the Southern Front had a unified operational command, its command-and-control centre was in Amman and almost entirely subordinated to Jordanian concerns. It was isolated from military operations in other Syrian regions. And when the Russian intervention began, it was sacrificed on the altar of an understanding with Moscow on the future of Jordan's role in Syria. Its component parts were subjected to reconciliation agreements and ultimately incorporated into the fifth column that Russia sought to establish.

Civil war

I did not try to define 'civil war' in this book, and I do not think efforts in this direction will be very productive. It is clear that what we are talking about is an internal war[42] between armed forces (one of them the regime) to take control of the country and its resources, or to take control of land and population in order to secede and establish a new entity. To those who insist on distinguishing between armed revolution and civil war – a distinction entirely absent from the literature on civil wars – I say that what distinguishes a civil war in this context is the involvement of large groups of the population in supporting the warring parties, including the regime. This is what happened in Syria. The regime did not stand alone against the revolution: it succeeded in mobilizing a social base that took up arms to defend it. Moreover, the war was not fought by a revolutionary army or armed forces that carried the values of the revolution; some major armed forces that fought against the regime held counterrevolutionary values and

---

[40] Hamzeh al-Moustafa, 'Facing ISIL: Reasons and Possible Impacts' [Arabic], *Siyasat Arabiya* 7 (March 2014), 119–25.

[41] Lina Khatib, 'Syria's Last Best Hope: The Southern Front', Malcolm H. Kerr Carnegie Middle East Centre, 6 July 2015, at: https://bit.ly/38dDDnH (accessed 17 April 2022).

[42] Stathis N. Kalyvas, 'Civil Wars', in *The Oxford Handbook of Comparative Politics*, ed. Carles Boix and Susan C. Stokes (Oxford: Oxford University Press, 2009), 417.

aims. This was not an armed revolution fought by the FSA. The Syrian revolution made the transition from *civil* revolution to *civil armed* revolution and then to *armed groups embroiled in a civil war* before degenerating into an effort to defend the besieged areas under their control. As this process progressed, the majority of the armed groups moved steadily away from the values of the revolution against despotism. Some of them had never believed in these values or taken part in the civil revolution. In the areas under their control, they practised their own form of despotism.

This civil war was always asymmetric. It was fought against a regime capable of deploying all the tools of conventional warfare, including air power, which it used to devastate its own cities – a first in the history of regimes making war against their own people. When the Russian air force joined the fight on 30 September 2015, this aspect of the war intensified. But alongside the regular army, the regime and its allies made extensive use of irregular forces, from the *shabbiha* of the NDF to the sectarian militias recruited from Lebanon, Iraq, Afghanistan and Pakistan. This gave the war a *symmetric, non-conventional* dimension, as Stathis Kalyvas calls it,[43] a kind of warfare distinguished by its primitive nature and its brutality. The regime and its allies prosecuted two wars: one conventional and the other unconventional.

The Syrian case is made even more complicated by the fact that it is not simply a matter of two sides at war – armed revolutionaries against the army and militia of the regime. Forces like ISIS have arisen that fight both sides and proclaim both of them to be infidels. Others have fought the regime not in order to defeat authoritarianism but in order to establish a totalitarian religious state: the Nusra Front, for example, or Ahrar al-Sham. Others still are hostile to the regime but have degenerated into gangs led by warlords that have no intention of taking power across Syria and whose ambitions are limited to specific areas. In mid-2012, the CIA estimated that there were around 1,000 groups active in Syria. A year later, the Carter Centre put the figure at somewhere between 1,050 and 3,500. For comparison, at the height of the Lebanese Civil War, there were no more than thirty different groups active.[44] Even in mid-2012, only half the groups were affiliated with the FSA.[45]

By the end of 2013 there were around 1,500 groups fighting the regime army. These varied widely in size: some were active only across a handful of districts or a neighbourhood or two, while others dominated whole districts. At the peak of the armed conflict, they commanded between them some

---

[43] Ibid., 428.
[44] Phillips, 127.
[45] Hokayem, 185.

150,000 fighters.[46] Salafi groups had been present since 2011, but after mid-2013 they began to become dominant: '[F]ive of them featured among the seven most powerful rebel groups [...] two of them were offspring of the Jihadi Islamic State in Iraq (*Jabhat al-Nusra* [...] and the Islamic State in Iraq and Sham, ISIS), and the three others would soon become the founding factions of the more pragmatic IF (*Ahrar al-Sham*, the Army of Islam, and *Suqur al-Sham*), along with the Islamist, but non-Salafi *Tawhid* Brigade.'[47]

There are other forces that seek to achieve the demands of particular ethnic groups. Here I am referring in particular to the SDF, which are dominated by the PYD. In 2012, the PYD took over large swathes of the majority-Kurdish Al-Jazirah region at the regime's invitation. The regime had various reasons for doing this: it needed to redeploy the Syrian army to protect 'useful Syria', that is the area between Damascus and the Mediterranean coast; it also hoped to create problems for Turkey around its borders (in this it was successful, and Turkey's main concern now in its Syria policy is the Kurdish issue), set the PYD against the opposition forces and prevent the Kurdish movement from joining the broader Syrian revolution. In any case, the PYD adeptly exploited the ISIS threat to secure US support that allowed it to expand its control over all parts of Syria between the Euphrates River and the Iraqi border, as well as the area around Menbij west of the Euphrates. It also rebranded, allying with local tribal Arab groups as the SDF, although the PYD remained the dominant force. Decisions continue to be made by the Stalinist organization of the PKK leadership in the Qandil Mountains in north-eastern Iraq. The PYD's control is strong in al-Hasakeh but weaker in ar-Raqqa and weaker still in Deir ez-Zor. The fight against ISIS produced a US-Kurdish alliance, which came at the expense of US-Turkish relations and further complicated the situation. US-Turkish coordination rapidly collapsed, and the US came to rely on the SDF, which considered Turkey its main enemy rather than the Syrian regime, with which it maintained warm relations.

On top of this long list of forces, militias[48] made up of thousands of foreign fighters have fought alongside the regime, most importantly

---

[46] Sherifa Zuhur, 'The Syrian Opposition: Salafi and Nationalist Jihadism and Populist Idealism', *Contemporary Review of the Middle East* 2, nos. 1 and 2 (2015), 144. A low estimate was 115,000, see: Christopher M. Blanchard, Carla E. Humud and Mary Beth D. Nikitin, 'Armed Conflict in Syria: Overview and U.S. Response', Congressional Research Service, 27 June 2014, 3, at: https://bit.ly/3RUg4CN (accessed 25 July 2022).

[47] Thomas Pierret, 'Salafis at War in Syria: Logics of Fragmentation and Realignment', HAL Archives, 29 March 2018, accessed at: https://bit.ly/36lw39G (accessed 17 April 2022); Joshua Landis, 'Syria's Top Five Insurgent Leaders', *Syria Comment*, 1 October 2013, at: https://bit.ly/3DEJ0bb (accessed 17 April 2022).

[48] I use the term 'militias' to describe irregular forces fighting alongside the regime against the insurgency, irrespective of whether they were established on the regime's initiative or as independent projects. See: Corinna Jentzsch, Stathis N. Kalyvas and Livia Isabella Schubiger, 'Militias in Civil Wars', *Journal of Conflict Resolution* 59, no. 5 (August 2015), 755–69.

Lebanese and Iraqi Hezbollah, the Abu'l-Fadl al-'Abbas Brigades and the Afghan and Pakistani Fatimid Militias, which have become more important since the majority of Iraqi fighters were forced to return home to confront ISIS after the occupation of Mosul. This is not to mention the thousands of foreign Salafi-jihadis who have fought for ISIS and other terrorist groups in the country. In September 2014, CIA estimates put the number of ISIS fighters between 20,000 and 31,500 (16,000 of them foreign), while the chief of the Federal Security Service of the Russian Federation (FSB) gave a figure of 30,000 to 50,000 (25,000 of them foreign).[49]

It is difficult to categorize these forces as part of a civil war[50]: a party to a civil war is a *local force* operating within the framework of a state. Nonetheless, these foreign forces have intensified the divisions within Syrian society more than anything else. They are largely sectarian forces which have made flagrant use of sectarian rhetoric to mobilize fighters from other countries to fight alongside or against the regime. The Shi'i militias have regularly presented themselves as protectors of Shi'i holy sites in Syria.

At the beginning of the armament, some of the factions that had not formed a central organization sought to establish control over a particular region of Syria that would play the role that Benghazi had played in Libya. But once it became clear that there would be no foreign intervention in Syria, the Benghazi model was no longer relevant, and taking control of populated areas became an end in itself, part of a civil war, despite the fact that this made no strategic contribution to the aim of bringing down the regime. After a bloody domestic conflict between the factions, the Islamists managed to seize most of these areas. As a result, cities, towns and villages became targets for brutal airstrikes. And there was no international attempt to protect the civilians now facing a war of extermination.

During the civil war, there was a power struggle between the major Islamist factions, in the course of which ISIS took over ar-Raqqa, expelling Ahrar al-Sham and the Nusra Front forces that had held the city previously (13 January 2014). It also managed to take control of areas southeast of the Euphrates, including Deir ez-Zor, Abu Kamal and al-Mayadin, while the Nusra Front took over Idleb.

---

[49] Vasiliev, 453.
[50] 'Civil war' is a long-standing but linguistically imprecise term. There is nothing 'civil' about a civil war except that it takes place between citizens of the same state and not between different states. The usual Arabic term, *harb ahliyya*, is closer in literal meaning to 'communal war'. This is not what the Syrian war is, at least not since 2014, when its nature changed. On this point I agree with Yassin al-Haj Saleh in his *The Impossible Revolution* [Arabic] (Beirut: Arab Institute for Research & Publishing, 2017), 24, who notes the change that happened when Hezbollah intervened directly in the Battle of Qusayr and sectarian militias began pouring into the country. At that point, what had been the Syrian revolution became part of the so-called 'Sunni-Shi'i conflict' and regional polarization (Ibid., 235–9). 'Sunni-Shi'i conflict' is another expression that substitutes an imaginary conflict for actual political and social conflicts.

Various international bodies maintain a quantitative definition of civil war. One such definition requires 1,000 people to be killed in a single year in fighting between armed forces. Using this classification, one-third of countries have witnessed civil wars over the last half-century. Another requires twenty-five people to be killed, in which case half of all countries have experienced civil wars in the same period.[51] But the Syrian civil war belongs to a much smaller group encompassing perhaps no more than 10 per cent of countries. And if we look more closely at its sheer duration and complexity, the scale of the losses and the crimes that have been committed, it may be a unique case.

The civil war was the regime's choice, as it stood firm against any political change. Its systematic oppression continued, culminating in what security officials and regime supporters called the 'starvation until submission campaign',[52] which involved starving densely inhabited areas held by rebels.[53] It went on while the regime was participating in negotiations, where it refused to offer any concessions but helped the international community to delude itself that a 'political process' was ongoing and won time for its violent everything-or-nothing policy. I agree that 'analyses arguing that the regime's good fortunes, at least until early 2015, can be solely attributed to massive support from Russia, Iran and Hizballah underplay the regime's own adaptability and, more specifically, its role in obtaining such foreign support and utilizing it to optimal effect'.[54] But the regime could not have survived without the persistent support of these parties and their direct military intervention. Its determination to hold on to the bitter end by using all manner of violence against its own people convinced its allies that the choice was to accept the regime as is or to lose the geostrategic battle over Syria: 'In short, the Syrian regime calculatingly embarked on a counter-revolutionary campaign that first helped to transform a largely peaceful uprising into an insurgency, and then derailed

---

[51] I could go into more detail on quantitative measures, but that would be beside the point here. In any case, the Syrian civil war has far exceeded all these measures and has become something of a laboratory for new ones. See: Christopher Blattman and Edward Miguel, 'Civil War', *Journal of Economic Literature* 48, no. 1 (March 2010), 3–4.

[52] Reinoud Leenders, 'Repression Is Not "a Stupid Thing": Regime Responses to the Syrian Uprising and Insurgency', in *The Alawis of Syria: War, Faith and Politics in the Levant*, ed. Michael Kerr and Craig Larkin (New York: Oxford University Press, 2015), 258; UNSC, 'Report of the Secretary-General on the Implementation of Security Council Resolution 2139 (2014),' 26 March 2014, at: https://bit.ly/38uRypu (accessed 17 April 2022).

[53] Allowing free passage of food and humanitarian aid is a duty under international law and should not require additional action. The UNSC unanimously adopted Resolution 2139 demanding that all parties fulfil their obligations in this respect. But since no country was willing to force the regime to comply, the resolution went unimplemented – further proof that international law and even UNSC resolutions do not mean much in the absence of coercive executive force.

[54] Leenders, 271.

the latter so that all that remained was a vicious civil war in which it stood [a] better chance of surviving.'[55]

Are there any winners in such a war? Is civil war likely to lead to the partitioning of Syria? Unlike the Balkan wars, no side in Syria seeks to secede. The only ethnic cause that has been politicized in Syria is that of the Kurds in northern Syria. Their best organized and most extreme nationalist party has been able to take control of a region in which Kurds do not constitute a numerical majority. But even that faction does not officially seek to secede. Nor would it be able to. It has none of the basic requirements that it would need to survive in the absence of US support. The areas controlled by other anti-regime forces, meanwhile, are areas of temporary control that likewise lack the requirements to survive long term unless they are literally annexed to Turkey, which would be unacceptable internationally and regionally. Russia continues to insist that the Syrian regime must rule *all* of Syria as a precondition for any solution.

There are those who believe that the regime has won the war, some of whom predicted this outcome from the very beginning because of the close ties between the Alawi community and regime.[56] The truth is that it is the sectarian nature of the regime that led it into civil war, and it was by no means inevitable that the regime would win. Military victory as represented by regime survival would not have been possible without Russia and Iran. Comparisons with Iraq and Lebanon, meanwhile, lead us to the conclusion not of a viable federal system but rather permanent crisis. The sectarian system in Lebanon has failed, as has the Iraqi system, which is not sectarian in itself but is run by sectarian parties on a quid pro quo basis. In 2019, young people in Lebanon and Iraq launched their own uprisings, calling for a state belonging to its citizens and not to representatives of confessional communities. It is my belief that the outcome of the conflict in Syria is still not decided and the tragedy continues. It is neither united nor partitioned, and there are no winners in the civil war. Everyone is a loser, and the Russo-Iranian intervention cannot transform a beleaguered regime that has lost its legitimacy and is unable to rule Syria into a winner.

The Russian intervention: A turning point

Despite the armed groups' lack of organization, between late 2014 and early 2015 the war nonetheless posed a genuine threat to the regime's existence.

---

[55] Ibid., 272.
[56] See: Joshua Landis, 'The Work of Fabrice Balanche on Alawites and Syrian Communitarianism Reviewed by Nikolaos van Dam', Syria Comment, 30 November 2013, at: https://bit.ly/3NZoV41 (accessed 10 April 2022).

A joint offensive by Ahrar al-Sham and the Nusra Front made extensive gains in the north and along the coast, including the provincial capital of Idleb in the northwest. Alongside a renewed offensive by other factions in the south, these advances alarmed the regime. In a speech on 6 May 2015, Assad conceded that not all was going as planned: 'War is not one battle but a series of many battles [...] When setbacks occur, it is our duty as a society to boost the morale of the soldiers and not wait for them to boost ours.' On 26 July, he added, 'Sometimes, under some circumstances, we are forced to give up areas to move forces to [other] areas that we want to hold onto [...] we must define the important regions that the armed forces will hold onto so as not to allow the collapse of the other areas.'[57] Russia began to deploy troops in April 2015 and began airstrikes in late September.[58]

Western countries did nothing to stop the intervention, which aimed both to save the regime and to re-establish Russia's reputation as a great power. No sanctions were imposed (in stark contrast to the response to its invasion of Ukraine). Moscow presented its actions as part of the US-led coalition's war on terror in Syria – part of the intervention already launched against ISIS. But the Russian idea of the 'war on terror' extended to all Islamist organizations that refused Russian-sponsored negotiations with the regime. And it did not launch airstrikes against ISIS or fight it on the ground, despite its notional aim being to support the regime against the organization.[59] That task it left to the US and its allies.

Samer Abboud writes correctly that the Russian intervention had nothing to do with ideological similarities or a desire to protect an ally. It was the product of a confluence of geopolitical, local and economic factors and a fear of the spread of extreme Salafi-jihadi ideas in the region (an analysis Russia shared with others). Russia was also anxious about the prospect of US intervention à la Libya.[60] The NATO intervention in Libya was the real reason for Moscow's use of its veto to scupper every UNSC resolution against the Syrian regime. But the Russian intervention was not intended to prevent a similar US intervention. It was launched once it was already clear to everyone that the US and NATO had no intention of getting involved militarily. Moreover, Russia was filling an international

---

[57] *Al Jazeera* (international), 6 May 2015, at: https://bit.ly/3JCnuoI (accessed 16 April 2022); *BBC* (international), 26 July 2015, at: https://bbc.in/3xyBGNi (accessed 16 April 2022).
[58] Guido Steinberg, 'Ahrar al-Sham – the "Syrian Taliban": Al-Nusra Ally Seeks Partnership with West', Stiftung Wissenschaft und Politik/Deutsches Institut für Internationale Politik und Sicherheit, 2016, at: https://bit.ly/36g9mUj (accessed 17 April 2022).
[59] Florence Gaub, 'Russian Non-War on Daesh', in *Russia's Return to the Middle East: Building Sandcastles?* ed. Nicu Popescu and Stanislav Secrieru, Chaillot Paper 146 (Paris: European Union Institute for Security Studies, 2018), 57–64.
[60] Samer N. Abboud, *Syria*, 2nd edn (Cambridge: Polity Press, 2018), 144.

vacuum left by its agreement with the US to destroy Syria's chemical weapons. Russia sought to reassert itself as a great power, a force that could not be treated like a Third World state and subjected to sanctions (as happened during its 2014 invasion of Crimea). It was worried about the spread of jihadi-Salafism to the North Caucasus, which in 2012 had been shaken by a wave of demonstrations in solidarity with 'Sunni brothers' in Syria. Economic concerns having to do with regional arms sales and gas exports to Turkey also played a role, albeit a secondary one. Abboud says repeatedly that the Russian intervention broke the stalemate and allowed the political process to begin.[61] But it is my view that Russia intervened at a critical moment for the regime and saved it from collapse. And this intervention has not ushered in any kind of meaningful political process at all. The regime has become even more intransigent and unwilling to consider any kind of reform or settlement, and has continued to treat the negotiations as a meaningless performance.

At this stage, the international community's fear of the fall of the regime overcame its fear of its survival. By this point, the regime controlled no more than 20 per cent of the country.[62] The armed groups' influence had expanded at the regime's expense and had driven back its forces in the north and south. Damascus had also lost control of the oil revenues, which were appropriated first by ISIS and then by the SDF: having taken in $4.7 billion on oil in 2011, it earned a mere $0.22 billion in 2014.[63] Anxieties about what would happen if the regime collapsed were rooted primarily in the outcome of the interventions in Iraq and Afghanistan and were compounded by developments in Libya and an inability to predict the geostrategic consequences of an unstable Syria (as the regime itself warned). Initial optimism about the Arab revolutions had also faded after the victory of the Muslim Brotherhood in the Egyptian elections and the coup that followed in July 2013. But foreign fears were truly exacerbated by the growing dominance of Takfiri Islamist groups like ISIS and the Nusra Front on the military scene – groups that made Salafi movements like Ahrar al-Sham look moderate by comparison. These groups not only proclaimed the regime and the democratic opposition to be infidels. They did the same to one another. And once the Russian intervention foreclosed the possibility of a regime defeat and made negotiations an inevitability, other countries became less willing to continue funding non-Islamist and non-Salafi groups. Western media became preoccupied with ISIS and its

[61] Ibid., 195.
[62] Vasiliev, 490.
[63] Anna Borshchevskaya, *Putin's War in Syria: Russian Foreign Policy and the Price of America's Absence* (London: I.B. Tauris, 2022), 159.

exhibitionist sadism, turning a blind eye to regime crimes that outstripped them both quantitatively and qualitatively: 'When, by mid-2013, it had become clear that not the regime but jihadist–salafists posed the greatest danger to journalists, the regime lifted some of its restrictions on Western journalists and granted them more visas. Far fewer now dare to visit rebel-held territory. As a result, the *Economist* noted, "coverage of the regime has become kinder".'[64] Syrian suffering became less telegenic.

Russia always sought to coordinate its military operations with the US. It wanted to be treated as a partner great power, without any preconditions concerning the nature of the regime in Syria. It considered its intervention to be a precursor to partnership with the US on Middle Eastern issues as a whole. Moscow became a regular destination for the leaders of Gulf countries, Turkey, Iran and Israel (whose existing relationship with Russia was strengthened). Israel agreed to coordinate its strikes on Iranian and Hezbollah targets in Syria with the Russian commanders at Homeimim Base.

After Aleppo had been besieged and pounded from air and land and restored to regime control in December 2016, Russia adopted a policy of de-escalation in several regions. This should not be understood as part of a political process intended to lead to negotiations, as it claimed. It was part of an all-encompassing military plan: strikes on supply routes into rebel-controlled areas, besieging those areas to the point of starvation, and then forcing them to agree to 'de-escalation zones'. A strategy of siege and starvation had already been adopted by the regime in 2013 in the towns around Damascus, but its military defeat in the north in 2014 had led it, along with Iran, to request Russian military intervention. The de-escalation agreements were in themselves a first step towards forcing fighters to accept evacuation to Idleb or co-optation by Russia, which was easier to stomach than cooperating with the regime. The regime thus gradually nibbled away at the areas under rebel control until it restored control over all but three areas: Idleb, a sort of Gaza Strip for the opposition; the northern border, under direct Turkish control since Ankara's intervention to reduce the size of the border zone controlled by the PYD; and the SDF areas in the northeast. It is one of the curious ironies of the confluence and contradiction of international interests that the Turkish intervention (direct and via Syrian proxies, the so-called National Army) was based on an understanding with Russia and a disagreement with the US, while the US intervention east of the Euphrates took place with Russian assent and Turkish irritation. Since 2015, the international forces active in Syria have all behaved as

---

[64] Leenders, 260–1; *The Economist*, 21 October 2013, at: https://econ.st/3Kea8zY (accessed 17 April 2022).

though there were no Syrian people, no just cause, only the pure logic of interests. It became difficult even to identify stable alliances.

The establishment of a new negotiations track with some of the armed groups in Astana in 2017 – a Russo-Turkish initiative with Iranian participation – was the first step towards the de-escalation zones and the removal of the opposition groups from the areas in which they had been entrenched. Since the Astana negotiations were formally based on UNSC Resolution 2254, which called for a transitional process including the drafting of a new constitution and the building of a new political structure, some have concluded that they are the best path to a solution. Since so many armed groups were involved (generally under Turkish pressure), it seemed to reflect the military reality on the ground.[65]

In reality, the Astana path has not led to any kind of political solution. Instead, it has given political embodiment to the military balance of power, removing the armed groups from many areas and concentrating them in Idleb or turning them into Russian collaborators. Contrary to many claims, the de-escalation areas[66] were not part of the peace process. They were part of an expansive military plan to re-establish regime control over Syria, which Russia considers a precondition for any solution in Syria.

All this ultimately led to the withdrawal of the countries that supported the opposition from the conflict. The MOC and the Joint Operations Centre (Müşterek Operasyon Merkezi or MOM) were closed down. President Donald Trump announced that the US would be withdrawing from Syria. The armed groups were cut down to size by Russia and then forced to accept de-escalation agreements. Finally, those members of the armed groups that had survived airstrikes and sieges were left running tiny, marginal bits of the country. The international forces that had backed the regime took centre stage in the disastrous scene that followed. The role of the political opposition abroad, which had in any case never been able to establish a strong central leadership capable of organizing even the civil forces of the revolution, began to diminish.

How did this happen?

The West was quicker than Turkey or the Gulf to put pressure on the Syrian regime. But in the West's case this was rooted in a negative baseline view of the regime with a long and well-known history, which had nothing to do with the suffering of the Syrian people or the nature of the regime itself.

---

[65] Abboud, 211.
[66] Ibid., 219.

This attitude had remained in place despite several crises during which the US had been forced to cooperate with Damascus (usually on security matters), particularly after the occupation of Iraq. But while officials began to affirm that Assad had lost his legitimacy and even to call for him to step down between July and August 2011, the US position remained just that: a position. It was not translated into a goal or a plan of any kind. The US expected the regime to fall – some officials even *hoped* that it would fall – but it made no effort to bring it about. Some scholars have suggested that its allusions to delegitimization and its calls for an Assad exit were based on a miscalculation: a failure to realize that, unlike in Egypt, the West had little influence over the regime in terms of trade or arms sales and the regime was used to sanctions and isolation in the West[67]; it was coup-proof and unlikely to fall quickly, unlike the Egyptian and Tunisian regimes, and its social base, now convinced that regime change was a threat to it, was fairly cohesive. These have continued to be the key elements explaining the regime's survival, along with Iran and Russia's decision to do everything necessary to prevent its collapse and the West's hesitancy and clear decision not to directly intervene.

At first, the Syrian opposition was sure that US intervention – whether direct or via NATO – was inevitable. Their allies supported this delusion, convincing them that Assad's days were numbered. The US did not want to intervene. It had an Iraq complex, and although it had overcome that complex, under French and Gulf pressure, in Libya, that adventure had ended in failure when the state-building exercise ground to a halt. But at the same time, it had no desire to clarify its anti-intervention position. This only added to the confusion.

Western countries had no love for the Syrian regime and resented being forced to work with it in Iraq and Lebanon. But it was not sympathy with the Syrian people's sufferings under despotism that was the main reason for this. That came very far down the list. Unlike in the 1960s, the regime was not hostile to the West or to imperialism, but it liked to make trouble for certain Western countries, particularly the US, either to extract concessions or as a reaction to pressure from those countries. This is why it supported Hezbollah attacks on US personnel in Lebanon and resistance to the US occupation in Iraq – until the UN realized that it was easier to cooperate with Damascus. In July 2006, during the Israeli invasion of Lebanon, it was reported that President Bush had told Tony Blair that they needed Syrian pressure to rein in Hezbollah. David Lesch, who met Assad personally during that period, reports that the president was ecstatic: 'I love

---

[67] Phillips, 77–8.

it. I love that he said that. It makes me feel great, because at least he is thinking about Syria. He is thinking about us.'[68]

These countries may have been sympathetic to the revolution. They may have hoped that the regime would fall. But they were also afraid of the consequences: a crescent of instability stretching from Iraq to Lebanon and along the Israeli border. Nor were they able to identify an alternative. And they were wary of the armed Islamist groups. The regime was the devil they knew, with whom it was possible to reach ad-hoc agreements. For these reasons, the US had no desire to intervene in Syria from the very beginning. But it left the door open. Even when it finally did deny categorically that there was any possibility of direct intervention, many were unwilling to recognize reality.

On 12 September 2005, years before the revolution began, the US ambassador to Iraq told a talk show audience that America's patience with Syria was 'running out [...] They must cooperate with the new Iraqi government, or they will have to face increased pressure, not only from the Iraqis but from us as well.'[69] He warned that 'all options are on the table', refusing to rule out military action.[70] But shortly thereafter, a State Department official announced that the US did not expect Syria to change its regime but to change its behaviour.[71] This position has long outlasted the brief neoconservative period and has shaped the US attitude ever since, despite statements from Obama and other officials about Assad's loss of legitimacy and their 'wishes' that he would step down. In July 2021, the acting assistant secretary of the Bureau of Near Eastern Affairs confirmed that the US was seeking not regime change but behavioural change.[72] As early as 2017, in fact, the last US ambassador to Syria stated, 'Assad has won and he will stay. He may never be held accountable, and Iran will be in Syria to stay. This is the new reality that we have to accept, and there isn't much we can do about it.'[73]

In the post-2014 period, the exigencies and alliances of the war on ISIS took precedence over the regime – at a time when the pro-regime states, however, did not think twice about intervening directly on its behalf. The US leapt on the excuse of the Russian veto to conceal its own hesitation and failure to reach a decision on Syria.[74] But since when does America wait for UNSC resolutions to take action? In any case, the Russian

[68] Lesch, *Syria*, 34.
[69] See Khalilzad's interview on *Talk of the Nation* [Radio programme]: *NPR*, 12 September 2005, at: https://n.pr/3r0xotF (accessed 5 April 2022).
[70] *The New York Times*, 12 September 2005, at: https://nyti.ms/3uVCc51 (accessed 5 April 2022).
[71] Wieland, 162.
[72] For Joey Hood's exclusive interview, see *Today's Interview* [TV pr ogramme]: *Al Jazeera*, 10 July 2021, at: https://bit.ly/3LGpQV2 (accessed 6 April 2022).
[73] *The National*, 28 August 2017, at: https://bit.ly/3KvxzoV (accessed 6 April 2022).
[74] Hokayem, 184.

intervention put an end to any lingering possibility of US involvement, saving Washington any further embarrassment. The greatest aspiration of the Western countries was the hope that Syria would resume its position in the Russian (rather than the Iranian) sphere of influence and carry out a handful of reforms under Russian pressure. With Moscow's encouragement, the idea spread that Russia could 'guarantee' that the oil kept flowing and that Israel would be safe, and that it could serve as a bulwark against extremist and extremist-adjacent groups – and this at a time when ISIS and ISIS-linked cells were carrying out violent attacks in Western countries. More significant still was the effect on Iranian influence. Western countries took the opportunity presented by the Russian intervention to turn their backs on Syria and all its complications. During the 2022 Russian intervention in Ukraine, on the other hand – which Western countries made no attempt to avoid or forestall – they confronted Russia and mobilized international public opinion against it.

In 2014, a year before the Russian intervention, the US announced a plan to intervene militarily against ISIS. During its strikes on ISIS positions, it avoided hitting regime forces, which had committed crimes no less horrific than those of ISIS. As the regime continued to pound the armed groups in densely populated cities and avoided fighting ISIS itself, the US judged these groups exclusively by whether they were fighting ISIS or not. This criterion was not accepted by the majority of the armed opposition, although they were all simultaneously victims of both ISIS and the regime.

A year earlier, on 31 August 2013, the regime had used chemical weapons against civilians in Ghouta, near Damascus, crossing the 'red line' that Obama had said in August 2011 would justify US intervention in Syria. A total of 1,729 civilians were killed in that attack, many of them children.[75] But the US did not keep its promise. Instead of the regime itself, it focused on the type of weapons that it was using, deciding to let the matter go so long as the regime was willing to give up its chemical weapons. The regime took this as a green light to use any other kind of weaponry it had available. And that is exactly what it has done ever since. Once Obama's red line had been crossed without any US response, and once the US had agreed to a chemical disarmament agreement instead of a military intervention,[76]

---

[75] Jasmine K. Gani, 'US Policy towards the Syrian Conflict under Obama: Strategic Patience and Miscalculation', in *The War for Syria: Regional and International Dimensions of the Syrian Uprising*, ed. Raymond Hinnebusch and Adham Saouli (London: Routledge, 2019), 217.

[76] Obama was always hesitant and became even more so after the British parliament voted against intervention. British Prime Minister David Cameron had not prepared the ground for a vote and lost as a result, a mistake he would repeat with the Brexit referendum. US Secretary of State John Kerry, when asked how Syria could avoid US intervention, answered that agreeing to give up its chemical weapons might be sufficient. It has been suggested that he agreed on this answer in advance with Sergei Lavrov, allowing them to present it as a US idea with Russian agreement.

there were no longer any limitations on the regime. Since 2013, there have been no more red lines. The regime made the transition to total war, and in the process, the forces that had pinned their hopes on foreign intervention were marginalized and replaced by more extreme alternatives.

Trump's position in this respect was no different from Obama's. In fact, during his campaign, he accused Clinton of seeking to embroil the US in a new war in Syria. Once in power, he showed himself quite content to allow Russia to play the leading role. The airstrikes he ordered on 13 April 2018 against what he claimed were 'chemical weapons plants' being used by the regime were for media consumption, an attempt to distinguish himself from Obama. He made sure to warn Russia in advance.[77] He even tried to withdraw the US forces fighting ISIS alongside the Kurds east of the Euphrates, on the grounds that ISIS had been defeated, although on that point US intelligence prevented him from moving forward with the plan.

Four UN envoys and a decade of failure

It is impossible to understand the failure of the UN special envoys except as a symptom of the inability of the great powers to achieve justice and a desire to shunt responsibility onto international officials. The significance of the work of the envoys is directly correlated with the great powers' support for them. The less support there is, the more their personal views and inclinations take centre stage in the media (pointlessly, of course).

The Arab League tried to give its first (November 2011) and second (January 2012) initiatives compulsory force by submitting them as a draft UNSC resolution under Chapter 6 of the UN Charter. But the Russian veto on 5 February 2012 scotched this plan, encouraging the regime to begin a military operation in Baba Amr in Homs that ended with the destruction of the whole neighbourhood. By early 2012, particularly after the Baba Amr offensive, the transition to armed action was complete.

The Friends of the Syrian People group, made up of seventy countries including the majority of Arab states, Turkey, the EU and the US, was established to 'find a solution to the Syrian crisis outside the Security Council'. At its first conference, held in Tunis on 24 February 2012, the group promised to provide all possible means of support for the Syrian people against the regime, including military support. In response, Russia proposed a 'political solution' based on the Arab League initiatives, to be implemented with UN sponsorship. The UN, in turn, appointed its first special envoy (shared with the Arab League) the same day.

---

[77] *BBC* (international), 14 April 2018, at: https://bbc.in/3rxXioX (accessed 17 April 2022).

As of this writing, there have been four special envoys appointed to 'find a political solution' for 'the tragedy of the Syrian people': Kofi Annan, Lakhdar Brahimi, Staffan de Mistura and Geir Pedersen. But the regime has proven very resistant to the Russian idea of a settlement, despite the fact that Russia's primary goal in this is to keep it in power – to the point that Russia has publicly expressed its frustration with Damascus's intransigence. In February 2012, Russian Foreign Minister Lavrov said Assad believed that 'history is on his side',[78] adding that Russia was not interested in 'personalities' but the 'fate of the Syrian people, the fate of Syria as a united sovereign, independent state' and that 'the authorities made many mistakes', failing to 'respond to the legitimate requests from the opposition for too long'.[79] But this did not mean that Russia was willing to give up on the regime. It was an attempt to force it to engage with the new rules of the game in some minimal way.

The regime has been a willing participant in all the meetings held by the four special representatives over the last decade, even as massacres were being committed and weapons, including chemical weapons, Scud missiles and vacuum bombs, were being used against populated areas. This has been a way of playing for time. There was no connection between what it was discussing and what was happening on the ground. More importantly, the regime's participation was proof of its legitimacy as *the Syrian state*. Its representatives gave speeches condemning the 'international conspiracy' (sometimes the 'universal conspiracy') against Syria, affirmed Syrian sovereignty, equated opposition with terrorism and refused to discuss any of the details.

The special envoys have failed to achieve any meaningful breakthrough, despite the 'passive neutrality' they have maintained in the face of calls to condemn the regime's crimes, even those, like the chemical weapons case, where the regime's involvement has been proven by an international investigation. In the absence of great power consensus on the need to protect civilians and impose justice – and with direct Russian involvement on the side of the regime unchallenged by the US – their efforts have been reduced to a gradual process of regime normalization. The most recent envoy, Geir Pedersen, has overseen a veritable rehabilitation of the regime internationally through his 'step for step' initiative, which treats the Syrian conflict not as a 'crisis of governance' – which would require a political transition capable of bringing to an end what the UN human rights chief has described as the 'worst man-made disaster the world has seen since

---

[78] See Lavrov's interview for the documentary film on Syria by Hubert Seipel: *ARD TV*, 13 February 2013, at: https://rb.gy/nkuidx (accessed 21 April 2022).
[79] Ibid.

A Critical Account of Developments Since 2013   339

World War II'[80] – but as a crisis of *government*, requiring only a political agreement on how to move ahead with electoral procedures.

1. Annan: Disagreement between the great powers on how to interpret Geneva 1

Kofi Annan, the Nobel Prize-winning former UN secretary general, was the fastest and most effective in putting forward a plan. When this plan failed, he left his position, refusing to allow himself to become a witness to negotiations or a 'political process' that failed to distinguish between victim and perpetrator and which in reality represented no more than an attempt to play for time.

Annan was named special envoy at the height of international concern with the Syrian crisis. He attempted to translate this concern into support for a six-point plan to end military escalation and build an international consensus around the essential parameters of any political solution in Syria. At the Geneva 1 Conference, which was held on 30 June 2012, he managed to put together a roadmap to end the war and carry through a political transition that 'would fulfil the legitimate aspirations of the Syrian people'. It was agreed that a transitional governing body with full executive power would be set up to provide a neutral environment within which the transition would take place. But without the full weight of international executive power behind him, Annan was unable to force the regime to implement the agreement, either directly or via its allies, especially with respect to reducing the level of violence, which had been rising steadily ever since his appointment. By refusing to comply with the timetable for a withdrawal of its forces from the cities, the regime torpedoed the first two points of the agreement, giving Annan the choice of either humouring it or announcing the plan's immediate failure. That the US refusal to allow Iran, Syria's major foreign backer, to participate in negotiations also helped scupper Annan's efforts.[81]

The main problem, however, was disagreement between the various signatory powers over what a transitional governing body exercising full executive powers was supposed to be. Was Assad to be excluded from it from the get go, as the US and the anti-regime states maintained, or would he oversee it as part of the 'institutions of government' that remained in place during the transition, as Russia insisted? This disagreement occasioned a fierce war of words between Clinton and Lavrov and derailed

---

[80] *UN News*, 14 March 2017, https://bit.ly/3LEjPb9 (accessed 23 May 2022).
[81] *The Atlantic*, 3 August 2012, at: https://bit.ly/36kokc4 (accessed 17 April 2022).

efforts to make the Geneva communique enforceable through the UNSC, ultimately leading to Annan's resignation on 2 August 2012 (citing 'finger-pointing and name-calling in the Security Council'). In a rare moment of candour, he told journalists that a transition meant 'there was going to be a change in government, the transition meant President Assad would have to leave sooner of [sic] later'.[82] In an editorial for the *Financial Times*, he said: 'It is clear that President Bashar al-Assad must leave office. The greater focus, however, must be on measures and structures to secure a peaceful long-term transition to avoid a chaotic collapse. This is the most serious issue. The international community must shoulder its share of responsibility.'[83]

It is true that there can be no political transition so long as Assad is present and controls the security forces and the army. This alone would be enough to thwart any transition. This has always been true. Annan's efforts failed because of the regime, although the opposition also bears part of the responsibility, having spent this period locked in internal competition and dismissing any diplomatic attempt that did not result in Assad's immediate removal as a distraction from the only real solution: a military intervention, despite the lack of any evidence that such an intervention was in the cards. The opposition refused to support the Geneva communique, and many opposition leaders made statements against it at the time. Of course, the opposition as represented by the SNC would not have been able to prevent its implementation had the international will been present – indeed, if the plan had been put into practice, its members would have scrambled to participate. But its rejection of the plan nonetheless gave the regime additional room to manoeuvre, allowing it to participate vocally while stymieing any effort to make the scheme a reality on the ground.

2. Brahimi: Mission impossible

On 17 August 2012, fifteen days after Annan's resignation, Brahimi, a former Algerian foreign minister and UN special representative to Iraq

---

[82] *UN News*, 2 August 2012, at: https://bit.ly/3yR7due (accessed 23 May 2022).
[83] In the editorial, Kofi Annan advised his successors, saying that 'Syria can still be saved from the worst calamity. But this requires courage and leadership, most of all from the permanent members of the Security Council, including from Presidents Putin and Obama'. In another article in *The Washington Post*, he repeated that without 'joint, sustained pressure from those with influence, including consequences for noncompliance' there could be no hope of a solution. Although he attacked all parties to the conflict, including the opposition, he saved his harshest criticism for the regime, which he described as '40 years of dictatorship'. See *Financial Times*, 2 August 2012, at: https://on.ft.com/38KEIDx (accessed 17 April 2022); *The Washington Post*, 28 June 2012, at: https://wapo.st/3uO6Az8 (accessed 17 April 2022).

and Afghanistan, was named as his replacement. Brahimi's mission, which he described as 'nearly impossible', was based on the Geneva communique. But during his tenure, far more destructive weapons, including Scud missiles and barrel bombs, were deployed for the first time, and as a result Brahimi adopted a strident tone, repeatedly stressing that 'there is no place for Assad in a transitional government'. After Assad's January 2013 suggestion of an 'alternative political initiative' based on 'national dialogue in order to preserve Syrian sovereignty and check terrorism' – dialogue, of course, that excluded the opposition, which he described as a 'handful of [foreign] agents and gangs that accept only the language of blood and terror' – Brahimi accused him of 'sectarianism' and 'one-sidedness' before withdrawing his comments and claiming it had been a 'slip of the tongue'. In a later interview, he predicted that Syria would become a 'second Somalia': 'It will not be divided, as many have predicted. It's going to be a failed state, with warlords all over the place.'[84]

At the same time, Brahimi described the Syrian conflict as a 'civil war'.[85] It was clear that Brahimi was trying to strike a balance between the various international powers. He used the term 'civil war' in a joint press conference held with Lavrov in November 2012 to convince Moscow, whose role in Syria was expanding as the US role shrank, to move forward with a political solution involving a transitional body with full executive powers, as provided for by Article 1 of the Geneva communique. Equipped with US-Russian support, Brahimi oversaw the second Geneva Conference in early 2014, attended for the first time by representatives of the regime and the opposition. Despite the optimism surrounding the conference, however, the negotiations were conducted without any effective timeframe or preconditions, and produced no meaningful results other than a week-long truce in partially besieged Homs. The logic that allows for a negotiating process with no preconditions, no timeframe and no agreed-upon foundation transforms it into an entirely superficial process, a fig leaf for agreements based on the military balance of power on the ground, or at best a media spectacle that remains important only until the attention of news teams turns elsewhere.

Brahimi agreed to allow discussion of the 'war on terror' as part of the political process alongside discussion of political transition. This allowed the political process to begin to move in a new direction and break off into side tracks. He also helped make Iran part of the political solution, which had been Russia's exclusive preserve over the previous years, saying in May 2014 (when he was already a former envoy) that Iranian suggestions on the

---

[84] *CNN Arabic*, 9 June 2014, at: https://cnn.it/3jS1GLm (accessed 20 April 2022).
[85] The term had already been used by the Red Cross in July 2012. See: *BBC* (international), 15 July 2012, at: https://bbc.in/38LWsOS (accessed 17 April 2022).

future of Syria were 'worth discussing', although these were substantively the same as Assad's own suggestions and coincided with the arrival of Iran-linked Lebanese and Iraqi fighters in Syria.[86]

Approximately two years into his 'nearly impossible' mission, Brahimi resigned on 13 May 2014, without no apparent successor.[87] This coincided with Assad's announcement that he intended to stand for a new presidential term.[88]

3. De Mistura: Stalemate

In June 2014, a few weeks before de Mistura took over as special envoy, ISIS seized Mosul, and international attention turned away from the crimes of the regime and its Iranian, Lebanese and Iraqi militias to ISIS atrocities and how to confront them. At the same time, Obama was focusing on securing a nuclear agreement with Iran, an achievement which he hoped would represent his foreign policy legacy. Meanwhile, the EU was growing increasingly concerned with the massive influx of refugees from Syria and increasingly willing to support any settlement that would stop that influx irrespective of whether the settlement was just or not. Under these circumstances, and with all the previous attempts to reach a solution having focused on the system of government, de Mistura decided to adopt a new approach, focusing on temporary settlements intended to 'freeze the conflict' or 'reduce its humanitarian effects'. His first step was to try and set up a 'freeze zone' in Aleppo, which if successful could be replicated across the country, in the hope of mobilizing international and regional support.[89]

'Freeze zones' were an entirely new idea, de Mistura's personal invention. They marked the beginning of the normalization of the idea that the regime would stay in place and the conflict would be deescalated under its supervision, first via disengagement in the various conflict regions. The zones were entirely in tune with the strategy of 'reconciliation' adopted by the regime (population displacement and demographic engineering): those who did not accept reconciliation in a particular area would be forced to leave, and the reconciliation itself would amount to no more than the return of traditional regime rule.

---

[86] In his interview with *Al-Monitor*, Lakhdar Brahimi said, 'If the Syrians are not capable of solving the problem alone, the first people who can help are the neighborhood, and definitely Iran is part of the neighborhood. So I think we have always been in favor of Iran being involved.' *Al-Monitor*, 18 May 2014, at: https://bit.ly/3jJSCbx (accessed 17 April 2022).
[87] *The Guardian*, 1 May 2014, at: https://bit.ly/3uPeSqF (accessed 17 April 2022).
[88] Ibid.
[89] *Al Jazeera* (international), 31 October 2014, at: https://bit.ly/3Lb1IKp (accessed 17April 2022).

The 'freeze zone' strategy also helped de Mistura to remain in post while awaiting new international and regional developments. Developments of this kind finally came in September 2015 with the Russian intervention. At the end of the year, the opposition restructured itself, forming the Higher Committee for Negotiations and expanding its membership to include representatives of both the domestic and emigre opposition; at the same time, the Cairo and Moscow Platforms were established. De Mistura's approach to the opposition was consistently patronizing: alongside the states allied with it, he sought to set the conditions under which it would reconstitute itself. He acted as if the whole issue were a question of intra-opposition negotiations, consistently avoiding discussing the issue of a transitional governing body capable of meeting Syrians' basic demands.

De Mistura gradually came to lean towards the Russian solution, particularly after the retaking of Aleppo in late 2016 and the beginning of the Astana Process in early 2017. This latter development saw the resurrection of the 'freeze zones' under a new name: 'de-escalation zones'. On 4 May 2017, the state sponsors of the process (Iran, Turkey and Russia) agreed to establish four de-escalation zones in Idleb, the areas to the east of Homs, Eastern Ghouta and the southern region.

During de Mistura's tenure, the UN vision of a political solution came to correspond to the Russian vision. Four 'agenda baskets' – political transition, fighting terrorism, the constitution and elections – were established as part of efforts to implement UNSC Resolution 2254.[90] Its only real outcome, however, was to pave the way for the establishment of the Constitutional Committee and to marginalize Geneva I and the main issue, which is political transition. The Higher Committee eventually suspended its participation in the political process and its cooperation with the special envoy until it was forced to restructure itself at the second Riyadh Conference in late 2017 after the resignation of the committee's leader, Riad Hijab.

De Mistura played for time, but despite eight rounds of negotiations, ten workshops outside the Geneva structure and the establishment of numerous consultative committees (including legal, constitutional, women's and communal committees), he made no serious breakthrough and focused on formalities far more than on the central problem. At the end of January 2018, he resigned for family reasons.

4. Pedersen: Managing, not solving, the crisis

In late 2018, the UN appointed the Norwegian diplomat Pedersen as the new special envoy, who remains in post at the date of writing. To the

[90] UNSC, 18 December 2015, at: https://bit.ly/3xtI2Mc (accessed 17 April 2022).

complication and fragmentation of the mission he inherited from de Mistura, Pedersen added his own fresh complications. He dedicated much effort to forming a Constitutional Committee (which de Mistura had failed to bring into being) comprising the opposition, the regime and civil society, whose task was to draft a new constitution in accordance with UNSC Resolution 2254, which provides for the formation of a transitional governing body and elections.

The special envoy has continued to hold meetings despite the regime's refusal to implement Resolution 2254. He has been unable to force any progress on the question of withdrawing foreign forces from Syria,[91] and he faces what he has described as a 'strategic stalemate' on the ground. As a result, the negotiations have become a meaningless façade, not even significant enough to qualify as dialogue. This is the reality of the constitutional committee. 'Reconstruction', which the US rejects out of hand and has sought to link to a political settlement, has gone nowhere: not a single refugee has returned home, despite the many conferences organized by the regime with Moscow's support.

The basic problem for the opposition is Pedersen's 'step for step' approach, which the SNC considers to be a distortion of Resolution 2254 and the roadmap based on it. This new approach boils down to a series of procedural steps by which other countries open up doors for the regime in exchange for corresponding steps towards a solution. It seeks to 'gradually change the regime's conduct' and create an appropriate environment for the 'voluntary return of refugees and displaced people'. The proposal included a timetable for the various fields that the 'step for step' approach would operate within: humanitarian issues, Resolution 2254, anti-terrorism and the withdrawal of foreign forces.[92]

Pedersen believes that the lack of change in the military situation on the ground since the Moscow agreement in May 2020 shows that there can be no military solution and that a political solution is the only option for international and local actors alike. His argument for the 'step for step' approach is based on the Joe Biden administration's discussions with Russia on the renewal of the aid mechanism, which allows aid to pass through areas under regime control to areas under opposition control and vice-versa. His team is very active in detainee swaps between the regime and the opposition, which he has cast as a new mechanism by which the detainee issue can be settled – an idea that Russia and the regime are opposed to.

---

[91] Maan Talaa, 'Sixth Round of Meetings of the Constitutional Committee: A Floating Agenda and Constant Deadlock' [Arabic], *Omran for Strategic Studies*, 2 November 2021, at: https://bit.ly/3M2Ob7w (accessed on 17 April 2022).

[92] *Al-Araby al-Jadeed*, 12 October 2021, https://bit.ly/3jxb46Y (accessed on 17 April 2022).

Pedersen has sought to develop a vision of the Syrian conflict as a domestic political crisis similar to crises in Lebanon, Iraq and Sudan: a governmental crisis, not a crisis over the nature of the regime. As such, this requires power-sharing arrangements – even this is rejected outright by the regime – rather than a political and democratic transition. Pedersen maintains that this can be achieved through the drafting of a new constitution that will pave the way for parliamentary or presidential elections in which all parties can take part, including Assad. This is his ultimate aim, which he hopes to achieve by taking advantage of war-weariness and international backers' conviction that there is no use continuing with an endless conflict, especially given events in Ukraine. This is ultimately Russia's vision, which it has not tried to force Assad to accept. It envisions a strong presidential system similar to Russia's in which the president controls the security forces and the army, with a degree of pluralism and formal and informal powers granted to the parliament, while allowing some parts of the opposition to participate. But the regime remains unwilling to accept anything other than the current model, which has remained unchanged by any of the constitutional amendments conducted in early 2012 despite the formal pluralism that they instituted. The security regime that has rallied around the president is not affected by constitutional amendments.

Since its intervention, Russia has redoubled its efforts to convince various countries (especially Arab states) to normalize relations with the regime, arguing that this will allow it to exercise greater political influence on Damascus, pressure it to introduce reforms in line with Resolution 2254 and separate it from Iran – or, at the very least, better cooperate on humanitarian issues and reconstruction. More significantly, it has tried to convince countries hosting Syrian refugees that better relations with the regime will make it easier to send them home. This is more or less the approach taken by Pedersen: he believes that it is possible to influence the regime and, by offering it step-by-step incentives, induce it to reform.[93] But normalization of the regime has never led to reforms. It has led only to *acceptance* of the regime, without the regime itself changing or adapting. Normalization has simply strengthened its belief that the only language that the international community understands, just like Syrian society, is force. It has concluded that ultimately the world will come crawling back.

For the regime, normalization is seen as a victory won by strength, whether its own or that of its allies. The same applies to the lifting of

---

[93] Steve Heydemann, 'Assad's Normalization and the Politics of Erasure in Syria', Brookings Institution, 13 January 2022, at: https://brook.gs/3JJq3Fy (accessed 17 April 2022).

sanctions, which Russia and China, among others, continued to advocate. When Jordan moved decisively towards normalization in July 2021 and reopened the Syrian-Jordanian border to bilateral and international trade – and when the UAE and Bahrain reopened their embassies in Damascus – regime media trumpeted the Arab 'surrender' to its will. Relations between Syria and the UAE have since developed to the point where private banks and other companies linked to the regime have opened special branches in Abu Dhabi and Dubai which help them avoid US and European sanctions. The crowning moment of the process came on 18 March 2022, when Assad himself made an official visit to the UAE.

Just as it had no compunction about targeting Syrian cities with barrel bombs, the regime does not think twice about holding Syrians hostage under painful sanctions that cover food, medicine and heating. It is quite happy to use them as a sort of human shield. The logic of normalization is to transform the hunger and cold that Syrians suffer from a lever of pressure on the regime into a means of pressuring others to normalize their relations with the regime by using it as a channel for humanitarian aid. Of course, the regime itself will distribute this aid through its network of corruption, turning it into both a source of income and a way of exerting pressure on Syrians: those who obey will receive aid, while those who rebel will be punished. The regime's allies, Russia and China, provide no significant aid to the Syrian people; they merely call on the regime's enemies to do so. They use the immiseration and starvation of Syrians to pressure those who imposed sanctions to lift them and recognize that they have been defeated, welcoming the Syrian regime back into diplomatic salons irrespective of the crimes against humanity that it has committed.

Normalizing the regime will not fix it. It may remove one of the last checks on its behaviour. And it is not only the Syrian regime that will get worse. If Assad escapes punishment, all other authoritarian regimes will realize that whatever crimes they commit, they will be able to get away with them.

Four regions of control

As of 2022, Syria is divided into four regions of control: 1) a regime-controlled area covering most of the country; 2) the areas under the control of the SDF; 3) the areas under the control of the Turkish-backed Syrian National Army (SNA); and 4) the areas under the control of HTS, dominated by the organization formerly known as the Nusra Front. This region is also within the Turkish sphere of interest.

Map C.1 Areas of Control

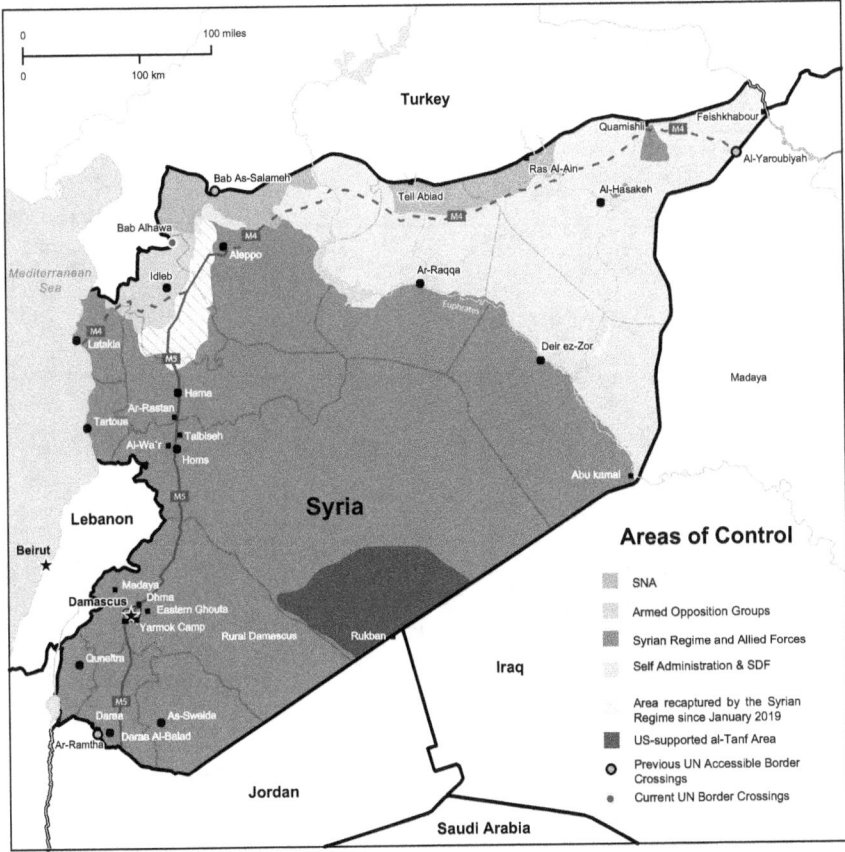

Source: adapted from the map created by Natasha Hall, 'Rescuing Aid in Syria', Center for Strategic and International Studies, February 2022, 3, at: https://bit.ly/3byuqs8 (accessed 24 April 2022).

In this section, I will try to give a brief sketch of each region. Because of the unverifiable and at times contradictory nature of available population and economic data, some circumspection is in order. While drawing on various published sources, I rely on field sources[94] and my own calculations and judgment to reach the estimates given here.

All four regions of Syria today are criss-crossed by a patchwork of military bases, positions and checkpoints, manned by 28 Coalition, 90 Russian, 119 Turkish and 277 Iranian detachments. This is in addition to the regime army, the NDF, and its many foreign militiamen.

---

[94] I am indebted to the Harmoon Centre and especially its director, Samir Seifan, for his assistance in collecting this information.

I. Regime-controlled areas

Map C.2 Regime-controlled Areas

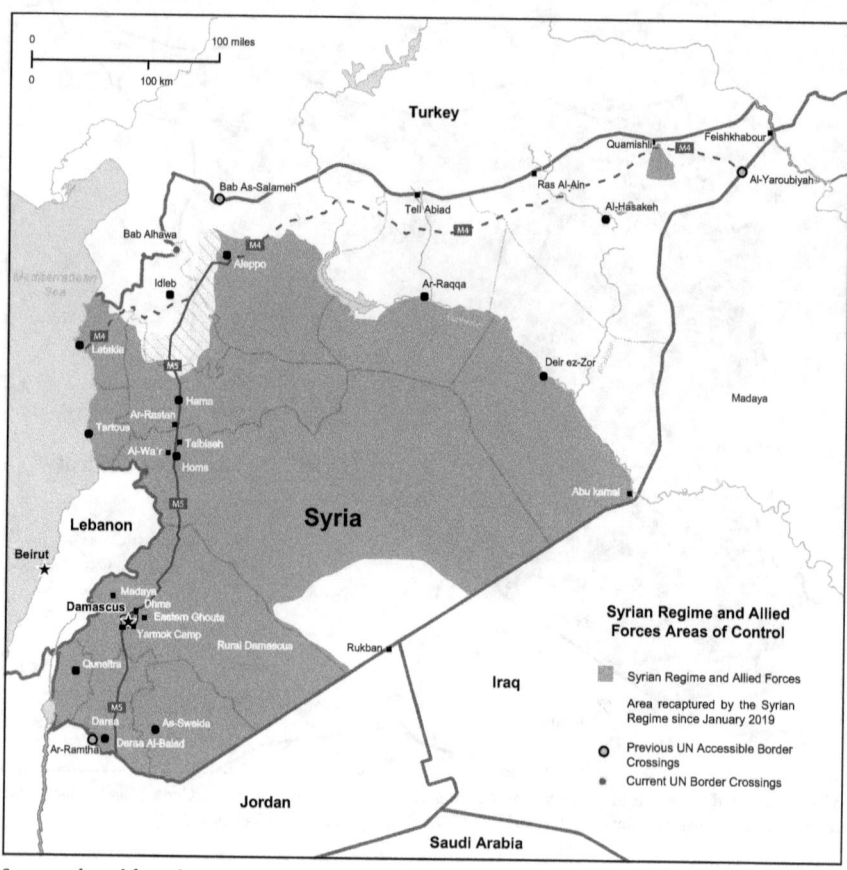

Source: adapted from the map created by Hall, 3.

Borders and governance

The regime has regained control of approximately two-thirds of the country (about 63 per cent of its 185,000 km²)[95]: the south, the centre, the coast, parts of the northern region around Idleb and Aleppo (including Aleppo itself) and those parts of Deir Ezzor and ar-Raqqa governorates north of the Euphrates. It holds the entire coastline and the borders with Lebanon, Israel and Jordan, with the exception of the small strip of al-Tanf, which sits close to the intersection of Syria, Jordan and Iraq.

---

[95] *Jusoor Studies*, 24 December 2021, at: https://bit.ly/3rxvdOS (accessed 23 April 2022).

Around 11.9 million Syrians are estimated to live in regions under regime control, including 3.3 internally displaced persons (IDPs)[96] who are unable to return home although the majority of them come from regime-controlled areas. In many cases, IDPs have been prevented from going home as part of the well-documented policy of demographic engineering implemented by Syria and Iran, which aims to reduce the size of the Sunni majority. In areas under regime control, Iran strengthened its military, political, economic, religious, cultural and educational involvement and purchased property. Attempts to Shiʿify the population in some locations have generated a great deal of controversy, although they have seen very little success.[97]

The system of government in the regime-controlled areas has not changed. It is a modified version of the system instituted by Hafez al-Assad in 1970. Although the 2012 constitution mandates a 'pluralist presidential system', Bashar al-Assad continues to control the legislature, executive and judiciary and act as commander-in-chief of the armed forces and secretary-general of the Baʿth Party. All the business of ruling the country revolves around him: the president is the central link tying together, individually and independently, all the other institutions of government, preventing any of them from developing an independent momentum that might threaten him or check his power. Within the regime itself the person of the president is more sacred than ever, despite the loss of all his popularity and prestige among the general population. Alongside Assad himself, his family now figure prominently in hagiographic regime propaganda. But war has given army commanders in the field more power and influence than they once

---

[96] Estimates of the current population vary because of the lack of a recent census and the incentive to meddle with the figures. Estimates include:

- 22.14 million (2022) according to the Central Bureau of Statistics (CBS), 'Compilation of Statistics for the Year 2020', Table 2.4, at: http://cbssyr.sy/;
- 19.6 million (2019) according to the Syrian Centre for Policy Studies, 'Determinants of Forced Displacement in the Syrian Conflict', 4;
- 16.5 million (2021) according to Jusoor Centre for Studies, 'The Demographic Change in Syria 2021–2011', March 2021, 4, at: https://bit.ly/3EJrIda;
- 10.23 million in the regions outside regime control, with 3.56 million in the SDF-controlled areas, 3.63 in the Hayʾat Tahrir al-Sham (HTS)-controlled areas and 1.83 million in areas under the control of the Turkish-backed Syrian National Army (SNA), according to the Assistance Coordination Unit (ACU), at: https://acu-sy.org;
- 21.7 million, according to OCHA. This includes 6.9 million IDPs, more than 2 million of whom live in one of the 1,760 camps scattered across Syria. The UN Coordination of Humanitarian Affairs (OCHA) also estimates that 14.6 million are in need of humanitarian aid. See: 'Humanitarian Needs Overview', 3, 8.

Based on these figures, I estimate that Syria has a current population of around 20 million people, 11.9 million of whom live under the regime, 3.7 million under the SDF, 1.5 million under the SNA and 3 million under HTS.

[97] See for example, Harmoon Centre for Contemporary Studies, 'Iran's Role in Re-Structuring the Syrian Society', 8 September 2021, at: https://bit.ly/3rID2kL (accessed 23 April 2022).

had. And the four great independent security organs have been tasked with keeping an eye on everything – even one another – without being subjected themselves to any oversight or accountability. The army is one of the central pillars of the regime – its strike force – overseen from above by military intelligence. Each primary subdivision of the army is linked in practice directly to the president, despite their formal subordination to the General Staff. The army has remained an institution dominated by Alawi officers: nearly 70 per cent of officers today are from that background, as are more than 90 per cent of top-ranking commanders in the security and military establishment (around 1,000 of 1,100 positions).

According to Hicham Bou Nassif's estimates, around 3,000 officers, all Sunnis, defected from the Syrian armed forces in the wake of the 2011 uprising. He adds that half of Syria's Sunni officers had defected by summer 2014. If his sources are correct, this means that out of the 50,000–60,000 Syrian officers (based on Nassif's estimates), only 3,000 Sunni officers remained in the Syrian armed forces. The percentage of military academy graduates who are Alawi has been 80–90 per cent since the early 1980s. Similarly, 90 per cent of Alawi cadets are accepted to the privileged military schools every year, whose graduates dominate command positions, while non-Alawi cadets are scattered among other schools.[98]

Sectarian discrimination within the army and the higher salaries and privileges enjoyed by elite units (the Republican Guard and the Fourth Armoured, for example) go some way towards explaining the defection of around 100,000 soldiers[99] and 3,000–5,000 officers over the course of the revolution. Although both individuals and groups defected, *whole units did not defect*, and the army as a whole – kept on a tight leash by the security forces and loyalist commanders – remained on the side of the regime.

Although the 2012 constitution removed the clauses making the Baʿth Party the 'leader of state and society' under pressure from the popular protests, the party remains the regime's sole political face, the main means of framing and integrating its social base. Assad has neglected the party throughout his time in power, showing far more interest in technocrats than ideologues. The neoliberal reforms have deprived it of much of its social base and its ability to drive social integration. Over the course of the revolution the party's power has been further eroded by the rise of the

---

[98] Hicham Bou Nassif, '"Second-Class": The Grievances of Sunni Officers in the Syrian Armed Forces', *Journal of Strategic Studies* 38, no. 5 (2015), 632, 644.

[99] There are no precise figures on defections from the army. Some put the figure as high as 40 per cent of manpower. Others give a figure of 170,000. See: Abdullah al-Najjar, 'Defection: Roles and Consequences' [Arabic], Harmoon Centre for Contemporary Studies, 2 June 2021, at: https://bit.ly/3gibHAC (accessed 24 April 2022).

shabbiha and the National Defence Committees. And despite all that has happened over the last eleven years, the regime has not changed its approach: suppression of freedoms, random arrests, and linking dictatorship to corruption.

The regions controlled by the regime are dotted with garrisoned Russian forces or Russian affiliates and Iranian militias. Russia and Iran exercise a great deal of influence on the regime.

The economy

The economy of the regime-controlled areas is fragile and reliant on Russian and Iranian support as well as UN aid and remittances from Syrians abroad. Russian and Iranian control has been extended to cover most significant economic activity (energy, phosphate, fertiliser, animal husbandry, major commercial centres) without spurring any real growth in the Syrian economy. The second Ukrainian crisis in 2022 has exacerbated already dismal economic conditions and living standards, a development particularly visible in rising prices, the fall of the lira against the dollar, the disappearance of basic goods from the marketplace and the uptick in migration out of regime areas.

The regime has replaced many of its old pre-revolutionary circle of businessmen with new figures who emerged unexpectedly during the war, most of them previously unknown.[100] Their rise has been expedited by the belief that they are fronts for the Assad family, which during the war has tried to centralize financial resources in its hands. But in general, the neoliberal turn and the alliance with businessmen remains in place, although the weight of the army, the security organs and the militias has increased within this alliance.

Even in a time of war, the 'development' strategy of turning poor zones into consumer hubs of shopping malls and luxury residential towers has continued, taking advantage of falling real estate prices and the confiscated property of 'absentees', for example in the poor areas on the outskirts of Damascus: 'These areas, due to their proximity to the wealthy parts of the city and to the Damascus-Beirut highway, were a target for large investors and real estate developers during the 2000s, but the displacement of many of their residents during the conflict enabled an easier acquisition of the area. Through a complex process that involved the creation of a holding

---

[100] These figures, who have taken over huge projects in manufacturing, tourism and property, include Khudor Ali al-Tahir, Samir al-Fawz, the Qatirji brothers, Muhammad Qaband, the Jabir brothers, Wasim Qattan, Himam Misouti, Sakr Tastam, Mortada al-Dandashi and the Berri family.

company owned by the Governorate of Damascus, the area was acquired at very low cost and is being leased out to private businesses.'[101]

The CBS' figures for 2020[102] give a current-price GDP for 2019 of SYP 11,904,318, less than $20 million (at a rate of 600 liras to the dollar[103]). There is no more recent official data, and the statistical compilations released by the CBS are often imprecise given war conditions. Economic conditions have worsened since 2019 due to the tightening of sanctions under the Caesar Act, dwindling cash inflows and the crisis of the Lebanese banking system, where Syrians and particularly Syrian businessmen had deposited an estimated $30 billion over the years.

Commodity imports in 2019, again the most recent official data available, stood at approximately $4.97 million, while exports in the same year were valued at $1 billion.[104] Around 80 per cent of exports go to Arab countries (Iraq, Saudi Arabia, the UAE, Jordan and Egypt). In 2021 exports were estimated at around €664 million and imports at €4 billion, making for a deficit of €3.33 billion.[105] Oil accounts for the majority of imports, around $3 billion annually,[106] with (Russian) wheat coming in second place; once a wheat exporter, Syria is now a net importer.

The regime's budget for 2022 was SYP 13.3 trillion (around $3.8 billion). The real value of state income is exaggerated in its accounts and it relies in practice on loans and credit facilities from Iran and Russia. The Damascus government is thus struggling to make ends meet – particularly now that the regime controls more than 63 per cent of the country and around 12 million people – and has steadily pared down the social safety net to an absolute minimum, exacerbating the poor living conditions of most citizens. It can no longer afford to pay its *shabbiha* or its soldiers and has thus given them carte blanche to steal from and extort the general population. During the war, the militias were allowed to loot with impunity and appropriate the property of those who had fled abroad, all with the collusion of the security forces. The decades of familiar corruption devolved

---

[101] Shamel Azmeh, 'Avoiding the Return to Conflict: Envisioning a Democratic Development State in Syria', in *Striking from the Margins: State, Religion and Devolution of Authority in the Middle East*, ed. Aziz al-Azmeh et al. (London: Saqi, 2021), 80. See also M. Al-Lababidi, *Damascus Businessmen: The Phantoms of Marota City* (Florence: European University Institute, 2019).
[102] Table 28.15, Central Bureau of Statistics, 2020 Statistical Compilation.
[103] The exchange rate at the beginning of 2019 was SYP 500 to the dollar. By the end of the year, it was 911.
[104] Table 9.1, Central Bureau of Statistics, Compiled Statistics for 2020.
[105] Statement of Rania Khodr, assistant to the Economy Minister: *Shaam Network*, 15 January 2022, at: https://bit.ly/3KctFQF (accessed 23 April 2022).
[106] The economy minister has put the bill for oil derivatives at $1 billion every four months, meaning that Syria is spending $3 billion every year. He said that Syria was able to carry on importing fuel thanks to Iranian credit. See: *al-Araby al-Jadeed*, 8 April 2021, at: https://bit.ly/3OvMth7 (accessed 5 June 2022).

into armed robbery pure and simple. These factors, taken together, have made life in the regime areas worse than any other area of Syria.

The Syrian lira is the only currency allowed to circulate in regime areas. Under Legislative Proclamation No. 3, issued by Assad on 18 January 2020, those who use other currencies are subject to serious criminal penalties: a minimum of seven years in prison plus steep fines.[107] As a result, most commercial transactions are still completed in Syrian lira, but based on the prevailing exchange rate on the free market.

Because of declining government revenue and continuing high military expenditure, the regime relies on other sources to fund its activities, primarily:

- Iranian support, particularly in the form of crude oil. The value of Iranian oil imports since 2019 alone is estimated at $4.5–$7.6 billion.[108]
- Russian support, primarily credit facilities making it possible to import wheat. At a press conference on 21 October 2021, Economy Minister Mohammad Samer al-Khalil estimated annual Syrian consumption of wheat (in regime areas) at 2.1 million tonnes and production at only 400,000 tonnes.[109] This means that regime areas need to import more than 1.5 million tonnes every year, most of which comes from Russia. Russia also provides Syria with oil derivatives, particularly those required to keep the Russian military machine running on the ground.
- High taxes aiming at increasing local revenues and secure more hard currency through various means, most significantly raising fees for government services such as issuing passports.
- Deficit funding: printing large amounts of money out of all proportion to the requirements of the growth of the economy (which in any case has been negative). One study estimates that newly printed money covers around 38 per cent of the shortfall in the public accounts every year.[110]
- Exploiting UN humanitarian aid, using some of it for its own financial ends or channelling large amounts of it to the military and (selectively) to its popular base.[111] On paper, the value of humanitarian aid to Syria exceeds the entire public budget, and most of this goes to the regime, thanks to its success (with Russian help) in imposing its own distribution mechanisms on others.

---

[107] *SANA*, 18 January 2020, at: https://bit.ly/3KT99FZ (accessed 17 April 2022).
[108] Karam Shaar and Ali Fathollah-Nejad, 'Iran's Credit Line to Syria: A Well That Never Runs Dry', Atlantic Council, 10 February 2020, at: https://bit.ly/3JPfKje (accessed 17 April 2022).
[109] Press conference given on 21 October 2021 to Syrian state TV, on: YouTube, 12 October 2021, at: https://bit.ly/3Olv36H (accessed 17 April 2022).
[110] 'Looking into Syria's national budgets over 2012–2016, we calculate that, on average, 38 per cent of Syria's government spending came from deficit funding by printing more money,' Shaar and Fathollah-Nejad.
[111] 'Some testimonies and evidence have suggested that some UN aid to Syrians in regime-controlled areas ended up with the regime's military forces or allied militias.' See: Syrian Association for Citizen Dignity, 'Weaponization of Aid, Interference and Corruption: Syrian Regime's Methods of Control of Humanitarian Sector', 11 November 2021, 18, at: https://bit.ly/3uLuEmq (accessed 17 April 2022).

According to SANA, the average monthly salary for a state employee in regime-controlled areas is around SYP 130,000,[112] less than $35; in the private sector it is only slightly higher, at $45. Even worse, there are very few job opportunities.

With the war effectively over, funding for armed groups – as well as aid money – has slowed considerably. The Syrian economy has been plunged into a deep crisis: no longer a war economy, it has also failed to make the transition back to a peace economy. Instead, it has become a *mafioso economy*. Slowly but surely, drugs have become one of the most important sources of income for many forces within or linked to the regime.[113] The latter have outstripped legal exports and are now valued in the billions of dollars, making Syria one of the world's leading narco-states.

Immiseration has reached such a point that medicine, food and heat are now beyond the means of many, and the regime areas, like everywhere else in Syria, are facing a near famine.

As a result of all this, and despite the fighting petering out, in the last two years the number of people leaving these areas – whether emigrating or moving to areas under SDF or opposition control – has risen steadily. The situation is still not safe enough to allow IDPs and refugees to return home. The regime is opposed to their return in any case, except within limits and subject to stringent conditions.

II. Areas under SDF control

Borders and governance

The SDF control all of the al-Hasakeh governorate apart from two regime security zones in Quamishli and al-Hasakeh itself and approximately eighty villages which remain under regime control. They also hold the ar-Raqqa and Deir ez-Zor governorates east of the Euphrates and part of the Aleppo governorate west of the Euphrates around Menbij. The area includes much of the northern border with Turkey and most of the eastern border with Iraq, and accounts for around 25 per cent of all Syrian territory. A largely symbolic US military presence on the eastern side of the Euphrates – around 900 soldiers associated with the forces in Iraq – prevents any

---

[112] *SANA*, 15 December 2021, at: https://bit.ly/3M5qYl6 (accessed 17 April 2022).

[113] According to a report by the Centre for Operational Analysis and Research, in 2020 'Captagon exports from Syria reached a market value of at least 3.46 billion USD', five times the value of the country's legitimate exports. Narcotics (mainly hashish and the amphetamine-based stimulant Captagon) are now a central part of the Syrian war economy. See: Centre for Operational Analysis and Research, 'The Syrian Economy at War: Captagon, Hashish, and the Syrian Narco-State', 27 April 2021, at: https://bit.ly/3vbrKr8 (accessed 24 April 2022); Ian Larson, 'Narcos: Syria Edition—and What the US Can Do About It', Atlantic Council, 14 June 2021, at: https://bit.ly/3xUP3Y7 (accessed 24 April 2022).

Map C.3 SDF Areas of Control

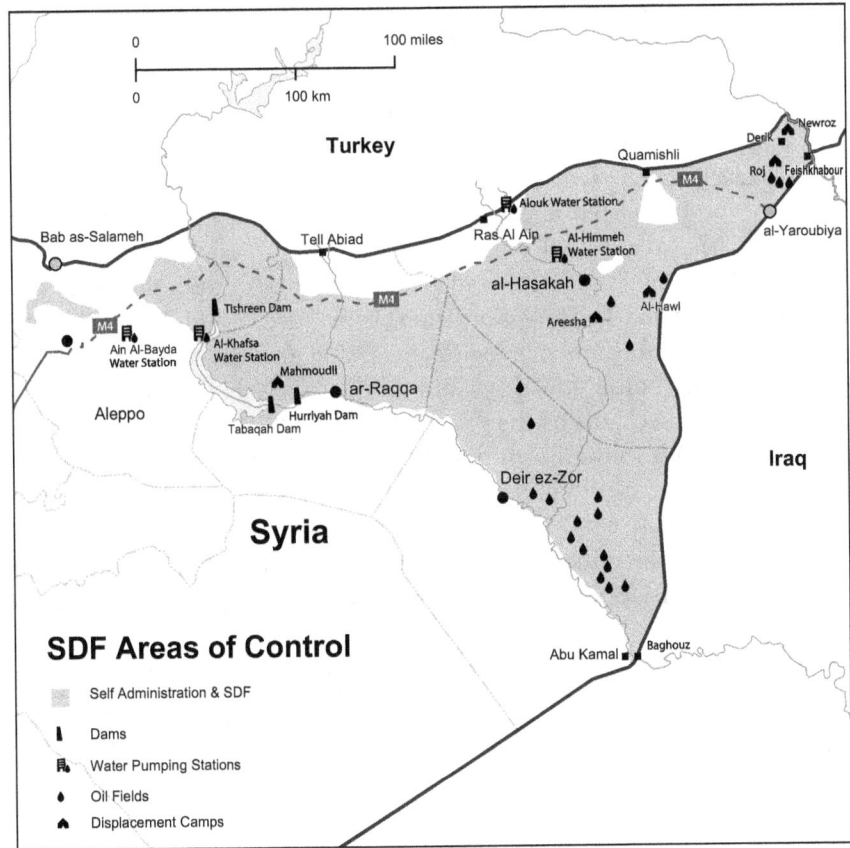

Source: adapted from the map created by Hall, 7.

other force in the country from thinking about trying to take over SDF territory. In some parts of the region there are also Russian forces, primarily in areas from which the coalition has withdrawn, as well as their major base at Quamishli airport. Only around 2.8 million people reside in the entire region, including 733,000 IDPs.

On 17 October 2017, SDF forces drove ISIS out of ar-Raqqa with the help of US special forces and air support. According to some estimates, the largely untargeted airstrikes on the city resulted in the death of at least 1,000 civilians and the flight of 270,000 more, practically levelling the city.[114] In October 2017, it was calculated that 12,707 houses had been partially or totally destroyed and that only around 7,000 people were living in the city; in 2016 it was home to some 300,000 people.[115] Not for nothing

[114] Phillips, 255.
[115] Relief Web, 2 November 2021, at: https://bit.ly/3vIG49B (accessed 23 April 2022).

was the Amnesty International report on the city titled *War of Annihilation*.[116] A great and terrible crime was committed. There is a veritable conspiracy of silence surrounding atrocities against civilians in the course of the war on ISIS, as though fighting ISIS justified anything. Some civil society organizations have provided detailed accounts from civilians who, having suffered horribly under ISIS rule, then fell victim to US strikes, displacement and arbitrary government. This applies in particular to the families of ISIS fighters, who have been put in internment camps with no prospects for their children. No good will come of this.

The SDF maintains a largely independent administration similar to the autonomous region in Iraqi Kurdistan. It has tried to build proto-state institutions of its own in this region, including an army, police force and security organs, border crossings into other areas of Syria, a judiciary, an executive and mechanisms for service provision. The Syrian Democratic Council (SDC) is 'the authority and political umbrella of the Autonomous Administration of North and East Syria (AANES) and the SDF, and the body empowered to conduct any negotiations'.[117]

The SDF are the militia of the Kurdish PYD, the Syrian branch of the Turkish PKK. Its leaders came to Syria in summer 2012, following an

Map C.4 North-Eastern Syria Oil Fields and Cross-Border Points (15 November 2019)

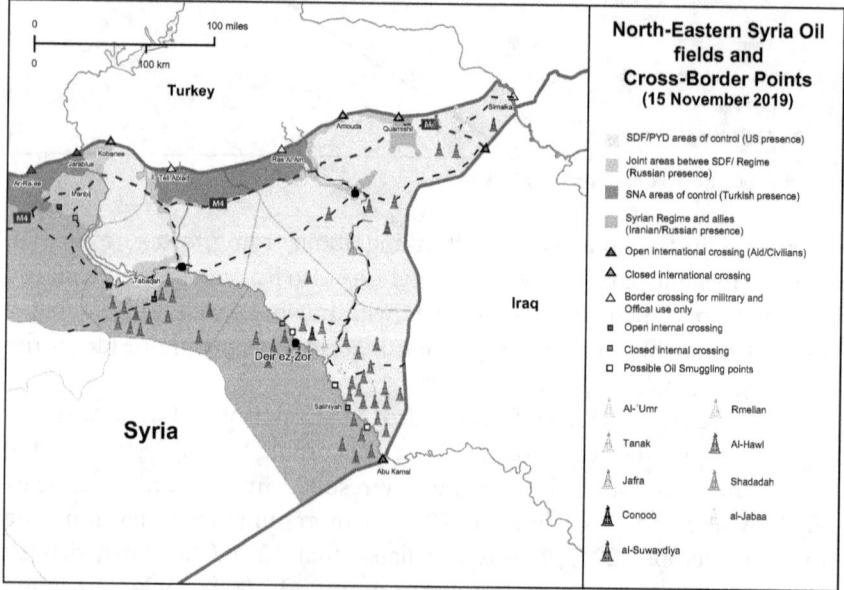

Source: adapted from the map created by Sinan Hatahet, 'The Political Economy of the Autonomous Administration of North and East Syria', Middle East Directions, 29 November 2019, 10, at: https://bit.ly/3ry07Xn (accessed 24 April 2022).

[116] Amnesty International, 5 June 2018. Archived copy at: https://bit.ly/38iFtU4 (accessed 23 April 2022).
[117] SDC website, at: https://bit.ly/3jQFPDS (accessed on 17 April 2022).

agreement with the regime, with the purpose of disciplining the general Kurdish population and ensuring that they would not take part in the ongoing demonstrations. The SDF managed to extend its control by joining the international coalition against ISIS. Today they include Arab tribal forces and representatives of other groups such as Syriacs and Turkmen.

Alongside the SDC, many other local councils run the smaller administrative divisions. The AANES acts as the executive arm, including 'ministries', service organizations and municipalities with powers limited to administrative and economic issues. There is also an internal security organization, the Asayish, subordinate to the SDF leadership but also closely linked to the PKK intelligence organization led from the Qandil Mountains, which also controls the oil fields and the revenue they generate. The AANES collects taxes as well, but how much and where they go is not clear.

Despite the ostensible alliances with other ethnic groups, the commanders of the PYD, the People's Defence Units (Yekîneyên Parastina Gel or YPG(and its female arm the Women's Protection Units (Yekîneyên Parastina Jin or YPJ) are all directly linked to the PKK leadership in Qandil. The same applies to the Asayish and the leaders of the civilian and economic administration. The PKK controls all military, security, political, administrative and economic decisions. The AANES is effectively a one-party state under the supervision of the PKK. Civil society organizations and media activity are tightly controlled. Syrians from other regions are treated as foreigners, described as 'migrants' (*wafidin*) and refused ID cards.[118]

The US is very influential east of the Euphrates. It is the protector and supporter of the AANES and has a limited military presence. Russia also enjoys some influence, thanks to its own military presence and its ability to sway the regime, and France has highly developed links with the PYD and PKK cadres in Syria. Were it not for these sponsors, the PYD could not continue to govern the region. Its relationship with Turkey is hostile, as is its relationship with the Kurdish Regional Government in Iraq, which supports the KNC founded during the revolution. The regime, meanwhile, has no desire to see a long-term autonomous or even semiautonomous region, and will be willing to cooperate with the SDF only as long as it takes to re-establish its own power (perhaps the only point of agreement between Damascus and Ankara).

---

[118] After the beginning of the protests in March 2011, the demands of Syrian Kurds of all ideological stripes became much more developed, some in a moderate direction and some more extreme. They were no longer content with cultural demands about using their language in education and media and showing their distinctiveness within the existing Syrian framework. The PYD has sought to make these demands a reality by creating an autonomous region along Iraqi lines – but in this case with an ideological framework derived from the Turkish PKK. It was encouraged by Assad's need for allies, the regime's weakness, and later US support for autonomy rooted in a need for partners on the ground and a sense that the SDF, unlike the opposition battalions, was a socially liberal force.

Economy

The economy of the SDF-controlled regions depends primarily on agriculture and animal husbandry (grains, vegetables and domesticated animals), oil production, government positions and service jobs. There is very limited manufacturing, most of it very small-scale or handicraft-focused. It is a region whose development has long been neglected by the regime.

The SDF's income is derived from several major sources. It controls all of Syria's major oil fields, in al-Hasakeh, Deir ez-Zor and ar-Raqqa.[119] It holds a monopoly on raw materials, such as wheat, cotton, sugar, as well as cement, construction materials, and fertiliser. It also levies customs duties at the Iraqi border, particularly at the Semalka crossing over the Tigris, which is the only crossing-point shared with the Kurdistan Regional Government (KRG). It taxes commercial activity and receives income from the various state properties in the region, including land, businesses, public buildings and farms.

The SDF-controlled regions produce an estimated 80,000 barrels of oil a day, mostly heavy oil from the al-Hasakeh fields, earning an estimated $1 billion every year.[120] Official sources place the figure slightly lower, at 70,000 barrels a day, and say that the oil is sold in neighbouring markets after local consumption has been satisfied.[121] On 18 January, the SDF published its 2022 budget, which disposes of around $981 million ($901 million on the current account and $80 million for investment), including $100 million for buying wheat and another $107 million for salaries. The budget for 2021 amounted to only $620 million ($580 million current account and $40 million investment).[122] There is inadequate information about how much revenue the SDC brings in and how it is spent, particularly given consistent claims from local sources that much of the money goes to the Turkish PKK. The lira is used in retail trade and to pay salaries, while the dollar is used for wholesale purchases. Table C.1 shows the sources of employment of the population in the SDF-controlled Areas.[123]

Pay in the SDF-controlled areas is lower than in other parts of northern Syria. Salaries vary depending on the employer, with the SDF's military

---

[119] The SDF control the As-Suwaydan, Rumeilan, Jabseh, Mulla Abbas, Yusefiyeh, al-Hawl, Shadadah, Conoco, al-'Umr, Tanak, Kamsheh, Ward, Tayyem and Jafra oil fields.
[120] Samir Seifan and Mahmood Alhosain, 'The Destruction of the Energy Sector in Syria During the War 2011–2020', Harmoon Centre for Contemporary Studies, 14 July 2021, 36, at: https://bit.ly/3rK4ZZm (accessed 23 April 2022).
[121] *Syria Oil*, 6 February 2022, at: https://bit.ly/37pOeMa (accessed 17 April 2022).
[122] *Watan*, 19 December 2021, at: https://bit.ly/3rwi7ky (accessed 17 April 2022).
[123] Based on a report from the ACU that investigated economic conditions in areas outside regime control. The study was based on 276 interviews with key informants, and perception surveys with employers and residents, in 135 towns and cities in 64 sub-districts affiliated with 21 districts in the governorates of Idleb, Aleppo, ar-Raqqa, al-Hasakeh and Deir ez-Zor. See: ACU, 'Economic Reality in Northern Syria', April 2021, at: https://bit.ly/3OANrcb (accessed 20 April 2022).

Table C.1 Sources of Employment in the SDF-controlled Areas

Sector	%
Public	33
Agriculture	21
Trades and services	13
Commercial	12
Construction	14
Other (day labourers)	7

Source: based on Figure 6 in ACU, 'Economic Reality in Northern Syria', April 2021, 16 at: https://bit.ly/3OANrcb (accessed 20 April 2022).

Table C.2 Population of Eastern Syria by Average Monthly Income

More than $300 (%)	$300–200 (%)	$200–100 (%)	$100–50 (%)	Less than $50 (%)	No monthly income (%)	Other (additional) sources of income (%)
5	5	16	51	18	5	28

Source: based on Figures 19 and 20 in 'Economic Reality in Northern Syria', 25.

and security forces paid better than average. Table C.2 shows the distribution of average monthly incomes.

The lowest salaries are earned by government employees at regime institutions still operating in eastern Syria, who receive an average of $25 each month and, like most Syrians, are dependent on remittances and humanitarian aid.

III. Areas under SNA control

Borders

The Turkish-backed opposition controls the portion of northern Syria between Ras Al Ain (al-Hasakeh governorate) and Tell Abiad (ar-Raqqa governorate) and north of the M4 international highway. This region can be divided into three smaller areas, all of them taken over by the so-called SNA with Turkish backing and direct Turkish intervention during Operation Euphrates Shield, Operation Olive Branch and Operation Peace Spring.[124]

---

[124] Turkey has taken great pains to avoid direct clashes with the regime, and has limited its operations to the PYD and (to a lesser extent) ISIS. The only direct engagement with regime forces took place in Idleb in February 2020, after an airstrike in which 33 Turkish soldiers were killed. In the ensuing tank battle, Turkey shot down two Syrian aircraft. See: *The Guardian*, 1 March 2020, at: https://bit.ly/3k9dkBJ (accessed 23 April 2022). Limited clashes also took place in Ras Al Ain in 2019 after regime forces advanced and took control of a series of villages along the Turkish border. See: *Al Jazeera* (international), 31 October 2019, at: https://bit.ly/39gjvSn (accessed 23 April 2022).

Map C.5 Areas under SNA Control

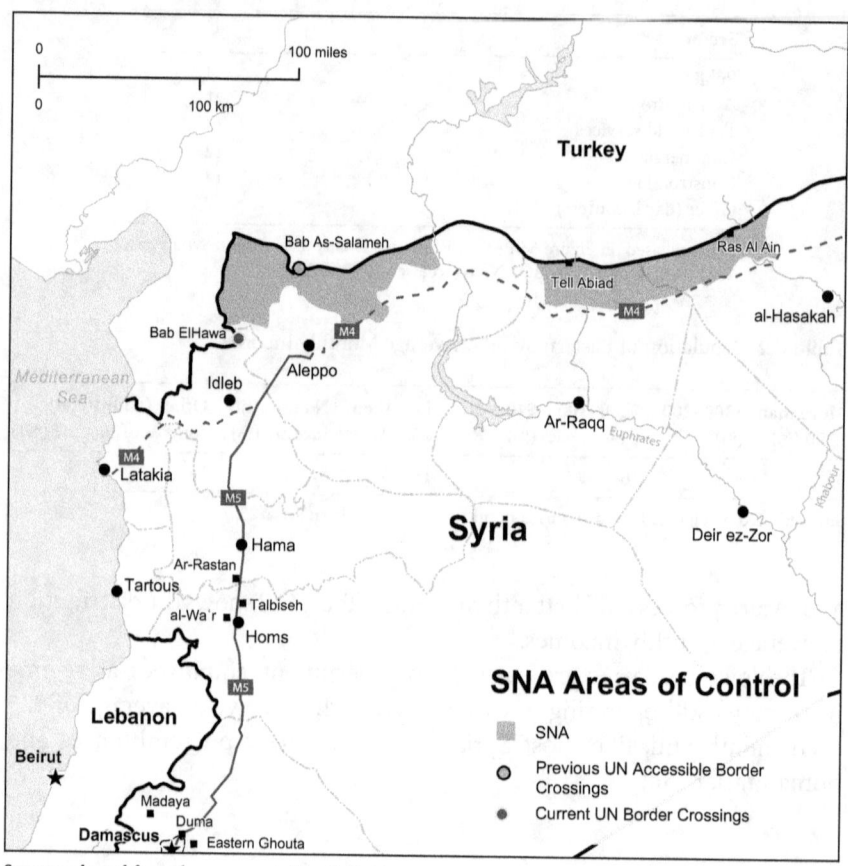

Source: adapted from the map created by Hall, 17.

Most of these areas had previously been under PYD control. The area taken during Operation Peace Spring is separated from the other two areas by the Ain al-Arab region (Kobani as it is called by the Kurds in the area), which remains under PYD control. All three areas have long borders with Turkey in the north and west and also border on areas under regime, HTS and SDF control in the south and east. Taken together, they comprise about 8,150 km^2 of Syrian territory.[125] The most significant urban centres are Afrin, from which unknown numbers of Kurds were expelled after the Turkish takeover, Tell Abiad, Ras Al Ain, al-Bab, A'zaz, Ar-Ra'ee, Dabeq, Jarablus, Jindaires,

---

[125] This estimate is based on the percentages given by Şaban, taking into account the regions retaken by the regime in March 2020. See: Navvar Şaban, 'Control and Influence Changes After Operation "Peace Spring"', *Omran for Strategic Studies*, 18 December 2019, at: https://bit.ly/3EIIKYZ (accessed 24 April 2022).

Raju and Sheikh El-Hadid. There are a few Yazidi Kurds. There are also a few Alawi villages, generally thought to be 'Bektashi' (as in the Sufi order), whose inhabitants have largely fled since the Turkish invasion. There are an estimated 1.5 million people living under SNA control, including 880,000 IDPs. Most of those who fled to this region came from Homs, the Damascus periphery, Daraa and areas to the north of Hama.

Governance

In theory, the SOC – headquartered in Istanbul – is the Syrian opposition's governmental body. The SOC consists of a General Commission, a Political Commission and a Presidential Bureau, and is also the force behind the Syrian Provisional Government set up in Gaziantep (which has offices inside Syria and operates independently of the SOC). But the SOC has no real power on the ground and has been increasingly insignificant even internationally since the establishment of the Higher Negotiating Committee (HNC) in December 2015. The Provisional Government, meanwhile, has only limited resources and is not very effective as a result. Local assemblies are responsible for day-to-day administration, and although formal 'consultative councils' do exist in some areas, their role is limited and there is no real legislature. Moreover, neither the SOC, the Provisional Government nor local councils enjoy freedom of action. They are unable to contradict Turkish policy in any respect.

Direct authority in all three areas is held by the twenty-eight armed groups of the SNA.[126] Although they are notionally organized into larger formations, each of these groups insists that it is a separate entity, and each controls a particular area and owns its own equipment. And while they are ostensibly subordinate to the General Staff, in practice they take their orders from the Turkish security authorities. Although there are civilian and military judiciaries formally run by the Ministries of Justice and Defence, both are subject to the influence of the armed groups and to Turkish oversight. There is also a police force, but its resources are limited and its authority extends only to civilians. Military and security matters are controlled exclusively by the armed groups. Each group has its own security apparatus, but all coordinate closely with Turkey.

---

[126] The groups are: Jaysh al-Islam, al-Hasakeh Shield, the al-Hamza, al-Muʻtasim, al-Mustansir Billah, Sultan Murad Brigades, Faylaq al-Majd, Liwaʾ al-Shamal, Liwaʾ al-Waqqas, the Revolutionary Liberation Committee, the Damascus Revolutionaries, Faylaq al-Sham, Suqur al-Sham, the Shami Front, Ahrar al-Sham, Suqur al-Shamal, Liwaʾ al-Shamal, Jaysh al-Sharqiyya, Ahrar al-Sharqiyya, the Suleiman Shah Brigade (known as the Amashat), the Mehmet the Conqueror Brigade, the Malikshah Brigade, the 9th and 20th Brigades, the 112th Brigade, Jaysh al-Nukhba and the Special Forces. There are four groups with Ottoman names: Suleiman Shah, Mehmet the Conqueror, Malikshah and Sultan Murad.

Citizens living in these areas face arbitrary government and complicated bureaucracy exacerbated by the absence of a single central government. Competition and struggle sometimes generate instability, and there is a huge body of evidence demonstrating the failure of the armed groups to competently administer these areas. Local councils are responsible for providing civilian services: education, health, utilities, post and the maintenance of the civil and property registries. Some of these are shared with Turkey, such as the post office (operated by the Turkish postal service), electricity (provided by a private Turkish company) and banking (in which Turkish banks are prominent). There is no single fiscal body, and each of the groups levies its own taxes at border crossings or checkpoints, a portion of which finds its way to the councils and the Provisional Government. The councils themselves also raise revenue from their areas of responsibility, although they are heavily reliant on foreign aid.

As a result of the great plurality of authorities, there is a margin of freedom in all three areas for political and civil society activity, union organizing and independent journalism, once licences have been secured from a local council. But it is not possible to criticise the armed groups or the Turkish authorities.

Over the course of the war, clerics and conservative forces have taken on an increasingly visible role in all aspects of public life, particularly in education. The predominant ideological movements are Sufi and Salafi Islam and Turkish nationalism. Although there are many independent political activists of a Syrian 'national' inclination, there is no movement binding them together or representing them.

Turkey exercises direct military and civilian oversight of all three areas. It enjoys far-reaching control, but it does not intervene directly in day-to-day affairs. Each area is subordinate to the Turkish provincial governor (*vali*) on the other side of the border. Turkish government bodies are responsible for many services, infrastructure and housing projects, and both the armed groups and government employees are paid by or via Turkey. The Turkish government shows a marked reliance on Turkmen groups within the SNA.

Economy

Public life throughout the SNA regions is chaotic. In the absence of a single central authority, the environment is not very welcoming either to commercial activity or to social life more broadly. The regional economy is mainly based on agriculture, government jobs and services. There is very little manufacturing, most of it small workshops or handicrafts; this area was long neglected by the regime. The high cost of agricultural inputs,

Table C.3 Sources of Employment in Northern Aleppo, ar-Raqqa and al-Hasakeh

Sector	%
Public	31
Agriculture	24
Trades and services	12
Commercial	12
Construction	13
Other (day labourers)	7

Source: based on Figure 4 in 'Economic Reality in Northern Syria', 15.

Table C.4 Population of Western Syria by Average Monthly Income

More than $300 (%)	$300–200 (%)	$200–100 (%)	$100–50 (%)	Less than $50 (%)	No monthly income (%)	Other (additional) sources of income (%)
6	11	33	27	10	14	42

Source: based on Figures 19 and 20 in 'Economic Reality in Northern Syria', 25.

including fertiliser, pesticides, seeds and animal feed, as well as irrigation, electricity and fuel, have made farming increasingly difficult, especially since Damascus stopped sending agricultural subsidies. The local market is also very limited. Public sector employment is the main source of income in the region, followed by farming, as shown in Table C.3.

Incomes in this region are higher than in the SDF regions, but prices are correspondingly higher because the market is closely linked to its Turkish counterpart. Table C.4 shows the distribution of average monthly incomes.

Like other parts of Syria, the inhabitants of this region suffer from high poverty rates and unemployment. They also have to deal with chronic instability due to the constant threat of regime or Russian attack and regular strikes on villages under various pretexts.

The SNA-controlled regions operate as a commercial intermediary zone, importing Turkish products for re-export to areas under the control of the SDF, HTS or the regime. They export some agricultural products of their own to the same areas and, to a much more limited extent, to Turkey. They also import products from other parts of Syria, particularly oil produced in the SDF regions and the illegal drugs manufactured on a grand scale in regime areas.

Since there is no central government, there is no central budget or plan to organize any aspect of public life in the areas controlled by the SNA. Despite the presence of Turkish banks in the region,[127] some 58 per cent of financial transfers in the region are made via local exchange bureaus, while the

---

[127] ACU, 'Economic Reality in Northern Syria', 25.

remainder are made through Turkish banks.[128] Although the Syrian lira and the dollar are both in use, it is above all else the Turkish lira that dominates.

IV. HTS-controlled areas

Map C.6 Areas under HTS Control

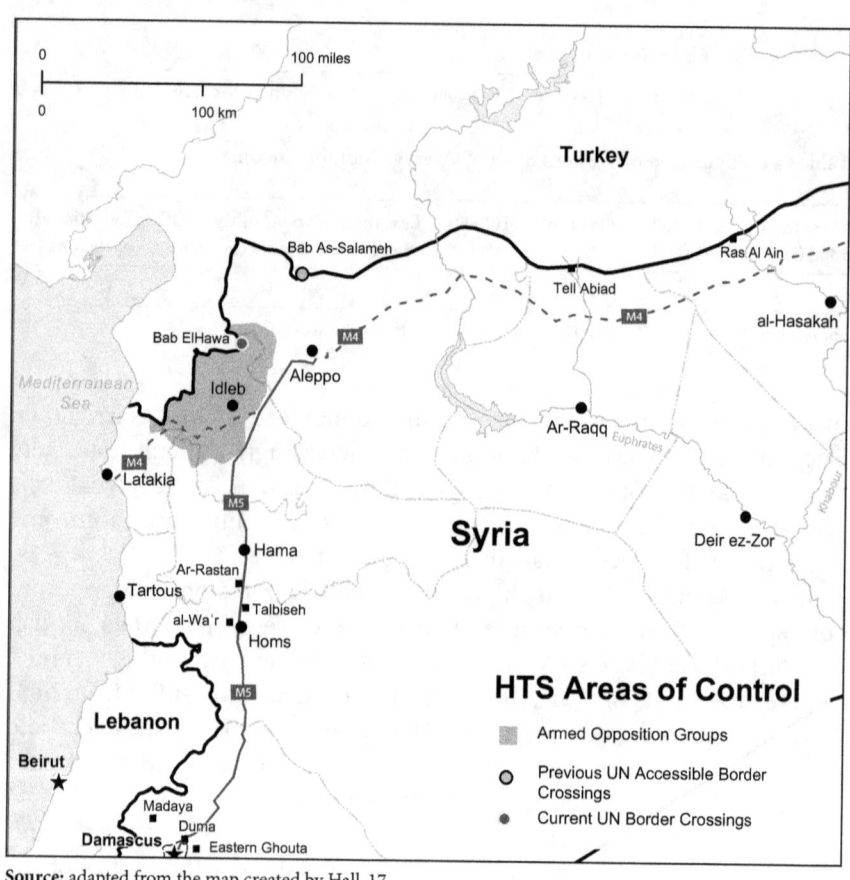

Source: adapted from the map created by Hall, 17.

Borders and governance

The region controlled by HTS falls almost entirely within the boundaries of the Idleb governorate in north-western Syria. It comprises the areas of Ariha, Harim, Idleb and Jisr ash-Shughur, and borders on the Latakia, Aleppo and Hama governorates in the west, east and south respectively; its northern limit is the Turkish border, of which some 129 km² are under

---

[128] Ibid., 55.

HTS control. Various independent local sources suggest that HTS controls around 3,000 km² of territory, approximately half of the Idleb governorate, while the regime and its affiliates control the remainder. A small portion of the Aleppo governorate, approximately 6 per cent of its 18,482 km², is also controlled by HTS.[129]

HTS runs an authoritarian government. In this respect, it is exactly like the SDF: a one-party system dominates that allows no form of political pluralism and throttles freedom of expression. The difference is that HTS governs according to its interpretation of the Shari'a – albeit in a fashion much less stringent than the supposed al-Qaeda model, in order to maintain good relations both with the general population and the international community. HTS have abolished the religious police (*hisbah*), which once oversaw every aspect of behaviour and dress. It interferes far less in the daily lives of inhabitants than it once did and is more accepting of local custom, a process which been made easier by the defection of many of the group's non-Syrian members. It tolerates a certain amount of civil society and political activism (although not the creation of parties other than the Islamist Hizb al-Tahrir) and union organizing (under governmental oversight). It also allows the operation of independent media outlets, although criticism of HTS itself is forbidden. But none of this has changed its basic nature, which is that of a religious movement that seeks to establish a religious state.

Although HTS is classified by the US as a terrorist organization and its leader is still on an international most wanted list, its centres are no longer targeted by US special forces, unlike members of schismatic organizations like Hurras al-Din. HTS has put much effort into remarketing itself, putting pressure on foreign fighters (in particular Uyghurs) in the areas under its control. Its policy is intended to put it at the intersection of various local and international intelligence services.

HTS has established a legislature, the General Consultative Council (GCC), appointed via 'directed' elections and including prominent local figures. But the council is largely ineffective. HTS has also created a National Salvation Government (NSG) responsible for services and civil affairs in the areas under its control, to which all civilian government bodies are subordinated. The NSG, however, has limited resources and no publicly available budget or action plan. Nor does it interfere in military, security or judicial issues, which are the sole province of HTS. The HTS security organs are powerful and capable and have generally been able to make the region more stable – from a security perspective – than other parts of the country.

---

[129] This estimate is based on Şaban's percentages, taking into account the regions retaken by the regime in March 2020. See: Şaban, 'Control and Influence Changes'.

HTS operates a religious judiciary governed by the Shariʻa. The NSG's Interior Ministry has its own civilian and traffic police, which do as much as they can given the lack of money, qualified personnel and clear jurisdiction (which often overlaps with that of the security forces). HTS itself controls all the revenue, and there is no public budget or oversight.

The Turkish authorities enjoy direct influence over HTS via the large Turkish garrison in Idleb[130] and for economic reasons: everything the HTS administration needs comes through Turkish border crossings, and it is only due to the understanding between Ankara and Moscow that it has been able to establish a degree of stable government in the region. Without this understanding it would face a full-on assault from the regime areas, supported by Iranian militias and Russian air power.

It is worth noting that the HTS areas and the SNA areas do not coordinate with one another or have any form of relationship. The borders between them are heavily policed, and those wishing to travel between them sometimes require prior agreement.

There are an estimated 3 million people in the areas under HTS control, 2 million of them IDPs. Most IDPs are from the area around Damascus and Qalamoun, then Hama and Homs, and to a lesser degree the area around Aleppo and al-Bab.

Economy

HTS has established a central fiscal body responsible for its financial affairs. A July 2021 study[131] shows that HTS funds itself from a variety of sources, primarily control of fuel sales and distribution (via the Watad company), money-changing and power generation; trade in various goods is restricted to paid-up licensees. It also controls the Bab Elhawa crossing, the most important gateway into Syria for Turkish imports, the queuing system for shipping, and border trade with other regions. It extracts tribute in the form of *zakat* payments (overseen by the Hisbah organization) and levies various taxes on commercial activity. It has also expropriated a great deal of property formerly owned by the Syrian state, regime loyalists (including soldiers and policemen) and emigre Christians, seizing around 550 houses and shops between 2018 and 2019, according to one report,[132]

---

[130] Comprising as of April 2021 no less than 63 military positions put in place in 2017 to maintain the de-escalation zone in north-western Syria (Idleb) as provided for by the Astana agreement between Russia, Iran and Turkey.

[131] Nisreen al-Zaraee and Karam Shaar, 'The Economics of Hayat Tahrir al-Sham', Middle East Institute, 21 June 2021, at: https://bit.ly/3OeZR9l (accessed 17 April 2022).

[132] Syrians for Truth and Justice, 'HTS Confiscates No Less Than 550 Homes and Businesses Belonging to Christians in Idleb', 14 January 2020, at: https://bit.ly/3OLWIhF (accessed 25 April 2022).

and another 500 in 2020.[133] It is involved in the illegal antiquities trade and in smuggling, and, via its Bank al-Sham, in exchanging the Turkish lira. It also monopolises internet services through SYR Connect and controls cigarette sales, water distribution and bakeries. It relies on aid money as well, appropriating some 30 per cent of payments into the region. Since an HTS proclamation banning the use of the Syrian lira, retail purchases are generally concluded in Turkish lira and wholesale trade in dollars.

According to Zaraee and Shaar, 'HTS's earliest attempts to generate revenues and income from NW Syria were mainly limited to spoils captured from the regime and opposition factions, estimated to be at least $149 million by early 2018. HTS has also received at least $94 million in a number of prisoner-exchange deals with several entities, including the regime, Iran, the Lebanese government, and the Italian government. In addition, unknown sums have been received from the families of detainees in regime prisons, paid in return for including demands for these detainees' release in the aforementioned deals. Along with kidnap ransoms, HTS demanded payments from Iran and Hezbollah in exchange for the bodies of their fighters who were killed in action.'[134]

The region's economy is based primarily on agriculture, a sector that has suffered a great deal as a result of the war and the destruction of waterways. Agriculture is not helped by the fact that the regime is constantly nibbling away at the region's borders: in its last major military campaign, conducted in March 2020 with Russian and Iranian support, it re-established control of a vast area of plain around Idleb and Aleppo. Agriculture receives no support, and in addition to drought suffers from high production prices, a problem compounded by the general ban on export of most agricultural products (generally with exceptions made for quantities surplus to local requirements).

Table C.5 Sources of Employment in Idleb Governorate

Sector	%
Public	33
Agriculture	20
Trades and services	13
Commercial	14
Construction	11
Other (day labourers)	8

Source: based on Figure 5 in 'Economic Reality in Northern Syria', 16.

---

[133] Zaraee and Shaar, 'The Economics of Hayat Tahrir al-Sham'.
[134] Ibid.

The instability of the region over the last decade has led to a decline in local manufacturing and its total replacement by imported goods. Local sources say that there are 140 manufacturing businesses registered with the NSG's Idleb Chamber of Commerce, most of them small workshops with a handful of medium-sized enterprises. There is some manufacturing investment in small- and small-to-medium-sized enterprises in relatively stable areas such as Dana and Sarmada near to the border (Bab Elhawa).[135] Table C.5 shows the distribution of the sources of employment in the region.

Like other regions, this area suffers from high rates of unemployment, with only 57 per cent of men and 24 per cent of women ages 20–45 years old having jobs.[136] The fall of the Turkish lira against the dollar has had significant repercussions for the living standards of inhabitants, since the lira is the main currency in circulation. According to OCHA, 90 per cent of locals live under the poverty line, 60–65 per cent of them in extreme poverty.[137] Alongside this difficult reality, the threat of attack from the regime, Iranian militias and the Russian air force makes living here constantly physically dangerous.

Not a final note

The last three regions discussed above are maintained by implicit and explicit understandings between Russia, Turkey and the US. Save for the redeployment of regime forces, including withdrawal from what has become SDF region of control, the regime (and Iran) is not a party to these understandings. These regions lack both legitimacy and the means for self-sustainment. Consequently, they could vanish if these controlling states strike another deal, or if they encourage Syrians to reach and accept an agreement on the nature of their political system after Assad. If the present circumstances persist, the latter scenario is impossible without Russian pressure on the regime, whether exerted for its own reasons, including the costs and ungovernability of Syria under the existing regime, or as a consequence of other states' actions or pursuant to the dictates of other states or geostrategic exigencies. Iran and the regime could not withstand such pressure and would be compelled to sign on to such an agreement, even if it included a post-Assad transitional phase. Until that time comes, the extension of Assad's rule and any violence among Syrians will alter nothing; they will just increase human suffering, prolong the nightmare and waste more human lives and resources.

---

[135] ACU, 'Economic Reality in Northern Syria,' 17.
[136] Ibid., 14.
[137] OCHA, 'Humanitarian Needs Overview: Syrian Arab Republic', March 2021, 6, at: https://bit.ly/3rObevj (accessed 24 April 2022).

Calculating the incalculable

By early 2019, when the fighting began to die down, more than half of the Syrian population – some 13 million people – had been displaced by the conflict. Of these, 6.6 million are refugees, 5.6 million of them residing in neighbouring countries or in northern and western Europe. Another 6.7 million people have been internally displaced, fleeing from areas destroyed or otherwise made unliveable by war.[1] Syria has become the largest forced displacement crisis in the world since the Second World War.[2] At least 350,000 Syrians have been killed, according to the World Bank.[3] The real figure is probably more than half a million: many deaths remain undocumented, and there is no tally of the indirect victims of war. According to a report from the World Health Organization (WHO) and Handicap International, '1.5 million people have been injured. An additional 1.5 million people are living with permanent disabilities, including 86,000 people whose injuries have led to amputations.'[4] Numbers, of course, do not adequately convey the real harm caused by permanent disability.

This human cost is the most horrific aspect of the war, one whose magnitude is difficult to fathom: every person killed, injured or disabled, physically or mentally, every refugee and prisoner has a story. The social and psychological effects and the moral ramifications of the Syrian tragedy are equally incalculable. But even from a purely economic perspective, studies on economic growth estimate that the effect of human losses on the economy outstrips that of the actual material destruction.[5] Other losses are

---

[1] Maha Yahya and Marwan Muasher, 'Refugee Crises in the Arab World', in *Arab Horizons: Pitfalls and Pathways to Renewal*, ed. Joseph Bahout et al. (Washington, DC: Carnegie Endowment for International Peace, 2018), 85–105; UN High Commissioner for Refugees, at: https://bit.ly/3LcB83r (accessed 23 April 2022); UN High Commissioner for Refugees, 15 March 2022, at: https://bit.ly/3OcZoEG (accessed 16 March 2022); UN High Commissioner for Refugees, January 2022, at: https://bit.ly/3jrt4zE (accessed 16 March 2022).
[2] World Bank, 10 July 2017, at: https://bit.ly/3OgoPVQ (accessed 17 April 2022).
[3] World Bank, at: https://bit.ly/3KSP6aG (accessed 17 April 2022).
[4] Relief Web, 11 December 2017, at: https://bit.ly/3L9yNGH (accessed 23 April 2022).
[5] Robert Barro and Xavier I. Sala-i-Martin, *Economic Growth*, 2nd edn (Cambridge and London: MIT Press, 2004 [1995]), 246.

harder to approximate in numbers: physical and psychological disabilities affecting children, the rising levels of illiteracy as a result of the breakdown of education in many areas, the immense damage to the country's social fabric. Catastrophic only begins to describe the situation.

According to OCHA, there are 21.7 million people living in Syria today, 32.7 per cent of whom (7.1 million) are 'in stress', and 14.6 million of whom are 'in need'. Of this latter category, 44.5 per cent (9.6 million people) are in severe need, 22.5 per cent (4.9 million) extreme need, and 3 per cent (60,000) catastrophic need. Some 76 per cent of families are unable to meet basic needs. The average household income only covers 51 per cent of expenses, and close to one-third of households report that their children cannot go to school because they need to work to support the household.[6] Between 2010 and 2017 the birth rate fell from 38.8 per thousand to 25 per thousand (a finding at odds with many studies which have found that fertility rates tend to rise during times of war, particularly among displaced people). According to a population survey, women account for 51 per cent of the general population, but 57 per cent of IDPs. The age pyramid has also changed: the cohort aged 15–39 has shrunk dramatically, particularly among IDPs, as other age groups, particularly children younger than 15, have grown proportionally.[7]

The Human Development Index (HDI), which measures three basic dimensions of human development (a long and healthy life, access to knowledge and a decent standard of living), reflects far greater deterioration. In 2011, Syria was classified as 'high' in the human development classifications, at an HDI value of 0.678. By 2019, it was classified as 'medium' nearly to 'low' with an HDI value of 0.567, falling from 109 of 189 countries on the HDI ranking in 2011 to 151 in 2019.[8]

The Syrian regime has been absolutely explicit in its almost fascist position on human losses, not only by making it more difficult for refugees to return home and arbitrarily confiscating their property, but also by using the population exodus to make Syrian society more homogenous. In a speech on 20 August 2017, shortly after the Russian intervention, Assad said, 'It is true that Syria has lost its youth and infrastructure, but it has won a healthier and more homogeneous society in the real sense.'[9] For him,

---

[6] OCHA, 'Humanitarian Needs Overview: Syrian Arab Republic', February 2022, 3, 6, at: https://bit.ly/3HtZvsx (accessed 17 April 2022).
[7] Syrian Centre for Policy Studies, 'Determinants of Forced Displacement in the Syrian Conflict: An Empirical Study', March 2021, 4, at: https://bit.ly/3y4jdbJ (accessed 23 April 2022).
[8] UNDP, 'Syrian Arab Republic', 15 December 2020, at: https://bit.ly/3HRDILD (accessed 20 June 2022).
[9] SANA, 20 August 2017, at: https://bit.ly/3k8GIIl (accessed 23 April 2022).

human losses – deaths and displacements – are a cleansing force leading to a healthier, more homogenous society.

In 2016, the UN Economic and Social Commission for Western Asia (ESCWA) estimated cumulative losses between 2011 and 2015 at $259.6 billion, $169.7 billion in GDP and $89.9 billion in capital stock.[10] A follow-up report four years later stated, 'By the end of 2018, damage to physical capital was estimated at $117.7 billion at 2010 prices, after discounting the annual damage value by the world inflation rate. As such, if the conflict had not taken place, Syrian counterfactual GDP would have reached $90.1 billion by the end of 2018, starting from $61 billion in 2010 (Figure S.1). The accumulated annual GDP loss is, therefore, estimated to have reached $324.5 billion by the end of 2018. However, since GDP, by definition, does not capture the damage that happens to physical capital outside the production process assets – like that incurred by the conflict – the value of the damage to physical capital ($117.7 billion) detailed has to be added to the GDP loss figure ($324.5 billion) to reach a realistic estimate for the macroeconomic cost of the conflict, which would come close to $442.2 billion.'[11] According to the Institute of Economics and Peace, Syria ranked first globally in terms of the economic cost of violence as a percentage of GDP, with the share in Syria standing at 68 per cent compared to 51 per cent for Iraq.[12]

Syrian experts put the total economic losses at the end of 2019 at $530 billion,[13] around nine times (898 per cent) 2010 GDP. Military spending accounts for $37.8 billion ($24 billion by the regime and $13.8 billion by armed groups),[14] as losses to economic growth have also resulted from the redirection of resources away from productive activity and into destructive military activity. The Syrian Central Bank has exhausted its entire $17.5 billion reserve and GDP fell from approximately $34 billion in 2010 to $16.3 billion in 2019.[15] And foreign debt – which in 2010 had been brought down after long effort to around 7 per cent of GDP – stood in 2019 at 116 per cent of GDP, not counting the colossal domestic debt, which has led to unprecedented inflation.[16] The Fragile States Index puts Syria in its 'very high alert' category, with a score of 110.7 in 2020 – above only South Sudan, Somalia and Yemen.[17]

---

[10] ESCWA, 'Syria at War: Five Years On', 2016, 14, at: https://bit.ly/3P7yCMW (accessed 7 August 2022).
[11] ESCWA, 'Syria at War: Eight Years On', 2020, 45, 52, at: https://bit.ly/3zrm26J (accessed 23 April 2022).
[12] Azmeh, 'Avoiding the Return to Conflict', 78; FAO, 'Counting the Cost'.
[13] Syrian Centre for Policy Studies, 'Syria: Justice to Transcend Conflict', May 2020, 8, at: https://bit.ly/3vhSwOZ (accessed 23 April 2022).
[14] Ibid., 58.
[15] World Bank, at: https://bit.ly/37Unm6Q (accessed 17 April 2022).
[16] Syrian Centre for Policy Studies, 'Syria: Justice to Transcend Conflict', 63.
[17] Fund for Peace, 'Fragile States Index: Annual Report 2020', 7, at: https://bit.ly/3JPbiB2 (accessed 17 April 2022).

Figure S.1 Actual and Counterfactual GDP change, 2011–2018 (per cent), and real GDP loss, 2011–2018 (billion dollars)

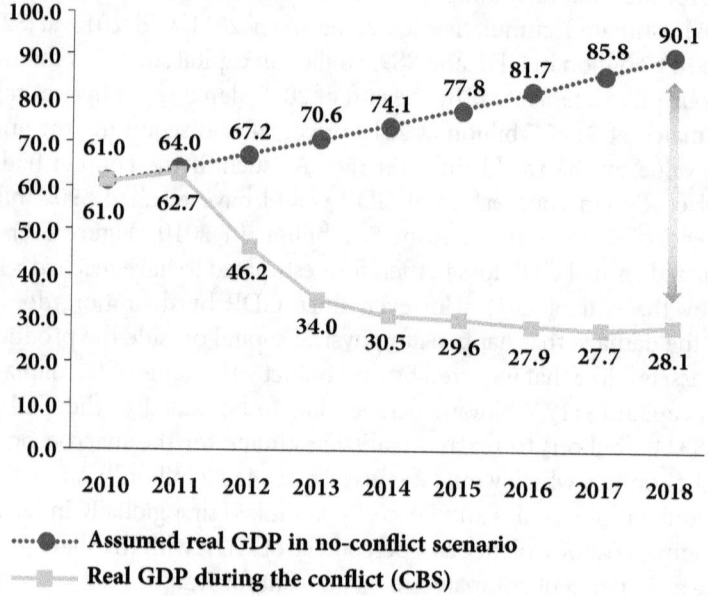

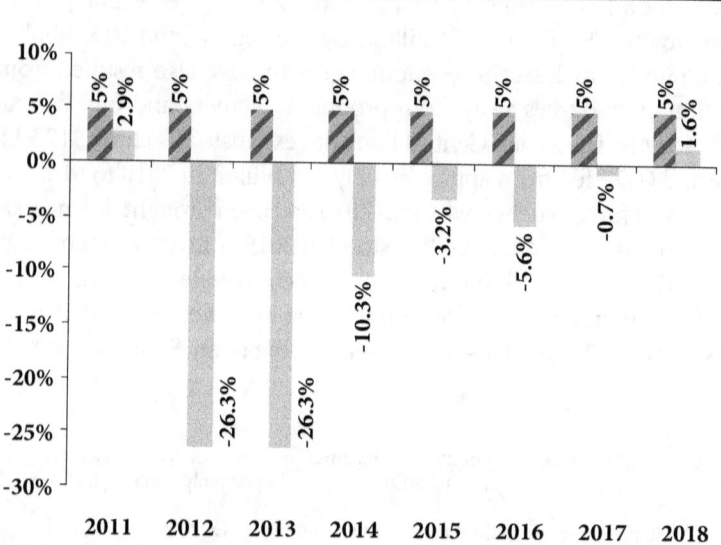

Source: 'Syria at War: Eight Years On', ESCWA, 2020, 52, at: https://bit.ly/3IMRcse (accessed 23 April 2022).

The armed groups, particularly ISIS and the SDF, have taken control of the oil wells in north-eastern Syria, extracting whatever they can by primitive means and selling it in neighbouring markets. Over the course of the revolution, oil production fell from 385,000 barrels a day in 2010 to a mere 24,500 barrels a day in 2019, a decline of around 93.6 per cent, as a result of the main wells passing out of regime control. Fuel usage, meanwhile, has risen to around 136,000 barrels per day – a gap between production and consumption that costs some $8.8 million a day. For the same reason, natural gas production fell by about 50 per cent over the same period, from 34 million cubic metres to only 17.5 million, and production of phosphate from 3.5 million tonnes to zero. The direct and indirect losses of the oil sector alone were estimated in October 2019 at no less than $81 billion.[18] Other official estimates in 2022 placed the figure at $100.5 billion.[19] The US Treasury estimates that ISIS made around $4 million a month from oil in addition to the money it seized from banks and its other sources of funding.[20]

After the revolution, the investment that had been pouring into Syria over the previous decade came to an abrupt halt. It was replaced by a new kind of money closely linked to ongoing political developments. Exactly how much of this new money came in remains controversial. But by Syrian standards, huge sums have entered the country from a range of sources and with diverse aims, including the purchase of weapons for armed groups or the regime, UN and international aid, and funding for NGOs like the White Helmets[21] or Doctors Without Borders. This is not to mention the continuing remittances from Syrians abroad, whose transfers to relatives back home are the only thing allowing many families to make ends meet.[22] We have no precise figures for any of this, but estimates place it at billions of dollars. Much of it entered the country in dollar form, which in purely monetarist terms explains how the Syrian lira avoided major deterioration until after the war, collapsing dramatically only in 2018–2019 when foreign funds ceased to pour into the war economy.

---

[18] *Syria Oil,* 2 October 2019, at: https://bit.ly/3JRquh7 (accessed 17 April 2022). Investigative reports have shown that this detail may be not accurate and that Russian companies have managed phosphate production and its export to Europe since 2018. See: *Lighthouse Reports,* 30 June 2022, at: https://bit.ly/3OCf8zL (accessed 6 July 2022).
[19] *Syria Oil,* 6 February 2022, at: https://bit.ly/37pOeMa (accessed 17 April 2022).
[20] Vasiliev, 453.
[21] The White Helmets were founded in October 2014, uniting seven branches of different National Defence groups trained in Turkey. Initially they operated across seven governorates. They have developed a huge network of workers who, alongside rescue duties, are also involved in construction and other social work: maintaining sewage systems, clearing roads, removing unexploded munitions and so on. See the group's official website at: https://bit.ly/39As3E7 (accessed 17 April 2022).
[22] Former Syrian Economy Minister Lamya Asi estimated remittances at $125–150 million a month, approximately $1.5–$1.8 billion a year. See: *Al Mashhad Online,* 13 April 2022, at: https://bit.ly/37u97pk (accessed 17 April 2022).

According to the former UN Special Envoy de Mistura, Iran has spent around $6 billion for every year of its war in Syria.[23] The *Financial Times* puts the figure for Iranian economic aid to the Syrian regime in 2012–2018 at $16 billion.[24] Qatar, meanwhile, has contributed $1–3 billion[25] (not including direct cash support), and official Saudi support to Syrians as a whole and to refugees and IDPs within Syria and beyond is estimated at $6.7 billion.[26] Spending on UN humanitarian aid in Syria from 2012 to 2021, whether in regime-controlled or opposition-controlled areas, has been estimated at $22.2 billion. The figure for NGO support, most of which has passed through regime organizations, is unknown. The Regional Refugee and Resilience Plan (3RP) is recorded as having received around $24.774 billion for refugees in the years 2012–2020. The UN bodies responsible for these figures stress that they are subject to constant amendment.[27]

Visible transfers in remittance form have risen steadily as conditions within the country deteriorated and were estimated by the official Syrian statistical agency at $2 billion in 2016, $3.8 billion in 2017 and more than $4 billion in 2018, before dropping to $3 billion in 2019.[28] Millions of Syrians abroad are also forced to pay considerable fees in order to renew their passports every two years at Syrian embassies and for the registration of births and the certification of all manner of documentation. These fees cover the expenses of the Foreign Ministry and fetch a surplus for the regime.

If we add these visible transfers to the other forms of new money flowing into the country – not to mention the growing number of invisible transfers made via alternative channels not recognized by the Central Bank,[29] generally because of differences between the black market and centrally set exchange rate – $100 billion seems like a very realistic overall figure, even allowing for a revision of de Mistura's figures for Iranian payments. This is a remarkable sum, more than five times what Syria received in aid, mostly from the Gulf states (mainly Saudi Arabia), during the period 1970–1994 ($20 billion total).

---

[23] *Bloomberg*, 9 June 2015, at: https://bloom.bg/3zJMtoJ (accessed 23 April 2022).
[24] *Financial Times*, 14 February 2018, https://on.ft.com/3ElwFbY (accessed 17 April 2022).
[25] Vasiliev, 457.
[26] See: KSrelief, at: https://bit.ly/3KQ7C3f (accessed 17 April 2022).
[27] Based on a discussion with Ali al-Zaatari, resident coordinator of humanitarian activity in Syria, by a researcher at the ACRPS on 12 April 2022. See also: Joseph Daher, 'The Deep Roots of the Depreciation of the Syrian Pound', 18 December 2019, Research Project Report, Middle East Directions, Wartime and Post-Conflict in Syria, 2019/18, 4, at: https://bit.ly/3KQ85m1 (accessed 17 April 2022).
[28] *Syria TV*, 5 July 2022, at: https://bit.ly/3yPUU0X (accessed 8 July 2022).
[29] Daher, 'The Deep Roots of the Depreciation of the Syrian Pound'.

This money has been spent not on construction and development but on basic needs, aid and destruction (war). And as long as it continued to flow in, it concealed the reality of the deteriorating purchasing power of the lira. The scarcity of productive employment made it easier for armed groups to recruit fighters, and an untold proportion of this money was used to pay their salaries, stimulating market demand and effectively creating a new profession. As the war drew on, so many Syrians became professional fighters that some of them are now being exported to work in Libya, Azerbaijan and Ukraine.

With the agricultural, industrial and services sectors paralysed, unemployment rose to shocking levels unprecedented in modern Syrian history. At the same time as financial support for the armed groups was tapering off, so was humanitarian aid. Saudi official support, for example, shrunk from $511 million in 2017 to $39.5 million in 2021.[30] As a result, the period between October 2019 and January 2020 saw a dramatic collapse of about 96 per cent in the value of the lira.[31] By early April 2022, the lira was trading at around 3,900 to the dollar – a catastrophic fall from 47 to the dollar in 2011. The poverty rate shot up to 90 per cent and the absolute poverty rate, whose most significant indicator is a lack of sufficient food, to no less than 50 per cent. According to the World Food Programme, around 12.6 million Syrians are not food secure, and 1.3 million suffer from severe food insecurity.[32] The fall of the lira has had terrible economic and social consequences in every sense of the word. The cost of just staying alive has risen precipitously.

Alongside the regime itself, the Western sanctions imposed on Syria bear a great deal of the responsibility for the current calamity; Syrians have paid far more than the regime itself, which through its relationships with allies and networks of mafioso businessmen (which it has reshaped as needed and occasionally shaken down for money[33]) can circumvent them, tightening its grip on a society that has lost control of its fate.

The regime bears primary responsibility for the catastrophic situation because of its refusal to accept any political settlement, even a partial

---

[30] This figure fell from $511 million in 2017 to $357.5 million in 2018, $281 million in 2019, $188 million in 2020, and finally $39.5 million in 2021. See: KSRelief, at: https://bit.ly/3KSTMNA (accessed 17 April 2022).
[31] Syrian Centre for Policy Studies, 'Syria: Justice to Transcend Conflict', 8.
[32] World Food Programme, at: https://bit.ly/37XiNbL (accessed 17 April 2022).
[33] The case of Rami Makhlouf is instructive. The backbone of the alliance of 'new businessmen' and Gulf and expatriate capital in Syria, he was the main driver of the formation of vast holding companies in Syria, and received a veritable licence to print money when he was granted a communications monopoly in the early 2000s. Like other big businessmen who owed their money to the regime, however, he was a serial tax evader, and when the regime found itself in desperate need of cash it confiscated his companies, which has allowed for the rise of a new class of businessmen with far fewer scruples.

settlement like the Constitutional Committee. It has made this committee into merely another means of wasting time, a way of pretending to accept the political process that allows hostile states (once known as the Friends of the Syrian People) to delude themselves – and Syrians – that something is happening. Each meeting follows the same process: one side makes demands, the other rejects them out of hand, and the meeting is adjourned until a new agenda can be found to justify another few weeks of pretence. Assad's refusal to respond to the demands of the civil revolution has cost far more than his abdication and a disciplined political transition would have.

Bibliography

Arabic Books

'Syria's Intellectuals Call for an End to the State of Emergency and the Release of Detainees'. In *The Damascus Spring: Issues, Currents and Endings* [Arabic]. Radwan Ziadeh (ed.). Reform Issues Series 17. Cairo: Cairo Institute for Human Rights Studies, 2007.

Abd al-Fadeel, Mahmud. *Arabs and the Asian Experience: Lessons Learned* [Arabic]. Beirut: Centre for Arab Unity Studies, 2000.

al-Arif, Arif. *The Nakba: The Nakba of Jerusalem and the Lost Paradise, 1947–1952* [Arabic]. vol. 2. Saida: al-Maktaba al-Asriya, 1956.

al-Hamash, Munir. 'An Arab Perspective on the Reality of Arab-Turkish Economic Relations' [Arabic]. In *Arabs and Turkey: The Challenges of the Present and the Wagers of the Future*. Muhammad Nureddine (pref.). Beirut and Doha: ACRPS, 2012.

al-Hut, Bayan Nwaihed. *Sabra and Shatila, September 1982* [Arabic]. Beirut: Institute for Palestine Studies, 2003.

Al-Jahmani, Yousef Ibrahim. *The Alawis in Turkey* [Arabic]. Beirut: Dar Al-Kunouz Al-Adabiyah, 2003.

al-Jameel, Sayyar. *The Modern History of the Arabs* [Arabic]. Amman: Al-Shuruq Publishing, 1997.

al-Kayyali, Nizar. *A Study in the Contemporary Political History of Syria, 1920–1950* [Arabic]. Damascus: Tlas Publishing, 1997.

Al-Lababidi, M. *Damascus Businessmen: The Phantoms of Marota City* [Arabic]. Florence: European University Institute, 2019.

al-Moustafa, Hamzeh. *The Virtual Public Sphere in the Syrian Revolution: Characteristics, Currents, Mechanisms for Shaping Public Opinion* [Arabic]. Doha and Beirut: ACRPS, 2012.

Al-Naimi, Saleh. *The Israeli Strategic Mind: Reading the Arab Revolutions and Predicting their Outcomes* [Arabic]. Doha: Al Jazeera Centre for Studies; Beirut: Arab Scientific Publishers, 2013.

Atassi, Suhair. 'The Damascus Spring: The Experience of Jamal al-Atasi's Forum for National Dialogue' [Arabic]. In *Democratic Transition in Syria and the Spanish Experience*. George Ayrani and Radwan Ziadeh (eds.). Reform Issues Series 23. Cairo: Cairo Institute for Human Rights Studies, 2009.

Barout, Muhammad Jamal. *The Arab Enlightenment Movement in the Nineteenth Century: The Aleppo Circle, a Study and Selections* [Arabic]. Issues and Debates of the Arab Nahda, 17. Damascus: Ministry of Culture, 1994.

Barout, Muhammad Jamal. *The First Basic National Report for the Syrian 2025 Project, the Axis of the Economy and Productivity: Surveying and Analysing Macroeconomic Trends in Syria (1970–2005)* [Arabic]. Syrian Arab Republic, State Planning Commission and the UNDP.

Barout, Muhammad Jamal. *The Last Decade in the History of Syria: The Dialectic of Stagnation and Reform* [Arabic]. Beirut and Doha: ACRPS, 2012.

Bishara, Azmi et al. *The Question of Syria's Kurds: Reality, History and Mythology* [Arabic]. Beirut and Doha: ACRPS, 2013.

Bishara, Azmi. 'The Arabs and Iran: General Remarks' [Arabic]. In *The Arabs and Iran: A Review of History and Politics*. Azmi Bishara and Mahjoob Zweiri (eds.). Beirut and Doha: ACRPS, 2012.

Bishara, Azmi. *Civil Society: A Critical Study* [Arabic]. 6th edn. Doha and Beirut: ACRPS, 2011.

Bishara, Azmi. *On the Arab Question: Preface to an Arab Democratic Manifesto* [Arabic]. 2nd edn. Beirut: Centre for Arab Unity Studies, 2010.

Bishara, Azmi. *Syria: A Path to Freedom from Suffering. An Attempt in Contemporary History (March 2011–March 2013)* [Arabic]. Beirut and Doha: ACRPS, 2013.

Bishara, Azmi. *The Glorious Tunisian Revolution: The Structure of a Revolution and its Evolution through Its Daily Chronicles* [Arabic]. Beirut: ACRPS, 2012.

Bishara, Azmi. *The Islamic State Organization 'ISIL': A General Framework and Practical Contribution to Understanding the Phenomenon* [Arabic]. Beirut and Doha: ACRPS, 2018.

Deeb, Kamal. *The Contemporary History of Syria: From the French Mandate to the Summer of 2011* [Arabic]. Beirut: Dar al-Nahar, 2011.

Dugin, Alexsandr. *The Foundations of Geopolitics: The Geopolitical Future of Russia* [Arabic]. Emad Hatem (trans.). Beirut and Tripoli, Libya: Dar Al-Kitab Al-Jadidah Al-Muttahidah, 2004.

Ghalioun, Burhan. *A Manifesto for Democracy* [Arabic]. 5th edn. Casablanca, Morocco: Arab Cultural Centre, 2006.

Ghalioun, Burhan. *Self-Destruction: The Realities of an Unfinished Revolution, Syria 2011–2012* [Arabic]. Beirut: Arab Network for Research and Studies, 2019.

Ghalioun, Burhan. *The Sectarian Question and the Problem of Minorities* [Arabic]. 3rd edn. Beirut and Doha: ACRPS, 2012.

Hakeem, Yusif. *Syria and the French Mandate* [Arabic]. Beirut: Al-Nahar Publishing, 1983.

Heydemann, Steven. *Authoritarianism in Syria: Institutions and Social Conflict* [Arabic]. Abbas Abbas (trans.) Beirut: Riad el-Rayyes, 2011 [1999].

Kassir, Samir. *The Lebanon War: From National Strife to Regional Struggle, 1975–1982* [Arabic]. Salim Anturi (trans.). Beirut: Al-Nahar Publishing, 2007.

Khalidi, Ahmed and Hussein J. Agha. *Syria and Iran: Rivalry and Cooperation* [Arabic]. Adnan Hassan (trans.). Beirut: Dar Al-Kunouz Al-Adabiyah, 1997.

Laurens, Henry. *The Empire and Its Enemies* [Arabic]. Bashir al-Sibai (trans.). Cairo: National Centre for Translation, 2010.

Nahar, Hazem. *Trajectories of the Regime and the Opposition in Syria 2000–2008: A Critique of Visions and Practices* [Arabic]. Reform Issues Series. Cairo: Cairo Institute for Human Rights Studies, 2009.

Nur al-Din, Muhammad. *Turkey in Changing Times: Concerns of Identity and the Conflict of Options* [Arabic]. London: Riad el-Rayyes, 1997.

Seif, Riad. *The Experience of Riad Seif: Issues in Industry and Politics* [Arabic]. Damascus: [n. p.], 1999.

Tlas, Mustafa. *Three Months that Shook Syria* [Arabic]. [n.p]: [n.p], [n.d].

Zakaria, Ahmad Wasfi. *The Clans of Syria: A Treatise on the Geography, History, Settlements, Ethics, and Customs of the Syrian Desert* [Arabic]. vol. 2. 3rd edn. Beirut: Dar al-Fikr al-Muʿasir; Damascus: Dar al-Fikr al-ʿArabi, 1997.

Foreign Language Books

Abboud, Samer N. *Syria*. 2nd edn. Cambridge: Polity Press, 2018.

Azmeh, Shamel. 'Avoiding the Return to Conflict: Envisioning a Democratic Development State in Syria'. In *Striking from the Margins: State, Religion and Devolution of Authority in the Middle East*. Aziz al-Azmeh et al. (eds.). London: Saqi, 2021.

Balanche, Fabrice. '"Go to Damascus, My Son": Alawi Demographic Shifts under Ba'th Party Rule'. In *The Alawis of Syria: War, Faith and Politics in the Levant*. Michael Kerr and Craig Larkin (eds.). Oxford: Oxford University Press, 2015.

Barro, Robert and Xavier I. Sala-i-Martin. *Economic Growth*. 2nd edn. Cambridge and London: MIT Press, 2004 [1995].

Batatu, Hanna. *Syria's Peasantry, the Descendants of its Lesser Rural Notables, and their Politics*. Princeton, NJ: Princeton University Press, 1999.

Bishara, Azmi. *On Salafism: Concepts and Contexts*. Stanford: Stanford University Press, 2022.

Bishara, Azmi. *Sectarianism without Sects*. Oxford: Oxford University Press, 2021.

Bishara, Azmi. *Understanding Revolutions: Opening Acts in Tunisia*. London and New York: I.B. Tauris, 2021.

Borshchevskaya, Anna. *Putin's War in Syria: Russian Foreign Policy and the Price of America's Absence*. London: I.B. Tauris, 2022.

Daoudy, Marwa. *The Origins of the Syrian Conflict: Climate Change and Human Security*. Cambridge and New York: Cambridge University Press, 2020.

Donker, Teije Hidde. 'Beyond Syria: Civil Society in Failed Episodes of Democratization'. In *Social Movements and Civil War: When Protests for Democratization Fail*. Donatella della Porta et al. (ed.). London and New York: Routledge, 2018.

Gani, Jasmine K. 'US Policy towards the Syrian Conflict under Obama: Strategic Patience and Miscalculation'. In *The War for Syria: Regional and International Dimensions of the Syrian Uprising*. Raymond Hinnebusch and Adham Saouli (eds.). London: Routledge, 2019.

Gaub, Florence. 'Russian Non-War on Daesh'. In *Russia's Return to the Middle East: Building Sandcastles?* Nicu Popescu and Stanislav Secrieru (eds.). Chaillot Paper 146. Paris: European Union Institute for Security Studies, 2018.

Haddad, Bassam. *Business Networks in Syria: The Political Economy of Authoritarian Resilience*. Stanford, CA: Stanford University Press, 2012.

Helberg, Kristin. *Brennpunkt Syrian: Enblick in ein Vershclossenes Land*. Freiberg, Basel, Wien: Heder, 2012.

Heydemann, Steven. *Authoritarianism in Syria: Institutions and Social Conflict 1946–1970*. Ithaca and London: Cornell University Press, 1999.

Hinnebusch, Raymond A. 'Democratization in the Middle East: The Evidence from the Syrian Case'. In *Political and Economic Liberalization: Dynamics and Linkages in Comparative Perspective*. Gerd Nonneman (ed.). Boulder: Lynne Rienner, 1996.

Hinnebusch, Raymond A. *Syria: Revolution from Above*. London and New York: Routledge, 2002.

Hokayem, Emile. *Syria's Uprising and the Fracturing of the Levant*. London: Routledge; the International Institute for Strategic Studies, 2013.

Kalyvas, Stathis N. 'Civil Wars'. In *The Oxford Handbook of Comparative Politics*. Carles Boix and Susan C. Stokes (eds.). Oxford: Oxford University Press, 2009.

Khaddour, Kheder. 'The Alawite Dilemma (Homs 2013)'. In *Playing the Sectarian Card: Identities and Affiliations of Local Communities in Syria*. Friederike Stolleis (ed.). Beirut: Friedrich Ebert Stiftung, 2015.

Leenders, Reinoud. 'Repression Is Not "a Stupid Thing": Regime Responses to the Syrian Uprising and Insurgency'. In *The Alawis of Syria: War, Faith and Politics in the Levant*. Michael Kerr and Craig Larkin (eds.). New York: Oxford University Press, 2015.

Lesch, David W. *Syria: The Fall of the House of Assad*. Updated edn. New Haven and London: Yale University Press, 2013.

Longrigg, Stephen Hemsley. *Syria and Lebanon under the French Mandate*. London: Octagon Books, 1972.

Mazur, Kevin. *Revolution in Syria: Identity, Networks and Repression*. New York: Cambridge University Press, 2021.

Meijer, Roel. 'Introduction'. In *Global Salafism: Islam's New Religious Movement*. Roel Meijer (ed.). New York: Columbia University Press, 2009.

Perthes, Volker. *The Political Economy of Syria Under Asad*. New York: I.B. Tauris, 1995.

Phillips, Christopher. *The Battle for Syria: International Rivalry in the New Middle East*. Revised and updated edn. New Haven and London: Yale University Press, 2020.

Pierret, Thomas. 'States Sponsors and the Syrian Insurgency: The Limits of Foreign Influence'. In *Inside Wars: Local Dynamics of Conflicts in Syria and Libya*. Luigi Narbone, Agnès Favier and Virginie Collombier (eds.). Florence: European University Institute; Robert Schuman Centre for Advanced Studies; and Middle East Directions, 2016.

Pierret, Thomas. *Religion and State in Syria: The Sunni Ulama from Coup to Revolution*. New York: Cambridge University Press, 2013.

Poelling, Sylvia. 'Syria's Private Sector: Economic Liberalization and the Challenges of the 1990s'. In *Political and Economic Liberalization: Dynamics and Linkages in Comparative Perspective*. Gerd Nonneman (ed.). Boulder: Lynne Rienner, 1996.

Rabinovich, Itamar. *Syria under the Ba'th, 1963–66: The Army-Party Symbiosis*. Abingdon: Routledge, 1972.

Sayigh, Yezid. *Armed Struggle and the Search for State: The Palestinian National Movement, 1949–1993*. Oxford: Institute for Palestine Studies, 1997.

Seale, Patrick. *Asad of Syria: The Struggle for the Middle East*. Berkeley: University of California Press, 1988.

van Dam, Nikoalos. *Destroying a Nation: The Civil War in Syria*. London: I.B. Tauris, 2017.

van Dam, Nikoalos. *Struggle for Power in Syria: Sectarianism, Regionalism and Tribalism in Politics, 1961-80*. London: Croom Helm, 1981.

van Dam, Nikoalos. *The Struggle for Power in Syria*. London: Croom Helm, 1979.

van Dusen, Michael H. 'Syria: Downfall of a Traditional Elite'. In *Political Elites and Political Decelopment in the Middle East*. Frank Tachau (ed.). Cambridge, Mass.: Schenkman Pub. Co, 1975.

Vasiliev, Alexey. *Russia's Middle East Policy from Lenin to Putin*. New York: Routledge, 2020.

Wedeen, Lisa. *Ambiguities of Domination: Politics, Rhetoric, and Symbols in Contemporary Syria*. London: University of Chicago Press, 1999.

Weiss, Michael and Hassan Hassan. *ISIS: Inside the Army of Terror*. New York: Regan Arts, 2015.

Wiarda, Howard. *Corporatism and Comparative Politics: The Other Great "Ism"*. Armonk, NY: M. E. Sharpe, 1997.

Wieland, Carsten. *Syria: Ballots or Bullets? Democracy, Islamism, and Sectarianism in the Levant*. Seattle, WA: Cune Press, 2006.

Wimmen, Heiko. 'The Sectarianization of the Syrian War'. In *Beyond Sunni and Shia: The Roots of Sectarianism in a Changing Middle East*. Frederic Wehrey (ed.). London: Hurst, 2017.

Yahya, Maha and Marwan Muasher. 'Refugee Crises in the Arab World'. In *Arab Horizons: Pitfalls and Pathways to Renewal*. Joseph Bahout et al. (eds.). Washington, DC: Carnegie Endowment for International Peace, 2018.

Yedlin, Amos. 'The Arab Spring a Year on'. In *One Year of the Arab Spring: Global and Regional Implications* [Hebrew]. Yoel Guzansky and Mark Heller (eds.). Tel Aviv: Institute for National Security Studies, 2012.

Arabic Journal Articles

Al-Labbad, Mostafa. 'The Kurdish Question in the Turkish Politics' [Arabic]. *al-Siyasa al-Dawliya* 42, no. 169 (July 2007).
al-Moustafa, Hamzeh. 'Facing ISIL: Reasons and Possible Impacts' [Arabic]. *Siyasat Arabiya* 7 (March 2014).
Kablan, Marwan. 'The Syrian Revolution/the Conflict over Syria: Fallout from an Imbalance of Regional Powers' [Arabic]. *Siyasat Arabiya* 18 (January 2016).
Muharib, Mahmoud. 'Israel and the Geostrategic Changes in the Arab World' [Arabic]. *Siyasat Arabiya* 1, no. 1 (March 2013).
Tabsi, Aziz. 'The *Shabbiha* Phenomenon: Early Indices of the Decline of the Military Clique' [Arabic]. *Damascus Journal* (London), no. 1 (March 2013).
Younis, Alexander Abi. 'Confused Relations between Turkey and the European Union' [Arabic]. *National Defence* (Beirut), no. 331 (January 2011).

Foreign Languages Journal Articles

Aldoughli, Rahaf. 'Departing "Secularism": boundary appropriation and extension of the Syrian state in the religious domain since 2011'. *British Journal of the Middle Eastern Studies* 49, no. 2 (2022).
Aldoughli, Rahaf. 'Securitization as a Tool of Regime Survival: The Deployment of Religious Rhetoric in Bashar al-Asad's Speeches'. *The Middle East Journal* 75, no. 1 (2021).
Balanche, Fabrice. 'Géographie de la révolte syrienne'. *Outre-Terre* 29, no. 3 (December 2011).
Batatu, Hanna. 'Some Observations on the Social Roots of Syria's Ruling Military Group and the Causes for its Dominance'. *Middle East Journal* 35 (Summer 1981).
Blattman, Christopher and Edward Miguel. 'Civil War'. *Journal of Economic Literature* 48, no. 1 (March 2010).
Bou Nassif, Hicham. '"Second-Class": The Grievances of Sunni Officers in the Syrian Armed Forces'. *Journal of Strategic Studies* 38, no. 5 (2015).
Bou-Nacklie, N. E. 'Les Troupes Speciales: Religious and Ethnic Recruitment, 1916–46'. *International Journal of Middle East Studies* 25, no. 4 (November 1993).
Devlin, John F. 'The Baath Party: Rise and Metamorphosis'. *American Historical Review* 96, no. 5 (December 1991).
Eiland, Giora. 'The Upheavals in the Middle East and Israel's Security'. *Strategic Assessment* 14, no. 2 (July 2011).
Ghadbian, Najib. 'The New Asad: Dynamics of Continuity and Change in Syria'. *Middle East Journal* 55, no. 4 (Autumn 2001).
Hinnebusch, Raymond. 'Syria: From "Authoritarian Upgrading" to Revolution?' *International Affairs* 88, no. 1 (2012).
Jentzsch, Corinna, Stathis N. Kalyvas and Livia Isabella Schubiger. 'Militias in Civil Wars'. *Journal of Conflict Resolution* 59, no. 5 (August 2015).
Landis, Joshua M. and Joe Pace. 'The Syrian Opposition'. *Washington Quarterly* 30, no. 1 (Winter 2006–7).
Landis, Joshua M. and Joe Pace. 'The Syrian Uprising of 2011: Why the Asad Regime is Likely to Survive to 2013? *Middle East Policy* 19, no. 1 (Spring 2012).
Lia, Brynjar. 'The Islamist Uprising in Syria, 1976–82: The History and Legacy of a Failed Revolt'. *British Journal of Middle Eastern Studies* 43, no. 4 (2016).

Madouni, Ali and Hichem Derradji. 'The Caesar Law for the Protection of Civilians in Syria: Objectives and Ramifications'. *Prizren Social Science Journal* 4, no. 3 (2020).

Moubayed, Sami. 'Lesson from Egypt: West Is Not Best'. *Forward Magazine*, no. 48 (February 2011).

Shaaban, Bouthaina. 'The Real Evils Plaguing the Region'. *Forward Magazine*, no. 48 (February 2011).

Walther, Olivier J. and Patrick Steen Pedersen. 'Rebel Fragmentation in Syria's Civil War'. *Small Wars & Insurgencies* 31, no. 3 (2 April 2020).

Yassin-Kassab, Robin. 'Revolutionary Culture'. *Critical Muslim* 11 (2017).

Zuhur, Sherifa. 'The Syrian Opposition: Salafi and Nationalist Jihadism and Populist Idealism'. *Contemporary Review of the Middle East* 2, nos. 1 and 2 (2015).

Interviews

Activist from Deir ez-Zor (anonymous).
Activist involved in the Ma'an movement (anonymous), 7 May 2013.
Ali al-Zaatari, 12 April 2022.
Ali Rahmoun.
Ali Sadr al-Din al-Bayanuni, 7 October 2012.
Bassam Yousef, 21 November 2011.
Bilal Turkiya, 13 March 2013.
Contracted private militiaman (anonymous), 10 November 2011.
Deiaa Dughmoch, 13 September 2011.
Fathi Bayoud.
Fayez Sara, 13 September 2011.
Hazem Nahar, 15 August 2011.
Ibrahim Abd al-Kareem, 10 May 2013.
Ibrahim al-Masri (known during the revolution as Omar al-Hourani), 29 September 2019.
Jihad Mahameed, 26 June 2019.
Khalid al-Jawabra, 19 March 2012.
Khuzama Udai, 3 August 2012.
Marwa al-Ghamian, 13 September 2011.
Mithqal Abazed, 9 September 2019.
Mohammad al-Haj Ali, 2 August 2012 and 25 May 2019.
Muhammad Saleh, 30 November 2011.
Najati Tayyara, 3 August 2012 and 7 November 2011.
Nasr, *nom de guerre* Abu Anas al-Shami, 13 March 2013 and 20 March 2013.
Nidal Darwish, 24 February 2012.
Nizar al-Haraki, 13 March 2013.
Omar Abdallatef.
Omar Edlbi, 3 August 2012, 5 August 2012 and 1 April 2013.
Omar Shaheen, 22 April 2011.
Police Officer (anonymous).
Protest organizer in Hama (anonymous), 10 September 2011.
Raed Abazeed, 13 September 2011.
Raja al-Nasser, 13 September 2011.
Riad Hijab, 12 March 2013.
Shams al-Deen al-Kilani.

Sheikh Muhammad Abdulaziz Abazed, 19 May 2019.
Tariq Abdel Hai, 18 July 2019.
Thaer Deeb.
Wael Abu Rshaidat, 25 February 2012.
Wael Salam (alias Khalid al-Umar).
Zahraa resident (anonymous), 27 January 2012.

Online Articles, Working Papers and Seminars

Abu Hilal, Firas. 'Iran and the Arab Revolutions: Positions and Repercussions'. ACRPS. September 2011. At: https://bit.ly/3spFNbW (accessed 3 February 2022).
ACRPS. 'Army of Islam: The Search for a Role in the Future of Syria' [Arabic]. July 2015. At: https://bit.ly/37qjcUr (accessed on 17 April 2022).
ACRPS. 'Effects of Sanctions on Syria's Macroeconomy in 2012'. 22 January 2012. At: https://bit.ly/3zPNxHZ (accessed 13 Jun 2022).
ACRPS. 'Is the Arab League Capable of Saving Syria?'. 21 November 2011. At: https://bit.ly/33i2AvY (accessed 14 February 2022).
ACRPS. 'Is the Syrian Revolution Entering a New Stage?'. 6 January 2013. At: https://bit.ly/3E7yPdS (accessed 3 January 2022).
ACRPS. 'Recurrent Israeli Aggressions against Syria'. 18 May 2013. At: https://bit.ly/3FgAi2E (accessed 3 February 2022).
ACRPS. 'The Arab Opinion Project: Arab Opinion Index 2011'. March 2012. At: https://bit.ly/3wYJuY7 (accessed 6 February 2022).
ACRPS. 'The General and the Particular in the Ongoing Syrian Popular Uprising'. 15 May 2011. At: https://bit.ly/3evkkpv (accessed 26 December 2021).
ACRPS. 'The Islamic Front: An Experimental Integration of the Largest Military Groups in Syria' [Arabic]. November 2013. At: https://bit.ly/3ElCpm5 (accessed 17 April 2022).
ACRPS. 'The Positions of the Syrian Opposition toward the Central Arab Causes'. 16 February 2012. At: https://bit.ly/3HgYlPL (accessed 26 December 2021).
ACRPS. 'The Reality of the Syrian Opposition and Current and Future Challenges'. October 2011. At: https://bit.ly/3e7aMRJ (accessed 13 March 2022).
ACRPS. 'The Recent Bombings in Syria: Do They Change Reality on the Ground?'. June 2012. At: https://bit.ly/3GTaYA4 (accessed 5 January 2022).
ACRPS. 'The Syrian National Coalition: Motivations for its Formation and Building Blocks of Success'. 11 December 2012. At: https://bit.ly/3mko95c (accessed 2 February 2022).
ACRPS. 'Turkey's Position on the Libyan Revolution'. 21 March 2011. At: https://bit.ly/3Hqebbc (accessed 3 February 2022).
al-Ahmad, Khalid. 'The Great Hama Massacre (1982)' [Arabic]. Arab Orient Centre for Strategic Civilization Studies. 6 February 2006. At: https://bit.ly/3mpJri3 (accessed 22 December 2021).
al-Ahmad, Khalid. 'The Massacre of Jisr ash-Shughur' [Arabic]. Arab Orient Centre for Strategic and Civilization Studies. 27 October 2005. At: https://bit.ly/3yNvbo8 (accessed 22 December 2021).
al-Najjar, Abdullah. 'Defection: Roles and Consequences' [Arabic]. Harmoon Centre for Contemporary Studies. 2 June 2021. At: https://bit.ly/3gibHAC (accessed 24 April 2022).
al-Radawi, Taysir. 'Shedding Light on the Eleventh Five-Year Plan'. Symposium, Syrian Economic Society. 5 January 2011. At: https://bit.ly/3b7nTEA (accessed 25 July 2022).

Atrissi, Talal. 'Iranian Goals and Interests in the Arab Order after the Revolutions' [Arabic]. Paper presented at 'Geostrategic Transformations in the Context of the Arab Revolutions' conference at ACRPS. Doha, 15–17 December 2012.

Barout, Muhammad Jamal. 'Sectarianism: Its Manufacturing and False Consciousness'. Paper presented at 'The Arab Revolution and Democracy: The Roots of Sectarian Conflicts and How to Combat Them' conference at ACRPS. Doha, 28 January 2012.

Centre for Operational Analysis and Research. 'The Syrian Economy at War: Captagon, Hashish, and the Syrian Narco-State'. 27 April 2021. At: https://bit.ly/3vbrKr8 (accessed 24 April 2022).

Cohen, Edy. 'Was the Assad Dynasty Good for Israel?' [Hebrew]. Begin-Sadat Center for Strategic Studies. 24 May 2017. At: https://bit.ly/3QGCyGL (accessed 22 June 2022).

Daher, Joseph. 'The Deep Roots of the Depreciation of the Syrian Pound'. Research Project Report. Middle East Directions. Wartime and Post-Conflict in Syria. 18 December 2019. At: https://bit.ly/3KQ85m1 (accessed 17 April 2022).

Harmoon Centre for Contemporary Studies. 'Iran's Role in Re-Structuring the Syrian Society'. 8 September 2021. At: https://bit.ly/3rID2kL (accessed 23 April 2022).

Heydemann, Steven. 'Assad's Normalization and the Politics of Erasure in Syria'. Brookings Institution. 13 January 2022. At: https://brook.gs/3JJq3Fy (accessed 17 April 2022).

Khaddour, Kheder. 'Assad's Officer Ghetto: Why the Syrian Army Remains Loyal'. Carnegie Middle East Centre. 4 November 2015. At: https://bit.ly/3qYNnZe (accessed 13 June 2022).

Khatib, Lina. 'Syria's Last Best Hope: The Southern Front'. Malcolm H. Kerr Carnegie Middle East Centre. 6 July 2015. At: https://bit.ly/38dDDnH (accessed 17 April 2022).

Landis, Joshua M. 'Syria's Top Five Insurgent Leaders'. Syria Comment. 1 October 2013. At: https://bit.ly/3DEJ0bb (accessed 17 April 2022).

Landis, Joshua M. 'The Work of Fabrice Balanche on Alawites and Syrian Communitarianism Reviewed by Nikolaos van Dam'. Syria Comment. 30 November 2013. At: https://bit.ly/3NZoV41 (accessed 10 April 2022).

Larson, Ian. 'Narcos: Syria Edition—and What the US Can Do About It'. Atlantic Council. 14 June 2021. At: https://bit.ly/3xUP3Y7 (accessed 24 April 2022).

Lund, Aron. 'Into the Tunnels: The Rise and Fall of Syria's Rebel Enclave in the Eastern Ghouta'. Century Foundation. 21 December 2016. At: https://bit.ly/3MdAVwS (accessed 17 April 2022).

Lund, Aron. 'Syria's Salafi Insurgents: The Rise of the Syrian Islamic Front'. UI Occasional Paper. no. 17. Swedish Institute of International Affairs. March 2013. At: https://bit.ly/3jK3qX9 (accessed 17 April 2022).

Lund, Aron. 'Syrian Jihadism'. UI Brief. no. 13. Swedish Institute of International Affairs, 14 September 2012.

Lund, Aron. 'The Politics of the Islamic Front, Part 1: Structure and Support'. Malcolm H. Kerr Carnegie Middle East Centre. 14 January 2014. At: https://bit.ly/3Mfsu4t (accessed 17 April 2022).

Marzuq, Nabil. 'Economic Sanctions: A Slow Stifling of the Syrian Regime' [Arabic]. Al Jazeera Centre for Studies. 19 November 2011. At: https://bit.ly/3glSNI8 (accessed 3 February 2022).

Pierret, Thomas. 'Brothers in Alms: Salafi Financiers and the Syrian Insurgency'. Carnegie Middle East Centre. 18 May 2018. At: https://bit.ly/3uPz1Ng (accessed 17 April 2022).

Pierret, Thomas. 'Salafis at War in Syria: Logics of Fragmentation and Realignment'. HAL Archives. 29 March 2018. At: https://bit.ly/36lw39G (accessed 17 April 2022).

Şaban, Navvar. 'Control and Influence Changes After Operation "Peace Spring"'. Omran for Strategic Studies. 18 December 2019. At: https://bit.ly/3EIIKYZ (accessed 24 April 2022).

Sadak, Youssef. 'The MOC's Role in the Collapse of the Southern Opposition'. Atlantic Council. 23 September 2016. At: https://bit.ly/3xzjlQb (accessed 17 April 2022).
Seifan, Samir and Mahmood Alhosain. 'The Destruction of the Energy Sector in Syria During the War 2011-2020'. Harmoon Centre for Contemporary Studies. 14 July 2021. At: https://bit.ly/3rK4ZZm (accessed 23 April 2022).
Shaar, Karam and Ali Fathollah-Nejad. 'Iran's Credit Line to Syria: A Well That Never Runs Dry'. Atlantic Council. 10 February 2020. At: https://bit.ly/3JPfKje (accessed 17 April 2022).
Shatz, Howard J. 'The Power and Limits of Threat: The Caesar Syrian Civilian Protection Act at One Year'. RAND Blog. 8 July 2021. At: https://bit.ly/3rw7mia (accessed 17 April 2022).
Steinberg, Guido. 'Ahrar al-Sham – the "Syrian Taliban": Al-Nusra Ally Seeks Partnership with West'. Stiftung Wissenschaft und Politik/Deutsches Institut für Internationale Politik und Sicherheit. 2016. At: https://bit.ly/36g9mUj (accessed 17 April 2022).
Talaa, Maan. 'Sixth Round of Meetings of the Constitutional Committee: A Floating Agenda and Constant Deadlock' [Arabic]. Omran for Strategic Studies. 2 November 2021. At: https://bit.ly/3M2Ob7w (accessed on 17 April 2022).
Wieland, Carsten. 'Syria: a Tale of Missed Opportunity'. *Open Democracy*. 4 October 2011. At: https://bit.ly/3LFo9qK (accessed 28 April 2022).

Documents and Reports

ACU. 'Economic Reality in Northern Syria'. April 2021. At: https://bit.ly/3OANrcb (accessed 20 April 2022).
Arab League. 'Syrian Revolution and Action Plan' [Arabic]. At: https://bit.ly/3IYA8i2 (accessed 3 February 2022).
Blanchard, Christopher M., Carla E. Humud and Mary Beth D. Nikitin. 'Armed Conflict in Syria: Overview and U.S. Response'. Congressional Research Service. 27 June 2014. At: https://bit.ly/3RUg4CN (accessed 25 July 2022).
BP. 'Statistical Review of World Energy'. June 2011. At: https://bit.ly/3J5ly9r (accessed 25 July 2022).
Carnegie Middle East Centre. 'The Syrian Constitution – 1973–2012'. 5 December 2012. At: https://bit.ly/3qqv9Pp (accessed 26 December 2021).
ESCWA. 'Syria at War: Eight Years On'. 2020. At: https://bit.ly/3zrm26J (accessed 23 April 2022).
European Centre for Kurdish Studies. 'Decree 49: A Tool for Confiscating the Property of the Kurds? Observations on the Political and Economic Repercussions of the Decree'. Report 6. August 2010.
FAO. 'Counting the Cost: Agriculture in Syria after Six Years of Crisis'. 2017. At: https://bit.ly/3MUGEb8 (accessed 13 June 2022).
Fund for Peace. 'Fragile States Index'. Annual Report. 2020. At: https://bit.ly/3JPbiB2 (accessed 17 April 2022).
Hall, Natasha. 'Rescuing Aid in Syria'. Center for Strategic and International Studies. February 2022. At: https://bit.ly/3byuqs8 (accessed 24 April 2022).
Hatahet, Sinan. 'The Political Economy of the Autonomous Administration of North and East Syria'. Middle East Directions. 29 November 2019. At: https://bit.ly/3ry07Xn (accessed 24 April 2022).
IMF. 'Syrian Arab Republic: 2009 Article IV Consultation'. Country Report. no. 10/86. March 2010. At: https://bit.ly/3PPy3s3 (accessed 25 July 2022).

IMF. 'World Economic Outlook Database: Syria'. October 2019. At: https://bit.ly/3nti1rS (accessed 25 July 2022).

Immigration and Refugee Board of Canada. 'Syria: Destruction of Hama and Hums in Syria'. Document no. SYR2294. 1 October 1989. At: https://bit.ly/3IOv27q (accessed 31 March 2022).

International Crisis Group. 'Popular Protest in North Africa and the Middle East (VI): The Syrian People's Slow Motion Revolution'. Middle East/North Africa Report. no. 108. 6 July 2011. At: https://bit.ly/3pbbSBY (accessed 3 January 2022).

International Crisis Group. 'Syria's Mutating Conflict'. Middle East Report. no. 128. 1 August 2012. At: https://bit.ly/3IUoGED (accessed 21 December 2021).

International Crisis Group. 'Tentative Jihad: Syria's Fundamentalist Opposition'. Middle East Report. no. 131. 12 October 2012. At: https://bit.ly/3EePzzQ (accessed 3 January 2022).

Malcolm H. Kerr Carnegie Middle East Centre. 'Charter of the Syrian Islamic Front'. 4 February 2013. At: https://bit.ly/3ECjG6c (accessed 17 April 2022).

OCHA. 'Humanitarian Needs Overview: Syrian Arab Republic'. February 2022. At: https://bit.ly/3HtZvsx (accessed 17 April 2022).

OCHA. 'Humanitarian Needs Overview: Syrian Arab Republic'. March 2021. At: https://bit.ly/3rObevj (accessed 24 April 2022).

OCHA. 'Syrian Arab Republic - Population Statistics'. At: https://bit.ly/3NAzHgV (accessed 31 March 2022).

Sharp, Jeremy M. and Christopher M. Blanchard. 'Armed Conflict in Syria: U.S. and International Response'. Congressional Research Service. 22 April 2013. At: https://bit.ly/3shSghL (accessed 3 February 2022).

Syrian Association for Citizen Dignity. 'Weaponization of Aid, Interference and Corruption: Syrian Regime's Methods of Control of Humanitarian Sector'. 11 November 2021. At: https://bit.ly/3uLuEmq (accessed 17 April 2022).

Syrian Centre for Policy Studies. 'Determinants of Forced Displacement in the Syrian Conflict: An Empirical Study'. March 2021. At: https://bit.ly/3y4jdbJ (accessed 23 April 2022).

Syrian Centre for Policy Studies. 'Syria: Justice to Transcend Conflict'. May 2020. At: https://bit.ly/3vhSwOZ (accessed 23 April 2022).

Syrians for Truth and Justice. 'HTS Confiscates No Less Than 550 Homes and Businesses Belonging to Christians in Idleb'. 14 January 2020. At: https://bit.ly/3OLWIhF (accessed 25 April 2022).

UNDP. 'Syrian Arab Republic'. 15 December 2020. at: https://bit.ly/3HRDILD (accessed 20 June 2022).

UNGA. 'Final Communiqué of the Action Group for Syria'. 30 June 2012. Archived copy available online: https://bit.ly/3NQrDZ6 (accessed 3 February 2022).

UNSC. 'Report of the Secretary-General on the Implementation of Security Council Resolution 2139 (2014)'. 26 March 2014. at: https://bit.ly/38uRypu (accessed 17 April 2022).

News Networks and Websites

Aksalser
Al Ahram
Al Arabiya
Al Jaml

Al Jazeera
Al Jazeera (international)
Al Jumhuriya
Al Manara Al Bayda'
Al Sbah (Palestine)
Al Watan Voice
Al-Akhbar (Lebanon)
Alanba (Kuwait)
Al-Araby al-Jadeed
Al-Ayam (Bahrain)
Al-Bab
Albawaba
Albayan
Al-Hayat (London)
al-Hiwar al-Mutamaddin
AlKhalij (Oman)
All4Syria
Almadenah News
Al-Monitor
al-Quds al-Arabi
Alrai Media
Alriyadh
Al-Thawra
Alwatan Voice
Ammon News
Amnesty International
Anadolu Agency
Anba Moscow
ANHRI
Annahar (Lebanon)
Arraee
Asharq Al-Awsat
Assafir (Lebanon)
Atlas News
BBC Arabic
BBC (international)
Bloomberg
Calcalist
Carnegie Middle East Centre
CBS News
CNN Arabic
CNN (international)
C-SPAN
Elnashra (Lebanon)
Facebook
Financial Times
Foreign Policy
FSA (Damascus)
Globes
Government of Israel – Prime Minister's Office

Haaretz
Human Rights Watch
Independent
Iraqibeacon
JDN
Jusoor Studies
Kassioun
KSrelief
Le Figaro
Le Matin
Lighthouse Reports
Maariv
Macrotrends
Mehr (Iran)
Middle East Transparent
Mivzakim
Moheb Jabhat al-Nusra
Moqawama (Lebanon)
N12 News
NRG
Reuters Arabic
Russia Today Arabic
Saaa 25
SANA
Sawt al-Kurd
SDC website
Shaam Network
Shahb News
Sham FM
Souryioun Net
SYRCU
Syria Islamic Liberation Front (SILF)
Syria News
Syria Noor
Syria Oil
Syria TV
Syrian Electronic Army
Syrian Ministry of Local Administration and Environment
Syrian Observatory for Human Rights
Syrian Safahat
Syrian Shuhada
Syrianoor
The Atlantic
The Economist
The Global Economy
The Guardian
The Jerusalem Post
The National
The New York Times
The Wall Street Journal

The Washington Post
The White Helmets
Time
UN High Commissioner for Refugees
UN News
UN Official Document System
UNSC
Wattan (Palestine)
World Bank
World Food Programme
Ynet
Youm7
YouTube
Zaman al-Wasl

Index

Page numbers in **bold** refer to figures, page numbers in *italic* refer to tables.

Abadi, Fayrouz, 256
al-Abdallah, Ali, 204
Abdel Aziz, Ahmad Khaled, 71n6
Abdullah bin Abdulaziz Al Saud, 264, 265, 267
al-Abidin, Muhammad Surur Zayn, 320, 322
Abu Kamal, 77
Abu Zlam Forum for Civilizational Studies, 200
Abu'l-Fadl al-'Abbas Brigades, 327
Action Group for Syria, 236–7
Adana Agreement, 251
ad-hoc initiatives and conferences, 206–9
Afghanistan, 96, 101, 183, 226, 242, 244, 245, 248, 299, 316, 325, 331, 341
Aflaq, Michel, 147
agriculture, 30, 31, 162, 164, 184, 292, 358, *359*, *362*, *363*
Ahrar al-Sham, 193, 194, 320–1, 327, 330
Ahmadinejad, Mahmoud, 275
Air Force Intelligence, 6n7
airstrikes, 105, 133, 283
 United States of America, 355
Al Arabiya, 226, 227–8, 229, 230, 278
Al Jazeera, 225, 226–31, 271, 273–4, 274–5
Alawis, 13, 136, 139, 159, 304, 305, 307, 309–10, 350
al-Albani, Muhammad Nasiruddin, 317n25
Aleppo, 46, 72, 85, 93, 110, 190, 192, 304, 317, 343, 348, 367
 airstrikes, 105
 Battle for, 93, 95, 104–7
 Battle of, 133
 civilian exodus, 103–4
 crime, 197–8
 demographic composition, 90
 economic factors, 90–2
 population, 89
 protests, 92–4
 regime escalation, 93–4
 reluctance to join the revolution, 90
 revolutionary movement, 89–94
 shabbiha, 136
 siege of, 332
 state policy, 90–1
 youth groups' failure, 92
Aleppo Military Council, 104–7
al-Ali, Louay, 40n6, 41n9
Aliyev, Heydar, 150, 150n15
Allawi, Ayad, 258
Alloush, Zahran, 108, 317, 321
Alwan, Jasim, 146
American-Syrian relations, 3, 21–2, 29, 239–44, 287–8
Ammar Foundation, 256
Amnesty International, 356
anger, 33, 34, 36, 52, 53, 58, 85, 184, 296
Annan, Kofi, 234, 236–7, 338
Annan plan, 245, 261
 see also Kofi Annan plan, 173
Annapolis peace conference, xvii, 240
Ansar al-Islam, 109, 193
Ansar Battalions, 193
Antalya conference, 207
anti-colonial struggle, 4–5
anti-imperialism, 125, 166
al-Aoudat, Hussein, 204, 207n14
Aoun, Michel, 239
Aqrab massacre, 175
Arab Action Plan, 235, 245
Arab Centre for Research and Policy Studies, 209, 226
Arab identity, 1
Arab Israeli conflict, 226
Arab League, 93–4, 100, 122, 218, 218–9, 244, 268, 313
 Council of Foreign Ministers, 217, 275–6, 277

first initiative, 211, 337
monitoring mission, 269
peace plan, 233–6
sanctions, 288, 290, 290–1
Saudi Arabia and, 268–9
second initiative, 337
Syrian membership suspended, 275–6
Arab Liberation Party, 145
Arab nationalism, 166
Arab Opinion Index survey, 226
Arab revolution, 4
Arab Socialist, 145
Arab Spring, the, xii, 1–3, 15, 26–7, 35, 40, 111–3, 117, 259–60, 263, 271, 273–4, 278, 295
Arabness, xvii–xviii
el-Araby, Nabil, 233–4
armed groups, opposition, 314–8
  aims, 318
  alliances, 317–8
  equipment, 315–6
  funding, 317–8, 318–9, 322
  integration attempts, 318–24
  local character, 316–7
  military aid, 316
  numbers, 325–6
  organization, 316
  tactics, 317
  weapons, 315–6, 317
  see also individual groups
armed revolt, 13, 95–113, 297, 303–4
  airstrikes, 105
  Battle for Aleppo, 93, 95, 104–7
  Battle for Deir ez-Zor, 113
  Battle for the Damascus periphery, 107–11
  Battle of the Border Crossings, 112
  Jisr ash-Shughur security headquarters attack, 95, 98–9
  militarization, 97–8, 104, 224
  spontaneity, 96
army, xii, xviii, 295, 350
  army defections, 98, 99, 101–4, 194, 350
  Bashar al-Assad's relationship with, 157–9
  command structure, 129
  competing blocs, 145–8
  discrimination, 149–50
  doctrinaire, 148–9

first operations, 85
French mandate, 143, 143–4
manpower, 133–4
rebuilding, 149–51
recruitment policies, 151
sectarianization, 140–53
strength, 152
Army of Islam, 317, 321–2
al-Aroor, Adnan, 168–9, 319
Artillery School massacre, Homs, 151
Artuz al-Balad massacre, 179n29
al-Asaad, Riad, 99, 102
Asharq al-Awsat, 19–20
Asi, Lamya, 373n22
al-Assad, Asma, 242n16
al-Assad, Bashar, xvii, 340, 349
  accession to presidency, 201, 305
  Aleppo policy, 90–1
  alternative political initiative suggestion, 341
  ambiguous messages, 129–30
  arguments against reform, 18–9
  in army command structure, 129
  army purge, 158
  ascent to power, 15–6
  attitude, 20
  concerns, 10–1
  conciliatory tone, 117
  consolidation of power, 23–7
  conspiracy narrative, 52
  the Damascus Spring, 17–8
  delegations to, 125
  Eid al-Adha prayers, 2011, 111
  extreme approach, 128
  first speech, 202
  foreign policy, 29
  geostrategic calculations, 238
  good president myth, 130
  inaugural speech, 16
  inherited status, 152
  intent, 19–20
  Israeli position, 278–9, 282
  language, 129
  Legislative Proclamation No. 3, 353
  legitimacy, 23–4, 25, 95–6, 203, 268, 334, 335
  lifestyle, 166
  loss of legitimacy, 268
  mandate renewed, 2007, 29
  narrative, 115–21

orders, 120
paternalistic discourse, 19–20
policy of brute force, 115
popularity, 117
populist discourse, 11
position on human losses, 370–1
prisoner of security strategy, 130
reformist rhetoric, xv–xvi, 16–7
refusal to respond to the demands, 376
rejection of reform, 10, 158–9
relationship with the army, 157–9
rhetoric of confrontation, 26–7
rule, 15–37
sanctions, 288, 289
Saudi Arabia and, 263–5
sectarian argument, 167–8
security solution, 127–8
social base, 157–9
speech, 3 June 2012, 117
speech, 10 January 2012, 116
speech, 16 April 2011, 52–4, 117
speech, 30 March 2011, 26–7, 115, 115–6
stability assurance, 35
strategy, 115–38
Turkish position, 254
ultimate decision-maker, 49
Umayyad Mosque appearance, 118
visits UAE, 346
Western values, 242n16
al-Assad, Bassil, 16n1, 150
al-Assad, Hafez, xvii, xviiin20, 11, 16, 18, 62, 90–1, 123, 147, 149, 150–1, 152, 155–6, 166, 200, 201, 263–4, 305, 349
al-Assad, Jamil, 136n64
al-Assad, Maher, 158, 243n17, 288, 289
al-Assad, Rifaat, 150–1, 152, 305
Astana Process, 333, 343
Atasi Forum, 204
Atassi, Suhair, 55–6
Atatürk, Mustafa Kemal, 144
al-Atrash, Sultan, 142n6
atrocities, 85, 88–9, 105, 173
authoritarianism, 18, 47–8, 162, 163, 305
Autonomous Administration of North and East Syria, 356, 357
Azadi Friday protests, 72–3, 77–8, 83

Baba Amr, Battle for, 131–2
Babacan, Ali, 290
al-Baghdadi, Abu Bakr, 192
Bahrain, 117, 273–4, 308
  Peninsula Shield intervention, 266–7
Baker-Hamilton Commission, 240
Balkan wars, 329
Bandar bin Sultan bin Abdulaziz Al Saud, 267, 270
Banyas, 50, 170–1
Baqqara clan, 75
Barada, 228
Barak, Ehud, 279–80, 281–2
Barakat, Ghiyath, 34
barrel bombs, xx, 316, 346
Basateen al-Waʿr, massacre, 180
al-Bashir, Nawaf, 75, 77
al-Bashir, Raghib, 75n19
Baʿth Party, 17, 349
  competing blocs, 145–8
  conference, 2005, 21
  foundation, 144
  leadership, 155
  militarization, 142–3
  military domination, 155
  monopoly on power, 222
  power, 350–1
  role, 199
  ruralization, 154–9
  sectarianism and sectarian violence, 142–3
  Sixth National Conference, 148
al-Bayanuni, Ali Sadr al-Din, 125
BBC (Arabic), 225, 227, 228
Beida, massacre, 171, 179–80
Beirut-Damascus Declaration, 205–6
Bekheitan, Mohammed Saeed, 132
Ben Ali, Zine el-Abidine, xii, 1, 10, 27, 35
Benghazi model, 327
Biden, Joe, 344
bin Baz, Abdulaziz, 321
birth rate, 370
Bitar, Salah al-Din, 149
Blair, Tony, 334
Border Crossings, Battle of the, 112
Bouazizi, Mohamed, 37
Brahimi, Lakhdar, 234, 237, 338
Brezhnevian period, xviii
Brigades and Battalions for the Purification of Syria, 109

Brothers in Alms, 320
Brussels, 208
brutality, 8, 99, 126, 274
Bush, George W., 23, 29, 334
business class, 164–6
Bustan Elbasha Association, 136
al-Buti, Muhammad Said Ramadan, 34, 53n38, 87

Caesar Act, xx, 352
Cairo conference, 215
Cairo Platform, 315, 343
Cameron, David, 336n76
Camp David Agreement, 257
capital losses, 371
capitalist class, 24
caricatures, 81
casualties, 120, 303, 369–71
    Alawis, 307
    Beida and Ras al-Naba', 180
    civilian, 187
    Clocktower Square protest, Homs, 57–8, 60
    Damascus periphery massacres, 179n29
    Daraa uprising, 45
    Deir ez-Zor, 76, 78
    Friday of Martyrs, 64
    Friday of Resilience, 50–2
    Good Friday, 2011, 66
    Hama massacre, 69–70, 72n9
    Houla massacre, 88–9
    Jdidet al-Fadl massacre, 179
    Jisr ash-Shughur, 82, 83–4
    Jisr ash-Shughur security headquarters attack, 98
    Karm az-Zaytoun massacre, 176–7
    Kherbet Elsawda massacre, 180
    official explanation, 52
    Qubayr/Maarzaf massacre, 178
    regime position, 370–1
    Rifai massacre, 177
    Shammas massacres, 178
    Thiyabiyeh massacre, 178
    Treismeh massacre, 178
Chamooun, Camille, 175
change, aspirations for, 2
chants, 63, 64, 81, 86
chemical weapons, 279, 285, 299, 331, 336–7, 338

Chevalier, Éric, 214
children, 40, 40n3, 41n8, 41n9, 41–2, 72, 88, 172, 173, 176, 177, 178, 179n29, 180, 336, 370
China, 100–1, 133, 236, 237, 246n25, 269, 346
Christians, 55n40, 59n59, 63, 90, 103n19, 140–1, 144, 146, 149, 151, 153, 165, 170, 175, 231n24, 307, 366
CIA, 316, 325, 327
citizenship, xviii, 5, 12
civic organizations, 12
civil revolution, xiv–xv
civil society, 171, 183, 203
civil society initiatives, xiv, 37
civil war, 324–9, 341
    Russian intervention, 325, 329–33
clerics, 87–8, 184, 307, 362
Clinton, Hillary, 243, 244, 308, 337, 339–40
Clocktower Square protest, Homs, 39, 50, 54–62
    begins, 58–9
    buildup, 57–9
    casualties, 57–8, 60
    causes, 54–6
    end of, 59–62
    Friday of Martyrs, 57–8
    leadership committee, 59n57
    National Unity Tent, 59n59
    outbreak, 56–7
    security force response, 57
    as turning point, 60–1
    violence, 60
Cold War, 16, 245, 249, 287–8
collective punishment, 69, 71
colonialism, 203
communal networks, 7–8
communications blackouts, 229
competitive monopolies, 165
concessions, 54
conspiracy narrative, 51–2, 115–7, 122, 124, 125, 137, 204, 244, 306, 308–9, 338
constitution, 54, 350
    Article 8, 17, 199
    Article 83, 201
    violation of, 16
Constitutional Committee, 343, 344, 376
consultation, as weakness, 18
containment strategy, 119–20, 296

coordination committees, 12, 43
    Local Coordination Committees, 224
    Syrian Revolution Coordinators Union, 224
coordination groups, 221-2
    General Commission of the Syrian Revolution, 224-5
    Local Coordination Committees, 222-3
    Syrian Revolution Coordinators Union, 223-4
Corrective Movement, 75, 155-6
corruption, xv, xxi, xivn3, 2, 7, 20, 23-4, 25, 128, 134-5, 155, 162-3, 195, 201, 352-3
Council of Arab Foreign Ministers, 235
counterespionage, 116
crime and criminal violence, 181, 182, 195-8, *196*
crimes against humanity, 346
Crisis Cell, 132
crony capitalism, 6-7, 24
cultural commonalities, 5
cultural identity, xvii-xviii
currency, 353, 375
current history, 13

Dalila, Arif, 200
Damascene Bloc, 145-6
Damascus, 46, 72, 85, 122, 228, 274
    airport siege, 109
    armed revolt, 97
    Battle for, 89, 108
    bombing, 18 July 2012, xix
    bringing the revolution to, 64-6
    crime, 198
    Good Friday protests, 39, 50, 62
    Hamidiyeh Market protest, 85-6
    Hariqa Market incident, 36-7
    Israeli airstrikes, 283
    jihadi violence, 183
    market strike, 89
    military operations, 88
    minibus drivers strike, 2010, 33
    National Security Bureau bombing, 132-3
    population, 154-6
    Powell visit, 239
    precursors to revolution, 31-3
    revolutionary movement, 85-9
    Rifai Mosque, 87
    riots, 1860, 140-1
    rural population, 154-5
    Samiramis Hotel meeting, 208
    satellite towns, 50, 62-3
    security situation, 87
    Sham Higher Institute for Religious Studies, 53n37
    Umayyad Mosque, 118
    Zaid Mosque, 87-8
Damascus Declaration, the 20-3, 204-6, 210, 211
    National Council of 205-6
Damascus periphery
    Battle for, 107-11
    massacres, 179n29
    satellite television coverage, 229
Damascus Spring, the, 17-8, 21, 81, 199, 199-204, 208
Damascus University Liberal Arts Faculty, sit in, 34
Damour massacre, 175
Daraa and the Daraa uprising, 1, 2, 12, 26-7, 39-48, 53, 54, 66, 206
    aims, 43
    armed revolt, 97
    army sent in, 128
    casualties, 45
    demands, 44
    detainees, 39-40
    funeral procession, 42
    general strike, 44
    al-Ikhtiyar addresses, 43-4
    Mekdad delegation, 43
    military operation, 85
    organizing committees, 44
    regime response, 42-4, 44-6
    satellite television coverage, 227-8, 231
    spreads, 46-8, 49-50
    torture, 41
    triggers, 40-1
    Umari Mosque attack, 44-6, 228
    Umari Mosque sit-in, 59, 70
Darayya, 107, 110
Darayya massacre, 179n29
Davutoglu, Ahmet, 250, 255-6
de Mistura, Staffan, 338, 374
Decree 49, 40n5
de-escalation agreements, 332
de-escalation zones, 343

Defence Battalions, 151
Deir ez-Zor, 50, 72, 74–8, 111, 112, 189, 192, 275, 304, 354, 358
    Battle for, 113
    first death, 76
    military bombardment of, 129–30
    military operation launched, 78
    protester numbers, 78
    protests, 75–8
    shabbiha, 136
    socioeconomic grievances, 74–5
democracy, xvi, xvii
democratic transition, 54, 234, 345
Democratic Union Party, xivn3, 136, 210, 312, 326, 356, 360
democratization, 19
demographic engineering, 349
Dempsey, Martin, 316n24
despotism, 2, 162
destabilization, fear of, 15–6
detainees, xx
development strategy, 351–2
Devlin, John, 143
dictatorships, longevity of, 4
diesel smuggling, 56
discrimination, 149–50
displacement crisis, 369
diversity
    politicization of, 5
    social, 139
doctrinaire army, 148–9
documentation efforts, xx
Doha Agreement, 211, 258–9, 265, 275
Doha Meeting, 209–12, 273
Dream of Homs project, 32–3, 55
drought, xvn4, 157
drug trade, 354, 363
Duba, Ali, 6n7, 152
Duma, 62, 63, 64, 317
    Battle for, 107–9, 110
Duma Martyrs Battalion, 108
Dummar Cultural Forum, 200
Dunya TV, 275

economic crime, campaign against, 56
economic crisis, 354
economic elite, 24
economic growth, 369–70, **372**
economic liberalization, 20, 29–31, 158–9, 163–4, 201, 292, 305, 307–8

economic losses, 369–71, **372**, 373–5
economic marginalization, 40
economic networks, 164
economic policies, 29–33
economic transformation, 24–5
Economist, 332
Economy and Transport, 164–5
education, 10, 157, 293, 298, 307, 362, 370
Egypt, xvi, 1, 2, 11, 15, 26, 28, 35, 47, 95, 103, 117, 135, 145, 164, 206, 224, 243, 245, 259, 273, 307, 331
elections, 200–1, 234, 345
emigre opposition, 3, 253, 313, 314, 343
endless conflict, 345
Erdoğan, Recep Tayyip, 247, 252n41, 254
Eshel, Amir, 279n107
European Union, 218, 249–50, 337, 342
    sanctions, 288, 289–90
evil, manifestations of, 174–6
evil advisors myth, 243n17
exchange rates, 353
executions, 186

fabrications, regime strategy, 122–3
Facebook, 35, 37, 78, 118, 225
Fahd bin Abdulaziz Al Saud, 264
Faisal bin Sultan Al Saud, 269
Fares, Nawaf, 75, 75n20
Farkash, Aharon Zeevi, 278
al-Farouq Battalions, 317, 322
Farouq Battalions, 194
Fateh Brigade, 105, 322
al-Fawzan, Saleh, 321
fear, 49
Fighting Vanguard organization, 151
Financial Times, 340
fitna, 115
Five-Year Plan, 2011–15, 118
food prices, 30
Ford, Robert, 214, 242
foreign debt, 371
foreign intervention, 22–3, 187, 212, 303
foreign investment, 373–5
foreign policy, 3, 29, 31
foreign pressure, popular pressure identification with, 115–7
Founding Document of the Civil Society Revival Committees, 202–3

Fragile States Index, 371
fragmentation, 310–1
France, 218
France 24, 228
Free Officers' Brigade, 82, 99
Free Syrian Army, xivn3, 88, 186, 216, 303, 317, 318, 318–9, 319, 321, 323
  Battle for Aleppo, 104–7
  command structure, 101–2, 255
  disunity, 101–4
  formation, 99–100
  high command, 101
  jihadi groups, 195
  Joint Staff, 102
  organization, 101, 316
freedom, xiv, 4, 312
freeze zone strategy, 342–3
French mandate, 141–3, 143–4
Friday of Defiance, 77
Friday of Determination, 50, 54, 58, 64–5, 70, 80, 82, 87, 126
Friday of Dignity, 42, 42–3, 56, 91
Friday of Honour, 56, 57, 63, 75, 87, 227, 231
Friday of Martyrs, 57–8, 63–4, 75, 81, 82
Friday of Opposition Unity, 212
Friday of Rage, 81, 82
Friday of Resilience, 50–2, 70, 75, 82, 91
Friday of the Children of Freedom, 73, 83
Friday of the Clans, 78
Friday of the Sons of Khalid bin al-Waleed, 78
Friends of Syria Conference, 214, 255, 260–1, 269
Friends of the Syrian People, 337
fuel subsidies, abolition of, 33–4
Furqan Brigade, 108

Gaza war, 2008–9, 121
Gemayel, Bachir, 174, 175, 176
General Commission of the Syrian Revolution, 36, 177, 224–5
General Consultative Council, 365
General Intelligence Apparatus, 6n7
Geneva 1 Conference, 339–40, 343
Geneva 2 Conference, 323, 341–2
Geneva Accords, 217–8, 218
Geneva communique, 261–2, 340, 341
geopolitical interests, 219–20

geostrategic calculations, 237–85, 298–300
  Iran, 238, 256–63
  Iraq, 299
  Israel, 277–85
  Qatar, 270–7
  Russia, 244–8, 298–9
  Saudi Arabia, 263–70
  Turkey, 238, 248–56, 299
  United States of America, 237, 239–44
Get Out Friday, 73–4
Ghalioun, Burhan, 213, 215, 312
Ghazal, Mohammad Eyad, 33, 55
al-Ghazali, Rustum, 43
Ghouta, chemical weapon attack, 336–7
Gilad, Amos, 278
global conspiracy, 122
Golan Heights, Israeli occupation, 107
Golan, Yair, 279n107
Good Friday, 62–7, 70–2, 76–7, 80–1, 82, 128
Good Friday protests, Damascus, 39, 50
graffiti, 37, 39
Great Arab Revolt, 141
Great Syrian Revolt (1920–5), 63
Greater Syria, xxi
Gross Domestic Production, 30, 31, 352, 371, **372**
gun ownership, 56, 61–2, 97

Habib, Ali, 96, 128
al-Habib al-Mustafa Brigade, 109
al-Hafiz, Amin, 147
Halevy, Efraim, 279
Hama, 117
  al-Assi Square, 70–2
  Azadi Friday protests, 72–3
  collective memory, 71
  defiance, 74
  Friday of Determination, 70
  Friday of Resilience, 70
  Friday of the Children of Freedom, 73
  Get Out Friday protest, 73–4
  Good Friday, 70–2
  population, 69
  protests, 69–74
  satellite television coverage, 229–30
  Umran Dweik beating, 72–3
Hama massacre, xii–xiii, 16, 17, 28, 69–70, 71n6, 71n7, 72n9, 105, 267, 275
Hama-Latakia road, 196

Hamad bin Khalifa Al Thani, 271
Hamas, 22, 206–7, 239, 272
Hamadi, Nazem, 322
Hamidiyeh Market protest, Damascus, 85–6
Hammouriyah massacre, 179n29
Handicap International, 369
al-Haraki, Nizar, 43
Harasta, 62, 107–8, 110
Hariqa Market incident, 36–7
al-Hariri, Nasr, 52
al-Hariri, Rafiq, 264
    assassination of, xvi, 1, 18–9, 23, 25, 29, 204, 239, 309
al-Hariri, Saad, 258–9, 266, 267, 268
Hassan, Jamil, 130
Hatoum, Salim, 148, **155**
Hawi, William, 175
al-Hawrani, Akram, 144
Hay'at Tahrir al-Sham, 309, 364–8
Hezbollah, 22, 51, 239, 259, 264–5, 268, 272, 273, 278, 279, 282, 283, 284, 285, 299, 327, 334
Higher State Security Court, abolition, 53n37
Hijab, Riad, 119, 129, 129–30, 170n6, 217–8, 343
al-Hinnawi, Sami, 144
historiographical war, xiv
Hitto, Ghassan, 217, 218
Hmadeh, Wael, 110n39, 322
Hobeika, Elie, 176
Homs, 32–3, 53, 105, 107
    armed revolt, 97
    Artillery School massacre, 151
    Clocktower Square protest, 39, 50, 54–62
    de-escalation zone, 343
    Friday of Determination, 58
    Friday of Martyrs, 57–8
    Good Friday, 2011, 66
    immigration, 54–5
    military operation, 85
    regime strategy, 131
    sectarian polarization, 61–2
    sectarian violence, 171, 172
    shabbiha, 137
    willingness to protest, 54–5
al-Homsi, Maamun, 168
Homs–Tripoli Road development, 55n42

al-Hoss, Salim, 131
Houla massacre, 88–9, 173, 282
household income, 370
HTS-controlled areas, 364–8, **365**, 367
human cost, 369–71
Human Development Index, 370
humanitarian aid, 101, 328n53, 353, 374, 375
humanitarian crisis, 30–1
Hussein, Saddam, 28–9, 105, 159, 257

identitarian diversity, 5
identity
    diversity management, 5
    local, 222
    national, 12–3
    shared, 4
    subnational, 5
ideology, xviii, xix, 12, 181, 182, 184, 267, 295, 300, 301
Idleb, 78, 110, 304, 348, 367
    central square protests, 84
    de-escalation zone, 343
    popular committees, 79
    protester numbers, 80–1
    protests, 79–84
    socioeconomic grievances, 79
al-Ikhtiyar, Hisham, 43
immiseration, xv, 346, 354
imperialist conspiracies, 18–9
imports, 31, 352, 363, 366
Independent Islamic Current, 209, 211, 213
infiltrators, 52
informers, 153
Institute of Economics and Peace, 371
institutes for the memorization of the Qur'an, 184–5
institution-building, 10
Interior Ministry, 52
Interior Ministry sit-in, 86, 121–2
Interior Security Directorate, 196
internal occupation, 22
Internal Security Branch, 6n7
internally displaced persons, 349, 369, 370, 374
international brigades, 189
International Crisis Group, 49n25
international isolation, end of, 25
internet, the, xiv, 308

internment camps, 356
intolerance, xivn3
investment, 24, 31
Iran, 253, 264–5, 269, 281, 282, 285, 301, 315, 339, 341–2, 342, 349, 374
  Arab Spring position, 259–60, 263
  financial support, 353
  foreign policy, 257
  and Geneva communique, 261–2
  geostrategic calculations, 238, 256–63
  hostility to US policy, 257, 258
  and Israel, 257, 263
  militiamen, xxi, 237
  national interest, 262
  relations with Turkey, 260–1
  and Saudi Arabia, 261
  Syrian revolution position, 260–1
Iran-Iraq War, 257
Iraq, xvi, 1, 2, 22n23, 23, 79–80, 159, 190, 238, 248, 329, 357
  geostrategic calculations, 299
  instability, 29
  occupation of, 334
  US occupation, 240–1, 251, 258
  US project, 29
Iraq war, 28, 76, 185, 250–1, 264
Islam Battalion, 317
Islam Brigade, 108, 317
Islamic Front, 322–3, 326
Islamic State of Iraq and al-Sham, xix, xivn3, 175, 181n1, 192, 194, 309, 311, 317, 322–3, 325, 326, 327, 331–2, 336, 337, 355–6, 357, 373
Islamism, 140
Islamist discourse, exclusionary character of, 323
Islamist terrorists, 120
Islamist uprising (1976-1982), 27–8
Islamization, 319
Israel, xvii, 25, 121, 122, 123, 125, 226, 239, 240, 273, 300, 305, 334–5
  factors influencing, 283–5
  geostrategic calculations, 277–85
  ideal scenario, 281
  and Iran, 257, 263
  military intervention, 282–3
  policy of ambiguity, 278–81
  pragmatism, 277
  US, EU policy alignment, 281–2
al-Issawi, Rafi, 260n61

Istanbul, 212, 214
Istanbul conference, 207
Istanbul Group, 210, 211

al-Jaafari, Bashar, 121n21
Jacquier, Gilles, 231
Jadaan, Manal, 76n24
Jadid, Ghassan, 145
Jadid, Salah, 80, 90, 147, 148-51, 148n13, **155**
Jamal al-Atasi Forum for Democratic Dialogue, 202n3, 203–4
Jazra, Hassan, 106n23
Jdidet al-Fadl, massacre, 179
Jews, 140, 141, 168n3
Jibril, Ahmed, 136
Jihadi Islamic State in Iraq, 326
jihadi violence, 181, 183–95
  first indicators, 183
  groups established after militarization, 194–5
  Nusra Front, 185–6, 187–92
  Salafi, 184, 185, 187–94
al-Jililati, Mohammad, 290
Jisr ash-Shughur, xix, 79, 82–4, 85, 230–1, 243
Jisr ash-Shughur security headquarters attack, 95, 98–9, 125
Joint Operations Centre, 314n22, 333
Jordan, 102–3
al-Julani, Abu Muhammad, 188, 190
al-Jundi, Abd al-Karim, 148-9
Justice and Development Party (AKP), 248–56

Kafr Batna, 107
Kafr Nobol, 81
Kalthum, Faysal, 40, 41n9
Karm az-Zaytoun, massacre, 172, 176–7
Katsav, Moshe, 240
Kerry, John, 240
Khaddam, Abd al-Halim, 201, 205
Khalidiyeh, Freedom Square, 60
al-Khalil, Mohammad Samer, 353
Khalil, Samira, 110n39, 322
Khamenei, Ali, 259, 259n60
Khan Shaykhun, 79, 81
al-Kharrat, Hasan, 63
al-Khatib, Ahmad Mouaz, 88, 215, 217–18
al-Khatib, Hamza, tortured to death, 73

Khayrbek, Muhammad Nasif, 6n7
Kherbet Elsawda, massacre, 180
kidnappings, 173, 197, 322, 367
Kilo, Michael, 205–6
Kissinger, Henry, 287
kleptocracy, 162
Kochavi, Aviv, 280
Kofi Annan plan, 173
    see also Annan plan, 245, 261
Kurdish Democratic Alliance, 206n13
Kurdish Democratic Party, 199
Kurdish Future Trend, 28
Kurdish National Council, 213
Kurdish uprising, 2004, 28–9
Kurdistan Workers' Party (PKK), 251, 254, 312, 357, 358
Kurds, xviii, 28, 54, 182, 206n13, 210, 214, 254, 309, 337, 357n118, 360–1
Kuwait, 270

Lahoud, Émile, 264, 265
Latakia
    massacre, 170
    protests, 49–50
    satellite television coverage, 228
Lavrov, Sergei, 256, 338, 339–40
Law 49, 21, 54, 199
Lebanese Civil War, 137, 174–6
Lebanon, xvi, 2, 31, 153, 205, 226, 239–40, 240, 248, 258, 264–6, 268, 271, 273, 280, 305, 329, 334–5
Lebanon war, 2006, 23, 25
Legal Committee, 106n23
Legislative Decree 49/2008, 31–2
Legislative Proclamation No. 3, 353
legitimacy crisis, 95–6
Libya, 2, 3, 37, 95, 117, 135, 209, 219, 229, 238, 251–2, 259, 273, 330, 334
Libyan embassy sit-in, 37
Lieberman, Avigdor, 280, 281–2
living conditions, 172
Local Coordination Committees, 222–3, 224
local identity, 222
looting, 352
al-Luhaidan, Saleh, 321

Maarouf, Jamal, 320
Ma'arrat An-Nu'man, 69, 80–1
macroeconomics, sanction impacts, 291–4

Madamiyet Elsham massacre, 179n29
Makhlouf, Rami, 136
al-Maliki, Nouri, 238, 240, 258, 260
Mamluk, Ali, 132, 133
manufacturing sector, 292–3
marginalization, 47
Marshall Foundation, 254
Masalma, Samira, 52
al-Masharqa, Zuhayr, 150n15
Maskanah, 198
mass mobilizations, 67
massacres, 174–6, 300, 338
    Damascus periphery, 179n29
    sectarian, 169–71, 176–80
    see also individual events
al-Mayadin, 77
Mazra'a Mosque suicide bombing, 34
media
    activism, 212
    Arab, 99
    attitude to violence, 182
    critical role, 230–1
    foreign, 122
    paternalistic discourse, 11
    pro-revolution, 89
    regime strategy, 121–5
    revolutionary, 98–9
    sanctions, 290
    satellite television, 225–31
    sectarianism and sectarian violence, 168–9
    shabbiha, 138
    Turkish, 254–5
media projects, xiv
Mediterranean Summit, 238
Medvedev, Dmitry, 236n7
Mehlis, Detlev, 239, 240
Mekdad, Faisal, 43
Meshaal, Khaled, 207n14, 253n43
migration, 55n40, 107, 153, 157
Mikati, Najib, 268
militarization, xiv, 97–8, 104, 140–53, 224
Military Committee, 154, *155*
military councils, 102
Military Intelligence Apparatus, 6n7
Military Operations Command, 314n22, 324, 333
military spending, 371
military strategy, 28n32
minibus drivers strike, 2010, 33

Ministry of Social Affairs, 204
Mirza, Wael, 209n21, 210
modernization, 201
moral position, xiii
Moscow Platform, 315, 343
mosques, 64, 71, 77, 87, 91, 169, 208
Mousavi, Mir-Hossein, 260n62
al-Muallim, Walid, 235
Mubarak, Hosni, xii, 1, 10, 27, 35
murders, 173
al-Murshid, Sulayman, xiin1
Musa, Badr Abu, 58, 97
Muslim Brotherhood, 21, 28, 63, 71, 79, 90–1, 117, 125, 142, 199, 204, 205, 206, 207, 209n22, 210, 211, 213, 214, 217, 253, 255, 305, 307, 314, 331
al-Mustapha Brigade, 193

An-Nahar, 22
Nahar, Hazem, 118, 204, 207n15, 210
Nahhas, Ubaidah, 210, 214n31
Najib, Atif, 40, 41, 51n31
Nasrallah, Hassan, 51
Nasser, Gamal Abdel, 145, 148n13
National Action Group, 209
National Coalition for Syrian Revolutionary and Opposition Forces, 215–6, 219–20, 312, 361
National Coalition to Support the Syrian Revolution, 208
National Command Council, 146–7
National Coordination Body for Democratic Change, 207, 210, 211, 213, 234
National Defence Army, 133–4, 135, 137
National Defence Committees, 351
National Democratic Rally, 17, 199, 205
National Democratic Renaissance Party, 23
National Dialogue Conference, 127, 128
National Dialogue Forum, 203–4
national identity, 12–3, 142, 171
National Initiative Commission, 215–6
national liberation discourse, 4–5
National Progressive Front, 199
national salvation conference, 208
National Salvation Government, 365–6
National Security Bureau, bombing, 132–3

national unity government, 234
National Unity Tent, Clocktower Square protest, Homs, 59n59
nationalization, 90, 154–5, 165
NATO, 227, 238, 246, 247, 248, 249, 252, 259, 330, 334
al-Nayef, Saad Abdelsalam, 107
neoliberalism, 10, 18, 25, 162
neo-Ottomanism, 256
Netanyahu, Benjamin, 278, 281–2, 282–3
new bourgeoisie, 155
new colonialism, 203
New York Times, 243
niqab ban, 34, 53, 88
Nixon, Richard, 287
no-go zones, 196
normalization, 345–6
Nusra Front, xix, 81, 106, 121, 125, 185–6, 187–92, 194, 309, 311, 317, 320, 323, 324, 327, 330, 331
  al-Qaeda affiliation, 192
  blacklisting, 190
  expansion, 188–9
  fighters, 190–1
  fighters by nationality, *191*
  flexibility strategy, 188–9
  founding statement, 190
  functional role, 190
  ideological vision, 188–90
  organization, 188
  splits, 192
  strength, 191
  suicide bombings, 188
  support, 189
  targets, 190

Obama, Barack, 3, 23, 233, 240, 242–3, 244, 282, 289, 308, 323, 336–7, 342
Öcalan, Abdullah, xvii
October (Yom Kippur) War, 149
Office for the Coordination of Humanitarian Affairs, 30, 368, 370
oil, 159, 162, 336, **356**, 357, 358, 373
  revenues, 331
  sanctions, 289, 290, 291, 292
  sectoral damage, 292
Olmert, Ehud, 240
Operation Peace Spring, 359–60

opposition, 199–220, 300
  ad-hoc initiatives and conferences, 206–9
  armed groups, 314–8
  attitude to violence, 182
  competition, 212
  conspiracy narrative, 309
  containment, 201–2
  Damascus Declaration, 20–3, 204–6
  Damascus Spring, 199–204
  demands, 202–3, 207
  dependence on foreign powers, 218
  Doha Meeting, 209–12
  domestic, 207, 208–9
  emigre, 3, 253, 313, 314, 343
  in exile, 207, 207–8
  foreign sponsorship, 313–5
  fragmentation, 218
  hopes, 204
  Islamist, 208
  Israeli position, 280–1
  key tasks, 219–20
  lack of unity, 311
  leadership, 207, 212, 311–2, 314–5
  media activism, 212
  National Coalition for Syrian Revolutionary and Opposition Forces foundation, 215–6
  parties, 199
  political, 311–2, 312, 312–8
  political forums, 200–4
  pre-revolution activism, 199–206
  provisional government, 216–20
  rejection of Geneva communique, 340
  during the revolution, 206–20
  satellite television channels, 228
  Syrian National Council foundation, 209, 211–2, 212–5
  Transitional National Council, 208–9
  Turkish position, 255–6
  weakness, 21
Orient TV, 228, 229
Ottoman Empire, 140–1
Özal, Turgut, 250

Palestine, 117, 166, 226, 258, 264–5, 277
Palestinian Liberation Organization, 117, 257, 277, 305
Palestinian refugees, 50
pan-Arabism, 143
pan-Arabist rhetoric, 306
Panetta, Leon, 316n24
pardon decree, 7 March, 119
paternalistic discourse, 11, 19–20
patronage, 4
peasants' and workers' union, 24
Pedersen, Geir, 338, 338–9
Peninsula Shield intervention, Bahrain, 266–7
People's Assembly, 201
Peres, Shimon, 281–2
permanent crisis, 329
Petraeus, David, 244
police force, 196, 356, 361
political actors, responsibility, 302
political detainees, 202
political forums, 200–4
political future, Local Coordination Committees vision, 223
political initiatives, failure, 298
political life, 28
political participation, xvii, 47
political parties, regulation, 127
political prisoners, 17, 86, 234
Political Security Apparatus, 6n7
political solution, distant, 300
political solutions, proposed, 233–7
political violence, 181–2
political-security complex, 120
Pope John Paul II in Rome, 240
popular committees, 12, 70, 135
Popular Front for the Liberation of Palestine, 136
popular movement, leadership, 12
popular pressure, identification with foreign pressure, 115–7
popular uprising, 48–54
populist discourse, 11
populist rhetoric, regime, 305–7
poverty, xx, 30, 46–7, 292, 363, 368, 375
Powell, Colin, 204n9, 239
power-sharing arrangements, 345
pre-revolution activism, opposition, 199–206
presidential elections, 2007, xvi
prisoners of conscience, 222
private sector, 165
proletarianization, 33

propaganda, 122–3
property rights, 31–2
pro-regime demonstrations, 73n15, 75
protection money, 166
protest suppression, brutality, 8
Provisional Government, 361, 362
provisional government, 216–20
  chair, 217, 217–8
  nature of, 217–8
  obstacles, 218–9
public debate, 17
public opinion, 267, 301, 313
public sphere
  closure, 312
  lack of, xii
purchasing power, 375
Putin, Vladimir, 236n7, 246–7

Qaboun, 107
Qaddafi, Muammar, 37
al-Qaeda, 96, 106, 125, 173, 188, 189, 190, 192, 317
Qandil, 357
al-Qaradawi, Yusuf, 168
Qatar, 102, 112, 216, 220, 227, 252, 308, 309, 314, 374
  flexibility, 271
  foreign policy, 272–3
  geostrategic calculations, 270–7
  leading role, 277
  political vision, 270–1
  population, 270
  post-revolution stance, 273–7
  Syrian position, 271
  Syrian-Qatari relations before the revolution, 271–3
  ties to the US, 272
Qatari Diyar Company, 32–3
Qatari-Saudi-Turkish conspiracy, 125
Qubayr/Maarzaf, massacre, 178
Qudsiyyah, Abd al-Fattah, 6n7
Qur'an circles, 184–5

racism, Western, 10–1
radical Islamists, 307
Ramadan, Ahmad, 209n21, 210, 214n31
ar-Raqqa, 103, 111–3, 136, 192, 304, 327, 354, 355–6, 358
ar-Raqqa–Damascus highway, 196
Ras al-Naba' massacre, 179–80

ar-Rastan, 97, 317
Rayyis Forum, 204
al-Rayyis, Suheir, 202n3
referendums, 16n1
reform, xvii, 24, 295, 296
  apparent openness to, 54
  arguments against, 18–9
  economic, 18
  limited, 127–8
  missed opportunities, 15–20
  promises of, 17–8
  regime attitude to, 10, 296–7
  rejection of, xiii, 10, 158–9
Reform Party of Syria, 23
reformist protest movement, 10
reformist revolutions, xvi
reformist rhetoric, xv
refugees, xiv, 107, 243, 248, 256, 313, 345, 369, 374
regime
  Aleppo policy, 90–1
  alienation from populace, 8, 301
  attitude to reform, 10, 296–7
  attitude to violence, 182
  brutality, 8, 99
  budget, 352
  business families close to, 164–5
  civil war policy, 328–9
  conspiracy narrative, 338
  cosmetic reforms, 296
  crimes, 48, 173–6
  crimes against humanity, 346
  cross-sectarian alliance, 305
  development strategy, 351–2
  factions, 125
  fear of reform, 10
  financial support, 353
  foreign positions, 308–9
  Iranian support, 259, 262
  Israeli position, 278–80, 282, 285
  legitimacy, 3, 95–6, 334, 338
  loyalty to, 9–10
  militias, 12, 32n47, 87, 96, 97, 115, 126, 134, 169, 172, 173, 174, 176, 177, 178, 179, 180, 188, 197, 198, 306n10, 325–7, 351, 352
  narrative, 51
  nature of, 159–66
  normalization strategy, 345–6
  populist discourse, 11, 305–7

position on human losses, 370–1
power base, 304–5
regions of control, 348–54, **348**
responsibility, xx–xxi, 375–6
revenue, 159, *160–1*, 162
sanctions, 288–91
self-defence strategy, 29
since 2013, 304–12
social base, 157–9
stability claims, 197
starvation until submission campaign', 328–9
transition to total war, 337
Turkish position, 251–6
value system, 163
West's negative baseline view of, 333–7
regime change, 236, 239, 251, 284, 335
regime strategy, 115–38, 183
    concessions, 120
    containment, 119–20
    diagnosis, 126–35
    differences of opinion, 125
    extreme approach, 128
    eyewitnesses, 122
    fabrications, 122–3
    force, 120
    goal, 125
    Homs, 131
    media, 121–5
    official discourse, 115–21
    precautions against revolution, 117–9
    provocation, 130–1
    revolutionary branding, 120–1
    security solution, 127–8
    shabbiha, 124, 130–1, 135–8
    small protests, 119–20
    social media, 124
    websites, 124
Regional Command Council, 227–8, 53n37
Regional Refugee and Resilience Plan, 374
regions of control, 346–7, **347**, 368
    borders and governance, 348–51, 354–7, **356**, 364–6
    development strategy, 351–2
    economy, 351–4, 358–9, *359*, 362–4, *363*, 366–8, *367*
    employment, *359*, *363*
    governance, 361–2
    HTS-controlled areas, 364–8, **365**, *367*

    incomes, 354, 358–9, *359*, 363, *363*
    legitimacy, 368
    oil fields, **356**, 357, 358
    population, 349, 355, *359*, 361, 366
    regime-controlled areas, 348–54, **348**
    SDF control areas, 354–9, **355**, **356**, *359*
    SNA control areas, 359–64, **360**, *363*
religiosity, xix, 110n37, 157, 171–2, 184, 189, 267
religious courts, 186, 188, 193
repression, 2, 16, 18, 20, 25, 96, 183, 221, 296, 299–300, 312
Republican Guard, 158
revolutionary branding, 120–1
Revolutionary Military Council, 109
Rice, Condoleezza, 3
Rifai massacre, 177
Riyadh Conference, 343
roving protests, 80–1
rumours, 124
Rumsfeld, Donald, 240
rural revolution, 304
ruralization, 154–9
Russia, 100–1, 133, 218, 236, 237, 244, 253, 256, 269, 276, 315, 344, 351, 357, 368
    arms sales, 246, 280
    financial support, 353
    Geneva 2 Conference, 341–2
    geostrategic calculations, 244–8, 298–9
    normalization strategy, 345–6
    primary goal, 338
    relations with Israel, 283
    vision, 345
Russian air force, 325
Russian intervention, xxi, 325, 329–33, 336, 343, 345, 370–1

Sabra massacre, 175–6
Sadr, Mohammad, 260n62
Saeed, Khaled, 41n8
Safar, Adil, 117, 128n45, 228n2
Sakr, Okab, 269
Salafism and Salafis, xix,, 96, 106, 108, 112, 121, 124, 171–2, 308, 317
    jihadi violence, 184, 185, 187–92
As-Salamiyeh, 186–7
Saleh, Ali Abdullah, 227, 235, 268n77
Salehi, Ali Akbar, 260
Samiramis Hotel conference, 127, 208

sanctions, xx, 287–94, 346, 352, 375
   Arab League, 288, 290
   European Union, 288
   Turkey, 288, 290–1
   US, 287–8
Saraqab, 79–80, 81
Sarkozy, Nicolas, 271
satellite television, 225–31
Saud bin Faisal bin Abdulaziz Al Saud, 268, 269
Saudi Arabia, 25–6, 102, 151, 215, 218, 243, 272, 273, 277, 308, 309, 314, 374, 375
   geostrategic calculations, 263–70
   and Iran, 257, 261
   military aid, 269
   Syrian revolution position, 266–70, 319
Saudi Monetary Authority, 266
Sawiris, Naguib, 165
al-Sayyid, Jalal, 75
scholarly Salafism, 317
sectarian grievance, xix
sectarian identity, 142
sectarian majority, the, 169
sectarian retribution, 125
sectarianism and sectarian violence, 9, 10, 13, 61, 139–53, 206, 300–1, 309–12, 329
   argument, 167–8
   Baʿth Party, 142–3
   channels of, 167–72
   competing blocs, 145–8
   core demands, 167
   French mandate, 141–3, 143–4
   loyalties, 169
   massacres, 169–71, 176–80
   media, 168–9
   militarization, 140–53
   Ottoman Empire, 140–1
   polarization, 168
   political consciousness, 169
   and ruralization, 154–9
   Syrian revolution, 167
   unleashed, 167–80
secular nationalist ideology, 139
security dilemma, 77
security establishment, 295, 305
   Alawi officers, xviii
   business involvement, 25
   chiefs, 126
   infiltration of every domain of life, 48–9
   level of control, 7
   loyalty, 9–10
   parallel state, 48–9
   popular uprising dilemma, 48–9
   power, 28, 120, 130
   role, 5–7, 48
   strategy, 49
   ultimate decision-maker, 49
   unaccountable, 36
security solution, 127–8
Seif, Riad, 200, 215
Shaaban, Buthayna, 26n30, 50n30
al-Shaar, Mohammad Nidal, 290
shabbiha, xxi, 97, 124, 130–1, 135–8, 170, 174, 182, 197, 325, 351, 352
Shalish, Dhu al-Himma, 130
Sham Higher Institute for Religious Studies, Damascus, 53n37
al-Shamat, Farouq Abu, 20n16
Shammas massacres, 178
al-Sharaa, Farouq, 128
Shariʿa, 190, 194, 366
Sharon, Ariel, 176
Shatila massacre, 175–6
Shawkat, Asef, 6n7, 243n17
al-Sheikh, Abu Issa, 320
al-Sheikh, Muhammad bin Ibrahim, 321
al-Sheikh, Mustafa, 102
al-Shishakli, Adib, 142, 144, 145
Sieda, Abdulbasit, 209n21, 210, 215n33
El-Sisi, Abdel Fattah, 61n62
Six Day War, 148, 149
Sixth Legislative Convention, 201
Skype, 109
Sleiman, Michel, 265
smuggling networks, 153
smuggling routes, 97
social development, 20
social media, 167, 308
   block lifted, 118
   regime strategy, 124
social mosaic, politicization of, 4–5
social solidarity, 7
solidarity demonstrations, 12, 37
Southern Front, 324
sovereignty, 234
Special Tribunal for Lebanon, 268
starvation, 328–9, 332, 346

state failure, 9
state of emergency, 17, 28, 54
state ownership, 8–9
state revenue, 159, *160–1*, 162
state-building, 5
Statement of the 1,000, 81, 202–3
Statement of the Ninety-nine, 81, 202
step for step approach, 344–5
Strategic Cooperation Agreement, 2010, 31
strategic crops, subsidy cut, 33–4
strategic stalemate, 344
subnational identity, 5
suicide bombings, 186, 186–7, 188
Sulayman, Bahjat, 6n7, 124
Suleimani, Qassim, 134
Sunnis, xix, 9n12, 13, 32, 55n40, 57n49, 61-2, 87, 90, 106, 137, 141, 146, 149, 151, 153, 165, 168–71, 174, 176, 187, 198n29, 268, 278, 306 307–8, 311, 327n50, 331, 349, 350
Support the FSA Friday, 100
Supreme Council of the Islamic Revolution in Iraq, 258
Supreme Military Council, 102
Suqur al-Sham, 320, 322
Suqur al-Sham in Idleb, 193
al-Suri, Abu Abdullah (Hassab Aboud), 194
surveillance, 49
As-Sweida, Political Security office, 41
Syria
    composition, 7–8
    political and geostrategic position, 8
Syrian Arab New Agency, 119
Syrian Central Bank, 289, 371
Syrian Communist Party, 22
Syrian Day of Rage, 35
Syrian Democratic Council, 356
Syrian Democratic Forces, 309, 312, 326
    demands, 20–1
    regions of control, 354–9, **355**, **356**, *359*
Syrian Economics Association, 200
Syrian Electronic Army, 124
Syrian Islamic Front, 112, 194, 322
Syrian Islamic Liberation Front, 195, 320, 322
Syrian National Army, regions of control, 359–64, **360**, *363*
Syrian National Council, 209, 215–6, 218, 223, 312–3, 340, 344
    decision-making, 214
    external factors, 214
    financial backing, 215
    first General Assembly, 276–7
    foreign relations, 214
    foundation, 212–5
    founding statement, 211–2, *212*
    membership, 213
    representation on, 214
    role, 213
    self description, 213
    Turkish position, 255
Syrian Network for Human Rights, 177
Syrian particularity (*Khususiyya*), 19
Syrian revolution, xiii–xxi, xiii–xiv, 295, 300, 301–2
    aims, 54, 183–4
    armed revolt, 95–113
    biggest threat to, 140
    channels of sectarianism, 167–72
    communal level, 311
    constituency, 47
    core activists, 48
    fragmentation, 310–1
    generation of, 16–7
    Iranian position, 260–1
    Islamization, 319
    Israeli position, 281–2
    leadership, 297, 298, 304, 313
    mass mobilizations, 67
    military aid, 269, 316
    motivation, 46–8
    opposition during, 206–20
    popular momentum, 295–6
    popular uprising, 48–54
    precursors, 27–33
    protest in the run-up to, 33–7
    Qatari position, 271, 274–7
    Saudi Arabian position, 266–70, 319
    sectarian rhetoric, 167
    shabbiha, 137–8
    strategy, 298
    transition to civil war, 324–5
    triggers, 1–12
    Turkish position, 251–6
    US reluctance to support the revolution, 241–2
    warlord phenomenon, 297–8

Syrian Revolution Coordinators Union, 36, 223–4, 224
Syrian Revolution Facebook page, 225
Syrian Revolutionaries Front, 193
Syrian Revolutionary Front, 319–24
Syrian Socialist Nationalist Party, 142
Syrian-Turkish relations, 248–56, 292
Syrian-Turkish Strategic Cooperation Council, 291
Syriatel, 289

Tabaqah, 112
Tabaqah airfield, 113
Takfiris, 52, 120–1
Tal al-Zaatar massacre, 175
Talbiseh, 97
at-Tall, 63
Tamim bin Hamad Al Thani, 274
Tawhid Brigade, 103–4, 105, 191, 193, 317, 322
taxation, 353
Tayeb, Mehdi, 256
television, satellite, 225–31
Temu, Mashaal, 28–9
al-Thawra, 121–2
Thiyabiyeh, massacre, 178
time factor, 54
Tishreen, 52
Tishreen University, 170
Tlas, Abdul Razzaq, 194
Tlas, Mustafa, 152
torture, xx, 41, 59, 73, 82, 116, 137, 302
totalitarianism, 11, 123
Transitional National Council, 208–9
Treismeh massacre, 178
tribal factor, 75, 76, 77–8
Trump, Donald, 333, 337
Tunisia, xvi, 2, 11, 15, 26, 28, 35, 46, 47, 95, 103, 117, 164, 206, 245, 259, 273, 295, 307
al-Turk, Riyad, 22
Turkey, 31, 90–1, 101, 102, 112, 121, 220, 237, 243, 247, 277, 308–9, 314, 315, 326, 329, 332, 337, 359–60, 361, 362, 363, 368
 geostrategic calculations, 238, 248–56, 299
 relations with Iran, 260–1
 relations with Syria, 248–56, 292
 sanctions, 288, 290–1

Turkmani, Hasan, 132
Twitter, 35

al-Ujail, Ujail Ahmad, 76
Ukraine, 345, 351
Umari Mosque attack, 44–6, 228
Umari Mosque sit-in, 59, 70
Umma Project, 323
Ummah Party, 320
Umran, Adnan, 203
UN Economic and Social Commission for Western Asia, 371
UN Food and Agriculture Organization, 30
UN special envoys
 Annan, 338, 339–40
 Brahimi, 338, 340–3
 de Mistura, 338, 342–3
 failure, 337–46
 passive neutrality, 338
 Pedersen, 338, 338–9, 343–6
unemployment, 30, 30–1, 363, 368, 375
Union of Soviet Socialist Republics, 145, 150, 155, 239, 287
United Arab Emirate, 215, 346
United Arab Republic, 63, 90
United Kingdom, 218, 237
United Nations Security Council, 88, 100–1, 133, 227, 236, 245, 248, 269, 276, 335–6, 337
 Resolution 1559, 239–40, 264
 Resolution 1644, 240
 Resolution 1973, 251–2
 Resolution 2139, 328n53
 Resolution 2254, 333, 343, 344
United States of America, xv, 100–1, 125, 315, 337, 339–40, 357, 368
 airstrikes, 355
 conspiracy narrative, 204, 244
 Geneva 2 Conference, 341–2
 geostrategic calculations, 237, 239–44
 intervention, 22–3
 Iranian hostility, 257, 258
 Iraq policy, 29, 240–1
 Middle East policy, 22–3, 239, 242
 occupation of Iraq, 240–1, 251, 258, 334
 Qatari ties with, 272
 rapprochement with, 21–2

reluctance support the revolution, 241–2
sanctions, 287–8, 288–9
and the SNC, 214, 215
Syria Accountability Act, 239
Syrian policy, 3, 29, 204n9, 216, 218, 220, 239–44, 287, 329, 333, 334–7
unity rhetoric, 306–7
USAID, 287
US-Kurdish alliance, 326

Velayati, Ali Akbar, 299n1
victimhood, 9
violence, xxi–xxii, 49, 50–1, 306
alternative offered, 134
attitude to, 182
Clocktower Square protest, Homs, 60
criminal, 181, 182, 195–8, *196*
economic cost of, 371
increase in, 182
jihadi, 181, 183–95
justification, 183
manifestations of, 181–98
political, 181–2
volunteer networks, 221

The Wall Street Journal, 35
war on terror, 330, 341–2
warlord phenomenon, xx, 297–8, 311
al-Watan, 37, 105
websites, regime strategy, 124
women, 88, 134, 172, 173, 176, 177, 178, 180, 217, 343, 368, 370
World Bank, 30
World Food Programme, 375
World Health Organization, 369

Yedlin, Amos, 280–1
Yemen, 73n15, 117, 135, 259
young wolves, 153, 166
'Your Silence Is Killing Us' Friday, 78
youth groups, 76–8, 92
YouTube, 35

az-Zabdani, xix, 107, 108, 95, 100
al-Zaim, Husni, 144
Zaitouneh, Razan, 110n39, 322
Zamalka, 107
Zamalka massacre, 179n29
al-Zawahiri, Ayman, 192
Zaytun, Muhammad Dib, 132, 133, 288n2